CROSS CURRENTS

CROSS CURRENTS

Family Law and Policy
in the United States and England

Edited by
SANFORD N. KATZ
JOHN EEKELAAR
MAVIS MACLEAN

OXFORD
UNIVERSITY PRESS

OXFORD

UNIVERSITY PRESS

Great Clarendon Street, Oxford OX2 6DP

Oxford University Press is a department of the University of Oxford.
It furthers the University's objective of excellence in research, scholarship,
and education by publishing worldwide in

Oxford New York

Athens Auckland Bangkok Bogotá Buenos Aires Calcutta
Cape Town Chennai Dar es Salaam Delhi Florence Hong Kong Istanbul
Karachi Kuala Lumpur Madrid Melbourne Mexico City Mumbai
Nairobi Paris São Paulo Shanghai Singapore Taipei Tokyo Toronto Warsaw
and associated companies in Berlin Ibadan

Oxford is a registered trade mark of Oxford University Press
in the UK and certain other countries

Published in the United States
by Oxford University Press Inc., New York

British Library Cataloguing in Publication Data

Data available

Library of Congress Cataloging in Publication Data

Cross-currents: family law and policy in the United States and England/[edited by]
Sanford N. Katz, John Eekelaar, Mavis Maclean.
p. cm.
Includes bibliographical references and index.
1. Domestic relations—United States. 2. Family policy—United States.
3. Domestic relations—Great Britain. 4. Family policy—Great Britain.
I. Katz, Sanford N., 1933– II. Eekelaar, John. III. Maclean, Mavis.
K670.C755 2000
346.4201′5—dc21
00–046504

ISBN 0–19–826820–3
ISBN 0–19–829944–3 (pb)

1 3 5 7 9 10 8 6 4 2

Typeset by J&L Composition Ltd, Filey, North Yorkshire
Printed in Great Britain
on acid-free paper by
Biddles Ltd., Guildford and King's Lynn

Preface

In 1957 the members of the law faculty of King's College, London published the book, *A Century of Family Law*, which was edited by R. H. Graveson and F. R. Crane. The work, introduced by Professor Graveson's chapter, 'The Background of the Century', was followed by chapters on marriage, illegitimacy and adoption, parental control and guardianship, and divorce and its economic consequences. There were also chapters on the substantive areas of tort, contract, evidence, criminal law, gifts, conflict of laws, focusing on the interface of family relationships with those areas, and one chapter on women in public law. The book, a superb publication and a historical document, provided more than a frozen picture of family law in Britain after the first fifty years of the century. It attempted to look to the future and to suggest the issues that would dominate the courts and scholarship during the concluding years of the century. What is so interesting is that while it hit the mark with regard to the issues women, and particularly married women, would face, it did not and could not foresee the effect of science and technology on the whole area of family life, nor could the authors imagine how the emergence of informal unions would affect marriage.

While Sanford was a Visiting Fellow at All Souls College, Oxford in 1997, he and John discussed using *A Century of Family Law* as a model for a book on family law, but expand it to include American family law. From time to time they met and began drafting an outline, each time deviating more and more from their original effort. Soon it became clear that family law in 1997 was so different from family law in Britain in 1957, that a totally new structure was needed. Further, there was a major omission in the 1957 work: a serious discussion of family policy and demography. It was then that Mavis Maclean joined the effort.

The end of World War II was taken to be a convenient point of departure for the contributions, partly because this provided a tidy method of following on from Graveson and Crane's volume. However, it soon became evident that from the point of view of demographic and social change, the immediate post-war years were less significant than those of the last quarter of the century, and a fuller picture often required looking back to a period many years before 1945. So, while the focus of the volume still rests upon the last half of the twentieth century, the contributions set this period within the sweep of longer-term historical trends.

In providing the structure for this book we have been influenced by Professors Joseph Goldstein and Jay Katz' monumental work, *The Family and the Law*, published in 1965. They saw family law as a process in which governmental decisions about the family are made. They perceived the cycle of state and family interaction in terms of three basic problems for decision: establishment, administration or maintenance, and reorganization. We have, however, modified this framework to allow more scope for issues that have arisen as a result of the re-thinking of the role of the state in determining social relations which have arisen in the last quarter of the century. We have also asked our contributors to concentrate primarily on the jurisdiction about which they were writing, and to keep comparative comments to a minimum. We wished readers to be able to draw their own conclusions about the relationships between respective developments in England and in the United States from reading the individual chapters. To assist them to reflect on the cross currents between these jurisdictions, we have constructed a pattern of chapter order which alternates between the American and English accounts. To further assist comparison, the index gives US references in italics and English references in roman type. English law discussed here applies also in Wales, but not in Scotland nor (fully) in Northern Ireland, which lack of space precludes us from covering. Readers will note that we have allowed contributors to employ the conventions of citation in use in their respective countries.

The project received financial assistance from The Oxford–NYU Institute on Law in a Global Society, an institute that has been set up and funded by a number of law firms to research into legal problems in a global society. We would particularly like to thank Manches & Co., a London firm with an Oxford office, which funded a meeting between almost all of the contributors in Oxford in March 1999. We wish to record our gratitude to them and to the Director of the Institute, Professor Dan Prentice, for making this possible. Sanford is grateful to Professor Aviam Soifer who, while Dean of Boston College Law School, encouraged his research; and to Dean John Garvey of Boston College Law School who funded his research during the writing of this book. He is grateful to Darald and Juliet Libby whose generosity made it possible for him to devote the summer of 2000 to continue his research. He also wishes to acknowledge the assistance he has received from Associate Dean Michael Cassidy and from the Revd William B. Neenan, S.J., Vice-President of Boston College, who has been extraordinarily supportive of his research for over a decade. In addition, two members of the class of 2000 at Boston College Law School, Gregory P. Connor and James P. Dowden, and Jeffrey D. Gaulin of the class of 2002 helped to prepare this book for publication. We recognize with special appreciation the considerable amount of research and editorial work which Jim Dowden performed on this book and his assistance at the March 1999 Oxford conference. We are also grateful to Ms Jackie Lewis of Pembroke College for her secretarial and computer assistance. Finally, it has been an honour and pleasure working with our distinguished contributors.

Sanford wishes to thank the Warden and Fellows of All Souls College, Oxford and the Master and Fellows of Pembroke College, Oxford for providing him the opportunity to work in Oxford, first organizing the book with John Eekelaar in 1997 and then writing his contributions in 2000. He is especially grateful to Dr Stephen Cretney, Fellow of All Souls and to John Eekelaar, Fellow of Pembroke College for their colleagueship and friendship. He is especially indebted to Jerome A. Barron, Mary Sarah Bilder, Mark S. Brodin, Ruth-Arlene W. Howe, and Elbert L. Robertson for acts of collegial generosity in commenting on early drafts of his chapter. In addition, Sanford expresses his special and affectionate gratitude to his wife, Joan, who was closely associated with the planning for this book.

Sanford dedicates his contribution to this book to the memory of his beloved college friend, Jerome E. Weinstein, who died in California in 1997. It was Jerry who introduced Sanford to the world of Oxford and Cambridge about forty years ago. Jerry held law degrees from Trinity Hall, Cambridge and Harvard Law School. Even though his interests and law practice were in intellectual property, he would have been enthusiastic about the publication of this book.

SANFORD N. KATZ
JOHN EEKELAAR
MAVIS MACLEAN
Pembroke College, Oxford
May 2000

Contents

C. Regulating and Reorganizing the Family

D. The Family and Governmental Agencies

E. Epilogues

Contributors

George J. Annas is the Edward R. Utley Professor of Health Law at Boston University School of Public Health, Boston, Massachusetts.

Jerome A. Barron is the Lyle T. Alverson Professor of Law at George Washington Univerisity, National Law Center, Washington, DC.

Grace Ganz Blumberg is Professor of Law at the University of California at Los Angeles, School of Law, Los Angeles, California.

Ruth Deech is Principal of St Anne's College, Oxford and Chairman of the Human Fertilisation and Embryology Authority.

John Dewar is Professor of Law at Griffith University, Nathan, Brisbane, Queensland, Australia.

Rebecca Dobash is Professor at the School of Social Policy and Social Work at the University of Manchester.

Russell Dobash is Professor at the School of Social Policy and Social Work at the University of Manchester.

Gillian Douglas is Professor of Law at Cardiff Law School, Wales.

John Eekelaar is Fellow at Pembroke College, Oxford.

Ira Mark Ellman is Professor of Law at Arizona State University College of Law, Phoenix, Arizona.

Michael Freeman is Professor of English Law at University College, London.

Barry L. Friedman is Professor of Social Welfare at the Heller Graduate School, Brandeis University, Waltham, Massachusetts.

Colin Gibson is a former member of the Department of Social and Political Science, Royal Holloway College, London.

Michael Grossberg is Professor of History at Indiana University, Department of History, Bloomington, Indiana.

Martin Guggenheim is Professor of Clinical Law and Director of Clinical Advocacy Programs at New York University School of Law, New York, New York.

Ruth-Arlene W. Howe is Professor of Law at Boston College Law School, Newton Centre, Massachusetts.

Sanford N. Katz is the Libby Professor of Law at Boston College Law School, Newton Centre, Massachusetts.

Jane Lewis is Barnett Professor of Social Policy at the University of Oxford.

Nigel Lowe is Professor of Law and Director of the Centre for International Family Law Studies at Cardiff Law School, Cardiff, Wales.

Mavis Maclean is Senior Research Fellow in Family Law and Policy at the University of Oxford.

Judith Masson is Professor of Law at Warwick University, Coventry.

Donna Ruane Morrison is Assistant Professor of Public Policy and Demography at Georgetown University Public Policy Institute, Washington, DC.

Stephen Parker is Dean of the Faculty of Law, Monash University, Melbourne, Australia.

Jessica Pearson is Director of the Centre for Policy Research, Denver, Colorado.

Martin Rein is Professor of Comparative Social Policy in the Department of Urban Studies and Planning at Massachusetts Institute of Technology, Cambridge, Massachusetts.

Elizabeth Schneider is Professor of Law at Brooklyn Law School, Brooklyn, New York.

Linda J. Silberman is Professor of Law at New York University School of Law, New York, New York.

Carol Smart is Professor of Sociology and Director of the Centre for Research on Family, Kinship and Childhood at the University of Leeds.

Walter J. Wadlington is James Madison Professor of Law, University of Virginia School of Law, Charlottesville, Virginia.

Barbara Bennett Woodhouse is Professor of Law at University of Pennsylvania Law School, Philadelphia, Pennsylvania.

A
Background to the Twentieth Century

1

How to Give the Present A Past?
Family Law in the United States

1950–2000

MICHAEL GROSSBERG

The purpose of this chapter is to place the last fifty years of United States family law in historical context in order to help introduce a series of substantive analyses of particular aspects of contemporary Anglo-American domestic relations law. The perennial difficulties posed by historical analysis of recent events are compounded in the case of the United States family law because the major problems are primarily analytical not empirical. That is, though critical new evidence emerges continually, an important body of information about American family law over the last fifty years already exists as does an established interpretation of changes in the era. It is, to use family law scholar Mary Ann Glendon's apt phrase, an era of transformation.[1]

This chapter, which introduces the American contributions to this book, is not intended to be read, however, simply as a preface unrelated to the contents of the chapters to follow. Instead, my goal is to present a historical analysis of the years from 1950 to 2000 that makes the recent past seem like a different, more complicated place. It seeks to provide new ways to think about the era and its major developments that do not simply act as stage setting, but also aid in understanding and interpreting recent events. In this way I want to suggest why looking backwards and thinking historically is more than background; it is a compelling, even vital way to think about current problems and future goals.

I argue that a series of fundamental changes in the United States family law during the early years of the era transformed American domestic relations by ending a nineteenth-century regime of family governance. The changes are worth recovering and analyzing because they have framed subsequent legal practice and disputes. At the same time, however, the nature of the new domestic relations regime was determined not simply by change, but also by continuities in family law and by reactions to the transformations. Thus, this chapter will be organized in three main parts: transformation, continuities, and reactions.

[1] See generally MARY ANN GLENDON, THE TRANSFORMATION FAMILY LAW: STATE, LAW AND FAMILY IN THE UNITED STATES AND WESTERN EUROPE (1989).

TRANSFORMATION

The contemporary era in American family law began with transforming change. The family governance regime in place in 1950 had its origins in the nineteenth century, particularly in the decades between the American Revolution and Civil War.[2] However, after 1950 many if not most of the key tenets of what now ought to be called the family law regime of the long nineteenth century were abandoned.[3] A partial listing of the repudiated rules document a range of family law changes clearly worthy of the label transformation: maternal preference, bans on inter-racial marriage, fault-based divorce, laws against abortion and birth control, refusals to accept charges of marital rape, circumscribed juve-nile rights, and even basic legal definitions of families. Each of these family law orthodoxies was replaced with a new rule and practice. We remain in the new era created by these changes.

As with any significant change, the transformation in American family law was the product of a diverse set of forces. These ranged from the emergence of a modern feminist movement and the increasing presence of the federal government, especially the federal courts, in family law to new attitudes about children and innovations in reproductive technol-ogy. Legal change also occurred in the midst of what historian Eliane Tyler May has called a 'demographic watershed.' By that she means that by the early 1970s the profile of American families had been altered in critical ways including the termination of almost half of all marriages by divorce, the rise in the number of single person households to a quarter of the population, the reduction of nuclear families to a third of the nation's households, and massive increases in the number of working married women with children.[4] At the same time, indeed symbiotically, legal change promoted a new sense of egalitarianism that created new ideas of families and family member rights. That change encouraged individual and group challenges to the existing denial of legal rights and habits of domination embedded in domestic relations rules that governed every aspect of family life from birth to death. These new beliefs and acts promoted the courtroom as an appealing forum for change and gave the equality-imposing phrases of the Fourteenth Amendment to the United States Constitution new meanings for families. Thus for the first time

---

[2] For a general assessment of the creation of American family law as a distinct legal category, see MICHAEL GROSSBERG, GOVERNING THE HEARTH: LAW AND THE FAMILY IN NINETEENTH CENTURY AMERICA (1985) [hereinafter GROSSBERG, GOVERNING].

[3] For a compelling use of the notion of the long 19th c, see HENDRIK HARTOG, MAN AND WIFE IN AMERICA, A HISTORY (2000).

[4] See *Myths and Realities of the American Family,* in 5 A HISTORY OF PRIVATE LIFE 583 (Philippe Aires and Georges Duby eds, 1991).

American family law was 'constitutionalized' in a series of dramatic decisions by the United States Supreme Court. The justices rewrote the law in the 1960s and 1970s by using the Fourteenth Amendment to recast rules governing marriage, procreation, children and parental rights, and the rights of non-traditional family members. As a result 'by the late twentieth century, the language of rights had become the dominant discourse in family law.'[5]

Equally important, these American developments were variants of a broader series of similar changes in the rest of West Europe and North America. As sociologist Frank E. Furstenberg, Jr has recently concluded, '[T]he rapidity and depth of the most recent period of family transformation which began in the wake of the Second World War rivals any in history. In most Western nations, marriage and family relationships have become more discretionary and variegated while at the same time become more precarious than at any time in recorded history.'[6] These transnational transformations ought to be considered as an example of what French theorists Michel Foucault and Jacques Donzelot have called 'discursive movements.' By that they mean that at particular moments new ways of perceiving social conditions give rise to new forms of knowledge, and that knowledge in turn compels attempts to apply it. Though the resulting efforts vary, they form a discursive movement because of shared priorities, assumptions, and tactics.[7] Such a discursive movement emerged during the mid-twentieth century in Western Europe and North America. American family law transformations are both a product and a source of the trans-Atlantic movements of this era. They illustrate many of the common priorities, assumptions, and tactics of these movements. Although beyond the scope of this chapter, they thus suggest the need to understand them within a broad framework of family law reconstruction and reform that occurred throughout Western Europe and North America.

Even without such a comparison, a few suggestive examples demonstrate the character of the transformation of United States family law and how it ranged across all of the categories of domestic relations to redefine the legal rights and status of all family members. Dramatic and visible changes in legal relations between husbands and wives are an apt initial

---

[5] Katherine L. Caldwell, *Not Ozzie and Harriet: Postwar Divorce and the American Liberal Welfare State*, 23 L & Soc Inquiry 40 (1998).

[6] Frank E. Furstenberg, Jr, *Is the Modern Family a Threat to Children's Health?* 36 Society 37 (July/Aug. 1999).

[7] See generally Michel Foucault, Power/Knowledge in Colin Gordon (ed), Selected Interviews and Other Writings, 1972–1977; see also Jacques Donzelot, The Policing of Families (1979). For an application of this approach, see Andrew Polsky, The Rise of the Therapeutic State (1991).

example. Basic assumptions of existing marital law orthodoxies were challenged and changed. Revealingly, for instance, courts in several states rearranged the balance of power in families and status of each spouse by decreeing that husbands and wives could sue each other, a husband could not give his children his surname without his wife's agreement, and that husbands could be prosecuted for raping their wives.[8] Changes like these were echoed throughout the law of marriage and divorce.

Legal changes that tilted the law toward limiting restrictions on the right to wed exemplify the methods and results of the era's family law transformations. The most dramatic and emblematic change was the elimination of the ban on interracial marriages. Several states had repealed the ban in the 1940s and 1950s, and then in 1967 the Supreme Court declared it unconstitutional in *Loving v Virginia*.[9] Calling marriage one of the 'basic civil rights of man,' the justices limited the regulatory power of the state by holding that unwarranted nuptial restrictions violated the principle of equality in the Fourteenth Amendment and thus deprived citizens of liberty without due process of law. Justice William O. Douglas made the new orientation of marriage law perfectly clear: '[T]he Fourteenth Amendment requires that the freedom of choice to marry not be restricted by invidious racial discriminations . . . To marry, or not to marry, a person of another race resides with the individual and cannot be infringed by the state.'[10]

Loving voiced the new primacy of contractual freedom and private ordering that transformed marriage law to make the right to wed a fundamental right. As a result, marriage restrictions came under new questioning. The consequences were evident in revealing decisions such as *Zablocki v Redhail* in which the Supreme Court struck down a Wisconsin statute that denied marital rights to those with existing child support debts. Treating the ban as class legislation, Justice John Paul Stevens objected that according to the statute: 'the rich may marry, the poor may not.' He argued that '[e]ven assuming that the right to marry may sometimes be denied on economic grounds, this clumsy and deliberate legislative discrimination between the rich and the poor is irrational in so many ways that it cannot withstand scrutiny under the Equal Protection Clause of the Fourteenth Amendment.'[11] Similar sentiments against states' restrictions on individual nuptial rights were codified in the Uniform Marriage and Divorce Act of 1970. It championed the elimination of nuptial curbs such as restrictions on the remarriage rights of the guilty party in a divorce. In their place the model act set minimal requirements

---

[8] See Steven Mintz, *New Rules: Postwar Families*, in Joseph M. Hawes and Elizabeth I. Nybakken (eds), AMERICAN FAMILIES: A RESEARCH GUIDE AND HISTORICAL HANDBOOK 189 (1991).
[9] 388 US 1 (1967).   [10] *ibid* at 12.   [11] *Zablocki v Redhail*, 434 US 384, 386 (1978).

for a valid marriage and even urged that marriages entered into in violation of its standards be considered valid unless formally declared void.[12]
Family law scholar Milton Regan captured the new orientation of marriage law: '[a]lthough the Court has been careful to proclaim the validity
of reasonable regulations that do not significantly interfere with the marriage decision, the clear message is that individual choice regarding marriage is an exercise of personal autonomy to which the state should defer
in most cases.'[13] The result was to make nuptial restrictions vulnerable to
charges that they interfered with constitutionally protected rights.

Equally dramatic changes occurred in the law of divorce. A new commitment to individual choice and private ordering transformed it as well.
In this case, the very notion of fault as the prime issue in marital breakups
lost its authority. No-fault divorce reform began in California in 1969 and
then swept the nation. By the 1990s all states offered some form of no-
fault divorce.[14] The new provisions allowed couples to dissolve their
marriages by claiming incompatibility, irretrievable breakdown, or
similar bases. Not only were specific fault grounds for divorce eliminated
but under the new divorce regime one spouse could terminate a marriage
without the consent of the other. The removal of fault as the basis for
divorce was also intended to dilute the moral stigma attached to the act,
a goal that served as its own commentary on family law change. As historian Roderick Phillips explains,

In short, since the 1960s, but especially since the 1970s, divorce has lost much of
its scandalous reputation, and is far less stigmatized as a result. The shift of legal
principles away from fault and the need to prove adultery or other matrimonial
offenses has undermined the association of divorce with scandalous and immoral
behavior. Even though divorce is still often viewed negatively—by no means is it
considered desirable for its own sake—it is treated more openly and not as something to be hidden from respectable society.[15]

The substitution of 'dissolution' for divorce expressed the transformed
orientation of the law.

And in 1971 the Supreme Court made divorce a constitutionally protected right by striking down mandatory filing fees. The justices considered
the fee a violation of the due process rights of impoverished but estranged
couples. The court declared that divorce was 'the adjustment of a fundamental human relationship' and the method by which 'two consenting
adults may mutually liberate themselves from the constraints of legal obligations that go with marriage, and more fundamentally the prohibition

---

[12] See 9A ULA 147 (1993).
[13] MILTON C. REGAN, JR, FAMILY LAW AND THE PURSUIT OF INTIMACY 37 (1993).
[14] For a general overview of these changes, see RODERICK PHILLIPS, TORN ASUNDER: A
HISTORY OF DIVORCE IN WESTERN SOCIETY 561–72 (1988).   [15] *ibid* at 626.

against remarriage.'[16] They thus elevated the right to divorce near to the status of the right to wed. Both rights had been produced by a transformed law of marriage that placed new limits on public nuptial control while clothing individual choice with greater authority. And once again the policy was incorporated in model statutes. Section 308 of the Uniform Marriage and Divorce Act rejected notions of marital fault entirely.[17]

The law of child custody underwent a similar transformation. Amid broad changes in gender roles and beliefs, the central tenet of orthodox custody rules—maternalism—came under attack as an ideal and a policy. As a result support for the presumed superior ability of mothers to raise children that undergirded the law began to erode. Psychologist Arlene Skolnick summarizes the situation by reminding us that maternal preference had 'remained unchallenged until the family upheavals of the 1960s and 1970s. In the wake of rising divorce rates, challenges to women's traditional roles, and men's claims of sex discrimination in custody awards, most states abandoned the maternal presumption in favor of a more gender neutral "best-interests" standard.'[18] Thus a New York appellate judge could declare in 1971: 'The simple fact of being a woman does not, by itself, indicate a capacity or willingness to render a quality of care different from that which the father can provide.'[19]

As a result of such sentiments basic custody doctrines like the tender years rule, which presumed that infants and young children were best cared for by their mothers, were eliminated or had their significance reduced in nearly all states. Similarly, the Uniform Marriage and Divorce Act urged the removal of marital fault in custody awards, one of the major props of maternal preference. It advocated state codes that distinguished between spousal conduct and parenting rights by suggesting the admonition that the 'court shall not consider conduct of a proposed custodian that does not affect his relationship to the child.' And the Uniform Parentage Act recommended the equal balancing of the claims of mothers and fathers.[20] Though most awards of physical custody went to women, the new rules enabled more fathers to secure custody than ever before. They also led to new custodial arrangements such as joint custody, shared custody, and divided custody. All of these would have been unthinkable in the previous family law regime.

---

[16] *Boddie v Connecticut*, 401 US 371, 374, 383, 376 (1971).

[17] See 9A ULA 147, 347 (1987); see also Barbara Bennett Woodhouse, *Sex, Lies, and Dissipation: The Discourse of Fault in a No-Fault Era*, 82 Geo L J 2537 (1994) [hereinafter Woodhouse, *Sex, Lies*].

[18] Arlene Skolnick, *Solomon's Children: The New Biologism, Psychological Parenthood, Attachment Theory, and the Best Interest Standard*, in Mary Mason *et al* (eds), All Our Families, New Policies for a New Century 242–3 (1998).

[19] *State ex Rel Watts v Watts*, 350 NYS 2d 285, 289 (1973).

[20] See 9A ULA 147, 561 (1987); 9A ULA 287 (1994).

Similar and similarly significant changes occurred in the laws governing illegitimacy. Though efforts to remove the penalties of illegitimacy had begun in the 1780s with historic reforms by Thomas Jefferson in Virginia and continued into the twentieth century, the mark of illegitimacy intentionally remained a social and legal stigma and illegitimate children continued to be deprived of many basic family rights.[21] However, Supreme Court's doctrines developed during the 1970s significantly remade the law amid rising rates of illegitimate births, fears of uncollected child support by putative fathers, concerns about the psychological impact of illegitimacy on children, increasingly reliable paternity tests, and broader revaluations of the social utility of illegitimacy as a means of policing sexual misconduct. Under the Court's tutelage illegitimacy became a constitutionally suspect classification and children earned a new 'right' to be treated as individuals and not punished for the sins of their parents, a goal of family law reform since Jefferson's day.

Change began in May 1968 when two cases involving Louisiana's wrongful death statutes compelled the court for the first time to address the constitutionality of state laws that classified children on the basis of legitimacy of birth. Overturning a decision by the state supreme court, the high court ruled in *Levy v Louisiana*[22] that there existed no rational basis for denying illegitimate children the right to recover for the wrongful death of their mothers. Focusing on the needs of children, a 6 : 3 majority challenged the logic of the policy, and declared that child welfare should be the law's central concern. Using similar reasoning, the court ruled in *Glona v American Guarantee & Liability Insurance Co.*[23] that a mother could recover for the wrongful death of her illegitimate child. Almost ten years later, the court directly repudiated the age-old policy of using illegitimacy to check immorality and sexual promiscuity by declaring that states must show more convincing arguments than the 'promotion of legitimate family relations' to support these policies.[24] This decision expressed the policy of the Uniform Parentage Act that, in 1973, urged states to jettison the concept of illegitimacy entirely and equalize inheritance, wrongful death, and workers' compensations rights of all children.[25]

---

[21] For an analysis of these issues, see Michael Grossberg, *Citizens and Families: A Jeffersonian Vision of Domestic Relations and Generational Change*, in James Gilreath (ed), THOMAS JEFFERSON AND THE EDUCATION OF A CITIZEN 3–27 (1999); see also GROSSBERG, GOVERNING, n 2 above, at ch 6.   [22] 391 US 68 (1968).

[23] 391 US 73 (1968).   [24] See *Trimble v Gordon*, 430 US 702 (1977).

[25] See generally EVA R. RUBIN, THE SUPREME COURT AND THE AMERICAN FAMILY 28–38 (1986); Robert L. Stenger, *Expanding Constitutional Rights of Illegitimate Children, 1968–1980*, 19 J FAM L 408–9 (1980–1).

Equally dramatically, for the first time, courts began to give custodial rights to unwed fathers in addition to their traditional obligation of support. In 1971, the United States Supreme Court considered the custodial rights of unwed fathers after the death of the mother in *Stanley v Illinois*.[26] Peter Stanley challenged an Illinois statute that made children wards of the court upon the death of the mother. He claimed that equal protection under the federal Constitution required that he be treated like married fathers, who were presumed fit custodians under Illinois law whether they were divorced, separated, or widowed. The Supreme Court agreed, and determined that there must be a fitness hearing to determine custody, as there would be for all natural parents in such circumstances. Justice Byron White maintained that the 'private interests here: that of a man in the children that he has sired and raised, undeniably warrants deference and, absent a powerful countervailing interest, protection.'[27] The court explained the new rules governing the custody rights of unwed fathers in a 1983 decision rejecting the adoption challenge of a man who had never lived with his daughter:

the significance of the biological connection is that it offers the natural father an opportunity that no other male possesses to develop a relationship with his offspring. If he grasps that opportunity and accepts some measure of responsibility for the child's future, he may enjoy the blessings of the parent–child relationship and make uniquely valuable contributions to the child's development. If he fails to do so, the Federal Constitution will not automatically compel a State to listen to his opinion of where the child's best interests lie.[28]

As a result of decisions like these, unwed fathers who demonstrated a willingness to act as parents could secure rights to visitation, consent to adoption, and inheritance unthinkable under the previous family law regime. Family scholar Mary Ann Mason captures the significance of the transformation of illegitimacy by linking it to changes in other categories of American family law:

Until very recently, the law controlled sex outside of marriage by punishing the doers . . . In the second half of the twentieth century, however, the state quit punishing sexual behavior outside of marriage. This trend mirrored the no-fault revolution in divorce; if the state was not going to consider adultery or other sexual misconduct in divorce and custody actions, then it could no longer legitimately punish illegitimacy.[29]

Finally the rights of children also became a central issue in this legal era. Children's rights were significantly enhanced, particularly for

---

[26] 405 US 645 (1972).   [27] *ibid* at 658, 651.
[28] *Lehr v Robertson*, 463 US 248, 262 (1983).
[29] MARY ANN MASON, FROM FATHER'S PROPERTY TO CHILDREN'S RIGHTS: THE HISTORY OF CHILD CUSTODY IN THE UNITED STATES 144 (1994).

adolescents, as a result of statutory changes, judicial decisions, and even a constitutional amendment. As Justice Harry Blackmun wrote in *Planned Parenthood v Missouri*, which granted a minor the right to an abortion without parental consent: 'Constitutional rights do not mature and come into being magically only when one attains the state-defined age of majority. Minors, as well as adults, are protected by the Constitution and possess constitutional rights.'[30]

Decisions like this one added a liberationist strain to discussions of children's rights. They recast the legal status of children by applying an adult model of rights to them for the first time. Corresponding statutory initiatives, such as medical emancipation laws and lowered drinking ages, spoke in the same liberationist language as did the Twenty-Sixth Amendment to the Constitution, which lowered the voting age to 18. The lure of children's rights was evident in the tendency to issue children's 'bills of rights.' The charter composed by lawyers Henry Foster and Doris Freed, for instance, included a child's right to emancipation from a troubled home and called for the abolition of minority status, which they likened to slavery and coverture.[31] And child rights advocate John Holt observed in 1974: 'Much is said and written these days about children's rights. Many use the word to mean something that we all agree it would be for every child to have: "the right to a good home" or "the right to a good education." ' But Holt discounted these paternalistic rights of a previous generation in favor of autonomous rights central to the rights claims of his time: 'I mean what we mean when we speak of the rights of adults. I urge that the law grant and guarantee to the young the freedom that it now grants to adults to make certain kinds of choices, do certain kinds of things, and accept certain kinds of responsibilities.'[32]

Declarations like Holt's underscored the anti-interventionist, anti-statist strain that ran through much of the children's rights movement and its use of rights as trumps to challenge special public protections for the young embedded in family law and other social policies. And legislative and judicial action on the part of children translated many of these sentiments into law. As legal scholar Frank Zimring noted in 1982:

Before 1966, the United States Supreme Court had never decided a case that could properly be filed under the rubric of 'juvenile rights'; in the last fifteen years, adolescence has been a major concern of the Court. The United States Reports are filled with cases adjudicating the rights of adolescents in matters as diverse as abortion, school suspension, involuntary civil commitment, corporal

---

[30] 428 US 52 (1976).

[31] Henry Foster and Doris Freed, *A Bill of Rights for Children*, in Sanford N. Katz (ed), THE YOUNGEST MINORITY: LAWYERS IN DEFENSE OF CHILDREN 318–50 (1974).

[32] Beatrice Gross and Ronald Gross (eds), THE CHILDREN'S RIGHTS MOVEMENT: OVERCOMING THE OPPRESSION OF YOUNG PEOPLE 321 (1977) (quoting Holt).

punishment, jury trials in juvenile courts, and political demonstrations ...
Federal district courts are flooded with constitutional challenges to regulations of
the young that have previously gone unchallenged. Legislative bodies, state and
federal, are rethinking public policy toward adolescent work and wages,
compulsory education, access to medical care, and the jurisdiction and mission of
the juvenile court ...[33]

Countless other examples could be offered to amplify these points.
They range from the judicial and statutory recognition of cohabitation to
the elimination of bans on birth control and abortion. The central point,
though, is that after 1950 American family law was fundamentally redefined. Its linked changes came to contain a new emphasis on private
ordering and individual rights that led to new balances in the law
between state interest and individual choice, family uniformity and
family diversity, and the roles and rights of individual family members.
In a 1976 review of a new edition of a family law casebook, William
Binchy expressed the depth and spirit of these legal changes:

If contract is dead, a strong case could be made that the law relating to marriage
is on the verge of extinction. Most of the distinctive functional and normative
congeries of rights and obligations traditionally associated with that institution
have been discarded as American family law disengages itself from policing
spousal and parental roles. Thus, the barriers to divorce on demand have been
substantially dismantled, the concept of illegitimacy has been discredited, marital
privileges in relation to sexual conduct have been overturned, spousal support
obligations in their restatement here have been restricted in scope, and parental
'rights' in regard to children have been greatly circumscribed.[34]

We continue to feel the aftershocks of these transformations.

CONTINUITIES

The nature and meaning of the post-1950 transformation of United States
family law, however, is not understandable simply in a chronicle of innovations and departures. On the contrary, such lists raise critical questions about the depth and permanency of the era's changes. In particular,
a focus on change hides the presence of continuities in domestic relations
law and their power to help determine the course of change and its
impact on lives and law. Giving analytical significance to persistent features of Anglo-American family law demonstrates that some critical components of domestic relations are subject to generational solutions rather

---

[33] Frank Zimring, The Changing Legal World of Adolescence 14 (1982).
[34] Book review, 15 Journal of Family Law 315–16 (1976–7) (reviewing C. Foote *et al*, Cases
and Materials on Family Law 2nd edn, 1976).

than permanent resolutions. So continuity is a second issue that must be added to a historical analysis of these years.

Examining family law continuities reveals the power of the past to determine the context of a particular period and thus some of the limits of change. Focusing on the recurring features of the law also raises questions about why particular policies and rules are long-lived and others are time-bound. And it highlights what legal historian James Willard Hurst called 'drift' and its power to order legal change and legal experience. By drift, Hurst meant the ongoing elaboration of dominant legal trends at work in every legal category. And drift was clearly critical to the character of family law even in this era of transforming change.[35] Consequently, continuities help us understand the basic lineaments of American family law and therefore the nature of its transformation in the years after 1950.

Family law continuities took a variety of forms. These ranged from the continued acceptance of corporal punishment by most parents and lawmakers to the persistent power of individual choice in matrimony.[36] I want to highlight several of the most significant instances of continuity because they demonstrate its power to order American family law during an era of transformative change.

Particularly significant is the fact that despite numerous successful challenges to orthodoxy, the basic framing mechanism of family law remained unchanged. Throughout the era, as in the past, Anglo-American family law framed disputes in metaphoric terms of balancing. That is, like a teeter-totter the law tends to depict household disputes as balances between individual and family rights on one side and autonomy and state regulation, interests, and regulation on the other. Examples fill the chapters of every domestic relations casebook: the right to wed balanced with state regulation of matrimony, the right to leave a troubled marriage versus state interest in family preservation, the parental right to her child's custody versus the public interest in child protection, and on and on. Equally long-lived has been the triggering device that alters the legal balance: tensions between ideal and functioning families. Ideal families are the forms of family life recognized in statutes, legal doctrines, administrative directives, and the other formal expressions of public authority. Functional families are the various ways women, men, and children actually live together. The two do not always coincide, and indeed they often occupy different sides of family law's teeter-totter.[37] Clashes over

---

[35] See James Willard Hurst, Law and Social Order in the United States ch 5 (1977).

[36] See eg Murray A. Straus, Beating the Devil out of Them, Corporal Punishment in American Families 6–7 (1994).

[37] See generally Note, *Looking for a Family Resemblance: The Limits of the Functional Approach to the Legal Definition of the Family*, 104 Harv L Rev 1640–50 (1991) [hereinafter *Family Resemblance*].

these family forms shift the legal balance in family law. Equally importantly, both find concrete expression in forms distinct to particular eras
but yet also persist as framing devices in domestic relations law.

Moore v East Cleveland[38] is an apt illustration of the continued use of
balancing tests to resolve tensions between ideal and functional families
within the post-1950s transformations of American family law. It is also
an example of a period-specific balance between the two. In this 1977
case, the Justices of the Supreme Court achieved a new balance between
state interest and functional families that granted greater legitimacy to
family diversity. The case involved claims by the city of East Cleveland
that a family composed of grandparents and grandchildren violated its
zoning ordinances requiring single families in that part of town and
limiting the number of relatives that could reside in one household. The
Court rejected the city's claims and declared: 'Ours is by no means a
tradition limited to the nuclear family. The tradition of uncles, aunts,
cousins, and especially grandparents sharing a household along with
parents and children has roots equally venerable and equally deserving
of recognition.'[39] The zoning law had clearly rejected that tradition. But in
this era its commitment to an ideal form of family gave way to a new
functional commitment to family diversity.

Similarly in 1989 New York state's highest court granted a gay man
protection against eviction from his deceased lover's rent-controlled
apartment by explicitly defining family in functional terms. The judges
ruled that the 'exclusivity of the relationship, the level of emotional and
financial commitment, the manner in which the parties have conducted
their everyday lives and held themselves out to society, and the reliance
placed upon one another for daily family services . . . it is the totality of
the relationship as evidenced by the dedication, caring, and self-sacrifice
of the parties which should, in the final analysis, control.'[40]

Most significant here, though, is not so much the results of cases like
these as the way they were framed. The continued use of balancing tests
that pit functional versus ideal families is one of the most persistent
features of American family law. And, equally significant, this legal
framing mechanism contains the possibility that future views of functional families and revised commitments to ideal families could result in
another tilt in the law. Indeed it is worth noting, as the authors of a
Harvard Law Review note suggested, that '[g]iven the relatively few statutory exceptions to the traditional legal definition of family, the formal
approach results in privileging the nuclear family over all alternatives.'[41]

---

[38] 431 US 494 (1977).   [39] *ibid* at 504; See also Rubin, n 25 above, at 144–6.
[40] Judith Stacey, In the Name of the Family: Rethinking Family Values in the Postmodern
Age 115 (1996) (quoting New York Court of Appeals).
[41] *Family Resemblance*, n 37 above, at 645.

In family law, as in so many other legal categories, form does indeed matter.

Though cases like *Moore* modified the basic family law preference for nuclear families, that commitment and related ones continued to govern many aspects of American domestic relations laws, and thus highlight another family law continuity. As legal scholar Wendy Maloney contends in a study of step-parents, 'A major purpose of many family-related doctrines is to safeguard the interests of individual family members, especially children, and also to protect the family unit. The traditional emphasis on the nuclear family has effectively prevented many individuals, who live in other family situations, from enjoying the same type of legal recognition and protection.'[42] Indeed after documenting the hold of the past on the present, Maloney bleakly concluded that the transformations of the era had left the rights of step-parents virtually unchanged even though the surging divorce rate produced more and more of them. Mason reached a similar conclusion and suggested its consequences: 'The revolution in divorce and custody laws that swept through the states in the late twentieth century almost totally ignored the growing presence of stepparents. Family law continued to view stepparents through common law lenses, giving them no legal rights over their stepchildren and imposing few obligations.'[43]

Equally potent has been the persistent preference for blood relations embedded in domestic relations rules. Foster parents, for instance, acquired few parental rights even though foster care had become the preferred form of placing children removed from their homes. The Supreme Court sanctioned the secondary status of foster families in *Smith v Organization of Foster Families For Equality and Reform*.[44] Though he lauded the contributions of foster parents, Justice William J. Brennan expressed a continued commitment to protect the rights of natural parents who had not fully relinquished their children: 'The usual understanding of "family" implies biological relationships, and most decisions treating the relationship between parent and child have stressed that element.' And he distinguished foster families from natural ones by declaring:

It is one thing to say that individuals may acquire a liberty interest against arbitrary governmental interference in the family-like associations into which they have freely entered, even in the absence of a biological connection or state-law recognition of the relationship. It is quite another to say that one may acquire such an interest in the face of another's constitutionally recognized liberty interest that derives from blood relationships, state-law sanction, and basic human right.[45]

[42] WENDY M. MALONEY, STEPFAMILIES AND THE LAW 1 (1994).
[43] MASON, n 29 above, at 136.   [44] 431 US 816 (1977).
[45] *ibid* at 843. For a full discussion of the case, see David L. Chambers and Michael S. Wald, in Robert H. Mnookin *et al* (eds,) IN THE INTEREST OF CHILDREN, ADVOCACY, LAW REFORM, AND PUBLIC POLICY 67–147 (1985).

Some of the most publicized and heart-wrenching family law cases of the era involved the longstanding preference for blood ties. Most notorious was the Baby Jessica case[46] in which the courts struggled between giving custody of a young girl to birth parents or the foster parents she had known since infancy. In awarding custody the court focused on whether the parental rights of the biological father had been correctly terminated. And the decision to take the child from the family that raised her and return to her biological parents provoked public outrage. Yet, as Skolnick observes,

Many commentators, though, believe that the child's best interests are in fact served by growing up with biological parents, and that parents not only have a right to their children but that 'natural bonds of affection' lead parents to care for their children in a way that no 'stranger' could. This biological slant of the legal system also reflects widespread, but usually unarticulated assumptions about ties based on blood and genes in American culture. Because they are so taken for granted, there is a danger that unless they are made explicit, these assumptions may well guide decision making and discussion of the issues in an unreflective way. The belief that family bonds are the natural and essential product of biological ties is deeply rooted in American kinship beliefs. The saying 'blood is thicker than water' tells us that ties not based in biological kinship cannot be as strong as those that are. This belief is enshrined in a host of tales in which children discover their real parents and live happily ever after.[47]

Furthermore, she asserts, 'For a variety of reasons, then, the facts of biological parenthood carry more legal weight than in the past. Courts have shown a strong preference for awarding custody to what they call "natural parents" whether or not a parent–child relationship exists. Large numbers of adults who have actually nurtured and raised children—relatives, stepparents, and foster parents—have no legal standing.'[48] Policies like these demonstrate that family law's transformations were selective. Not all doctrines were repudiated or even substantially revised. And, of course, such selectivity raises compelling questions about the depth of family law change in the new era.

Institutional continuities also persisted amid the legal transformations. United States family law has become a body of rules primarily codified in statutes. Nevertheless, in this period as in the past judges continued to dominate its articulation and conceptualization by playing an oracular role. The major change has been that while in most of the history of the republic, state judges served as the nation's primary family law oracles, in this era federal judges often delivered seminal family law declarations.

---

[46] See *DeBoer v Schmidt*, 502 NW2d 649 (Mich 1993).
[47] Skolnick, n 18 above, at 238–9.
[48] *ibid* at 242.

And yet even this judicial shift underscores the continuing power of federalism in American family law that makes state–federal tensions central to all legal debates and changes including those involving domestic relations.

Since the mid-nineteenth century judicial family law hegemony has been reinforced by the way lawyers learn family law through treatises and casebooks that give a privileged place to appellate opinions. Despite the determination of states to protect their domestic relations powers, these tendencies have been abetted by the organizing power of legal writers, especially the ideal of a national family law promoted with increasing success in casebooks, law review articles, and model uniform statutes.[49] For example, Christopher P. Manfredi's recent study of juvenile justice and the Supreme Court points out the authoritative role of law reviews in this kindred field. 'Historically rooted in the sociological and economic studies first introduced into constitutional jurisprudence by Louis Brandeis, the strategic and tactical use of law reviews and other publications was perfected by the NAACP in its constitutional struggles against racially restrictive covenants and segregated education.' Manfredi maintains that the arguments promulgated in legal books and periodicals were used with strategic success in pivotal juvenile justice cases such as *Kent v US*[50] and *In re Gault*.[51] 'Not surprisingly, given the developing trends in the legal literature concerning juvenile justice and courts,' he contends, 'most of this material found its way into the briefs submitted by the organizations seeking to constitutionalize juvenile justice procedures. With the prevailing law against these reformers, such extrinsic sources provided the authority necessary to support their program of legal change.'[52] In juvenile justice as in all categories of American family law, though the results of decisions altered the substance of legal doctrines, reliance on the methods of legal change had been established long before this era of transformation.

A continued reliance on social science in the analysis and application of family law also marked the era. Psychological and clinical studies as well as the empiricist reverence for statistics as a way of knowing about family life have been influential in family law from around 1900.[53] For example, in 1974 Professor Homer Clark explained the legitimacy of no-fault divorce and the move away from fault-based marital

---

[49] For a discussion of these issues, see HARTOG, n 3 above, at ch 10.

[50] 383 US 541 (1966).   [51] 387 US 1 (1967).

[52] CHRISTOPHER P. MANFREDI, THE SUPREME COURT AND JUVENILE JUSTICE 42 (1998); see also generally *ibid* at 36–45.

[53] For a call for better family law statistics, see PAUL H. JACOBSON AND PAULINE F. JACOBSON, AMERICAN MARRIAGE AND DIVORCE 1–14 (1959); see also generally JOHN HENRY SCHLEGEL, AMERICAN LEGAL REALISM AND EMPIRICAL SOCIAL SCIENCE (1995).

offenses by citing the work of sociologists and psychologists who had argued that 'such activities as adultery, cruelty and desertion were merely symptoms, not causes, of marital failure.'[54] Instead, they contended that 'fault itself was out of place in divorce, and that marriages broke up in a context of conflicts in attitude, personality, or other difficulty on both sides, rather than as a result of fault by one spouse and innocence by the other.'[55] Such a reliance on social science theories and findings both encouraged and legitimated legal change in this era as it had in previous ones.

Child custody law is a particularly revealing and contested example of the sway of social science over family law. As Mason explains, 'Dependence upon the social sciences accelerated late in the century. The abolition of fault-based divorce and the maternal presumption, both of which fostered vague standards for judicial decision making, promoted this dependence.'[56] It expressed itself in a number of ways such as the use of psychological theories by legislators and judges to support the primacy of one or both parents in custody disputes following divorce and the use of expert witnesses drawn from the ranks of mental health professionals to testify about parental capacity in contested custody cases. Revealingly, the use of experts in child custody trials rose from 10 per cent of appealed cases by the 1960s to a third of such cases by 1990. Equally significantly, though initially parents had employed experts, by 1990 judges appointed them in most cases.[57]

In custody law itself the psychological authority most frequently cited by the appellate courts in the middle of the era was the 1973 book, *Beyond the Best Interests of the Child* by law professor Joseph Goldstein, child analyst Anna Freud, and psychiatrist Albert Solnit. The authors created the concept of the 'psychological parent': the one individual, not necessarily the biological parent, with whom the child was most closely attached. In their opinion this person should have total and, if necessary, exclusive custodial rights, including the power to refuse visitation to non-custodial parents. This book became the centerpiece of many custody decisions by encouraging legal expressions of 'psychological parenthood' that stressed the importance of continuity and stability in caretakers and led jurists to frown upon joint and divided child custody arrangements.[58] For instance, lawyers for the foster parents in *Smith v OFFER* relied on the book and Goldstein filed a brief on their behalf with the Supreme Court.[59] Yet *Beyond the Best Interests* also became a

[54] HOMER H. CLARK, JR, CASES AND PROBLEMS ON DOMESTIC RELATIONS (2nd edn, 1974).
[55] *ibid* at 9.   [56] MASON, n 29 above, at 161.   [57] See *ibid* at 161–2.
[58] For a general analysis of this issue, see LYNNE CAROL HALEM, DIVORCE REFORM, CHANGING LEGAL AND SOCIAL PERSPECTIVES ch 6 (1980).
[59] See Chambers and Wald, n 45 above, at 101–3, 110–11.

target as new theories rose to challenge its assumptions and thus engulf family law in social science debates. Critics argued that children could and had thrived within multiple family forms, and they challenged the notion of a 'psychological parent.' They encouraged lawmakers to develop strategies for divorced parents to share the custody of their off-spring.[60] Such changes revealed part of the consequences of the dependence on the authority of social science experts and raised questions about the wisdom of grounding legal rights on the changing theories and findings of social scientists.

More broadly, the growing reliance on social science represents a family law variant of a larger quest for an objective basis for legal rules that stretches back at least to the early years of the long nineteenth-century domestic relations regime. Wendy Fitzgerald explains the continuing appeal of the seeming certainty of scientific theories with custody law as an example:

Courts have entertained empirical evidence of children's 'best interests' with understandable desperation. Absent some empirical basis for a 'best interest' determination, after all, the court's decision must manifest little more than idiosyncratic and subjective conclusions about what living arrangements are 'best' for children. Courts' selection of empirical evidence itself entails a value judgment; whether to value, for example, that which is financially 'best' for children or spiritually 'best' for children. Courts usually select 'psychological health' as the most valued criterion for 'best interests' determinations. Psychological evidence appears to courts as objective and unassailable, vastly simplifying courts' Solomonic custody decisions and permitting reliance on a class of seemingly disinterested experts.[61]

Such evidence is particularly appealing in times of change and conflict such as the early years of this new era in American family law.[62]

Finally, family law in this new era was also characterized by the persistence of what legal scholar Jacobus Ten Broek called a dual system of family law that first emerged in the Elizabethan poor laws. It promotes liberationist policies for the middle and upper classes and repressive ones for the lower classes.[63] Even though a transformed family law granted greater recognition to functional families and increased the rights of

---

[60] See Skolnick, n 18 above, at 244–9; see also generally CAROL B. STACK, ALL OUR KIN: STRATEGIES FOR SURVIVAL IN A BLACK COMMUNITY (1974).

[61] Wendy Fitzgerald, *Maturity, Difference, and Mystery: Children's Perspectives and the Law*, 36 ARIZ L REV 56 (1994).

[62] For an exchange over these issues, see Martha Fineman and Annie Opie, *The Uses of Social Science in Legal Policy-Making: Custody Determination at Divorce*, 1987 WIS L REV 107–58; David Chambers, *The Uses of Social Science: A Reply to Fineman and Opie*, 1987 WIS L REV 159–63; Martha Fineman, *A Reply to David Chambers*, 1987 WIS L REV 165–9.

[63] See Jacobus Ten Broek, *California's Dual System of Family Law: Its Origin, Development, and Present Status [Parts I & II]*, 16 STAN L REV 257 (1964).

indigent household members in cases like *Zablocki* and *Boddie*, the dual system remained a crucial part of family law's balancing acts.

Family privacy is a prime example. Family privacy came to have dual meanings. It provided increased protection from the state for middle and upper class families, but was often rendered meaningless for poor ones dependent on public assistance. Informational privacy is a case in point. It involves the right of family members to withhold information about their households from state inquiries, a more and more critical issue as new forms of invasive technology engulf the persistently anti-statist republic. In *Wayman v James*[64] the United States Supreme Court upheld a New York state welfare department's regulations requiring claimants of Aid to Families with Dependent Children to consent to home visits in order to maintain benefit eligibility. The Justices reasoned that even if the visits could be characterized as 'searches' under the Fifth Amendment's proviso against illegal search and seizure, the consent of a recipient to be visited was a fair trade-off for the aid sought from the state. Welfare recipients thus could not avoid disclosing intimate information, no matter what havoc it wreaked on their lives. Equally important is the popular support for such disclosures as protection against welfare fraud. The limits imposed on the informational privacy of poor families are in stark contrast to those demanded by other classes. Such differing rules and policies illustrate how class has continued to be used to distinguish privacy rights. The limits imposed on the informational privacy of the economically poor are echoed in other privacy decisions such as those that uphold the Hyde Amendment denials of publicly funded abortions to indigent women.[65] Similar balances occur in statutory privacy. And they demonstrate how state surveillance remained a reality for certain American families.

Continuities like these and others such as the continued role of individual litigants in the construction and application of United States family law and the persistent power of male dominion in domestic relations law conditioned and mediated change in American family law.[66] They helped determine the meaning and experience of the legal transformations. In doing so, they imposed limits on those changes and thus in critical ways defined the scope and content of the new domestic relations law regime that emerged after 1950.

---

[64] 400 US 309 (1971); see also Rubin, n 25 above, at 147–8.

[65] For an assessment of the Hyde Amendment, see Donald T. Critchlow, Intended Consequences: Birth Control, Abortion, and the Federal Government in Modern America 202, 206–7 (1999).

[66] See eg Steven L. Nock, *The Problem with Marriage*, 36 Society 20–8 (July/Aug, 1999); Barbara Bennett Woodhouse, *Children's Rights: The Destruction and Promise of Family*, 82 BYU L Rev 503 (1993).

REACTIONS

Finally, I want to probe the consequences of change and continuity by examining the reactions to the transformations of United States family law. If this chapter had been written late in 1979, transformation would have been its primary and perhaps singular theme. The emphasis would have been on the triumph of private ordering in family law evident in the legal recognition of cohabitation rights in cases like *Marvin v Marvin*[67] or in the ongoing secularization of domestic relations rules. Even continuities would have been obscured by the overwhelming sense of change that dominated those years and encouraged the conviction that it would continue. But the view at the turn of the twentieth-first century is quite different. The trajectory of change is neither as clear nor as uniform as it seemed just twenty years ago. Looking backwards now reveals very clearly that each major family law change generated not simply acceptance and support, but also opposition and resistance. And the importance of those reactions for the meaning and practices of American family law have grown over time.

Consequently, reactions like continuities raise critical questions about the depth and permanency of the transformations that marked the first part of the era. They remind us that every departure from orthodoxy spurs resistance. Indeed each family law controversy sparked pitched battles for and against change. However, if the breadth and power of opposition grows to such an extent that it begins to have an impact on the law itself then the reaction is more than mere resistance. That is what has happened to family law as the innovations of the recent past have themselves become targeted for change. Increasingly strident calls demanded a shift in the balance of family law away from an emphasis on equality and individual rights and toward greater state regulation of parents and children, husbands and wives. As Judith Stacey has argued, these demands were part of a larger reaction to legal and family change: 'Backlash sentiment against the dramatic family transformations of the past four decades have played an increasingly pivotal role in national politics in the United States since the late 1970s, when the divorce rate peaked, and a national White House Conference on the Family that was planned during the Carter administration fractured into three deeply polarized, regional conferences on families convened during the first year of the Reagan administration.'[68] Thus an assessment of the reactions to family law change is critical to any effort to construct a historical framework for understanding this new era in the history of United States domestic relations law.

[67] 557 P 2d 106 (Cal 1976).
[68] STACEY, n 40 above, at 3.

Though the reactions to family law change had multiple sources, two are particularly significant. The first is another persistent feature of American family law: crisis. In this era, as in the past, a sense of crisis among various groups of Americans spurred reactions to intertwined social and legal change. As in the past, powerful if ephemeral movements rose to ventilate deeply felt social anxieties that often centered on the fate of families and children. As historian Linda Gordon has observed, 'Over at least 150 years there have been periods of fear that "the family"—meaning a popular image of what families were supposed to be like, by no means a correct recollection of any actual "traditional" family—was in decline; and these fears have tended to escalate in periods of social stress.'[69] Recent decades have been just such an era. Indeed after the first years of transforming change, the family and its law became central battlegrounds in the cultural wars and memory battles that engulfed American society. Conflicts erupted over both the legitimacy of new rules such as abortion rights and over proposed extensions of family law changes to include relationships such as same-sex couples.

Critical to all the reactions was a second defining feature of American family law: the ongoing presence of civil society as an alternative source of power to the state. This was manifested in the emergence of groups like the Moral Majority and the National Abortion Rights Action League as critical actors in family law controversies. The agents and agencies of civil society have held a prominent place in the construction and application of Anglo-American family law since the late nineteenth century. And they did in this era as well. Indeed abortion law became a major battlefield of conflicting associations that used litigation and lobbying as their primarily tools of legal action.[70]

Reaction manifested itself in a number of ways. One of the most significant was the emergence of self-designated communitarians as searching critics of a transformed American family law. They charged that legal change had tilted domestic relations rules too far toward individual autonomy and away from common social interests. Sociologist David Popenoe, for instance, argues:

Marriage has become less a well-established and revered *social* institution, one shaped by moral imperatives and in which all people are expected to participate over the course of their adult lives, and more a private relationship based on

---

[69] LINDA GORDON, HEROES OF THEIR OWN LIVES : THE POLITICS AND HISTORY OF FAMILY VIOLENCE: BOSTON, 1880–1968 3 (1988).

[70] For 19th-c examples, see GROSSBERG, GOVERNING, n 2 above. For a full analysis of role of organized interest groups and foundations in one area of family law, family planning, see CRITCHLOW, n 65 above.

personal choice and the needs for personal fulfillment. It might be said that 'till death do us part' has been replaced by 'so long as I am happy.'[71]

Communitarian advocates like Glendon contended that the transformed family law rules promoted atomistic individuals and a contractual perspective that only recognized obligations produced by consent and thus undermined a needed sense of family loyalty and responsibility. She and others feared that as a result family responsibilities were understood as far less binding than they had been under the previous family law regime.[72]

Reactions to family law change like these affected every category of American domestic relations law. They generated not simply opposition, but also legal revisions that altered the newly transformed rules and practices. Abortion is a particularly evocative example of the rise and impact of reaction because it generated some of the most intense and even violent resistance to family law change. *Roe v Wade*'s sanction of early term abortions made one issue become a rallying point for resistance to the transformed family law. As Eva R. Rubin explained,

The abortion issue provided a moral rallying point for cultural fundamentalists who were unnerved by the pace of social change. The fetus has become a symbol of larger concerns—family dissolution, morality, secularism. Abortion intersected with a number of specific social issues with which social conservatives were concerned: sex education, women's rights, teenage promiscuity and pregnancy, divorce, changing sex and family roles, the secularization of society, pornography and the loss of religious values. To all of these dissatisfactions, the abortion issue had given a focus.[73]

As a result, opposition to abortion helped generate broader movements of reaction that treated the family law changes as linked policies and thus common objects of attack.

Anti-abortion agitation also had direct legal consequences. Indeed, the law, particularly judicial rulings, framed both resistance to abortion rights and their defense. Historian Donald Critchlow maintains that the 'abortion issue transformed American politics, as proabortion and antiabortion groups carried their fight to state legislatures and the federal courts. These battles on the state level and subsequent court rulings provided the backdrop for federal abortion policy in Congress and the presidency. So poignant was the abortion issue that it affected every facet of American political life.'[74] Nationally, foes of abortion tried to

---

[71] David Popenoe, *A Demographic Picture of the American Family Today—and What It Means*, in Christopher Wolfe (ed), THE FAMILY, CIVIL SOCIETY, AND THE STATE 73 (1998).

[72] For a broad statement of communitarian concerns, see Jean Bethke Elshtain, *A Call to Civil Society*, 36 SOCIETY 11–20 (July/Aug 1999).   [73] RUBIN, n 25 above, at 75–6.

[74] CRITCHLOW, n 65 above, at 200.

repeal *Roe* by championing the enactment of a constitutional amendment banning abortion and by campaigning to limit its use through prohibitions on federal funding for abortion. In the states they tried to
prescribe its use through restrictive regulations. Their efforts resulted in
the introduction of hundreds of legislative acts, many of which were
passed. By 1990 thirty-eight states had imposed restrictions on abortion
designed to limit its use through such tactics as bans on advertising and
public funding, rules that required informed consent from parents or
spouses of women seeking abortions, and mandates for special licenses
and reporting rules for doctors who performed abortion. These acts,
along with the continued anti-abortion agitation, also led many hospitals to refuse to perform abortions. And yet legislative restrictions
turned the courts into the central arenas of struggle for opponents and
supporters of abortion rights. And the courts, the primary authors of
the new family law regime, could not satisfy either group even though
the Supreme Court had issued over twenty major abortion decisions by
the mid-1990s. These rulings upheld the central doctrines of *Roe*, but
they also granted state legislatures the right to impose many of the new
regulatory controls on abortion. And thus the 'entangling web of litigation on both the state and federal levels during the next two decades
placed the Supreme Court in the role of a regulator, minutely determining which state laws were acceptable or unacceptable.'[75] Yet despite
the intense reaction and tightened regulations, the previous bans were
not reimposed and abortion remained a central tenet of the new family
law regime.

Resistance also arose to the notion of autonomous children's rights and
thus renewed the debate over the legal status of the youngest members
of families. Amid fears of mounting risks for the young—parental abuse,
teenage pregnancy, suicide, and drug addiction, gang membership—the
children's rights movement itself faced growing opposition. Critics
reversed the terms of debate and argued that more rights put children at
risk instead of helping them. A growing number of opponents charged
that increased rights had undermined child welfare by fostering adversarial family relations and weakening necessary parental and school
authority. In 1976 law professor Bruce Hafen warned: 'serious risks are
involved in an uncritical transfer of egalitarian concepts from the
contexts in which they developed to the unique context of family life and
children.' He argued, 'the most harmful of the potential consequences is
that the long-range interests of children themselves may be irreparably
damaged as the state and parents abandon children to their rights.' He

---

[75] CRITCHLOW, n 65 above, at 200–1; see also Gerald N. Rosenberg, *The Hollow Hope: Can
Courts Bring About Social Change?* 173–201 (1991).

even asserted that the right not to be abandoned to rights may well be the young's most basic right.[76]

Once again reaction led to legal change. States began to revise some of their earlier policies. For instance, in 1971 Michigan had lowered the minimum age for purchasing alcoholic beverages from 21 to 18 as part of a larger revision of children's rights in order to align state policies with the newly enacted Twenty-Sixth Amendment that had lowered the voting age to 18. Seven years later, though, Michigan voters reconsidered the issue and hiked the drinking age back up to 21. And in 1980 they turned back a proposal to lower the minimum age, this time to the nineteenth birthday.[77] Similarly, the rights of young women were circumscribed in many states by new abortion restrictions that were premised on the conviction that abortion is a family matter and not simply one for an individual child. The courts backed away from initial support of minors' rights to uphold statutes that required parental or judicial consent before a minor could obtain an abortion.[78] Legal changes like these occurred amid stories of children suing their parents, calls for the return to *in loco parentis* at colleges and universities, and renewed defenses of corporal punishment that included a backlash from parents who felt that an Orwellian state had used child abuse laws to overreach itself and tilt state regulation of parents too far. As a result, restriction took center stage in debates over children's rights.[79]

Escalating divorce rates and fears for family stability also fed reactions to family law change and led to renewed disputes over the legal regulation of marriage and divorce. Opposition groups contended that no-fault divorce tilted the law too much toward individual choice and too much against marital permanence. In addition, according to historian Stephen Mintz, some critics complained that the no-fault divorce system 'does a poor job of protecting the welfare of children, who are involved in about two-thirds of all divorces.' And some feminist legal scholars argued that under the new rules divorced women were 'deprived of the financial support they need. Under no-fault laws many older women, who would have been entitled to lifelong alimony or substantial child support payments under old fault statutes, find it extremely difficult to support their families.'[80] Equally significant in understanding the depth and

[76] See Bruce Hafen, *Children's Liberation and the New Egalitarianism: Some Reservations about Abandoning Children to their 'Rights'*, 1976 BYU L Rev 607, 656.

[77] See ZIMRING, n 33 above, at 3–4.

[78] See *Ohio v Akron Center for Reproductive Health*, 110 S Ct 2972 (1990); *Hodgson v Minnesota*, 110 S Ct 2926 (1990); *Planned Parenthood v Ashcroft*, 462 US 476 (1983); *HL v Mathewson*, 450 US 398 (1981).   [79] See RUBIN, n 25 above, at 70, 110–11.

[80] MINTZ, n 8 above, at 194; see also generally MARTHA L. FINEMAN, THE ILLUSION OF EQUALITY: THE RHETORIC AND REALITY OF DIVORCE REFORM (1991); HERBERT JACOB, SILENT REVOLUTION: THE TRANSFORMATION OF DIVORCE LAW IN THE UNITED STATES (1988).

implications of the reaction to family law changes have been studies that document popular resistance to no-fault. Phillips concluded that

[i]t is questionable how far the no-fault principles of modern divorce laws have penetrated spouses' perceptions of marriage breakdown. They are still predominately expressed in terms of fault, and in many cases, such as where there is violence and exploitation, quite rightly so, even if neither spouse can be exonerated entirely. The social implications of marriage breakdown have been mitigated as the social stigma attached to divorce has declined and as husbands and wives are no longer required to give details of their marriages in court. But within the private sphere of marriage, the pain and bitterness of marriage breakdown persists.[81]

Studies of divorcing men and women reveal the consistent determination of divorcing spouses to seek public declarations of fault. After surveying such studies, Law Professor Barbara Bennett Woodhouse decided that 'spousal hostility and blaming have a life of their own, regardless of whether the law looks to substantive standards of fault.' She found that most couples often settled out of court with the 'guilty' spouse compensating the 'innocent' spouse with a relatively generous settlement, and that those husbands and wives unable to dissolve their unions out of court fought on until a winner was named or judges called a draw and awarded joint custody.[82] A New Jersey divorce attorney captured this reality with declaration: 'My angry clients need closure. They will not quit until they get the judge to tell them who was right and who was wrong.'[83] Similarly, socio-legal scholars William Felstiner and Austin Sarat discovered that clients wanted personal validation for their marital behavior from their attorneys despite the lawyers' advice that such pronouncements were now irrelevant to the process of marital dissolution.[84]

Covenant marriage has been another revealing reaction to mounting concerns about individual marital responsibility. Under that system in Arizona[85] and Louisiana,[86] a couple can elect one of two marriage regimes: the traditional one based on no-fault divorce rules, and covenant marriage that requires premarital counseling and is governed by traditional fault ground for divorce. As sociologist Steven L. Nock notes, 'Covenant marriage laws are the first in over 200 years in America designed explicitly to make marriage more permanent and divorce more restrictive.'[87]

---

[81] PHILIPS, n 14 above, at 627.   [82] See Woodhouse, *Sex, Lies*, n 17 above, at 2548–9.
[83] Cited *ibid* at 2549.
[84] See generally WILLIAM FELSTINER and AUSTIN SARAT, DIVORCE LAWYERS AND THEIR CLIENTS, POWER AND MEANING IN THE LEGAL PROCESS (1995).
[85] See Louisana Act 1380 (1977), amending LA CIV CODE arts 102, 103 and LA REV STAT § 9: 245 and adding § 9: 225 (A)(3), §§ 9: 307–9: 309.
[86] See S 1133, 43d Leg, 2d Reg Sess (Ariz 1998) (codified at ARIZ REV STAT ANN § 9 (West 1998).   [87] Nock, n 14 above, at 26.

Same-sex marriage has become an even more contentious issue than no-fault divorce. It has provoked the fear that even more family law change will occur if gay and lesbian unions are considered the logical result of a transformed marriage law that places individual choice at its center and state restrictions at its periphery. It too has stirred strident reactions. Opponents of same-sex marriage argue that recognizing such unions would undermine the institution of marriage and the role it plays in maintaining social stability. Thus Walter Burns insists that gay and lesbian leaders 'are obviously after bigger game' than equal treatment alone. Rather, he maintains, 'they want to change the marriage laws because they want to change the culture . . . [T]hey view themselves as part of the broader counterculture movement,' whose purpose 'is to undermine the traditional idea of the family: The family is the building block of society, the family of mothers and fathers who naturally care for their children' and who 'care for the society in which those children will have to live.'[88] Some opponents dismiss same-sex unions as unnatural, immoral, or sinful. Still others argue that recognizing such marriages would promote the spread of homosexuality and present an unhealthy, confusing environment for children.

Such sentiments have meant that same-sex couples, like interracial, polygamous, bohemian unions, and other outsider unions before them, have borne much of the reaction to family law change. For those who resist further family law change, same-sex unions have become the 'other' of marriage law, held up to define unwanted marital partners and unwanted marriages. They have spurred demands for a return of orthodoxy. Hafen, for instance, asserts, 'My central point is that American society should more clearly, consistently, and forcefully articulate a position that reenthrones heterosexual marriage as a crucial and highly preferred element in perpetuating both personal liberty and social stability.'[89] The impact of this reaction was evident in a recent symposium commemorating the thirtieth anniversary of *Loving v Virginia*, which overturned bans on interracial marriage. The implications of the decision for same-sex marriage quickly became a focal point of discussion with participants arrayed on both sides of the question.[90]

Again reaction has been translated into legal conflict and legal revisionism that have modified the apparent trajectory of family law change. This was particularly apparent in the wake of decisions by the Hawaii Supreme Court in the 1990s on the legality of same-sex marriage.

---

[88] Quoted in Bruce C. Hafen, *The Legal Definition and Status of Marriage, in* Christopher Wolfe (ed), THE FAMILY, CIVIL SOCIETY, AND THE STATE 107 (1999).   [89] *ibid* at 111.
[90] See *Symposium: Law and the Politics of Marriage: Loving v Virginia after 30 Years*, 47 CATH U L REV 1207 (1998).

In *Baehr v Lewin* the court ruled that the state's refusal to grant marriage licenses to three same-sex couples violated the Hawaii's constitutional ban on discrimination. The justices concluded that the ban amounted to discrimination on the basis of sex and sexual orientation, and thus that it could only be justified on the ground of a valid state interest in denying such unions.[91] Then in *Baehr v Miike* the court concluded that the state had not met this requirement.[92] State voters responded with a constitutional amendment exempting marriage from the state's equal protection clause. Fears that conflict of law rules and the Full Faith and Credit Clause of the United States Constitution would compel other states to recognize such unions led to state and congressional actions around the republic. Tellingly, the congressional 'Defense of Marriage Act,' promulgated by Republicans in 1996 and signed immediately by President Clinton, was directed primarily at same-sex marriage, not the more common marital experience of divorce. It defined marriage exclusively in heterosexual terms as 'a legal union between one man and one woman as husband and wife.' It also permitted states not to recognize marriages from any states not following this model.[93] As of April 2000, thirty-one states had passed legislation barring same-sex marriage.[94]

Reaction challenged and even modified the new American family law. And it clearly had a major impact on the trajectory of change in the law. However, it did not overturn the fundamental tenets of the new domestic relations regime. Nevertheless, reaction dominated family law debate and conflict in the final decades of the twentieth century as Americans struggled to incorporate the legal transformation of the era into their lives and their law.

CONCLUSIONS

I have tried to meet the challenge of writing a relevant historical introduction to recent United States family law by analyzing the era in terms of family law transformations, continuities, and reactions. Of necessity I have had to traverse some rather familiar terrain. My intent in doing so has been to suggest ways of thinking about the emergence of a new family law regime over the last several decades by making this era a part of the past.

[91] See 852 P 2d 44 (Hawaii Sup Ct 1993).
[92] See 23 FAM L REP (BNA) 2001 (Dec 10, 1996).   [93] See 28 USCS Sec 1738c (1996).
[94] These states are: Alabama, Alaska, Arizona, Arkansas, California, Colorado, Florida, Georgia, Idaho, Illinois, Indiana, Iowa, Kansas, Kentucky, Louisiana, Maine, Michigan, Minnesota, Montana, Mississippi, North Carolina, North Dakota, Oklahoma, Pennsylvania, South Carolina, South Dakota, Tennessee, Utah, Virginia, Washington, West Virginia. See Lambda Legal Defense and Education Fund, *State-by-State Anti-Marriage Laws* (visited Apr 10, 2000) <http://www.lambdalegal.org/cgi-bin/pages/states/antimarriage-map>.

Since 1950 basic changes have clearly altered the governance of the family and the content of family law. A new era began because change outweighed continuities and has not been significantly displaced by reactions. And yet the interaction of transformation, continuity, and reaction is critical to understanding the period and how it has framed the present and will help determine the future. Change was consistently tempered by continuities and reactions that limited the breadth and depth of family law innovation by challenging, modifying, and changing emerging legal rules and practices. As a result, the domestic relations transformation was not a wholesale renovation of the law, but rather a selective alteration that left much in place. Most importantly, the underlying structure of the law persisted and acted to channel change and thus link the law's present to its past. And that reality suggests that the changes of the era produced a new regime that must itself be understood as contingent and subject to further change.

Transformation, continuity, and reaction framed the major family law debates of the years 1950–2000. They remain important critical sources of the current pressures and predicaments facing American families. Only by viewing all of these forces can we begin to acquire a full understanding of the republic's new domestic relations law regime and why it makes American family law seem like such a more complicated place than it was in 1950.

2

Changing Family Patterns in England and Wales over the Last Fifty Years

COLIN GIBSON

This chapter aims to set down and examine the major demographic trends and social changes within the family structure of England and Wales between 1950 and 1999. The current population of England and Wales is some fifty-two million. The two countries form some nine-tenths (91 per cent) of the population of the three countries (England, Scotland, and Wales) that constitute Great Britain (henceforth Britain for brevity). Some important official sources of data refer only to Britain (ie *The General Household Survey*); it is proper to relate such information to the changing social structure of England and Wales (henceforth England). However, text and table figures refer to England unless otherwise stated.

Changing social mores have helped modify the traditional attitude that the nuclear conjugal family was the expected setting in which to raise children. An increasing proportion of dependent children will experience family settings with one parent present, or within partnerships formed by unmarried couples, or households formed by parent and step-parent families. And, of course, the permutations can be extended.

HOUSEHOLD PATTERNS

The proportion of households comprising a couple with children has been steadily falling in Britain since 1960. This period has seen the percentage of all households formed by single-family households with dependent children living in the home decline by 61 per cent between 1961 (38 per cent) and 1998 (23 per cent).[1] The same period has experienced a noticeable move towards people living alone; the proportion formed by such single households has increased from 11 per cent to 28 per cent. This change towards single-residence housing is partly explained by the growing propensity for younger people to live alone; the mounting number of casualities of failed partnerships; and the increasing longevity among older widowed citizens. Over the same time the proportion of households

---

[1] Office of National Statistics, *Social Trends* 29. London: The Stationery Office (1999) 42.

headed by a lone parent with dependent children has increased from 2 per cent to 7 per cent. These movements appear likely to continue.

PARTNERSHIP MOVEMENTS

Marriage

The last quarter century has seen a noticeable movement away from traditional patterns. Marriage is now a less-accepted institution, as reflected in the following interrelated trends. Comparison is made between current figures and those for 1971; the latter being a time when marriage formation was recording historically high popularity.

1. The number of marriages in which both spouses are single has declined to the lowest number this century; and has halved since 1971 (Table 2.1). Four out of ten marriages link at least one spouse who has been previously married; second marriages mainly involve the divorced.

TABLE 2.1. *Marriage changes: 1951–1997*

Features	1951	1961	1971	1981	1991	1997
Number: first marriages for both parties (,000)	293	294	320	228	192	156
Number: all marriages (,000)	361	347	405	352	307	271
Proportion: 'first' to 'all' marriages (%)	81	85	79	65	63	58
Spinster: mean age at marriage	24.4	23.3	22.6	23.1	25.5	27.5
Spinster: age under 20 at marriage (%)	17	29	31	24	8	5

2. The above former pattern incorporates an expanding minority's readiness to reject marriage in preference for either the single state or extramarital cohabitation. This belief is given credence by calculations from the Office of Population, Censuses and Surveys which forecasts that 5 per cent of girls aged 16 in 1974 will be unmarried at 50; a similar-aged 1991 cohort projects 26 per cent.[2] This fivefold increase in less than two decades indicates rapidly changing social attitudes towards the appropriateness of traditional marriage. Yet the British experience of the 1990s suggests that 30 per cent could be a more realistic estimate of the 1991 cohort of women remaining unmarried. Men are showing a similar

[2] OPCS *Monitor* FM2 No 18.

propensity to remain single. Half of all men aged between 30 and 44 in 2021 will have remained single; though many will have experienced extramarital relationships. One in seven (14 per cent) of all households in Britain in 1998 consisted of single adults under pensionable age; this proportion has doubled since 1971. This evidence reflects an increasing trend for men and women to choose single-state lives, a reflection of an individualistic society in which the risk of a partnership commitment is less willingly embarked upon. The flight from the early marriage patterns of the 1970s is associated with a greater likelihood that adult children will continue to live at home with their parents.

3. The average age at first marriage is increasing rapidly for both men and women. Today's spinster bride is now marrying at an older average age (1997: 27.5 years) than at any time since official figures were first published in 1846. Similar trends have occurred in mainland Europe. This is linked to the increasing rate of premarital cohabitation.

We are witnessing important demographic and social changes in long-held habits, and it is as yet uncertain where they will lead. What is clear is that couples are increasingly living together in stable relationships and raising children out of wedlock.

Extra-marital Cohabitation

Extra-marital cohabitation has now become an important constituent of modern-day family life. *The General Household Survey* shows that the proportion of non-married women aged 18 to 49 who were cohabiting in Britain has doubled between 1981 and 1996–7 to 25 per cent.[3] This movement is a partial reflection of the flight from marriage enrolment that is most evident among the single category. Current evidence for England from the Office for National Statistics suggests that the popularity of cohabitation as a partnership arrangement will significantly increase over the next two decades. The number of cohabiting couples is forecast to double, rising from 1.56 million in 1996 to nearly 3 million by 2021.[4] This trend once again raises both family policy and legal questions concerning rights and obligations within extra-marital relationships. For instance, in inheritance legislation our current taxation policy provides financial advantage to the wife upon her husband's death. By 2021, 6 per cent of men over 55 will be cohabiting.

In broad terms, cohabitation can lead to the couple either: marrying, ending the relationship, or continuing together for a long period. Each

[3] Office of National Statistics, n 1 above, 46.
[4] C. Shaw and J. Haskey, 'New Estimates and Projections of the Population Cohabiting in England and Wales', (1999) 95 *Population Trends* 7.

group displays different characteristics, but there is also variation in practice and attitude within the individual groups. In the new patterns of
family life it is clear that extramarital cohabitation has also become a
partial replacement for marriage. In Scandinavian countries many cohabiting couples no longer consider marriage as the necessary outcome for
pregnancy or child rearing. Such attitudes are now being established in
England. One in sixteen of all dependent children are now being raised
by couples living together in stable extramarital relationships.[5] This feature of contemporary family life means that marriage and parenthood are
no longer inextricably linked for an increasing proportion of society. The
majority of unmarried cohabiting parents will eventually marry, though
a significant minority either continue cohabiting or separate. A characteristic of long-term cohabiting mothers found in McRae's 1992 survey[6]
was that a quarter of the households lacked a wage-earner, and a fifth of
all the fathers had been unemployed for two or more years. The low-
income, poorly educated mother has less economic incentive to marry
when the man cannot, or will not, offer long-term support.

Premarital Cohabitation

Premarital cohabitation has now become the customary route into marriage. Such arrangements in the supposedly liberal 1960s were a very
uncommon practice. Evidence for Britain shows that only 5 per cent of
spinster brides who married in the mid-1960s had lived with their husbands before marriage; this increased steadily to 70 per cent for those
who married in the early 1990s.[7] The date of marriage has become an
increasingly unsatisfactory boundary mark to record such matters as
duration of the couple's overall cohabitation or child-spacing patterns.

The highest rates of premarital cohabitation occur among the previously divorced. For the latter, memories of marital unhappiness and an
increased worldliness have helped cohabitation to become an institutionalized part of premarriage selection patterns. By the early 1990s nine out
of ten women marrying for the second time in Britain (consisting largely
of the divorced) had previously lived with their husbands. It is also the
case that postmarital cohabitation as a long-term alternative to marriage
is becoming a mutual choice for the divorced. Figures for 1991–2 indicate
a quarter (26 per cent) of all divorced British women under 60 were in
consensual unions. Within the age group 35–49 previously divorced

---

[5] J. Haskey, 'Population Review (6) Families and Households in Great Britain', (1996) 85 *Population Trends* 10.

[6] S. McRae, *Cohabiting Mothers: Changing Marriage and Motherhood*. London: Policy Studies
Institute (1993).

[7] J. Haskey, 'Trends in Marriage and Cohabitation, The Decline in Marriage and the Changing Pattern of Living in Partnership', (1995) 80 *Population Trends* 5.

women were far more likely to be in such a union (29 per cent) than were widows (4 per cent).[8] This variation in lifestyles might be an indicator of the divorcees' more unorthodox attitudes and weaker commitment to the institution of marriage.

Ending cohabitation

Marriage is the most likely outcome for couples in an extramarital partnership. Some six out of ten women in Britain who leave a cohabiting relationship do so to marry their partner; for the remaining women the partnership ceases.[9] An increasing number of men and women will experience a succession of long-term relationships that end in breakdown. Within many households there will, of course, be children. Upon separation, cohabiting couples experience similar emotional, economic and legal problems as the divorced. It is no longer demographically feasible to examine the impact of relationship breakdown upon both adults and children without giving study to extramarital cohabitation and its repercussions on family life and habit. It is a contentious question as to how the lawmakers should react to the new lifestyles that have emerged in western industrial society.

Breakdown Risk

Cohabitation as a lifestyle generally does appear to have greater risks of breakdown compared with marriage. Survey findings suggest children of a cohabiting relationship have an increased likelihood of experiencing parental breakdown than if they had been born within marriage.[10] Further evidence found that, after controlling for all economic and other factors, the risk of breakdown experienced by cohabiting parents still remained twice that of married parents.[11]

This increasing tendency to live together before marriage should theoretically brush apart some couples whose unsuitability for life membership of the marriage club would have emerged after enrolment. In practice, however, premarital cohabiting couples do appear to have greater vulnerability to marital breakdown—though the imputing features need to be qualified. Evidence from the 1989 *General Household Survey* of Britain found that the divorce risk of premarital cohabitants narrows, but does not disappear, when the duration period for compari-

---

[8] Office of National Statistics, Social Trends, London: The Stationery Office (1995) 39.
[9] Office of National Statistics, n 1 above, 47.
[10] Office of National Statistics, n 1 above, 51.
[11] P. Morgan, 'An Endangered Species?' in M. David (ed), *The Fragmenting Family: Does It Matter?* London: The IEA Health and Welfare Unit (1996) 76. See also M. Maclean and J. Eekelaar, *The Parental Obligation,* Oxford: Hart Publishing (1998), showing higher and quicker breakdowns between unmarried than between married parents.

son with traditional couples becomes the premaritally cohabiting couples' total time together. For example, when duration of fifteen years' *de facto* union together becomes the contrast point, the premaritally cohabiting couples still record a 20 per cent higher divorce level.[12] The initial British Household Panel Survey data reported that those in the study who were divorced or separated were about a third more likely to have lived together before marriage than were the still married. This latter conclusion has been modified by recent work on the National Child Development Study (a longitudinal survey which interviewed a sample of people now aged 33). The NCDS material suggests that those experiencing premarital cohabitation are no more at risk of marriage breakdown than those who are not. Rather, the risk-producing element is whether either partner has already experienced one or more earlier similar relationships.[13] The relevance of these findings is the qualified association between premarital cohabitation and the increased probability of divorce (though it is not being argued that the former causes the latter). Within the contemporary demographic recipe the increasing likelihood of earlier premarital cohabitations is an ingredient which, by itself, suggests an increase in the rate of divorce.

The evidence of this section underlines that these contemporary changes in marriage are a fundamental amendment to earlier custom. The turnabout has occurred within a relatively short period, and it is increasing rapidly in momentum.

FAMILY FORMATION AND PARENTHOOD

Fertility Patterns

Women are experiencing smaller families and later motherhood compared with their mothers. Data for births in England show that women born in each decade since 1937 have given birth to fewer children on average than those born in the preceding decade, and that births occur later in a woman's life.[14] Childbearing and marriage no longer have the strong association of fifty years ago. Births outside marriage now make a significant input to our overall fertility rate (annual live births per 1,000 women).

---

[12] J. Haskey, 'Pre-marital Cohabitation and the Probability of Subsequent Divorce: Analyses Using New Data from the General Household Survey', (1992) 68 *Population Trends* 10, at 16–17.

[13] K. Kiernan and G. Mueller, 'Who divorces?' in S. McRae (ed), *Changing Britain: Families and Households in the 1990s*. Oxford: Oxford University Press (1999) 396–7.

[14] Office of National Statistics, n 1 above, 34.

Fertility Decline

The last forty years have recorded a significant decline in the propensity of women to bear children as indicated by Table 2.2, which reports a one-third decline in the overall fertility rate between 1961 (90) and 1997 (60). The rate substantially fell between the end of the baby boom years of the early 1960s and 1977.[15] It has remained fairly stable since 1980, though fluctuations have occurred in different age groups. If current British fertility rates continue to operate throughout a woman's childbearing span, the completed family size would be 1.7 children. There has been a steady rise in the number of women who have never had a child. The majority of these women remain childless through choice. Attitude surveys indicate a significant minority of younger women declaring that they do not intend to have children; the evidence shows that they mean it. Only 11 per cent of women born nearly sixty years ago (1942) remained childless at 45; for women born thirty years later it is projected that the proportion will increase to almost a quarter.[16]

TABLE 2.2. *Fertility changes: 1961–1997*

Features	1961	1971	1981	1991	1997
Live births (,000)	811	783	634	699	642
Extramarital rate (as % of live births)	5	8	13	30	37
Fertility rate (per 1,000 women aged 15–44)	90	81	62	64	60
Average age of married mother*	27.7	26.4	27.2	28.9	30.4
Child deaths under 1 year (per 1,000 live births)	21	18	11	7	6
Mothers under 20 years: (*a*) births (,000)	66	92	63	58	52
(*b*) extramarital rate (as % of *a*)	20	26	46	83	88

* For Britain.

A partial consequence of contemporary marriage patterns is the deferment of childbearing leading to a later age in marital motherhood. In 1971 only 22 per cent of marital births in Britain were to wives aged 30 or more; by 1997 the proportion had become 53 per cent. The movement to later child rearing has led to the mother's child-bearing age now averaging 30 years (Table 2.2), a figure below that of most West European countries.

[15] B. Armitage and P. Babb, 'Population Review: (4) Trends in fertility', (1996) 84 *Population Trends* 7.

[16] Office of National Statistics, n 1 above, 53.

Contraception and Abortion

The vast majority (some 90 per cent) of women under 50 who are sexually active utilize some form of contraception.[17] Development of oral contraceptives and IUDs has allowed women to be mistresses of their own fertility and time of mothering, and this reformation in demographic pattern and familial habit has modified motherhood so that it now occupies only a small part of their lives.

Abortion is available as a safety net against unwanted pregnancies; it is the ultimate method of birth control. With the introduction of the 1967 Abortion Act in 1968, the number of abortions rapidly rose to 167,000 in 1973. Since then the annual number has never fallen below 130,000. Following a medical warning over the contraceptive pill in October 1995 abortions increased to 170,000 in 1997. These figures suggest that one in five conceptions (excluding spontaneous abortions) are medically terminated. Such numbers and rates reflect ignorance, or unwillingness, by a significant minority of adults always effectively to use reliable methods of pregnancy prevention. The ethical, medical and feminist debates concerning the justification for abortion continue. The increasing survival of very premature babies has once more focused minds on basic questions concerning the foetal form.

Parenthood

Very few parents now experience the grief of losing their child through death in its vulnerable first year. Improved standards of child rearing, health, and environmental conditions have helped reduce infant mortality to the lowest recorded rate of 6 deaths per 1,000 live births (Table 2.2). It remains the case that two parents continue to raise the majority of dependent children. Four-fifths (79 per cent) of children in Britain lived in such families in 1998; though this is a noticeable decline from 1972 when over nine-tenths (92 per cent) of children lived in couple families.[18] However, a larger proportion of dependent children will experience a single-parent household than are presented by such statistics because of the possibility of later parental breakdown.

It is not only that family size is now smaller, but also that women reach their desired completed family size more quickly than did mothers fifty years ago. Today, nine out of ten couples will complete their family size within ten years of marriage. Parental desire to control the spacing and size of their families, linked with the promotion of acceptable and

---

[17] Calculations based upon Office of National Statistics, n 1 above, 52.
[18] Office of National Statistics, n 1 above, 43.

efficient methods of family planning, have resulted in couples generally having wanted children.

Extramarital Families

The last quarter-century has witnessed an escalation in the rate of extramarital births in England (Table 2.2). In 1961 extramarital births formed 5 per cent of all live births (a percentage, excepting the two war periods, that had hardly fluctuated since 1900), and 1971 recorded a relatively low 8 per cent. The 1980s experienced a particularly steep rise, increasing from 13 per cent in 1981 to 30 per cent in 1991. This leap was largely a consequence of the input of extramarital cohabiting unions to the existing social and demographic patterns. By 1999 almost four in ten children were born outside marriage.

The majority of mothers experiencing births outside marriage do have the father providing some acknowledgement of his new status and paternity. At the birth's registration some four-fifths of the fathers jointly record their name with that of the mother.[19] Three-quarters of such registrations recorded a similar parental address; this strongly suggests an ongoing relationship in six out of ten births. It is probable that many of these couples will eventually marry; none the less it remains the case that unmarried pregnancy no longer creates the social pressures towards marriage that still existed in the early 1970s.

It is the younger (under 20) unmarried mother who is most likely to lack meaningful links with the father. In 29 per cent of such births the mother solely registered the birth. Survey findings present the low level of paternal commitment; half the interviewed mothers reported that within one year of birth the earlier ongoing relationship with the baby's father had ceased.[20] Whereas in 1971 an extramarital pregnancy would generally lead to marriage, today only a tenth of such infants will be born into a marital union. (Though with younger age at marriage comes the associated increased risk of divorce.) As well as cohabitation, some of the associated characteristics that facilitate the high rate of lone parenthood among younger vulnerable women are: changing attitudes among both under-achieving younger men and women and their parents, greater range of life choices, high unemployment among younger males, fatalistic attitudes among sexually active teenagers, welfare support structures, the mothers' low levels of education with limited career choices and a general disdain, and unprotected sex. Young unmarried mothers have

---

[19] Office of National Statistics, n 1 above, 50.

[20] I. Allen and S. Dowling, 'Teenage Mothers: Decisions and Outcomes', in S. McRae (ed), *Changing Britain: Families and Households in the 1990s*. Oxford: Oxford University Press (1999) 351/; M. Maclean and J. Eekelaar, n 11 above.

helped to make the single lone mother family group increase at a faster rate during the 1990s than any of the other family forms.

Step-parenting

The increase in lone parenthood and subsequent new partnerships means that about 8 per cent of children in Britain live in stepfamilies; this compares with 5 per cent in 1979.[21] Two-thirds of such families are a consequence of either marriage or remarriage; while a third are headed by cohabiting couples, with the associated higher breakdown risk than if married.

The New Technologies

New medical and genetic knowledge and techniques have extended the nature and meaning of parenthood. The new technologies have allowed post-menopausal women to bear children, dead men to sire children, genes to be manipulated, while human cloning cannot be far away. The rapid and radical developments witnessed in the last twenty years suggest that the overused concept of revolution can properly be applied to this enormous arena of private and public choices. It is inescapable that the exponential expansion of discovery and capability in reproductive technologies and genetic engineering will present the new century with awesome moral and bioethical quandaries.

The full impact of the new technologies upon demographic patterns has yet to come, and it remains uncertain to what extent these new skills will transform future family choices. This argument can be seen in the area of in vitro fertilization (IVF), which became available in the United Kingdom in 1978. IVF—where the egg is removed from the woman for fertilization before being returned to the womb—highlights the expansion of medical advances in, and individual recourse to, infertility therapy. The number of treatment cycles has increased dramatically in the United Kingdom (Britain and Northern Ireland), the 33,520 cycles in 1996–7 being nearly five times the 1986 figure. Improved techniques over the ten-year period have doubled the chances of treatment generating births to 17 per cent.[22] These recent figures suggest that parenthood has been laboratory-conceived for some 5,000 happy couples. One consequence of IVF treatment has been an increase in multiple births, with health and social care implications for both parents and society.

---

[21] P. Newman and A. Smith, *Social Focus on Families*. London: HMSO (1997) 27.
[22] Office of National Statistics, n 1 above, 53.

Birth rates in Western Europe have fallen below replacement levels and we are experiencing a generalized ageing process. It is not that the maximum lifespan has been extended as yet, but that a larger proportion of men and women than ever before are experiencing longevity. This is particularly noticeable for women; a woman aged 60 can expect to live a further twenty-three years, an increase of four years compared with 1961. The same actuarial tables underline nature's discrimination in matters of life and death. Newborn girls have a lifespan of 80 years, five years longer than their brothers. A fifth of the population is now aged 65 or over. The ageing population, and the linked reduction in the income-tax paying workforce, has led the government to announce the equalization of the age at which men and women receive the state old age retirement pension to be 65, starting in April 2010. The pension policy of earlier times has meant woman receiving this pension five years before their menfolk.

Longevity and its Impact

Longevity has lead to 7 per cent of the population having reached their seventy-fifth birthday, this proportion having doubled since 1951. There remain social class variations in mortality patterns that are a consequence of differing class life patterns in such areas as occupational and environmental hazards, housing, smoking, diet, and ignorance of medical provision. The elderly, defined as those aged 75 or more, are predominately women (65 per cent). The majority (some 60 per cent) of elderly women live alone; the majority (62 per cent) of similarly aged men still have their wives for companionship and mutual care. The increased divorce rate since 1960 has begun to influence the marital status of the elderly; Table 2.3 suggests this trend will intensify until a tenth of both elderly men and women will be divorced in 2021 compared to the current 3 per cent.

TABLE 2.3. *Distribution of the elderly by marital condition, 1971–2021*

Marital condition of those 75+	Males			Females		
	1971	1996	2021	1971	1996	2021
	(Percentages)			(Percentages)		
Never married	6	6	6	16	9	4
Married	58	62	62	19	24	33
Widowed	36	29	22	65	65	52
Divorced	(0.4)	3	10	(0.4)	3	11
Total number: (,000)	750	1,315	1,917	1,615	2,454	2,832

Longevity also allows a growing proportion of contented unions to continue to the fourth-age, though the partnerships increasingly begin later!

Care of the Very Elderly

One of the issues of the new century will be the responsibility placed by the very elderly (85+) on the scarce young. The very elderly have increased from less than a half per cent of the population of England fifty years ago to 2 per cent. These citizens number some one million, of whom three-quarters (74 per cent) are women. The propensity to be ill or disabled rises exponentially with advancing age. This means that the very elderly are far more likely to incur some need of care and attention than those aged between 60 and 85. Mental capacity can also become impaired: of all persons aged 80 or more, over one in five will suffer from some degree of dementia. This does not imply that the majority of the very old experience constant extreme dependency, but it does mean that outside assistance and help becomes necessary at regular intervals. Many of these same elderly are likely to be living alone. Their dominant source of caring continues to be the family, and it remains the case that daughters are expected to provide the major attention and services necessary to help the very elderly carry on within the community. Reduced family size produces a further reality: at least a quarter of the very elderly have no surviving children of either sex to provide care for them.

Policy Issues

Demographic certitude raises many questions concerning future policy towards the elderly, one of which is who will provide the care and under what conditions? Further related policy issues of care in old age that have disturbed our governments in the 1990s are the questions of who should meet the costs, and where obligations should lie. Should the provision of assistance for the elderly in need fall upon the state, the family or a mixture of both? There is no legal obligation upon children either to care for their parents or even to ensure their financial respectability. Such obligation—which was limited to elderly claimants for poor relief—was removed in 1948 with the dissolution of the Poor Law and the introduction of what we knew as the welfare state. Today, care of elderly parents by their children is a voluntary act of solicitude: bonds of attachment have displaced legal obligation. It is also the case that most older people requiring help do not wish to be a burden on kin but prefer to have professional carers.

From a family law perspective the analysis raises the question of who should speak for and protect the interests of those vulnerable elderly who are unable to decide their future. This is part of a broader issue of a person's capacity to give consent. These concerns can be seen in such fields as medical advancement and the ability to prolong life; or the coerced transfer of a house title to save inheritance tax for the children rather than continuing control by the elderly owner. Abuse of the elderly at home and in institutions and hospitals continues to give concern.

DIVORCE

The Divorce Reform Act 1969 instituted irretrievable breakdown as the new ground for divorce. The Act's introduction in 1971 led to an immediate surge of petitions. But the 1960s had already experienced an annual rise of 9.5 per cent to 70,575 petitions in 1970. Unchanged continuation of this yearly increase would have led to over 200,000 petitions by 1990 compared to the recorded 189,000 petitions. The 1969 legislation was partly an acknowledgement of the steadily increasing propensity to divorce, but its introduction did not lead to a long-term change in resort. Demographic analysis of English divorce patterns over the twentieth century shows that each succeeding age cohort registered a higher rate of divorce than the preceding generation.[23] The evidence suggests that the impact of liberal divorce legislation on the divorce rate has been of a short-term nature.

Numbers and Rates

Between 1970 and 1996 the number of divorces doubled. The decade 1981–90 displayed a fairly constant picture of around 150,000 divorces annually. The early years of the 1990s saw a slight increase on the 1980s pattern, peaking in 1993 with some 163,000 divorces. Since then the numbers have dropped to 146,000 in 1997, though this recent decline reflects the fall in the younger married population. Over the last half-century the marked trend towards divorce intensifies with more recent marriages. For instance, spinster brides aged 20–4 in 1961, when followed up twenty-five years later, had experienced twice the level of divorce (19 per cent) compared with a similar-age cohort who had married in 1951 (9 per cent).[24]

---

[23] C. S. Gibson, 'Contemporary Divorce and Changing Family Patterns', in M. Freeman (ed), *Divorce: Where Next?* Aldershot: Dartmouth (1996) 31.

[24] J. Haskey, 'Trends in Marriage and Divorce, and Cohort Analyses of the Proportions of Marriages Ending in Divorce' (1989) 54 *Population Trends* 21.

Divorce rates, by using the ongoing married population as a base for comparison with divorce numbers, provide a firmer indication of trends in the propensity to divorce. There has been a fivefold rise in the divorce rate in the thirty-five years between 1961 and 1996 (Table 2.4). From 1980 the divorce rate records some 13 in every 1,000 ongoing marriages being dissolved annually. Such a rate, if it continues at the 1993–4 divorce level and pattern, implies that around four in every ten newly formed marriages will ultimately end in divorce.[25] The United Kingdom now sustains the highest divorce rate within the European Union. Over the next two decades the rate of divorce seems set to remain at current levels; though divorce numbers are projected to fall further to around 110,000 in 2021.[26]

TABLE 2.4. *Annual number and rate of divorce: 1945–1997*

Year	Average*	Rate†
1946–50	40	3.7
1951–60	27	2.4
1961–70	40	3.3
1971–80	122	9.8
1981–90	151	12.6
1991–95	160	13.7
1996	156	13.8
1997	146	13.0

* Decrees absolute: dissolution and nullity, rounded to nearest thousand.
† Rate of divorce to every 1,000 of ongoing married population.

Divorce Facts

Proof of breakdown at the beginning of the new century continues to require establishing the occurrence of one of the following five supporting facts: adultery, 'ureasonable behaviour', desertion, separation for two or more years and consent, and separation for five or more years. Divorce reformers expected the three fault facts continuing within the 1969 Act—adultery, behaviour, and desertion—to decline in usage. The quarter-century since the implementation of 1971 of the Divorce Reform Act 1969 has shown this to be a false hope. In 1996 seven out of ten divorces were granted for either unreasonable behaviour (44 per cent) or adultery (26 per cent).[27] The 1969 Act had brought divorce by agreement into the statute book by

[25] Office of National Statistics, *Social Trends* 28. London: HMSO (1998) 51.
[26] C. Shaw, '1996-Based Population Projections by Legal Marital Status for England and Wales', (1999) 95 *Population Trends* 23.
[27] Office of National Statistics, *Marriage, Divorce and Adoption Statistics*, FM2 series 24 (1999).

way of the new two years separation fact. This way was intended to be the conciliatory civil approach to divorce for couples who recognized their relationship had irretrievably come apart. Yet the mutual consent fact has for most of the time since 1971 been used by no more than a quarter of all petitioners; in 1996 it was 23 per cent.

Wives were granted seven out of ten decrees obtained in 1996. Half the wives were granted divorce on the ground of their husband's unreasonable behaviour. It is the most commonly used fact because it allows the homemaker quick progress to court. Yet this same fact creates most bitterness and acrimony, and this can continue long after the divorce in situations where spousal association is maintained through paternal contact with the children. Criticism of the efficacy of the existing divorce process, and in particular its failure to encourage reconciliation, and its tendency to exacerbate hostility and conflict, led to new legislation in the form of the Family Law Act of 1996, not yet implemented.[28]

Demographic and Social Associates of Divorce

Age at Marriage

Those who marry at an earlier age not only experience greater risk of divorce but also are significantly more prone to earlier breakdown. However, it has already been seen how the habit of early marriage has rapidly declined over the last twenty-five years. Young bridal age (under 20) at marriage is numerically declining as a precipitating factor towards divorce. This changing pattern is reflected in the diminishing proportion of young brides within the overall divorcing population, from 38 per cent in 1980 to 19 per cent in 1996.

Age at Divorce

The age at divorce pattern has remained fairly constant over the last thirty years, with wives' median age at divorce rising slightly from 32.4 years in 1970 to 32.9 years in 1980, and 35.6 years in 1996. The more recent rise in the general population's age at marriage suggests that divorce age will show a slow but steady increase. The older wife is especially vulnerable to the financially debilitating consequences of marriage breakdown and divorce. Pressure to improve the claims of the divorcing wife upon the husband's pension scheme has led to remedying equitable legislation. In demographic terms this issue of financial support and compensation will grow because of the input of later marriage age and the build-up of

---

[28] See Smart, Ch 16 and Maclean, Ch 24 of this volume.

future failed marriages where the wife does not marry again. The proportion of women who are divorced and not remarried in the 65 or more female age group is likely to increase significantly between 1996 (4.1 per cent) and 2021 (14.3 per cent).

Social Class

Surveys report that marriages in which the husband is an unskilled worker have the highest risk of divorce within the Registrar General's social class groupings of employed men.[29] A similar pattern has been reported for America.[30] The highest rate occurs among marriages where the husband is, or has recently been, unemployed. This association between low income and greater propensity to marriage breakdown has policy implications when discussing financial issues such as support for mother and child.

Children

In the ten years 1986 to 1995 some 1,600,000 children under 16 experienced parental divorce. An additional unknown minority were witnesses to parental separation. Current divorce trends suggest that one in four of all children will have first-hand knowledge of parental divorce before reaching the school-leaving age of 16. Between the years 1970 and 1996 the proportion of divorcing couples with dependent children has fallen from 62 per cent to 55 per cent; there has been a linked small rise in childless divorces (Table 2.5). These movements are a reflection within all marriages of older entry age and smaller family size, and shorter marriage duration for those who will ultimately experience divorce. But since 1966 the annual numbers of dependent children incorporated as both audience and cast within their parents' marital drama have more than doubled to some 162,000 in 1996 as a consequence of the rising divorce numbers. For many children the reality of being raised in a lone-parent household is a short-term setting that will be replaced by a new family form of parent and step-parent. The formation of new adult relationships contained within extramarital cohabitation and remarriage are now significant life events within contemporary family life.

[29] C. S. Gibson, *Dissolving Wedlock*. London: Routledge (1993) 136.
[30] W. Goode, *World Changes in Divorce Patterns*. London: Yale University Press (1993) 154.

TABLE 2.5. *Family patterns in divorce, 1970–96*

Year/period*	Divorcing couples (a) Childless	(b) With children One or more −16	All 16+	Numbers of children −16
	[Percentages]			[,000]
1970	26	62	12	71
1971–5	26	59	15	124
1976–80	29	60	11	156
1981–5	30	58	12	156
1986–90	31	55	14	150
1991–5	30	56	14	166
1996	31	55	14	162

Note: Calculations based upon ONS, FM2 series, table 4.10.
* Yearly average.

REMARRIAGE

Since 1947 there has been a steady rise in the proportion of new marriages registering a divorced person (Table 2.1). This is a consequence within the under 60 married population of both the growing probability of divorce and the reduced mortality threat; it is linked with their greater propensity to marry again compared with those of a more senior age. The divorce explosion of the 1970s intensified this trend by returning increasing numbers of the unhappily married back to the single population. Linked with this status transportation has been the desire of many divorced men and women to marry once again. This movement has had consequences for both marriage and divorce.

The move away from marriage within all segments of single society has had a noticeable impact on the divorced. Official marriage rate tables (the number of persons out of a 1,000 within a status group who have married in that year) record the overall decline in remarriage likelihood for divorced women from a rate of 116 in the year 1956, rising to a peak of 171 in 1972, falling to 69 in 1986, and 43 for 1996. This rate shows a decline of 37 per cent over the period 1986–96. These figures underline the increasing distaste for remarriage over the last quarter-century. Yet divorced women are still, within each age group, more likely to re-enter matrimony than their single sisters.[31] A demographic consequence is that four out of ten contemporary weddings (1996: 40 per cent) unite a spouse who has been divorced. An additional 2 per cent involve combinations of widowed and single (the remaining 58 per cent being first marriages for

---

[31] Office of National Statistics, n 27 above, 13.

both). Though the remarriage rate is in decline, the numbers of divorced women remarrying has remained fairly stable (1986: 80,000, 1996: 79,000). This helps to explain why, over the half-century, the number of married-couple stepfamilies has risen sharply.

The decline in remarriage has been partially matched by increasing cohabitation within the divorced population. A significant minority of divorced cohabitants see and refer to their relationship as a marriage.[32] The *General Household Survey* findings for 1996–7 show that since 1981 cohabitation has become a more common form of living for divorced women under 50, increasing from 20 per cent to 32 per cent over this period.[33] Premarital cohabitation has now become the standard precursor to marriage when one or both spouses have been previously married.[34] The increasing popularity of extramarital cohabitation, linked with the general trend to a delay—or rejection of—marriage entry helps to explain why recorded remarriage rates for divorced men and women have declined from their 1972 peak. An increasing proportion of the divorced are neither marrying again nor cohabiting but are either remaining single or living with their children in lone-parent households.

Remarriage Chances

Men have a greater probability of remarriage than do women, and men who remarry do so within a shorter time than women. Though remarriage rates decline with age for both sexes, it is women's chances that fall most rapidly. This gender remarriage rate differential widens with each increasing year, so that at 60 a divorced woman records only a quarter of the probability for similarly aged divorced men. The differential will intensify through the increasing age at both the time of divorce and within the residual divorcing population. The same pattern helps to lower still further current remarriage rates. The majority (1996: 53 per cent) of divorcing mothers with dependent children (under 16) are in the relatively high remarriage group aged under 35. The rates of remarriage and cohabitation recorded in surveys indicate that divorce is a transitional event for the majority of disunited couples and their children. Most dependent children experiencing breakdown of parental marriage are likely to find themselves in a reconstituted family unit of mother and stepfather. The formation of these new family webs creates new kin associations and bonds of attachment and obligation.

---

[32] K. Dunnell, *Family Formation 1976*. London: HMSO (1979) 39.
[33] Office of National Statistics, n 1 above, 46.
[34] J. Gregory and K. Foster, *The Consequences of Divorce*. London: HMSO (1990) 15.

Instability in Second Marriages

The complexities and problems facing those who marry again is a feature helping to explain why it is that second marriages have a greater risk of divorce. The probability is double that of a first marriage.[35] Those who divorce again also experience shorter durations of marriage compared with those both divorcing for the first time.[36] Such trends, linked with the increasing number of non-marital household relationships, affect the stability and continuity of parental socialization. One in twenty of the 1980s newborn are likely to share the confusing childhood experience of at least two more partners taking up residence with the custodial parent.

Serial divorces are having an increasing influence upon the overall divorce pattern of England and Wales. Over a quarter (28 per cent) of all divorces in 1996 contained a previously divorced spouse. At the level of individual divorce experience, 19 per cent of all 1996 divorcing spouses were undergoing their second (or more) divorce. A similar calculation for 1970 produces 5 per cent. Of greater relevance to future breakdown trends is the rapid rise in serial divorce numbers that has helped to produce this new marital facet. The men and women experiencing a further divorce in 1996 (58,673) totalled more than all the spouses divorcing in 1956 (52,530). Some reasons for the previously divorced spouse's vulnerability to further breakdown emerges from studying the interaction between the structural, institutional, and behavioural features that affect family life.

The increasing numbers experiencing a further divorce means that it has become too simplistic to equate reconstituted families with a second marriage (or cohabitation). We now have several parallel structures of family life cycles (first, second, third or more) with their own demographic (age, fertility), social (kinship, multiple parentage), and legal (support obligations, custody) life-course characteristics.

---

[35] J. Haskey, 'Marital Status before Marriage and Age at Marriage: Their Influence on the Chance of Divorce' (1983) 32 *Population Trends* 4; D. Coleman, 'The Contemporary Pattern of Remarriage in England and Wales', in Grebenik, E. et al. (eds.), *Later Phases of the Family Cycle*. Oxford: Clarendon Press (1989); Office of Population, Censuses and Surveys, *General Household Survey* 22. London: HMSO (1993) 76.

[36] J. Haskey, 'Trends in Marriage and Divorce, and Cohort Analyses of the Proportions of Marriages ending in Divorce', (1989) 54 *Population Trends* 21, Table 5.

LONE-PARENT FAMILIES

Numbers and Status

The last three decades have witnessed a rapid increase of single parent-hood within the family. The number of lone-parent families in Britain had doubled in the twenty years between 1971 and 1991; in the latter year 1.3 million lone parents were responsible for raising 2.2 million dependent children (Table 2.6). The 1990s have seen the numbers continue to rise to some 2.9 million children in 1998. These figures mean that a lone parent is now raising one in four of all dependent children, though this may not be a permanent setting. The daily caring and rearing, the associated longer-term realities, issues and problems of heading a lone-parent family largely fall upon women, for only a tenth of such households are headed by a man.

TABLE 2.6 *Lone-parent families in Britain: distribution and numbers, 1971–1991*

Lone-parent family	Percentage of all families with dependent children		
	1971	1981	1991
Mother			
Single	1.2	2.3	6.6
Divorced	1.9	4.4	6.5
Separated	2.5	2.3	4
Widowed	1.9	1.7	1
Total Mothers	7.5	10.7	18.2
Father	1.1	1.4	1.6
All lone parents	8.6	12.1	19.8
Numbers		(millions)	
(i) LPFs	0.6	0.9	1.3
(ii)Dependent children	1.0	1.5	2.2

Source: J. Haskey, 'Estimated Numbers of One-Parent Families and their Prevalence in Great Britain in 1991', (1994) 78 *Population Trends* 5, 6–7.

Reasons for the increase

The advancing count of lone mothers largely results from the growing ranks of single and divorced mothers. The rising numbers of divorced mothers and falling remarriage rates were the main features behind the gradual increase in the total of lone mothers until the mid-1980s. Since then the surge in both the numbers, and the proportion of all families headed by a lone-parent, has been noticeably aided by the rapid increase in single lone mothers (that is, with non-marital children and not cohabitating). Single lone mothers were responsible for some 600,000 dependent children in 1991. Their rising numbers are but one consequence of the increasing numbers of extramarital relationships that fail. But a second factor is that more women from all classes feel they have the right to choose motherhood without necessitating the father's household presence. This movement is associated with changing attitudes towards family life, motherhood, and independence. Though the sum of lone mothers has increased, their growing proportion within dependent children families is also a demographic result of the reduced numbers of children being born and raised in two-parent families through later marriage entry and smaller family size.

   Marital breakdown is still the most common reason for a lone-parent family despite the increase in the proportion of single mothers; divorced or separated mothers headed 10 per cent, while single, never married, mothers headed 7 per cent, of all families with dependent children in 1991 (Table 2.6). The great majority of mothers classified as separated will proceed on to divorce. The growth in divorce is, of course, the demographic facet that accounts for the increasing percentage of divorced mothers. It has already been noted that the levels of remarriage among the divorced have fallen sharply. In the past marriage was the only appropriate means by which a divorced mother could shield herself and her children from the harsh realities of being a lone-parent family. The last thirty years have seen a reduction in prejudice against divorcees, and this has helped diminish remarriage as the set institutional process towards respectability. Changing structural patterns have especially helped divorced mothers by allowing them greater freedom of choice when considering the possible benefits and disadvantages of a new marriage. The availability of improved welfare services, government financial provision, better employment opportunities, and equal pay have provided other viable alternatives for women than a new partnership. And more men are opting either to remain single or not to remarry, thereby reducing the field of partnership opportunity.

Transitional Situation

The lone-parent families that mass to form the cold statistics of numbers and trends are, when observed as individuals, constantly changing in their social pattern and status. As new lone parents increase the total at a particular time, so extramarital cohabitation, marriage, remarriage, and the youngest child becoming dependent are significant life events that reduce overall numbers. An analysis of the Britain Household Panel Survey found that over the period 1991 to 1997 the most common route into lone-parenthood was through the breakdown of a partnership (72 per cent); followed by the birth of a child to a lone single mother (18 per cent).

The least common event was the death of a partner (4 per cent). Following through life-course events showed, on average, that annually around one in six lone parents with dependent children moved out of this family setting. For seven in ten the change was caused by marriage or forming a new partnership.[37] The findings suggest that over half of lone parents leave this status within five years.[38]

Non-marital Births

Non-marital births have risen from 5 per cent of all births in 1961 to 37 per cent in 1997 (Table 2.2). The majority of these mothers are in an on-going relationship with the father; over half of all non-marital births are jointly registered by the mother and father who live together (as shown by the same address) and form a dual-parent family unit. This facet excludes them from lone-parent family surveys. Only a small proportion of the remaining lone single mothers place their children for adoption.

A fifth (21 per cent) of all non-marital births are to young mothers aged under 20. Their conception and abortion rate have both remained relatively stable since the mid-1980s; this suggests a probable future increase in births to young women. Those that do form partnerships with the father have a high failure rate. There is a strong association between high level of early motherhood and low educational achievement. Susan McRae[39] succinctly sums up the evidence concerning young mothers: 'having an early birth damages life chances: . . . (they) are more likely to leave home early, to live in social or subsidized housing, to be in a manual job or unemployed, and to be welfare-dependent.'

Ethnicity

The varying ethnic minority groups—forming 5 per cent of the British population—show a wide variation in their propensity to be a lone-parent family. In 1998 lone-parent families formed 22 per cent of all British families with dependent children. Just over half (55 per cent) of the Black (largely African or Caribbean in origin) group recorded lone-parent status; the White group: 22 per cent; the Pakistani/Bangladeshi group: 17 per cent; the lowest likelihood being recorded by the Indian group: 9 per

---

[37] Office of National Statistics, n 1 above, 45.

[38] K. Kiernan, 'Family Change: Issues and Implications' in M. David (ed), *The Fragmenting Family: Does It Matter?* London: The IEA Health and Welfare Unit (1996).

[39] S. McRae, 'Introduction: Family and Household Change in Britain', in S. McRae (ed), *Changing Britain: Families and Households in the 1990s*. Oxford: Oxford University Press (1999) 11.

cent.[40] A partial explanation of the very high level of lone-parent families within the Black group is the greater relevance of consanguineous ties.

Socio-economic Situation

Findings from the ONS Longitudinal study report that lone mothers were more likely to come from a less advantaged background, as indicated by access to a car and the nature of their housing tenure, than mothers with partners. The analysis also found, when looking at early life factors, that lone mothers were more likely to come from a lone-parent household.[41] Once again the question arises as to how relevant the concept of a 'cycle of deprivation', whereby disadvantage is transmitted from one generation to the next, is to the analysis of the contemporary family?

EMPLOYMENT OF WOMEN

Married and cohabiting women have come to occupy a significant part of the overall labour force. In the 1950s fewer than a quarter of married women were in paid employment, this has now grown to over 70 per cent for married women under 60; the dual-income family has become the standard pattern. Motherhood no longer acts as an insurmountable block to a woman's employment; it is now a lesser part of her life cycle. Evidence from the British Household Panel Survey on the working histories of 30-year-old women with children shows just how much has changed even over the last thirty years. Mothers born in the 1930s (and recalling 1960s experiences) record a 38 per cent employment activity level during the year they were 30; for mothers turned 30 in the 1990s this figure is 68 per cent. For mothers with partners the presence of young children is no longer a brake to employment, as seen by the fact that in 1998 six out of ten married or cohabiting women with pre-school children were economically active. Lone mothers with similar-aged children are much less likely to be in employment; just over a third were economically active. Within the lone-mother group it is single lone mothers who are less likely to have employment than are the older divorced lone mothers.[42] Three consequences follow from these trends.

---

[40] Office of National Statistics, n 1 above, 44.

[41] Office of National Statistics, 'Who Becomes a Lone Mother?' (1998) 91 *Population Trends* 3.

[42] J. Bradshaw and J. Millar, *Lone Parent Families in the UK*. London: HMSO (1991) 36; J. Haskey, 'Birth Cohort Analyses of Dependent Children and Lone-Mothers Living in Lone-Parent Families in Great Britain', (1998) 92 *Population Trends* 15, 20.

1. As the family expenditure broadens to incorporate two incomes, so the relative decline in the accepted and expected standard of living if the partnership dissolves is greater.

2. Many households where the father has low—or no—income have been insulated from poverty by the additional wages of the mother.

3. Lone-parent households—and especially those of single lone mothers—are falling further adrift from the economic standards presented by two-parent households. Over half of lone-parent families in Britain in 1996–7 had less than half the average household income.[43]

PROSPERITY AND INEQUALITY

Much of the poverty debate focuses on the nature and relevance of the concept of relative poverty and deprivation. Though standards of living may be rising for many, those at the bottom end of the economic ladder are being denied a proper slice of improving overall prosperity. Yet home and environmental conditions have undoubtedly improved over the half-century. An England of 1950 recorded 6 per cent of all households without piped water, 6 per cent lacking a kitchen sink, and as many as 37 per cent were without a fixed bath.[44]

Post-war Britain saw the introduction of the 'welfare state'; fifty years later the evidence suggests that inequality has been increasing since the early 1980s. The number of people living in households on or below half average income rose from 4 million in 1982 to 10.5 million in 1996/7. In the latter period one-third of all children lived in households that fell below half average income. Children within lone-parent families are especially at risk of experiencing poverty; in the early 1990s some seven out of ten lone mothers were receiving Income Support.[45] Over the preceding twenty years both the numbers of lone-parent families on government support and the proportion in poverty had increased from that of 1971 when half of all lone mothers (excluding widows) were receiving Supplementary Benefit, the predecessor of Income Support.[46] Low-income households extend to two-parent families. The number of children living in couple families experiencing incomes at or below the level of Income Support in 1989 was almost the same as that in lone-parent

---

[43] C. Howarth, P. Kenway, G. Palmer, and C. Street, *Monitoring Poverty and Social Exclusion: Labour's Inheritance*. York: Joseph Rowntree Foundation (1998).

[44] A. M. Carr-Saunders, D. Carodog Jones, and C. A. Moser, *A Survey of Social Conditions in England and Wales as Illustrated by Statistics*. Oxford: Clarendon Press (1958).

[45] J. Bradshaw and J. Millar, *Lone Parent Families in the UK*. London: HMSO (1991).

[46] Report of the Committee on One-Parent Families (Finer Committee), Cmnd 5629. London: HMSO (1974) 244.

families. Family poverty significantly reduces both the quality of life and the life chances of both parent and child, as is seen in the educational sphere. Whilst educational outcomes are generally improving, the attainment of children in schools with more than a third of pupils on free school meals fell between 1997 and 1998.[47] Their adult life opportunities are thereby reduced while the likelihood of social exclusion is extended.

At the same time that poverty has widened the gap between groups, inequality has also increased within groups. This pattern is observed among the elderly. Pensioners are the largest single group on means-tested benefits; yet many recently retired pensioners (through occupational pensions, investment incomes, and owner occupied homes) are quite comfortably off, and far more economically secure than were their parents.

CONCLUSION

It might be that we are witnessing only a temporary aberration from traditional life-long marriage form, though this is unlikely. The evidence points to continuing transformations in family patterns. Parenthood is increasingly being separated from marriage. The evidence indicates that various alternative forms of family life have become more commonplace over the last thirty years. Nevertheless, the fact that seven out of ten children in 1995 were living with their married parents confirms that the most popular form of parenthood remains that which regularizes the relationship between family members, and formalizes bonds between family and society. Marital parenthood continues, yet today's evident and accepted non-conventional patterns will be more prevalent in tomorrow's families.

[47] C. Howarth, P. Kenway, G. Palmer, and R. Miorelli, *Monitoring Poverty and Social Exclusion 1999*. York: Joseph Rowntree Foundation (1999).

3

A Century of the American Family

DONNA RUANE MORRISON

INTRODUCTION

The present state of the American family is commonly interpreted as a 'sign of the times,' a by-product of contemporary values and culture and the economic forces that shape modern life. Taking a longer view, however, reveals that many aspects of current family demography reflect patterns that have been under way since the beginning of the twentieth century, while others are newer developments. The aim of this chapter is to highlight the major demographic trends that have shaped family life in the United States since 1900. With an understanding of the historical origins of today's demographic realities we can better predict those which will continue to challenge families, communities, policy makers, and the courts of tomorrow. Moreover, this historical vantage point allows for a more realistic appraisal of the contemporary family and what can be done to support and strengthen it.

FAMILY TRENDS OF THE CENTURY

If the major trends in twentieth-century family life were featured as newspaper stories there would be three front-page headlines: 'RETREAT FROM MARRIAGE GAINS LATE-CENTURY MOMENTUM,' 'TIES WEAKENED BETWEEN CHILDBEARING/CHILD-REARING AND MARRIAGE,' and 'MOTHERS MOVE FROM HOME TO MARKETPLACE.' Each of these major trends not only came about by a combination of forces, but is also interrelated with the others. Before delving into the details of each story, I will show that there are two other demographic trends that set the stage for them.

First, Americans are living significantly longer now than in the past. Improved standards of living and scientific advances have pushed back the clock on life expectancy by roughly thirty years—from 46 years for men in 1900, to nearly 74 years in 1996; for women from roughly 48 years to 80 years over the same interval.[1] Second, the twentieth century

I gratefully acknowledge Michelle Waul for her creation of graphics for this chapter and Jennifer Trombley for library research.

[1] US BUREAU OF THE CENSUS, HISTORICAL STATISTICS OF THE UNITED STATES: COLONIAL TIMES TO 1970 (1989) and US BUREAU OF THE CENSUS, STATISTICAL ABSTRACT OF THE UNITED STATES (1999).

continued an already well-established pattern of lower fertility. In 1800, the average number of children per family was a little over 7 children, whereas the mean number of births per woman in 1903 was 2.4,[2] partly in response to declining mortality and partly in response to changing economic and social opportunities to improve the conditions of people's lives.[3] This decline in the total fertility rate continued throughout the twentieth century, surging to 3.6 again in the post-war baby boom and reaching a low of 1.7 in 1976. In recent decades, the average number of children born to American women has ranged from 1.8 to 2.[4]

Social historians and demographers argue that longer life spans and declining fertility have significantly affected the cycle of family life because as societies gain a stronghold over mortality and fertility there is a shift from involuntary demographic trends influencing family life to voluntary demographic decision-making.[5] This type of shift paves the way for control over other domains in family life as well, such as the timing of marriage and the participation of women in the labor force. Second, the longer the life span the greater the importance placed on marriage in its own right, the potential length of marriage, and its duration over more phases of the family life course (eg family formation, child-rearing, 'empty nest').[6] According to the demographer Peter Uhlenberg it was not until 1900 that a sizeable percentage of American women experienced a common family cycle of leaving the parental home, getting married, having and raising children, and surviving into their fifties alongside their spouses. Still, about 60 per cent of women either never married, never reached marriageable age, died before childbirth or were widowed while their offspring were still young children.[7]

Hence, demographically speaking, the nature of family life in America was ripe for change. So it is not surprising that family-related behavior made significant shifts during the twentieth century. We will see how economic and social forces have shaped these trends as well. Three of the most dramatic of these changes are profiled in turn.

---

[2] Tamara K. Hareven, *American Families in Transition: Historical Perspectives on Change* 40–57 in ARLENE S. SKOLNICK and JEROME H. SKOLNICK (eds), FAMILY IN TRANSITION (1992), and ANDREW J. CHERLIN, MARRIAGE, DIVORCE, REMARRIAGE (1992).

[3] Kingsley Davis, *The Theory of Change and Response in Modern Demographic History*, 29 POPULATION INDEX 345 (1963) cited in JOHN R. WEEKS, POPULATION: AN INTRODUCTION TO CONCEPTS AND ISSUES 196 (1999).

[4] Suzanne M. Bianchi and Daphne Spain, *Women, Work, and Family in America*, 51 POPU-LATION BULLETIN (1996). [5] Hareven, n 2 above at 40–57.

[6] *ibid* at 40–57.

[7] Peter R. Uhlenberg, *Cohort Variations in Family Life Cycle Experiences in United States Females*, 36 JOURNAL OF MARRIAGE AND THE FAMILY 284 (1974) cited in Hareven, n 2 above at 40–57.

Retreat from Marriage Gains Late-Century Momentum

To set up the first big demographic story of the twentieth century, let us suppose we wished to submit the institution of marriage to an imaginary physical fitness check. To examine its current condition would be informative, but it would be even better to look for stability or change in important indicators of the vibrancy of the institution over time. Measures might include the centrality of marriage in the life course (age at marriage could be thought of as an indicator), the level of participation in marriage found in society (perhaps compared to the level of participation in any available alternatives to marriage), the level of divorce, and the level of remarriage among people who had married previously. Just as assessments of a person's fitness over time would have to account for the influence of external factors, such as changing occupational demands, ageing, and other situational issues, our hypothetical 'fitness check' of the institution of marriage would have to be imbedded in an understanding of changing cultural norms and expectations; economic and societal trends, especially as related to education, employment, and the economic independence of women, would have to be considered.

So what would such a fitness check reveal? Although the complete picture is somewhat more complicated, the general assessment is that the institution of marriage has weakened. America has moved increasingly toward a 'retreat from marriage' over the century, reflected in a sharp rise in cohabitation, high levels of marital instability, the marked postponement of marriage by recent cohorts, and decreasing remarriage rates. Family formation changes have been particularly pronounced among African Americans, who as a group are less likely to marry today and have postponed marriage to a greater extent than either Hispanics or whites.[8] Although some of the trends contributing to this overall retreat from marriage got under way more than a hundred years ago, the trends have been somewhat uneven across time. In fact, an unmistakable aspect of the pattern of aggregate marriage behavior in the twentieth century is its responsiveness to the economic, political, and cultural imperatives of given eras, or what demographers refer to as period effects.

Cherlin, a social demographer who chronicles trends in American marriage patterns in detail in his book, *Marriage, Divorce, Remarriage*,[9] notes that two time periods in particular stand out from the trend lines. These are the 1950s and the period from the late 1960s to the 1970s. In the 1950s, Americans were unusually centered on the nuclear

---

[8] M. Belinda Tucker and Claudia Mitchell-Kernan, The Decline in Marriage among African Americans: Causes, Consequences, and Policy Implications (1995). (Note, however, that African American divorce rates have mirrored the trends of the general population.)   [9] Andrew J. Cherlin, Marriage, Divorce, Remarriage (1992).

family of married parents and young children. With a prosperous post-war economic recovery in place, marriage and birth rates were at an all-time high and divorce rates were uncharacteristically low. The emphasis in family life shifted more to the companionship and fulfill-ment of the married couple away from legal responsibilities and obli-gations. In fact, while this era is often idealized now, the redirection of attention during the 1950s from the 'collective' (ie the concerns of the extended family and society) to the self-contained nuclear family of married couple and children caused consternation among some social scientists of the day.[10]

The next historical anomaly occurred after this atypically family-centered period, but in the opposite direction. From 1965 through the 1970s, Americans made an unprecedented departure from the family, with lower birth rates, increasing delays in age at marriage and skyrocketing divorce rates, beyond what would have been predicted from even pre-1950s trends. Consequently, by the end of the century, despite some recent stabilization in divorce rates, the concerns of commentators have come full circle to grappling with whether the now very highly prized nuclear family is in peril. Let us turn to the details of how this retreat from marriage came about.

Timing of Marriage

In the first place, Americans are postponing marriage to a greater extent now than at any other time during the past hundred years.[11] Figure 3.1 shows that in 1900 the median age at marriage (the midpoint in the distribution of ages where half marry earlier and half marry later) was 21.9 for women and 25.9 for men. By 1998, the figures were 25 years for women and 26.7 years for men. But, this comparison of the start to the end of the century masks a deep dip that occurred during the mid-part of the century. The median age at marriage changed little over the first forty years of the century for women, but slowly declined over the same period for men. By 1940, half of first marriages among women and men occurred by ages 21.5 and 24.3 years, respectively. Most people are well acquainted with images of young post-World War II brides and indeed, a sizeable drop in the median age at marriage occurred at this time, for example to 20.3 years for women and 22.8 years for men in 1950. Most young adults continued to enter into marriage quickly until 1964, when marriages began to be postponed again.

---

[10] Frank F. Furstenburg, Jr, *The Future of Marriage*, 18 AMERICAN DEMOGRAPHICS 34 (1996).
[11] Available at US Bureau of the Census website, http://www.census.gov/population/socdemo/ms-la/tabms-2.txt.

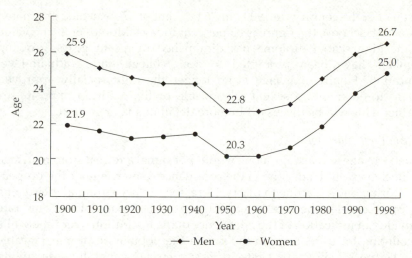

FIGURE 3.1. Median age at first marriage, by sex: 1900–1998. Source: US Bureau of the Census, Table MS-2, Estimated Median Age at First Marriage, by Sex, 1890 to the Present (January 7 1999). http://www.census.gov/population/socdemo/ms-1a/tabsms-2.txt.

The subsequent change has been dramatic. Over the next thirty-five years, the span of time necessary for a single birth cohort to reach middle adulthood, the median age at marriage rose by nearly five years for women and four years for men, to well past the typical ages for college completion.

Some interesting shifts occurred among minority sub-groups as well. While at the start of the century, African Americans married at younger ages than whites, the pattern completely reversed after World War II. Since that time, African Americans marry at later ages than whites.[12]

The natural question is, why has marriage lost its immediacy among recent cohorts? There are demographic, social, and economic explanations. Longer life spans and changing societal norms have elongated the transition into adulthood so that unlike early in the twentieth century, young people are more likely in recent years to leave their parental homes at earlier ages and set up an independent residence before marriage.[13] Marriage is not the only ticket to adult independence as it once was. Moreover, the population as a whole is significantly better educated and therefore spends more time in formal schooling. For example, whereas earning a high school diploma was uncommon throughout the

---

[12] See CHERLIN, n 9 above.

[13] FRANCES GOLDSCHEIDER and LINDA J. WAITE, NEW FAMILIES, NO FAMILIES?: THE TRANSFORMATION OF THE AMERICAN HOME (1991).

first half of the century (in 1900 only 6 per cent of 17-year-olds graduated from high school), the figure is 83 per cent today.[14] Moreover as the value of the high school diploma has diminished in recent years, growing numbers have been prompted to seek college and graduate-level education. Finally, marriage is no longer the only socially approved means to enter into a sexual relationship or live with an opposite-sex partner. This will be discussed in more detail in a later section.

Rate of First Marriage

A delay in age at marriage alone would not signal a retreat from marriage as much as would a decline in the prevalence of marriage or the propensity during one's lifetime to marry. Here, too, we see strong evidence of a retreat. Consider the rate of marriage per 1,000 population. This rate provides an indication of the prevalence of the institution over time while accounting for differences in the size of the population of marriageable age. Figure 3.2 shows that rates of first marriage generally rose among single women aged 15 years and older in the first part of the century, with the exception of the period when the country was in the throes of the Great Depression. By 1945–7 first marriage rates had rebounded to an all-time high of 143 per 1,000 single women aged 15 to 44 years of age and remained high during the 1950s.[15] In the 1960s, marriage rates began to decline, eventually dipping during the 1970s to levels below the unprecedented trough of the Depression and remaining lower until the present. Although rates of marriage have remained fairly constant over the past few decades, they remain at the century's lowest level, 76 per 1,000 single women ages 15 to 44 years of age for 1987 to 1989.[16]

The pattern among African Americans tells a different story. While in any given year during the first half of the century a greater share of white women aged 20 to 24 years were single than black women of the same age, this trend turned around after 1950.[17] More recently, black women have been increasingly less likely both to marry early as well as to ever marry.[18] For example, in 1990, 75 per cent of African American women had married by their late thirties, compared to 91 per cent of white women.

This growing disparity in black–white marriage patterns has heightened the interest of scholars and policy makers in discovering why. There

---

[14] Data are contained in US Census Bureau Press Release, Dec. 20 1999, *Facts for Features* CB99–FF.17, A Century of Change: America 1900–1999, available at http://www.census.gov/Press-Release/www/1999/cb99–101.html.

[15] ARTHUR J. NORTON and LOUISA F. MILLER, *Marriage, Divorce and Remarriage in the 1990s*, CURRENT POPULATION REPORTS, Series P-23, No 180 (1992).

[16] *ibid*. (Note that more recent data are unavailable as the National Center for Health Statistics stopped tabulating final marriage, divorce, and remarriage statistics in 1990.)

[17] See CHERLIN, n 9 above.   [18] See TUCKER and MITCHELL-KERNAN, n 8 above.

FIGURE 3.2. Rates of first marriage, divorce and remarriage for US women: 1921–1989 (three-year averages). Source: National Center for Health Statistics, Table A, Numbers and Rates of First Marriage, Divorce, and Remarriage: 3-Year Averages. 1921–1989. Data on first marriages and remarriages are not available for 1989. The proportions for 1988 were applied to 1989 marriages.

  * First marriages per 1,000 single women 15–44 years old.
  † Remarriages per 1,000 widowed or divorced women 15–54 years old.
  ‡ Divorces per 1,000 married women 15–44 years old.

are generally two types of explanations. Proponents of a demographic view maintain that women are more likely to marry when the ratio of men to women is relatively balanced. Among blacks in recent decades, both a lower ratio of male to female births as well as relatively high mortality rates for young black males have created a surplus of black women during the ages when people typically marry. Alternatively, proponents of an economic perspective look to the relatively weak labor market position of African American men (eg low wages, poor job security) caused in part by America's move away from a manufacturing to a service-oriented economy. These diminished prospects have made many black males economically unattractive marriage partners. Under either scenario, there is a shrinking pool of 'marriageable' African American men, deemed so on the basis of either their age and or their economic position.[19]

[19] William P. O'Hare, Kelvin M. Pollard, Taynia L. Mann, and Mary M. Kent, *African Americans in the 1990's*, 46(1) POPULATION BULLETIN (1991).

Rate of Divorce

Perhaps no other component of the retreat from marriage resonates more with families, the general public, and policy-makers than the high level of divorce in the United States today. What perhaps is less well understood is that high divorce rates are not only a recent societal lament. Figure 3.2 shows that the rate of divorce rose steadily for most of the century, following a pattern that had been in place since the Civil War.[20] Even though by today's standards divorce at the beginning of the twentieth century was rare,[21] Americans were registering concern even then. A marriage begun in 1910 had a 1 in 7 chance of ending in divorce, compared to 1 in 12 in 1880.[22] Even so, the divorce trend has not been a linear one, but rather temporarily fluctuating in response to atypical periods in the country's economic and social circumstances.

In his analysis of divorce patterns over the century, Cherlin describes how divorce rates rose briefly after the century's major wars, but fell when many were reluctant to divorce during the hard economic times of the Great Depression.[23] During the post-war era of the 1950s the trend in divorce took a dramatic and more lasting departure from its uphill trajectory. During the decade from 1950 to 1960, the rate of divorce was considerably lower than would have been expected based on the historical trend. But this period of high marital stability did not last. In the late 1960s the rate of divorce made a sharp ascent which continued through the late 1970s. Like the 1950s downturn that preceded it, this surge was more radical than would have been predicted from the trend line over time. Given that during this span of fifteen years divorce rates more than doubled from 17 per 1,000 single women ages 15 to 54 in 1963 to 1965 to 40 in 1978 to 1980, it is not surprising that this pattern was dubbed the 'Divorce Revolution.'[24] Observers attribute the rise in divorce rates during this period to several things, including the sexual revolution, the availability of modern contraception to control fertility via artificial means, and the legalization of abortion, each of which may have increased marital infidelity. Moreover, both the introduction of no-fault divorce laws and the increased labor market involvement of women (and hence their improved economic independence) may have made it easier for couples to sever their marital ties.[25] The rate of divorce began to level

---

[20] Samuel H. Preston and James T. McDonald, *The Incidence of Divorce within Cohorts of American Marriages Contracted since the Civil War*, 16 DEMOGRAPHY 1 (1979).

[21] Fewer than 1% of the nation's men and women (age 15 and over) were divorced in 1900 according to the US Bureau of the Census, *Statistical Abstract of the United States, 1999*, Table No. 1418 Marital Status of the Population, by Sex: 1900 to 1998.

[22] See CHERLIN, n 9 above.   [23] *ibid.*   [24] See Norton and Miller, n 15 above.

[25] See FURSTENBERG, n 10 above; CHERLIN, n 9 above; and Patricia H. Shiono and Linda S. Quinn, *Epidemiology of Divorce*, 4 THE FUTURE OF CHILDREN 15 (1994).

off in the 1970s and actually declined during the 1980s. More recently, the divorce rate has remained high, but steady.

As this emerging plateau in divorce rates began to take shape in the mid-1990s, many cautioned against undue optimism. They reasoned that the leveling off may have more to do with changes in the composition of the population than with fundamental shifts in the attitudes of Americans about the permanence of marriage.[26] The compositional explanations include several possibilities, including that: broken cohabiting unions may be filtering out some of the marital unions that would have ended in divorce; [27] the ageing of the baby boom generation may be altering the share of married couples who are older and have marriages of longer duration, which lessens the risk of divorce;[28] a decline in remarriage rates may be removing a historically less stable form of union from the potential pool; and finally, increases in both age at first marriage and average levels of educational attainment are diminishing two potent risk factors for divorce.[29]

A recent empirical test of these explanations using historical data on divorce gives a more sanguine view. Joshua Goldstein showed that neither compositional factors, such as the age structure of the population, age at marriage, and order of marriage, individual or behavioral factors, such as age at marriage, educational attainment, number of children, and timing of childbearing, nor selectivity factors (traits of those who are choosing to marry) accounted for the leveling off of divorce rates since 1980.[30] Hence, he maintains that the current plateau may not only be 'real,' but it may also help to create different expectations regarding divorce for children born in the late 1970s and later that may affect their later propensity to divorce.

This would be welcome news to the extent that divorce in America increasingly affects the life course of children. Sociologists Frank Furstenberg and Andrew Cherlin estimate that roughly 7 to 8 per cent of children in 1900 experienced parental separation or divorce before reaching their teen years.[31] Over the century, the pattern of the number of

[26] See CHERLIN, n 9 above; and Julie DaVanzo and M. Omar Rahman, *American Families: Trends and Correlates*, 59 POPULATION INDEX 350 (1993).

[27] Larry L. Bumpass and James A. Sweet, *National Estimates of Cohabitation*, 26 DEMOGRAPHY 615 (1989).

[28] Larry L. Bumpass, Teresa Castro-Martin, and James A. Sweet, *The Impact of Family Background and Early Marital Factors on Marital Disruption*, 12 JOURNAL OF FAMILY ISSUES 22 (1991).

[29] Teresa Castro-Martin and Larry L. Bumpass, *Recent Trends and Differentials in Marital Disruption*, 26 DEMOGRAPHY 37 (1989).

[30] Joshua R. Goldstein, *The Leveling of Divorce in the United States*, 36 DEMOGRAPHY 409 (1999).

[31] FRANK F. FURSTENBERG, JR and ANDREW J. CHERLIN, DIVIDED FAMILIES: WHAT HAPPENS TO CHILDREN WHEN PARENTS PART (1991). (See p 123, n 19 for more details on the derivation of this estimate.)

children affected by divorce has largely mirrored the overall trends in divorce. Patricia Shiono and Linda Sandham Quinn observe that fluctuations in the numbers of children involved are attributable to decreases in family size, increases in births outside of marriage, and the shorter duration of marriage.[32] Prior to the 1960s fewer than 400,000 children experienced a parental divorce each year, but this figure grew as the number of divorces grew because of larger family sizes. Since the late 1970s, more than one million children under age 18 are affected by divorce each year.[33] The majority of children reside with their mothers following divorce, and despite the fact that most fathers have visitation rites, only a minority see their fathers on a regular basis, although this pattern may have improved somewhat in recent years.[34] In 1995, about 70 per cent of custodial mothers and fathers who were eligible for child support payments received at least a portion of their awarded amount, an annual figure averaging $3,732. The propensity to receive child support payments is positively related to having joint custody or visitation rights. Failure to receive child support payments is significantly associated with poverty. About one in three custodial parents not receiving child support payments were classified as poor, compared to 22 per cent of those receiving at least partial payments of their child support awards, and 16 per cent of all parents with children.[35]

Remarriage

A third indicator of the vibrancy of marriage are remarriage patterns (shown in Figure 3.2). It is interesting to note that rates of remarriage, which once provided a counter-point to the perception that the institution of marriage was breaking down, are now part of the combination of trends that make up the current retreat from marriage. Remarriage rates have generally paralleled marriage rates over the century with two exceptions: a sharp spike in remarriages during the 1960s (the cause for optimism) and more recently, a more rapid decline in the rate of remarriages compared to first marriages, especially among younger people (the cause for pessimism). During high rates of divorce in the late 1960s, the remarriage rate soared to an all-time high (166 per 1,000 single women ages 15 to 54 from 1966 to 1968), increasing the confidence of

---

[32] See SHIONO and QUINN, n 25 above.

[33] National Center for Health Statistics, *Advance Report of Final Divorce Statistics, 1988*, 39 MONTHLY VITAL STATISTICS REPORT (1991).

[34] Frank F. Furstenberg, Jr, Christine W. Nord, James L. Peterson, and Nicholas Zill, *The Life Course of Children of Divorce: Marital Disruption and Parental Contact*, 48 AMERICAN SOCIOLOGICAL REVIEW 656 (1983).

[35] Public Information Office, US Bureau of the Census, Press Release. CB99–77. Friday, Apr. 23, 1999, available at http://www.census.gov.

demographers that Americans were not turning away from the institution of marriage, just their current marriages.[36] More recently, however, rates of remarriage have declined and a sizeable share of previously married women enter cohabiting unions.[37] In 1987–9 the rate of remarriage per 1,000 single women ages 15 to 54 was 109. Living with a partner is actually more common among separated and divorced adults than among those who have never married.[38] The median duration between divorce and remarriage is roughly three years, but this may be increasing as cohabitation rates increase.[39]

Among African Americans rates of remarriage traditionally have been lower, and when they do remarry, it is less quickly following divorce.[40] For example, social demographers James Sweet and Larry Bumpass found that only 32 per cent of black separated and divorced women would remarry within ten years, compared to 72 per cent of non-Hispanic whites.[41] This means that African Americans spend considerably less time in marital unions than do whites, the obvious implication being that black children spend a large share of their life course living apart from two biological parents.

A noteworthy demographic characteristic of remarriages is their instability, partly attributable to their being less completely institutionalized in terms of norms and role expectations than are first marriages.[42] Cherlin reports that the proportion of couples who will marry, divorce, remarry, and redivorce has risen eightfold during the course of the century, climbing from barely 2 per cent of those born in the first decade of the twentieth century to 16 per cent of those born after 1970.[43] This often puts children involved in remarriages into a cycle of multiple marital transitions. A discussion of the consequence associated with this comes later in the chapter.

Cohabitation

Finally, critical to an assessment of the centrality of marriage is the extent to which Americans are involved in non-marital unions, perhaps in lieu of marriage or remarriage. A dramatic rise in the prevalence of cohabitation over the past twenty-five years makes it clear that non-marital unions have become an increasingly acceptable: 1. alternative to

---

[36] See *Norton and Miller*, n 15 above.

[37] Larry L. Bumpass, James A. Sweet, and Andrew J. Cherlin, *The Role of Cohabitation in Declining Rates of Marriage*, 53 JOURNAL OF MARRIAGE AND THE FAMILY 913 (1991).

[38] *ibid.*   [39] See CASTRO-MARTIN and BUMPASS, n 29 above.

[40] Barbara F. Wilson and Sally C. Clarke, *Remarriages: A Demographic Profile*, 13(2) JOURNAL OF FAMILY ISSUES 123 (1992).

[41] JAMES A. SWEET and LARRY L. BUMPASS, AMERICAN FAMILIES AND HOUSEHOLDS (1987).

[42] Andrew J. Cherlin, *Remarriage as an Incomplete Institution*, 84 AMERICAN JOURNAL OF SOCIOLOGY 84 (1978).   [43] See CHERLIN, n 9 above.

marriage; 2. step in the progress toward first marriage (by giving couples the opportunity to size each other up as potential spouses); as well as 3. a substitute for marriage after separation and divorce. Moreover, the widespread acceptance of cohabitation, in turn, diminishes the 'imperative' of marriage. Lynn Casper and her colleagues at the US Census Bureau estimate a steep and nearly linear increase in unrelated couple households from 1 million in 1977 to more than 4 million in 1997, a figure that is even higher when other data sets are used for the estimates.[44] Thus, despite a significant postponement in marriage, the prevalence of cohabitation makes contemporary young adults nearly as likely to be sharing a household with a partner as those in previous decades.[45]

The rise in cohabitation is of course facilitated by the aforementioned loosening social mores about non-marital sex, contraception, and abortion, and changes in the importance placed on the institution of marriage, but also by the wariness on the part of young people whose own parents have divorced to enter more permanent unions. In addition, the oft-cited emphasis of contemporary Americans on self-fulfilment contributes to the prevalence of cohabitation. Cohabitation is a way to have some of the benefits of marriage, without the legally binding aspects. Cohabiting couples can stay together so long as it proves personally rewarding, but the door is implicitly always open if either party becomes dissatisfied.

Using data from the National Survey of Families and Households (NSFH), to examine cohabitation trends across American cohorts, Larry Bumpass and James Sweet found that the share of persons who lived in a non-marital union before first marriage increased fourfold from the 1965–74 marriage cohort (11 per cent) to the 1980–4 marriage cohort (44 per cent). They estimate that well over half of more recently formed marriages were preceded by cohabitation. When comparing successive birth cohorts from 1940–4 and 1960–4, they showed an increase from 3 to 37 per cent of females who had cohabited before age 25. Comparing data from the late 1980s to the early 1990s, cohabitation increased in every age category, particularly among the youngest women. For example, while 17 per cent of single women ages 25 to 29 years cohabited in the first wave of the survey, 23 per cent did so by the second wave. Strikingly, almost one-quarter of unmarried 25 to 29-year-olds, 30 to 34-year-olds, and 35 to 39-year-olds were currently cohabiting in 1992–4.[46] Blacks are more likely than whites to live with a non-married partner, but this is largely attributable to distinctive demographic characteristics such as low education, family background, and timing of marriage.[47]

---

[44] Lynn Casper, Phillip N. Cohen, and Tavia Simmons, *How Does POSSLQ Measure Up? Historical Estimates of Cohabitation*, 36 POPULATION DIVISION WORKING PAPER (1999).
[45] See CHERLIN, n 9 above.   [46] See Bumpass and Sweet, n 27 above.   [47] *ibid.*

Available evidence makes it clear that cohabiting unions and marriages are not equivalent. Both the characteristics of those who choose to live together as well as the character of the unions themselves are distinctive.[48] For example, those who live together outside of marriage have traits more in common with single persons than with married persons.[49] Cohabiting unions are generally briefer and less stable than marriages. Specifically, it is estimated that 60 per cent of cohabiting unions dissolve within the first two years.[50]

For some, cohabitation is a step in the courtship process. Larry Bumpass and his colleagues report that slightly less than half of cohabiting couples (who had not previously married) in the NSFH stated that they had definite plans to marry and 74 per cent of the couples either had definite plans or thought that they would marry their partners.[51]

Significantly, a growing number of cohabiting unions involve children. In 1960, of the 439,000 unmarried-couple households, 197,000 contained children under 15 years of age.[52] By 1998, the number of unmarried-couple households had grown to over 4 million (4,236,000) with over 1.5 million of those (1,520,000) containing children. Because these data have not been collected at the national level until very recently, we know very little about how non-married and remarried partners share their incomes and assets, which has important implications for the economic standing of children in these unions.[53] One possibility is that cohabiting couples do not pool their financial resources as much as married couples do, but income-sharing may be more common in relationships of longer duration or when the relationship has produced children.[54] Alternatively, mothers rely exclusively on their own incomes in short-term cohabiting relationships.[55] This makes cohabitation a risky enterprise for children in terms of economic standing and stability. Moreover, children whose mothers cohabit are also at risk of behavioral and emotional difficulties owing to the instability of these arrangements and the ambiguous parental role of non-marital partners.

---

[48] Linda J. Waite, *Cohabitation: A Communitarian Perspective*, THE COMMUNITARIAN NETWORK available at http: //www.gwu.edu/ccps/Waite.html; See also DaVanzo and Rahman, n 26 above.

[49] Ronald R. Rindfuss and Audry VandenHeuvel, *Cohabitation: A Precursor to Marriage or an Alternative to Being Single?*, 16 POPULATION AND DEVELOPMENT REVIEW 703 (1990).

[50] Arland Thorton, *Cohabitation and Marriage in the 1980s*, 25 DEMOGRAPHY 497 (1988).

[51] See Bumpass, Sweet, and Cherlin, n 37 above.

[52] Located at the US Bureau of the Census website: http: //www.census.gov/population/socdemo/ms-la/tabad-2.txt.

[53] For a discussion on this point, see CONSTANCE F. CITRO and ROBERT MICHAEL, MEASURING POVERTY: A NEW APPROACH (1995).

[54] Ann E. Winkler, *The Living Arrangements of Single Mothers with Dependent Children: An Added Perspective*, 52 AMERICAN JOURNAL OF ECONOMICS AND SOCIOLOGY 1 (1993); and ROBERT SCHOEN and ROBIN M. WEINICK, *Partner Choice in Marriages and Cohabitations*, 55 JOURNAL OF MARRIAGE AND THE FAMILY 408 (1993).   [55] *ibid.*

Ties Weakened Between Childbearing/Child Rearing and Marriage

The second major demographic story of the century is closely related to the first and involves the markedly changing context of childbearing and child rearing in the United States. As Goldscheider and Waite put it, 'the axis of the family may be shifting away from men, both as spouses and as parents, and more toward women and children.'[56] This is seen in both the century-long rise in non-marital childbearing (no longer seen as socially deviant), which has been especially swift over the past fifty years, and the rise in separation and divorces involving children. Both trends have combined to create unprecedented increases in the numbers of children who spend at least part of their childhoods in single-parent families.[57]

At the turn of the century the primary route through which children entered a single-parent family was parental death, something experienced by nearly a quarter of all children.[58] Adding to parental deaths the incidence of separation and divorce, perhaps as many as a third of children lived in a single-parent family. As death rates declined over the first half of the century, divorce ascended as the primary cause of single parenthood for children. In the 1950s about 22 per cent of children resided in a single-parent family via the combination of parental death, separation and divorce, and births outside of marriage.[59] In 1998, the percentage of children living with a single parent had risen to 32 per cent, but a dramatic shift in the reasons for this living arrangement had also occurred.[60] While separation and divorce still accounted for 55 per cent of the children living with their mothers only in 1998, a full 40 per cent of the remaining children in this category were born to never married mothers.[61] In 1994, 32.6 per cent of all births were to unmarried mothers, nearly twice the percentage of less than fifteen years ago (18 per cent in 1980).[62]

Since the mid-1990s, the ratio of out-of-wedlock childbearing to overall births has slowed a bit, actually registering a modest decline and remaining fairly stable at 32.4 per cent of all births in 1997. Table 3.1 shows the percentage of births to unmarried mothers, by race, from 1985 to 1997. Among African Americans, the figures are striking. A sizeable

---

[56] See GOLDSCHEIDER and WAITE, n 13 above.

[57] Larry L. Bumpass and James A. Sweet, *Children's Experience in Single-Parent Families: Implications of Cohabitation and Marital Transitions*, 21 FAMILY PLANNING PERSPECTIVES 256 (1989); See also BUMPASS, SWEET, and CHERLIN, n 37 above.

[58] See FURSTENBERG and CHERLIN, n 31 above.   [59] See BUMPASS and SWEET, n 57 above.

[60] Available at the US Bureau of the Census website: http: //www.census.gov/population/socdemo/hh-fam/htabFM-2.txt.

[61] Available at the US Bureau of the Census website: http: //www.census.gov/population/socdemo/ms-la/tabch-5.txt.

[62] US BUREAU OF THE CENSUS, STATISTICAL ABSTRACT OF THE UNITED STATES (1999), Table 99; and US BUREAU OF THE CENSUS, STATISTICAL ABSTRACT OF THE UNITED STATES (1997), Table 97.

TABLE 3.1. *Percentage of births to unmarried mothers, by race: 1985–1997*

	1985	1990	1991	1992	1993	1994	1995	1996	1997
Total	22.0	26.6	28.0	30.1	31.0	32.6	32.2	32.4	32.4
White	14.5	16.9	18.0	22.6	23.6	25.4	25.3	25.7	25.8
Black	60.1	66.7	68.2	68.1	68.7	70.4	69.9	69.8	69.1
Hispanic	29.5	36.7	38.5	39.1	40.0	43.1	40.8	40.7	40.9

Source: US Bureau of the Census, *Statistical Abstract of the United States*. 1998 and 1999.

majority—69 per cent—of all births among African Americans occur to women who are never married, divorced, or widowed.[63] But here too, the share of all births that occurred outside of marriage declined very slightly in 1994 from what had been a consistently upward trend. To understand the significance of these trends, and whether there is room for optimism in these recent signs of slowing, we must consider the underlying factors.

The ratio of non-marital births is affected by a composite of demographic factors.[64] The first is the size of the population 'at risk' of a non-marital birth, which in this case means the number of single men and women of childbearing age. The second and third are the birth rates among both married and unmarried women. Consequently, the aforementioned delays in age at marriage, increases in marital disruption, the growing acceptability of sex outside of marriage, as well as cohabitation have all considerably expanded the risk of pregnancy among unmarried persons. Moreover, differentials in the birth rates of married versus unmarried women also help to fill out the explanation.

After a period of high marital fertility rates from the 1940s through the early 1960s, which produced the baby boom, fertility among married women began to decline markedly. From 1960 to 1975 alone, birth rates among married women dropped from 157 births per 1,000 married women ages 15 to 44 to 92 births per 1,000 women ages 15 to 44 years. More recently, in 1993, the married birth rate was 87 per 1,000 married women ages 15 to 44 years.[65] Birth rates among unmarried women, in contrast, increased from 7 live births per 1,000 women ages 15 to 44 in 1940 to 21.6 in 1960. Non-marital birth rates remained steady for a period of years, but began rising again in the late 1970s through the 1980s. The rate has increased even more quickly from the 1980s, reaching 44 per 1,000 in 1990.[66] Thus, while increases in the ratio of out-of-wedlock births may have been largely influenced by declining marital fertility in the

[63] *ibid*.
[64] US DEPARTMENT OF HEALTH AND HUMAN SERVICES, REPORT TO CONGRESS ON OUT-OF-WEDLOCK CHILDBEARING (1995).   [65] *ibid*.
[66] See DaVanzo and Rahman, n 26 above.

1960s through mid-1970s, since that time, there is little question that *actual increases in non-marital fertility* explain a large part of the rise in the ratio of births occurring to unmarried mothers. Demographers speculate that the ageing of the baby boom generation accounts for the recent modest slowing in out-of-wedlock childbearing, and will be looking to the family-formation behaviors of the 'baby boom echo' generation to see if they imitate the lifestyles of their parents or choose more traditional living arrangements.[67]

Out-of-wedlock childbearing is the culmination of a series of decision points once pregnancy occurs, however, including whether to abort, relinquish the baby for adoption, or marry.[68] Table 3.2 presents historical data regarding first births among relatively young women—ages 15 to 29—detailing the proportion of these births which were premarital births, premarital conceptions, and postmarital conceptions. The first thing to note is the remarkable increase in the share of first births to women of this age group which are premarital births—8 per cent in 1930–4 to 41 per cent in 1990–4. The final column provides the percentage of premaritally pregnant women who marry before the birth of their first child. Here too we see the increasing separation of births from marriage over the century. While the majority (53.6) of 15- to 29-year-olds with an out-of-wedlock conception in 1930–4 got married before the child's birth, this was true of less than one-quarter of similar young women in 1990–4.

National-level data on adoption are not readily available, but the NSFG provides some information on both adoption as well as relinquishment for adoption. The demographers William Mosher and Christine Bachrach report that the percentage of women who ever adopted a child remained at roughly 2 per cent during the 1970s and 1980s. Relinquishment of babies for adoption among white women declined dramatically over the same time period, however, from 19 per cent of all non-marital births in 1965–72 to 3 per cent of all non-marital births in 1982–8. Rates of relinquishment among African American women, which have been historically low (less than 2 per cent of non-marital births) showed little change. Demographers attribute the initial drop among white women to the legalization of abortion in 1973, but more recently the decline is more likely to be related to the greater social acceptance of births outside of marriage.[69]

---

[67] Lynn Casper and Ken Bryson, *Household and Family Characteristics: March 1998 (Update)*, CURRENT POPULATION REPORTS P20–515 (1998).

[68] Amara Bachu, *Trends in Premarital Childbearing: 1930–1994*, CURRENT POPULATION REPORTS P23–197 (1999); See also US DEPARTMENT OF HEALTH AND HUMAN SERVICES, n 64 above.

[69] William D. Mosher and Christine A. Bachrach, *Understanding US Fertility: Continuity and Change in the National Survey of Family Growth, 1988–1995*, 28 FAMILY PLANNING PERSPECTIVES 4 (1996).

TABLE 3.2. *Marital status of women ages 15 to 29 at first birth, 1930–34 to 1990–94*

Period of first birth	% of first birth			% premaritally pregnant women marrying before the birth of their first child
	Premarital birth	Premaritally conceived birth	Post-maritally Conceived birth	
1930–4	8.2	9.5	82.2	53.6
1935–9	8.5	9.0	82.6	51.4
1940–4	7.0	7.5	85.5	51.8
1945–9	7.6	7.9	84.6	50.9
1950–4	7.9	9.3	82.8	53.9
1955–9	10.0	10.9	79.1	52.3
1960–4	10.3	15.5	74.3	60.0
1965–9	15.1	18.0	66.9	54.4
1970–4	18.0	17.1	64.8	48.7
1975–9	25.7	12.0	62.2	31.8
1980–4	29.6	12.3	58.1	29.4
1985–9	32.7	10.7	56.5	24.7
1990–4	40.5	12.3	47.2	23.3

Source: Bachu, Amara, 1999. *Trends in Premarital Childbearing 1930 to 1994*, Special Studies, Washington, DC: US Bureau of the Census, Table 1.

The issues for child well-being raised by living in a single-parent family in some ways differ according to whether the situation was prompted by marital disruption or unmarried parenthood. Regardless of the route into single parenthood, however, children who live in mother-headed families lack the access to their parents' economic resources that children raised by two biological parents have counted upon in the past. Moreover, children in mother-only families score lower on a wide array of indicators of well-being, including high school graduation, teen parenthood, and finding and maintaining jobs, and they are five times more likely to be poor than those in the average two-parent married families.[70] Among children with never-married mothers, even those who share their households with their mothers' non-marital partners, are not economically equivalent to married couple households.[71] Finally, cohabitation among the never-married is highly selective of women with less advantageous economic backgrounds.[72]

In the case of marital disruption, separated and divorced mothers and their custodial children experience a roughly 21 to 30 per cent decline in family income.[73] Remarriage can be a promising route to economic recovery following divorce.[74] For example, using the 1984 Survey of Income and Program Participation (SIPP), Suzanne Bianchi and Edith McArthur (1991) observed that children whose mothers remarried or reconciled at some point during the panel had almost double the income to needs ratio as those who remained in a mother-only family throughout.[75] Cohabitation, on the other hand, does not compare favorably with remarriage as a route for economic recovery for separated and divorced mothers and their children.[76] Children whose mothers cohabit following marital

[70] Irwin Garfinkel, Jennifer Hochschild, and Sara S. McLanahan (eds), Social Policies for Children 1–32 (1996); and Sara McLanahan and Gary Sandefur, Growing up with a Single Parent: What Hurts, What Helps (1994).

[71] Wendy D. Manning and Daniel T. Lichter, *Parental Cohabitation and Children's Economic Well-Being*, 58 Journal of Marriage and the Family 998 (1996).

[72] See Furstenburg and Cherlin, n 31 above; and see Sweet and Bumpass, n 41 above.

[73] Suzanne Bianchi, L. Subaiya, and Joan Kahn, *The Gender Gap in the Economic Well-Being of Non-Resident Fathers and Custodial Mothers*, 36 Demography 195 (1999); Suzanne Bianchi and Edith McArthur, *Family Disruption and Economic Hardship: The Short-Run Picture for Children*, Current Population Reports P70–23 (1991); Saul D. Hoffman and Greg J. Duncan, *What are the Economic Consequences of Divorce?*, 25 Demography 641 (1988); and Richard Peterson, *A Re-Evaluation of the Economic Consequences of Divorce*, 66 American Sociological Review 528 (1996).

[74] Greg Duncan and Saul D. Hoffman, *Economic Consequences of Marital Instability*, cited in Martin David and Timothy Smeeding (eds), Horizontal Equity, Uncertainty and Economic Well-Being 427–67 (1985); see Peterson, n 73 above; and Donna Ruane Morrison and Amy R. Ritualo, *Routes to Children's Economic Recovery after Divorce: Are Remarriage and Cohabitation Equivalent?* (forthcoming), American Sociological Review.

[75] See Bianchi and McArthur, n 73 above.

[76] See Morrison and Ritualo, n 74 above.

disruption have lower absolute incomes potentially available to them, greater levels of poverty, more reliance on AFDC, and lower receipt of child support than those whose mothers remarry. These differences can be attributed to two factors: that marriage is associated with a real improvement in stability as well as the fact that cohabitation is highly selective of women who are already economically disadvantaged. The level of economic support potentially available from non-married partners is apparently insufficient for pulling children's families off of AFDC and out of poverty to the extent of the decline in AFDC receipt that accompanies remarriage.

Mothers Move from Home to Marketplace

The third major demographic story of the twentieth century is the considerable increase in the participation of women in the workforce, a trend which edged upward slowly in the first half of the century and then accelerated.[77] The changes over time are striking. As Table 3.3 shows, roughly one-fifth of women were in the labor force in 1900, one-third in 1950, over half in 1980, and 60 per cent in 1998. Not only has the level of labor force participation changed, but also the composition of the female workforce. Once primarily the domain of young, unmarried women, the labor market now employs a majority of women, including those who are married and have young children. Let us look at the trend in mothers' labor force participation among the sub-group of children who live in two-parent families. Seventy-eight per cent fit the breadwinner father–stay at home mother model in 1940, 73 per cent in 1950, 66 per cent in 1960, 53 per cent in 1970, 38 per cent in 1980.[78] More recently, the figure is 25 per cent. This shift in women's labor market behavior is the result of changing attitudes about women's roles as well as changes in the demand for female labor at the macro level.[79]

In pre-industrial America, the majority of children lived on family farms on which parents and children worked together to support the family. With the Industrial Revolution, a growing share of fathers began taking jobs located away from the home.[80] Industrial and commercial enterprises had increasing demands for workers, including women. Moreover, as the service sector grew, from about 1890 to 1920, women were also drawn in to perform clerical jobs.[81] In each instance, however,

---

[77] Suzanne M. Bianchi and Daphne Spain, *Women, Work and Family in America*, 51 POPU-LATION BULLETIN (1996).

[78] DONALD J. HERNANDEZ, AMERICA'S CHILDREN: RESOURCES FROM FAMILY, GOVERNMENT AND THE ECONOMY (1993).   [79] See Bianchi and Spain, n 77 above.

[80] See HERNANDEZ, n 78 above.

[81] VALERIE K. OPPENHEIMER, THE FEMALE LABOR FORCE IN THE US (1970) cited in BIANCHI and SPAIN, n 77 above.

TABLE 3.3. *Women's labor force participation by presence of children and as a share of the total labor force, 1900–98*

Year	Women's labor force participation rate	Labor force participation rate of married women with children ages 6 to 17	Labor force participation rate of married women with children under age 6	% total labor force made up by women
1900	18.8	–	–	18.3
1910	23.4	–	–	21.2
1920	21.1	–	–	20.5
1930	22.0	–	–	22.0
1940	25.4	–	–	24.5
1950	33.9	–	–	29.6
1960	37.7	39.0	18.6	33.4
1970	43.3	49.2	30.3	38.1
1980	51.5	61.7	45.1	42.5
1990	57.5	73.6	58.9	45.3
1998	59.8	76.8	63.7	46.3

Source: For 1900–60: US Bureau of the Census, *Historical Statistics of the United States, Colonial Times to 1970*; for 1970–98: US Bureau of the Census, *Statistical Abstract of the United States: 1998*, Tables 650 and 659.

the typical female candidates were young and unmarried. Social historians explain that despite opportunities and conveniently available
transportation, the prevailing ideology of domesticity kept the vast
majority of middle-class married women out of the workforce.[82] As time
went on and labor market demands outgrew the supply of young single
women, so married women began filling the need.[83] This continued until
economic downturns and some employer prohibitions against the hiring
of married women slowed the pace. During the 1950s and 1960s the composition of the female workforce was once again modified. Older women
with grown children began to fill the clerical positions being abandoned
by younger women who were at home raising their children. In the
decades of the 1970s and 1980s, another shift occurred. The economic
benefits of employment began to increase for women, relative to the costs
of remaining at home.[84] America saw its biggest labor force increase
among young, married women with children, the group historically least
likely to enter the market. In 1998, 77 per cent of married women with
children were in the job market. And, of the subset with children under
age 6, the figure was 64 per cent, although full-time, full-year work is not
typical for this group.[85] With the economic status of US workers at a
historic high point, it appears unlikely that women will leave the labor
force in large numbers in the near future.

The experiences of low-income and minority-group women have been
quite different. African Americans have been historically more likely to
be in the paid workforce and their full-time, full-year participation has
been less influenced by the presence of children.[86] Moreover, mothers
who are heads of households, either by virtue of never having married,
separation, or divorce, not surprisingly are more likely to be in the paid
workforce so that they can support their families.

If one were to tabulate how the large-scale entry of women into the labor
force has affected the well-being of children, the ledger sheet would show
pluses and minuses. On the one hand, with smaller family sizes, the typical
child gets more parental time than they did in an era of many siblings. On
the other hand, maternal employment directly affects the time that mothers
have available to children. The average children with employed mothers
receive six hours per day of primary care time from them including being
dressed, fed, talked to, and played with, which is roughly half the time
children with non-employed mothers receive on those same activities.[87]

---

[82] See HAREVEN, n 2 above.　　　[83] See OPPENHEIMER, n 81 above.
[84] PAULA ENGLAND and IRENE BROWNE, *Trends in Women's Status*, 35 SOCIOLOGICAL
PERSPECTIVES 17 (1992).
[85] Howard V. Hayghe and Suzanne M. Bianchi, *Married Mothers' Work Patterns: The
Job–Family Compromise*, MONTHLY LABOR REVIEW 24 (June 1994).　　　　　　[86] ibid.
[87] John P. Robinson, *Caring for Kids*, 11 AMERICAN DEMOGRAPHICS 52 (1989).

This is in part because to accommodate their employment schedules many mothers use day care of some kind. While the effects of day care on child well-being have been hotly debated,[88] few would question the uneven quality of the American child care system, due in part to a lack of national standards for day care centers and a lack of guidelines by many states.[89]

On the plus side, children at the top of the income distribution benefit from an increase in time spent with and being cared for by their fathers.[90] And, the greater economic independence of working women has allowed mothers and children to exit more readily harmful and/or dangerous unions. Finally, some benefits have been documented for the daughters of working mothers,[91] and for both girls and boys when mothers are deriving satisfaction with their employment roles.[92]

CONCLUSION

This chapter has identified the major demographic developments affecting family life during the twentieth century. Some trends such as lower fertility, increases in age at marriage, and elevated divorce levels took root early on in the century, making patterns in family life ripe for change. Other developments, such as the large-scale participation of mothers with young children in the labor force, the prevalence of cohabitation, and sharp increases in out-of-wedlock childbearing, have only recently gained momentum. What is most noteworthy is that these trends have combined into a retreat from marriage in American society and the separation of childbearing from marriage. Consequently, many varieties of family life have been created beyond traditional married-couple families, and women have been given wider role options and greater economic independence than their counterparts in the past. However, while many applaud this current lifestyle diversity, it is also associated

---

[88] Martha J. Zaslow and Carol A. Emig, *When Low-Income Mothers Go to Work: Implications for Children*, 7 THE FUTURE OF CHILDREN 110 (1997). They report that most existing research on the effects of maternal employment on child well-being examine children whose mothers are voluntarily in the paid labor force, and many early studies relied upon middle-class samples. In general, no consistent pattern of negative effects has emerged from the accumulated findings, but some difficulties have been observed among middle-class boys with employed mothers. While research has focused less upon children in low-income families, there is evidence of positive effects of maternal work, including higher reading achievement and receptive vocabulary scores.

[89] See GARFINKEL, HOCHSCHILD, and McLANAHAN, n 70 above.

[90] MICHAEL E. LAMB, THE FATHER'S ROLE (1987).

[91] L. M. Jones and J. L. Bride, *Sex-Role Stereotyping in Children as a Function of Maternal Employment*, 111 JOURNAL OF SOCIAL PSYCHOLOGY 219 (1980).

[92] See eg Lois W. Hoffman, *Maternal Employment and the Young Child* in M. PERLMUTTER (ed), MINNESOTA SYMPOSIUM IN CHILD PSYCHOLOGY 101–28 (1984).

with new and often troubling social realities, particularly for children. Marital disruption (and dissolutions of other unions) is commonplace in the lives of children, and in many instances they must adjust to multiple separations and divorces by their parents. Children are also over-represented among the poor (mainly for reasons of family structure). In addition, both emotionally and financially, the centrality of parenthood has diminished for fathers because of out-of-wedlock childbearing and marital disruption. Moreover, children have declining access to their mothers' full-time care, owing in part to the fact that a majority of women with young children not only work (often full time) but also when they do, they return to work within the first year of their infants' lives. Finally, many of the new family forms are ill equipped to perform the functions typically expected of families. Some child rearing and socialization functions have shifted to other institutions, such as schools and day care centers, but with regard to the unique demands of dual-earner families, there are still only weak institutional supports available.

The evidence presented in this chapter supports the conclusion that marriage as an institution has weakened. Although the holders of this view are sometimes described as being on a 'nostalgia trip,' the data presented here shows that it is not even necessary to view the current circumstances of families through the lens of the baby boom era to arrive at this conclusion. While the period from 1945 to 1964 was historically anomalous for its unprecedented focus on the nuclear family of married couples and children, the roughly thirty years that followed it were atypical as well. From 1965 to 1994, family-formation behavior took a marked departure from the past, even beyond what would have been predicted from the trend line prior to the baby boom days.

The chapter detailed the complex components of demographic change and showed that from this vantage point, there may actually be room for some optimism regarding the continued importance of marriage, especially for its childbearing and child-rearing functions. Modest declines in recent years in rates of divorce and out-of-wedlock childbearing may well represent real attitudinal change at the societal level. However, even if stabilization of these forces is simply the consequence of the ageing of the baby boom cohort, the retreat from marriage may be quelled because demographic behavior often becomes self-justifying.

What can be done to support and protect the diverse families of the twenty-first century? The list of possibilities is too long to delve into in any depth here. However, at least four general goals are key. First, social policy needs to direct attention to preserving the institution of marriage. Marriage is good for society and is unquestionably good for children. Second, institutional supports for working parents need to be put into place along with a greater urgency in ensuring safe and high-quality day care. Third, the emotional and economic involvement of fathers in their children's lives needs to be encouraged and, in the case of child support, strictly enforced. And fourth, efforts are needed to increase economic security for children, including those of the working poor. The challenge that this chapter makes clear is that future legislative and public policy efforts will have to accommodate to the demographic complexities of present-day family lives.

4

Family Policy in the Post-War Period

JANE LEWIS

In the European context, it has long been thought that family policy is something that the continental European countries (especially France) had and Britain did not. Not until the 1990s did government, first Conservative and then Labour, attempt to formulate a family policy. However as Land and Parker[1] pointed out twenty years ago, the absence of an explicit family policy does not mean that governments do not have one. This chapter begins with the assumptions underlying policies and seeks to show how the story of the development of family policy in Britain has been the movement away from a relatively firm and coherent set of (implicit) assumptions about what the family looks like and how it works. Only with the dawning realization as to the profound and rapid change in family patterns over the past twenty-five years and especially over the last decade has government put the family on the policy agenda.

Not surprisingly, historically government has assumed the existence of a two-parent family, in which the husband and father's primary task is to earn and maintain and that of the wife and mother to care. This rendered the woman dependent on a male breadwinner, and women gained entitlements in respect of modern welfare policies chiefly as wives rather than as mothers. Indeed the early feminist literature on the post-war welfare state[2] emphasized the extent to which social policies represented 'the state organisation of domestic life'. Certainly, the assumptions about female dependency were the same ones that made it possible for the vote to be confined to male 'heads of families' throughout the nineteenth century and part of the twentieth.

However, the social reality is more complicated. Women's position in the modern welfare state is more complex than that of men, and has also undergone more change. Broadly speaking, the proportion in the labour market of women with children has increased dramatically, but the amount of unpaid domestic work (housework and caring work for young and old) carried out by men has changed very little. The mix of work (although not necessarily the kind of work) performed by women has changed much more than the mix of work performed by men. The sources of income for women have therefore also changed. During the twentieth

---

[1] H. Land and R. Parker, 'Family Policy in Britain: The Hidden Dimensions', in A. Kahn and S. Kamerman (eds), *Family Policy in Fourteen Countries*. New York: Columbia University Press (1978).
[2] E. Wilson, *Women and the Welfare State*. London: Tavistock (1977).

century there was a major shift away from dependence on individual male relatives (especially husbands), and towards increased dependence on the labour market for married women and for single women without children, and dependence on the state for lone women with children. In the case of the latter, modern social welfare policies have permitted the transformation of traditional family forms and the formation of autonomous households by lone mothers, while at the same time attempting to enforce assumptions about men's obligation to maintain. Thus state policies have in practice often been Janus-faced in this respect.

The nature of the relationship between the increase in women's employment, the development of state benefit programmes, and the increasing autonomy of women is a highly fraught subject. The position of the family as a mediating institution between the individual and the state has undergone huge change. The fundamental dilemma for government at the end of the twentieth century has become how far it can or should treat adult family members as independent individuals. In face of the increasing proportion of adult women in the workforce, should it completely abandon any notion of dependency inherent in the male breadwinner model? In face of changing family forms, with less marriage, later marriage, more cohabitation, and more lone motherhood, should it abandon the attempt to regulate family life via the law of husband and wife? If so, does this not mean that new measures are needed to secure the position of children? Family policy in the form of public *and* private law has never been entirely coherent in its treatment of family members at the level of either principles or practice.[3] The trend in terms of the social reality has been towards greater 'individualization', although this does not mean that women have become fully individualized. In the closing years of the twentieth century the problem for government has become how far to recognize the changing social reality, the problem being that in taking steps to recognize it, the law may also promote it.

1940s–1970s: MAINTAINING THE TRADITIONAL FAMILY MODEL IN PUBLIC AND PRIVATE FAMILY POLICY

Given that in modern societies independence derives primarily from wage-earning,[4] the assumption that women were located mainly in the

---

[3] This was emphasized in the *Report of the Committee on One-Parent Families* (The Finer Report). London: HMSO, Cmnd 5629 (1974) hereafter referred to as the Finer Report.

[4] C. Pateman, 'The Patriarchal Welfare State', in A. Gutman (ed), *Democracy and the Welfare State*. Princeton: Princeton University Press (1988).

private sphere as wives and mothers, supported by male breadwinning husbands, also meant that women were only partially individualized. In regard to social policies, the liberal dilemma first described by Okin,[5] whereby for the purposes of determining political citizenship 'individual' effectively meant 'male head of household', has persisted. Most modern welfare states have subscribed to some degree to the idea of a male breadwinner model and have therefore treated women as dependants of men, although the persistence of this assumption in the late twentieth century has varied considerably between countries.[6]

In its pure form, the male breadwinner model predicts that married women will not engage in paid work, but rather will undertake the work of caring for children and other dependants at home without the support of collectively provided services, and that they will be subordinated to their husbands for the purposes of social security entitlements and tax. In reality, such a model never existed, although it most closely matched the social reality of middle-class women at the turn of the century. For the late nineteenth-century social theorist Herbert Spencer, for example, society was 'progressing' towards a position whereby all women would be able to stay at home in their 'natural sphere'. It is no coincidence that the foundations of most Western European welfare states were also laid down at this time, when the ideology of 'separate spheres' for men and women was at it height. Thus Skocopol[7] has argued that social insurance for sickness and unemployment, the central programme of the modern welfare state (adopted in Britain in 1911), was fundamentally paternalist. Women were only covered if they were in full-time, insurable employment, a status achieved by only about 10 per cent of adult women prior to World War II. After World War I, provision was made for allowances for the 'dependants' of unemployed men, that is, women and children. Nevertheless, it was broadly accepted, by trade unionists and by women themselves, as well as by politicians, that the male breadwinner model 'ought' to characterize the way in which families organized themselves. For policy makers, this family form was considered above all to be the best way of securing male work incentives. Thus, Helen Bosanquet, a leading light in the Charity Organisation Society and a member of the 1909 Royal Commission on the Poor Laws, wrote in 1906: 'nothing but the considered rights and responsibilities of family life will ever rouse the

---

[5] S. M. Okin, *Justice Gender and the Family*. New York: Basic Books (1989).

[6] J. Lewis, 'Gender and the Development of Welfare Regimes', (1992) 2 *Journal of European Social Policy* 159; J. Lewis, 'Gender and Welfare Regimes: Further Thoughts', (1997) 4 *Social Politics* 160.

[7] T. Skocopol, *Protecting Soldiers and Mothers*. Cambridge, Mass.: Harvard University Press (1992) .

average man to his full degree of efficiency, and induce him to continue working after he has earned sufficient to meet his own personal needs'.[8]

The post-war social security settlement in Britain also rested on the male breadwinner model. The Beveridge Report of 1942[9] tried to secure a system of social insurance 'for all and everything'. But Beveridge experienced great difficulty in trying to fit women into an insurance scheme necessarily tied to the labour market. Sir William Beveridge saw adult women primarily as wives; marriage rather than motherhood constituted the touchstone of his proposals for social policies in respect of women. He saw marriage as a partnership and followed Muller Lyer (whose work on marriage was translated from the German in 1930) in his belief that marriage was evolving from a second stage, in which nuclear families were dominated by the economic power of the man, to a third stage, described as a 'personal stage', in which the personalities of wives and children claimed independent recognition.[10] He believed that husbands and wives did work of equal importance, albeit that their roles were very different. He sought to give recognition to the caring work that women performed in the home, not least for eugenic reasons (like many of his contemporaries, Beveridge was very worried about the fall in the birth rate during the 1930s), but in so doing he also sought to make social security law consistent with the social reality in which married women were, for varying periods of time, dependent on a man's wage. In fact, in 1943, 40 per cent of married women were in paid employment, but Beveridge took as his social reality the number of married women who were economically inactive during the inter-war period (90 per cent). Thus, Beveridge's perception of the 'is' became an 'ought', notwithstanding the acknowledgement he gave to the emergence of more companionate marriages in which husbands and wives decided for themselves how paid and unpaid work would be distributed. In the case of married women, he decided to give them a new insurance status on marriage whereby they would be insured via their husbands, paying less by way of contributions and receiving less by way of benefits. This differential treatment of men and women under social insurance was not reformed until the passing of the equality legislation of the 1970s, which in turn was prompted by European law. However, the depth of assumptions regarding women's position may be gauged by two pieces of legislation that were passed at the very same time as the equality legislation

---

[8] H. Bosanquet, *The Family*. London: Macmillan (1906) 206.

[9] *Report of the Committee on Social Insurance and Allied Services* (The Beveridge Report) Cmd 6404. London: HMSO (1942).

[10] H. Glennerster and M. Evans, *Squaring the Circle? The Inconsistencies and Constraints of Beveridge's Plan*, Welfare State Programme Discussion Paper 86. London: London School of Economics (1993).

(centring on equal pay and sex discrimination). The housewife's non-contributory invalidity pension defined women's incapacity as an inability to do housework; and the invalid care allowance was denied to married women because such unpaid caring work was deemed to be part of their 'natural' responsibilities. The latter was eventually judged to be discriminatory by the European Court of Justice in 1986.

The post-war welfare settlement assumed that adult women would be married and would be supported by men. Indeed, the whole framework was premised on full male employment and stable two-parent families. Beveridge had endeavoured to address the problem of women who were not supported by men, whether by reason of widowhood, divorce, or unmarried motherhood, but social insurance could only work for women claiming as workers in their own right, or as the wives and widows of insured men. From the first, Beveridge excluded unmarried mothers from the possibility of insurance cover unless they could claim as workers in their own right, just as widows were firmly included so long as their husbands had been in insurable employment. Beveridge tried hard to find a way of including divorced women in an insurance scheme. In his view, on marriage a woman undertook 'to perform vital unpaid service to the community and becomes exposed to new risks, including the risk that her married life may be ended prematurely'. He swung between making marriage breakdown a risk analogous to industrial accident and seeing it as 'leaving work without just cause'.[11]

The attempt to assimilate the risk of marital breakdown to risks associated with the labour market, around which social insurance was constructed, failed. The problem in relation to the principles of insurance was threefold: first there was the issue of whether it was possible for women to profit from an insurance paid for by their husbands when they were at 'fault' in the process of marriage breakdown, and whether it was possible for men to have insurance cover in respect of their wives if they were at fault; second, the issue of the possibility of double cover for women in respect of the public law of social security and the private law of divorce; and third, the problem of proving the status of a deserted or separated wife. Given the way that Beveridge conceptualized women's place within marriage as equal and yet different, and given the way in which he made marital status the determinant of women's social insurance status, it was well nigh impossible for him to provide a single insurance-based benefit for once-married women. As feminist commentators complained at the time, unmarried mothers were never serious contenders for fear of rewarding immorality, although Beveridge was

---

[11] Cited in J. Lewis, 'The Problem of Lone-Mother Families in Twentieth Century Britain', (1998) *Journal of Social Welfare and Family Law* 251.

quite keen to provide some benefits to an unmarried woman 'living as a wife', something that had been accepted during World War I under unemployment insurance and which lasted until 1927.[12] However, he did not feel that female cohabitants should qualify for their male partners' pensions; some distinctions between the legally married and cohabiting had to be preserved.

The Finer Committee on One-Parent Families, which reported in 1974, neatly summed up Beveridge's problems in constructing the post-war framework for social security as stemming from both his failure to give married women a separate insurance status independent of their husbands, in other words, his failure to 'individualize' women, and, in the case of separated and divorced women, the impossibility of insuring against something for which one of the parties had to be deemed to be 'at fault'.[13] The only remaining hope for women in respect of the post-war social security system was family allowances (introduced in 1945) which attached to them as mothers rather than as wives, but these were never generous and nothing was paid in respect of the first child, which effectively ruled out support for the majority of lone mothers. Thus unmarried and divorced women, who had children and who by definition lacked male breadwinners, were bound to seek support, as mothers, from the social assistance authorities if they were not themselves in insurable employment. Widows of insured men were covered by social insurance.

Social assistance has been described as a 'second class' benefit by American feminist commentators on social policy.[14] This was true in Britain, but the stigma attaching to social assistance faded substantially in the post-war period. In the first place, Britain did not develop the kind of comprehensive, social insurance-centred system envisaged by Beveridge. Low benefits meant that means-tested social assistance always played a large part in the social security system for men and for women. Furthermore, social assistance was nationally determined, a rarity within Europe, and paid the same amount to men and to women. After 1980, social insurance entitlements were dramatically curtailed and 'targeted' social assistance came to occupy an even larger place in the social security system.[15] This has meant that gender differentials have been slight. Everyone gets the same mean level of benefit. This is in contrast to an

---

[12] S. Parker, *Informal Marriage, Cohabitation and the Law, 1750–1989*. London: Macmillan (1990).

[13] Finer Report, n 3 above, Appendix 5, para 108.

[14] B. Nelson, 'The Two-Channel Welfare State: Workmen's Compensation and Mothers' Aid' in L. Gordon (ed), *Women, the State and Welfare*. Madison: University of Wisconsin Press (1990).

[15] T. Eardley, *Social Assistance in OECD Countries*, i. DSS Research Report no. 46. London: HMSO (1996).

otherwise more generous insurance-based system of public provision such as that of Germany, where gender differentials in terms of benefit levels are high, because it is women (and primarily lone mothers) who fall through the insurance net.[16]

Notwithstanding the assumptions of policy makers about the desirability and existence of the traditional family form, the possibility of a measure of economic autonomy increased for all women in the post-war period. Married women entered the labour market in increasing numbers, albeit that almost all the post-war increase in their employment can be accounted for by part-time work.[17] Lone mothers, who were not obliged to register for employment until their children reached the age of 16, were able to draw social assistance benefits and, from the late 1970s, were also more likely to qualify for social housing.[18] Thus even though the post-war settlement failed to 'individualize' women for the purposes of social security, and indeed persisted in treating them as the dependants of men, social assistance nevertheless made an independent existence possible for women with children and without men.

The degree of autonomy achieved by lone mothers under the post-war social security was certainly not intended by post-war policy makers. But in the 1970s, there was no significant protest against it. Changes in family forms were noted, but the sociological accounts were optimistic in the 1960s and 1970s, stressing the fundamental stability of marriage.[19] Chester[20] was one of a very small minority to draw attention to the (slowly) rising divorce rate of the 1960s and to see it as the product of something more than easier access and availability. He insisted that it was part of a new pattern of behaviour which also included rising illegitimacy rates. He predicted that these patterns would continue and attributed the changes to a more permissive approach to personal behaviour. Much more dominant, however, were the calls for 'sex reform', with freer access to birth control and a more relaxed attitude to premarital sexual experimentation.[21]

---

[16] M. Daly, 'The Gender Division of Welfare: The British and German Welfare States Compared'. Unpublished PhD. Thesis, Florence: European University Institute (1996).

[17] C. Hakim, 'Notes and Issues: The Myth of Rising Female Employment', (1993) 7 *Work Employment and Society* 97.

[18] K. Kiernan, H. Land, and J. Lewis, *Lone Motherhood in Twentieth Century Britain*. Oxford: Oxford University Press (1998).

[19] See esp R. Fletcher, *The Family and Marriage in Britain*, Harmondsworth: Penguin (1966); G. Gorer, *Sex and Marriage in England Today. A Study of the Views and Experience of the Under-45s*, London: Nelson (1971); M. Young and P. Willmott, *The Symmetrical Family: A Study of Work and Leisure in the London Region*, London: Routledge and Kegan Paul (1973).

[20] R. Chester, 'Contemporary Trends in the Stability of English Marriage', (1971) 3 *Journal of Biosocial Science* 389.

[21] See esp G. M. Carstairs, *This Island Now*, London: Hogarth Press (1962); A. Comfort, *Sex in Society*, London: Gerald Duckworth (1963); H. Wright, *Sex and Birth Control*, London: Allen and Unwin (1968).

Most influential were the changing views of churchmen, who while they did not give their approval to extramarital sex, nevertheless reformulated ideas about morality such that they could be used to justify more radical, hedonistic, and individualistic behaviour. Oppenheimer was typical in suggesting that personal relationships based on duty gave rise to lower-level claims than those based on love.[22] Many felt that the most invidious aspect of the traditional, rule-bound morality (typified by fault-based divorce) was the fact that coercive behaviour inside marriage did not stand condemned. In the most influential text, the Bishop of Woolwich rejected the traditional Christian thinking on marriage and divorce and advocated a position 'based on love', whereby nothing could be labelled as 'wrong'—not divorce, nor premarital sex—unless it lacked love.[23] The changing views of Christian writers on matters of sexual morality were part of a much broader questioning of the relationship between law and morality. Lord Devlin's Second Maccabean lecture, delivered in 1958 after the Wolfenden Committee reported in favour of reform to the law on homosexuality, examined the boundary between public and private morality. Devlin's argument that it was possible to identify and enforce a common morality aroused a storm of criticism from those who believed that morality in mid-twentieth-century England was necessarily pluralist and that external regulation would effectively impose the behaviour of the majority.[24] Most crucially, the dominant strand in the 1960s literature on sexual morality stressed its private nature and the need for morality to come from within the individual rather than being imposed from without.

The fundamental shift on the part of policy makers to questions regarding sexual morality had a profound effect on the private law of the family. In the immediate post-war years, policy in this area was as conservative in respect of its view of the family, as that of social security settlement. A Royal Commission on Marriage and Divorce,[25] appointed in the wake of a 1951 attempt to make marriage breakdown a new ground for divorce, feared that relaxing the divorce law would result in an increase of what it called 'divorce mindedness', and stressed the 'insidious' nature of the tendency to take marriage less seriously. The Commission recommended—in 1956—against any change in the law of divorce, and yet ten years later a group appointed by the Archbishop of Canterbury advocated reform. The group concluded that the concept of matrimonial offence or fault embodied in the law of divorce committed the courts to a superficial idea of the relationships between husbands and

[22] H. Oppenheimer, 'Moral Voice and Divine Authority' in I. R. Ramsey (ed), *Christian Ethics and Contemporary Philosophy*, London: SCM Press (1966).
[23] J. A. T. Robinson, *Honest to God*. London: SCM Press (1963).
[24] See esp H. L. A. Hart, *Law, Liberty and Morality*. Oxford: Oxford University Press (1963).
[25] *Report of the Royal Commission on Marriage and Divorce*, Cmd 9678. London: HMSO (1956).

wives and made it impossible for the couple to say honestly that their marriage was at an end. It recommended that the concept of marital breakdown replace that of offence. However, because it was impossible for the church to countenance divorce by consent (which would have the effect of turning a sacrament into a mere contract that could be terminated at will), it favoured 'breakdown with inquest'.[26] The Law Commissioners moved swiftly to point out the impracticability of interrogating couples about the state of their marriages. The Law Commission's own proposals, while asserting that the aim was 'to buttress, rather than to undermine, the stability of marriage', were based on the aim of enabling 'the empty shell to be destroyed with the maximum fairness, and the minimum bitterness, distress and humiliation' when a marriage had irretrievably broken down.[27] Divorce law reform in 1969 was based on a compromise between church and state. Marital breakdown was made the sole ground for divorce, but in order to avoid any suspicion of a move towards treating marriage as a contract that could be broken at will, it had to be established by reference to one of five 'facts': adultery, unreasonable behaviour, two years' desertion, two years' separation if both parties agreed, or five years' separation if one party did not. Thus Britain moved in 1969 only to partial no-fault divorce. Most couples, 76 per cent of those divorcing in 1986, continued to use the old fault-based grounds—adultery and unreasonable behaviour—as proof of marriage breakdown.[28]

As with the post-war reform of public law which affected the support of men and women in the family, policy makers did not intend to deregulate and individualize the private law of the family. The profound shift in ideas about sexual morality among churchmen was inspired by the search for a 'higher morality'. At the end of the day, their belief was always that progressive reform, whether in the form of greater access to contraception or easier divorce, would strengthen marriage and personal relationships. Nevertheless, as the Finer Committee on One-Parent Families recognized, ideas about sexual morality had shifted significantly. In the view of the members of this Committee: 'Once it is conceded that the law cannot any longer impose a stricter standard of familial conduct and sexual morality upon the poor than it demands from others, it follows inexorably that part of the cost of breakdown of marriage, in terms of the increase of household and dependencies, must

[26] Archbishop of Canterbury, *Putting Asunder: A Divorce Law for Contemporary Society*. London: SPCK (1966).
[27] Law Commission, *Reform of the Grounds of Divorce: The Field of Choice*, Cmnd 3123. London: HMSO (1966) 15.
[28] Law Commission, *Facing the Future. A Discussion Paper on the Ground for Divorce*, HC 479. London: HMSO (1988).

fall on public funds'.[29] The Committee felt that it was impossible to restrict the freedom to divorce, remarry, and reproduce, that is for government fundamentally to change the marriage system: 'The fact has to be faced that in a democratic society, which cannot legislate (even if it could enforce) different rules of familial and sexual behaviour depending on the ability to pay for the consequences, the community has to bear much of the cost of broken homes and unmarried motherhood.'[30] In the case of private law, divorce rates increased dramatically after the move to a partial no-fault regime. After 1969 the interest of the state in the reasons for ending a marriage receded to 'vanishing point'.[31] In 1973, a 'special procedure' was introduced to enable couples to dispense with legal representation in simple cases and this was extended to all undefended cases in 1977. As Cretney noted,[32] it is unlikely that Parliament would have been willing to pass the 1969 legislation if it had been known that within ten years there would be so little attempt to impose morality from without.

1980s and 1990s: FROM POLICY BASED ON MARRIAGE TO POLICY BASED ON PARENTHOOD

By the 1980s, research findings were drawing much more pessimistic conclusions about family change than had the sociologists of the late 1960s and 1970s. British research followed the American in providing evidence of the detrimental impact of divorce on the educational achievement, employment, and personal relationships of children and young adults.[33] Looking at high rates of family breakdown, the rapid increase in extramarital births, and the move towards later marriage and less marriage, policy makers increasingly feared that behaviour was becoming more individualistic and more selfish. This fear was clearly articulated during the parliamentary debates over the 1996 Family Law Act, during the course of which many Members of Parliament sought to make the legislation more of a vehicle for saving marriages. In the House of Lords, Baroness Young said that 'for one party simply to decide to go off

[29] Finer Report, n 3 above, para 4.49.

[30] Finer Report, n 3 above, para 4.224.

[31] G. Davis and M. Murch, *Grounds for Divorce*. Oxford: Clarendon Press (1988), 13.

[32] S. Cretney, 'Divorce Reform in England: Humbug and Hypocrisy or a Smooth Transition', in M. Freeman (ed), *Divorce Where Next?* Aldershot: Dartmouth (1996).

[33] eg M. P. M. Richards and M. Dyson, 'Post-Divorce Arrangements for Children: A Psychological Perspective', (1982) *Journal of Social Welfare Law* 133; M. Maclean and M. E. J. Wadsworth, 'The Interests of Children after Parental Divorce: A Long Term Perspective', (1988) 2 *International Journal of Law and the Family* 155; K. Kiernan, 'The Impact of Family Disruption in Childhood on Transitions made in Young Adult Life', (1992) 46 *Population Studies* 213.

with another person . . . reflects the growing self-first disease which is debasing our society'.[34]

In fact, pessimism about the growth of selfish individualism as the driver of rapid family change, which policy makers tend to feel profoundly uneasy about, has had an impact on both the public and private law of the family. Observing the high rates of divorce and of extramarital births, policy makers have first blamed opportunistic, selfish behaviour on the part of men and of women, and second, feared the extent to which policy has fuelled these changes. However, new policy initiatives have been mixed and are not easy to characterize. Certainly politicians in the 1990s have learned how difficult it is to promote 'family values'. Putting the clock back such that policy makes assumptions about the existence of a male breadwinner family has proved impossible when first, successive Conservative governments since 1979 and now Labour have pursued the American path towards a flexible, low-wage economy that makes women's earnings crucial to the two-parent family economy;[35] and second, so many families either consist of cohabiting couples or are headed by lone mothers. Neither traditional roles nor marital status can be assumed in the late twentieth century. In addition, the determination of successive governments to curb public expenditure has made it impossible to continue to support a traditional caring role for lone mothers with the state stepping in to fill the role of male breadwinner. Lone mothers in Britain, as in The Netherlands and the United States, have been encouraged to become paid workers, and yet the increased participation by mothers in the labour market has also been viewed as a manifestation of women's greater economic autonomy which in turn has fuelled family change. The assumptions that governments can or should make about relationships and behaviour in the family are no longer clear. As a result, policy makers have increasingly focused on an aspect of responsibility that most can agree upon, the responsibility of adults as parents. However, the trend towards making this the only focus of public and private law has not been unambiguous.

By the early 1990s, the political debate was dominated by those who stressed the irresponsibility and selfishness of men as well as of women. Michael Howard, then Home Secretary, said in a speech to the Conservative Political Centre in 1993: 'If the state will house and pay for their children the duty on [young men] to get involved may seem removed from their shoulders . . . And since the State is educating, housing and

---

[34] *House of Lords Debates (Hansard)*, 29 Feb 1996, col 1638.

[35] For an account of the extent to which men's contribution to family economy has diminished, see S. Harkness, S. Machin, and J. Waldfogel, 'Women's Pay and Family Incomes in Britain, 1979–1991', in J. Hills (ed), *New Inequalities: The Changing Distribution of Income and Wealth in the UK*. Cambridge: Cambridge University Press (1996).

feeding their children the nature of parental responsibility may seem less immediate'.[36] Men's traditional duty to maintain was argued not only on the grounds of the importance of the role model it provided for children, but also in terms of fairness to the taxpayer: '. . . when a family breaks up, the husband's standard of living often rises whereas that of his wife and children falls, even below the poverty line. Taxpayers may then be left to support the first family, while the husband sets about forming another. This is wrong. A father who can afford to support only one family ought to have only one.'[37] Such views stood in stark contrast to the attitudes expressed some twenty years earlier in the Finer Report,[38] which had recognized the difficulty in a liberal democratic society of determining who had the right to procreate and which, in the absence of any capacity to stop further reproduction on the part of men, recommended that the state was bound to support the mothers and children they left behind.

The prime concern of political commentators about men's obligation to maintain was often allied with a more generalized concern on the political Right,[39] and the political Left,[40] among politicians[41] and the media,[42] about an increase in male irresponsibility. All argued that the successful socialization of children required the active involvement of two parents. Dennis and Erdos[43] sought to trace the rise of the 'obnoxious Englishman' to family breakdown. Their chief concern was the effect of lone motherhood on the behaviour patterns of young men. Lone motherhood was in their view responsible for at best irresponsible and at worst criminal behaviour in the next male generation. In fact such convictions about the link between absent fathers and rising crime rates have not been tested for any large-scale British sample. Morgan,[44] while not blaming individualism, argued for more incentives, for example in the form of tax allowances, to the formation of two-parent families based on marriage. Despite their explicit commitment to the traditional family, the married man's tax allowance withered under the Conservative governments of the 1980s and 1990s.

The assumption of much of this literature is that men are instinctively uncivilized and that family responsibility is the only thing that ties them

---

[36] Picking up the Pieces, Mimeo, Conservative Political Centre Fringe Meeting, Blackpool (1993).

[37] *The Economist*, Editorial, 9 Sept 1995.

[38] n 3 above.

[39] P. Morgan, *Farewell to the Family: Public Policy and Family Breakdown in Britain and the USA*, Choice in Welfare series, no 21. London: Institute for Economic Affairs (1995).

[40] N. Dennis and G. Erdos, *Families without Fatherhood*, Choice in Welfare Series, no 12. London: Institute for Economic Affairs (1992).

[41] *House of Commons Debates (Hansard)*, 3 Dec 1993.

[42] eg BBC *Panorama* 20 Sept 1993.

[43] n 40 above.

[44] n 39 above.

into communal living. Dench[45] has argued strongly that family responsibilities are an indispensable civilizing influence on men:

If women go too far in pressing for symmetry, and in trying to change the rules of the game, men will simply decide not to play . . . Many women are now setting great store by the coming of New Man . . . the current attack on patriarchal conventions is surely promoting almost the exact opposite, namely a plague of feckless yobs, who leave all the real work to women and gravitate towards the margins of society where males naturally hang around unless culture gives them a reason to do otherwise. The family may be a myth, but it is a myth that works to make men tolerably useful.

The influential journalist Melanie Phillips[46] has also concluded that it is the erosion of the male role that has created 'yobbish men'. The identification of male behaviour as problematic during the 1990s was new in the post-war period, although it had been common at the beginning of the twentieth century. The fear in both historical periods was similar: given the opportunity, men would pursue their own selfish interests and ignore those of their families to the cost of both women and children, and the *polis*.

Women have also been seen as pursuing a more individualist course that is sometimes construed as a search for self-fulfilment at the expense of other family members. Above all, women's changing pattern of labour market participation has been highlighted. As Oppenheimer[47] has pointed out, the idea that women's increased economic independence has an effect on their marital behaviour is widespread, possibly because people with very different politics can buy into it. Both Gilder[48] in the United States and Dench[49] in Britain have seen the increase in adult women's labour force participation and attachment as something that has stripped men of their traditional breadwinning role within the family, and they blame women for pursuing self-fulfilment in the form of a career at the expense of their families. But feminists are as likely to endorse a theory that stresses the importance of women's economic independence as are right-wing polemicists, while of course stressing women's right and/or need to work. Other commentators have also stressed the democratic potential of relationships in which both partners have a measure of economic independence.[50] The fact remains that policy

---

[45] G. Dench, *The Frog, the Prince and the Problem of Men*. London, Neanderthal Books (1994) 16–17, citing the work of the American commentator, George Gilder.

[46] M. Phillips, *The Sex Change State*. London: Social Market Foundation (1997).

[47] V. K. Oppenheimer, 'Women's Rising Employment and the Future of the Family in Industrialised Societies', (1994) 20 *Population and Development Review* 293.

[48] G. Gilder, 'The Collapse of the American Family', (1987) *The Public Interest* (Fall) 25.

[49] n 45 above.

[50] eg A. Giddens, *The Transformation of Intimacy. Sexuality, Love and Eroticism in Modern Societies*. Cambridge: Polity (1992).

makers in Britain have remained somewhat suspicious of married mothers undertaking full-time work,[51] while being increasingly ready to push lone mothers into paid employment. Desmond King[52] highlighted the division among Conservatives between the libertarian and authoritarian Right on the question of married women's work.

For policy makers, the proof of growing selfish individualism, whatever its cause, lay in the statistics documenting the rapid pace of family change. During the 1960s, sex was increasingly separated from marriage, and increased sexual activity resulted in a rise in both the extramarital and marital birth rates, but there was still a marked tendency for pregnant women to marry. A majority of births to women under 20 were conceived outside marriage in the 1960s, but the majority of premaritally conceived births took place inside marriage. In 1969, 55 per cent of extramarital conceptions were legitimized by marriage, 32 per cent resulted in 'illegitimate' births, and 14 per cent were aborted (the abortion law was liberalized in 1967). Divorce rates also remained low. Taken together, these statistics explain in large measure the optimism of family sociologists in the 1960s and early 1970s. Since the beginning of the 1970s, there have been marked changes in marriage patterns, characterized by older marriage and substantial declines in marriage rates; a dramatic rise in divorce rates, which plateaued from the 1980s; and the emergence of widespread cohabitation. From the late 1970s, the proportion of births outside marriage began to increase slowly at first and then rapidly throughout the 1980s, with signs of stabilization in the early 1990s at about one in three of all births. It is in the main the broad trend associated with the seeming decline in marriage and the rise of cohabitation that has produced the *fin de siècle* anxiety about the future of marriage and the family.

As the Finer Committee Report pointed out in 1974, it is enormously difficult for liberal democratic governments to do anything about family change. Nevertheless, by the end of the 1980s British politicians were following their American counterparts in questioning whether social policies were providing incentives to the kind of change, namely, the increase in lone motherhood, that was considered undesirable. Charles Murray's arguments[53] about the causal relationship between the benefit system proved influential on both sides of the Atlantic. Both American and British critics of Murray effectively demolished the notion of a causal

---

[51] The 1995 *General Household Survey* showed that between 1993 and 1995, 74% of married women with dependent children aged 5 or over were working, compared with 53% whose youngest child was under 5.

[52] D. King, *The New Right: Politics, Markets and Citizenship*. London: Macmillan (1987).

[53] C. Murray, *Losing Ground: American Social Policy 1950–1980*. New York: Basic Books (1985).

relationship between social provision and family change.[54] State benefits and access to social housing might facilitate the formation of lone-mother families, but they do not cause it. The possibility of being able to achieve autonomous living via wages or benefits is crucial but is unlikely to be the only or even the decisive factor influencing behaviour. Rationalities other than the economic have been shown to be important for understanding the behaviour of lone-mothers.[55] Nevertheless, at the end of the 1980s and during the 1990s British politicians turned their attention to the social assistance system that supported lone-mother families as part of a much wider attack on what became known as 'welfare dependency'. Indeed, the term 'welfare' only achieved common currency in Britain in the 1990s, largely replacing reference to 'benefits' and even 'social security', which in Britain had always been used to cover both social insurance and social assistance.

The desire of the Conservative governments of the 1980s and 1990s to roll back public expenditure, together with the conviction that state benefits enabled the formation of lone-mother families and the growing unease about the pace of family change, made the idea of reducing benefits to lone mothers attractive. The possible sources of income for lone mother families are threefold: the state, the labour market, and men. In accordance with the logic of post-war assumptions about the male breadwinner model family, the state had stepped in to provide the lone mother with income on the condition that no man was present in the household (the cohabitation, or 'man-in-the-house' rule). If the state was to reduce provision, then lone mothers would have to be encouraged to turn either to the fathers of their children or to the labour market. By the late 1980s, only one out of three lone mothers was receiving regular maintenance and 59 per cent were receiving state benefits. Sixty per cent of children in families receiving income support (social assistance) were members of one-parent families.[56] The British Government turned first to fathers as an alternative provider to the state, in keeping with its

[54] I. Garfinkel and S. McLanahan, *Single Mothers and their Children: A New American Dilemma*, Washington, DC: Urban Institute (1986); D. Ellwood and M. J. Bane, 'The Impact of AFDC on Family Structure and Living Arrangements', in R. G. Ehrenberg (ed), *Research in Labor Economics VII*, Greenwich. Conn: JAI Press (1985); M. J. Bane and P. A. Jargowsky, 'The Links between Government Policy and Family Structure: What Matters and What Doesn't' in A. Cherlin (ed), *The Changing American Family and Public Policy*, Washington, DC: Urban Institute Press (1988); R. Ford, A. Marsh, and S. McKay, *Changes in Lone Parenthood*, Department of Social Security Research Report, no 40, London: HMSO (1995).

[55] R. Edwards and S. Duncan, 'Rational Economic Man or Women in Social Context?' in E. Bortolaia Silva (ed), *Good Enough Mothering? Feminist Perspectives on Lone Motherhood.* New York: Routledge (1995).

[56] J. Bradshaw and J. Millar, *Lone-Parent Families in the UK*, Department of Social Security Research Report no 6. London, HMSO (1991).

ambivalence about the desirability of women with young children engaging in paid work.

The ill-fated Child Support Act of 1991 created a single government agency to deal with child support, and sought to make all fathers responsible for maintaining their biological children.[57] The legislation is open to many interpretations, but it provoked an opposition from (mainly middle class) men and their second families similar to that to the equally ill-fated 'poll tax' (local taxation) legislation of the 1980s. In the words of the then Secretary of State, Peter Lilley, the legislation was intended to reverse 'the inadvertent nationalization of fatherhood'.[58] In this, the legislation paralleled the 1989 Children Act, in which responsibility defined in terms of a preference for parental over state responsibility bulked as large as the simple desire to enforce parental responsibility for children.[59] The emphasis on personal responsibility in the child support legislation was designed to reduce collective provision and thus to increase that of individuals, but it may *also* be construed as a measure that effectively recognized the way in which the family was changing. After all, late twentieth-century Conservatism favoured individualism; the only problem was how to enforce individual responsibility, which of course opened the way for what Lawrence Mead[60] has called a 'new paternalism'. The child support legislation did not attempt to bolster marriage, but rather moved towards enforcing parental responsibility, albeit that the responsibility attributed to fathers was the traditional one of financial support rather than care. Indeed, the child support formula introduced in 1991 took no account of the travelling expenses incurred by fathers who maintained contact with their children. The child support formula was modified considerably in 1994 and again in 1995. In practice, the child support agency has focused its attention on mothers in receipt of state benefits, and, given that money collected from fathers has been deducted pound for pound from benefits, the Treasury, rather than mothers and children, has stood to benefit most. In 1996 the penalty for lone mothers who refused to cooperate with the child support agency was increased to 40 per cent of the parent's allowance for three years with the possibility of renewal.

The child support legislation may be criticized as part of a 'new paternalism' designed to enforce individual responsibility, but it was also a means of addressing the problem of support for lone-mother families that did not attempt to reverse the trend of family change. The approach of the agency was undoubtedly often experienced as punitive by lone-mothers as

---

[57] See further Maclean, Ch 24 of this volume.

[58] BBC Radio 4, *World at One*, 6 Mar 1993.

[59] J. Eekelaar, 'Parental Responsibility: State of Nature or Nature of the State', (1991) *Journal of Social Welfare and Family Law* 37.

[60] L. Mead, *The New Paternalism*. Washington, DC: Brookings (1997).

well as by fathers. Furthermore, in the late 1990s, the British Government moved further in the direction of actively attempting to discourage lone motherhood by reducing state benefit levels. In 1996 it was announced that after April 1998 no new claims for one-parent benefit (part of the British provision of child benefit (the old family allowances)) would be accepted and those newly claiming social assistance would no longer qualify for the one-parent premium. While nowhere near as draconian as the 1996 US Personal Responsibility and Work Opportunity Act, this represented a major departure from the immediate post-war definition of lone mothers as 'mothers' and therefore entitled to benefits. At the same time, government announced a new incentive to assist lone mothers into paid employment by setting up pilot schemes to provide individual help with job search and assistance with training for work. The New Labour Government that took office in May 1997 upheld the benefit cut for lone mothers and extended the idea of 'welfare to work', making lone mothers part of its 'new deal' for the unemployed, albeit without the measure of compulsion that has been applied to getting the young unemployed into the labour market.

The labour market is the only remaining source of income for lone mothers, now that the fiasco of the child support agency has put back the attempt to make fathers pay up for some considerable time (some suggest as much as a generation).[61] But it is an irony that the solution to the problems faced by lone mothers is now seen in terms of behaviour that in the case of married mothers has been interpreted by many as selfish. The story of recent policy towards lone mothers shows policy makers acting to enforce individual parental responsibility in the face of the breakdown of the traditional two-parent, male breadwinner family. However, the aim of the policy has been more to limit state responsibility than fully to individualize the treatment of men and women in the family. In the case of lone mothers, government has been constrained in its choice of policy instruments by its aim of limiting public expenditure. But this does not mean that it has effectively accepted family change and moved away from any attempt to underpin marriage.

During the 1980s, it seemed that Government was inclined to accept the idea of increasing individualization. Independent taxation was finally introduced in 1990 and the tax incentives to marriage were substantially eroded throughout the 1980s and 1990s. The 1984 Matrimonial and Family Proceedings Act moved further in the direction of separating the position of the divorcing adults as husbands and wives from their position as parents. The attempt to leave the parties to the divorce in the

---

[61] J. Bradshaw, C. Stimson, C. Skinner, and J. Williams, *Absent Fathers?* London: Routledge (1999). See Maclean, below at 544–5.

same position as they would have been in had the marriage not broken down (the position after reform in 1969), which arguably involved some notion of compensaiton for women as unpaid carers, was abandoned. This, of course, had the effect of acknowledging that the private law of divorce relied on public law and the benefits system to provide an income for divorced women caring for children.[62] In the debates leading up to the 1984 legislation, no mention was made of the problem of securing the economic well-being of women and children after divorce. The aim for the adults was to promote a 'clean break' and to facilitate remarriage, which entailed the assumption that men and women could be independent.[63] Smart and Neale[64] have commented on the way in which this legislation in fact assumed that marriage had become more individualistic. Nevertheless, primary consideration was to be given to the children of the marriage, even though the debate proceeded without much reference to them.[65] As O'Donovan[66] commented, the focus in the 1980s was above all on adults as the 'consumers' of divorce.

The attempt to continue to liberalize family law in respect of adults while prioritizing children also characterized the proposal finally to introduce full no-fault divorce in the mid-1990s. Initially, the Lord Chancellor announced his intention of introducing measures to cut the rate of divorce. However, in a 1995 White Paper on mediation and the ground for divorce he proposed instead a collection of measures intended to make divorce less expensive and more amicable. According to *The Independent* of 28 April 1995, he had 'recognized an important truth—that the state has limited ability and little right to intervene in the personal relationships of private individuals'. The justification for what became the Family Law Act 1996 was that the use of fault-bred conflict and 'ritualized hostility', which was unlikely to foster the post-divorce contact necessary to ensure the welfare of children. Thus the Law Commission[67] recommended that divorce be treated more as a process and that a 'consideration and reflection' model be employed. It was during the parliamentary debate on the 1996 Act that considerable anxiety was voiced by Members of Parliament about the growth of what Baroness Young called 'the self-first disease'. As a result, the legislation

[62] G. Davis, S. Cretney, and J. Collins, *Simple Quarrels*. Oxford: Clarendon Press (1994).

[63] G. Douglas, 'Family Law under the Thatcher Government', (1990) 17 *Journal of Law and Society* 411.

[64] C. Smart and B. Neale, 'Wishful Thinking and Harmful Tinkering? Sociological Reflections on Family Policy', (1997) 26 *Journal of Social Policy* 301.

[65] J. Eekelaar, and M. Maclean, *Maintenance after Divorce*. Oxford: Clarendon Press (1986).

[66] K. O'Donovan, *Family Law Matters*. London: Pluto Press (1993).

[67] Law Commission, *Facing the Future. A Discussion Paper on the Ground for Divorce*, HC 479, London: HMSO (1988); Law Commission, *Family Law. The Ground for Divorce*, HC 636, London: HMSO (1990).

ended up putting considerably more emphasis on the importance of marriage and marriage saving. Problems on its practical implementation meant that the Act had only been partially implemented by the end of 2000.

The Labour Government has been as concerned as the Conservatives about the fate of marriage. But like the Conservatives, its rhetoric seems to be stronger than its will to act in this difficult area. In 1998, for the first time in the post-war period, government announced a national child care strategy, which meant a move away from the position (held also in the US) that child care is a private responsibility, and towards the continental European view that the state has a responsibility to try to reconcile the work and family responsibilities of adult citizens. This entails recognition of the increased labour market participation of all adult women. Labour has firmly supported 'family values', but its 1998 Consultative Paper used the word 'families' in the title rather than 'the family'.[68] The line seems to be: 'we are only concerned about families with children; where children are present, marriage is best; but we acknowledge the importance of supporting all families with children.' Thus government has returned to a position which recognizes the reality of family change, without abandoning support for more traditional forms.

CONCLUSION

The longstanding position of British policy makers has been to make implicit assumptions about family form and functions, which have had a profound effect on policy, but not to adress family questions explicitly. Towards the end of the 1980s, this changed as policy makers became increasingly concerned about the nature of family change and increasingly convinced as to a simple causal relationship between law and behaviour, something that remains problematic for a majority of social scientists.

The debate over 'the family' is peculiar to the English-speaking countries. It is noteworthy that lone-mother families exist in considerable numbers in other northern European countries, but that they have not become the focus for social anxieties in the same way as in Britain. In Denmark and Sweden, for example, the debate centres on the problems of one-earner as opposed to two-earner families. Having drawn adult women into the labour force such that their participation rate is virtually the same as that of men, these countries do not have to choose between

---

[68] Home Office, *Supporting Families*. London: Home Office (1998).

defining lone mothers as mothers or workers. All adults share a common worker-citizen status. In this context, one-earner families, whether headed by a lone mother or a male breadwinner, are recognized as being likely to have financial problems. Furthermore, it is recognized that the vast majority of adult women face difficulties in reconciling family and employment responsibilities. Lone mothers benefit from the generous social security and child care provisions made for *all* women with young children. The ability of lone mothers in other European countries to 'package' (the term is that of Rainwater, Rein, and Schwartz[69]) income from earnings *and* from state benefits means in turn that they tend to be significantly better off than their British counterparts.

What is most marked in the British system has been the absence of any firm commitment to integration and social inclusion on the part of successive governments in the 1980s and 1990s. In both Britain and the US, inequalities have grown sharply[70] and the position of lone mothers has deteriorated. Between 1979 and 1991 the number of children living in households with below 50 per cent of average income trebled to 3.9 million. In the early 1990s one child in three was growing up in a poor household compared with one in ten in the late 1970s.[71] Compared to continental European countries, both the UK and the US have a high rate of young motherhood, married and unmarried. One of the most convincing explanations for this is the polarization of wealth and income in both countries and the relative lack of investment in children.[72] Selfish individualism has been blamed by policy makers for increased family breakdown, but it is also the case that the New Right governments of the 1980s and 1990s have been hoist by their own individualist, in the sense of anticollectivist, petard. In introducing its 1999 Budget, the Labour Government talked at length about the importance of addressing the welfare of children; much will depend on how effective it is in this respect.

[69] L. Rainwater, M. Rein, and J. Schwartz, *Income Packaging in the Welfare State*. Oxford: Clarendon Press (1986).

[70] J. Hills (ed), *New Inequalities: The Changing Distribution of Income and Wealth in the UK*. Cambridge: Cambridge University Press (1996).

[71] J. Bradshaw, *Child Poverty and Deprivation in the UK*. London: National Children's Bureau (1990).

[72] K. Kiernan, 'Family Change: Parenthood, Partnership and Policy' in D. Halpern, S. Wood, S. White, and G. Cameron *et al* (eds), *Options for Britain: A Strategic Policy Review*. Aldershot: Dartmouth Press (1996).

5

The Evolution of Family Policy in the United States after World War II

BARRY L. FRIEDMAN AND MARTIN REIN

Families have changed substantially over the last half-century in the US, and family policy has evolved in response. Many kinds of policies have emerged over the years that affect families. Policies in their early stages tend to be directed at specific problems. There are policies relating to marriage and divorce, others concerned with child care, some with work by mothers, and others with income support for families. These policies initially tended to be specialized, each concerned with its own aspect of family behavior. But family behavior itself is not compartmentalized. One aspect of behavior is interrelated with others. Once policies were established, it turned out that one kind of policy could affect not only its intended area, but other kinds of behavior as well. The result has been that policy has also become more complex as the separate strands of policy and behavior have become more interdependent.

To provide a framework for tracing the evolution of policy over time, we associate a policy with its initial area of specialization and refer to this as a domain. A domain involves first a particular aspect of family behavior. Second, it involves the policies that emerge to deal with problems relating to this aspect of behavior. Thus, a domain combines an aspect of behavior with the associated policies initially targeted at it. We identify four domains that are useful in tracing the various aspects of family behavior and policy. One is women's work. A second is child care. A third is family structure, including issues such as marriage and divorce. Each of these reflect basic family decisions. The fourth is family income, which is an outcome of these and other choices on and off our list. There have been major changes in behavior in each of these domains in the last half-century, and there have been important developments in policy in each. Although policies initially tended to specialize in domains, they could not continue to do so over time because the domains are interrelated. Nevertheless, the separation by domains is a useful analytic device because it allows us to keep track of interdependencies.

Interdependencies arise on more than one level. At one level, the underlying behavior is likely to be linked across domains, and a change in one domain is likely to affect others. For example, the long-term trend toward marketization of household activities continued into this half-century, which saw major shifts of women's work into the market. But increased market work by mothers may require child care by non-mothers, including the possibility of market child care. The marketization of women's work is linked in some degree to the marketization of child care. A second level of linkage occurs at the policy level. Policies in one domain are intended to affect the behavior in that domain. However, the policies in one domain are likely to affect others, sometimes favorably, sometimes adversely. Because of the cross-effects of policies, it may be possible to use policies from one domain to obtain (or minimize) effects in another.

A third level is political and results from the fact that researchers, policy makers, and the general public may not agree on what the linkages are. To illustrate the interdependencies in both behavior and policy as well as the disagreements, single parenting, a behavior in the family structure domain, may increase the risk to family income and the likelihood of poverty. In one view, this connection justifies an income support policy in the income domain to improve outcomes in the child care domain for children in single-family households. Another view, however, argues that there is an additional form of interdependence, that welfare benefits themselves induce single parenthood. In this view, welfare creates, rather than cures the problem. The disagreements are resolved by political compromises that determine which policies are adopted and which linkages are to be used (or avoided). There is no dominant paradigm underlying family policy in the US. There are competing paradigms, each of which influences policy, but no one of them dominates. There are periodic shifts in the political balance between the advocates of different paradigms, leading to adjustments, but generally not to total upheavals in US policy.

In the first part of the paper, each of the four domains will be introduced separately. Behavioral trends will be examined along with the emergence of public policies in each domain. The second part of the paper deals with the links between domains. Since there are so many links, the paper will focus on links centered on the family income domain. We consider what is known about the links, but also the gaps in knowledge. The uncertainty concerning links in turn permits disagreements and political struggles, and we trace the resulting evolution of policy.

INTRODUCTION TO THE DOMAINS AND THE EVOLUTION OF POLICY WITHIN EACH

Women's Work

The movement of women from work at home to work in the market reached its peak during this half-century. Women have always worked, often at home and without receiving a market wage. But, to focus on paid labor outside of the home, the United States has witnessed both a remarkable trend in the persistent increase in women's paid work, and a striking change in the composition of women who are at work. Indeed, adult women are the only demographic group whose labor force participation has continuously increased over the century in comparison to the decline in employment among males, particularly among male teenagers, young adults, and older persons before the normal age of retirement.

This section first looks at trends in the paid work by women, examining differences among categories of women. Second, it looks at policies that responded to problems within this domain. Primarily, these policies attempted to open the demand side of the market to women.

Trends in Paid Work

Between 1890 and 1940 only between 5 and 14 per cent of married women were considered participants in the female labor force. The figure for white women, no doubt the reference group at the time of the passage of the Social Security Act, was even lower, from 3 to 13 per cent.[1]

Consider next the long-term trend and the changing composition of women's work. It is useful to separate daughters, wives, and mothers. Single women, mainly daughters, both living at home and living away from home, sometimes sending remittances back home, were the main female workers for pay at the beginning of the twentieth century in urban areas. In 1890, single women accounted for three-fourths of the white female labor force. By 1960, they were only about one-quarter, not because they worked less, but because there were so many more married women in the labor force. Around 1890 the median age of these single daughters working in manufacturing was about 20, but by 1960 it was 40 years.[2] Policy issues then concerned the plight of these daughters, their working conditions, and their lives apart from their families.

After World War II, wives became a growing component of the labor force. Before 1950 the increase in the married women's labor force was very gradual. After 1950 there was a virtual explosion in the employment rate, not only of married women, but later of wives who were also mothers. Before this, there had been barriers against the employment of married women. For example, there had been a prohibition against employing married women as teachers in local public school systems. Wives were also barred from clerical employment in most large firms. But after the 1950s the cultural norms and rules about the employment of married women changed and the barriers diminished.

---

[1] See CLAUDIA GOLDIN, UNDERSTANDING THE GENDER GAP: AN ECONOMIC HISTORY OF AMERICAN WOMEN 17 (1990).   [2] See GOLDIN n 1 above, at 26.

One additional change relates to the employment of single mothers, including both those who were never married and those who were divorced and separated. By the 1990s this group consisted mainly of never-married mothers. But what are especially interesting are the trends in the employment rates of women aged 18–44 with children, both married and unmarried. The employment rate of married mothers increased from 27 per cent in 1963 to 65 per cent in 1997. By sharp contrast the single mothers' employment rate was quite stable during the 1970s and the 1980s when about half of these mothers worked. To step for a moment out of this domain, the welfare policy debate began to notice that married mothers were more likely to work than single mothers. The result was increased pressure for the employment of unmarried mothers who received welfare payments. During the 1990s the employment rate of unmarried mothers did change from the rather stable level of about 50 per cent to a figure approaching the 65 per cent level of employment achieved by married mothers. It has been argued that this change was induced by welfare policy, but whatever the cause, it was an important change in female work patterns.[3]

Public Policies in the Women's Work Domain.

Policy interventions did not become important in this domain until the marketization of women's work was well under way. When they did emerge, interventions focused on altering the demand side of the market. Eliminating barriers to employment was always a concern. The most notable policies centered on issues of discrimination, the unequal outcomes in earnings and employment by gender, given identical inputs. The 1963 Equal Pay Act and Title VII of the 1964 Civil Rights Act brought these issues of discrimination onto the legislative agenda. There have also been policies aimed at more indirect barriers to women's employment such as sexual harassment. Over time the legislative agenda has again shifted to creating a family friendly or supportive work environment not only for mothers with young children, but for families with caring responsibilities for their aged parents. Parental leave was a very contentious issue in American politics, but a parental leave law was finally passed in 1993. The controversy left its mark on this law. Unlike similar laws in other countries, the US law neither provides child care benefits nor mandates that employers do. Its main accomplishment is to protect the job rights of parents who take time off for care responsibilities. Although parental leave laws with benefits would fall in both the

---

[3] See David Ellwood, *The Implications of the Earned Income Tax Credit and Other Social Policy Changes on Work and Marriage in the United States*, Remarks at the Australian National University (Nov 25 1998).

domains of women's work and child care, the American law leans more into the women's work domain.

Child Care

The change in the work behavior of mothers changed the situation of their children. If the mother had been the primary caregiver, a new form of child care would be needed for the time that the mother was at work. This adjustment took place on its own as each family made the arrangements for the care of its children. Public policy became involved first in the 1960s out of a concern that the child care arrangements parents were choosing were not conducive to child development. In particular, policy was concerned with the child care arrangements of poor children, and the Head Start program was the response.

Since then, care for the children of mothers at work has remained a policy issue with multiple concerns. Continuing in the tradition of Head Start, one approach emphasizes developing forms of care that focus on child development. Another approach focuses primarily on the cost of care to the family and would subsidize care while letting families make their own choices about the form of care. In addition to the child care needs that arise when the mother works, policy has also been involved with care for disabled children, an area that emerged in the 1960s around the same time as Head Start. Finally, policy has been drawn into the issue of care for abused children.

We begin with care for the children of working mothers. We examine the demand for care by families and the various forms it has taken. Then we turn to the supply of care, the problems in the care market, and policy responses to these problems. Other parts of this domain that we do not cover in this paper concern policies related to disability and abuse.

Demand for Child Care by Families

The work decisions of mothers are closely related to the child care decisions of the family. Models of child care choice have long recognized the interdependence. There is a trade-off between work in the market and the combination of leisure and work at home. But there is also a simultaneous trade-off between household production and the purchase of household goods and services in the market. For some household goods such as food and clothing, there have been technical advances, which either reduced cost relative to home production or increased variety, quality, or convenience. Such changes facilitated the decisions by mothers to seek market work. However, in the case of child care, technical change is not so evident. But families do face a market offering a variety of forms of care, each with a different price and perceived quality. Family choices are constrained not only by price, but also by beliefs about the quality of care.

Looking at the outcomes, one can see that many choices are made, and these differ significantly for different ages of children. About two-thirds of the care to children of working mothers is in some form of informal arrangement. In 1991, for example, over one-third were cared for at home: 41 per cent of those less than 1 year old; 39 per cent of those 1 or 2; 31 per cent of 3- and 4-year-olds; and only 10 per cent of school-age children.[4] The extent of care at home fluctuates over time, but is around a rate close to one-third. It was one-third also in 1977. Nearly 60 per cent of the care at home is by fathers, although this is far less likely for lone mothers. Grandparents give about one-fifth of at-home care, while other relatives and non-relatives give the rest. The other major informal mechanism is care in another home, accounting for a little less than one-third in 1991, although it had been 40 per cent in 1977. In 1991, only 23 per cent of children were in organized child care facilities, but this did represent a substantial increase from 13 per cent in 1977. Relatively few of the youngest children were in organized facilities, but 33 per cent of 3- and 4-year-olds were. Among grade school children, nearly 8 per cent were latchkey children who cared for themselves at least part of the time their mothers were working.

In view of the extent of informal arrangements, it is not surprising that only one-third of mothers report making a monetary payment for child care. Of course, others give much of the care within the family. But it is likely that informal arrangements do involve some sort of exchange, even if not monetary or not reported. Since the full amount of compensation may not be knowable, it is difficult to assess the impact of cost on child care choices. But for the kinds of care with monetary charges, it appears that cost has remained stable in real terms over long periods. At the same time, women's wages have risen in real terms. This combination has probably facilitated the movement of women into market work.[5]

It is difficult for researchers to assess but, of course, each family makes its own judgment. Researchers and government regulations have focused on structural measures of quality such as child–provider ratios, group size, and educational levels of providers. However, research has not found a relationship between these characteristics and the prices that

[4] See Lynn M. Casper, *et al*, *Who's Minding the Kids? Child Care Arrangements: Fall 1991*, US BUREAU OF THE CENSUS, CURRENT POPULATION REPORTS: HOUSEHOLD ECONOMIC STUDIES, P70–36 (1994).

[5] See Arleen Leibowitz, *Child Care: Private Cost or Public Responsibility?*, in Victor Fuchs (ed), INDIVIDUAL AND SOCIAL RESPONSIBILITY (1996).

parents pay.[6] In other words, there is no price premium for such characteristics. Studies have found an association between price and expanded
measures of quality such as teacher qualifications and turnover. When
parents were asked what they valued, the most common response was
the quality of the interactions between caregivers and children.[7] Actual
choices depend on the combination of cost and quality. But it has been
noted that the children in centers with the highest measured quality
tended to come from low-income and high-income families. The low-
income families are eligible for subsidized programs like Head Start,
while the high-income families can afford quality care. This leaves the
middle-income families to make the difficult trade-offs between cost and
quality.

The Market for Child Care and Public Policy

Public policy has been concerned with access and affordability of child
care. The main approach to this problem has been subsidization. It has
been estimated that the largest government child care program is the
child care tax credit, available to working mothers, and which absorbed
60 per cent of all federal spending on child care in 1988.[8] Policy has also
been concerned with child development, particularly among children
growing up in poverty. Head Start was the initial response, and debates
continue over whether it should be expanded. Although policies evolved
as responses to problems, the policies did not always fully solve the problems, leading to further efforts at policy development.

Consider first subsidization and its appropriateness as a tool to
improve access and availability. Among all families paying for child care,
the average cost was $63 per week in 1991, and this was almost the same
for families above and below the poverty line.[9] For poor families, this
would be a higher proportion of income, but fewer women in poverty
paid for child care than those above the poverty line (24 per cent versus
36 per cent). Moreover, this cost has remained constant in spite of increasing demand for care. Studies have concluded that overall the supply is
highly elastic.[10] This suggests that care is available and at an average price
that is stable and modest. Of course, even a low cost can be a relatively

---

[6] See Linda Waite *et al*, *What Parents Pay For: Child Care Characteristics, Quality, and Costs*,
47 J Soc Issues 33–48 (1991).
[7] See Sandra Hofferth, Child Care Quality Versus Availability: Do we have to Trade One
for the Other? (1994).
[8] See Philip K. Robins, *Federal Financing of Child Care: Alternative Approaches and Economic
Implications*, 9 Population Res Pol'y Rev 65–90 (1990).
[9] See Casper, *et al*, n 4 above.
[10] See Ellen Kisker and Rebecca Maynard, *Quality, Cost, and Parental Choice of Child Care*,
in David M. Blau (ed), The Economics of Child Care 127–44 (1991); see also David M. Blau,
The Child Care Labor Market, 26 J Hum Resources 19–39 (1992).

large burden for a poor family. Moreover, if the issue is not just care, but quality care, the tax credit may not be well targeted. As we have seen, poor families participate in high-quality programs because they are subsidized and high-income families because they can afford them. But the tax credit may not be sufficient to induce middle-income families to participate in high-quality formal care. On the other hand, families do not necessarily agree on what constitutes quality, nor do they necessarily concur with standards set by government agencies. Subsidization will result in a diversity of outcomes. Some families may even substitute other goals such as convenient location for quality.

Considering the goal of child development, an early concern was that care not given by mothers might even be detrimental to children. By now, evidence has accumulated that child care can have at least some positive developmental outcomes. Program quality does seem to have a positive effect on outcomes for children.[11] There has been evidence that care is particularly beneficial for children facing health risks or lack of family resources.[12] Not surprisingly, such findings have stimulated proposals for expansion of Head Start.

One more strand in child care policy has been an outcome of welfare reform. In the effort to get mothers into jobs, welfare programs have tended to incorporate a child care benefit. The goal of such benefits has been more to get mothers to work than to promote child development. Thus, these programs are less costly than Head Start.

Finally, the market itself has been slow to increase quality. The quantity of day care has expanded readily, although it is not clear that there has been any corresponding increase in quality. Cost has remained stable over time largely because of a ready supply of low-wage workers rather than because of improved productivity. It is hard to imagine a technological advance in child care. However, other service areas have been able to improve productivity even with unchanged technology, largely by exploiting economies of scale and economies of scope. In the child care market, such developments have not proceeded as rapidly as in other service areas, nor have policy makers found ways to stimulate productivity.

Family Structure

While marketization spawned new policies in our first two domains, the domain of family formation had always been a matter of public policy.

---

[11] See Martha Zaslow, *Variation in Child Quality and Its Implications for Children*, 47 J Soc Issues 125–38 (1991).

[12] See Alison Clarke-Stewart, *A Home is Not a School: The Effects of Child Care on Children's Development*, 47 J Soc Issues 105–24 (1991).

The state had always set rules for marriage, divorce, and some aspects of childbirth such as abortion. In this domain, the old rules began to change. The changes in rules were accompanied by changes in values and norms. The rule and norm changes were followed by major changes in behavior as well, particularly the emergence of lone-parent families. Eventually, concerns arose about the adverse effects of the behavior changes on other domains. And there has been a search for policy remedies for the adverse effects. Here we can only sketch some highlights of this process.

In the United States the evolution of divorce law varies from state to state, but nevertheless, there are common patterns to the changes. Public policy was initially based on the assumption that marriage is a lifetime arrangement and within marriage common law doctrine about coverture shaped legal practice. According to this doctrine a married woman lost her legal identity after marriage, including the right to own property, to enter into contracts, to conduct business, to sue. She was expected to reside in the place chosen by the husband. In return for these legal disabilities, common law required a husband to provide his wife with the 'necessaries' for performing the wiving and mothering roles. Two broad legal movements slowly made these common law doctrines obsolete. From the second half of the nineteenth century to the 1970s the Married Women's Acts gradually conferred on wives a series of rights which removed the legal disabilities imposed by common law practice.

Subsequently, the state's interest in the preservation of marriage dwindled as evidenced by the rapid spread of no-fault divorce. Divorce became accessible on the grounds of incompatibility rather than the misbehavior of one of the parties. No-fault divorce is now available in some form in all states. Whatever grounds are statutorily specified, most states in effect allow unilateral divorce on demand.[13] The change in divorce laws was accompanied by and perhaps induced by changes in values concerning marriage. There was a growing sentiment to allow people choice in many areas including family relationships. There was also a new egalitarian movement, which emphasized particularly the rights of women, ushered in by the rise of feminism. A change in social norms may be followed by a change in behavior. As Sunstein observed, 'People may publicly support an existing norm not because they are genuinely committed to it, but because they fear social sanctions. When those sanctions diminish or disappear . . . the result can be astonishingly rapid social change.'[14]

Following the change in divorce laws and the modifications in norms concerning divorce, marriage, and family, there were, indeed, notable

---

[13] See M. Margaret Conway, Women and Public Policy 132 (1999).
[14] Cass Sunstein, Free Markets and Social Justice 47–8 (1997).

changes in behavior. Perhaps the most significant was the increase in the number of lone-parent families. Lone parents are a distinctively new social category that has emerged in both England and the United States over the last thirty years. This category brings together a very heterogeneous group including widows, divorced (half of all marriages end in divorce), separated, never-married women, cohabiting couples, grandparents, and newly emerging patterns where lone parents raise children of whom neither paternity nor maternity is known. To consider just the sub-category of female-headed families: in 1970 there were 5.6 million such families with no man present and by 1995 the number had increased to 12.2 million. The social category of lone parents is large, heterogeneous, and represents a change in the traditional view that married couples are the appropriate institutional form in which to raise children.

As marriage and parenting behavior changed, society gradually had to deal with external effects from the new family forms. The new behavior patterns had undesired effects on family income and hence on the well-being of children. One side effect of divorce is the tendency toward a decline in the living standards of divorced women. Income problems can be dealt with through income supports. But there are options even in this domain within divorce law. Divorce settlements may include alimony payments to offset the income loss. However, such payments have become relatively uncommon. In the 1990s, alimony awards occurred in only 15 per cent of divorces and the former wives actually received payments in only two-thirds of the cases where awards were made. While alimony has fallen into disfavor, there has been growing public concern about child custody and child support. In 1975 Congress created the Child Support Enforcement (CSE) program. The welfare reform law of 1996 strengthened the tools available for collecting child support in a determined effort to make fathers responsible for the financial support of the children they have fathered.[15]

In addition to the adverse effects on income for lone mothers, demarriage has also brought problems for men. Ackerloff observed a decline in the proportion of young men who marry, and explored the consequences.[16] He noted that between 1968 and 1993, the fraction of men 25–34 who were householders living with children declined from 66 per cent to 40 per cent. Concerning the causes, he argued that there has been a technological change in which women have access to birth control and abortion and therefore are in a position to control conception, if they choose. Men have responded in two important ways. First, there has been a sharp decline in 'shot-gun' marriages since men no longer feel fully

---

[15] See CONWAY n 13 above, at 139.
[16] See George A. Ackerloff, *Men without Children*, ROYAL ECON SOC'Y J (1998).

responsible for the outcome of an unwanted pregnancy. Accompanying the decline in coerced marriage, there has been a decrease in overall marriage rates. This could have a beneficial effect if the men instead of marrying spent more time at school and pursuing a career. But by and large this has not happened. For those who do marry, marriage continues to symbolize the adoption of a new identity by both the bride and the groom, a rite of passage from one stage of the life course to another. In particular, marriage presages an increased attachment to work. As evidence, married men earn more when at work; their earnings increase more rapidly compared to single men; and they accumulate more financial assets since they are likely to invest in buying a home in preparation for raising a family. In Ackerloff's interpretation, the fact that men do not marry is a causal factor in the increase in crime and drugs and other forms of deviant behavior. Although the change in behavior may have resulted from changes in cultural norms, the old norms cannot be restored. Adverse effects have been unleashed, but it may take new forms of policy to get them back under control.

Family Income

In each of the previous domains, policy initially tended to focus on the domain itself and only later came to respond to linkages with other domains. In contrast, the family income domain has been linked to others from the beginning. Behaviorally, family income is the result of the work decisions of all family members, non-earned income, and external market circumstances. Other domains such as women's work and family formation decisions have external effects on it. The principal policy response in this domain has been anti-poverty programs. From the beginning, income support programs have been attentive to the other domains. There was an initial concern over the support of children in poor families. Over time, policy discussions have become more involved with the interdependencies between this domain and the others. This section introduces early trends in federal anti-poverty policy in the US and some of the value conflicts that grew up around it.

The original federal welfare policy included in the Social Security Act of 1935 was income support with special concern for children. It was designed to make sure that children were not separated from their parents solely for reasons of poverty. The program made available a cash grant to families of dependent children (those under 16 who are deprived of parental support because of death, continued absence from home, or physical or mental incapacity of one parent). At the time of the passage of the legislation, it was assumed that these benefits were to be provided to mothers with young children, probably widows. These mothers were expected by prevailing public norms to care for their children and not to be actively engaged in paid employment in the labor market. That is, it was not only income support, but also the basis of a child care policy. The anti-poverty frame was accepted as the best guarantor of the development of healthy children. This early crossing of the boundaries between the income and child support domains preceded the emergence of the specialized child care policies discussed above.

In contrast to the early goal of child care for single mothers rather than work, welfare programs have come to expect and even require work of recipients. The change in focus has been driven by values and conflicts over them, by changing norms concerning work behavior, and by a concern over the behavioral consequences of welfare programs. We consider here changing values and norms, while the second part of the chapter explores further behavioral consequences.

There were, and still are, individuals who believe that society has an unconditional obligation to help children in need. But there is also a sizeable segment of American society that has a value conflict in helping mothers who have violated social norms by being unmarried, even if they are raising their children in poverty. In 1936, this was not a major issue since it was assumed that welfare benefits would go largely to orphaned children whose fathers had died. There was differentiation of treatment of families even in the original Social Security Act, but it was motivated more by practical concerns rather than values. The Social Security pension system included survivor benefits for the children of workers who would have been eligible for pensions, and for their mothers. Children could receive benefits up to age 16 and, if a full-time student, to a higher age, which was eventually raised to 25. Aid to Families with Dependent Children (AFDC) was set up at the same time to cover other lone-parent families in need. It was not restricted to widows, but they and their families were probably expected to be the main beneficiaries, in particular those not eligible for the survivor benefits. Even today, aggregate spending for children through survivor benefits is greater than that under AFDC.

Changing facts heightened the value conflict. The composition of the welfare caseload by and large shifted from orphaned children whose fathers had died to fatherless children whose mothers were never married. The changes in women's work and in family structure have already been discussed. For those who disapproved of unmarried parenthood, there was growing reluctance to 'reward' unmarried mothers with unconditional support for their children. The matter was compounded by race. For white women, the rate of unmarried parenthood is not dramatically different than that in France and other European countries. However, the higher rate for black mothers has played an important role in the politics of welfare. The public perception of the program was that it largely served unmarried black mothers.

Values concerning appropriate family behavior had implications for work. The value conflict between helping children and not rewarding their mothers was dealt with by setting the goal that these mothers should work. If mothers did not receive welfare at all, their means of support would likely be work. Instead of going this far, AFDC was preserved over the years, and it helped families with children even if their mothers were unmarried. But the American system, instead of providing unconditional support for children, made that support in the case of AFDC conditional on work or at least job-seeking. There were other programs where children or their families could receive a benefit without a work requirement. Social Security survivor benefits continued without a work requirement. In addition, the Supplemental Security Income program, SSI, has come to provide benefits to disabled children without a work requirement. It was originally designed for those with a disability severe enough to prevent or restrict the ability to work, presumably excluding children. However, the Supreme Court in 1990 ruled that excluding disabled children was too restrictive. Since then, children who did not function as well as others their age have been classified as disabled and qualified for benefits, and work is not required. SSI and survivor benefits are targeted at special populations—disabled or orphaned children—who have not posed the kind of value conflict related to unmarried mothers in AFDC. The issue concerning unmarried mothers was heightened by the realization that increasingly, married mothers were working. If wives with young children worked, should solo mothers on welfare be expected to do the same? It became a question of fairness, of treating working and non-working poor families equally.

POLICY AND THE INTERDEPENDENCE BETWEEN DOMAINS

A Schematic Representation Centered on the Family Income Domain

We separated the domains because policies in their early stages sometimes were specialized responses to the problems within them. However, behavior is interrelated across domains. Policies have eventually begun to take account of the linkages across domains. Many of the controversies in family policy relate to the linkages. Figure 5.1 illustrates possible linkages involving the family income domain.

It is necessary to distinguish the underlying behavior in a domain from the policy interventions intended to correct problems within the domain. The principal problem within the family income domain is low income

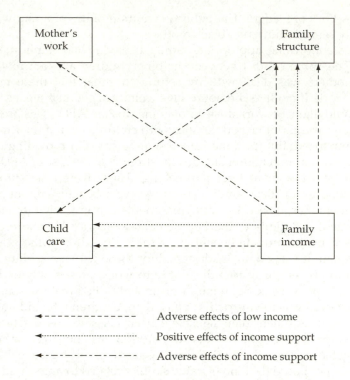

FIGURE 5.1. External effects from the family income domain.

(which may in turn be the result of behavioral issues in other domains, but we will refer to it as the underlying problem in this domain, whatever its source). Low income may have adverse effects on other domains, for example on the quality of child care (indicated by the horizontal dashed line in Fig. 5.1). The policy response within the family income domain is income support programs. Their direct effect is to relieve the problem of low income, but in so doing, they may also counteract the adverse effects of the low income on other domains. The horizontal dotted line illustrates the possibility of a beneficial effect on child care, offsetting the dashed line. The welfare may allow mothers to clothe, feed, and care for their children better.

Similarly, there is a pair of lines linking the family income and family structure domains. Low income may have an adverse effect on family stability, increasing the risk of divorce or perhaps of abuse within a bad marriage (vertical dashed line). Income support programs may have a positive effect, helping to stabilize a difficult family situation (vertical dotted line). Again, the income support may help to offset the adverse effects of low income.

While the dashed lines represent the adverse effects from low income, another set of adverse effects may result from welfare programs themselves. Income support creates a potential moral hazard problem in which people come to take advantage of the program. In Figure 5.1, the dash-dot lines illustrate the main channels for moral hazard where adverse effects may emerge. There may be an adverse effect on family structure if women are induced to have more children or to leave marriages, knowing that welfare will support them. This line from the family income box to the family structure box then continues on to the child care box, on the assumption that the adverse family structure developments in turn have adverse effects on children. There may also be an adverse effect on work (assuming that work for mothers is desirable) if women believe that welfare will support them.

All of the arrows shown in Figure 5.1 are empirical possibilities. These arrows represent, first, research questions, and there have been considerable efforts to estimate the magnitude of each of these effects. Second, political factions have prior beliefs on the magnitudes of the effects represented by the arrows. As a simplified sketch, liberals are particularly concerned about the adverse effects of low income (dotted arrows). Conservatives are concerned about the adverse effects of welfare policies (dash-dot arrows). These are partly value positions, but there is also an empirical aspect. Each side tends to emphasize evidence supporting the strength of its preferred arrows. The research has provided much information, but there remains a region of uncertainty about the relative magnitudes of the links (arrows) between domains. In the political world, this allows different factions to espouse different, even conflicting, views on how the links work and what should be done about them. What begins as an information problem becomes a conflict over information as political factions struggle to interpret evidence in line with their views. Moreover, political processes work out policies even when information is incomplete. People with diverse views can compromise and agree on policy even if they do not agree on the underlying information. As Sunstein argues, 'Incompletely theorized agreements on particular results are an important part of democratic deliberation; they are a distinctive solution to the problem of social pluralism and disagreement.'[17]

Uncertainty and the Political Interpretations of Information: Illustrations for the Family Income Domain

Several kinds of research have provided information on the linkages originating in the family income domain. Welfare caseloads have shown ups

[17] Cass R. Sunstein, *Incompletely Theorized Agreements*, 10 HARV L REV 1733 (1995).

and downs, which have fueled the political debates without resolving fully the questions of the magnitudes of the linkages. A large body of research on the effects of welfare programs generally shows effects on work, although usually not large ones. The work on welfare spells opens the largest information gap and has played an important role in political discussions.

Caseloads provide aggregate data from which it is difficult to distinguish causes. Rising caseloads could result from increased poverty or from increased attempts by individuals to take advantage of welfare programs. Nevertheless, as trends have gone up and down, people have seized on the trends as evidence to support their views. When the program first began in 1940, only 1 in 83 families received AFDC. By 1960 the numbers had increased to 1 in 38, still relatively small. But from the mid-1960s to the mid-1970s the caseload more than doubled and so too did the numbers of female-headed families with children. Conservatives used these numbers as evidence of growing welfare dependency. Liberals argued that the change was not a result of increased dependency. Rather, access to the welfare system had opened as more people who were already poor applied (a norm change) and of those who applied, more were accepted (a change in administrative practice). Then between 1973 and 1984 the growth slowed. The welfare caseload increased from 3.2 million to only 3.7 million, even though the number of female-headed families with children increased from 4.6 to 6.8 million. The value of a welfare benefit in real terms declined from 204 dollars to 169 dollars per recipient. These developments fueled a liberal counterattack. But between 1988 and 1994, the welfare caseload once again began to increase precipitously from 3.7 million to over 5 million. At the same time, only a small fraction of recipients reported work, about 10 per cent.[18] Again welfare reform was back on the political agenda, leading to a period of state welfare reform legislation and ultimately the federal welfare reform program. Of course, the ups and downs in caseloads were also associated with ups and downs in the economy. It was often difficult to distinguish moral hazard arguments from these trends.

With welfare reform in 1996, caseloads have continued to change. But the change has been not so much an overall cut in benefits, but a change in their form. Consider the percentage of single mothers receiving AFDC, Medicaid, Housing Assistance, Food Stamps, and the Earned Income Tax Credit (EITC). Between 1990 and 1994, about 18 per cent received public housing or rent subsidies, about 33 per cent of single mothers received AFDC, about 40 per cent received Medicaid, 45 per cent Food Stamps,

[18] See US Committee on Ways and Means, 1996 Green Book: Background Material and Data on Programs Within the Jurisdiction of the Committee on Ways and Means 474 (1996).

and about half EITC. During this period there was clear evidence that the share of mothers receiving these benefits rose modestly, except for EITC, which was relatively stable. However, in the four years after 1994 the pattern changed sharply. The share of mothers receiving AFDC declined to about 22 per cent and so did all other social benefits. However, the population receiving EITC increased to over 62 per cent during this period. While the means-tested programs based on need such as AFDC and its successor TANF declined, other benefit programs based on work increased. These recent trends may show as much about policy changes as about the underlying causes of welfare participation. Arguably, the overall level of welfare spending has been stable over this time period, but the composition of spending has changed sharply in response to the new policies.[19]

Formal tests of the effects of welfare on work give more direct evidence. There have been numerous studies using data from both experiments and existing programs. A review article by Moffitt concluded that welfare programs do have statistically significant impacts on work effort. He concludes, however, that these impacts do not explain the extent of poverty among female heads. They would still be poor even if AFDC were not present to induce them to reduce work effort.[20]

The work of Bane and Ellwood on welfare dynamics was a landmark in advancing knowledge and stimulating other work, but also in revealing the remaining region of uncertainty. It looked at dynamic responses, transitions out of welfare, rather than single period effects. It looked at varieties of responses rather than at the mean effect, finding a mixed story. Bane and Ellwood found that half of all welfare spells last less than two years.[21] That is, half of recipients are able to find an alternative such as work, which allows them to get off welfare in a relatively short period of time. Of course, some of the alternatives prove not to be stable and people do return to welfare. Periodic support from welfare can help these women, who can then find alternatives. On the other hand, 48 per cent of recipients currently on welfare will be on it for ten or more years. These amount to only 14 per cent of all welfare recipients, but they are heavily represented among those currently on welfare at any time. Alongside the people who cycle in and out of welfare fairly quickly, there is thus a sizeable minority of the welfare population who are in the midst of very long spells.

---

[19] See Christopher Jencks, *Briefing on Welfare Reform*, Presentation before the Ways and Means Committee (Feb 24 1999).

[20] See Robert Moffitt, *Incentive Effects of the US Welfare System*, 30 J ECON LIT 56 (1992).

[21] See MARY JO BANE and DAVID ELWOOD, WELFARE REALITIES 29 (1996).

Politically, the numbers on the long durations alone had a strong effect. As one observer commented, 'I think the finding that 65 per cent of recipients [currently on welfare] are on welfare for eight years or more astonished almost everyone and was the clear winner in the battle for people's understanding of whether dependency was a serious problem.'[22] Of course, this finding is only part of the story, since those with eight years or more are only 19 per cent of all those who ever go on welfare.[23] But the figure does suggest a dramatic possibility. If benefits to all those on welfare for eight or more years could be terminated, in a steady state the caseload at any point in time could be lower by 65 per cent. This is, of course, a mechanical result. But it raises the question of what accounts for the long spells. As Bane and Ellwood point out, there are multiple possibilities, and this is where the uncertainty comes in. One is that the long-term recipients are people with special problems who are somehow not capable of working. Another is that they are initially the same as other welfare recipients, but the longer they stay on welfare, the more their job-finding and work skills deteriorate, and the less likely they are to find jobs. If this were the case, they would benefit from a policy designed to get them off welfare quickly. Some characteristics of recipients are associated with the risk of long durations including single motherhood, being a high school dropout, and little work experience.[24] But these characteristics do not explain the long durations. As Pavetti found for welfare recipients as a whole, there are recipients with the same characteristics as other women who work.[25] The data do not distinguish whether there is some unmeasured problem that is a barrier to work and that distinguishes those with long durations, or whether there is a group, admittedly disadvantaged, which ends up taking advantage of the welfare system.

Politics and the Evolution of Policy in the Family Income Domain

Research on welfare has produced extensive information, but has not resolved the political disputes. Given the regions of uncertainty, each faction has found evidence to support its views, but has not been able to deal a decisive blow to the other. However, although the intellectual disputes are not fully resolved, policy decisions are made. The political process plays a role in the evolution of policy that research and analysis cannot. Although the political factions cannot agree on the facts concerning domain linkages, they can reach compromises on policy. This section will

[22] Ron Haskins, Liberal and Conservative Influences on the Welfare Reform Legislation of 1996 (1998).   [23] See Bane and Ellwood n. 21 above, at 32.   [24] See *ibid* at 50.
[25] See LaDonna Pavetti, *How Much More Can They Work? Setting Realistic Expectations for Welfare Mothers*, Urban Inst Rep 25 (1997).

provide illustrations of the recent compromises that have arisen in response to changes in the political balance between the factions.

One conservative view, argued forcefully by Charles Murray, was that the adverse effects of welfare are so powerful and so deleterious to the functioning of recipients that they overwhelm any positive effects. Murray concluded that the dependence created by welfare could be eliminated only by the elimination of welfare. This view drew considerable attention and influenced the welfare reform debate, but in the end did not prevail in its simplest form. In terms of our Figure 5.1, even many conservatives conceded that there was some merit to our dotted and dashed lines and that there may be some value or even necessity for a welfare program. In the end, a welfare program did survive. Conservatives agreed to a compromise on the basis of the argument that the need for welfare is temporary. Indeed, the program that emerged from the welfare reform of 1996 is called Temporary Assistance to Needy Families (TANF). The idea is that welfare will be eliminated for individuals, but only after time limits. The debate switched from one over eliminating welfare altogether to one over whether welfare needs are temporary or permanent. Is the issue resolved that they should be treated as temporary? As of now, it would seem so. But policy continually evolves. The program has begun in a favorable time with low unemployment. Moreover, the program has not yet matured, so that many recipients have not yet reached their time limits. If there is a notable increase in hardship, it is conceivable that exemptions from the time limits may increase, or the limits might be modified altogether. Political currents do shift over time, but it is difficult to make predictions.

Just as conservatives have had to compromise, so have liberals. Liberals have had to deal more explicitly with the possibility of adverse effects from welfare programs. There was reluctance at first, but more attention and research have been devoted to the adverse effects on work and on family structure as represented by the dot-dash arrows in Figure 5.1. Bane and Ellwood consider themselves liberals, but were convinced that a long spell on welfare is itself a barrier to getting off. They saw a need to focus particularly on young mothers to make sure that they do not become long-term recipients. They were in the Clinton administration when it proposed its version of welfare reform with the provision, 'two years and you work.'[26] They hoped to limit the time on welfare by assisting recipients into jobs. Politically, it was just a small step from there to time limits, limiting time by terminating benefits. In both cases the outcome might be

---

[26] David Ellwood, Winners and Losers in America: Taking the Measure of the New Economic Realities 22–9 (1999).

work, but in the liberal view, through assistance, and in the conservative view, through the more coercive procedure of termination.

Even this story does not capture the extent of the compromises on both sides. Eligibility for traditional income support for those not working has, indeed, become more restrictive under TANF. As already noted, TANF is not the only form of income support. The Clinton administration wanted to reward work and also to deal with the low wages of many who did work. Thus, in 1993 it introduced a significant increase in the existing Earned Income Tax Credit (EITC). This was an earnings subsidy conditional on work and paid as a credit through the income tax system. In 1997, an existing employer tax credit was raised, increasing the subsidy to employers who hire long-term welfare recipients. Within TANF, there are provisions for child care and transportation benefits (temporarily), both of which are supports that make work more attractive. Medicaid and state programs have been expanded to provide health care to most low-income, uninsured children, easing the concern that work would eliminate health care eligibility in Medicaid. Many of these changes have been initiated by liberals, but in fact have restructured our welfare system in a direction that could be considered more conservative. We have not eliminated income support, but have increasingly made it dependent on work.

CONCLUSION

We have argued that family policies initially responded to changes in behavior in areas such as mothers' work, child care, family structure, and family income. But these domains of family behavior are not independent. While programs initially may have targeted particular problems, it soon became clear that behavior in one domain had external effects on other domains. Similarly, a policy in one domain was likely to have external effects on the other domains. As policy makers became aware of the interdependencies, policies have been reshaped to take account of them. However, the process was complicated by the fact that there was disagreement over the nature, direction, and importance of the various external effects. There has thus been continual political struggle over the direction of the set of policies directed at families.

Out of this process of conflicting pressures over many policies, could it be said that there is a coherent American view or style of family policy? If one thinks in terms of traditional ideological views, the answer would appear to be no. Liberals have emphasized basic needs in the various domains and have looked to government policy as a way to meet the needs. Conservatives have emphasized the adverse effects of government policies and have sought to limit them. In the absence of government actions, they have tended to emphasize the personal values that might result in productive behavior relating to work and to family. Considering the role of government, there appears to be a sharp ideological divide. But over time, the two sides have had to share power. It has not been possible for one side to ignore the views of the other. Conservatives have not been able to eliminate many of the programs targeted at needs, and liberals have not been able to ignore the adverse effects of the programs they espouse.

Both sides are deeply concerned over the interdependencies between our domains. Each side on its own would tend to ignore the forms of interdependence emphasized by the other. However, the political process has not permitted this to happen. Thus, if there is a characterization of American family policy, it is that it has had to deal with all the forms of interdependence. It is eclectic in a way that does not fit any ideology. Government policies continue to address the needs of families and their children and to support the incomes of those who are poor. But the policies have also become very attentive to their own adverse effects. Indeed, the need to address adverse effects has often helped shape the direction of support in fundamental ways. For example, we have been moving away from unconditional income support for those who do not work while expanding income supplementation for those who work but are poor. We have not eliminated income support, but have transformed it. American family policy may not be ideologically appealing, but it does have a coherence of a sort in its attention to the wide range of interdependencies among domains.

6

English Family Law since World War II:
From Status to Chaos

JOHN DEWAR AND STEPHEN PARKER

INTRODUCTION

This chapter offers a survey of developments in legal ideology and policy in family law in England and Wales since World War II. It does so by identifying three ideological and policy 'eras', or schemas, in family law: the 'formal', the 'functional', and the 'complex' (or, less politely, the 'chaotic'). Although our starting point is the mid-twentieth century it is necessary to go back earlier for the purpose of establishing what we mean by the formal era.

We suggest that the history of family law during our period can be understood as a period of transition between these eras—from the first to the second era in the middle decades of the twentieth century; and from the second to the third era, over a period starting in the late 1980s and continuing today. Each era can be understood as characterized by a different set of balances struck between four dichotomies: rights–utility, form–substance, principle–pragmatism, and public–private.[1] We explain these terms in more detail below, and attempt to substantiate our claim that they successfully capture the successive phases of legal ideology and policy in this area.

We do not suggest that there is a neat real-time division between each era, nor that the point at which family law tipped from one into another can be precisely identified. Indeed, it could be argued that one of the chief characteristics of the current, third era is that there are lingering traces of the previous two, but overlaid by something new and different from what preceded it. A metaphor to illustrate this might be the sliding balance knob on a stereo radio, which controls the speaker from which the sound comes. In the first era of family law, the knob was well over to one side, although there was still some sound coming from the other channel. In the second, it was well over to the other side. The metaphor runs out on us when we try to describe the state we are in at the moment. Maybe the stereo is picking up several stations, including the local taxi firm, like short wave radio on a clear night.

---

[1] This typology originates in S. Parker, *New Balances in Family Law*, Family Law Research Unit Working Paper No 2, http://www.gu.edu.au/centre/flru/content2b.html (1998).

THE TERMS DEFINED

Historically, we think, one can make sense of change in family law by reference to four dichotomies.

Rights–Utility
Form–Substance
Principle–Pragmatism
Public–Private

We concede some doubts about the whole exercise of reducing complex bodies of thought to sets of dichotomies, particularly if one loses the capacity to observe that there is no body of thought there at all—for example, that 'family law' is a wholly artificial shaping of some regulatory policies. On the whole, however, we think there is some point to it. Law generally is made up of competing and changing ethical impulses and we need some way of netting the butterflies for long enough to observe them. Also, these impulses may help to tell us something about the very process whereby areas of law, such as 'family law', are constructed: provided, that is, one can tame the information for long enough to be able to reflect on it.

We suggest that the successive eras in family law can be charted by looking at which of the two poles in each of these dualities is emphasized. In the first era the first is emphasized, in the second era the second is emphasized. Probably at no time was there ever exclusive reliance on one alone, but in each there was a basic orientation in one direction or the other. In the third era, which we suggest has been emerging since the late 1980s, matters become more complex. It is characterized by further shifts in these dichotomies, but unlike previous shifts, these are not uniform across all four, and the poles of each dichotomy have taken on new meanings. In some cases, it is possible to see both poles of a dichotomy in evidence.

We have called these three eras the *formal* era, the *functionalist* era, and the *complex* era. Because our focus is on the period 1950 onwards, we do not dwell long on the first era, save in so far as is necessary to set the scene for the second and third.

THE FORMAL ERA

This era we take to refer to the period from 1857 (the introduction of civil divorce) to the introduction of the divorce reforms in the late 1960s, although in practice it had been petering out from the end of World War II. This era saw family law emerge from ecclesiastical law to become centrally a matter for the civil state. The marital relationship was seen basically as a form of contract, albeit a contract of adhesion, because the terms were not freely negotiable. It was more accurately a contractually acquired status, with the terms of that status set out by law. Of course, many changes took place during the period: for example, to the law concerning married women's property, or to the rules governing custody and guardianship of children following divorce.[2] Nevertheless, the period can be characterized as emphasizing the first term in each of the pairs set out above.

Rights

There was a strong sense of spouses as right-holders, using rights in the sense of claims that need no other justification for their enforcement. Rights had correlative duties. Breach gave rise to a remedy in the other, or the forfeiture by the guilty party of relief. Marriage was dissoluble only by showing breach, in the form of a matrimonial offence that had not itself been condoned, connived at, or conduced.[3] A wife's entitlement to maintenance was affected by her 'guilt' or 'innocence';[4] and decisions about the custody of children were resolved either by reference to the assumed superiority of the father's right to custody[5] or, latterly, by reference to moral evaluations of the parties' conduct.[6]

Form

Family law was made up of fixed categories that gave rise to predictable legal consequences. There were grounds of divorce and other relief. There

---

[2] For an account of these legislative changes, see M. L. Shanley, *Feminism, Marriage and the Law in Victorian England 1850–1895*, Princeton: Princeton University Press (1989).

[3] See M. Finer and O. MacGregor, 'The History of the Obligation to Maintain', in *Report of the Committee on One Parent Families*, Vol 2, Appendix 5, London: HMSO (1975); C. Gibson, *Dissolving Wedlock*, London: Routledge (1994) ch 4 for accounts of the development of the law of divorce during this period.

[4] See J. Barton, 'The Enforcement of Financial Provisions', in R. H. Graveson and F. R. Crane (eds), *A Century of Family Law*, London: Sweet & Maxwell (1957) ch. 14; J. Eekelaar and M. Maclean, 'The Evolution of Private Law Maintenance Obligations: The Common Law', in M. Meulders-Klein and J. Eekelaar (eds), *Family, State and Individual Economic Security*, Brussels: Story Scientia (1988) ch 6 for a discussion of the development of the law of maintenance and financial claims.

[5] At common law, a father had the right to the legal custody of his legitimate children, subject to limited exceptions: see *Re Agar-Ellis* (1883) 24 Ch D 317. This common law principle was gradually displaced during the late 19th and early 20th centuries by the principle that custody was to be resolved by reference to the 'welfare of the child' as the paramount consideration: see Guardianship of Infants Act 1925.

[6] For an analysis of the moralistic case law on child custody, decided under the auspices of the 'welfare principle', see C. Smart, *The Ties that Bind: Law, Marriage and the Reproduction of Patriarchal Relations*, London: Routledge & Kegan Paul (1984) ch 4.

were technical bars to relief, such as connivance, condonation, and conducement. The analogies with classical contract law, and even tort and criminal law, were close. Discretionary powers addressing the *substance* of the relationship were anathema, just as judicial variation of a contract was anathema to the common lawyer. For example, as late as 1969, the House of Lords held that there was no judicial power to reallocate property on divorce under the Married Women's Property Act 1882; instead, there was merely a power to declare existing rights.[7]

Principle

One could divine a coherent edifice of thought in family law, discordant though that edifice might seem today. The lack of reciprocity in the grounds of divorce available to men and women,[8] the limited and conditional availability of maintenance, and decision-making about children, all pointed to a legal edifice founded on patriarchal assumptions: the sexual double standard, the assumed economic dependence of women, and the idealizing of motherhood. The ecclesiastical origins of secular law had a continuing influence and reflected many centuries of principled development, expressed in such ideologies as the doctrine of unity of husband and wife, and of *consortium vitae*. These doctrines had far-reaching consequences for the civil status of married couples, especially in relation to property ownership, contractual capacity, tortious liability, and the protection of the criminal law from physical harassment or abuse.[9]

Public

Proceedings took place in public and there were clear public policy goals about deterring misconduct through punishment, stigma, and public shaming.[10] The frequently humiliating and intrusive nature of divorce proceedings was one of the factors leading to demands for a change in the law.

---

[7] *Pettitt v Pettit* [1970] AC 777 (HL).

[8] Under the Matrimonial Causes Act 1857, a husband could divorce his wife for adultery alone (subject to the statutory bars to a decree), whereas a wife could divorce her husband only on proof of adultery coupled with another 'aggravating' offence, such as incest, bigamy, cruelty, or desertion. The grounds were equalized in 1923 and extended in 1937.

[9] Many of the consequences of these doctrines outlasted the end of the formal era. For example, a husband's common law immunity from prosecution for raping his wife was abolished only as recently as 1991: see *R v R* [1991] 4 All ER 481 (HL).

[10] It is instructive to read some old accounts, such as H. E. Fenn's *Thirty-Five Years in the Divorce Courts*, London: T Werner Laurie (date unknown) to remind oneself of the theatrical nature of divorce proceedings.

THE FUNCTIONALIST ERA

In the middle decades of the twentieth century, changes were evident in the conception of marriage itself, and of the role of marriage and the family in the wider society. A growing ideological belief in personal individualism was taking place, catching up with earlier beliefs in economic and political individualism.[11] There was an increased faith in the power of social science to explain, predict, and control human behaviour. Legislation for the purpose of deliberately bringing about social change became an accepted part of government, with a consequent growth of an administrative state, and later a welfare state, with a broad range of utilitarian functions. At the same time, there was increased recognition that the concept of matrimonial fault drew the courts into issues that were either impossible or inappropriate to resolve judicially, or simply irrelevant. If adjusting to the future was what mattered, the concept of fault hardly seemed to fit.[12]

Through a mix of case law and statutory reform from the mid-1940s to the mid-1970s a new family law was put into place that emphasized the second poles of the dichotomies. Perhaps the most obvious point of transition from the first era to the second was the passage of the Divorce Reform Act 1969 and the Matrimonial Proceedings and Property Act 1970. This legislation was characterized by a number of features, open to generalization.

First, the new laws largely eradicated the concept of 'fault' or matrimonial offence as the basis of divorce and ancillary relief. The new divorce law itself was not 'pure' no-fault. Although the sole ground for divorce was stated to be the 'irretrievable breakdown' of the marriage, some of the closed list of bases, or 'facts', from which irretrievable breakdown could be inferred were still fault-based.[13] However, the adjustive consequences of divorce were to be reckoned largely without reference to fault. Thus, the parties' conduct was taken into account in relation to property and maintenance only in extreme cases;[14] and traces of fault-based reasoning in child custody decisions quickly disappeared during the 1970s. Yet the removal of fault from property matters left open the question of what principles were to underlie court orders, especially those dealing with financial provision.[15]

---

[11] See generally S. Parker, *Informal Marriage, Cohabitation and the Law, 1750–1989*, London: Macmillan (1990), ch 5.

[12] See Gibson, n 3 above, ch 7; L. Stone, *Road to Divorce: England, 1530–1987*, Oxford: Oxford University Press (1992) 401-22; Lewis, ch 4 and Smart, ch 16 of this volume.

[13] S 1 Matrimonial Causes Act 1973, which is still in force following the decision to postpone implementation of the Family Law Act 1996. The three fault-based facts are adultery, unreasonable behaviour, and desertion.

[14] *Wachtel v Wachtel* [1973] 1 All ER 829.   [15] See Eekelaar, Ch 18 of this volume.

In the case of financial provision, the answer lay in widening the court's powers both in the range of property covered and the orders available to redistribute it on divorce, and then subjecting the exercise of those powers to a statutory list of factors and general principles. The only general principle stated,[16] however, was that the court should seek to place the applicant spouse in the position he or she would have been in had the marriage not broken down.[17] The effect of this was to vest in the courts a wide-ranging discretion, but with very limited guidance as to how it was to be used. This placed judges at centre stage, and set a premium on legal-professional predictions of how that judicial discretion would be exercised on a particular set of facts. Public funding for legal advice was freely available through the legal aid system. Moreover, the centrality of the court process was emphasized by the fact that the right to go to court to seek a judge-made solution could not be bargained away by pre- or post-nuptial agreement.[18]

Second, although the primary objective of the reformed divorce law was to 'buttress the stability of marriage',[19] it was not to engage in marriage-saving in relation to *particular* marriages. Indeed, the preservation of marriage as an institution was thought to require the decent burial of individual marriages that were dead, so that the parties to it could then remarry. As Carol Smart has put it, '[t]he main purpose of the new divorce law ... was to facilitate remarriage ... [so as] to ease the redistribution of men, women and children around units that were capable of legal recognition'.[20]

Third, marriage and its dissolution remained the primary focus of legal remedies and procedures in the legislation but case law developments and minor amendments to various statutes not directly to do with 'family law' were increasingly treating marriage-like relationships in similar ways to marriages. In effect, some forms of cohabitation were seen as functional equivalents to marriage and a process began of according to them similar legal consequences.

Finally, the universal safety net of the welfare state was considered a legitimate source of support for family members in need after divorce. In

---

[16] With very little discussion: see Law Commission, *Financial Provision in Matrimonial Proceedings*. London: HMSO (1969) 40-1.

[17] This was said to reflect pre-existing judicial practice as exemplified by *N v N* (1928) 44 TLR 324 and *Moy v Moy and White* [1961] 1 WLR 552.

[18] Although parties were free, and were encouraged, to resolve court proceedings *once initiated* by consent order. However, the explicit and self-conscious promotion of private ordering is more obviously a feature of the complex era: see below.

[19] Law Commission, *Reform of the Ground of Divorce—The Field of Choice*. London: HMSO (1966) 15.

[20] C. Smart, 'Regulating Families or Legitimating Patriarchy?: Family Law in Britain', (1982) 10 *International Journal of the Sociology of Law* 129 at 141.

choosing between individual responsibility on the one hand, and individual freedom coupled with collective responsibility on the other, the system opted decisively for the latter. In short, the functionalist regime introduced by the shift from the first era to the second was marriage-focused (within the context of an extended conception of marriage), heavily discretionary, reliant on judges and professionals (whose services were freely met from public funds), concerned to preserve marriage as an institution rather than individual marriages, and presupposed that any economic casualties of divorce would be supported at state rather than private expense. The term 'functionalist' seems an apt description of this regime, because it was a regime that invested considerable faith in the power of experts, and the power of the state, to reconcile respect for individuals' freedom of choice with finding solutions for the problems that the exercise of that choice would create. In short, it was optimistic and ambitious in the social change it sought to bring about.

How, then, does all of this relate to the dichotomies outlined above? We can now track the second term in each of the pairs listed earlier.

Utility

The focus of legal policy came to be more on the needs and futures of the parties, and of children. For much of this period, a reference to rights, other than perhaps procedural rights, was out of place or beside the point. Family law had functions, and courts were vested with wide-ranging powers with which to discharge them. John Eekelaar wrote a comparative law book called *Family Law and Social Policy*, the first edition of which in 1978 was built around family law's three supposed functions in various countries: adjustive, protective, and supportive. Modern family law's focus on producing welfare outcomes rather than vindicating rights sat comfortably with a utilitarian ethic.

Substance

There was a recognition that legal forms were incapable of capturing the true dynamics of a relationship. Instead, there was a belief in the power of courts to exercise discretion in a way that would maximize outcomes in individual cases.

Pragmatism

There was a realization that the courts were ill equipped to inquire into causation in complex situations like marriages. The fault-based law had fallen into disrepute, because its requirements were easily satisfied by collusion between the parties, or because it was becoming very costly to everyone, with the rise in marriage breakdown following World War II. The focus of legal regulation of divorce shifted from using divorce as a site of moralistic prescription, to assisting the parties to adjust to, or come to terms with, life after divorce.[21] The price to be paid for this, however, was uncertainty over what principles underlay the new regime. Matrimonial fault had been removed, but no equivalent guiding principle had been put in its place.

Private

We see the development of a concern that individual dignity was sacrificed in intrusive family law proceedings. Although we tend to think of reforms to laws on homosexuality, abortion, and perhaps prostitution as the major privacy reforms of the twentieth century, changes in family law's content and procedures have arguably been the privacy measures affecting most people. This is not to say, however, that how to resolve the consequences of divorce, was entirely a matter for the parties to decide. As we have seen, the functionalist era placed judges, armed with discretionary powers, at the centre stage, and gave parties very limited autonomy to make their own private agreements without court sanction. In other words, the 'privacy' that was preserved by the functionalist era was one concerned to keep the matrimonial history out of the public eye, while preserving the central role of the legal process to determine the future consequences of the divorce itself.

Looking back, family law seemed appropriate to the political times. Technocratic decision-making, implementing future-oriented utilitarian policies, promised to make the world a better place. There was a form of egalitarianism at work, but it was of the 'equal but different' kind. Men and women had their functions and roles in 'the family'. The family had its functions in society. Given continued economic growth and high quality administration by governments, all would be well.

THE COMPLEX ERA

Against this background, then, we can start to outline the ways in which a different set of assumptions, objectives, and techniques has emerged since the late 1980s —to chart, in other words, the uneasy transition to the

[21] See Smart, n 20 above, who refers to the shift from the 'punitive obsession' (characteristic of what we have called the formal era) to a new and more positive form of regulation that focused on the economic and psychological well-being of family members (characteristic of what we have called the functional era).

present complex era of family law. Unlike the two eras that preceded it, however, the complex era is not easily captured by reference to a simple oscillation in the dualities already identified. Instead, there are a number of different ways in which the shift can be described, none of which is decisive or definitive, but which when taken together begin to compose a picture that is identifiably distinct from the one that preceded it. Alternative labels to 'complex' might be 'postmodern' or 'chaotic'.

We suggest that the following perspectives offer a way of understanding the nature of the shift under way:[22] (*a*) a shift in the organizing concepts of family law, away from pre-eminent emphasis on marriage and quasi-marriage; (*b*) a change in the normative types encountered in family law, and particularly a move away from discretion towards a more rule-like framework; (*c*) the emergence of new sources of, and audiences for, family law norms; and (*d*) a fragmentation or horizontalization of the family law system.

A Shift in Organizing Concepts: The Growth in the Significance of Parenthood

The functional model just outlined gave centre stage to marriage as a means of linking law to families. In defining obligations of family members towards each other, the law now pays less attention to marriage and more to parenthood.

Two separate factors have driven this shift towards parenthood as a significant legal status.[23] The first has been the pursuit since the early 1980s of a policy of eliminating discrimination affecting children based on the marital status of their parents. One logical consequence of this policy has been that children have the same financial claims against their parents on relationship breakdown whether the parents are married to each other or not. The second arises from a concern to improve the financial position of all children after parental separation and to reduce reliance of family members on state welfare. The growth in the numbers of children being born outside marriage has meant that any private legal obligation of support would have to be constructed on the basis of something other than marriage, and parenthood was the obvious alternative.

---

[22] For more detailed elaboration of these arguments, see S. Parker, 'Rights and Utility in Anglo-Australian Family Law', (1992) 55 *Modern Law Review* 311; J. Dewar, 'Family Law and its Discontents', (2000) 14 *Int J Law Policy Fam* 59.

[23] See M. Maclean, and J. Eekelaar, *The Parental Obligation: A Study of Parenthood across Households*, Oxford: Hart Publishing (1997) ch 3 for a detailed discussion of the importance of parenthood in contemporary family law, by comparison with marriage and home-sharing.

The growing importance of parenthood can be seen chiefly in three statutes, clustered around the late 1980s and early 1990s. In 1987, a series of Law Commission Reports culminated in legislation removing any legal discrimination against children flowing solely from the marital status (or lack of it) of the child's parents.[24] This involved, amongst other things, giving all children the same private law claims against their parents to property transfers and maintenance.[25] The Children Act 1989 created the framework for the formal recognition of the legal status of the unmarried father, while the Child Support Act 1991 imposed statutory obligations of child support on 'absent parents' that rested solely on proof of parenthood, rather than on marriage between the parents. Indeed, marriage plays no part in the conceptual structure of the Act.

All of this means that marriage and parenthood now co-exist as significant statuses in family law, with their relative importance hinging on a range of interacting factors. This is especially true in relation to financial obligations between family members, where much now depends on the assets available to the parties.

Take, first of all, couples with few, if any, capital assets, but with at least one earning capacity. The existence of children will make a big difference to the parties' legal and practical liabilities, because the parent with whom the children are not living after separation will be obliged, directly or indirectly, to pay child support under the legislative scheme. It will make no difference to either the existence or extent of this liability whether the parents are married to each other. Further, the private law powers to order transfers of property by parents to or for the benefit of their children have been interpreted as authorizing a court to order a transfer of a tenancy from one parent to the other, which may be the only significant asset (other than income and earning capacity) available to many couples.[26] To couples falling into this category, then, being a parent will be more important than being married. To put it another way, the fact that parents are married will not add anything to the liabilities already generated by the fact of parenthood. This does not mean that marriage is redundant for all purposes (for example, treatment under the tax or welfare systems, or under private pension schemes)—although even here, marriage is less important than it used to be.

Yet marriage retains a significance in other cases, especially where the parties' assets are greater. Liabilities attaching to parenthood relate primarily to income or, in the case of property, extend only to provision for a child during minority; so where these liabilities do not exhaust the available income and asset pool, the privileged status of marriage

---

[24] Family Law Reform Act 1987. See further Douglas, ch 10 of this volume.
[25] Sch 1, Children Act 1989.   [26] *K v K* [1992] 2 FLR 220.

becomes more apparent. The reasons for this are that spouses can access the wide-ranging redistributive powers of the divorce court, whereas unmarried couples (even those who are parents) cannot; and that spouses owe duties of mutual support that unmarried couples (even those who are parents) do not. All of this makes it tempting to suggest that parenthood has become the primary source of legal obligation for poor families with few assets, while marriage retains its significance exclusively for wealthier, middle-class, couples. Yet, at the same time, there will be many couples for whom obligations stem from a mixture of the marriage and parenthood. It is the multiplicity of the ways in which families are visible to law that contributes to the complexity of the current law.

There is, perhaps, another process at work in this increased emphasis on parenthood. As we have seen, functional family law was concerned to preserve the stability of the institution of marriage, rather than specific marriages. Divorce was one way of promoting that policy, by ensuring that dead marriages could be buried and new ones entered into. 'Looking to the future' meant embarking on a new life freed from the constraints of the old. In the complex era of family law, however, things are not so straightforward. Instead, there is evidence of an attempt to strengthen family ties across households after separation—that is, to preserve family ties long after the household in which they were formed has ceased to exist. This might be called a new form of 'institutionalism'.

The evidence for this lies in the child support legislation, which requires parents to pay support to children with whom they no longer reside, and the emphasis in the Children Act 1989 on shared parenting and the importance of maintaining contact between children and the non-resident parent after divorce or separation.[27] As Smart and Neale have suggested, there has been

a shift away from a presumption that families co-reside or that they can be found in one spatial location. Rather, fragments of families are found in various households linked by biological and economic bonds, but not necessarily by affection or shared life prospects . . . [F]amily law is trying to hold the fragments together through the imposition of a new normative order based on genetics and finances, but not on a State-legitimated heterosexual union with its roots in the ideal of Christian marriage.[28]

---

[27] The 1989 Act introduced the concept of 'parental responsibility' to describe the legal position of parents with respect to children, and states that natural parents who are married to each other automatically acquire parental responsibility for their children: Children Act 1989, s 2(1). There appears to have arisen a judicial presumption in favour of contact, even though no such presumption appears on the face of the legislation itself: see eg *Re O (Contact: Imposition of conditions)* [1995] 2 FLR 124.

[28] C. Smart and B. Neale, *Family Fragments?* Cambridge: Polity Press (1999) 181.

New Types of Norm: From Discretion to Rules?

We have seen that the technocratic model of family law was characterized by extensive use of judicial discretion—that is, a legally sanctioned authority to make a choice between a range of outcomes.[29] This was especially true of the law governing financial provision. Decision-making in relation to children, being governed by the welfare principle since 1925, has been characterized by a large degree of discretion for some time.[30] Yet one of the most noticeable features of family law legislation since the late 1980s has been the tendency to reduce or eliminate discretion from family law decision-making, and to replace that discretion with rules permitting little or no choice at the point of application.

Examples of this include: the introduction of the child support scheme by the Child Support Act 1991, which significantly reduced the role of judicially exercised discretion in fixing levels of child support; the introduction of the concept of shared parental responsibility by the Children Act 1989 and the associated judicial shift towards presumptions in favour of contact between parents and children; and recent debates surrounding reform of ancillary relief, which posit judicial discretion as, in one way or another, problematic.[31] This trend can be explained, in part, in terms of a dissatisfaction with the technocratic model; but at the same time, that model has not been entirely displaced. Instead, we have a discretionary system, underpinned by certain assumptions, objectives, and concerns, being overlaid by a more rule-bound family law, in turn stemming from a different set of assumptions and concerns. This too contributes to the complexity of the current law.

The functionalist model was strongly attached to discretion for two reasons. The first was underpinned by an assumption that the best way of approaching the questions raised by family dissolution was to invest experts with wide-ranging powers to reach the optimal solution in a given case. The varied circumstances of each case meant that discretion was required, so that the decision-maker had a range of choices open at the point of application: outcomes could not be prescribed in advance, because there were too many unknown factors that might be relevant.

---

[29] The literature on the meaning of discretion is extensive. For an analysis in the context of family law, see C. Schneider, 'Discretion and Rules: A Lawyer's View', in K. Hawkins (ed), *The Uses of Discretion*, New York: Oxford University Press (1992), ch 2, and J. Dewar, 'Reducing Discretion in Family Law', (1997) 11 *Australian Journal of Family Law* 309.

[30] Even though that discretion may have been exercised in accordance with rule-like principles, such as allocating custody to the 'innocent' parent.

[31] In a Consultation Document issued in 1998, the government suggested that the existing law of ancillary relief meant that 'the Court's discretion to allocate property means that the outcome of the case is hard to forecast, even with the advice of experienced lawyers' (Home Office, *Supporting Families: A Consultation Document*. London: HMSO, Home Office (1998) 37).

The second was that discretion allowed difficult questions about the principles of justice applicable between family members to remain
unanswered. As Katherine O'Donovan has put it, '[s]ince, in liberal
society [which is ideologically attached to privacy], the law's role in
personal relations is under attack it must retreat into discretion'.[32]

Those assumptions have increasingly been called into question, for
three main reasons. First, discretion is increasingly seen as being too
costly as a way of resolving disputes. It is too costly to the state, in that
decision-makers may not have in mind when making decisions the implications of those decisions for public expenditure (eg the extent to which
parties would be reliant on state benefits), or if they did, they did not
attach sufficient weight to those implications.[33] It was also too costly in
that it has been suggested that it is harder to settle disputes against a
backdrop of discretionary law as opposed to one of clear rules. Creating
a clearer framework of rules, so it is argued, will make cases easier to
settle, thereby reducing the burden on the courts, the legal aid fund, and
the parties' own resources.[34]

The second reason arises from a growing interest in reviving questions
of normative or justificatory frameworks governing the rights and obligations of family members to each other. This too has been associated
with a shift to rules and away from discretion, because there is an affinity
between rights on the one hand and rules as their mode of normative
expression on the other: rules appear to offer a guarantee of an
outcome—a vindicated claim—in a way that discretion does not.[35] The
factors leading to this growth in rights claims are complex, and include
domestic political pressure from organized groups (such as fathers' rights
groups seeking greater 'equality' in legal treatment, especially in matters
concerning children); the increased relevance of human rights instruments, especially those dealing with children's rights;[36] and a growing
perception that women have faired poorly under a discretionary regime,[37]

---

[32] K. O'Donovan, *Sexual Divisions in Law*. London: Weidenfeld & Nicolson (1985) 205.

[33] See M. Maclean and J. Eekelaar, 'Child Support: The British Solution', (1993) 7
International Journal of Law and the Family 205 on the policy background to the 1991 Act and
Maclean, Ch 24 of this volume.

[34] See Home Office, n 31 above, 37.

[35] This is not to suggest that the functionalist era was not also concerned to vindicate
rights, merely that rights claims, if successful, are more likely to find themselves enshrined
in rule-like legislative provisions.

[36] On the increasing 'constitutionalization' of modern family law, see below at 137.

[37] Empirical evidence for this emerged from the researches of L. Weitzman, *The Divorce
Revolution: The Unexpected Social and Economic Consequences for Women and Children in
America*, New York: The Free Press (1986) (in the US); J. Eekelaar and M. Maclean,
Maintenance after Divorce, Oxford: Oxford University Press (1986) (in the UK); and, in
Australia, the Australian Institute of Family Studies,: P. Macdonald, *Settling Up*, Melbourne:
Prentice Hall (1986). See Eekelaar, Ch 18 of this volume.

and that one response to this is to frame women's claims in terms of rights (eg in the case of financial provision, to compensate for relationship-induced losses or lost returns on investment in human capital) rather than discretionary determinations of 'need'.[38]

Discretion, which was in many ways the cornerstone of the pragmatic, utilitarian, functionalist era of family law, has come under increasing attack from a variety of quarters. The search for a more principled, rule-like, framework of family law is on—but given the wide constellation of forces driving that process, the prospects of finding a framework of principle that satisfies all rights-demands, as well as serving the needs of the state for an internally and externally more efficient system, appears remote.

New Sources of, and New Audiences for, Family Law Norms

Another important feature of the functionalist model, and one that still persists, is that almost all aspects of the lives of divorcing parties are potentially subject to the adjustive powers of the law. Although parties are encouraged to reach their own agreements on matters once in dispute,[39] agreements were made against the background of this all-embracing adjustive power, and only once the divorce process has begun. Divorcing parties have virtually no scope to exclude in advance the adjustive intervention of the legal system, since they are unable to bargain away their right to have their case considered in court. Paradoxically perhaps, this allows unmarried couples greater scope to make binding private arrangements[40] than their married counterparts—although the growing significance of parenthood has meant that many unmarried parents have also been drawn into this realm of restricted private ordering.

There is now growing pressure to permit married couples to order their own affairs in advance of marriage itself by means of premarital agreement. This has been proposed in the Government's Consultation Paper on family policy, entitled *Supporting Families*.[41] It reflects trends

---

[38] In some jurisdictions, this has translated into proposals for more structured, less discretionary, legal regimes: see eg K. Funder, 'Australia: A Proposal for Reform', in L. Weitzman and M. Maclean (eds), *Economic Consequences of Divorce: An International Perspective*, Oxford: Oxford University Press (1992); American Law Institute. *Principles of the Law of Family Dissolution: Analysis and Recommendations, Proposed Final Draft Part 1.* Philadelphia: American Law Institute (1997). See Blumberg, Ch 17 of this volume.

[39] Some liabilities, such as child support, are non-negotiable—although, even here, the legislation permits some degree of private ordering.

[40] These may include declarations of trust or contractual arrangements. In the case of the latter, any doubts about enforceability on grounds of public policy seem to have been resolved.   [41] n 31 above.

elsewhere—for example, the introduction in the United States of Uniform legislation, in New Zealand, and proposed legislation in Australia to permit binding pre-nuptial agreements.[42]

This trend towards the *contractualization* of family law— that is, the increased scope given to the parties themselves to define their own relationship terms—means that there will no longer be a single central source of legal norms governing all aspects of a relationship. This implies a fragmentation of norms, as each relationship becomes a potential source of 'proper' law for itself. Of course, the process of contractualization of relationships will not be uniform, for there will still be some matters that will be non-negotiable (eg payment of child support), or from which the courts will not be excluded as ultimate decision-makers (eg matters involving children).

Taken together with the decline in the centrality of the status of marriage (see above), we might say that there is a shift under way from status to contract in the legal understanding of marriage. At the same time as marriage has become contractualized and less a matter of status, so too have non-marital relationships acquired some legal visibility through the use of voluntarily made arrangements. Obvious examples include declarations of trust or conveyances; and there now seems little doubt about the enforceability of cohabitation contracts or living together agreements. Yet just as marriage has become a matter less of status and more of contract, we could say that the legal treatment of non-marital relations is becoming one of *both* contract and status, especially the status of parenthood. It may be that the logical end result of this is that marriage becomes invisible as a status-conferring institution, to be replaced by parenthood and, perhaps, dependence or co-residence.

Parallel to the trend towards contractualization is the trend towards the *constitutionalization* of family law—that is, the increased invocation of constitutional or human rights instruments as potential sources of norms relevant to families. Examples of this have been limited to date in the UK, the best perhaps being the use of Articles of the ECHR in relation to transsexual marriages. The implementation of the Human Rights Act in the UK will have further, and perhaps as yet unseen, ramifications for family law.[43] The potential power of this source of norms in family law should not be underestimated. It has already been suggested that rights-thinking has been responsible in part for the growing importance of parenthood as a legal status (ie, a consequence of removing legal discrimination against children whose parents are not married, or

---

[42] Family Law Amendment Act 1999 (*Cth*).

[43] J. Fortin,'Rights Brought Home for Children', (1999) 62 *Modern Law Review* 351; H. Conway, 'The Human Rights Act 1998 and Family Law', (1999) 29 *Family Law* 811.

of conceptualizing children as having rights to support from parents), and for the growth of a more rule-based family law. Human rights instruments are a significant source of further rights-talk in family law.

Allied to this growing diversity in the sources of family law norms is a self-conscious redefinition of the actual and potential audiences for family law legislation. Functionalist family law speaks directly to the technicians—the lawyers and the judges. The development of case law, and of professional rules of thumb about how judges might exercise their discretion on a particular set of facts, means that it is not always clear from the face of the legislation what principles are actually applied by decision-makers to cases. Indeed, some research evidence on the law of financial provision suggests that decision-makers do not regard the legislation as containing any clear set of principles at all.[44] This means that the principles, such as they are, are not transparently clear to a lay observer.

Modern family law legislation, on the other hand, seeks to speak directly to the parties themselves, over the heads of the technicians,[45] and onwards to the electorate.[46] One instance of this is the concept of parental responsibility contained in the Children Act 1989, a change of terminology from parental rights that was intended to have as much of an educative as a legal effect. It was designed to send out the message that it is children rather than parents whose rights and interests are primarily at stake in family disputes, that parents have a 'responsibility' to agree matters for themselves wherever possible, and to co-operate in parenting. In the same vein, the opening sections of the Family Law Act 1996 contain a statement of principles and objects, exhorting parties (amongst other things) to end their marriage and sort out their affairs by the cheapest means possible.[47]

Similar tendencies can be seen in government proposals for reforms to the law of financial provision. According to *Supporting Families*, 'the court's discretion in property cases means that the outcome is hard to forecast [and that] it is not possible, from the existing legislation for the lay person to get a clear view of what they can expect to receive on divorce'.[48] In view of this, the paper proposes measures that would offer parties 'greater certainty and clarity'—in other words, the law should be

---

[44] J. Eekelaar, *Regulating Divorce*. Oxford: Oxford University Press (1991).

[45] Child support legislation does not, of course, fit this pattern, being barely comprehensible to many lawyers.

[46] Since the mid-1980s, family law in the United Kingdom has taken on a party political aspect and, for some purposes, been subsumed within wider debates about welfare policy. See G. Pascall, 'UK Family Policy in the 1990s: The Case of New Labour and Lone Parents', (1999) 13 *International Journal of Law, Policy and the Family* 258.

[47] Family Law Act 1996, s 1(c)(iii). At the end of 1999, the implementation of the 1996 legislation was put on hold by the current Labour Government.

[48] n 31 above, para 4.46.

more readily understood by the parties affected by it without needing translation by a lawyer.

There are a number of possible reasons for this new style of legislation. One is that politicians seek to use legislation to perform an overtly educative role, or to create the illusion that there exists a set of 'organically' shared values around divorce and family life. As noted above, legislators seem to have overcome their reticence about prescribing models of behaviour in matters of separation and divorce. Family law statutes increasingly set out a vision of how to 'divorce well': parties must be rational, co-operative, cost-conscious, be able to take responsibility for their own affairs, and be willing to place the interests of others ahead of their own.[49] The return of a new institutionalism, referred to above, is one instance of this.

Another reason for this new style of legislating is that the emphasis is now on out-of-court agreement as the primary method of settling matters on divorce. This means the legislation must assume as its primary audience, not judges sitting in court or even lawyers advising clients, but those who are engaged in settlement activity. In short, this new legislative style (which, as we have seen, is also characterized by changing norms as well as changes in intended audiences) is broadly consistent with the policy of facilitating out-of-court agreement. Its role is to state principles that operate tone-setting for mediation or negotiation, rather than as conferring measurable entitlements. Private ordering is encouraged but against a backdrop of clearly articulated principles of public policy which dictate how that bargaining freedom should be used. Either way, the style and objectives of the legislation are observably different from those which characterized the technocratic regime.

MAKING SENSE OF COMPLEXITY

Returning to our four dichotomies, one sees now an oscillation within each of them rather than a consistent emphasis on one side, and a degree of independent operation (mixed signals) between them. Thus, there is now a greater emphasis on rights, but the rights-claims are more diverse and stem not from marriage itself, as under the formal model, but from other states, mainly to do with childhood or parenthood—hence children's rights, father's rights. Associated with this is a gradual return to formal rules, more reliance on general principles, and less use of judicial discretion or expert adjudication. There is a reduced emphasis on pragmatically attuning the outcome to the individual circumstances of each case, and a

---

[49] J. Dewar, 'The Normal Chaos of Family Law', (1998) 61 *The Modern Law Review* 467.

greater attention to vindicating claims regardless of their outcome or consequences. There is still an emphasis on privacy, as under the functionalist
model, but now privacy is associated with private *ordering*, either of disputes or by prenuptial agreements. Private ordering nevertheless takes
place against the background of *public* legislative statements of 'how to
divorce well' and of explicitly articulated public policies, mainly designed
to unburden the state.

Evidence for these shifts can be seen in child support legislation, the
proposed but yet-to-be-implemented divorce changes under the Family
Law Act 1996, mooted changes to laws on property distribution, and the
developing law on post-separation parenting under the Children Act
1989. Each exemplifies a greater attention to rights, more use of rules and
less reliance on discretion, and encouragement of private ordering. Yet
these changes have not entirely superseded the previous two eras, and do
not themselves cohere into an ordered whole. Instead, we have a chaotic
complex, which continues to exhibit strong tensions between rights and
utility, rules and discretions, and autonomy and coercion.

B
Establishing the Family

7

The Shadowlands: The Regulation of Human Reproduction in the United States

GEORGE J. ANNAS

The prospect of human cloning and germline genetic engineering has finally pushed the infertility industry into the domain of public policy.[1] Although it is too early to tell, there is for the first time in the United States some hope that the industry's thirst for growth and profits, and its aversion to public accountability, will be tempered by meaningful regulation designed to protect the interests of the children of assisted reproduction. As matters stand, however, the subtitle of this chapter can be seen as ironic, since there is virtually no governmental regulation of human reproduction in the United States.

There are three reasons for this regulatory vacuum, a historic, an economic, and a political one. Historically, although physicians have been licensed by the individual states for almost a hundred years, states have permitted the medical profession itself to define the 'practice of medicine,' including what procedures (such as new reproductive technologies) are medical. Economically, the United States is in the grips of free market medicine, and has been since the demise of the Clinton Health Care Plan in 1994. Under free market ideology, physicians offer services to consumers, who decide whether or not to accept them on the basis of their personal desires and income.[2] Politically, the continuing national debate on abortion, most recently focusing on so-called 'partial birth abortion' statutes aimed at outlawing a specific method of abortion, has profoundly diluted public support for governmental regulation of anything related to pregnancy.[3] All three reasons are important; but because abortion politics continues to dominate anti-government interference with reproduction rhetoric, I begin this chapter with an overview of US abortion law since 1973, the year the most important health case in the history of the US, *Roe v Wade*,[4] was decided.

---

[1] See GEORGE J. ANNAS, SOME CHOICE: LAW, MEDICINE AND THE MARKET 3–24 (1998) [hereinafter ANNAS, CHOICE]. Portions of this chapter are adapted from George J. Annas, *The Shadowlands: Secrets, Lies and Assisted Reproduction*, 339 NEW ENG J MED. 935 (1998); George J. Annas, *The Supreme Court, Liberty and Abortion*, 327 NEW ENG J MED. 651 (1992); George J. Annas, *Fairy Tales Surrogate Mothers Tell*, 16 LAW MED AND HEALTH CARE 27 (1988).

[2] See ANNAS, CHOICE, n 1 above, at 44–51.

[3] See George J. Annas, *Partial-Birth Abortion, Congress, and the Constitution*, 339 NEW ENG J MED 279 (1999).

[4] 410 US 113 (1973).

144 George J. Annas

ABORTION

Feelings, beliefs, and opinions are strong and divided on the 1973 US Supreme Court decision in *Roe v Wade*, the Court's 1989 decision in *Webster v Reproductive Health Services* that signaled a retreat from *Roe*, and the Court's 1992 compromise decision in *Casey v Planned Parenthood of Southeastern Pennsylvania.*[5] Opinion polls on abortion since 1973 show that Americans are deeply ambivalent on the issue. A consistent majority believe abortion is immoral in most cases. None the less, overwhelming majorities believe abortion should be available in cases of rape, incest, and severe genetic handicap, and more than two-thirds consistently say that even though they believe abortion is either wrong or immoral the ultimate decision should be made by a woman and her physician rather than by government decree.[6]

In *Roe v Wade*, and in all of the abortion cases that followed it (other than the financing cases), the Court was faced with a *criminal* statute designed to limit access to abortion. In *Roe*, the Texas statute it was reviewing made it a crime to perform or to attempt an abortion, except to save the life of the mother. Justice Harry Blackmun, formerly legal counsel to the Mayo Clinic, wrote the opinion of the Court. One of his major goals was to prevent the government from interfering with the practice of medicine and in the doctor–patient relationship.[7]

The decision was seven to two, with Justices William Rehnquist and Byron White dissenting. Building on a series of cases, including a leading one dealing with contraception, that had described a 'right to personal privacy, or a guarantee of certain areas or zones of privacy,'[8] the Court determined that a fundamental 'right to privacy' existed 'in the Fourteenth Amendment's concept of personal liberty and restrictions upon state action.' The Court went on to hold that this fundamental right 'is broad enough to encompass a woman's decision whether or not to terminate her pregnancy.'[9]

The detriment that the state would impose upon the pregnant woman by denying this choice altogether is apparent. Specific and direct harm medically diagnosable even in early pregnancy may be involved. Maternity, or additional offspring, may force upon the woman a distressful life and future. Psychological

---

[5] *Casey*, 505 US 833 (1992); *Webster*, 492 US 490 (1989).

[6] See Mary Ann Lamanna, *Social Science and Ethical Issues: The Policy Implications of Poll Data on Abortion* in S. Callahan and D. Callahan (eds,) ABORTION: UNDERSTANDING DIFFERENCES (1984); see also E. J. Dionne, *Poll Finds Ambivalence on Abortion Persists in US*, NY TIMES, Aug 3 1989, at A18.

[7] See generally BOB WOODWARD and SCOTT ARMSTRONG, THE BRETHREN: THE INSIDE STORY OF THE SUPREME COURT (1979).

[8] *Roe*, 410 US at 153.   [9] *ibid*.

harm may be imminent. Mental and physical health may be taxed by child care ... All these factors the woman and her responsible physician necessarily will consider in consultation.[10]

Although granting the abortion decision a very high degree of constitutional protection, the Court stopped short of declaring that a woman's right to an abortion was absolute, that she had a right to abortion on demand. Instead, the Court recognized that the state also has interests that may at times be compelling enough to limit abortion. The Court identified two such interests: the protection of maternal health and the protection of fetal life. The protection of maternal health has always been a legitimate state interest. In the case of abortion, however, the Court ruled that this interest could never be so 'compelling' as to prohibit abortion prior to the stage in pregnancy when it is less dangerous for the woman to carry the fetus to term than to have an abortion (in 1973, about the end of the first trimester). The Court decided that during the first trimester the state could only regulate abortions to protect the woman's health by requiring that they be performed by a physician. Thereafter it could only regulate to protect women in ways reasonably calculated to enhance the woman's personal health, rather than in ways really designed to protect the fetus or simply to discourage abortions.

The second state interest the Court identified was the interest in 'protecting the potentiality of human life.'[11] The Supreme Court did not decide that the fetus is not human, but only that a fetus is not a 'person' as that term is used in the Fourteenth Amendment. The Court also properly noted that 'the pregnant woman cannot be isolated in her privacy;'[12] her interests in privacy must be weighed against the state's interest in the life of the fetus. The question is: when does the state's interest become so 'compelling' that the state can justifiably interfere with the woman's constitutional right to have an abortion? No satisfactory answer to this question can be garnered from science, and any line of demarcation during pregnancy is inherently arbitrary. The Court decided to choose fetal viability, the interim point between conception and birth, at which the fetus 'is potentially able to live outside the mother's womb, albeit with artificial aid,'[13] apparently because at this point the fetus is biologically identical to a premature infant.

After viability, which continues to occur near the end of the second trimester, but whose actual determination is a function of medical technology and skill, the state 'may, if it chooses, regulate, and even proscribe, abortion except where it is necessary, in appropriate medical judgment, for the preservation of the life or health of the mother.'[14]

---

[10] *ibid.*   [11] *ibid* at 162.   [12] *ibid* at 158.   [13] *ibid.*   [14] *ibid* at 165.

Efforts to amend the US Constitution to change or overturn the decision were unsuccessful and have been all but abandoned. A parallel strategy is ongoing: the passage of state abortion statutes that are as restrictive as possible under the *Roe v Wade* framework in the hope that the Supreme Court will permit some state restrictions and ultimately modify or abandon *Roe* altogether.

By 1992, it looked as if the votes existed on the Supreme Court actually to overrule *Roe*. When the Court refused to reverse *Roe*, most observers were surprised. Three Reagan–Bush appointees joined together to reinterpret and uphold *Roe*, making it clear that the twelve-year attempt to overturn *Roe* by packing the Court with ultraconservative, anti-*Roe* Justices had failed. In the twenty years since *Roe* was decided, only two Justices willing to vote to reverse *Roe* had been appointed (Antonin Scalia and Clarence Thomas). At issue in *Casey*[15] was a Pennsylvania statute that required, among other things, that women wait twenty-four hours after giving informed consent before having an abortion, and that a married woman must notify her husband prior to having an abortion.

Three Justices, Sandra Day O'Connor, Anthony Kennedy, and David Souter, wrote a joint opinion reframing *Roe*, and under *Roe*'s new contours, upheld the constitutionality of all the provisions of the Pennsylvania law except spousal notification. Since Justices Harry Blackmun and John Paul Stevens agreed that the aspects of *Roe* that these three Justices retained should be retained (they would have retained it all), there were five votes for retaining what the joint opinion called the 'essential holding' of *Roe*.[16] As recast by the joint opinion's authors, *Roe* now stands for the proposition that pregnant women have a 'personal liberty' right to choose to terminate their pregnancies prior to viability that the state cannot 'unduly burden.'[17]

The nature of the constitutional right to choose an abortion is seen as not only being derived from the 'right of privacy' regarding family and personal decision-making, but also from cases restricting the government's power to mandate medical treatment or to bar its rejection. These post-*Roe* medical treatment cases protecting bodily integrity 'accord with *Roe*'s view that a state's interest in the protection of life falls short of justifying any plenary override of individual liberty claims,'[18] and prohibit the state from forcing either continued pregnancy or abortion on a pregnant woman.

The joint opinion concludes this substantive due process approach by holding that a woman's constitutional 'right to choose to terminate her pregnancy'[19] continues to fetal viability. Viability is chosen because it was

---

[15] See *Casey*, 505 US 833.   [16] *ibid* at 834.   [17] *ibid* at 837.   [18] *ibid* at 835.
[19] *ibid* at 870.

the most important line drawn in *Roe*, because 'there is no line other than viability which is more workable,'[20] and because at viability 'the independent existence of the second life can in reason and all fairness be the object of state protection [although *not* a person under the constitution] that now overrides the rights of the woman.'[21] The joint opinion continues: 'The woman's right to terminate her pregnancy before viability is the most central principle in Roe v. Wade. It is a rule and a component of liberty we cannot renounce.'[22]

The joint opinion, however, rejects the Court's post-*Roe* decisions that struck down most attempts by states to ensure 'that a woman's choice contemplates the consequences for the fetus . . . ' as misconceiving 'the nature of the pregnant woman's interest; and . . . undervalu[ing] the state's interest in potential life.'[23] In this regard, the joint opinion insists that not every law that makes a right more difficult to exercise 'is, *ipso facto*, an infringement on that right,'[24] even if such laws make the actual exercise of the right more difficult by increasing its expense or even decreasing the availability of the procedure: 'Only where state regulation imposes an *undue burden* on the woman's ability to make this decision does the power of the State reach into the heart of the liberty protected by the Due Process Clause'[25] (emphasis added). The phrase 'undue burden' is 'a shorthand for the conclusion that a state regulation has the *purpose or effect* of placing a substantial obstacle in the path of a woman seeking an abortion of an nonviable fetus.'

The twenty-four hour waiting period was found by the lower court to be burdensome for poor, rural women who must travel long distances to a clinic. The joint opinion, however, concluded that a 'particular burden is not of necessity a substantial obstacle'[26] and the waiting period, as part of the informed consent requirement which 'facilitates the wise exercise'[27] of the right to choose, is not an undue burden on the exercise of that right. Likewise, the requirements of having one-parent consent or judicial review for a woman under 18 years of age, and of requiring the reporting of certain information to the Department of Health, were found not to be undue burdens on a woman's right to choose.

On the other hand, the joint opinion found that the requirement of spousal notification could not meet the undue burden test. Because its exceptions were so narrow (not including, for example, psychological abuse, and assault not reported to the police), it would 'likely prevent a significant number of women from obtaining an abortion.'[28] This is because 'the significant number of women who fear for their safety and the safety of their children are likely to be deterred from procuring an

---

[20] *Casey*, 505 US at 870.   [21] *ibid.*   [22] *ibid* at 871.   [23] *ibid* at 873.
[24] *ibid* at 874.   [25] *ibid.*   [26] *ibid* at 887.   [27] *ibid.*   [28] *ibid* at 893.

abortion as surely as if the Commonwealth had outlawed abortion in all cases.'[29] As to the husband's undoubted interest in the pregnancy (when he is the father), the joint opinion concluded: 'A State may not give to a man the kind of dominion over his wife that parents exercise over their children . . . Women do not lose their constitutionally protected liberty when they marry.'[30]

Justices John Paul Stevens and Harry Blackmun both wrote opinions concurring in the affirmation of *Roe*, but dissenting from the approval of the provisions of the Pennsylvania law. The remaining four Justices all would have overturned *Roe* and upheld all of the provisions of the Pennsylvania law. They expressed themselves in two opinions, one by Chief Justice William Rehnquist and the other by Justice Antonin Scalia, each of which was concurred in by the four dissenting Justices (the two authors and Justices Byron White and Clarence Thomas).

Of these two opinions, the most illuminating portions are their remarks on *Roe* and on the undue burden test. In the Rehnquist opinion, the four dissenters say bluntly: 'We believe that Roe was wrongly decided, and that it can and should be overruled consistently with our traditional approach to stare decisis in constitutional cases.'[31]

In their view, the state should be able to prohibit abortion, or to regulate it in any 'rational' way, throughout pregnancy. The undue burden test is dealt with in Justice Scalia's opinion. He argues (persuasively, I think) that the test is ultimately 'standardless' and 'has no principled or coherent legal basis,' noting that 'defining an "undue burden" as an "undue hindrance" (or a "substantial obstacle") hardly "clarifies" the test.' Justice Scalia then tries to define the test operationally. He concludes that as applied in the joint opinion the 'undue burden' standard means that 'a State may not regulate abortion in such a way as to reduce significantly its incidence.'[32]

Justice Scalia's reading of the undue burden test seems correct: under *Casey* states cannot regulate abortion in ways that will prevent a significant number of women from obtaining them. It is in this sense that the Court has affirmed *Roe v Wade* in *Casey*. In addition, the always problematic emphasis in *Roe* on the right of the physician to practice medicine has been replaced by emphasis on the pregnant woman and her right to make the abortion decision. In *Roe*, for example, the Court had said: 'The decision [*Roe*] vindicates the *right of the physician* to administer medical treatment according to his professional judgment [prior to viability] . . . the abortion decision in all its aspects is inherently and primarily, *a medical decision*, and basic responsibility for it must rest with the physician'

[29] *Casey*, 505 US at 894.   [30] *ibid* at 898.   [31] *ibid* at 944.   [32] *ibid* at 992.

(emphasis added).[33] It is primarily for this reason, I believe, that the Court had previously consistently struck down detailed informed consent requirements, waiting periods, and reporting requirements: they interfered with the physician's judgment and discretion.

Casey properly focuses on the pregnant woman. It is *her* decision that the constitution protects, not her physician's. This makes requiring an informed consent conversation with the physician perfectly reasonable: 'Whatever constitutional status the doctor–patient relationship may have as a general matter, in the present context it is derivative of the woman's position. The doctor–patient relation does not underlie or override the two more general rights under which the abortion right is justified: the right to make family decisions and the right to physical autonomy.'[34]

This shift in emphasis, from doctor to patient, should be applauded by physicians. It *is* the woman, not the physician, who is pregnant, the woman who is making the decision, and the woman who is responsible for the decision. The problem with the joint opinion is not its emphasis on women, but its view of women. The Pennsylvania informed consent requirements are based on the supposition that women who decide to have abortions do not think very much about their decision, and if they had some additional information about the procedure and the development of the fetus, as well as twenty-four hours to think about it, many would continue their pregnancies to term. This view is extraordinarily patronizing to pregnant women, has no empirical support, and these consent requirements apply to no other medical procedure.

The Court's approval of the Pennsylvania informed consent requirements also highlights two major flaws in the approach of the joint opinion. First, the joint opinion seems to rest on the proposition that it is acceptable for the state to require physicians to inform women that childbirth is much preferable to abortion, as long as this does not inhibit many women from actually choosing abortion. This suggests that this value judgment and the inculcation of guilt feelings based on it are a legitimate state function in the abortion arena—an inconsistent, bureaucratic, and pointless position. Second, the Pennsylvania rules *will* affect some women—notably the rural poor and the very young. This is, however, consistent with prior abortion related opinions of the Court: government action that in its application is restrictive only to the poor and disadvantaged will be assumed to be constitutionally acceptable absent very specific evidence of its impact on this group. The only way out of this discriminatory impact on the poor is to ensure that birth control services as well as abortion are fully covered in any national system of health care.

[33] *Roe*, 410 US at 165–6.   [34] *Casey*, 505 US at 884.

In the summer of 2000, the United States Supreme Court issued *Stenberg v Carhart*,[35] the Court's most important abortion decision since *Casey*. In a five to four opinion, the Court ruled that Nebraska's 'partial-birth abortion' statute, which was substantially similar to state statutes in thirty states and a federal statute twice vetoed by President Clinton, was unconstitutional. The Nebraska statute made it a crime, punishable by twenty years in prison, for a physician to perform a partial-birth abortion defined as 'an abortion procedure in which the person performing the abortion partially delivers vaginally a living unborn child before killing the unborn child and completing the delivery.'[36] The Court gave two reasons for finding this criminal statute unconstitutional: the ban on this procedure did not have an exception for the woman's health (and thus violated *Roe v Wade*) and the procedure itself was so similar to another very common procedure (dilation and extraction abortion) that physicians might be afraid to offer this standard procedure to women, thus creating an 'undue burden' (under *Casey*) on their right to choose abortion.

Most of the majority opinion, written by Justice Breyer, was devoted to a description of the various forms of abortion and how physicians view the need and safety of each. The considerable debate in the medical profession about whether so-called partial-birth abortion is ever medically necessary was resolved by concluding that the 'division of medical opinion about [the added health risks of doing a different abortion procedure] at most means uncertainty, a factor that signals the presence of risk, not its absence.'[37] Justice Stevens, in a concurring opinion, noted that since *Roe* was decided in 1973, all but four of seventeen Justices on the US Supreme Court had endorsed it. He argued that banning this particular abortion procedure was irrational because it could not promote the state's interest in fetal life because it did not save one fetus.

The lesson from *Stenberg v Carhart* is that the right to choose to have an abortion is in no danger from the Court. This is because the anti-abortion forces had their best argument to ban a rarely used abortion procedure many saw as inches and moments away from infanticide (at least in a post-viability abortion) and a procedure that relied on the physiology of birth (thus the name, 'partial-birth abortion'), and even in this case the Court would not permit the states to ban the technique if 'substantial medical authority' thought it might be the safest procedure for some women seeking an abortion. The five to four vote, of course, is close; but it is not as close as it seems. This is because one of the four dissenters, Justice Kennedy, based his dissent solely on his view that the *Casey* joint opinion, which he co-authored, should permit states to ban this gruesome, rare, and probably never medically necessary abortion procedure.

---

[35] 120 S Ct 2597 (2000).   [36] *ibid* at 2605.   [37] *ibid* at 2612.

As he made clear in *Casey*, he supports the core holding of *Roe*, and would not vote to overturn it.

The other three dissenters, Justices Rehnquist, Scalia, and Thomas, who have always opposed *Roe*, understand that *Stenberg* looks more like *Roe* than *Casey*. Justice Thomas, joined by Justices Scalia and Rehnquist, for example, argued that in Stenberg the Court actually went far beyond *Casey* and returned to *Roe* and 'a reinstitution of the pre-*Webster* [1989] abortion-on-demand era in which the mere invocation of "abortion rights" trumps any contrary societal interest.'[38] This is overblown rhetoric, but it is none the less true that the bottom line of *Stenberg* and *Roe* is that the decision about whether and how to terminate a pregnancy prior to fetal viability can only be determined by the woman in consultation with her physician.

Justice O'Connor, concurring, does opine that it would be constitutional for the states to outlaw partial-birth abortions if they were uniquely and clearly defined, and if there was an exception to the ban if the physician believed the health of the woman required it. The dissenters, however, totally rejected this view. They argued that giving physicians this kind of discretion is tantamount to no ban at all. The dissenters are correct in observing that *Stenberg* is a strongly physician-centered (rather than woman-centered) opinion; but they are wrong to think that there is any substantial likelihood that the core of *Roe v Wade* will ever be overturned.

SURROGATE MOTHERHOOD

The highly publicized case of *Baby M*[39] involved a custody dispute between a father and a mother. The father, William Stern, had contracted with the mother, Mary Beth Whitehead, to bear him a child using artificial insemination. The contract, among other things, provided that she would receive a fee of $10,000 upon terminating her parental rights and giving up the child to him. The New Jersey Supreme Court had no problem concluding that payment to place a child for adoption (even with the spouse of its father) violated the state's adoption law. The court declared that 'the evils of baby bartering are loathsome for myriad of reasons.'[40] There is coercion, lack of counseling, and exploitation of all parties (including desperate infertile couples), as well as the fact that 'the child is sold without regard for whether the purchasers will be suitable parents'[41] and the lack of any protection of the natural mother. Making money

---

[38] *ibid* at 2636–7.   [39] Matter of Baby M, 537 A2d 1227 (NJ 1988).   [40] *ibid* at 1241.
[41] *ibid*.

takes precedence even over predictable human suffering. For example, the broker in the *Baby M* case failed to make further inquiry when a psychological evaluation of Mrs Whitehead revealed that she might change her mind. In the court's words, 'It is apparent that the profit motive got the better of the Infertility Center . . . to inquire further might have jeopardized the Infertility Center's fee.'[42]

The selling of babies that had been so slickly glazed over by others properly disgusted the court. The court noted that the originator of this scheme to circumvent the law by private contract is 'a middle man, pro- pelled by profit'[43] who 'promotes the sale. . . . The profit motive predom- inates, permeates, and ultimately governs the transaction.'[44] What's wrong with profit and using money as the sole measure of the value of children? The court did not hesitate to say: 'There are, in a civilized soci- ety, some things that money cannot buy. . . . There are . . . values that society deems more important than granting to wealth whatever it can buy, be it labor, or life.'[45] Not the least of these values is the protection of children from the vicious exploitation that treating them as commodities would bring, exploitation of the poor by the rich, and the demeaning of pregnant women by treating them as breeders indentured to their employers.

There has been much confusion about constitutional rights in the sur- rogacy arrangement. The only real parental right at stake is the right to custody of a child resulting from an unwed pregnancy, and in this contest the interests of the child properly take precedence. There is no constitu- tional right to purchase a child, even your own. And whatever procre- ation rights might be raised to a constitutional level in the area of custody, the rights of the mother must be at least as strong as those of the father. Indeed, they should be stronger, since fertile men need a nine-month commitment on the part of a woman to procreate, whereas fertile women only need sperm to procreate.

The constitutional right of privacy is founded on liberty interests in intimacy and freedom of association, along with notions of self-identity and self-expression. Privacy is *not* a technocrat's toy that requires the government to keep its hands off any method of procreation inventors can devise. Treating men and women equally in the realm of non-coital reproduction might require egg donation to be treated like sperm dona- tion, but no principled argument can equate (as the trial judge in *Baby M* did) nine months of gestation and ultimate childbirth with sperm dona- tion. As the US Supreme Court has ruled, states cannot even permit hus- bands to prohibit their wives from having abortions since, among other

---

[42] Matter of Baby M, 537 A2d 1227 (NJ 1988) at 1247.   [43] *ibid* at 1249.   [44] *ibid.*
[45] *ibid.*

things, 'it is the woman who physically bears the child and she is the most directly affected by the pregnancy.'[46] An Oklahoma court has also noted that husbands have no right to prevent their wives from becoming sterilized. In the court's words:

We have found no authority and the plaintiff has cited none which holds that the husband has a right to a childbearing wife as an incident to their marriage. We are neither prepared to create a right in the husband to have a fertile wife nor to allow recovery for damage to such a right. We find the right of the person who is capable of competent consent to control his own body paramount.[47]

If husbands have no constitutional right to fertile wives, it follows that they have no constitutional right to contract with unrelated women for purposes of reproducing themselves. The *Baby M* court saved for another day the question of whether a woman can irrevocably waive her constitutional right to the companionship of her children by a preconception contract (assuming such a contract is 'legalized' by legislation). But there would seem to be no basis that would allow the courts to enforce such an agreement. Even the lower court *Baby M* judge, for example, recognized that a woman could not irrevocably waive her right to terminate her pregnancy under the US Constitution because judicial enforcement of such an agreement would be an intolerable burden on the woman.[48] The argument against permitting an irrevocable pre-birth waiver of maternal rearing rights is at least as strong. Both decisions are so intimately related to the individual's personhood and human dignity that it would be an intolerable violation of personal integrity to force compliance with either. This is because pregnancy and childbirth may predictably and radically change self-image and self-fulfillment aspirations that are central features of identity and personhood.

Baby M involved no new medical technology, just old-fashioned artificial insemination, a practice that has never been regulated in the US, and that takes no medical technology to employ. IVF, however, for the first time, raised the possibility of separating the genetic from the gestational mother, and forced the California Supreme Court to choose between them. Crispina and Mark Calvert hired a young, single, black nurse to gestate an embryo composed of their egg and sperm and to give the resulting child to them for a fee of $10,000. Mrs Calvert was unable to bear a child because of a hysterectomy. Near the end of her pregnancy, Anna Johnson sought to retain custody of the child. Genetic testing confirmed that the child, Christopher, born September 19 1990, had no genetic relationship to Ms Johnson. Following a hearing, Judge Richard

---

[46] *Planned Parenthood of Central Missouri v Danforth*, 428 US 52 (1976).
[47] *Murray v Vandevander*, 522 P 2d 302, 304 (Okla App 1974).
[48] See In the Matter of Baby M, 217 NJ Super Ct 313, 525 A3d 1128 (1987).

N. Parslow, Jr, rendered an oral opinion from the bench, concluding that Crispina alone should be considered Christopher's mother: 'Anna Johnson is the gestational carrier of the child, a host in a sense. . . . She and the child are genetic hereditary strangers. . . . Anna's relationship to the child is analogous to that of a foster parent providing care, protection and nurture during the period of time that the natural mother, Crispina Calvert, was unable to care for the child.'[49]

The opinion was unanimously affirmed by an intermediate appeals court that concentrated exclusively on determining which of the two women was 'the child's "natural" mother, the woman who nurtures the child in her womb and give birth—or the otherwise infertile mother whose egg [embryo] is implanted into the woman who gave birth?'[50] The court decided that a blood test should determine maternity, just as it could determine paternity under California's 1975 Uniform Parentage Act:

We must 'resolve' the question of Anna's claim to maternity as we would resolve the question of a man's claim to (or liability for) paternity when blood tests positively exclude him as a candidate. . . . In light of Anna's stipulation that Crispina is genetically related to the child and because of the blood tests excluding Anna from being the natural mother, there is no reason not to uphold trial court's determination that Crispina is the natural mother. She is the only other candidate![51]

The court also concluded that California law violates no constitutional liberty interests in any relation with the child that Anna Johnson might have gained through pregnancy and childbirth. The California Supreme Court, relying on both the Uniform Parentage Act and the contract, affirmed, saying of the split between the genetic and gestational mother: 'when the two do not coincide in one woman, she who intended to procreate the child—that is, she who intended to bring about the birth of a child that she intended to raise as her own—is the natural mother under California law.'[52] These opinions contribute little to the resolution of whether the genetic or the gestational mother should be considered the legal mother of a child. Calling the genetic mother the 'natural' mother simply begs the question; it does not answer it. The court's equation of paternity testing with maternity testing is, of course, correct if one is trying to determine who the genetic parent is, but in this case that was never an issue. In human reproduction men contribute only genes; women contribute both genes and gestation. The question is what rule society should adopt now that these maternal contributions can be separated.

Anna Johnson never claimed to be the child's genetic mother. The only question she asked was whether her pregnancy and childbirth gave her a

---

[49] *Johnson v Calvert*, Cal Super Ct, Orange Co, Dept 11, No X633190 (Oct 22 1990).
[50] *Anna J. v Mark C.*, 286 Cal Rptr 369 (Ct App, 4th Dist 1991).   [51] *ibid* at 376.
[52] *Johnson v Calvert*, 851 P2d 776 (Cal 1993).

mother–child relationship with Christopher. Thus, the court's exegesis on statutes defining parenthood that were passed before the advent of *in vitro* fertilization is as irrelevant as the statutes concerning motherhood that were passed before *in vitro* fertilization and the statutes concerning artificial insemination, passed before embryo transfer, that the court discounted. The relevant question was the relation of Ms Johnson to Christopher; labeling Mrs Calvert Christopher's 'natural mother' does not answer it.

We currently live in an age when genes are seen, as all of the California judges in this case saw them, as the key to human existence. But what is the status of women who are capable of carrying a child to term but who cannot produce ova? They now rely on donated ova (rather than gestational surrogacy) to enable them to give birth to children. If the California judges are correct, the 'natural' mothers of these children are the donors of the ova, not the women who gave birth to them. This counter-intuitive conclusion would make current ovum donation programs unworkable. A related question involves fatherhood. Under California's Uniform Parentage Act, if we consider the donor of the ovum the natural mother, then her husband, and not the husband of the woman who gives birth (who is also the genetic father), is the natural father of the child. Likewise under the Act, if Ms Johnson had been married, Christopher would have been 'conclusively presumed'[53] to be a child of her marriage. These results are, of course, the very type of 'crazy making' the judges thought they were avoiding by ignoring the claims of the gestational mother. They have done even worse than ignore her, however. They have taken part in exploiting her. As in virtually all 'surrogate motherhood' arrangements, Ms Johnson was poor and needed the $10,000 fee literally to pay her rent. Poor women will probably continue to be used by middle-class couples to perform this 'service' for them.[54]

---

[53] *ibid* at 780.

[54] The reality of this case and others like it is that the child has two mothers, a gestational mother and a genetic mother. Society should acknowledge this biological fact and take it into account in allocating the rights and responsibilities of parenthood. We might decide to treat donors of ova the same way we treat sperm donors, but we cannot treat gestational mothers this way. My own preference is to acknowledge legally the existence of all three parents (two mothers and one father) in the case of ova donation followed by embryo transfer. If these three individuals could not work out a mutually agreeable living arrangement for themselves and their child, a custody hearing would have to be held. During this hearing, the gestational mother should have temporary custody of the child. Permanent custody should be determined on the basis of the best interests of the child. Because custody does not determine parenthood, however, the non-custodial mother should continue to have her status as gestational or genetic mother legally recognized, and should be granted specific visitation rights as well. As we work out the proper approach, all physicians and clinics must maintain careful records of the identities of donors of both sperm and ova. Public policy must acknowledge the complexity of gamete donation and ultimately take into consideration the best interests of the child.

ASSISTED REPRODUCTION

It is impossible to summarize all of the continuing problems in the assisted-reproduction industry in the United States. None the less, two recent court cases, one in California and the other in New York, and the report of the New York State Task Force on Life and the Law do a pretty good job, and all suggest that existing practices are inadequate to protect the interests of the clinic patients and their children.

Parentless in California

The California case involved Luanne and John Buzzanca, who used *in vitro* fertilization (IVF) with donor eggs and donor sperm. The embryos were subsequently implanted in a genetically unrelated woman (the 'surrogate' mother) for gestation and birth. The Buzzancas intended to rear the resulting child as their own. Before the child, Jaycee, was born, the couple separated and John wanted to have nothing to do with the child.

At a trial held to determine the legal parents of Jaycee, the identity of the genetic parents remained secret, and the gestational mother disclaimed any interest in the child. Because neither John nor Luanne was genetically or biologically related to Jaycee, the judge concluded that Jaycee was parentless. In my view, the conclusion—that a child with six potential parents (assuming the gestational mother was married) was legally parentless—was untenable. This decision was properly reversed on appeal.

The appeals court decided that because under California law, a husband who consents to his wife's artificial insemination becomes the legal father of the child, 'a husband and wife [should be] deemed the lawful parents of a child after a surrogate bears a biologically unrelated child on their behalf [since] in each instance a child is procreated because a medical procedure was initiated and consented to by intended parents.'[55] Thus, the court concluded that Luanne and John were Jaycee's legal parents.

To make sure no one missed the analogy, the court expanded on it, stating that gestational surrogacy and artificial insemination are 'exactly analogous in this crucial respect: both contemplate the procreation of a child by the consent to a medical procedure of someone who intends to raise the child but who otherwise does not have any biological tie.'[56] The court did not like the idea of people who are responsible for the creation of a child 'turning around and disclaiming any responsibility after the child is born.'[57] Since the court believed that John 'caused' the birth of

---

[55] *Buzzanca v Buzzanca*, 61 Cal App 4th 1410 (1998).   [56] *ibid* at 1418.
[57] *ibid* at 1420.

Jaycee simply by signing a contract, the court had no problem concluding that the same logic that made him the legal father made Luanne (his
wife at the time the contract with the surrogate mother was signed) the
legal mother, since she agreed to the 'procreative project' at the start.

The appeals court none the less concluded that it would be preferable
for the legislature to set the rules in this arena: 'We still believe it is the
Legislature . . . which is the more desirable forum for lawmaking.'[58] And
at the end of its opinion, the court tried to reassure John, now the legal
father, that things might work out for the best. The court conceded that
John may have agreed to the surrogate-mother arrangement simply 'as
an accommodation to allow Luanne to surmount a formality'[59] but
observed that 'human relationships are not static; things done merely to
help one individual overcome a perceived legal obstacle sometimes
become much more meaningful.'[60] Of course, there is no legal basis for
such musings, and the court resorted to citing literature to bolster its
opinion. It referred approvingly to *Shadowlands*, a play about the life of
C. S. Lewis and his marriage to an American citizen, Joy Gresham,
which was arranged so that she could stay in England.[61] Just as a deeper
relationship developed between Lewis and Gresham, the court seemed to
be saying, a deeper relationship might develop between John and Jaycee,
if not between John and his former wife, Luanne.

New York's Frozen Embryos

The New York case involved an attempt by Maureen Kass and her husband, Steven, to have a baby by means of IVF.[62] Maureen had previously
undergone five egg-retrieval procedures and nine embryo transfers; none
resulted in a live birth. Before the tenth and final attempt, for which
Maureen's sister agreed to try to carry the couple's embryos, the couple
signed four consent forms. Included in an addendum to one of the forms
was the statement that if the couple 'no longer wish to initiate a pregnancy or are unable to make a decision regarding the disposition of our
stored, frozen pre-zygotes . . . [they] may be disposed of by the IVF
program for approved research investigation as determined by the IVF
program.'[63] Maureen's sister failed to become pregnant, and the couple
subsequently decided to divorce.

Maureen then sought sole custody of the remaining frozen embryos so
that she could undergo another implantation procedure. Steven opposed

---

[58] *ibid* at 1429.   [59] *ibid* at 1430 n 22.   [60] *Buzzanca*, 61 Cal App 4th at 1430 n 22.
[61] See generally WILLIAM NICHOLSON, SHADOWLANDS (1991).
[62] See *Kass v Kass*, 91 NY 2d 554 (1998).
[63] See *Kass v Kass*, 235 AD 2d 150, 663 NYS 2d 559–60 (App Div 2d Dept 1997).

her request. The trial court granted custody of the embryos to Maureen, but an appeals court reversed this ruling in a split decision; the majority of the judges held that the provision that the embryos be turned over for research should be enforced.[64] This decision was appealed to New York's highest court, the Court of Appeals, which affirmed the decision that the couple's prior agreement, including the provision in question, should be enforced. The basic reason for this conclusion was that 'advance directives, subject to mutual change of mind that must be jointly expressed, both minimize misunderstandings and maximize procreative liberty by reserving to the progenitors the authority to make what is in the first instance a quintessentially personal, private decision.'[65] If such a document evidences informed, mutual consent, the court ruled, it should be honored by the courts. In the court's concluding words:

As they embarked on the IVF program, appellant and respondent—'husband' and 'wife,' signing as such—clearly contemplated the fulfillment of a life dream of having a child during their marriage. The consent they signed provided for other contingencies, most especially that in the present circumstance the pre-zygotes would be donated to the IVF program for approved research purposes. These parties have clearly manifested their intention, the law will honor it.[66]

Similarities and Lessons

These cases illustrate the two primary ways in which clinics and courts have tried to avoid the new legal issues raised by assisted-reproduction techniques: application of the sperm-donor model of secrecy to all aspects of infertility treatment, and dependence on contracts. Both clinics and courts like contracts, because they seem to put private, procreation-related decision-making in the hands of the married couple and permit the courts simply to interpret and enforce voluntary agreements. The problem, however, is that much more than contract law is at stake in these cases. The courts are not simply affirming the contents of a contract but are implicitly making profound and wide-ranging decisions about the status of embryos, the interests of children, and the identification and responsibility of their parents. The inadequacy of contract analysis in this area can be seen by the fact that no court has ever forced any person to fulfill the terms of a surrogate-mother contract, a custody contract, or a marriage contract by requiring that the parties be bound by the contractual terms regardless of their current wishes or the best interests of the children involved.[67]

---

[64] See *Kass*, 91 NY 2d at 581.   [65] *ibid* at 565.   [66] *ibid* at 569.
[67] See MARGARET J. RADIN, CONTESTED COMMODITIES (1996).

The California appeals court seemed to be simply honoring a surrogate-mother contract made before Jaycee's conception. In fact, however, the court was implicitly holding that the determination of motherhood would be governed by the same rules that the legislature has adopted to determine fatherhood in the case of sperm donation. The court seemed to see this as a neutral approach with respect to sex, but applying the model of sperm donation to women devalues both pregnancy and childbirth, since according to the court's analysis, not only the genetic mother (who as a donor of the egg used in the 'procreative project' could arguably be considered analogous to a sperm donor, even though donating eggs is much more painful and risky than donating sperm) but also the gestational mother is eliminated from consideration as the child's mother. Likewise, the court decided that because sperm donors have historically had their identities kept secret even from the children conceived as a result of their 'donations,'[68] keeping the identities of both the egg donor and the gestational mother a secret is appropriate.

Because both the primacy of the contract and the value of secrecy can be disputed, it is not surprising that the court concluded its opinion with a reference to *Shadowlands* rather than to the law. *Shadowlands* is a strong play, and its main character, C. S. Lewis, was a great writer, but to cite the play as a basis for the proposition that 'a deeper relationship' may develop between a man and a woman than that contemplated at the time of a marriage of convenience misses the point not only of the play itself (which is about the meaning of suffering) but also of the case itself (since the marriage had already ended in divorce). For Lewis, the real world was no more than 'the shadowlands' from which we will emerge, like Plato's cave-dwelling prisoners, into the afterlife, where we will finally see reality clearly.[69]

The California court's most important insight was that courts have an extremely difficult time making meaningful public policy in the realm of assisted reproduction because they are limited to deciding individual disputes after the fact, and that the legislature, which ideally can foresee and prevent disputes, is therefore the preferred law-making body in this area. The New York Court of Appeals did not do much better. The judges seemed to be especially proud of themselves for affirming the contract (consent form) the couple had signed (even though it was a technical, boilerplate form that was difficult to understand). But in affirming the contract, the court failed to examine the implications of its terms for public policy. For example, although informed consent is necessary for

---

[68] George J. Annas., *Fathers Anonymous: Beyond the Best Interests of the Sperm Donor*, 14 FAM LQ 1 (1980).

[69] See C. S. LEWIS, THE LAST BATTLE (1994) (originally published in 1956).

research involving human embryos, the gamete donors retain the right to withdraw their consent at any time. To the extent that the consent of both parties is necessary for valid consent to research (and this is what the consent form required), the withdrawal of consent by either party should mean that the research cannot proceed.

It may be that the New York court missed this point because it adopted the language of the consent form, with its meaningless term 'pre-zygotes'[70] (instead of embryos). Other clinics have used the euphemistic term 'pre-embryos,' but virtually everyone has now abandoned the prefix because the most meaningful distinction is between extracorporeal embryos (over which male and female gamete providers have equal say) and implanted embryos (over which the pregnant woman has the ultimate decision-making authority). The terms used often determine the outcome. It is evidence of the court's confusion that even though the court said it was adopting the terms used in the consent form, in the opinion, three different terms are used for the same entities: embryos, fertilized eggs, and pre-zygotes.

Finally, to the extent that the New York court was correct in concluding that the couple embarked on IVF and signed the consent form contemplating 'the fulfillment of a life dream of having a child during their marriage,'[71] their divorce put an end to this dream and radically altered their circumstances. Divorce would seem to be a sufficient change to call into question the embryo agreement, like the marriage agreement itself, and to provide each former spouse with the opportunity to revoke it.

In 2000, the Massachusetts Supreme Judicial Court decided *A.Z. v B.Z.*[72] and became the first state supreme court specifically to repudiate prior agreements as to the disposition of frozen embryos when one of the gamete providers changes his or her mind. Like the New Jersey decision in *Baby M*, the Massachusetts court noted that there were other family contracts courts would not (or at least should not) enforce. The court held that 'as a matter of public policy . . . forced procreation is not an area amenable to judicial enforcement.'[73] The court continued, 'We would not order either a husband or a wife to do what is necessary to conceive a child or to prevent conception, any more than we would order either party to do what is necessary to make the other happy.'[74]

These courts arguably did as well as they could, and reliance on prior contracts as a way to resolve controversies in assisted reproduction has also been espoused by leading legal commentators.[75] None the less, the

---

[70] *Kass*, 91 NY 2d at 556.   [71] *ibid* at 569.

[72] 725 NE2d 1051 (Mass 2000). See also George J. Annas, *Ulyssess and the Fate of Frozen Embryos: Reproduction, Research, or Destruction*, 343 New Eng J Med (2000).

[73] *A.Z.* at 1057–8   [74] *ibid* at 1058.

[75] See John A. Robertson, Children of Choice (1994).

California court is correct in asking that the legislature establish rules in this arena. The court's opinion, for example, gives no guidance on what should happen if the gestational mother or the egg donor changes her mind and wants to be designated the legal mother with the rights and responsibility to rear Jaycee. Must obstetricians and hospitals locate and interpret contracts to determine who a child's legal mother is at the time of the birth? Do commerce, money, and contracts really have more to say about motherhood than pregnancy and childbirth? If we consider the best interests of children more important than the best interests of commerce, children will be best protected by a universal rule that the woman who gives birth to the child is the child's legal mother—with, among other things, the right to make treatment decisions on behalf of the child and the responsibility to care for the child.[76] I believe this not because it is the traditional or natural rule but because the gestational mother is the only one of the three potential mothers who must be present at the child's birth and available to make decisions on behalf of the child. She is also the only one of the three potential mothers who has a personal relationship with the child. Decisions about treatment and care of the child must often be made immediately; the issues of long-term care, relinquishment of parental rights, and adoption can be dealt with later.

Similarly, the New York court acknowledged in its opinion that the New York State Task Force on Life and the Law recently 'issued a comprehensive report . . . together with recommendations for regulation . . . addressing a wide range of relevant subjects.'[77] The court, however, took no position on the recommendations themselves, and it is unclear from the opinion whether the judges actually had an opportunity to read the report (which was released only a week before the court's opinion was published).[78]

The New York State Task Force

The New York Task Force issued the first comprehensive legislative report on assisted reproduction in the United States in 1998. Similar reports were issued in the United Kingdom,[79] Australia,[80] and

---

[76] See generally S. Elias Sherman and George J. Annas, *Social Policy Considerations in Noncoital Reproduction*, 255 J AM MED ASSOC 62 (1986).

[77] *Kass*, 91 NY2d at 563 n 2.

[78] See NEW YORK STATE TASK FORCE ON LIFE AND THE LAW, THE ASSISTED REPRODUCTIVE TECHNOLOGIES: ANALYSIS AND RECOMMENDATIONS FOR PUBLIC POLICY (1998); see also Altman L. Health, *Panel Seek Sweeping Changes in Fertility Therapy*, NY TIMES, Apr 29 1998 at A1.

[79] See DEPARTMENT OF HEALTH AND SOCIAL SECURITY, REPORT OF THE COMMITTEE OF INQUIRY INTO HUMAN FERTILIZATION AND EMBRYOLOGY (1984).

[80] See COMMITTEE TO CONSIDER THE SOCIAL, ETHICAL AND LEGAL ISSUES ARISING FROM IN VITRO FERTILIZATION, REPORT ON THE DISPOSITION OF EMBRYOS PRODUCED BY IN VITRO FERTILIZATION (1984).

Ontario[81] more than a decade ago, and Canada issued a national report in 1993.[82] The United States has been reluctant to regulate the assisted-reproduction industry because of continuing controversies over abortion and embryo research, as well as our basic belief that, to a large extent, decisions about assisted reproduction should be left to couples and their physicians.[83] But certain aspects of these decisions have such a strong impact on matters of concern to society—such as child support and care, decisions about medical treatment and education for children, the social identity and responsibility of parents, basic informed-consent requirements, and record keeping—that they require public scrutiny and regulation.

The assisted-reproduction industry caters to the wishes of adults, and their wishes consistently trump the interests of children. The abortion model of private decision-making has been used to resist the regulation of assisted reproduction (even though what is sought is the birth of a child, not the termination of a pregnancy), and the sperm-donor model has consistently been applied to egg donation, pregnancy, and childbirth, even though none of them are equivalent. Perhaps the most disturbing aspect of the application of the sperm-donor model to virtually all assisted-reproduction techniques is the insistence on secrecy—to such an extent that records about sperm donors and their 'donations' are routinely kept from the children conceived as a result of the donations, who are intentionally and systematically deprived of knowledge of their genetic parents.[84] Secrecy has been the norm in donor insemination since its introduction. Worse, parents may be counseled to lie to their children about their genetic heritage, even though family secrets can adversely affect the entire family.[85]

The New York State Task Force recommended approximately sixty changes in state regulation of gamete banks, and eleven new state laws. It is not necessary to agree with all these recommendations to appreciate

---

[81] See ONTARIO LAW REFORM COMMISSION, REPORT ON HUMAN ARTIFICIAL REPRODUCTION AND RELATED MATTERS (1985).

[82] See ROYAL COMMISSION ON NEW REPRODUCTIVE TECHNOLOGIES, PROCEED WITH CAUTION (1993).

[83] US House of Representatives, *Hearings on the Extracorporeal Embryo* before the Investigations and Oversight Subcommittee of the Science and Technology Committee, Aug 8–9 1984. Washington, DC: Government Printing Office, 1984; see also George J. Annas *et al*, *The Politics of Human-Embryo Research—Avoiding Ethical Gridlock*, 334 NEW ENG J MED 1329 (1996).

[84] Ethics Committee, American Fertility Society. Ethical Considerations of Assisted Reproductive Technologies. Fertil Steril 62: Supp 1: 1S-125S (1994).

[85] See generally ANNETTE BARAN and REUBEN PANNOR, LETHAL SECRETS: THE SHOCKING CONSEQUENCES AND UNSOLVED PROBLEMS OF ARTIFICIAL INSEMINATION (1989); see also Sandra R. Leiblum and S. E. Hamkins, *To Tell or Not to Tell: Attitudes of Reproductive Endocrinologists Concerning Disclosure to Offspring of Conception via Assisted Insemination by Donor*, 13 PSCYHOSOM OBSTET GYNAECOL 267 (1992); Robert D. Nachtigall *et al*, *Stigma, Disclosure, and Family Functioning among Parents of Children Conceived through Donor Insemination*, 68 FERTIL STERIL 83 (1997).

the number of areas that may require regulation. The Task Force was concerned, for example, about the growing number of multiple pregnancies resulting from the use of fertility drugs and the implantation of multiple embryos, which are associated with increased risks of prematurity and low birth weight, or in fetal reduction (selective abortion of some of the fetuses). The Task Force ultimately could not agree on how to regulate multiple pregnancies. A private multidisciplinary group has recently recommended federal legislation to limit the number of implanted embryos per cycle to four.[86] The Task Force was also concerned about the lack of uniform standards for record keeping, consent procedures and forms, counseling, screening, reporting of success rates, egg donation, and embryo research.

The Task Force's most important decision was to adopt a child-centered perspective that takes seriously the protection of the interests of the children born as a result of assisted-reproduction techniques—for example, by identifying the children's legal parents and requiring clinics to keep records on behalf of the children. The most important specific recommendation was that 'New York law should clearly provide that the woman who gives birth to the child is the child's legal mother, even if the child was not conceived with the woman's egg.' If this rule had been in effect in California, the dispute there would not have occurred, since the gestational mother and her husband (if she was married) or the genetic father (if she was single) would have been Jaycee's legal parents, and they would have had to relinquish their parental rights to give her up for adoption. The Task Force's recommendation could also have resolved the dispute in the New York case, since it recommended that use of frozen embryos always requires the agreement of both gamete providers, thus giving each veto power.

CONCLUSION

More important than the rules proposed by the Task Force is its attempt to move the regulation of assisted reproduction out of the shadowlands of private clinics and the public realm of private disputes (the courts) into the light of public democratic lawmaking. Both the regulation of medicine and family relations have historically been dealt with under state law, not federal law because the states are responsible for family law and medical law. It has seemed reasonable for the states to handle these issues themselves and for the law to develop on a state-by-state basis.

---

[86] See ISLAT Working Group, *ART into Science: Regulation of Fertility Techniques*, 281 SCIENCE 651 (1998).

None the less, to the extent that assisted reproduction has become big business and to the extent that it is more accurately characterized as a commercial enterprise than as a medical or family-related enterprise, federal regulation of at least its interstate commercial aspects is desirable.

Other countries that have developed uniform standards for the infertility industry have appointed a committee or commission to study the issues and make legislative recommendations. It seems likely that if we want to consider establishing uniform commercial standards in the United States, a similar panel will have to be appointed by the President. The Advisory Committee on Human Radiation Experiments provides the best recent model, since it was given a specific charge, had an adequate budget, and received the co-operation of the relevant federal agencies.[87]

The states will, of course, continue to have jurisdiction over determining motherhood, fatherhood, child custody, and related issues of family law. But national standards of commerce could be developed for assisted reproduction, as they have for organ transplantation. A national advisory committee on the new reproductive techniques should consider uniform national rules that address the following issues: the content of informed consent in terms of the risks to parents and children; standard screening and record-keeping requirements for egg and sperm donation; the ability of children born as a result of assisted reproduction to learn the identity of their genetic and gestational parents; research on human embryos; time limits on the storage of human embryos; the use of gametes from deceased persons to produce children; and the addition of eggs and embryos (and possibly sperm as well) to the list of human tissues that cannot be purchased or sold in the United States.

C. S. Lewis, who also wrote children's books, believed that a 'bad way' to write for children is to do so as a special category of 'giving the public what it wants.'[88] Likewise, a bad way to protect the children who have been conceived and born with the assistance of the new reproductive techniques is simply to provide the adults involved with what they want. In late 1997, President Clinton signed a federal law designed to shift the emphasis in adoption practices from the rights of the biologic parents to the welfare of the children.[89] The assisted-reproduction industry should move in this direction as well. As with adoption, however, it will probably take federal action to move children to the center of consideration in the infertility business.

---

[87] Advisory Committee on Human Radiation Experimentation, *Final Report*. Washington, DC: Government Printing Office, 1995.

[88] C. S. Lewis, Of Other Worlds: Essays and Stories 22–34 (1966).

[89] See Katherine Q. Seelye, *Clinton to Approve Sweeping Shift in Adoption*, NY Times, Nov 17 1997 at A20.

8

The Legal Regulation of Infertility Treatment in Britain

RUTH DEECH

The history of the regulation of IVF in Britain reveals movement from control of embryo research to the regulation of infertility treatment in IVF centres and the monitoring of new assisted reproductive techniques (ART). Regulation was rooted in the need to allay widespread fears expressed by politicians, the media, the public and the professions about embryo research, its morality and its direction. It was the spread of IVF treatment and clinics that drove regulation and even then perhaps only because the National Health Service, under both Labour and Conservative governments, has declined to fund the generality of such treatment, giving it the potential to become big business and an area that needed regulation. The Human Fertilisation and Embryology Act 1990 (the Act), was the first piece of legislation in Britain to regulate research and IVF clinics. Its origins can be found in the Warnock Report, commissioned by the Government in response to public concern about IVF.[1] Under the legislation the Human Fertilisation and Embryology Authority (HFEA) was established 'to reconcile the technical perspective of the scientists with the social and moral requirements of the wider population'.[2] The purpose of the HFEA was 'to monitor and to regulate research and the provision of infertility services involving IVF and artificial insemination'.[3] This chapter will discuss the history that led to the legislation, the role of the HFEA, and how the HFEA has responded to the moral and ethical dilemmas that have arisen in its eight-year history of regulation.

REGULATION PRIOR TO THE HUMAN FERTILISATION AND EMBRYOLOGY ACT 1990

The Warnock Committee Report 1984 was not, as is often supposed, the starting point for regulation, but rather took up an already existing but

---

[1] *A Question of Life: Report of the Committee of Inquiry into Human Fertilisation and Embryology*, Cmnd 9314 (1984) (Warnock Report).
[2] M. Mulkay, *The Embryo Research Debate, Science and the Politics of Production*. Cambridge: Cambridge University Press (1997) 150.   [3] *ibid* at 16.

shadowy position created by the professional bodies themselves. By the end of 1983, the professional bodies had already been regulating research on embryos voluntarily, with sets of safeguards in existence to monitor medical and scientific developments. The Warnock Committee's terms of reference were 'to consider recent and potential developments in medicine and science related to human fertilisation and embryology; to consider what policies and safeguards should be applied, including consideration of the social, ethical and legal implications of these developments; and to make recommendations'.[4] The building blocks that constituted the HFEA and its policies, and which were recommended by the Warnock Committee, were already in place owing to the regulation by the professional medical bodies.

The Medical Research Council (MRC), which had rejected the application of the IVF pioneer Dr Edwards for funding in 1971, reacted to the birth of Louise Brown by setting up its own ethical group in 1979 to consider IVF in general, and in particular, species mixing, consent, and the need for a register, thus giving its approval to ART. At a later meeting in 1982 it considered preimplantation genetic diagnosis and the freezing of gametes and embryos.[5] In 1983 the Ethics Committee of the Royal College of Obstetricians and Gynaecologists (RCOG) reported on the same topic. It suggested a statutory body to advise the Secretary of State for Health on regulations, but was not willing to see statutory interference with practice.[6] In the same year the British Medical Association Working Group on IVF issued an Interim Report.[7] It was opposed to surrogacy, but introduced the notions of assessment of a couple before the offer of treatment, and storage of gametes for a year.

In the 1980s there was a real possibility that research would be prohibited and so the MRC and the RCOG established the Voluntary Licensing Authority (VLA), to ensure that their work could continue with responsibility. Five non-scientists joined four representatives from each of the two bodies, and the VLA gave itself the tasks of approving a Code of Practice on research and subsequently treatment; of inviting clinics, clinicians and scientists to submit their work for licensing; of visiting each clinic prior to licence; of reporting to the parent bodies; and of publicizing the work that was taking place. There were at that date twelve cen-

---

[4] Warnock Report, n 1 above, para 4

[5] Medical Research Council, 'Statement on Research Related to Human Fertilisation and Embryology', (1982) 285 *British Medical Journal* 1480.

[6] Royal College of Obstetricians and Gynaecologists, Ethics Committee, *Report of the RCOG Ethics Committee on in vitro fertilisation and embryo replacement or transfer*. London: RCOG (1983).

[7] British Medical Association Working Group on IVF, 'Interim Report on Human IVF and Embryo Replacement and Transfer', (1983) 286 *British Medical Journal* 1594.

tres in Britain carrying out IVF work. The VLA succeeded in showing in its six years of existence that embryo research and IVF treatment could be controlled and responsibly carried out and that the profession was capable and willing to control itself. Most clinics voluntarily conformed and the VLA became a successful model for the later HFEA and an effective weapon in fending off the parliamentary attempts of those years to end embryo research. It had the non-statutory advantage of flexibility in shaping itself to new demands as they arose but it was also dominated by the professionals, without sufficiently visible public and patient interest.

The Warnock Committee was able to extend its inquiry to the broader social and ethical issues of the debate. It considered all the current techniques, namely, donor insemination (DI), IVF, donation, surrogacy, storage, and research, and made sixty-three recommendations. The recommendations were that there should be established a statutory licensing authority to regulate research and treatment, with lay representation and a lay chairman; that all practitioners and premises should be licensed; that embryo research should be permitted as should the creation of embryos for research; that embryos could be kept outside the body for fourteen days, and that payment of donors should be allowed. Donor anonymity was favoured, together with a limit of children to ten from any one man. Adults were to be given non-identifying information about the donor. Storage periods were recommended, as was counselling. The collection of statistics on treatment was recommended, as was the organization of IVF within the NHS. Criminal sanctions were recommended for the unauthorized use of embryos and certain other practices; the legal status of the IVF child was considered and surrogacy was disapproved except in the most limited circumstances.[8]

The subsequent Bill faced a difficult, emotional, and delayed passage in both Houses of Parliament, but the time involved allowed pro-research groups to enter the field and persuade the public in the same way that anti-embryo research and anti-abortion groups had long done. The link between embryo research, fertility, and the eradication of genetic disease was successfully implanted in the public consciousness. The Bill sensitively combined prohibitions on the most feared types of research (cloning, genetic manipulation, mixing of species) with permission for wide and carefully controlled research and treatment. The parliamentarians were well aware of the ground-breaking nature of the legislation of 1990. In the House of Lords Lord Houghton described the Bill as 'a turning point in medical research and in the destiny of mankind. Nothing like this Bill has previously been placed before Parliament.' In the House of Commons, Kenneth Clarke described it as 'one of the most significant

---

[8] Warnock Report, n 1 above, 80–6.

measures to be brought forward by a government in the last 20 years. It is a complex and sensitive Bill that deals with matters that are fundamental to the wellbeing of our society.'[9]

There will always be some extra hesitation about reopening that particular piece of legislation for amendment when the time comes, because it can be used as a vehicle for the amendment of abortion law. This occurred during its passage when an amendment to the abortion law was made, with the effect of lowering the upper limit of general abortion from twenty-eight to twenty-four weeks. Those involved in ART and embryo research are understandably reluctant to make an association between abortion laws and embryo research and ART, but it has been forged and anti-abortion legislators are ready to seize any relevant opportunity to reopen the debate on abortion and its limits.

British abortion law is governed by the Abortion Act 1967, passed in the great law-reforming era of the 1960s, which saw liberalizing changes in the divorce law, capital punishment abolished, and homosexuality and contraception legalized. The Abortion Act was somewhat restricted in the course of the passage of the Human Fertilisation and Embryology Act 1990. The law is now that if the continuation of the pregnancy would involve risk greater than if it were terminated of injury to the physical or mental health of the pregnant woman or any existing children of her family, an abortion may be performed up to the end of the twenty-fourth week of pregnancy.[10] There are three other grounds not limited by the twenty-fourth week provision: to prevent grave permanent injury to the physical or mental health of the woman;[11] if the risk to her life is greater than if the pregnancy is terminated;[12] and if there is a substantial risk that the child would suffer such physical or mental abnormalities as to be seriously handicapped.[13] This law is also applied to the selective reduction which is sometimes contemplated when a multiple pregnancy has resulted after IVF, so that one or two children may survive at the cost of the others. Two doctors must provide the necessary certification of the grounds under the Abortion Act.

THE HUMAN FERTILISATION AND EMBRYOLOGY AUTHORITY

The Act followed the Warnock Report in broad outline although not in every detail. It established the HFEA with the duties of licensing centres,

---

[9] *House of Lords Debates (Hansard)*, Human Fertilisation and Embryology Bill vol 514, col 244 (20 Mar 1990); *House of Commons Debates (Hansard)*, Human Fertilisation and Embryology Bill vol 170, col 915 (2 Apr 1990).
[10] Human Fertilisation and Embryology Act 1990, s 37 (1)(a).   [11] s 37 (1)(b).
[12] s 37 (1)(c).   [13] s 37 (1)(d).

providing information, keeping a register of donors and treatments, publishing a Code of Practice, monitoring new situations, and then advising the Secretary of State if requested. The difference between the HFEA and the professional bodies is that the HFEA is a statutory and autonomous body, with a broad frame of reference. The HFEA fulfils many of the requirements laid down by Dr Edwards in the 1970s. The establishment of an independent body such as the HFEA, with its responsibility for policing work under the Act, has been crucial in maintaining public confidence while allowing medical research and treatment to continue within controlled parameters.

The HFEA is answerable to Parliament through the Health Minister, who appoints the twenty-one members after advertisement. It produces an Annual Report to Parliament with general information about the number of licensed centres, the range of research, statistics about IVF, and new developments in ART. The current budget of £1.5 million is set by the Government and the HFEA is required to raise 70 per cent by charging fees to the centres. The centres usually pass on the fees to the patients, and the need to collect fees has been used by critics to compromise the neutrality of the Authority. Far better, it seems, to have a regulatory system that is wholly publicly funded, leaving the Government to collect a compensatory tax directly from the clinics if necessary. The HFEA is left with a large measure of discretion but its decisions, including removal of a licence, are subject to judicial review. More than half the members, including the chair and the deputy chair, must not be medical practitioners, or involved in ART or embryo research. One-third are required to be specialists in the field; others are co-opted to subcommittees and patients' representatives and counsellors are also involved. The HFEA holds monthly meetings, conferences, and public consultations (making use of the Web as well), for example on sex selection, cloning, and payment to donors.

The first three years of the HFEA were preoccupied with the administrative base: designing a national regulatory system, having an extensive body of secondary legislation drafted; persuading professional people not much used to legislative control to accept regulation, and production of the first Code of Practice. In the first year a total of 121 IVF centres were inspected and licensed. The HFEA devoted much effort to getting in accurate data from centres and compiling a register of donors that retained the anonymity of the persons involved. This database is the largest of its kind in the world and could allow children conceived through IVF to determine their genetic origins. The success and outcome of treatments can also be derived from the register.

The Code of Practice, now in its fourth edition,[14] started as the short VLA 'guidelines' based on recommendations by the Warnock Committee, the MRC, and the RCOG. They dealt with research, treatment, licensing, and consents and are immediately recognizable as containing the same fundamental rules of good practice as the now seventy-page-long Code of Practice of the HFEA. The Code is 'voluntary' but failure to observe it would lead to scrutiny by a Licence Committee and possible removal of the licence to practise; and it might also expose the clinician to a malpractice action were anything to go wrong. It is constantly being updated and currently covers staffing of centres; their facilities; the assessment of donors, patients, and the welfare of their potential offspring; information to be given; consents to be obtained, together with model forms; counselling; the use of gametes and embryos; storage; research; records and complaints. It is careful not to trespass into the areas of good clinical practice which are properly the province of the professional bodies, but there are grey areas, such as the HFEA's emphasis on the placing of no more than three embryos in a woman in any one treatment in order to avoid multiple births with their cost and dangers to health.

PRINCIPLES OF THE HFEA

Four working principles of the HFEA can be discerned that have developed partly from practice and partly from statute.[15] Two derive directly from the Act, that is respect for the embryo and its protected status, and the need to consider the welfare of the potential child. Two others have consistently been considered, and they are safety, and the protection of human autonomy and dignity. Respect for the embryo is illustrated by the limited categories of research allowed in the Act and by the care exercised by the HFEA in permitting research and demanding explanations for the need to use embryos and how they are being used, following peer review. Care in disposal of unused embryos, and prohibitions on splitting and cloning are additional examples, and preimplantation genetic diagnosis (PGD) control may be included. These principles are the threads that run through the determinations of the HFEA. Decisions made by the HFEA are a careful assessment and balancing of these interests, along with an analysis of the implications of allowing procedures to take place.

---

[14] Human Fertilisation and Embryology Authority, *Code of Practice*, 4th edn (1998) 1–70.
[15] Ruth Deech, 'Infertility and Ethics', (1997) 9 *Child and Family Law Quarterly* 4.

The Regulation of the Use of Embryos

The morality of carrying out research on embryos was the issue that sparked off the debate that ultimately led to the Human Fertilisation and Embryology Act 1990. It is now difficult to recall that in the 1970s and 1980s in Britain, embryo research came close to being totally prohibited and that scientists may have accepted legal regulation as the price of being able to continue their work at all. Recent public discussion about cloning and associated cell nuclear replacement research has revealed that there is still significant opposition across all religious and social divisions to any form of embryo research on the ground that the embryo possesses the full moral status of a human being. The status of the embryo and the type of research that can be carried out on embryos have been settled by the Human Fertilisation and Embryology Act 1990, although the religious and ethical debate continues. The following activities may be undertaken only with a licence: creation of an embryo, using an embryo, placing an embryo in a woman, storing gametes, using donated gametes, mixing human and animal gametes for diagnostic purposes. The most severe penalties contained in the 1990 Act pertain to embryo research, which is hedged about by restrictions difficult to alter, by external control over scientists not found in any other field, and by criminal penalties for infringement of the permitted procedures.

The solution to the controversy over the status of embryos is contained in s. 3 (3)(a) of the Act: there is to be no retention out of the body of the live embryo after the appearance of the primitive streak, which is taken to be no later than the end of fourteen days from the mixing of the gametes (s. 3 (4)). This formulation accepts the argument put forward in the Warnock Committee Report,[16] that before the primitive streak appears there is only a collection of cells, any of which could become any part of the body ('totipotential'), and not all of which will take part in the subsequent development, if any, of the embryo.

Legal regulation in Britain also probably serves to protect clinicians and scientists not only from legal action for malpractice (where they have followed the HFEA Code of Practice) but also gives them a shield against accusations of ethical malpractice, for they are acting within the parameters agreed by Parliament and the HFEA. But the excitement has not vanished from this area. So fundamental are the questions raised by the success of the science, that after nearly thirty years of public awareness, there is more moral and ethical discussion than ever before and a new profession of bioethics has arisen.[17]

---

[16] Warnock Report, n 1 above, para 11.2–9
[17] J. Gunning and V. English, *Human in Vitro Fertilisation*. Dartmouth: Aldershot (1993).

Welfare of the Potential Child

The need to protect, as far as possible, the welfare of the potential child has given rise to much of the detail in the Code of Practice and to some difficult issues of privacy. How should the undoubted need to protect the child from the possibility of abuse be balanced against the patients' entitlement to confidentiality in their treatment and the unwillingness of some general practitioners to provide information about their patients to the infertility centre? Some general practitioners are unwilling to do this because they do not wish to give away confidential information; others because, as they say, since nature allows the most unsuitable of people to become parents if they are fertile, what right is there to prevent those who have to seek help from becoming parents on social grounds? There is an unresolved debate as to why it should be legal to license parenthood under the Act with its strict provisions if the intending parents are infertile by chance, and whether lesbian and single parents are intrinsically less good parents than heterosexual couples. Many clinics refuse *ab initio* to treat such women on principle, while even those who will consider them have to assess them under the provision of the Act instructing them to consider the child's need for a father. This was an amendment introduced in the House of Lords[18] in order to make it possible, but more difficult, for such women to receive treatment. Some research has shown that children do no worse when brought up by single or lesbian women, but there is still strong public reaction to it, and when medical resources in the field are perceived to be scarce, there is resentment against their being used on such persons. Amongst practitioners, there is no dissent from the premiss of the legislation that where there is state intervention, then there is a right to decide who may have access to treatment and who may not. This may be justified either by analogy to adoption (the use of a scarce resource needs rules about allocation) or by the sensitivity to the very topic of IVF which, it is agreed, needs controlling in a way that makes it acceptable to the public. Public and media reaction to cases of insemination of older women and lesbians bears that out, and should not be dismissed as the work of the media in stirring up reaction, because the respectability and acceptability to the public of research on embryos and advances in ART are crucial to their continuation and funding by politicians and research councils.

In considering and interpreting the welfare provision, the HFEA has taken the line that there is no 'right to a baby', even though this is sometimes taken up by the media when there is a heart-rending case. This age is sometimes described as one in which everyone has rights and every

---

[18] *House of Lords Debates (Hansard)*, 20 June 1990, col 1019.

want must be met. Clinicians have frequently supported the 'right to a baby' line of thinking, as it meets their professional requirements and wish to expand the possibilities of treatment and research. The Act, however, imposes 'the ethics of the nation' rather than the ethics of the profession.[19] The existence of regulation denies the absolute right to a baby, which is not to be confused with one 'reproductive autonomy' espoused by jurists. The latter 'right' represented a reaction against the discriminatory laws of apartheid South Africa and Nazi Germany that denied the rights of persons of different races to marry or cohabit. The HFEA has been anxious, in, for example, stressing the truth about the relatively low rates of success of IVF treatment, to ensure that no woman should feel inferior or worthless if she cannot or does not want to have a child by infertility treatment. Every woman is valuable in her own right, not just as a mother or a potential mother, and her life is as valuable if she is without children, whether by choice or not, as it is with children. There has to be balanced the rights of access to the portals of treatment and to all reasonable and appropriate technology on the one hand, against refraining from promising 100 per cent success, so that women and their partners know that science cannot always deliver a baby and that there is a limit to the attempts. Women must not be made to feel that if only they tried again or spent more resources, they could be mothers, and that their childlessness is the result of their own lack of effort. To quote from the Human Genetics Advisory Committee (HGAC)/Human Fertilisation and Embryology (HFEA) report on Cloning:

The relief of the pain of infertility is, in general, a good end, but it is not an absolute end to be achieved without regard to the ethical acceptability of the means employed for that achievement. The wish for genetic offspring is a natural human aspiration, but this has to be held in balance with other desirable aspects of human well being and it cannot be given an overriding priority above all other considerations.[20]

Safety

Safety has been a major, perhaps the major consideration in HFEA decisions regarding new forms of treatment and limits on existing forms—for example its ruling that only three embryos may be transferred at any one time. This consideration has informed its thinking about sex selection, use of spermatids, cloning, screening of sperm and import of gametes, and the licensing of intracytoplasmic sperm injection (ICSI). This is not

[19] J. Gunning and V. English, n 17 above, 131.
[20] HGAC/HFEA, *Cloning Issues in Reproduction, Science and Medicine.* London: Human Genetics Advisory Committee (Dec 1998), para 4.6.

surprising in view of the severe consequences that could arise if defective children were born from IVF. Not only would the whole science and its practitioners suffer a setback, possibly a permanent one, but the human consequences would be unimaginable, as would the cost and litigation, even bearing in mind the inadequacy of compensation when lives are destroyed. This was learned from the thalidomide tragedy of the 1960s and the more recent legal aspects of the link between cancer and cigarettes. A regulatory authority simply cannot be too cautious in this area, lest it is blamed by future generations for tragic results. So the HFEA is keeping under review any possible link between drugs used in infertility treatment and cancer, and is encouraging follow-up studies of IVF children.

Autonomy

Consent to medical treatment is a fundamental ethical, legal, and social principle which has governed medical practice for decades, if not longer. It has taken on an added force in the days of (much-needed) testing of new drugs and medical procedures on human subjects, and the existence of a wide range of emergency medical treatments. It is reinforced by respect for the incapacitated and freedom of choice,[21] as defined by bills of human rights, and most recently by the Council of Europe Convention on Human Rights and Biomedicine.[22] Perhaps the one ethical principle that unites those who disagree about medical experimentation on volunteers, new medical treatments, and work involving human gametes is that the subjects should have full information and be enabled to give their free, withdrawable consent. This was an issue from the earliest days of IVF, when Drs Steptoe and Edwards were accused of being cavalier about consent.[23]

British law attempted to deal with all foreseeable circumstances by requirements of consent in the Human Fertilisation and Embryology Act. Under Schedule 3, consent must be given in writing and may be withdrawn at any stage before use of the gamete or embryo. The person consenting must be given the opportunity to receive counselling and information. Consent must specify whether use is for treatment or research. Consent to storage of gametes or embryos must specify the maximum period of storage, if less than the statutory maximum period of ten years, and state what is to be done with the gametes or embryos if

---

[21] *St George's Healthcare NHS Trust v S, R v Collins and others, ex parte S* [1998] 3 All ER 673.
[22] European Treaty Series, no 164, 4 Apr 1997.
[23] P. Ramsey, 'Shall We Reproduce? The Medical Ethics of IVF', (1972) 220 *Journal of the American Medical Association* 1346.

the person who gave the consent dies or becomes incapacitated. So a party to divorce, a situation which has given rise to litigation over embryos in other countries, can withdraw his or her consent to the storage or use of an embryo that had come into existence by the act of the former parties to the marriage. The British attitude is very insistent on consent as the key to dignified and independent use of a person's genetic material. The preservation and protection of the autonomy and dignity of the individual and the embryo are held thereby to be protected. The preservation of bodily integrity and control over the destiny of one's own genetic material is paramount. The additional genetic confusion that would be caused if persons were allowed control over and to authorize the removal of another person's genetic material is profound and potentially very damaging. The Act is perhaps not complete however, as it does not resolve the question of donation of gametes or tissue by minors facing cancer treatment which threatens their sterility. While the *Gillick* rules[24] allow consent by competent minors to *operations*, or consent by their parents, the specific requirements of the Human Fertilisation and Embryology Act for written consent cannot be waived for minors.

WORK OF THE HFEA AND THE NEW ASSISTED REPRODUCTIVE TECHNOLOGIES

It is now proposed to give an overview of the topics that the HFEA has regulated in its eight years of existence, treating four of them.

Regulation of New Assisted Reproductive Techniques

The HFEA has had to consider the desirability and safety of new techniques for the treatment for infertility. These have involved the techniques of intracytoplasmic sperm injection (ICSI) with sperm or spermatids, sorting sperm by sex, egg freezing, storage of testicular and ovarian tissue, and advanced forms of embryo culture.

Storage of Testicular and Ovarian Tissue

After the first three years or so of the HFEA's existence, which were dominated by organizational and regulatory principles, the new techniques and ethical problems seemed to proliferate, along with media attention. In 1995 the question of tissue storage for cancer patients was considered. Young men facing treatment for cancer might be rendered sterile by that treatment and clinicians presented them with the possibility of donating

---

[24] *Gillick v West Norfolk Area Health Authority* [1986] AC 112.

sperm for cryopreservation. The problems were the need to explain this situation and gain informed consent at the very time when the young patient was having to come to terms with the knowledge that he had cancer and had to undergo immediate treatment; and requiring him to think about what should be done with his frozen sperm in the event of his death.

Modern treatments for cancer have presented interesting infertility conundrums. In 1997 there occurred the case of a 2-year-old boy called Oskar who was faced with emergency treatment for cancer that might destroy his future fertility. The surgeon suggested the removal of a small piece of his testicular tissue with a view to performing an experimental preserving procedure. Oskar's testicular tissue would be frozen until he was an adult, when it would be possible to reimplant it into him and hope that normal sperm production would be restored, or that by then there would be other as yet undiscovered methods of restoring his fertility. The question was whether the entire procedure was legal. Certainly Oskar's parents could consent to the operation that would remove his testicular tissue because parents may consent on behalf of minors to operations. The problem was that under the Human Fertilisation and Embryology Act no one but Oskar would be able to consent to the *storage* of his gametes and that would have to be in writing. By the time he was old enough for reimplantation to be considered, he would be able to sign his own consent to further procedures. The problem was not a barrier, however, for medical evidence showed that the testicular tissue of a prepubertal boy did not contain gametes, and would therefore not be subject to the provisions of the HFE Act until it did. It could therefore be stored on the consent of his parents, but restoration would need Oskar's consent. The Authority went on to consider the parallel situation with girls. It ruled that if ovarian tissue were to be removed and stored, it would fall under the provisions of the Act only if it contained an egg, and that this was never the case with prepubertal girls, and in the case of women would depend on whether the particular piece of ovarian tissue happened to contain an oocyte or not. Guidelines for the storage of ovarian and testicular tissue are in preparation.

Use of Spermatids

The HFEA warned patients of the dangers of treatment abroad by spermatids (or in an effort to select their future child's sex), but ultimately could not prevent people going abroad for that reason, although a clinic could be penalized if it encouraged or facilitated these journeys. Spermatids are immature sperm, and while there were reports of babies born in Europe by the injection of a spermatid into an egg, the HFEA for a time continued to insist on more proof of research before considering licensing such treatment. The spermatid has not undergone the same lengthy process of maturation as the sperm and there are reasonable fears of defects in a child's development until it is proved safe by animal experimentation Likewise, the process used to sort sperm into those that will produce girls and those that will produce boys may involve its exposure to fluorescent dye, and there is no proof that this is safe for the baby's development.

The Use of ART for Convenience and Preference

ART has been used not just for cases of infertility but has also been extended to matters of convenience and preference. For example, the insemination of older mothers past the age of menopause, posthumous insemination, choice of sex of the baby, egg freezing with a view to postponement of childbearing for personal reasons, and the insemination of single women.

Treatment of Older Women

Several controversial ethical issues emerged in 1994, some of which continue to trouble: should there be an upper age limit for treatment of a woman? Because of the varying ages of menopause, the Act provided no upper age limit (nor did it specify that a woman had to be married, heterosexual, or living in a stable union), and so to impose an age limit might well be ultra vires. On the other hand, the public did not seem to approve the expenditure of resources, even privately paid for, on women over 50 or so, all the more so if waiting lists or public expenditure were involved. In 1997 there occurred the case of Mrs Buttle, aged 60, who gave birth. At first it was reported that this was a natural birth, and the media reaction seemed to be one of congratulatory wonder. Subsequently it emerged, although it was never officially confirmed for reasons of confidentiality, that this may have been a case where a woman concealed her age when seeking treatment, the egg may not have been her own, and the provenance of the sperm was likewise unknown.

The age question should ideally be included in the assessment of the welfare of the child which is required by s. 13 (5) of the Act to be undertaken before treatment may be offered. A very old mother would not serve the welfare of her unborn child because she might not survive into the child's adulthood and she might not be fit enough to undertake its care in its demanding baby years. One of the factors about Mrs Buttle that caught media attention was her apparent bad health and unusual living conditions on a farm without modern facilities. The Code of Practice requires that the infertility clinician who proposes to treat a woman should contact her medical general practitioner to determine whether there is any reason why a woman or couple should not be treated.[25] A refusal to name the general practitioner, or to provide proof of age and identity, ought to alert an infertility clinician to circumstances demanding investigation. This understandable need to inquire into private life for the sake of the potential child has to be balanced against the British tradition of privacy. There is no universal ID card in Britain, and no compulsion to register with a general practitioner. Indeed, efforts to make proof of identity more thorough have been resisted both in the name of freedom and for reasons of convenience. Some further identifying factors are now being required, for the sake of children who may one day inquire about their origins, but no general restrictions have been imposed despite the media outrage over the 60-year-old mother. Since 1991 only twenty-seven mothers over 51 years have given birth so it is not a widespread problem; with the spread of freezing techniques, especially of eggs, this may become more of a problem but one that would demand a parliamentary decision.

Sex Selection

Another major issue of convenience has been sex selection. There are groups and individual persons who would like to be able to choose the sex of their future child, maybe for religious reasons, or because they prefer to have a boy or a girl, possibly already being the parents of children of the other sex, or for inheritance or succession reasons, or because they may carry an inheritable disease, such as haemophilia, which could be passed on to a child of one sex but not the other.

The issue of sex selection first came to public attention in 1993. The HFEA carried out a public consultation on the matter,[26] the result being that 67 per cent of the respondents disapproved of sex selection for social reasons. Consequently the HFEA banned sex selection in licensed treatment centres for social reasons, but allowed it for medical reasons to avoid transmission of an inheritable disease, such as haemophilia.[27] The reasons for the ban were that there was a danger of reinforcing sexual stereotypes to the disadvantage of women; that it would be the start of a slippery slope towards treating children as consumer goods; that it would affect family relationships and gender balance within certain ethnic communities; that it would be a misuse of medical resources for non-medical purposes; and because it was morally offensive. Nevertheless, the desire to choose a baby's sex remains strong within some groups and they may well be taking advantage of such services abroad.

---

[25] Human Fertilisation and Embryology Authority, *Code of Practice*, 4th edn (1998), para 3.24.   [26] Human Fertilisation and Embryology Authority, *Third Annual Report*, 1994.
[27] Human Fertilisation and Embryology Authority, *Code of Practice*, 4th edn (1998), para 7.20.

The Blood Case

The most striking use of infertility treatment for convenience so far in the British history of regulation has been the case of Diane Blood.[28] It raised the whole issue of consent to treatment, but it also disguised an even deeper ethical issue, if that were possible, namely, consent to the removal of gametes from the unconscious or dying body.

In the *Blood* case, Diane and Stephen Blood had been married for five years when Mr Blood died suddenly after contracting meningitis. They had no children but were a normal couple receiving no form of fertility treatment. In the last moments of Mr Blood's life just before the life support machinery was turned off, his wife asked the doctors to remove his sperm so that she could have the child that, she subsequently alleged, they were planning before his death to have. By chance, the hospital had on its premises a doctor experienced in the technique of removing sperm from the comatose and quadriplegics, known as electro-ejaculation, which involves the insertion of electrical equipment into the rectum and the ejaculation after shock of sperm into the bladder, from where it can be removed. The doctor performed this technique on Mr Blood, without asking the HFEA for advice, although the Authority was informed shortly after the procedure was completed. The advice would have been that, although not specifically covered in the Act, the removal of gametes from someone who was unconscious would be unlawful, not only because he was unable to consent but also because he would not be able to sign the necessary storage and use consent forms, let alone receive counselling and information, because he did not know what was being done to him. The law on consent to operations is that where someone is unconscious there may only be carried out on him or her that which is necessary in an emergency to make him or her better.

The HFEA subsequently refused permission for the stored sperm to be used, on the ground that there was an infringement of the Act by the keeping of it, and that use would be a further infringement. Mrs Blood sought to have the law overturned after a national media campaign in her favour, under the headlines of 'Grieving widow seeks husband's baby'. She alleged that although there was no sign of written consent to use or storage, she and her late husband had discussed the issue of posthumous birth and he would have wished this to take place. The court case concerned the issue of consent to use and storage, and also judicial review of the HFEA's refusal to use its discretion to allow export of the sperm to Belgium or another country where no such rules existed.

The High Court[29] and the Court of Appeal[30] found for the HFEA on the issue of written consent. The law was clear on that issue, and the sperm

---

[28] *R v Human Fertilisation & Embryology Authority, ex parte Diane Blood* [1997] 2 All ER 687.
[29] [1996] 3 WLR 1176.   [30] [1997] 2 All ER 687.

could not be stored (as would be inevitable in any form of proper infertility treatment) or used without informed written consent. The only exception in the Act to the requirement of consent is when a man and woman are being treated together,[31] and a man who was unconscious or dead could not be regarded as being treated 'together' with his wife. Any weakening of the law of consent would have thrown the whole regulatory system into disarray, opening the door to unauthorized research and experimentation and, not least, upsetting the accuracy of the register of treatment and outcomes.

The HFEA lost the second legal ground in the Court of Appeal.[32] Under s. 24 (4) of the Act, the HFEA has discretion to allow the import and export of gametes into and out of the country subject to conditions, and has the power to waive the requirements of ss. 12–14 (concerning sale, records, welfare, and consent) on those occasions. The HFEA refused Mrs Blood's request to have the sperm exported to Belgium largely on the ground that the request was being made in order to evade British law on consent and the taking of the sperm, and that it had always been the HFEA's policy not to allow export simply to overcome British regulations. If that were not its policy, then serious unethical breaches of the Act could be sustained by the all too simple expedient of exporting the gametes or embryos to another country where there were not such regulations, of which the most notable in Europe are Belgium and Italy and, further afield, the USA. While the HFEA was conscious that European law calls for freedom of movement in relation to goods and medical services, it did not consider that those principles[33] could possibly override the benefits of strict maintenance of the British regulatory system. Individual European countries have the right to diverge from European provisions where there are strong national reasons relating to cultural and social matters best dealt with by the host nation and which seem to it to outweigh the benefit of the European provisions. The Court of Appeal found that the HFEA had not sufficiently weighed the European principle of freedom of movement to seek medical services in reaching its discretionary decision not to allow Mrs Blood to export her husband's sperm, and that it should reach its decision afresh in the light of the judgement. It also held that if she were permitted to take the sperm abroad, the fact that it was unlawfully obtained and stored would not be an impediment. A significant feature in the Court of Appeal's finding was that the factual situation was and always would remain unique. In response to the HFEA's fears that the grant of judicial review would mean that every widow in similar circumstances would seek to circumvent the law, the Court stated that no doctor would ever be likely to remove

---

[31] Sch 3, para 5(3) and s. 4 (1)(b).   [32] [1997] 2 All ER 687.
[33] Treaty establishing the European Community, 25 Mar 1957.

gametes in such circumstances again, as all would know that the laws on consent in the Act could not be fulfilled and that storage and use would be illegal.

In actuality, in the wake of the publicity surrounding the *Blood* case, many telephone calls were received by the HFEA staff at all times of day and night seeking advice or permission to remove sperm from a dying and unconscious man, usually after a traffic accident. All were told that this would be illegal. It seemed to the HFEA that the Court of Appeal's judgement avoided the real issue of consent in the facts of the case, namely, whether it should be legal for gametes to be removed from the many thousands of young people who die unexpectedly every year from accident or illness, at the request of a bereft widow or widower, fiancé or fiancée, parents, grandparents, or partners. The practical difficulties of having to decide, in the few hours available for the procedure to be carried out effectively, whether the person calling for the removal of the gametes was entitled to do so, and what category of persons that should be, and whether the same considerations should apply to the removal of eggs from a dying woman as sperm from a dying man, and whether an unconscious woman should be kept alive on a ventilator in order to give birth or whether her eggs should be fertilized and stored, and for how long storage should continue, are major, and fraught with the greatest ethical issues imaginable.

International Trade in ART

This has sometimes been termed 'procreative tourism'. For example, if a couple in Sweden seek donor insemination (DI) but do not wish to be subject to the Swedish regime of identified sperm donors, they might choose to come to Britain for treatment with anonymous sperm donation. If a couple are not allowed treatment with spermatids in Britain they may go abroad to a country that does permit it and return home for the birth. Is the risk that presumably pertains to procreative tourism a price worth paying for the freedom of choice that it brings, or should countries be more stringent in seeking to control it and looking for international agreement to uphold certain basic standards in order to safeguard the health of the persons involved? After all, it is the home society that will have to bear the burden should ill health or a disabled child result from a particular treatment.

Sperm banks in the US are now advertising their wares on the Internet. For a relatively modest price the buyer may select the sperm of an identifiable individual for delivery. It was thought that some women in Britain who had been denied treatment by British clinics because they were deemed unsuitable might try to import sperm from the US for home insemination. The dangers of this course of action were primarily lack of access to identification of the donor if a resulting child should ever need or wish to know something about him, and safety. Under British law it is illegal to have sperm delivered to a private address, and it may only be legally delivered to a licensed clinic. Carriers and Customs and Excise were warned of this by the HFEA.

Future Trends

The fourth foreseeable development will be the elimination of disease and the addition of desirable characteristics to babies by use of pre-implantation genetic diagnosis, and currently prohibited techniques of cloning and genetic manipulation.

Preimplantation Genetic Diagnosis (PGD)

Preimplantation genetic diagnosis is used at the moment only by couples with a significant risk of passing an inheritable disease on to their babies, of such significance that it is worth undertaking the technique of IVF with its very low pregnancy success rate. It involves the creation of an embryo *in vitro* for a couple who are not otherwise infertile, with the aim of examining the embryo at the eight-cell stage, that is a day or two after fertilization, to see if it carries the defective gene. A defective embryo will be allowed to perish, but one that is tested clear of the inheritable disease will be transferred to the womb. Further genetic manipulation is illegal under British law, as is cloning, but the issues are worth discussing because they are currently colouring the public's view of the general scientific techniques involved.

Some may see the already well-established technique of preimplantation genetic diagnosis as the first step on the road to 'designer babies', that is children programmed to have certain characteristics. Certainly that belief has grown in reaction to the possibility of cloning, which is banned. Currently PGD has been used only in a limited fashion to avoid the passing-on of certain diseases which can be recognized in the embryo. The demand may grow. How far should this testing go?

The procedure is regulated by the HFEA, falling under ss. 3 and 14 of the Act. This procedure has caused grave ethical concerns. Genetic tests reveal information not just about the potential parents but also about their relatives. People who know that they risk passing on a serious genetic disorder to their children face a number of difficult choices. They must consider whether they wish to risk having children who may be affected by the disorder and whether they wish to have prenatal diagnosis, once a pregnancy exists, which may bring with it a difficult decision about terminating a pregnancy. The perceived danger is that increases in

PGD might create a climate where disability becomes avoidable; hence there would be pressure to avoid having a disabled child, guilt, and unwillingness to accept the condition.

Some of the conditions for which PGD is used affect the child from birth. Others appear only in later life. So there will be a period when affected individuals enjoy life free from the disorder. An example of such a condition is Huntington's disease, which usually has an onset of between thirty and sixty years with a small proportion of cases having an onset at less than fifteen years. Can an individual lead a normal life knowing that they will, or are likely to, develop a life-threatening or degenerative disease? Is it ethical to discard an embryo that might develop a disease in fifty years' time? Once the technology exists to detect multiple gene defects in an embryo quickly, will there be pressure to test all embryos to eliminate all inheritable diseases in a drive for a healthier population, or should PGD be limited to couples where serious diseases feature in the family medical history? Step by step the HFEA and other bodies are considering these significant questions and ruling on them.

Cloning and Genetic Manipulation

The final significant new technique is cloning. This possibility, which is all that it is for humans at the moment, has reopened world-wide discussion and interest in regulation of ART, and has filled books and columns of newspapers with fear and fantasies arising from the existence of Dolly the sheep, and first cloned mammal. The announcement of Dolly's birth prompted an inquiry by the British House of Commons Science and Technology Select Committee, which published its findings in March 1997 in a report, *The Cloning of Animals from Adult Cells*.[34] The report was clear that the reproductive cloning of human babies should not take place, as was the Minister of State for Public Health on 26 June 1997, when she indicated that there was an effective legal ban on such a procedure. The Select Committee also indicated that further inquiries should be undertaken into the potential benefits of the cell nucleus replacement technique when confined to the embryonic stage. Accordingly, a public consultation was carried out in 1998 by the HFEA and the Human Genetic Advisory Commission jointly. The consultation found that there was almost universal rejection of cloning by the public, even as a last resort for infertility.[35]

The HGAC/HFEA report[36] recommended that s. 3 of the Human Fertilisation and Embryology Act should be recognised as sufficient to ban

---

[34] HC 373–I, Mar 1997.

[35] HGAC/HFEA, *Cloning Issues in Reproduction, Science and Medicine*. London: Human Genetics Advisory Committee (Dec 1998), para 4.3.

[36] HGAC/HFEA, *Cloning Issues in Reproduction, Science and Medicine*. London: Human Genetics Advisory Committee (Dec 1998).

cloning, even though the Government might wish to introduce a specific ban. This recommendation rested on the ambiguity of the wording of s. 3, referring as it did to an older cloning technique, but legal
advice was given that the courts would take a purposive approach, and
accept that the intention of s. 3 was to ban cloning, regardless of the
detail of the technique. The ban on cloning referred to the production of
babies. The report explained that the word cloning had more than one
meaning, and that one of them was a reference to a type of technique
that did not necessarily lead to reproductive cloning. The phrase 'therapeutic cloning' refers to a technique designed to produce a cultured cell
line for the purposes of cell or tissue therapy. This sort of research in
cloning with a non-reproductive aim might be considered favourably by
the HFEA but further research in animals would be required to demonstrate its viability before the use of human embryos would be considered appropriate. Moreover, the use of human embryos for research
pertaining to general disease does not come under the five permitted
heads of embryo research in Schedule 2 of the Act. Accordingly the second recommendation of the report on cloning was that Schedule 2, para
3 of the Act should have two further research categories added by Regulation, if the Secretary of State considered it appropriate. Those two
heads would be 'developing methods of therapy for mitochondrial disease' (a way of eradicating an imperfection existing in the part of the
egg immediately surrounding the nucleus, which would not involve
cloning in the sense of producing a child with only one genetic parent,
but would enable women with imperfect eggs to reproduce with a partner); and 'developing methods of therapy for diseased or damaged tissues or organs'.

In banning reproductive cloning, Britain has followed the international trend, indeed, led it. The process of cloning with reproductive
aims is banned by the UNESCO Declaration on the Human Genome
and Human Rights (1997), the Council of Europe Convention on Human
Rights and Biomedicine,[37] the European Commission Directive on the
Legal Protection of Biotechnological Inventions,[38] the European Group
of Ethics in Science and New Technologies,[39] and the World Health
Assembly.[40]

[37] European Treaty Series No 164, 4 Apr 1997.
[38] 98/44/EC, OLJ 213, 30 July 1998, 13–21
[39] http://europa.ev.int/comm/sg/biotech/en/biotec12.htm
[40] 51st World Health Assembly, Resolution WHA 51.10, *Ethical, Scientific and Social Implications of Cloning in Human Health.* May 1998.

SURROGACY

Surrogacy throws up some of the most complex problems concerning truth about genetic origins versus the happiness of infertile couples. Surrogacy was grudgingly accepted by the Warnock Committee,[41] and law to control it was the first result of the report because of the notoriety of Kim Cotton. She was Britain's first media surrogate mother and gave birth to a child for an American couple. The Surrogacy Arrangements Act 1985 banned commercial surrogacy agencies, although voluntary ones are allowed to operate. Expenses without limit may be paid to the carrying mother by the commissioning couple. There is a ruling in favour of the surrogate mother as being the legal mother, entitled to security of status, even though she may not be the genetic mother of the child.[42] She cannot be required by the commissioning parents to hand over the child under any contractual arrangement. Welfare of the child is therefore rated more highly than the enforceability of any contract between the commissioning couple and the surrogate mother. The commissioning couple may, however, acquire full parenthood, akin to adoption, under section 30 of the 1990 Act, provided that they have the child, the surrogate mother and the child's father agree and that no payment other than expenses has been made. The court may well make the order even if unlawful payments have changed hands as there may be no alternative if the welfare of the child is considered. The origins of the child may be kept from him or her because surrogacy is perfectly possible on a do-it-yourself basis, and no information may ever be available to the child about paternity or maternity. Some surrogacies are full, that is, the surrogate carries an embryo created by the commissioning couple; others are partial, where the surrogate is fertilized by the commissioning father.

In 1998 a review of surrogacy was carried out for the Department of Health.[43] This indicated that, while in recent years there were some eleven surrogate births known to have been carried out in clinics licensed by the HFEA, there were about forty section 30 orders a year, indicating that most surrogate births take place outside the regulatory scope of the Agency. It also suggested that some commissioning couples were failing to seek section 30 orders and become the child's legal parents, and that sums of £10,000 or more were being paid to surrogates in a small minority of cases. The review proposed a new Surrogacy Act which would continue the provisions relating to non-enforceability of

---

[41] *Warnock Report*, n 1 above, paras 8.10–20.

[42] Human Fertilisation and Embryology Act 1990, s. 27.

[43] *Surrogacy: Review for Health Ministers of the Current Arrangements for Payments and Regulation: Report of the Review Team (Brazier Report)* Cm 4068 (Oct 1998).

surrogacy contracts and the prohibition on commercial arrangements, provide for the promulgation of a Code of Practice and the registration of not-for-profit surrogacy agencies with the Department of Health. In particular, the review took the view that rewarding surrogates financially was tantamount to sale of children, and proposed therefore to confine lawful payments to surrogates to specifically defined expenses. The model should be one of gift. The existing voluntary agencies dissented from the proposals, which they claimed would render their work unviable, particularly with respect to the limitation of payments to surrogates.

CONCLUSION

Some have claimed that regulation prevents research in Britain from being at the forefront because no new practice will readily be licensed. Intracytoplasmic sperm injection and the thawing of frozen eggs were practised abroad before being permitted in Britain. Yet the existence of the strictest regulatory system in the world has not denied British scientists and clinicians acclaimed practice and results, even though they have not always been first in the field. It may be that the confidence engendered by the existence of a regulatory system has helped the prestige and respectability of the associated professions, not least in pursuit of funding and patients.

The history of regulation shows that work on embryos might never have been permitted in Britain at all had it not been for the first, voluntary, professional self-regulation and subsequent statutory controls. It has progressed with reliability and in tandem with public and peer acceptability. Judged by those criteria, regulation in principle has been a successful move, although some bureaucracy is inevitable. In issues which raise public fears, and which concern the family and personal safety, regulation has been more of a success than a failure.

9

Parenthood in the United States

RUTH-ARLENE W. HOWE

INTRODUCTION

During the turbulent years preceding World War II, the American family was 'vital to the nation's survival, both as a symbol of democracy and as a counterpoint to the autocratic families of the Third Reich.'[1] After America entered the war, social scientists agreed 'that the traditional family, with its homebound mother and wage-earning father, would best maintain the domestic stability needed to win the war' and insisted that '[o]nly strong families . . . could provide the order and stability necessary for the inculcation of the fundamental values at the heart of democratic life—individualism, freedom, tolerance.'[2]

According to social science scholars Arlene and Jerome Skolnick, the popular stereotype of the traditional family was premised on five key propositions:

1. The nuclear family—a man, a woman and their children—is universally found in every human society, past, present, and future.

2. [It] is the building block of society. Larger groupings—the extended family, the clan, the society—are combinations of nuclear families.

3. [It] is based on a clear-cut, biologically structured division of labor between men and women, with the man playing the 'instrumental' role of breadwinner, provider and protector, and the woman playing the 'expressive' role of housekeeper and emotional mainstay.

4. A major 'function' of the family is to socialize children; that is, to tame their impulses and instill values, skills, and desires necessary to run the society.

5. Unusual family structures, such as mother and children, or the experimental commune, are regarded as deviant by the participants, as well as the rest of the society, and are fundamentally unstable and unworkable.[3]

Financial support from the gift of Peter F. Zupcofska, Esquire, in memory of his parents Patrick and Josephine, is gratefully acknowledged. I thank Theodore H. Howe, Sanford N. Katz, and Elbert L. Robertson for helpful comments on earlier drafts, and James P. Dowden and Bryan Sullivan for research assistance.

[1] ROBERT L. GRISWOLD, FATHERHOOD IN AMERICA: A HISTORY 162 (1993) [hereinafter GRISWOLD].

[2] *ibid.*

[3] EVA R. RUBIN, THE SUPREME COURT AND THE AMERICAN FAMILY: IDEOLOGY AND ISSUES 14–15 (1986) (quoting Arlene S. Skolnick and Jerome H. Skolnick (eds), FAMILY IN TRANSITION 7–8

But the Great Depression of the 1930s and the war years of the 1940s unleashed forces that ultimately made this stereotype *passé*.[4]

During the war many families were separated not only by the eventual drafting of fathers, but also by adults migrating from rural to urban areas in search of jobs in the defense industry. Many women entered the work-force for the first time, leaving the care of young children to grand-parents, especially those on the mothers' side, or to other friends and relatives. Although one sociological study[5] of 135 Iowa families found that most families coped well and father–child difficulties were minimal, studies by child psychologists concluded that 'the separation [of] GIs from their war-born children had a lasting and negative impact.'[6] Indeed, '[t]he war . . . confirmed that children [needed] the type of fathers who had been summoned by psychologists over two decades before: nurturant, sensitive, companionate fathers secure in their own identity who could help to shape the personalities of their children.'[7]

Black's Law Dictionary defines *parent* as '[o]ne who procreates, begets, or brings forth offspring,' without reference to marital status or age. A parent is not just 'an autonomous political person with rights against the government,'[8] but is a person involved in a 'parent–child' relationship with his or her offspring to whom obligations are owed. Generally, unless proven unfit, unable, or unwilling to fulfill those obligations, a parent:

is deemed to have a legal right to the custody of his or her child . . . [that] includes the right to give or withhold any required consents to adoption, marriage, or enlistment in military service, to name the child, and to make decisions covering all aspects of a child's upbringing—all routine daily care and supervision, education, medical care and religious training.[9]

(1971))[hereinafter RUBIN]. Rubin notes: 'This family type is as much an ideal, an idea of what ought to be, as it is a description of existing reality, past or present. It is part of a system of beliefs, about male and female roles, about the correct relationships between men and women, parents and children, as well as about the structure and functions of the family unit and it represents a vision of the family that developed and matured in the nineteenth century' (p 15).

   [4] GRISWOLD, n 1 above, at 160.
   [5] *ibid* at 177 (citing RUBIN HILL, FAMILIES UNDER STRESS: ADJUSTMENT TO THE CRISES OF WAR SEPARATION AND REUNION 64 and nn 69, 74 1949) (reporting 289 children coped well, but in 21 families (15%) children maladjusted).
   [6] *ibid* at 182.   [7] *ibid* at 183.
   [8] RUBIN, n 3 above, at 6 ('Constitutional doctrine is not entirely congenial to family problems because it is primarily concerned with the relationship of individuals to the state. The categories of constitutional law . . . do not always supply suitable solutions to family problems, where individual rights are intertwined and the family itself has a certain collective personality.').
   [9] Ruth-Arlene W. Howe, *Legal Rights and Obligations: An Uneven Evolution* (citing A. SUSSMAN and M. GUGGENHEIM, THE RIGHTS OF PARENTS (1980), in Robert L. Lerman and Theodora J. Ooms (eds), YOUNG UNWED FATHERS: CHANGING ROLES AND EMERGING POLICIES 142 (1993) [hereinafter *Legal Rights and Obligations*].

Before new reproductive technologies, every child had not one, but two parents, although every male parent may not have been a father to whom the law accorded legal rights or on whom it imposed legal obligations.[10]

The broad aims of this chapter are twofold: (1) to track changing conceptions and presumptions regarding parenthood in America during the last half of the twentieth century in response to changing lifestyles, social attitudes, and new reproductive technologies; and (2) to consider whether these developments mandate redefining legal parenthood.

US PARENTHOOD: MID-TWENTIETH-CENTURY PROFILE

At mid-century, most American parenting occurred in households headed by married couples, raising their biological, adopted, or foster children and sometimes stepchildren. During the decade of the 1950s, roughly nine out of every ten families with children under 18 were headed by a married couple.[11] By 1960, owing to the post-war baby boom, the percentage of the population under 15 rose sharply to 31 per cent. The median age (one half older and one half younger) of the American population dropped slightly from 30.2 years in 1950 to 29.5 in 1960 and 27.9 in 1965.[12]

Single-parent families were few—just 10 per cent of all families with children. The overwhelming majority of these were mother-only families, created more likely by a marital dissolution or separation, or the early death of a spouse, than by an unwed mother's decision to raise her child herself. Indeed, the social stigma attached to illegitimacy was so strong that never-married white women voluntarily relinquished their newborns for adoptions[13] arranged by child welfare agencies or private brokers.

---

[10] See *ibid* at 143, 149–54 (reviewing common law status of unwed fathers and discussing four significant US Supreme Court decisions: *Stanley v Illinois*, 405 US 645 (1972); *Quilloin v Walcott*, 434 US 246 (1978); *Caban v Muhammed*, 441 US 380 (1979); and *Lehr v Robertson*, 463 US 248 (1983)); see also Janet L. Dolgin, *Just a Gene: Judicial Assumptions About Parenthood*, 40 UCLA L Rev 637, 650–72 (1993) (analyzing these four key cases and arguing that the post-Lehr decision of *Michael H. v Gerald D.*, 491 US 119 (1989) interpreted those cases to accord protection only to those biological fathers who maintained a relationship with the child's mother in a 'family unit').

[11] BUREAU OF THE CENSUS, US DEP'T OF COMMERCE, CURRENT POPULATION REPORTS, SERIES P20–515, HOUSEHOLD AND FAMILY CHARACTERISTICS (FM-1, Families, by Presence of Own Children Under 18: 1950 to Present (March 1998)) (Internet Release Dec 11 1998) (visited Mar 1 2000)<http: //www. census.gov1998Current.Pop. Survey>.

[12] *Population*, in 22 ENCYCLOPÆDIA BRITANNICA 691 (200th anniversary edn 1969).

[13] See Sanford N. Katz, Ch 13 in this volume.

Parental Legal Rights and Obligations

In the few family law cases[14] decided by the US Supreme Court before the 1950s, the Court accepted the Victorian family as the ideal, viewing it as 'a small government in its own right, authoritarian and paternalistic, with women and children in a subordinate position.'[15]

'While the US Constitution makes no mention whatsoever of either parents or families . . . the legal rights of parents to bear children, raise their offspring, and guide their family according to their own beliefs are firmly rooted in the first ten amendments to the Constitution (otherwise known as the Bill of Rights).'[16] Additionally, Section 1 of the Fourteenth Amendment,[17] in pertinent part, declares:

[N]or shall any State deprive any person of life, liberty, or property, without due process of law; nor deny to any person within its jurisdiction the equal protection of the laws.

The first quoted clause is popularly known as the due process clause; the second, as the equal protection clause.

The Due Process Clause

Two distinct rights are recognized to flow from the due process clause: a *substantive* right protecting an individual's liberty or property interests and a *procedural* right requiring that notice and a hearing be held before a protected interest can be taken away by the government.

In 1923, the Supreme Court first defined 'liberty' to include the right 'to marry, establish a home and bring up children' in *Meyer v Nebraska*.[18] Two years later, referring to the doctrine of *Meyer*, the Court declared:

The fundamental theory of liberty upon which all governments in this Union repose excludes any general power of the State to standardize its children by forcing them to accept instruction from public teachers only. The child is not the mere creature of the State; those who nurture him and direct his destiny have the right, coupled with the high duty, to recognize and prepare him for additional obligations . . .[19]

---

[14] For a seminal article regarding parental rights and obligations and the law's adherence to an exclusive view of parenthood premised on the nuclear family, see eg Katherine T. Bartlett, *Rethinking Parenthood as an Exclusive Status: The Need for Legal Alternatives When the Premise of the Nuclear Family Has Failed*, 70 VA L REV 879, 883–93 (1983).

[15] RUBIN, n 3 above, at 16.

[16] *Legal Rights and Obligations*, n 9 above, at 145 (citing A. SUSSMAN and M. GUGGENHEIM, THE RIGHTS OF PARENTS (1980).

[17] US CONST. amend. XIV, § 1.   [18] 262 US 390, 399 (1923).

[19] *Pierce v Society of Sisters*, 268 US 510, 535 (1925).

And later, the Court described the custody rights of parents to be 'far more precious . . . than property rights.'[20]

To determine what due process may be required in a proceeding concerning a parent–child relationship, since 1976 the Supreme Court has weighed and considered three distinct factors:

(1) the *private interest* that will be affected by the official action; (2) the *risk of erroneous deprivation of such interest* through the procedures used, and the *probable value*, if any, of *additional or substitute safeguards*; and (3) the *Government's interest*, including the function involved and the fiscal and administrative burdens that the additional or substitute procedural requirement would entail [emphasis added].[21]

Depending on the time, place, and circumstances of the particular case before it, the Court has reached seemingly conflicting conclusions in applying this balancing approach.[22]

The Equal Protection Clause

The mandate of the equal protection clause of the Fourteenth Amendment for family law can be summarized as requiring 'that legislation must operate equally upon all members of a group that is defined reasonably and in terms of a proper legislative purpose. The clause does not forbid "unequal laws" and does not require every law to be equally applicable to all individuals.'[23] Since gender was not a suspect class,

[20] *May v Anderson*, 345 US 528, 533 (1953). In its 1972 landmark *Stanley* decision, the Court stated: '[i]t is plain that the interest of a parent in the companionship, care, custody, and management of his or her children "come(s) to this Court with a momentum for respect lacking when appeal is made to liberties which derive merely from shifting economic arrangements." ' *Stanley v Illinois*, 405 US 645,651 (1972) (alteration in original) (citation omitted). 'Nevertheless, under the common-law concept of *parens patriae*, parents' substantive rights to the custody and control of their child may be subordinated to the state's interest in the child's welfare. In resolving conflicts between parental rights and the state's interest in the welfare of a child, courts apply a "best interest of the child" standard.' Ruth-Arlene W. Howe, *Redefining the Transracial Adoption Controversy*, 2 DUKE J GENDER L & POL'Y 131, 153–4 and n 121 (1995) [hereinafter *Redefining the TRA Controversy*].

[21] *Mathews v Eldridge*, 424 US 319,335 (1976).

[22] Cf *Lassiter v Department of Social Servs. of Durham County*, 452 US 18 (1981) (concluding that lack of appointed counsel for incarcerated mother during proceeding to terminate her parental rights did not render proceedings fundamentally unfair) with *Little v Streater*, 452 US 1, 13 (1981) (holding denial of free blood tests to indigent defendants in paternity actions would abridge due process, as parent–child relationship is at issue) and *Rivera v Minnich*, 483 US 574, 580 (1987) (affirming Supreme Court of Pennsylvania's ruling that preponderance standard was constitutionally permissible in paternity proceedings because 'the putative father has no legitimate right and certainly no liberty interest in avoiding financial obligations . . . validly imposed by state law') with *Santosky v Kramer*, 455 US 745 (1982) (concluding that established legal parent–child relationship was entitled to due process protection and requiring state to show by clear and convincing evidence that grounds existed to justify termination).

[23] HARRY D. KRAUSE, FAMILY LAW: IN A NUTSHELL § 2.2, at 23 (3rd edn 1995).

gender-based distinctions passed muster under traditional equal protection review because of the relative ease of showing some relationship to a permissible state purpose.[24]

When living together, neither parent was deemed to have any greater legal standing to determine issues concerning their children than the other. Yet, courts routinely accepted and, upon the parents' separation or divorce, followed a maternal preference presumption rule that the welfare of a child of 'tender years' was best served by giving custody to the mother.[25] And as between unmarried parents, most unwed fathers just were not deemed to be 'similarly situated' as the child's mother.

Prevailing Normative Context

After World War II, some, like sociologist Willard Waller, '[f]earing that women had gotten "out of hand" during the war, . . . worried about the future of the family and called for a restoration of traditional patriarchal relationships: "Women must bear and rear children; husbands must support them."'[26]

During the 1950s post-war era, many young men married at much younger ages than their fathers or grandfathers had. Social commentator Barbara Ehrenreich suggests that 'the rush to fatherhood came in no small part because to do otherwise courted suspicion about one's sexual identity and maturity. To marry and sire children was "mature," "responsible," a sign of adulthood; to remain a bachelor signified immaturity, irresponsibility, and perhaps even worse, homosexuality.'[27] A 'reproductive consensus' or 'procreation ethic' existed during the 1950s. '[M]ost Americans assumed that marriage was the ideal adult state, that parenthood was preferable to nonparenthood, and that having at least two children was superior to having only one.'[28]

---

[24] See nn 29–31 below and accompanying text.

[25] HOMER H. CLARK, Jr, THE LAW OF DOMESTIC RELATIONS IN THE UNITED STATES §§ 19.1, at 787 and 19.4 at 799 (Hornbook Student 2nd edn 1988). But, see MARY ANN MASON, FROM FATHER'S PROPERTY TO CHILDREN'S RIGHTS: THE HISTORY OF CHILD CUSTODY IN THE UNITED STATES 121–33 (1994) [hereinafter MASON] (describing replacement of maternal preference with new gender-neutral preferences, such as joint custody and primary caretaker during later third of 20th c.).

[26] GRISWOLD, n 1 above, at 187 and nn 3–4 (citing Waller as quoted in WILLIAM CHAFE, THE AMERICAN WOMAN: HER CHANGING SOCIAL, ECONOMIC, AND POLITICAL ROLE 1920–1970 174–95 (1972); see also RUTH MILKMAN, GENDER AT WORK: THE DYNAMICS OF JOB SEGREGATION BY SEX DURING WORLD WAR II 99–127 (1987).

[27] *ibid* at 189 and n 9 (citing BARBARA EHRENREICH, THE HEARTS OF MEN: AMERICAN DREAMS AND THE FLIGHT FROM COMMITMENT 14–17 (1984).

[28] *ibid* at 190 and n 15 (citing LANDON JONES, GREAT EXPECTATIONS: AMERICA AND THE BABY BOOM GENERATION 31 (1981).

Fatherhood joined motherhood as a junior partner in the manufacture of the domestic mystique of the 1950s. Mature men supported their families and played an important role in socializing their children. 'Movies and especially the new medium of television prompted this equation of manhood and fatherhood. . . . The occupations of men like Ward Cleaver and Ozzie Nelson were either vaguely defined or unknown. . . . [T]hese men's "work" was the resolution of the minor crises that beset their children.'[29] Women, however, were still regarded as the center of home and family life, responsible for family maintenance and child care; although during the 1950s, 23 per cent of married women with children under 6 and 28 per cent of women with children ages 6 to 17 worked for wages.

Gender-based role assignments, a hallmark of the traditional nuclear family since the mid-nineteenth century, had yet to be challenged. For example, in *Hoyt v Florida*,[30] the US Supreme Court unanimously upheld an all-male Florida jury's second-degree murder conviction of Gwendolyn Hoyt for the 1959 killing of her husband with a baseball bat. The Court rejected her claim that systematic, discriminatory exclusion of women from the jury violated her right to due process. Justice John Marshall Harlan, writing for the Court, found it reasonable that the Florida legislature thought women should be at home with their families, rather than sitting in courthouses.[31] Scholars assert that the decision was proper and dictated by prevailing constitutional doctrine, precedent, and traditional equal protection rules.[32] However, ruling Florida's automatic exemption of women from jury service constitutional assigned all women to the private world of the family and the home. The Court took no judicial notice of the fact that one-third of the civilian labor force in 1960 was female.

US PARENTHOOD: CHANGING OPTIONS AND CHOICES

During the last third of the century, a confluence of demographic trends, shifting societal attitudes and expectations about gender roles in the family, and reproductive technology breakthroughs created new parenting options and choices for Americans.

---

[29] *ibid* at 191. Ward Cleaver and Ozzie Nelson were the lead actors in two popular television series, *Leave it to Beaver* and *The Ozzie and Harriet Show*. These shows appeared on the ABC and CBS networks from 1957 to 1963.

[30] 368 US 57 (1961).   [31] *ibid* at 62–3.

[32] RUBIN, n 3 above, at 3 ('The Court held, as it had before, that equal protection of the laws did not forbid the differential treatment of men and women as long as a rational basis for a gender classification was asserted.').

Demographic Trends

Significant changes in fertility and birth rates, the entry of more women into the work force, and the prevalence of new family types reshaped the landscape of American parenthood.

Fertility and Birth Rates

While the US 'fertility rate fell from 3.8 children per woman in 1957 to 1.9 by 1974; . . . the percentage of children born to unmarried women [rose] from 5 per cent in 1960 to 13 per cent in 1973.'[33] By 1996, 32.4 per cent of all births were to unwed mothers—just about one out of every three births.[34] This increase in the number of births to unwed mothers included a phenomenal rise in births of mixed-race children.[35]

Increased Presence of Women in the Labor Force

By the mid-1970s, more than a third of all mothers with pre-school children had entered the labor force[36] and were full-time homemakers no longer. Over half of all mothers with school-age children, aged 6 to 17, also were gainfully employed. Among non-white groups, an even higher percentage of mothers aged 16 and over were gainfully employed.[37]

By 1995, an unprecedented number of women (55 per cent of all aged 15 to 44) who had had a child in the preceding twelve months were gainfully employed, a jump from 31 per cent in 1976.[38] US Census Bureau data reveal a correlation between labor force participation and educational achievement. Seventy per cent of these baby-boomer mothers with new-born children 'had at least a bachelor's degree, compared with 48

[33] Marvin B. Sussman, *Family* in 1 ENCYCLOPEDIA OF SOCIAL WORK 358 (17th edn 1977).

[34] New Strategist Editors, *Newborns Show Diversity to Come*, THE AMERICAN MARKETPLACE, Jan 1999, at 65, *available in* LEXIS, Busref Library, AMMKTP File (reporting 70% of babies among blacks born out of wedlock: among Hispanics 41% and among whites 26%).

[35] See *Redefining the TRA Controversy*, n 20 above, at 148 ('According to the National Center for Health Statistics (NCHS), which has tracked mixed race births since 1968, "birthrates of children with one black and one white parent have been climbing. In 1991, 52,232 such births were recorded, compared to 26,968 in 1981, and 8,758 in 1968."' (citing LISE FUNDERBURG, BLACK, WHITE, OTHER: BIRACIAL AMERICANS TALK ABOUT RACE AND IDENTITY 11 (1994) (recounting lives of adult children of black–white unions)).

[36] Marvin B. Sussman, n 33 above, at 360 ('[F]rom 1940 to 1969, the percentage of mothers who entered the labor force with children under 6 increased from 13 percent to 30 percent, and mothers of schoolage children, aged 6 to 17, increased from 31 percent to 51 percent.').

[37] *ibid* (noting 64% non-white working mothers, 47% white working, 44% non-white with children under 6 to 27% white).

[38] See BUREAU OF THE CENSUS, US DEP'T OF COMMERCE, CURRENT POPULATION SURVEYS (H4. Women 15 to 44 Years Old Who Have Had a Child in the Last Year and Their Percentage in the Labor Force: Selected Years, June 1976 to 1995; H5. Women 15 to 44 Years Old Who Have Had a Child in the Last Year and Their Percentage in the Labor Force By Selected Characteristics: June 1990 and 1995) <http://www.cdc.nchshome.html>.

per cent who had completed only high school and 34 per cent with less than a high school diploma.'[39]

Family Types

The nuclear family model (so prevalent in the 1950s) was just one of many types by the end of the century. By 2000, parenting of children under 18 no longer occurred almost exclusively in nuclear families consisting of a first-time married couple with birth, adoptive, or foster children, living together apart from either set of in-laws, with a gainfully employed husband-father and a stay at home, full-time homemaker wife-mother. Indeed, the percentage of such families had dropped from a high of 93 in 1950 to 73 in the mid-1990s.

Other prevalent family types by 2000 included: 'dual-career' or 'multi-worker' families; 'single-parent' families; 'multi-parent' or 'step-parent' families created by the growing incidence of divorce and remarriage; and 'intergenerational' families.[40] A growing number of households maintained by cohabiting non-marital heterosexual, as well as gay and lesbian, partners during the 1990s had children under 18. In 1997, 6.7 per cent of families with children under 18 were headed by grandparents. And, because of adjudicated abuse and neglect, non-related foster parents and others cared for more than 550,000 children in state-supervised individual foster homes and group institutional facilities.

Because each year the parents of one million children divorce, '[i]t is projected that between 50% and 60% of children born in the 1990s will live, at some point, in single-parent families, typically headed by mothers. Currently, [given the number of divorced parents who remarry,] stepfamilies make up approximately 17% of all two-parent families with children under 18 years of age.'[41] By the late 1990s, 14.5 million children under the age of 18, almost triple the number in 1960, lived in a female-headed family,[42] created not by the death of a parent, but rather by divorce, separation, or out-of-wedlock conception. The number of

[39] BUREAU OF THE CENSUS, POPULATION DIVISION, FERTILITY OF AMERICAN WOMEN: JUNE 1994 (last modified Mar. 31 1999) <http://www.cdc.gov/nchswww/nchshome.html> (reporting approximately 12% living in families whose reported total income was $75,000 and over; similar percentage of working women with children under 1 year of age living in low-income families making under $10,000 a year).

[40] See Esther Wald, *Family, Multiparent*, in 1 ENCYCLOPEDIA OF SOCIAL WORK 258 (17th edn 1977) (discussing other names for stepfamilies, such as 'blended,' 'merged,' 'reconstituted,' 'remarried').

[41] E. Mavis Hetherington, Margaret Bridges, and Glendessa M. Insabella, *What Matters? What Does Not? Five Perspectives on the Association between Marital Transitions and Children's Adjustment*, 53(2) AM PSYCH 167 (1009) reprinted in (Margaret F. Brinig *et al* (eds), FAMILY LAW IN ACTION: A READER 116 (1999).

[42] See Laura M. Morgan, *Family Law in 2000: Private and Public Support of the Family: From Welfare State to Poor Law*, 33 FAM LQ 705, 710 (1999) [hereinafter Morgan].

male-headed one-parent families also increased, stabilizing in the mid-1990s at between 4 and 5 per cent of all households with children.[43]

Societal Changes

After the 1950s, American social attitudes and lifestyles changed. Out-of-wedlock births rose sharply from 5.3 per cent of all births in 1960 to 22 per cent of the 3.7 million births in 1985. Teen pregnancy rates climbed rapidly during the 1970s and 1980s. Many of the unwed fathers of children born to teen mothers were young men ages 19 to 25, many black and Hispanic.[44] Early establishment of paternity and rigorous enforcement of child support became policy priorities pushed at both federal and state levels.[45] The clear societal preference was to hold parents—especially unwed and divorced fathers—financially responsible for the care of their children rather than to have such costs totally assumed by the public.[46]

Non-marital cohabitation also steadily increased. By 1988 'about 31 per cent of unmarried cohabitants, or 802,000, had children under 15 in their households[,] a fourfold increase over the 196,000 cohabitants counted in the 1970 census.'[47] At its August 1988 Annual Meeting, the National Conference of Commissioners on Uniform State Laws (NCCUSL)[48]

---

[43] See Bureau of the Census, US Dep't of Commerce, Statistical Abstract, P20–506, No 84. Current Population Reports, Children Under 18 Years Old, by Presence of Parents: 1980 to 1997 (Sept 16 1998).

[44] See Bureau of the Census, US Dep't of Commerce, 1989 Statistical Abstract of the US (108th edn), p. 62, tbl 87. Births to unmarried women, by race and age of mother; 1991 Statistical Abstract (110th edn), p 66 tbl 87, Live births by race and type of Hispanic origin—Selected characteristics, 1985 and 1987, and p 67, tbl 90, Births to unmarried women, by race of child and age of mother: 1970 to 1987.

[45] See nn 86–91 below and accompanying text; see generally Harry D. Krause, Child Support in America: The Legal Perspectives (1981).

[46] See eg *Rivera v Minnich*, 483 US 574, at 579–80 (1987) (holding that 'causal connection between an alleged physical act of a putative father and the subsequent birth of the plaintiff's child sufficient to impose financial liability on the father will not trammel any pre-existing rights'); also see nn 86–91 and accompanying text.

[47] *Legal Rights and Obligations*, n 9 above, at 141 and n 1.

[48] The purpose of the National Conference of Commissioners on Uniform State laws (NCCUSL) is to promote uniformity in state law on all subjects where uniformity is desirable and practicable. Since its founding in 1892, NCCUSL has drafted over 200 uniform laws, many of which have been widely enacted, like the Uniform Commercial Code (UCC) and Uniform Child Custody Jurisdiction Act (UCCJA).

Commissioners from each state, the District of Columbia, and Puerto Rico, usually four in number, serve pro bono and are appointed by state governors and by other legislative sources, in some states. Commissioners are lawyers, judges, legislators, and law professors who are members of the bar. According to NCCUSL Executive Director Fred R. Miller, Professor of Law, University of Oklahoma: 'they are usually people whose experience and position allow adequate flexibility to do pro bono work. They are usually politically experienced, and have records reflecting good judgment and the ability to furnish astute

adopted the Uniform Putative and Unknown Fathers Act (UPUFA).[49] Recognizing that 'there [was] an expanding population of unwed men who wish to play a role in the upbringing of their children' and that unmarried fathers should not simply 'be categorized as absent or uncaring,' UPUFA's intent was to clarify certain aspects of the legal status of putative and unknown fathers, determination of their parental rights, and requirements for notice of adoption, custody or other proceedings concerning their child.[50]

Legalization of abortion by the United States Supreme Court in 1973,[51] ready accessibility of contraceptives, and the rapid spread of state no-fault divorce reform legislation[52] enabled women during the 1970s and 1980s to make new decisions about child bearing and child rearing. Shifts in social attitudes (such as waning traditional stigma attached to out-of-wedlock birth) contributed as much to the rapid rise in the number of single-parent mother only families as did divorce. Also, increased enrollment of women in undergraduate and graduate professional programs enabled many to be financially independent.

Because of these social trends and developments, very few single birth-mothers voluntarily relinquished their babies for adoption.[53] As the pool

---

advice. In short, they are people who have gotten things done and have the capacity to get things done.' Fred H. Miller, *Professor Carlson's Article: The Future of Uniform State Legislation in the Private Law Area*, 79 MINN L REV 861, 866 (1995).

[49] UNIF PUTATIVE & UNKNOWN FATHERS ACT, 9B ULA 17 (1988) (declaring the right of a man to bring an action to establish his paternity of a particular child (Section 2); addressing both procedural and substantive due process considerations for putative and unknown fathers in proceedings to change or establish legal or physical custody or visitation rights with respect to his child (Sections 3 and 4); and specifying fourteen factors for courts to weigh in determining when a sufficient father–child relationship is established). See *Legal Rights And Obligations*, n 9 above, at 160–3.

Although no state has adopted UPUFA, language from it appears in NCCUSL's 1994 Uniform Adoption Act 9 ULA Part I (1999) and the current working draft of the Proposed Revision of the Uniform Parentage Act, available at <http://www.nccusl.org.>.

[50] See UPUFA Prefatory Note, 9B ULA, at 92 (Sup. 1999).

[51] See *Roe v Wade*, 410 US 113 (1973).

[52] For background on the 'divorce revolution'—launched in 1969 by California's passage of its landmark no-fault divorce statute, followed by enactments in other states—that introduced de jure unilateral no-fault divorce to most states and de facto in all, see LENORE WEITZMAN, THE DIVORCE REVOLUTION: THE UNEXPECTED SOCIAL AND ECONOMIC CONSEQUENCE FOR WOMEN AND CHILDREN IN AMERICA (1985); see also FRANK F. FURSTENBERG, Jr, *History and Current Status of Divorce in the United States*, 4 THE FUTURE OF CHILDREN 29 (Summer/Fall 1994). But, for a critical assessment of 'no-fault' divorce and call for reform at the dawn of the third millennium, see Lynn D. Wardle, *Divorce Reform at the Turn of the Millennium: Certainties and Possibilities*, 33 FAM LQ 783 (1999).

[53] See generally Christine A. Bachrach *et al*, *Relinquishment of Premarital Births: Evidence from National Survey Data*, 24 FAM PLAN PERSP 27, 29 (1992) (reporting on analysis of data drawn from the 1982 and 1988 cycles of the National Survey of Family Growth (NSFG), indicating a drastic drop in the number of relinquishments by white, unmarried women from before 1973 (approximately 33,269 annually), to only aproximately 13,000 in 1982–8).

of adoptable white infants (a most desirable product) shrank, a new business opportunity in our market economy was created for those able to meet the demand. 'As the number of 'adults (mostly white) seeking to adopt began by far to exceed the number of available healthy white infants, many people, frustrated by the long waiting lists of agencies, began to obtain babies privately, via independent adoptions arranged by lawyers, doctors, the clergy, or other persons.'[54] Many middle- and upper-class white prospective adopters sought children from other countries through intercountry adoption (ICA) or finalized a domestic transracial adoption (TRA).[55]

By the end of the century, a growing acceptance of parenting across racial, ethnic, religious, and cultural lines was diluting the high premium once accorded biological parenting. During the 1990s the constitutionality of the traditional child welfare adoption practice of 'matching' child and adoptive parents (in terms of physical, intellectual, and even some social characteristics) was challenged. 'Same-race' preferences and policies were alleged to be especially harmful to the rapidly growing numbers of African American and other children of color entering and remaining in the foster care system for longer periods of time than white children because of a lack of approved 'same-race' homes.[56]

New Reproductive Technologies

Sterility among persons of childbearing ages in the US seems to be increasing, 'perhaps as a result of yet to be identified environmental factors or pollutants.'[57] However, recent 'innovations in technology have given hope of parenthood to [those] who in earlier times would have had to accept infertility as a sad fact of life,'[58] if artifical insemination did not result in a pregnancy or they were unable to adopt a child.

---

[54] Ruth-Arlene W. Howe, *Adoption Laws and Practices in 2000: Serving Whose Interests?* 33 FAM LQ 677, 681 and nn 13–14.   [55] *ibid* at 682.

[56] For challenges by legal scholars, see eg Elizabeth Bartholet, *Where Do Black Children Belong? The Politics of Race Matching in Adoption,* 139 U PA L REV 1163, 1248 (1991) and David S. Rosettenstein, *Trans-racial Adoption and the Statutory Preference Schemes: Before the 'Best Interests' and After the 'Melting Pot,'* 68 St John's L Rev 137, 197 (1994); for judicial challenges, see eg *Reisman v State of Tenn. Dep't of Hum. Services,* 843 F Supp 356 (WD Tenn 1993).

Federal legislation in the mid-1990s first attempted to limit race matching by prohibiting the use of race to delay or deny foster or adoptive placements and then imposed an absolute ban against any consideration of race as a factor in adoptive or foster care placement decision-making. On Tuesday Aug 20 1996, President Clinton signed Section 1808, *Removal of Barriers to Interethnic Adoption,* amending §§ 471(a) and 474 of the Social Security Act (42 USC. §§ 671(a) and 674)

[57] Ruth-Arlene W. Howe, *Adoption Practice, Issues, and Laws 1956–1983,* 1983, 17 FAM LQ 171, 195 (1983).

[58] Twila P. Perry, *Race Matters: Change, Choice, and Family Law at the Millennium,* 33 FAM LQ 461, 461 (1999).

A 1983 *Boston Globe* Science, Health and Technology Report[59] announced advances in fertility drugs and microsurgery that could treat successfully half of all infertility, but expressed 'worry that a frozen "embryo bank" would open the door to more exotic developments such as transfer of the embryos to the wombs of surrogate mothers.'[60] Now, just seventeen years later, there are various procreative procedures[61] in which a woman's womb is used just for gestation, with her having no genetic tie to the resulting child.

Parenthood is now possible for gay and lesbian partners and single persons. Chambers and Polikoff, writing in a Special Millennium issue of the American Bar Association *Family Law Quarterly*, state:

By the late 1970s, numerous factors coincided to encourage a new form of lesbian and gay parenthood not tied to heterosexual marriage. . . . While it may have initially appeared that parenthood would never be an option for such men and women, other cultural and medical phenomena soon resulted in a new frame of mind. Specifically, births of out-of-wedlock children no longer carried the stigma they did in earlier decades, and medical technology opened the possibilities for conception without sexual intercourse.[62]

Marsha Garrison, another family law scholar writing in the same Millennium issue, asserts '[n]ew technologies now make it possible to conceive a baby without sex and to both predict and witness the process of fetal development. A baby may have as many as six "parents"—sperm donor, egg donor, gestator, gestator's husband, and a couple who has "commissioned" the pregnancy.'[63] Garrison calls this 'purchased parenthood. Today's would-be parents can select and buy sperm, egg, and a human incubator for "their" baby just as they might choose furniture and hire an interior decorator to design the baby's room.'[64]

---

[59] Knox, *New Hope for Infertile Couples*, BOSTON GLOBE, Apr 4 1983, at 39, 46 as quoted in Howe, n 57 above, at 195.   [60] Howe, n 57 above, at 195.

[61] Procedures in 2000 include: *in vitro fertilization (IVF)*—an egg and sperm are combined in a laboratory dish; fertilized eggs are transferred into the uterus; *gamete intrafallopian transfer (GIFT)*—eggs and sperm are [transferred] directly into a fallopian tube; resulting embryos float into the uterus; *zygote intrafallopian transfer* (ZIPT)—eggs are fertilized in the laboratory, as in IVF; fertilized eggs (zygotes) are transferred directly into a fallopian tube. Dolores Kong, *What Price Pregnancy? Clinics Get Little Oversight*, BOSTON GLOBE, Aug 5 1995, at A1, A8 (highlighting many problematic consequences of treatment and low rates of success).

[62] David L. Chambers and Nancy D. Polikoff, *Family Law and Gay and Lesbian Family Issues in the Twentieth Century*, 33 FAM L Q 523, 532–41 (1999).

[63] Marsha Garrison, *The Technological Family: What's New and What's Not*, 33 FAM LQ 691, 691 (1999) [hereinafter Garrison].

[64] *ibid* at 692. See, Kevin Cullen, *Furor welcomes gays' newborns home to Britain*, BOSTON SUNDAY GLOBE, Jan 9 2000, at A1, A8–9 (reporting a Dec 9 1999 birth of twins in California to a gestational surrogate mother as the result of implantation of a donated egg fertilized by the mixed sperm of a British gay couple who were legally barred in England from hiring a surrogate and who had been turned down for adoption). Cullen wrote, in part: 'A California

And yet another procreative option—'cloning'—looms on the reproductive technology horizon. In the Summer 1999 issue of the *Louisiana
Law Review*,[65] David Orentlicher very persuasively argues the benefits of
cloning. The creation of a new person with the genetic material of just one
parent eliminates the risk 'that the other person's egg, sperm or placenta
will transmit undesired infections, genetic or toxic disease. By relying
on cloning, infertile couples—and single persons—can have children
without having to involve someone else in their procreative activities.'[66]

Orentlicher forthrightly states that '[c]loning turns on its head our view
of reproduction,' but asserts 'that this reconfiguration is in fact one of the
most compelling reasons to permit cloning.'[67] The possibility of
unwanted third persons claiming a right to play a role in the lives of their
genetic children is avoided.[68] Hence, cloning avoids the legal conundrum
of determining legal parenthood. It also would protect both the integrity
of the marital (or other intimate) relationship and the sanctity of the
parent–child relationship.

US PARENTHOOD: IN 2000 AND BEYOND

The US parenting landscape in 2000 bears little resemblance to the mid-
twentieth-century profile described at the beginning of this chapter. The

---

court says that Barrie Drewitt and Tony Barlow, millionaire businessmen from Danbury,
England, are the legal parents. . . . But under English law, the parents are the American
surrogate mother who gave birth to the twins and her husband, whose only connection to
the arrangement is that he happens to be married to her. . . . Anglican Bishop Tom Butler of
the Southwark diocese in London accused Drewitt and Barlow of creating "designer
children," part of a trend in which, he said, selfish adults are experimenting with a whole
generation.' Cullen, *ibid* at A1, A8.

[65] David Orentlicher, *Cloning and the Preservation of Family Integrity*, 59 LA L R 1019 (1999).
See, generally, articles exploring whether the law should regulate or prohibit reproductive
cloning technology in *Symposium on Human Cloning: Legal, Social, and Moral Perspectives for
the Twenty-First Century*, 27 HOFSTRA L REV 479 (Spring 1999).

[66] Orentlicher, *Cloning*, at 1020. Nevertheless, Orentlicher states: 'There is genetic material
not only in the nucleus of a cell, but also in the mitochondria (the "energy factories" of the
cell), which reside outside the cell's nucleus. . . . If a woman clones herself and uses one of
her own eggs, then all of her child's genetic material will come from her. If a man clones
himself, or a woman clones herself with the eggs of another woman, then the child will have
genetic material from two "parents." It is not known at this time the extent to which
mitochondrial genetic material affects a person's development' (citations omitted). 1019 n.1.

[67] *ibid* at 1020.

[68] See *Jhordan C. v Mary K.* 224 Cal Rptr, 530 (Cal App. 1986) (holding in favor of male
sperm donor) (ruling if women having children by artificial insemination want to prevent
sperm donor from having paternal rights, state statutory requirement of physician involvement must be observed).

nuclear family of married parents and children is no longer the most prevalent type.

Today, some children are being reared by persons who, having no biological or genetic relationship to them, fall outside of *Black's Law Dictionary* definition of *parent*. These adults do not 'procreate, beget, or bring forth offspring' as a natural consequence of sexual intercourse. Societal attitudinal and demographic changes, and the new reproductive technologies (discussed in the preceding section) have created not only new options and choices for Americans wishing to parent a child, but also new dilemmas for society and the law. As one family law scholar notes, '[b]oth commercial and delayed parenthood present difficult questions relating to the ownership of genetic materials and the status of preembryos that may—or may not—become human lives. Courts and legislatures have only begun to grapple with these genuinely novel aspects of the technological revolution in reproduction.'[69]

Determining Legal Parenthood

The changed and changing landscape of American parenting is posing questions for American family law: (1) Are traditional rules and presumptions based on biology still viable for determining whom to recognize as the legal parent of a particular child? (2) Given the trend of greater societal tolerance for private ordering in the intimate realm of family relations, should the interests, desires, and intent of adults to become parents be the controlling factor when parties use surrogacy and new reproductive technologies to have children?

Traditional Rules and Presumptions

Old rules and presumptions for the establishment of paternity grounded in biology may no longer work in all situations. Legal motherhood and maternity can no longer be presumed because a woman delivers a live baby. Indeed, when as many as six adults[70] (living and deceased) may play a role in the creation of new life, can it not be said that the proverbial 'genie is out of the bottle?'

So, are new rules and presumptions needed for determining the legal parents of a child born as the result of surrogacy and assisted conception?

---

[69] Garrison, n 62 above, at 692. See eg, In re Marriage of Buzzanca, 61 Cal App 4th 410, 72 Cal Rptr 2d 260 (1998) (holding a divorcing couple who had during the marriage engaged a gestational surrogate to carry to term a non-related child for them the child's legal parents); for analysis of case and demand for regulatory legislation, see Laura A. Brill, *When Will the Law Catch up with Technology? Jaycee B. v Superior Court of Orange county: An Urgent Cry for Legislation on Gestational Surrogacy*, 39 Cath Law 241 (1999).
[70] See n 63 above and accompanying text.

Some scholars, like Professor Garrison, say no. She views 'the various forms of technological conception . . . [as] novel ways of having babies, that require [only] extension of current legal doctrine.' She acknowledges that 'IVF . . . offers one genuinely new relationship, that of the gestational mother who is biologically unrelated to the child that she carries to term.' And, while 'recourse to traditional doctrines like estoppel and the marital presumption of legitimacy' may not resolve 'a legal contest between a gestational and genetic mother,' she asserts:

that is not to say that the determination of parental rights in such a case must rely on novel methods of analysis; the simplest— and, I would argue—best approach in these cases is to say that the genetic mother is the legal mother because she is the one biologically related to the child. Biology has been, after all, the primary determinant of parenthood both in our law and culture.[71]

But, given all the revolutionary advances to date and those expected in the future, I wonder if the twentieth-century rights-based paradigm for conceptualizing legal parenthood in terms of protectable individual 'liberty' interests needs overhauling or retooling? Should courts, when hearing the claims of parties seeking custody of a particular child or frozen embryos, or legislative bodies, when drafting statutory parent definitions, perhaps focus more on what basic societal interests are at stake?

While inclined to agree that new novel methods of analysis may not be required, I do contend, when determining legal parenthood, that there is a strong societal imperative to shift from focusing upon just individual rights to giving greater consideration to whether persons will honor and fulfill the obligations of parenthood owed to their children and to the state.

No society can have a future if its children are not reared, socialized, and prepared to be good, productive citizens upon attaining their adulthood. Of the five key propositions identified by the Skolnicks to describe the mid-twentieth-century stereotypical nuclear family, only two (2 and 4) have any currency fifty years later. The basic building block for our society is still the family, even though the rules governing formation and membership no longer narrowly limit this unit to 'a man, a woman and their children.'[72] Sustaining family units of whatever composition that

---

[71] Garrison, n 62 above, at 699. See also John Lawrence Hill, *What Does it Mean to be a 'Parent'? The Claims of Biology as the Basis for Parental Rights*, 66 NYLU L Rev 353 (1991).

[72] See nn 3, 40–3, 65–9 above and accompanying text. Indeed, legitimate family constellations in the 21st c (at least in some states) will include same-sex unions. On Apr 26 2000, Vermont Governor Howard Dean signed Vermont HB 847 which: 'creates state recognition for civil unions between two persons of the same sex who are excluded from marriage in Vermont; allows couples to apply for a civil union license . . . through a process that parallels that for obtaining a marriage certificate; entitles couples to the same benefits and privileges as spouses; provides for the dissolution of a union to be handled by family courts.' Lexis, Legislation Library, VTTRCK File.

undertake and perform the major societal function of childrearing is vitally important.

An Intent to Parent

More private ordering in the intimate realm of family relations is indisputable. According to Professor Garrison,[73] 'purchased parenthood' is now possible, raising the unsettling specter of commodification of human life,[74] if no biological or genetic tie exists between parent and child. From the perspective of either society or the child, should legal parenthood ever be based just on an adult's professed 'intention' to be a parent? Is this all that is necessary to resolve disputes between parties to a surrogacy arrangement who may have no biological or genetic link to the child?[75]

In 1989 NCCUSL adopted the Uniform Status of Children of Assisted Conception Act (USCAC)[76] to give state legislatures guidance in defining the legal status of children conceived through the use of assisted conception techniques and in determining who would be their legal parents. Section 1 of the Act provides that 'Intended parents'[77] shall be the legal parents of any child born as a result of a surrogacy agreement. During the 1990s, a few states,[78] while not enacting USCAC, passed legislation authorizing commercial surrogacy and providing for parenthood based on

[73] See n above 63.

[74] See eg, Margaret Jane Radin, *Market-Inalienability*, 100 HARV L REV 1849 (1987) (claiming some intrinsic capacities or properties of an individual; and also Christine L. Kerian, *Surrogacy: A Last Resort Alternative for Infertile Women or a Commodification of Women's Bodies and Children?* 12 WIS WOMEN'S L J 113 (1997).

[75] See case cited n 69 above. Justice Sills, in reversing a trial court's decision that Jaycee, born to a gestational surrogate, had no lawful parents wrote: 'Just as a husband is deemed to be the lawful father of a child unrelated to him when his wife gives birth after artificial insemination, so should a husband *and* wife be deemed the lawful parents of a child after a surrogate bears a biologically unrelated child on their behalf. In each instance, a child is procreated because a medical procedure was initiated and consented to by intended parents. The only difference is that in this case—unlike artificial insemination—there is no reason to distinguish between husband and wife (emphasis in orginal).' In *re Marriage of Buzzanca*, at 1412.

[76] UNIF STATUS OF CHILDREN OF ASSISTED CONCEPTION ACT §§ 1–16, 9B ULA 191 (1999). More closely resembling a model than a uniform act, USCAC offers two alternative approaches to surrogacy. Alternative A, adopted in 1991 by Virginia (VA CODE ANN §§ 20–156 to 20–165), provides that surrogacy agreements are valid if procedures for obtaining judicial approval are followed. Alternative B, adopted by North Dakota in 1989 (N D CENT CODE § 14–18–01 to 14–18–07), prohibits surrogacy and makes any agreement unenforceable.

[77] 'Intended parents' means a man and a woman, married to each other, who enter into an agreement with a surrogate under the terms of which they will be the parents of any child born to the surrogate through assisted conception regardless of the genetic relationships between the intended parents, the surrogate, and the child.' USCAC § 1.

[78] See Garrison, n 63 above, at 702, n 25 (citing FLA STAT § 63–212 (West 1997 & Supp 1999); N H STAT ANN §§ 168–B: 1 to B: 32 (1994 and 1999 Supp) (recognizing judicially approved contracts, specifying allowable payments, and allowing surrogate to rescind agreement within seventy-two hours of child's birth; NEV REV STAT. § 127.267 (Michie 1993) (excluding from baby-selling prohibitions a 'lawful contract to act as a surrogate'

'intention'. Other states[79] have statutes that prohibit surrogacy outright or declare the surrogacy contract to be unenforceable. It is interesting to note that biology is still of utmost importance in at least one state. Florida requires not only that the intended parents be a married couple, but that the assisted reproductive technology use 'the eggs or sperm of at least one of the intended parents.'[80]

But, should simple 'intention' ever be enough? Are not other procedural requirements and safeguards needed, such as requiring judicial approval before finalizing an enforceable contract? Such in theory would allow for the equivalent of an adoption home study and prescreening of applicants to determine fitness and suitability to parent. Some might even urge the licensing of parents.[81]

Parenting: A Private or Public Responsibility?

Whether parenting is a private or a public responsibility is an important question. Many family types once considered 'deviant' and 'fundamentally unstable' are today expected—like the once dominant nuclear family—to perform the major function of raising and socializing children to be healthy, productive adult citizens. I believe that to achieve this societal goal, parenting cannot be just a private responsibility; there is a public responsibility that government should not shirk.

The growing number of single-parent families face many stresses, especially given the greater involvement of mothers in the workforce. Children need close attention and affection. Whenever a mother works outside the home, roles and tasks within the two-parent family must be reallocated. For the single parent, mother or father, the availability of appropriate child care and easy access to a wide-range of supportive social, counseling, education, and other services is vitally important.

Statutes in every state impose a duty of support on all legal parents— mothers *and* fathers—whether unmarried, married, or divorced 'in accordance with their respective abilities to earn and pay, to render ser-

---

while 'not prohibit[ing] a natural parent from refusing to place a child for adoption after its birth')).

[79] See eg, IND CODE § 31–20–1–7 (1999); MICH COMP LAWS § 722.859 (1999).

[80] FLA STAT ch 742.13(2) (1999) (defining 'commissioning couple' for purposes of determining parentage).

[81] See Hugh LaFollette, *Licensing Parents*, 9 PHIL & PUB AFF 182 (Winter 1980) (arguing licensing of parents not only theoretically desirable but workable and offering social and philosophical justifications without focusing on the legal implications). For discussions of LaFollette's thesis, see generally Lawrence E. Frisch, *On Licentious Licensing: A Reply to Hugh LaFollette*, 11 PHIL & PUB AFF 171 (Spring 1982); see also Claudia Mangel, *Licensing Parents: How Feasible?* 22 FAM L Q 17 (1988); cf Michael J. Sandmire and Michael S. Wald, *Licensing Parents—A Response to Claudia Mangel's Proposal*, 24 FAM LQ 53 (1990).

vices, or other relevant circumstances.'[82] Other statutory provisions in all states mandate that: parents provide adequate food, clothing, shelter, and care in a manner that does not subject the child to physical or emotional harm, or expose the child to the risk of imminent danger; suspected abuse and neglect be reported, investigated, and if adjudicated, specify a range of civil and/or criminal sanctions—of fines, imprisonment, and possible temporary or permanent loss of parental rights.

While the financial support obligation of all parents is very clear, enforcement has been and continues to be problematic. The harsh realities of the late 1990s are that: '65 per cent of absent fathers contribute no child support or alimony and only 5.5 per cent of absent fathers contribute as much as $5,000 per year, while 91 per cent of married fathers contribute earnings of at least $5,000 to the total family income.'[83]

A disturbingly large number of children whose parents and families fail to provide adequately for them are placed in foster care each year. According to available data on the incidence of reported maltreatment in 1997:

the number had swelled to nearly 3 million annual reports (or forty-two children reported per 1,000 children in the population). Close to 1 million children annually are now officially identified by public child protective services (CPS) agencies as confirmed victims of unlawful abuse or neglect, with an estimate of over 1,000 children annually dying as a result of such maltreatment.[84]

Sadly, American federal and state policy initiatives and programs have failed to remedy either the problems of uncollected child support or child maltreatment. Moreover, the Personal Responsibility and Work Opportunities Act (PRWORA)—popularly known as the Welfare Reform Act of 1996[85]—ended public support of the family that had started with passage of Title IV-A of the Social Security Act of 1935.[86]

---

[82] Krause, n 23 above, § 15.1, at 244. Professor Krause notes: 'As a practical matter, however, so long as the tradition of favoring the mother in matters of custody proves resistant to change . . ., "equality" in terms of support obligations continues to mean that most fathers pay dollars, whereas most mothers fulfill their obligation by rendering personal care. As the incidence of custodial awards to husbands increases along with the ability of divorced wives to earn meaningful incomes, we may one day see financial support obligations imposed on mothers as often as on fathers.'

[83] Morgan, n 42 above, at 710.

[84] Howard Davidson, *Child Protection Policy and Practice at Century's End*, 33 Fam LQ 765, 767 and n 8 (1999) (citing government publications but noting some believe true number of deaths is even higher).

[85] Pub L 104–93, 110 Stat 2105 (1996). Signed by President Clinton on Aug 22 1996, this legislation eliminated the guarantee of federal welfare as an entitlement and replaced the cornerstone program of Aid to Families with Dependent Children (AFDC) with a block-grant program to states, giving them the power to fashion their own plans, setting an even stricter cap than the five-year maximum lifetime limit imposed by this Act.

[86] Title IV-A of the Social Security Act of 1935, Pub L No 74–271, 49 Stat. 620 (codified at 42 USC §§ 601–17 (1935)).

Federal legislative processes that resulted in child support and child protection initiatives passed between 1974 and 1996 failed fully to assess how difficult it is for some American families to rear their children to be well-adjusted adult citizens. Too little attention was paid to the negative consequences of chronic unemployment and underemployment, or to the triangular interrelationship between housing, education, and employment. As concern over welfare costs and caseloads increased, Congress in 1974 passed the Family Support Act (FSA)[87] which started a twenty-year retreat from public support of the family.

In the years between 1988 and 1998, 'federal and state action . . . increasingly focused on making fathers, mothers, and even extended family members such as grandparents, pay for the support of those in need in an effort to decrease the welfare burden on the federal government.'[88] First, states were mandated to enact child support advisory guidelines for the judicial determination of orders, then to make them presumptive and to institute a panoply of child support enforcement procedures.[89] Finally, willful failure to pay child support owed to a child in another state was *criminalized* by the Child Support Recovery Act of 1992.[90]

PRWORA's 1996 repeal of AFDC clearly shifted the cost of support of children from the public taxpayer to private parents, making it 'the apotheosis of the public enforcement of private responsibility in modern times. As such, it is to be regarded as the modern equivalent of the Elizabethan Poor Laws.'[91]

Parenting Without the Legal Status

As other family types replaced the once-dominant nuclear family, some American children in 2000 and beyond are and will be reared by persons not accorded legal parental status. Should legal parenthood be redefined to include persons such as step-parents, foster parents, grandparents or

---

[87] Social Security Amendments of 1974, Pub L No 93–647, 88 Stat. 2337 codified as amended at 42 USC §§ 651–65 (1974)).

[88] Morgan, n 42 above, at 705.

[89] *ibid* at 707–14 (describing Child Support Enforcement Amendments of 1984 (CSEA), Pub L No 98–378, 98 Stat 1305, amending 42 USC §§ 657–62 (codified as amended in scattered sections of 26 USC and 42 USC (1984); the Family Support Act of 1988, Pub L No 100–485, 102 Stat. 2343 (codified primarily at 42 USC. §§ 654, 666–7 (1988)). For comprehensive discussion of child support guidelines, see LAURA W. MORGAN, CHILD SUPPORT GUIDELINES: INTERPRETATION AND APPLICATION (1996).

[90] Pub L No 102–521, 105 Stat 3403 (codified at 18 USC § 228).

[91] See n 42 above, at 706 n 6 and 718 (citing Elizabethan Act of 1601 for the Relief of the Poor, 43 Eliz 1, ch 2, § VI (1601) (as amended)).

others, who actually perform all the important social functions of parenting youngsters in their care for significant periods of time?

Step-parents

Given the continuing high incidence of divorce, remarriage, and sometimes redivorce, large numbers of step-parents play central nurturing roles in the lives of the children who live in their homes. But, for the most part, family law 'continue(s) to view stepparents through common law lenses, giving them no legal rights over their stepchildren and imposing few obligations.'[92]

Ironically, but clearly consistent with the policy of making child support more a private than a public responsibility, the law has looked anew at step-parents. Congress, in an effort to be reimbursed by non-custodial unwed and divorced fathers for AFDC payments for their children, required states to consider the income of step-parents who lived with recipients. This action forced states to consider the obligations they impose on step-parents.[93]

Foster Parents

Like step-parents, foster parents may have physical custody of a child in their care, but only a minimal protectable 'liberty' interest.[94] Their true legal status is that of a service vendor under contract to the supervising state or county placement agency. Federal initiatives begun in the 1970s to promote permanency for children with special needs via adoption have accorded foster parents preferential consideration if they have developed significant emotional ties to a child and are willing to adopt.[95]

---

[92] Mason, n 25 above, at 136. For summary discussion of stepparent obligations, see MNOOKIN and WEISBERG, CHILD, FAMILY AND STATE: PROBLEMS AND MATERIALS ON CHILDREN AND THE LAW 258–60 (3rd edn 1995). In some jurisdictions: 'stepparents are under a statutorily imposed support obligation *only if* their stepchildren are, or will be likely to become public charges ... [In contrast ...] on the federal level the AFDC program ... required states to take stepparent income into account to determine eligibility since OBRA [Omnibus Budget Reconciliations Act] was enacted in 1981 ... Before OBRA, states were required, for AFDC purposes, to consider steparent income *only if* state law imposed a support obligation on all stepparents. 45 CFR §233.90(a) (emphasis added)' (*ibid* at 258–9).

[93] See Application of Slochowsky, 342 NYS2d 525 (1973) (holding New York law imposing a support liability only for stepchildren receiving AFDC consistent with 45 CFR §233.90(a).

[94] For a thoughtful opinion, exploring in some depth the complex relationship between foster parents, child, and child welfare agency, see *Smith v Organization of Foster Families For Equality and Reform*, 431 US 516 (1977). While not definitively resolving the foster parents' claim to a constitutionally protected liberty interest because the New York procedures were deemed adequate, Justice Brennan, writing for the Court, noted 'the limited recognition accorded to the foster family by the New York statutes and the contracts executed by the foster parents argue against any but the most limited constitutional "liberty" in the foster family' (*ibid* at 846).

[95] The first such preference appeared in Section 4 [Eligibility] of the Model State Subsidized Adoption Act and Regulations approved by DHEW Secretary Matthew in July

Grandparents

Perhaps the fastest growing new type of household is that maintained by a grandparent. Increasing numbers of grandparents today are rearing their children's children because the parents are deceased (a result of AIDS), ill, or incarcerated. Sometimes, but not in all instances, a grandparent may be the child's legal guardian. More often, they are not the legal guardian and may not be accorded any legal parental status. This makes it very difficult to access needed services and resources—medical, housing, schooling, respite care. Grandparents have united and now constitute a vocal political lobby.[96] Although statutes in all fifty states accord grandparents visitation rights, their constitutionality is being challenged.[97]

CONCLUSION

Since World War II, the landscape of American parenthood has been reconfigured. The mid-twentieth-century profile description is no longer accurate. What is unchanged, however, is the necessity to assure the future survival and viability of our society. American children need to be nurtured, socialized, and educated to become contributing, productive adult citizens. Although parenting is still the primary function assigned to the family, there is also a public responsibility that government should not shirk.

From this fifty-year review of American parenting, it should be clear that we stand on the threshold of a 'brave new world.' Scientific advances in reproductive technology are testing our ethics and values, as well as traditional legal rules and presumptions for determining parenthood.[98] It

1975. The full text is reproduced in Sanford N. Katz, *Subsidized Adoption in America*, 10 Fam LQ 3, 11–20 (1976). Other preferences appear in the Model Act to Free Children for Permanent Placement (reproduced in Sanford N. Katz, *Freeing Children for Permanent Placement through a Model Act*, 12 Fam LQ 203 (1978) and in NCCUSL's 1994 Uniform Adoption Act, found in 9 ULA Part I (West Supp 1999).

[96] In 1983, the US House of Representatives passed a resolution calling on the states to enact generous laws allowing visitation to grandparents (HR Con Res 45 , 98th Cong (1983)).

[97] On June 5 2000, a divided US Supreme Court ruled a Washington statute unconstitutional that gave child visitation rights to grandparents or other non-parental parties over the objection of a custodial parent. See *Troxel v Granville*, US, No 99–138 (discussed by Barbara Bennett Woodhouse, Ch 19 in this volume). For concise overview of grandparent visitation, see Krause, n 22 above, § 18.17 at 322–3; John DeWitt Gregory, *Whose Child is it, Anyway: The Demise of Family Autonomy and Parental Authority*, 33 Fam LQ 833, 834–5 (1999).

[98] See eg, Gregory R. Triber, *Growing Pains: Disputes Surrounding Human Reproductive Interests Stretch the Boundaries of Traditional Legal Concepts*, 23 Seton Hall Legis J 103, 115–16 (1998) ('Because the issues surrounding reproductive rights are emotional and controversial, most lawmakers are hesitant to enact laws that regulate assisted reproduction or restrict an individual's fundamental right to procreate').

is unclear what the end result may be. But, barring any collapse of our democratic system, we should expect in the future to see many different ways of creating and structuring families, of allocating and assigning gender roles and responsibilities between and among family members that lead to diversified norms and new conceptions of legal parenthood.

The reality today is that many children may spend a considerable portion of their childhood being raised by persons who are not generally accorded the full legal status given biological parents. The definition of legal parenthood needs to be expanded to include and recognize the roles played by those, such as step-parents, grandparents, or other adult relatives and foster parents, who on a daily basis perform all the tasks of parenting.[99]

The possibility of 'purchased parenthood' indicates a subtle shift toward according greater weight to the interests and desires of adults to become parents by having a surrogate bear them a child who is not biologically or genetically related to them. Is this perhaps a natural consequence of the trend toward more private ordering in the realm of family relations? What may be the impact on racial and social class dynamics and interactions, if new procreative options and choices are only available to white persons of the upper-middle and upper classes?

But, alas, what may be the consequences of the current attempt to make parenting a private rather than a public responsibility? There is a 'super-parent' role for the state that includes: legislating clear procedures to regulate and oversee the use of surrogacy, but also appropriately funding programs that provide universal support and assistance for families with children so that they can fulfill their parenting tasks; and rethinking the definition of legal parenthood—who should be accorded this status and what rights and obligations does a parent owe the child and the state? I believe that greater emphasis on the social duties and responsibilities that a parent assumes for a child in their care and less on the biological or genetic relationship between them is long overdue.

It is my hope that this occurs in ways that not only respect the basic values of democratic life—respect for the individual rights of each family member, freedom and tolerance—but that make promotion of 'the best interests of the child' the salient value and standard.[100] Without this clear priority, the state's fundamental interest in ensuring its future survival and viability is not well served.

[99] See eg Leslie Joan Harris, *Reconsidering the Criteria for Legal Fatherhood*, 1996 UTAH L REV 461 (exploring the law's continued reliance on biology to define legal parenthood and arguing for recognition of functional parenthood).

[100] *ibid* at 461 n 3. Harris observes that there is a strong tendency for discussions about child support and child custody, the major component of the parent–child relationship, to be couched in terms of advancing the interests of adults. There is substantial risk, though, that if problems are examined in this way, children will be objectified and their interests ignored.

10

Marriage, Cohabitation, and Parenthood— from Contract to Status?

GILLIAN DOUGLAS

INTRODUCTION

In 1950 the United Kingdom was instrumental in the drafting of the European Convention on Human Rights.[1] One of the key Articles in this Convention, for the purposes of this paper, is Article 12, which provides that

Men and women of marriageable age have the right to marry and to found a family, according to the national laws governing the exercise of this right.

Interpretation of this provision, especially by the European Court of Human Rights, suggests that Article 12 guarantees one right only, which links marriage to procreation. Under the Convention, marriage is seen as a relationship entered into by two persons of the opposite biological sex, for the purpose, *inter alia*, of having children.[2] And although a family may be founded through adoption or the use of donated gametes, the Convention organs have not (so far) considered this to be a right exercisable separately from, or outside the context of, marriage.[3]

Fifty years after its drafting and entry into force (in 1953), the European Convention became part of English domestic law through the enactment of the Human Rights Act in 1998. Yet just when it will become possible for the first time to rely directly on Article 12 in the English courts, it is increasingly clear that, contrary to the assumptions of Article 12, marriage and procreation are now regarded, both socially and legally, as two quite distinct activities, with no necessary links between them. Over the last fifty years there has been a gradual separation of these two aspects

---

[1] The full title is the Convention for the Protection of Human Rights and Fundamental Freedoms. For a thorough analysis see D. Gomien, D. Harris, and L. Zwaak, *Law and Practice of the European Convention on Human Rights and the European Social Charter*. Strasbourg: Council of Europe (1996).

[2] *Rees v UK* Series A, No 106 (1986) 9 EHRR 56; *Cossey v UK* Series A, No 184 (1990) 13 EHRR 622; *Sheffield and Horsham v UK* (1997) 27 EHRR 163, [1998] 2 FLR 928—all European Court judgments (cf the *Commission*'s view in *Cossey v UK* Commission Report, 9 May 1989).

[3] *Van Oosterwijck v Belgium* Series B, vol 36; Application 6564/74, 2 D & R 105. Families constituted by unmarried couples, and even by same sex (albeit one party a transsexual) couples, may have a 'family life' for which there is a right to respect under Article 8 of the Convention—*Johnston v Ireland* Series A, vol 112; (1987) 9 EHRR 203; *X, Y and Z v UK* [1997] 2 FLR 892.

of family life, with parenthood replacing marriage as the organizing principle and cornerstone of family law in England and Wales. This paper traces the legal developments which demonstrate this trend, and suggests possible ways in which the law will further develop in the wake of the social changes which have been experienced in the post-war period in Britain.

The starting point of the analysis is to consider the many and varied legal reforms which have occurred as none the less reflecting a continuing policy goal throughout the period—the achievement or recovery of stability in family relationships. As the Royal Commission on Marriage and Divorce (usually known as the Morton Commission) explained in 1956: 'It is obvious that life-long marriage is the basis of a secure and stable family life, and that to ensure their well-being children must have that background.'[4] A similar view was expressed by the Labour Government in 1998, in a consultation paper, *Supporting Families:* 'Families are at the heart of our society . . . children need stability and security . . . marriage is still the surest foundation for raising children and remains the choice of the majority of people in Britain. We want to strengthen the institution of marriage to help more marriages to succeed.'[5] Indeed, one of the striking features of the period under review is the extent to which the perceived concerns, diagnoses, and even remedies for solution have remained much the same despite enormous social change. Again, it is instructive to compare the Morton Commission with the New Labour consultation paper. The Royal Commission was established to

inquire into the law of England [and Scotland] concerning divorce and other matrimonial causes . . . into the powers of courts . . . in matters affecting relations between husband and wife, and to consider whether any changes should be made in the law or its administration, including the law relating to property rights of husband and wife, both during marriage and after its termination . . . having in mind the need to promote and maintain healthy and happy married life . . .[6]

By contrast, the title of the 1998 document, which refers to *families*, is significant. The Government was proud to claim this report as the first ever produced by a British government to focus upon the needs of families. It was at pains to avoid the public relations disaster which befell the previous administration's ill-fated 'back to basics' campaign[7] and

---

[4] *Royal Commission on Marriage and Divorce Report 1951–1955* (Morton Commission), Cmd 9678. London: HMSO (1956).

[5] Home Office, *Supporting Families*. London: the Stationery Office (1998) 4.

[6] Morton Commission, n 4 above, at iii.

[7] Discussed by A. Bainham, 'Family Law in a Pluralistic Society: A View from England and Wales', in N. V. Lowe and G. Douglas (eds), *Families Across Frontiers*. The Hague: Martinus Nijhoff (1996).

carefully eschewed any overt criticism of 'non-traditional' families such as single-parent families or even gay couples. Hence, the document deals with 'families'—not 'the family'. Yet in both reports, there is a firm view that family breakdown is due to the stress of modern living and the pace of social change (although the Royal Commission was prepared to criticize a reluctance to 'work' at relationships, which is only hinted at obliquely in the more recent document).[8] The remedy, both reports agree, lies in a set of measures designed to support marriage (with the Labour Government paying due service to its acknowledgement that Britain is now a pluralistic society, stressing that non-marital families also deserve support), ranging from greater education and information about what marriage entails, to the provision of more relationship counselling and mediation facilities.[9]

When the attention of reformers turns to the law, the goal of stability becomes translated into two legal objectives—the promotion of harmony and certainty. The former is not discussed in this paper, other than to note that many of the legal developments concerning family justice and process are geared towards inducing less adversarial and hence[10] more amicable stances in the task of dismantling legal ties. Harmony overlaps with certainty, however. If the terms and conditions of a relationship, relating to its formation, conduct, and termination, are certain, there is assumed to be less room for argument and dispute and hence more chance of resollution of problems in a more co-operative (and less expensive) way. The use of contracts is seen as the pre-eminent model capable of achieving this goal, at least where relationships between *adults* are concerned.[11]

The goal of certainty will form the main subject discussed here. It is the desire to draw clear boundaries, from within which legal consequences can be drawn and outside which other relationships can be excluded, which has been a major policy objective for legal developments concerning marriage, cohabitation, and parenthood. The difficulties involved in producing such certainty help explain why, even though cohabitation has grown enormously over the period under study, it is parenthood instead which has become the dominant concept and why, notwithstanding the apparent simplicity of using parenthood in this way, there continue to be major inconsistencies and confusions in the shape and functioning of the

[8] See Morton Commission, n 4 above, paras 46–9); Home Office, n 5 above, paras 4.10, 4.11, 4.27, 4.28.
[9] Morton Commission, note 4 above, paras 50–4; Home Office, n 4 above, *passim.*
[10] The causal link is deliberately, though not necessarily conceded as correctly, made here.
[11] For critiques of the use of the contractual approach, see M. Regan, *Family Law and the Pursuit of Intimacy*, New York: New York University Press (1993), who argues in particular for renewed recognition of status as a means of promoting stability in family relationships; W. Wagner, *The Contractual Reallocation of Procreative Resources and Parental Rights: The Natural Endowment Critique*, Aldershot: Dartmouth Publishing (1995).

legal code. The search for certainty also explains the attraction of two distinctly different legal concepts—contract and status—as the bases for legal ties, with contract being promoted as the model to be used in adult relationships, and status as the key to establishing adult–child links.

DEVELOPMENTS IN MARRIAGE

The very title of the Morton Commission demonstrates, as noted above, that fifty years ago, the prime concern of family policy lay in ensuring that marriage remained the pre-eminent legal relationship underpinning family life. The virtue of marriage, from the point of view of establishing certainty, lies in the obvious fact that it is a *legal* concept with generally clear rules governing its formation. We can usually determine, without major difficulty,[12] who is married to whom. We can also lay down the rules governing what can go on within a marriage, and what consequences may flow as a result. Reforms concerning each of these have taken place with the intention of modernizing marriage and hence making it more attractive to those who would either avoid it or seek to terminate it.

Entry Into Marriage

For example, a continuing issue has been the question of who can marry whom. Old taboos drawn from religious prescription have faded from public consciousness. Since the 1960s, as couples have increasingly been prepared to form relationships outside previously accepted social norms, it has been regarded as necessary to seek to 'legitimate' their union through marriage where possible. In this way, the ideology that marriage is the primary relationship to be preferred above any other can be sustained, rather than forcing couples to cohabit. Thus, when proposals to reform divorce law were put forward in the 1960s it was suggested that many cohabiting couples would marry once free to do so and that the number of 'stable illicit unions' would therefore decline.[13] Similarly, when

---

[12] But it may sometimes be difficult to determine *whether a lawful marriage has taken place*: see *Chief Adjudication Officer v Bath* [2000] 1 All ER 8 where the Court of Appeal rediscovered the common law doctrine of presumption of marriage to preserve the rights of a Sikh widow who appeared to have undergone a ceremony of marriage which had not conformed with the requirements of the Marriage Act 1949.

[13] See Law Commission, Report No 6, *Reform of the Grounds of Divorce: the Field of Choice*, Cmnd 3123, London: HMSO (1966) paras 33–7 and see the comment: R. Deech, 'Divorce Law and Empirical Studies', (1990) 106 *Law Quarterly Review* 229; response by J. Eekelaar and M. Maclean, 'Divorce Law and Empirical Studies: A Reply', (1990) 106 *Law Quarterly Review* 621.

the age of majority (and the age at which one could marry without parental consent) was lowered to 18 in 1969, it was regarded as impossible to raise the minimum age of marriage from 16. This was because, having accepted that one could not raise the minimum age of lawful sexual intercourse, it was felt to be wrong to require young couples to remain unmarried—and their offspring to be born illegitimate—simply because they had formed sexual relationships under the age of 18.[14]

But the view that there is an 'essence' of marriage—hard to elucidate but centring on 'acceptable' sexual activity and the possibility of procreation—sustained opposition to extending the rules of entry into marriage to transsexuals or homosexual couples. The problem of defining just what constitutes a 'man' or a 'woman' in law was dealt with in *Corbett v Corbett*.[15] In a famous—if increasingly criticized—judgment, Ormrod J held that a person's sex is determined by his or her biological sex at birth and that alteration of secondary sexual characteristics cannot affect this. The precedent was challenged unsuccessfully several times before the European Court of Human Rights.[16] There were also unsuccessful attempts to legislate to overturn its effects.[17] But the best hope for transsexuals may lie in the use of the Human Rights Act 1998 to mount a challenge in the domestic courts which will be freed from the constraints of old precedents and which could go beyond the boundaries drawn by the European Court if they chose to do so. Whether the courts would be as bold in response to a claim brought by homosexuals is hard to predict. Sympathy with their position was strikingly demonstrated by the House of Lords in a case concerning rights to succeed to a tenancy under housing law.[18] There, a majority of their Lordships were prepared to hold that, for the purposes of the legislation, a same-sex partner is capable of being 'a member of the other partner's family'. However, they were not ready to go so far as to accept that such a couple could be regarded as living together 'as husband and wife'. None the less, the case lends some support to the view that improvement of the legal position of homosexuals may come about more easily from the gradual equalization of the rules governing the *consequences* of relationships rather than in extending the right to marry, *per se*.

---

[14] *Report of the Committee on the Age of Majority* (Latey Committee), Cmnd 3342. London: HMSO (1967), paras 166–77. The proposals were enacted in the Family Law Reform Act 1969. The 'age of consent' for sexual intercourse is widely ignored and the number of teenage marriages is in sharp decline, suggesting that young people pay little or no attention to legal norms governing sexual activity.   [15] [1971] P 83.
[16] See n 2 above.   [17] eg the Gender Identity (Registration and Civil Status) Bill, 1995.
[18] *Fitzpatrick v Sterling Housing Association Ltd* [1999] 4 All ER 705.

Conduct During, and Consequences of, Marriage

The more overt aspects of the traditional sex-based division of labour and responsibility within marriage have been eroded since the start of female emancipation in the nineteenth century, and this process continued through a variety of reforms after the 1950s. The effect was to create a more formally equal marital relationship and to remove the husband's pre-emptive rights.

Reproductive and sexual rights

A key area was that relating to reproductive and sexual rights. Notwithstanding the views of the European Court and of Ormrod J in *Corbett v Corbett* that one of the essential purposes of marriage is procreation, proof of the ability to procreate has never been a requirement of a valid marriage in English law. In *Baxter v Baxter*[19] the House of Lords held that a marriage was consummated although the husband had used a condom. This separation of sexual intercourse from procreation was coupled with an eventual recognition that neither spouse—in reality, the husband—has a pre-emptive right to determine when the couple will seek to procreate or when they will have sexual relations. For example, abortion was legalized by the Abortion Act 1967 and it was held in *Paton v BPAS*[20] that a husband could not prevent his wife from seeking an abortion by means of an injunction. A wife is not legally required to consult, or even inform, her husband that she intends to undergo a termination. Strangely, it took rather longer for the courts to recognize a wife's *sexual* autonomy. It was not until 1991 that the House of Lords finally rejected the idea that a husband could have immunity from liability for rape of his wife.[21] Both the *Paton* and *R* rulings were subsequently challenged at Strasbourg under the European Convention on Human Rights. Both challenges failed, and the tenor of judgments on both occasions reflects a clear view that in a civilized, modern society, marriage must be seen as a partnership of equals.[22]

The right to occupy the marital home

The other major area where wives' inequality was recognized related to the occupation of the family home. During the immediate post-war period, there was a growing awareness of the vulnerability of married women who, having no legal title to the family home, found themselves deserted by their husbands and liable to eviction by landlords or mortgagees. The common law right of a wife to occupy the matrimo-

---

[19] [1948] AC 274.   [20] [1979] QB 276.   [21] [1992] 1 AC 599.
[22] See *Paton v UK* (1980) 3 EHRR 408 (European Commission); *CR v United Kingdom; SW v United Kingdom* [1996] 1 FLR 434, 448–9 (European Court).

nial home was held, by the House of Lords in *National Provincial Bank v Ainsworth*,[23] to be a personal right only, not enforceable against bona fide third parties. Legislation[24] was therefore brought forward to provide some protection to spouses (usually wives) in this situation. It clarified their rights in the property as against those of their spouses, and enabled them to be joined as parties to possession proceedings and to register their 'matrimonial home rights'[25] so as to provide statutory notice of their occupation to any third party. Although the latter remedy was of limited utility, the first formed the basis of improved rights to occupy the home against the spouse's will, in situations of domestic violence and family crisis.[26]

Taking the Law Out of Marriage

Another trend in the law was to remove legal consequences from the fact of marriage. This trend reflected two major social developments during the period. The first was the increasing view of marriage—or any other intimate relationship—as existing for the emotional and psychological benefit of each party, and only for as long as that benefit is experienced.[27] With romantic love seen as the essence and justification for marriage, the role of marriage as a form of economic organization diminished in significance (even while it continued to mask, and mitigate, the enduring economic inequality of women).[28] Hence, the action for breach of promise of marriage, which enabled either disappointed party to sue for damages, was abolished in 1970.[29] It was no longer felt right to face a reluctant fiancé(e) with the choice of marry or pay. Once the success of marriage was seen as dependent upon the parties' emotional commitment, it became impossible for the law to dictate that they should be legally bound together.[30]

---

[23] [1965] AC 1175 rejecting a series of cases which had created the 'deserted wives' equity'.   [24] Matrimonial Homes Act 1967.

[25] So called since the implementation of Part IV of the Family Law Act 1996.

[26] Through use of the Matrimonial Homes Act as the key to determining whether a court had jurisdiction to oust the spouse from the home—*Richards v Richards* [1984] AC 174, HL and now Part IV of the Family Law Act 1996. See Ch 22.

[27] A. Giddens, *Modernity and Self-Identity*, Cambridge: Polity Press (1991); U. Beck and E. Beck-Gernsheim, *The Normal Chaos of Love*, Cambridge: Polity Press (1995).

[28] See C. Roberts, 'The Place of Marriage in a Changing Society', address to the Lord Chancellor's Conference on *Supporting Marriage into the Next Century*, 3 Apr 1996, who notes that we may have underplayed the economic aspects of marriage and that people may be loath to admit that they married, even in part, for the mutual interdependence and exchange of goods and services that goes on in most marriages.

[29] Law Commission Report No 26, *Breach of Promise of Marriage*, London: HMSO (1969); Law Reform (Miscellaneous Provisions) Act 1970, s 1.

[30] Similarly, the action for restitution of conjugal rights was abolished: Law Commission Report No 23, *Proposal for the Abolition of the Matrimonial Remedy of Restitution of Conjugal Rights*, London: HMSO (1969); Matrimonial Proceedings and Property Act 1970, s 20.

Making Marriage More Individualistic—the New Marriage?

While policy makers' attention was focused upon 'modernizing' the ongoing marriage relationship, a dramatic demographic change took place whereby the popularity of marriage was seen to be in sharp decline.[31] Policy makers' attempts to revive the popularity of marriage in the face of this change appear to have focused as much upon making the *wedding*, as the *marriage* itself, more attractive to prospective entrants.

The detailed rules governing the formalities of marriage were amended many times to reflect religious pluralism and increased secularity on the one hand, and the needs of a bureaucratic state on the other.[32] A series of Acts from 1949 to 1994 modernized registration requirements, and most importantly liberalized the place and mode of ceremony. Some of these changes were impelled by adverse rulings by the European Commission of Human Rights, in response to complaints that the limitations on place of marriage broke the right to marry under Article 12.[33] But the Marriage Act 1994 reflected a desire to enable couples to have a wedding ceremony tailored more to their own—probably romantic—conception of marriage. This Act permits couples wishing to have a *civil* ceremony to marry in a variety of 'approved premises' rather than in the often uninspiring surroundings of the local register office. This has permitted stately homes, plush hotels, and more unusual venues such as the Brighton Pavilion and football stadiums (as long as the ceremony takes place off the pitch), to become the setting for couples to play out their wedding dreams. They may also add their own words to the ceremony and involve the guests in it.

The view of marriage as a contract involving an exchange of personal vows chosen by the parties themselves is evident in this development. There are further echoes of it in proposals that couples be given clear statements of their rights and responsibilities in marriage (*and* cohabitation); that they be encouraged to undergo marriage preparation courses in which they can discuss and decide on matters such as finances, children, and living arrangements during the marriage; and that they be permitted to enter into prenuptial agreements concerning disposal of property in the event of divorce.[34]

All these proposals may be seen to illustrate a view of marriage as a contractual commitment between the two parties themselves, and which

[31] See Gibson, Ch 2 of this volume.

[32] See N. V. Lowe and G. Douglas, *Bromley's Family Law*, 9th edn, London: Butterworths (1998) for detailed discussion.

[33] *Hamer v UK* (1982) 24 DR 5; *Draper v UK* (1980) 24 DR 72 (detained prisoners could not marry since the prison governor would not authorize their temporary release to marry outside the prison, and there was no legal provision to marry within prison).

[34] Home Office (1998: paras 4.13–4.23).

they make, and end, according to their own wishes and circumstances. Such a model of marriage removes it from a position as the pre-eminent legal and social institution, to a choice among many. In particular, it becomes difficult to distinguish it from cohabiting unions.

COHABITATION

While marriage apparently declined in popularity, cohabitation grew spectacularly over the period.[35] Seventy per cent of first marriages in the early 1990s were preceded by cohabitation, over 70 per cent of first part-nerships are cohabitations, and it is the dominant form of repartnering after a divorce.[36]

Cohabitation as a Status

Legal developments in the light of this growth were even more piecemeal than those in relation to marriage. Two basic approaches can be dis-cerned. The first was to give cohabitation some recognition as a distinct *status*, and to equate it with marriage by giving to cohabitants the same legal benefits and burdens as are given to spouses. This approach is mainly to be found in statute law, and, given past judicial reluctance to extend the meaning of statutory words to include cohabitants,[37] usually required express provision to be made in the statute. One example can be found in aspects of the law relating to inheritance and succession. A per-son who was living in the same household with the deceased as husband and wife may be entitled to succeed to a tenancy,[38] or, if the period of cohabitation had lasted for two years or more immediately prior to the death, to a claim to provision from the deceased's estate,[39] or under the Fatal Accidents Act 1976.[40] The aim of such measures is to give 'due' recognition to the claimant's relationship with the deceased as compared with the claims of other relatives by blood or marriage.

---

[35] See Gibson, Ch 2 of this volume.

[36] J. Ermisch and M. Francesconi, *Cohabitation in Great Britain: Not for Long, but Here to Stay*, Working Paper 98–1. Colchester: ESRC Research Centre for Micro- Social Change (1998).

[37] See eg *Gammans v Ekins* [1950] 2 KB 328, CA: 'To say of two people, masquerading, as these two were, as husband and wife—there being no children to complicate the picture—that they were members of the same family, seems to me an abuse of the English language', *per* Asquith LJ. But cf *Dyson Holdings Ltd v Fox* [1976] QB 503, CA. The reluctance was more recently mirrored (albeit in more sympathetic language) in the refusal to regard gay couples as living together as husband and wife in *Fitzpatrick v Sterling Housing Association Ltd* [1999] 4 All ER 705, HL discussed above.   [38] Rent Act 1977 Sch 1 paras 1, 2 (as amended).

[39] Law Reform (Succession) Act 1995 s 2, amending the Inheritance (Provision for Family and Dependants) Act 1975 s 25. But a cohabitant, unlike a spouse, can only claim provision for his or her maintenance.   [40] Section 1 (as amended).

There was also recognition of cohabitation as a status relationship giving rise to rights as against the other cohabitant, most notably in cases of
family violence. This example is important because the history of the relevant legislation and case law reveals a continuing conflict between property and personal protection. Notwithstanding the clear words of the
statute, which provided that an application for an injunction could be
made by either a party to a marriage or by a person living with the other
in the same household as husband and wife,[41] it was only after a House
of Lords majority ruling that it was accepted that a (man) could be
excluded from his own home at the behest of a partner to whom he owed
no legal duty of support or accommodation.[42] Continuing discomfort
with this state of affairs, and a fear that such a remedy 'downgrades' the
significance of marriage, led Members of Parliament to impose additional
criteria for the grant of this kind of order on the application of cohabitants, and to limit its duration, in Part IV of the Family Law Act 1996.[43]

The equation of cohabitation with marriage has been most striking in
the field of social security (welfare) law. Here, no distinction is drawn
between marriage and cohabitation for the purposes of determining a
family unit for means-tested benefit claims. Even though social security
law does not impose a liability to support a partner, it is assumed that
cohabitants support each other. Hence, where a person claims certain
types of benefits, the 'family's' resources are aggregated and payment is
made only where the partner is unable to support the claimant out of
his own income.[44] (By contrast, contributory benefits such as retirement
pension are not payable to cohabiting partners, but only to spouses.)[45]

Cohabitation as a Contractual Relationship

An alternative means of recognizing cohabitation was to view it, or more
accurately, aspects arising from it, as contractual, or quasi-contractual.
Here, the impetus came in the case law rather than statute, and was limited to the resolution of property disputes. The approach was facilitated
by the separate property regime which applies to all family property
under English law. Since there have been few special rules governing
marital property, remedies were developed which could apply regardless
of the personal status of the parties. The use of constructive trusts,[46]

---

[41] Domestic Violence and Matrimonial Proceedings Act 1976 s 1(2).
[42] *Davis v Johnson* [1979] AC 264.   [43] Section 36(6), s 41, s 36(10).
[44] Social Security Contributions and Benefits Act 1992 s 136.
[45] Social Security Contributions and Benefits Act 1992 ss 83, 84, to be substituted by s 83A,
inserted by the Pensions Act 1995 s 126, Sch 4 para 2, with effect from 6 Apr 2010 (!).
[46] The leading cases are *Gissing v Gissing* [1971] AC 886, HL; *Lloyds Bank v Rosset* [1991] 1
AC 107, HL.

underpinned by agreement, known, in the case law, as a 'common intention' (either implicit or explicit) as to the shares which the parties take in the property, may be seen as a quasi-contractual remedy to the problem of dissonance between title and substance. Similarly, a contractual licence was established where it could be shown that the defendant to possession proceedings had given consideration, in the form of relinquishing tenancy rights to another property, in order to move in with the plaintiff.[47] But the status of true 'cohabitation contracts' regulating the aspects of the parties' relationship, and the question whether old obstacles to recognition based on immorality or lack of consideration would continue to apply, have yet to be authoritatively tested,[48] and it is unclear how common such agreements are.

Defining Cohabitation

Neither of these approaches wrestled clearly with the problem of defining the nature or boundaries of a cohabitation relationship.[49] The statutory, status-based approach merely required that the parties be 'living together as husband and wife' (sometimes, as seen, for a minimum period of time). This gave rise to problems of interpretation.[50] For example, in *Adeoso v Adeoso*,[51] a domestic violence case, it was held that a couple who were living at arms' length from each other, albeit under the same roof, could be regarded as none the less living in the same household as husband and wife, even though, for the purposes of the old divorce law of desertion, they might well have been regarded as having separated into two households. The requirement to be living 'as husband and wife' was also held to prevent homosexual couples from relying on the same definition in other legislation.[52] The appropriate duration of cohabitation qualifying for legal recognition is also open to argument. A two-year qualifying period may be suitable in the inheritance context but may be inappropriate

---

[47] *Tanner v Tanner* [1975] 3 All ER 776, CA.

[48] Although it is most doubtful that courts would now attach weight to such arguments.

[49] Dame Brenda Hale has commented that the Law Commission, from which most family law reforms emanated during the 1960s to 1990s, deliberately chose to find ways of bringing cohabitants within the scope of remedies provided for spouses rather than create a fundamentally new form of 'de facto' marriage relationship: B. Hale, 'Family Law Reform: Whither or Wither?' in M. D. A. Freeman (ed), *Current Legal Problems 1995: Vol 48, Part II, Collected Papers* 217. Oxford: Oxford University Press (1995).

[50] Such problems are ignored by Regan, n 11 above, 126, who, in advocating a status-based approach to the recognition of cohabitation, suggests that such recognition be given where a couple's relationship 'substantively resembles formal marriage'.

[51] [1981] 1 All ER 107, CA.

[52] *Harrogate Borough Council v Simpson* [1986] 2 FLR 91, CA; *Fitzpatrick v Sterling Housing Association Ltd* [1999] 4 All ER 705, HL.

where the claim is to a share of property or to financial support on the breakdown of the relationship.

The Significance Attached to Cohabitation

The reforms noted here may in fact have more to do with equating cohabitation with recognized family relationships in general, than with putting it on a par with marriage.[53] In the inheritance context, for example, cohabitants were given rights to claim alongside the deceased's other relatives, but were not equated directly with surviving spouses.[54] In the housing field, they rank, *along with other members of the deceased's family*, as having a claim to succeed to the tenancy. The only area in which they, along with spouses, have a claim superior to that of other family members, is in relation to ouster from the family home in the case of domestic violence.[55] Yet even in this context, reformers have chosen to extend the range of potential beneficiaries of the law well beyond spouses and cohabitants. The more limited remedy of a non-molestation order[56] may be sought, in appropriate circumstances, by anyone who is 'associated with' the respondent, a categorization including homosexual couples who have lived together, relatives, fiancé(e)s, and parents of dependent children.[57]

Such reforms suggest that cohabitation has been viewed, not necessarily as akin to marriage, but as yet another intimate family relationship, deserving recognition because of the moral obligations taken on during its existence. The problems of achieving fairness and 'due' recognition of such obligations make it unlikely that a uniform definition of cohabitation, and hence a uniform status, could be arrived at. The goal of legal certainty therefore becomes difficult to realize. A uniform status (and the uniform legal consequences which could flow from this) may also be undesirable given the instability and variety of cohabitations and the uncertainty underlying their significance. On the other hand, greater reliance on a contractual model may not redress the basic economic inequalities that persist between cohabiting men and women.[58] It none

[53] Though see the prediction by Michael Freeman that marriage and cohabitation will become more alike in the future: M. D. A. Freeman, 'Family Values and Family Justice', in Freeman (ed), *Current Legal Problems 1997; Law and Opinion at the End of the Twentieth Century*. Oxford: Oxford University Press (1997), 357.

[54] See Inheritance (Provision for Family and Dependants) Act 1975 s 1(2).

[55] And the level of protection offered has more to do with the applicant's property rights than her cohabitation status: cf Family Law Act 1996 s 33 with ss 36 and 38.

[56] An order under Family Law Act 1996 s 42 prohibiting the respondent from molesting (ie using violence, pestering, or harassing) the applicant or a child.

[57] Family Law Act 1996 s 62(3) (4).

[58] As pointed out by J. Lewis, *Marriage, Cohabitation and the Law: Individualism and Obligation*, Lord Chancellor's Department Research Series 1/99. London: Lord Chancellor's Department (1999).

the less seems likely to assume greater significance in future legal policy as a means of embracing marriage, homosexual relationships, and other intimate associations within a unified model of adult relationships, with little to privilege one over another.

However, children are now born in about one in six cohabiting unions, and such unions tend to be economically more disadvantaged, much less likely to be converted into marriage than cohabiting unions with no children, and more likely to dissolve.[59] The implications of these statistics are not easy to determine. What should be the policy goals given the instability of cohabiting unions with children? It is not surprising that, faced with such a picture, coupled with increasing marriage breakdown and a rise of non-married, non-cohabiting, parenthood, reformers have sought to redefine family relationships and family law in the context of the parent–child, rather than adult, relationship.

PARENTHOOD

On first consideration, the concept of parenthood appears to avoid the pitfalls noted in relation to marriage and cohabitation. With marriage apparently in decline and cohabitation still in a state of flux, it would seem that the parent–child relationship is the only clearly ascertainable family relationship to which legal consequences can be attached. As Margaret Thatcher famously proclaimed, 'parenthood is for life', and unlike marriage, which is clearly a legal concept, and cohabitation, which is dependent upon uncertain social and cultural attitudes and practices, parenthood is seen as 'natural'. It may therefore seem both obvious and right that it be used as the central relationship underpinning family law, and there is less room for argument over whether rights and obligations should attach to it. Furthermore, parenthood can be regarded as distinct from the adult relationship, which enables legal consequences to be kept uniform regardless of the status of that relationship.

A decline in the legal significance of birth outside wedlock[60] over the post-war period reflected this change. Moves to equate all children regardless of the status of their parents had two consequences, however. On the one hand, the position of the child was improved. On the other, the position of the parents became more complicated. Once the law no longer associated children's status with the marital status of their parents, the question of parenthood—meaning, at this point, *fatherhood*—became one of deciding which father to attach to a child, rather than, as under the

---

[59] Ermisch and Francesconi , n 36 above.
[60] See Eekelaar, Ch 29 of this volume .

old affiliation rules, which children to attach to a father. The conundrum demonstrates that, contrary to initial perception, parenthood is far from being a 'natural' concept. Rather, as became increasingly clear, it is just as much a social construct as marriage. Indeed, it is a social construct with more dimensions than marriage, since it can be divided into biological, legal, and social parenthood, with different ramifications each time. The question for reformers has been to determine whether *legal* parenthood should be based upon biological, or social parenthood; a question to which conflicting answers have been given.

Biological Parenthood

'This is My Truth: Tell Me Yours'

On the one hand, there was a clear trend towards seeking to ascertain the biological 'truth' regarding a child's origins and fixing parenthood accordingly. This view went hand in hand with the diminishing stigma attached to illegitimacy[61] and hence the diminished importance attached to the longstanding legal presumption that the husband of a married woman is the father of her child. In a landmark case,[62] the House of Lords held that a blood test to ascertain paternity should be directed[63] *unless* it could be shown that this would be against the child's interests. In other words, the burden is on the person resisting the test to establish positively that the truth would harm the child. Although there have been decisions where the court has ruled that a test should be refused since it would be harmful to permit a 'stranger' to upset an established family unit,[64] the general tenor of decisions has been to favour the discovery of the truth. And with the development of DNA testing, biological parenthood could at last be established with certainty,[65] thus achieving one legal policy goal. This emphasis upon the blood tie also appeared to be com-

---

[61] Even at the end of the 20th c, birth within wedlock remains important for the transmission of hereditary titles however. For a fascinating insight into the life of one hereditary peer, and the legal issues resulting from his complicated domestic arrangements, see *Re Barony of Moynihan* [2000] 1 FLR 113 (House of Lords Committee for Privileges).

[62] *S v S, W v Official Solicitor (or W)* [1972] AC 24.

[63] Power to direct, but not to *order* a test to be taken by the relevant parties, is contained in s 20 of the Family Law Reform Act 1969. Adverse inferences should be drawn from a refusal: s 23 and *Re G (Parentage: Blood Sample)* [1997] 1 FLR 360, CA.

[64] See, in particular, *Re F (A Minor) (Blood Tests: Parental Rights)* [1993] Fam 314, CA and the comment by J. Fortin, '*Re F*: The Gooseberry Bush Approach', (1996) 57 *Modern Law Review* 296.

[65] Or at least, as certain as one can be: for details regarding DNA testing, see A. Grubb and D. Pearl, *Blood Testing, AIDS and DNA Profiling*, Bristol: Family Law (1990); K. O'Donovan, 'Who is the Father? Access to Information on Genetic Identity' in G. Douglas and L. Sebba (eds), *Children's Rights and Traditional Values*, Aldershot: Ashgate (1998).

patible with international law and opinion, most clearly in Article 7 of the United Nations Convention on the Rights of the Child.[66] Judges keen to assert the child's 'right' to know the identity of the biological father have relied upon this Article,[67] but sperm donors to licensed clinics are guaranteed anonymity; in 2000 the government indicated that certain non-identifying information might be released.

The Unmarried Father and His Child

Moves to reform the legal position of such fathers were an important aspect of the shifting focus towards parenthood.[68] When the Law Commission first proposed abolishing the status of legitimacy, they assumed that this would require placing all fathers in an equal position regardless of their marital status.[69] This view found little favour and the proposal was abandoned.[70] Following further consideration of the question, legislation was enacted in 1987 whereby unmarried fathers could apply to a court for a 'parental rights and duties order' which would give them the same legal rights as a married father.[71] But the Law Commission considered that there should be a simpler method of obtaining what, under the Children Act 1989, was to become known as 'parental responsibility' than having to take court proceedings. They recommended that it should be possible for the parents to make a 'parental responsibility agreement', with the safeguard against mothers being coerced into agreeing, of having the agreement checked by the court.[72] This recommendation was enacted in s 4(1)(b) of the Children Act 1989, though without requiring such scrutiny. Agreements were simply filed with the Principal Registry of the Family Division. However, following concern that the mother's signature might be forged by the father, the procedure was tightened to require that signatures be witnessed by a Justice of the Peace, justices' clerk, or court official authorized by a judge.

The introduction of an overtly contractual mechanism for allocating parental responsibility looks like yet another illustration of the trend from status to contract. The problem, however, is that, even though the formalities are minimal and there is virtually no cost involved, few agreements are actually entered into. For example, in 1996, some 3,590 agreements were made, compared with around 200,000 births outside

[66] This gives the child 'the right from birth to a name, the right to acquire a nationality and, as far as possible, the right to know and be cared for by his or her parents'.

[67] See eg *Re H (Paternity: Blood Test)* [1996] 2 FLR 65, CA.

[68] A. Bainham, 'When is a Parent not a Parent? Reflections on the Unmarried Father and his Child in English Law' (1989) 3 *Int J of Law and the Family* 208; N. V. Lowe, 'The Meaning and Allocation of Parental Responsibility—A Common Lawyer's Perspective', (1997) 11 *Int J of Law, Policy and the Family* 192.

[69] Law Commission, Working Paper No 74, *Illegitimacy*. London: HMSO (1979).

[70] Law Commission, Report No 118, *Illegitimacy*. London: HMSO (1982).

[71] Family Law Reform Act 1987 s 4.   [72] Law Commission (1988: para 2.18).

marriage.[73] The main reason for the low take-up is probably simple ignorance of the availability of the procedure and of the legal consequences of having, or not having, parental responsibility.[74]

Such ignorance is not helped by an apparent inconsistency of view among the judiciary on this very point. Where an unmarried couple do not make an agreement, the father may apply to the court for a parental responsibility *order*. This gives him parental responsibility ('all the rights, duties, powers, responsibility and authority which by law a parent of a child has in relation to the child and his property')[75] and, since he is already regarded as the child's parent as a matter of law, it must be assumed that having parental responsibility gives him an entitlement to exercise the rights, powers, and authority said to be vested in it. But seeking an order is usually a hostile act, undertaken where the relationship with the mother has broken down, and usually coupled with an application for contact with the child.[76] Judges appear to have been at pains, therefore, to play down the significance of obtaining the order, by suggesting, for example, that 'It is wrong to place undue and therefore false emphasis on the rights and duties and the powers comprised in "parental responsibility" and not to concentrate on the fact that what is at issue is conferring upon a committed father the status of parenthood for which nature has already ordained that he must bear responsibility.'[77]

Since applying for an order signals a breakdown in the relationship between the parents, and since making agreements has proved unpopular, if unmarried fathers were to be placed in the same position as married fathers and mothers, another mechanism had to be found. Bolstered by appeals to international law, where both Article 18 of the United Nations Convention on the Rights of the Child and Article 8 of the European Convention on Human Rights can be used to support their position,[78] and by the demographic picture, unmarried fathers appear to have won the intellectual argument for this. Much store, for example, was set by the Government on the finding that four-fifths of births outside marriage are registered jointly by both parents. This may be taken

[73] Children Act Advisory Committee, *Final Report 1997*. London: Lord Chancellor's Department (1997) Appendix 2.

[74] See R. Pickford, *Fathers, Marriage and the Law*. London: Family Policy Studies Centre (1999). The possibility that a number of fathers *deliberately* wish to avoid obtaining rights and obligations in respect of the child cannot be ruled out, although they may still be required to support a child regardless of whether they have parental responsibility—Child Support Act 1991, s 1.   [75] Children Act 1989 s 3(1).

[76] I. Butler *et al*, 'The Children Act 1989 and the Unmarried Father', (1993) 5 *J of Child Law* 157.

[77] Ward J in *Re S (Parental Responsibility)* [1995] 2 FLR 648, CA at 657; see J. Eekelaar, 'Parental Responsibility—A New Legal Status?', (1996) 112 *Law Quarterly Review* 233.

[78] But contrary arguments can also be made; see, in particular, the judgment by Hale J in *Re W, Re B (Child Abduction: Unmarried Father)* [1998] 2 FLR 146.

to signify assent by the mother to the father's inclusion on the birth entry and hence, presumably, a degree of recognition by both parents of his role in the child's life. Furthermore, of these jointly registering parents, three-quarters apparently live together at the same address, thus signifying an ongoing relationship. The Government therefore proposed that automatic parental responsibility should be vested in the father whenever he is so registered on the birth entry, thus eliminating the need, in the vast majority of cases, for either party to do anything extra to establish his legal position.[79] Full legal status (and the powers that go with it) is therefore imposed, or bestowed, rather than negotiated, illustrating the trend, once more, towards status as the mechanism for the establishment of parenthood, rather than contract.

Social Parenthood

Simultaneously with the increased attention paid to blood ties, there was a greater willingness to recognize the claims of social parenthood. However, a *contractual* approach to so doing has not found favour. The reason is the fear that allowing people to assign parental rights to others by private agreement may be detrimental to the welfare of the child. Instead, the prospective parent must establish his or her worthiness to be a parent. Such worthiness may derive from two arguments. First, a right to be a parent may be asserted, either as a human right (although, as we have seen, this has not yet been conceded in international law as existing separately from marriage) or as a moral or psychological right to be a 'complete' and fulfilled human being. Second, a claim may be based upon having proved one's fitness to be a parent by having fostered or cared for a particular child. The rights-based argument has been used in seeking access to techniques of human assisted reproduction. The 'fitness' argument finds expression most clearly in claims to adopt.

The 'Right to be a Parent'

Provisions relating to parenthood enacted in the Human Fertilisation and Embryology Act 1990[80] reflected social reality but also broke new ground. It had been apparent, at least since 1979,[81] that children born to married women after donor insemination were being falsely registered as the children of the mother's husband. Where the sperm had been donated to a clinic, the donor remained anonymous and the clear intention of all

---

[79] Lord Chancellor's Department, *1. Court Proceedings for the Determination of Paternity: 2. The Law on Parental Responsibility for Unmarried Fathers.* London: Lord Chancellor's Department (1998).   [80] See Deech, Ch 8 of this volume.
[81] See Law Commission (1979), n 69 above, para 10.7.

involved was that the child should be brought up within the family comprised of the mother and her husband. It was therefore sensible to enable the husband lawfully to be registered as the father of the child, and to remove the donor from the scene by terminating his parental status. This position was achieved, in respect of children born by donor insemination to married women, in the Family Law Reform Act 1987,[82] and was extended to the use of donor sperm in IVF and other high-tech treatments by the 1990 Act.

Attempts to limit access to treatment to married couples failed during the passage of the legislation, reflecting the recognition of the growth in cohabitation documented above. It was provided that where donated sperm is used in the course of *licensed*[83] treatment services provided for a woman and man together, that man shall be treated as the father of the child, once more displacing the donor. This convoluted formulation avoids the difficulties noted in defining cohabitation, but leaves open the possibility of 'sham' couples presenting for treatment, perhaps in situations where a woman would be refused treatment (eg because of her sexual orientation) if she sought it on her own. It does, however, for the first time in English law, enable a man to whom the child has no genetic links, and who has not married the mother, to obtain full parental status without any court scrutiny of his suitability or the needs of the child. It is simply his willingness to be classed as a father, as demonstrated by his presenting for treatment with the woman, which qualifies him for such status.

Similarly, in the case of women who receive donated *eggs*, it is the woman who gives birth to the child who is granted parental status,[84] and the egg donor's genetic link receives no recognition. This causes complications where surrogacy arrangements are used, and has necessitated a simplified adoption procedure to be introduced, whereby the intending parents in a surrogacy arrangement involving egg or embryo donation using their *own* gametes may acquire parental status by court order, subject to the agreement of the surrogate mother.[85] The choice of a court procedure, rather than automatic qualification based on the prior surrogacy agreement, reflects ambivalence over the legitimacy of surrogacy as a means of having children, the reluctance to permit children to be the subject of contracts, and a concern to ensure some control over the process. At this point, access to social parenthood begins to move away from a rights-based focus, towards a consideration of fitness and qualification, as demonstrated most sharply in claims to adopt.

---

[82] s 27.
[83] Where donor sperm are obtained privately, the donor remains the legal father. The aim is to encourage the use of licensed clinics rather than DIY arrangements.   [84] s 27.
[85] s 30. See Deech, Ch 8 of this volume.

Qualifying to be a Parent

Where a child is already in existence, the only means of achieving full parental status in respect of her is through adoption, or a parental order after a surrogacy arrangement. Both are controlled by the courts, but the former requires the prospective parent to undergo detailed scrutiny by a local authority social services department, approval by an adoption panel, and finally approval by the court, before parental status is bestowed.[86] The process is slow, uncertain, and stressful.[87] It is far removed from the automatic ascription of parenthood achievable by the other means noted here, and is the opposite of a contractual model[88] although the agreement (or dispensation thereof) of the birth parent is a prerequisite. Such agreement, however, relates to the relinquishing of parental rights rather than the grant of these to another couple.

But this tells only half the story of adoption. In fact, about half of all adoptions involve step-children.[89] Despite attempts to reduce this proportion, on the basis that step-parent adoption distorts family relationships and undermines the blood tie,[90] it remains an option favoured by some step-families, whether to cut the birth father out of the picture or for other reasons. It reflects the continuing view, in attitudes if not in law or policy, that social parenthood, the practical caring for children, should be recognized through the grant of parental status.

Biology as Destiny?

This section has demonstrated the extent to which parenthood in English law has come to be seen as a status-based concept, to be achieved either automatically on the basis of genetic links, or upon proof of fitness to carry out the social role and functions it entails. The complication caused

---

[86] See Lowe, Ch 14 of this volume and G. Douglas and N. V. Lowe, 'Becoming a Parent in English Law', (1992) 108 *Law Quarterly Review* 414. As noted above, a parental order is a simplified adoption, where there is no check prior to the court hearing on the suitability of the proposed parents, and where full agreement of the surrogate (and her husband or partner if he is classed as the legal father) is required. This process is clearly more akin to the judicial endorsement of a contract, although surrogacy arrangements are legally unenforceable: Surrogacy Arrangements Act 1985 s 1A (inserted by the Human Fertilisation and Embryology Act 1990).   [87] See M. Murch *et al.*, *Pathways to Adoption*. London: HMSO (1993).

[88] For further detailed consideration of the contractual model in the adoption context, see S. M. Cretney, 'From Status to Contract?', in F. D. Rose (ed), *Consensus ad Idem: Essays in the Law of Contract in Honour of Guenter Treitel*. London: Sweet & Maxwell (1996); N. V. Lowe, 'The Changing Face of Adoption—The Gift/Donation Model versus the Contract/Services Model', (1997) 9 *Child & Fam Law Quarterly* 371.

[89] Lord Chancellor's Department, *Judicial Statistics 1998*, Annual Report Cm 4371. London: The Stationery Office (1999). Table 5.4.

[90] For a concise history, see N. V. Lowe and G. Douglas, n 32 above, 630–1, and the references cited therein.

by social parenthood, as with cohabitation, lies in the range of circumstances it might cover, and the consequential apparent need to scrutinize
these to ensure suitability. Biological parenthood appears more certain.
Where it is in doubt, it can be resolved, in effect conclusively, by means
of DNA tests, and a genetic link is permanent—it can be legally broken
but its inheritance remains for ever. Where the legal goal of stability is
therefore in issue, the certainty of biology appears to trump the varieties
and vagaries of social parenthood. It also reinforces the heterosexual
'norm' of parenthood and obviates the need to consider whether alternative models such as homosexual parenting, or group parenting, should be
accommodated by law.

Alas, this happy steady state is probably destined to be a short-lived
interlude in the continuing twists and turns of legal policy. First, the
apparent legal preference for biological parenthood does not always
reflect what people want—hence the necessity to supersede it through
displacement provisions where donated gametes are used or through
adoption processes.[91] Second, biology may become as uncertain a basis
for parental status as marriage. Genetic and gestational motherhood can
already be separated through egg donation and womb leasing. The ability (albeit not lawful in Britain) to harvest egg cells from aborted fetuses[92]
engenders the possibility of a child being born whose biological mother
never lived, compounding the ethical dilemma already confronted by
the use of sperm (and eventually eggs) taken from a dead donor.[93] Scientific advances in gene modification, most dramatically through
cloning, will render the neat heterosexual basis of conception merely an
option. If human cloning becomes a reality, new problems concerning
who can be classed as one's parent will emerge. Who is the mother of a
clone? And who, if anyone, is the father? Once one reaches this point of
scientific innovation, social parenthood becomes the only sensible basis
for legal status.

CONCLUSIONS

This paper has traced legal developments since the 1950s which demonstrate a shift of focus from adult relationships to that between parent and
child. Marriage came to be seen, at least legally, as a partnership of

---

[91] Or, as described below, through the allocation of parental responsibility rather than
status.
[92] See Human Fertilisation and Embryology Authority, *Donated Ovarian Tissue in Embryo
Research and Assisted Conception: Report*. London: HFEA (1994).
[93] *R v Human Fertilisation and Embryology Authority, ex parte Blood* [1997] 2 All ER 687, CA.
See Deech, Ch 8 of this volume.

equals, with the purpose of marriage as the provision of emotional satisfaction, and the possibility of repudiation once such satisfaction ceases to
be forthcoming. These trends enabled the reconceptualization of marriage as a true contractual relationship, freely entered into, as it was
always said to have been. In the future this is likely to give rise to an individual shaping of its terms and conditions, including the consequences of
breach. Once marriage assumes this shape, it will become no more than
one (even if still the officially favoured) form of relationship giving rise to
legal consequences, to be chosen by the parties from a number of others.
Once marriage becomes optional, the certainty which it can provide as to
the ambit and scope of its ramifications will become irrelevant. Such certainty must be equally on offer when other forms of intimate relationship
are chosen.

Cohabitation became a legitimate alternative to marriage. It can, of
course, be hetero- or homosexual in nature. Anti-discrimination provisions in international law, as well as moral sentiment, may eventually
lead to an increased recognition of homosexual relationships as giving
rise to the same legal consequences as heterosexual cohabitation. But
cohabitation is essentially hard to delineate if justice is to be done to the
wide range of circumstances it embraces. The search for certainty in legal
terms risks the drawing of arbitrary lines in different contexts, with consequential confusion, complexity, and unfairness. The ability to draw up
individual contracts for cohabitation could help to remedy this situation,
if couples could be persuaded to resort to them. The problem is the ap-
athy, ignorance, or incomprehension of so many couples.

Parenthood has appeared to offer a more promising approach to determining the family relationships that should receive legal attention. Concentration upon the parent–child relationship reflects the major
demographic, social, and cultural trends in modern British society. There
remains a consensus that parents should act responsibly towards their
children and remain responsible for them.[94] Parenthood is a status
granted by law regardless of any agreement between the parties, and its
automatic grant avoids the problem of otherwise expecting people to take
active steps to acquire it. Its conception as a status would meet the concerns of those, such as Regan,[95] who fear that a contract-based approach
to the family risks further fragmentation of identity, commitment, and
responsibility. But parenthood itself is a label that can be persuasively
attached to very different forms of relationship. The biological basis,
which at first appears most likely to achieve the certainty being sought, is
found to have its own complications, and in any event to be unsuitable

---

[94] J. Eekelaar, 'Parental Responsibility: State of Nature or Nature of the State?', [1991]
Journal of Social Welfare & Family Law 37.   [95] n 11 above.

and unwanted in certain contexts. There has to be scope for the recognition of social parenthood, yet this has opened up the field to uncertainty.

One way round this dilemma, is to focus upon a new concept in English law—the concept of parental responsibility introduced by the Children Act 1989. As noted above, this embodies 'all the rights, duties, powers, responsibilities and authority which by law a parent of a child has in relation to the child and his property'.[96] It is automatically vested in all mothers, and in married fathers,[97] but it may be acquired by others through guardianship or court order.[98] Grant of parental responsibility to one person does not remove it from the parents who had it originally. It is capable of being shared among several people simultaneously.[99] It is therefore free from the assumption that parenting is carried out by, at most, two people, who are heterosexual. For example, in *G v F (Contact and Shared Residence: Applications for Leave)*[100] the applicant had played a full part in caring for and raising the child of her lesbian partner during their cohabitation. The court granted her leave to seek a shared residence order, which would vest her with parental responsibility for the child, to be shared with the birth mother (and, potentially, with the birth father as well).

Parental responsibility may not be *relinquished* without a court order, but it may be shared by *agreement*, between the mother and unmarried father.[101] It has also been proposed that it be similarly shared by agreement between parents and a step-parent,[102] and a person with parental responsibility may 'arrange for some or all of it to be met by one or more persons acting on his behalf'.[103] It is therefore a concept which could ultimately be used to grant the effects of parenthood, if not the status, to as many different people as are appropriate to the child's needs—by employing a *contractual* mechanism rather than court order—and avoiding the problems involved in privileging certain forms of relationship over others in attempts to prioritize certain 'family values'.

It may be that the next development in this area of the law will therefore be the reassertion of the contract approach, even in relation to

---

[96] s 3(1). Unhelpfully, these are not eludicated further in the statute; for a full discussion see Lowe and Douglas, n 32 above, 350–72.   [97] s 2(1)(2).

[98] Children Act 1989 s 4 (unmarried fathers), 5 (guardianship), 8 and 12 (residence order).

[99] Although how far a holder of parental responsibility may exercise the powers that go with it unilaterally is unclear. While s 2(7) of the Children Act 1989 provides that 'each may act alone and without the other . . . in meeting that responsibility' the courts appear to regard the exercise of some powers as requiring consent. See in particular the issues relating to choice and change of a child's surname, reviewed by the House of Lords in *Dawson v Wearmouth* [1999] 2 WLR 930.   [100] [1998] 2 FLR 799.

[101] Children Act 1989 s 4(1)(b).

[102] Department of Health and Welsh Office, *Adoption Bill—A Consultative Document*. London: Stationery Office Department of Health and Welsh Office (1996), cl 85.

[103] Children Act 1989 s 2(9).

parent–child relationships, through increased and varied use of the concept of parental responsibility. Whether this would ultimately provide certainty and stability in establishing legal family relationships, and whether it would mean that families could shape the legal consequences of their parenting and caring arrangements to fit their own preferences, as is becoming increasingly likely where marriage and cohabitation are concerned, remains unclear. None the less, it is arguable, at least, that in England and Wales the concept of parental responsibility may one day replace the 'institution' of marriage as the prime example of a 'status-contract' in the family sphere.

11

Marriage: An Institution in Transition and Redefinition

WALTER J. WADLINGTON

Surprisingly few states of the US have enacted legislation specifically defining marriage. Early courts introduced Lord Penzance's nineteenth-century language, addressing a potentially polygamous union, that described marriage as the voluntary union of one man and one woman for life.[1] To 'for life' has been added the obvious qualification 'unless sooner dissolved through law.' Although sometimes described as a civil contract, it has long been clear that despite possible contractual analogies and the fact that agreements to enter marriage may be largely contractual, marriage is a special institution regulated by the states with respect to who may enter into the relationship, the legal and economic incidents that may flow from it, and how it can be terminated.[2] In 1970 the Uniform Marriage and Divorce Act, an influential though not widely adopted model for state legislation, defined marriage in more contemporary fashion as

a personal relationship between a man and a woman arising out of a civil contract to which the consent of the parties is essential. A marriage licensed, solemnized, and registered as provided in this Act is valid in this State. A marriage may be contracted, maintained, invalidated, or dissolved only as provided by law.[3]

Regulation of family law in general, and marriage specifically, has long been within the nearly exclusive purview of the individual states.[4] Not until its 1967 decision in *Loving v Virginia*[5] did the Supreme Court of the United States clearly pronounce that the federal constitution could be used by courts as a yardstick to measure the validity of state marriage regulation to any significant degree. Describing marriage as 'one of the "basic civil rights of man," fundamental to our very existence and survival,' the court in *Loving* invalidated a Virginia statutory ban on miscegenous marriages, effectively ending such restrictions then existing in a third of the

---

[1] See the opinion of Lord Penzance in *Hyde v Hyde and Woodmansee*, 1 P & D 130, 35 LJP 57 (1866).
[2] See *Maynard v Hill*, 125 US 190 (1888).
[3] UNIFORM MARRIAGE AND DIVORCE ACT § 201, 9 ULA 100 (1979).
[4] For greater discussion of the constitutional dimensions of family law in the United States, see Jerome A. Barron, Ch 12 in this volume.
[5] 388 US1 (1967).

other states as well.[6] Initial reactions to the decision included suggestions by some that it would be limited to racial discrimination and concern by others that almost all state regulation of marriage had been rendered constitutionally vulnerable. Neither interpretation proved to be correct but realization that many antiquarian restrictions, at the least, were of questionable constitutional validity[7] provided a catalyst for significant legislative change that obviated some otherwise inevitable legal attacks on some plainly unnecessary (and often unfair) provisions. Further attacks on state marriage regulation under the federal constitution have followed, but questions still remain about the ultimate effect of greater ease of judicial challenges stemming from characterization of marriage as a 'fundamental right' by the Supreme Court. In *Zablocki v Redhail,*[8] the Supreme Court invalidated a Wisconsin statute forbidding a resident to marry within its territory without judicial permission unless he was in compliance with an outstanding child support order and could establish that the children under the order were unlikely to become public charges. In a concurring opinion, Justice Powell expressed the view that 'the majority's rationale sweeps too broadly in an area which traditionally has been subject to pervasive state regulation.'[9] He referred specifically to bans on incest, bigamy, and homosexuality as well as such preconditions to marriages as blood testing. Although concern has been expressed by others that application of a true fundamental rights/strict scrutiny approach might have far-reaching and unanticipated implications,[10] there seems to be current acceptance of less inclusive state restrictions in such areas as kinship, age, and marital status. However, limitations of same-sex marriage currently are under attack.[11]

COURTSHIP

Until several decades ago it was much easier to enter a marriage than to terminate one. Regulation of the courtship process has been minimal except for potential exposure to civil damage actions based on conduct such as breach of a marriage promise or seduction under breach of such

---

[6] See Walter Wadlington, *The* Loving *Case: Virginia's Anti-Miscegenation Statute in Historical Perspective,* 51 Va L Rev 1189 (1966).

[7] See Robert Drinan, *The Loving Decision and the Freedom to Marry,* 29 Ohio St L J 358 (1968).

[8] 434 US 374 (1978). Earlier, in the *Loving* case, the Court had described marriage as 'one of the "basic civil rights of man," fundamental to our very existence and survival.' *Loving,* 388 US at 12.

[9] *Zablocki,* 434 US at 396.

[10] See Cathy Jones, *The Rights to Marry and Divorce: A New Look at Some Unanswered Questions,* 63 Wash. ULQ 577 (1985).

[11] See nn 33–5 below, and accompanying text.

a promise. Some jurisdictions also enacted criminal sanctions for breach of promise, usually with the defense that if the promise were renewed and the parties married or the promise was declined, the action could be dropped.[12] The latter provisions, never widespread, have largely disappeared. The civil suits, known as 'heart balm' actions, still remain in some jurisdictions but a majority of the states have either abolished[13] or sharply limited[14] them because of the perception of their widespread misuse or the belief that they are social anachronisms. Concern about misuse stemmed from the hybrid contract/tort nature of the actions which took on the characteristics likely to be most favorable to the plaintiff regarding matters such as damages or statutes of limitation.

LEGAL QUALIFICATIONS FOR MARRIAGE

Each state establishes its own rules about who can enter a valid marriage. They have been fitted into several basic categories below for discussion, but it is important to understand that individual state provisions can vary significantly both in specific details and in the effect of non-compliance with them.

Undissolved Pre-existing Marriage

In our monogamous society, marriage long has been limited to the union of one man and one woman. In *Reynolds v United States*,[15] the Supreme Court of the United States upheld a federal statute criminalizing polygamy in what was then the Utah Territory (before Utah achieved statehood), rejecting a constitutional challenge based on freedom of religion under the First Amendment.[16] One might speculate whether subsequent judicial development of the Establishment Clause would strengthen such an argument today, but there still seems little likelihood that such a challenge would prevail. However, it is important to understand that although *Reynolds* upheld state legislative power to define

---

[12] See Walter Wadlington, *Shotgun Marriage by Operation of Law*, 1 GA L REV 183 (1967).

[13] Although they were common law actions, their demise has come largely through legislation. Other 'heart balm' actions that have met the same fate include criminal conversation and alienation of affections. See, eg NY CIVIL RIGHTS LAW § 80–2 (1992).

[14] There may be limits on the type or elements of damage, the time for bringing an action, or the nature of the proof or scope of the pleadings. Illinois permits only actual damages and requires notice within three months from the date of the breach of promise. See 740 ILL COMP STAT 15/2 *et seq* (West 1993). For a recent strict construction of the statute, see *Wildey v Springs*, 47 F3d 1475 (7th Cir 1995).   [15] 98 US 145 (1878).

[16] The accused was a Mormon and he asserted that male members of his church had a duty to practice polygamy if circumstances permitted this.

marriage as monogamous, it did not address whether a state law defining marriage to permit polygamy or polyandry would be invalid.[17] When Utah became a state after *Reynolds*, a provision that 'polygamy or plural marriages are forever prohibited' was included in its new constitution.[18]

The more typical case that reaches the courts involves remarriage to someone with a living spouse of an undissolved prior union. To deal with long absence or disappearance of a spouse under circumstances indicating probable death, many states have adopted so-called Enoch Arden statutes, named after Tennyson's famous character.[19] These statutes can take several different shapes. Some simply preclude a prosecution for bigamy after reappearance of the presumably deceased spouse,[20] while others provide that such a remarriage is not void.[21] Others provide procedures for declaring that the absent spouse is presumed dead; a remarriage after such a declaration may be considered valid even if the first spouse returns.[22] A further approach provides an action for dissolution—generally not labeled divorce—based on long absence or other circumstances; its protection only applies if the legal steps to dissolve the first union are taken before the reappearance.[23]

A device that can breathe life into a second marriage when one party may in fact have another living spouse is the widespread presumption that the most recent marriage is valid. This presumption requires a party challenging the current union to offer enough evidence that the earlier union was never dissolved to at least shift the burden of proof. Meeting this requirement can be simple if the parties had maintained contact with each other or lived steadily in only one or two communities. However, if they lost contact many years previously and one or both lived a peripatetic existence afterward, the proof requirement can be difficult or impossible to meet.[24]

---

[17] The potential problems of permitting only polygamy or polyandry would raise serious gender discrimination issues today.

[18] Utah Const, Art III, § 1.

[19] When Tennyson's character returned from a voyage seven years after being shipwrecked and discovered that his wife had found another companion, he remained quiet. Today's Enoch would be more likely to announce his presence loudly and go to great lengths to assert his rights. For a general discussion, *see* Walter Wadlington, *Divorce without Fault without Perjury*, 52 Va L Rev 32, 52 (1966).

[20] See eg Va Code Ann § 18.2–364 (Michie 1996).

[21] See SC Code Ann tit 8, § 20–1–90 (Law Co-op 1985).

[22] See eg 23 Pa Cons Stat Ann §§ 1701, 1702 (West 1991).

[23] See NY Dom Rel Law §§ 220, 221 (McKinney 1999).

[24] See eg Estate of Booker, 557 P2d 248 (Or 1976); *DeRyder v Metropolitan Life Insurance Co*, 145 SE2d 177 (Va 1965).

Minimum Age

Requirements of a minimum age for marriage continue to present confusion. Determining their impact in some states can require careful review of judicial opinions even in the face of statutory provisions. Some of those provisions are deeply rooted in the past and often were based on reasons long forgotten or never fully understood. Until the second half of the twentieth century, some states maintained different minimum marriage ages for males and females. A higher age (usually 21) was commonly fixed for males.[25] Today the usual age of majority for marriage is 18 for both sexes[26] but many states allow persons to marry earlier, typically at 16 with parental consent. This has produced questions about the validity of the marriage of a person between 16 and 18 without parental consent that conforms in all other respects with state marriage provisions. In some states such a marriage is valid, while in others it is voidable if an annulment action is commenced before the under-age party reaches majority. Further confusion can arise from a rule in some jurisdictions allowing only the under-age party to bring an annulment action in such circumstances. Finally, some state statutes provide that such a union is absolutely void,[27] precluding any subsequent ratification by the parties after both reach full majority.

Some states permit a woman to marry at an age as low as 14.[28] Although a parent may be eligible to bring an action for annulment on behalf of an under-age party, in some jurisdictions the parent cannot do so over the objection of the minor. Some states provide a possible 'escape hatch' through which a court may be able to consent in the absence of parental permission.

The constitutionality of minimum age statutes and requirements for parental consent below a certain age have been upheld on the theory that such laws do not constitute a total bar to marriage but merely impose a delay.[29]

---

[25] One explanation given for this was that 21 was the age when a male could be expected to saddle up with full armor.

[26] There may be other limitations, such as purchasing alcoholic beverages, which extend until 21. This can produce the anomalous situation in which a male can marry but cannot legally purchase champagne for the wedding reception.

[27] See Va Code Ann § 20–45.1 (Michie 1995). The Virginia statute (§ 20–45.1) confusingly provides that such a marriage is void while § 20–48 provides that only the under-age party can bring an annulment action. See Va Code Ann § 20–48 (Michie 1995).

[28] South Carolina allows a female to marry at age 14 with parental permission but a male must be 16. See SC Code Ann § 20–1–260 (Law Co-op 1985).

[29] See *Moe v Dinkins*, 538 F Supp. 623 (SDNY), *aff'd* 669 F2d 67 (2nd Cir 1982), *cert. denied* 459 US 827 (1982).

Kinship

Restrictions on intermarriage based on kinship were widely revised in the wake of the *Loving* decision. Many states eliminated all or most restrictions based on affinity-based relationships, or on consanguineous relationships carried out to a large number of degrees (such as to cousins). Bars to marriage between siblings by either half or whole blood, and marriages between persons in ascending lines generally were retained. In most states marriages contravening such limitations are absolutely void.

Statutes detailing who cannot intermarry are of several varieties. Some speak in terms of degrees of kinship calculated according to the civil law rule. Others list specifically related categories of persons (eg father and daughter) who may not intermarry. The latter, more cumbersome approach occasionally has created problems under ejusdem generis construction principles. Most statutes on criminal incest and intermarriage restrictions are phrased in terms of relationship through consanguinity or affinity, which do not include adoption. However, some jurisdictions have chosen to follow Uniform Marriage and Divorce Act § 207(2)[30] and include persons related only by adoption in their definitions of siblings and members of ascending and descending lines. Such a restriction was declared unconstitutional by the Colorado Supreme Court in a challenge involving siblings related only by adoption.[31] The court found that the law did not meet even a requirement of minimum rationality and did not further a legitimate interest in furthering intrafamily harmony. It has been suggested that a good case can be made for distinguishing between whether the adoptive relationship is effected when children are older rather than infants, but this argument has been unsuccessful. It is generally difficult to 'undo' an adoption, though in one state a divorced father and his adopted daughter (who had borne a child by him) recently were permitted to vacate their adoption so that they could marry and legitimate their child.[32]

Gender

Challenges to the requirement that parties to a marriage must be of different sexes are by no means new. Until recently, such restrictions were upheld against constitutional attack on the rationale that same-sex unions fall outside the traditional definition of marriage.[33] In *Baehr v*

---

[30] 9B ULA 108 (1979).   [31] See *Israel v Allen*, 577 P2d 762 (Colo 1978).
[32] See *In re Adoption of M*, 317 NJ Super 531 (1999).
[33] See eg *Singer v Hara*, 522 P2d 1187 (Wa 1974); *Baker v Nelson*, 191 NW2d 185 (Minn 1971).

Lewin,[34] the Supreme Court of Hawaii, applying the Hawaii constitution, held that the fundamental right to marry extended to gender discrimination. The practical effect of this was to require the state to justify its refusal to issue single-gender couples a license to marry under a 'compelling interests' test. On remand, the Circuit Court of Hawaii rejected the state's attempt at justification but issued a stay on single-gender marriages while the case was appealed. A series of unusual events, including an abortive attempt to convene a state constitutional convention, ultimately culminated in legislative adoption of a provision for 'reciprocal beneficiary' relationships through which same-sex couples can participate in health benefits plans, hold property as tenants by the entirety, and be entitled to various other provisions that previously flowed only from the traditional marriage relationship.[35]

Sex Transfer Through Surgery

Determining the effect of successful sex transfer surgery on eligibility to marry has been a special problem for courts both in the United States and abroad. Such an operation can involve a transfer from either sex to the other, but male to female procedures are more common and have reached the courts more frequently. After a successful procedure, heterosexual intercourse can take place though conception and childbirth cannot. However, because infertility normally does not disqualify a party from marriage (though fraudulent misrepresentations about fertility might lead to annulment), this alone seemingly should not preclude marriage eligibility. A widely cited 1970 English case held that a post-operative transsexual had not proved that her sex was changed from male to female, in effect deciding that true sex was determined at birth.[36] That approach was rejected by a New Jersey Appeals Court which held that after a successful surgical procedure 'the transsexual's gender and genitalia are no longer discordant; they have been harmonized by medical treatment.'[37] Accordingly, it was held that the party was eligible to marry as a female.

In the United States a substantial number of states have enacted statutory provisions allowing a person to obtain a new birth certificate after a successful sex transfer procedure.[38] These statutes usually do not refer specifically to marriage eligibility, though ordinarily a birth certificate is adequate to obtain a marriage license. The statutes do not address the effect that such an operation might have on an existing marriage that was

---

[34] 852 P2d 44 (Hawaii 1993).   [35] See HAW REV STAT ANN § 572C–1 *et seq* (Michie 1999).
[36] See *Corbett v Corbett*, [1970] 2 WLR 1306.
[37] *M.T. v J.T.*, 355 A2d 204, *cert denied* 364 A2d 1076 (NJ 1976).
[38] See eg CAL HEALTH & SAFETY CODE § 103425 (West 1996); LA REV STAT ANN 40: 62 (West 1999).

celebrated when the party's birth certificate and the medical conditions indicated a different sex.

Physical Capacity

Specific bars to marriage by persons with conditions such as epilepsy or Hansen's disease were largely eliminated several decades ago. However, impotence existing at the time of entry into marriage can be a ground for annulment under statutory provisions in some jurisdictions.[39] In this context impotence refers to inability to copulate rather than infertility, and it may stem from psychological as well as physical causes and be limited to inability to have intercourse with a specific person such as the other spouse.[40]

In assessing the restrictions in this category one also should recognize that fraudulent misstatements about certain health conditions such as sexual capacity may be a ground for annulment. In earlier times, concealment or denying existence of a 'loathsome disease' was another example of this.

Mental Capacity and Voluntariness of Consent

The early judicial decision mentioned at the outset of this chapter as influential in the definition of marriage described the necessary consent as 'voluntary'. This concept has been used by courts to permit annulment when the consent of a party was procured by fraud or duress, or in cases in which a party lacked sufficient mental capacity to understand the nature of the proceeding or the meaning of marriage.

A marriage that might be voidable for fraud or duress nevertheless can be ratified by continuing cohabitation of the parties after the duress ends or the fraudulent misrepresentation becomes known to the defrauded party. Some courts insist that the fraud go to the essentials of the marriage. This requires more than mere 'puffing' about one's general abilities and qualities, and goes more typically to matters such as basic sexual capacity.[41] However, occasionally successful actions have included misstatements about matters such as firmly held religious convictions or prior divorce that might be of such deep concern to the other party that the marriage clearly could not continue.[42] Fraud once was a near omnibus

[39] See eg VA CODE ANN § 20–89.1 (Michie 1995). This statute only permits an action by the aggrieved party (presumably the one who is not impotent).

[40] See *Rickards v Rickards*, 66 A2d 425 (Del 1960).

[41] In this regard it is important to understand that impotence is a specific ground for annulment only if it has been so designated by statute.

[42] See eg *Wolfe v Wolfe*, 389 NE2d 1143 (Ill 1979).

ground for dissolution in states such as New York when divorce grounds there were extremely limited. Some jurisdictions developed two tiers of fraud: if a marriage had not been consummated, simple fraud could be enough but in other instances gross fraud would be required. As a practical matter, if both parties wanted an annulment, there were no children, and the marriage was of short duration, courts once might find fraud in what might be regarded as a precursor to no-fault divorce. This led to substantial variance between the 'law of the books' and the law in practice. With the advent of breakdown divorce, the need for such expansive use of annulment is not so pressing and courts have no good reason to expand their annulment grounds. In fact, it is highly questionable whether the concept of voidable marriage is necessary any longer in many jurisdictions which provide for simple, breakdown divorce.

Several recurring fact situations have surfaced most frequently regarding the degree or type of mental incapacity required for annulment. One involves mentally retarded persons while another focuses on senility or dementia. Some states have tried to use the marriage license system to flag cases for referral to a court to determine capacity.[43] An applicant might be asked whether he or she has been declared legally incompetent, placed under guardianship, or hospitalized at length for mental illness. Except in cases where there has been a formal adjudication or appointment of a guardian, the licensing mechanism simply was not designed to determine whether an applicant might not possess adequate mental capacity, and therefore challenges based on this ground more frequently have been launched after parties have undergone a marriage ceremony. Judicial responses have often borrowed concepts from trusts and estates law to determine whether a party understood the nature of the ceremony and the definition of marriage rather than attempt to develop any functional test of the capacity of a party to function as a spouse at any particular level.[44] This approach is followed in cases of senility as well as retardation.[45]

A final category is temporary incapacity of a person of normal intelligence that is induced by alcoholism or drugs. If the party was so disabled as not to know the nature of the ceremony, the potential for timely annulment is high, based on the absence of voluntariness.[46] However, it is important that annulment be sought without delay and that no steps are taken that might be considered as ratification of the marriage once the party has returned to competence.

---

[43] See 23 PA CONS STAT ANN § 1304(c) (West 1991).
[44] See eg *Edmunds v Edwards*, 287 NW2d 420 (Neb 1980).
[45] See eg *Fischer v Adams*, 38 NW2d 337 (Neb 1949).
[46] See eg *Mahan v Mahan*, 88 So2d 545 (Fla 1956).

ACHIEVING MARITAL STATUS

Unlike obtaining a divorce, getting married does not require that either party have a special nexus with the state where the ceremony takes place, though it may be necessary to complete a brief waiting period and obtain a license there. Some states also require a physical examination, largely to test for venereal diseases such as syphilis and gonorrhea. This once widespread requirement has been eliminated in many jurisdictions, though the prospective spouses may be given information about further testing and the potential of genetic counseling when they obtain a marriage license.

The requirement of a formal ceremony is widespread but not universal. Usually certain civil or religious officials will be legislatively identified as agents who can perform marriages. Though perhaps treading close to the edge of First Amendment limitations, some states have defined who qualifies as a minister or religious official for such a purpose. For example, the Virginia Supreme Court determined that ministers of the Universal Life Church, Inc did not qualify under the Virginia statute establishing who could celebrate marriages because all of the church's members could be ministers and its only dogma was to 'believe that which is right as one defines it for himself.'[47] The court explained that 'The interest of the state is not only in marriage as an institution, but in the contract between the parties who marry, and in the proper memorializing of the entry into, and execution of, such a contract. In the proper exercise of its legislative authority it can require that the person who performs a marriage ceremony be certified or licensed.'[48] The North Carolina Supreme Court[49] refused to recognize a marriage conducted by a member of the same group, which had the effect of voiding a bigamy conviction based on a later ceremonial remarriage by one of the parties.

Informal or Common Law Marriage

In states where a formal ceremony is not required, an informal or common law marriage may take place. It is important to understand that this is a means for achieving marital status rather than a distinct type of marriage. The parties must meet the basic state qualifications on who can marry. There is no common law procedure for ending a common law marriage and thus it can be terminated only through death or judicial divorce. Many states that once permitted common law marriage long ago abolished it prospectively through legislation. But even though less than

---

[47] *Cramer v Commonwealth*, 202 SE2d 911, 915 (Va 1974).   [48] *ibid* at 914.
[49] See *State v Lynch*, 272 SE2d 349 (NC 1980).

a quarter of the states now permit common law marriages to take place within their territory, the doctrine still can have broad impact through the basic conflict of laws rule that a marriage valid where celebrated generally will be recognized in other jurisdictions.[50] Controversies continue to reach the courts over whether a valid common law marriage was effected in another jurisdiction or before its statutory abolition in the particular state. The stakes can be high; if there was a valid common law marriage that has not been dissolved, a later ceremonial union would be bigamous.

The common law marriage process can fall under two basic categories regarding the proof required. One is the case in which the parties go through a ceremony of some sort that is flawed under the law of the state of celebration. Proving the parties' present agreement to marry is simple to establish in such a situation. More difficult proof problems exist in the other category which extends to parties who never undergo a ceremony but who hold themselves out to the community as married to each other. The Supreme Court of Alabama has described the latter as 'public recognition of the relationship as a marriage and public assumption of marital duties and cohabitation.'[51] The assumption is that the parties agreed to be married at some point that may not need to be proven specifically. To establish the necessary 'holding out' or public recognition, courts have used evidence ranging from filing taxes jointly or opening joint bank accounts under a married name, to ordering joint tombstones with their married names on them. Because of the currently prevalent practice of married women to keep their surnames, this is not specially probative that there was no marriage.

Common law marriage once was used in some states to superimpose marital status on couples who might not consider themselves legally married. A key reason was to fix economic rights and duties between such cohabitants, and between the cohabitants and their children. Discrimination sometimes was alleged because common law marriage was most prevalent among persons with low income, and minorities. A major argument for maintaining the doctrine is that it can 'cure' some defective marriages by recognizing a new union after continued cohabitation of the parties following removal of a legal impediment, such as a pre-existing spouse. Absolutely void marriages ordinarily are not ratifiable, and in situations where the parties were unaware of a prior spouse's death or divorce it can be questioned whether they intended to enter a common law marriage after removal of the impediment. Where there was knowledge of

---

[50] Although there can be an exception to this in cases of strongly opposed public policy, this generally is not a problem with regard to this method for achieving marital status.

[51] *Boswell v Boswell*, 497 So2d 479, 480 (Ala 1986).

the changed situation, there must be recognition of a new agreement to uphold the creation of a common law marriage.[52]

The Uniform Marriage and Divorce Act remained neutral on whether to provide for common law marriage, offering optional provisions from which states could choose. However, the Act includes a separate curative proviso that certain marriages prohibited at the time of ceremonialization (including those where there was a pre-existing spouse) will be valid if the parties continue to cohabit after removal of the initial impediment to a valid union.[53] Other curative provisions provide for validity of marriages celebrated in good faith before an unqualified person who professes to have such authority.[54]

Acknowledgment Statutes and Confidential Marriage

A few states have adopted statutes that provide a means for parties jointly to acknowledge an informal union as a marriage and thus create a formal record of its existence.[55]

Several others have provisions for confidential marriage, which permit persons to obtain a license and go through a ceremony to achieve marital status without public notice. In California, for example, all records of a confidential marriage are sealed and can be accessed only by court order.[56] A key practical effect of such a provision is to allow parties who have been living as husband and wife in a jurisdiction that does not recognize informal marriages to achieve marital status with minimal, if any, publicity.

Proxy Marriage

Proxy marriage can allow two persons to go through a valid ceremony even though they are in different jurisdictions at the time. It is important to fix the place where the ceremony takes place and whose law will control because some jurisdictions do not recognize the doctrine as applying to unions that take place within their boundaries. In the absence of a specific judicial opinion or statute,[57] it is not always easy to determine whether a jurisdiction can be validly used as the situs for a proxy marriage. Some

---

[52] See *Byers v Mount Vernon Mills, Inc* 231 SE2d 699 (SC1977).

[53] See UNIF MARRIAGE AND DIVORCE ACT § 207(b), 9 ULA 108 (1979).

[54] See eg UTAH CODE ANN § 30–1–5 (1998).

[55] See eg TEXAS FAM CODE ANN §§ 2.401–2.405 (West 1998); UTAH CODE ANN § 30–1–4–5 (1998). The acknowledgment must take place within a limited time after the parties separate from each other.

[56] See CAL FAM CODE §§ 500 *et seq* (West 1994).

[57] The Uniform Marriage and Divorce Act includes model language for such an enabling provision. See UNIF MARRIAGE AND DIVORCE ACT § 206(b), 9 ULA 107 (1979).

states specifically require that both parties must be physically present together. A typical procedure is for one party represented by an authorized 'stand-in' at the site where the marriage ceremony will take place, with the absent spouse participating also by telephone. Not surprisingly, proxy marriage has been more popular during wartime conditions when one spouse is in another country and easy travel is not an option.

Use of proxy marriage for immigration purposes to marry someone in another country, often labeled 'picture marriage', is limited by a federal statute stating that 'the terms spouse, wife or husband do not include such a mate if both parties were not physically together at their marriage ceremony unless the marriage shall have been consummated.'[58] Ironically, even though parties to such a picture marriage might be validly married (consummation ordinarily is not an essential for validity of a marriage), the spouse abroad may not be eligible for special immigration status.

Putative Marriage

The doctrine of putative marriage can serve some of the 'curative' effects of common law marriage, though with much less sweeping effect.[59] Unlike common law marriage, parties to a putative union are not legally married. Putative marriage is a creature of legislative rather than judicial action. Its effect is to create spousal economic rights in favor of one who in good faith believed that he or she was validly married. Once it is discovered that there was no marriage, further creation of duties is ended.

Once confined largely to community property states in the US, putative marriage legislation recently has been introduced by legislation in some other states, often along with provisions on equitable division of property on divorce.

INVALIDATING A MARRIAGE

An attempted marriage in defiance of one or more of the rules on eligibility, capacity, or procedure for celebration may variously be deemed valid, absolutely void without even a judicial declaration, or voidable so that it can be set aside through timely judicial action commenced by a party with legal standing. Just which result will take place can depend on the strength of the public policy behind such a rule, the timing of the contest, the post-celebration conduct of the parties, or the person who brings the

---

[58] 8 USCA § 1101(a)(35).
[59] See Christopher Blakesley, *The Putative Marriage Doctrine*, 60 Tul L Rev 1 (1985).

action. Application of these variables, as well as confusion over terminology, has produced a morass of judicial gloss for more than a century.

Annulment[60] is the action seeking to declare a marriage invalid because of some legal impediment existing at the time of the ceremony or the purported inception of the relationship in the case of an informal or common law marriage. A decree of annulment means that a valid marriage was never formed and, in the absence of ameliorative provisions to the contrary, that no property or other rights were created. It is thus distinct from divorce, which terminates a valid marriage on a specific date after its inception.[61] The rules on eligibility and procedure for marriage are important because some unions in defiance of them are treated as void while others are only voidable. A void (sometimes labeled 'absolutely void') union is deemed invalid, even in the absence of a judicial declaration of annulment, because it offends some major public policy. Courts will nevertheless entertain actions to annul void marriages for the sake of certainty. A voidable marriage offends some lesser policy, but it will be deemed valid unless it is set aside through a timely annulment proceeding. 'Timely' may be determined by a specific statute of limitations in some jurisdictions. However, it also refers to the doctrine of ratification, under which continued cohabitation of the parties after removal of the impediment rendering the marriage voidable can end any prospect of annulment based upon it.

In theory at least, a void marriage can be challenged even after the death of a party to it. It cannot be ratified by the parties' continued cohabitation after removal of the legal impediment. For example, a bigamous union, in which one party has an already existing marriage, would not be ratified simply by the parties continuing to live together after the death of the partner's pre-existing spouse.[62] Some impediments, such as close kinship (eg brother–sister relationship), cannot be removed.

---

[60] The Uniform Marriage and Divorce Act replaced the term 'annulment' with 'declaration of invalidity', though the model Act's basic approach is similar to that of traditional annulment law. See UNIF MARRIAGE AND DIVORCE ACT § 208, 9 ULA 108 (1979).

[61] Several states still include as divorce grounds what are conceptually annulment grounds that refer to conduct or conditions in existence before the marriage. See eg GA CODE ANN § 19–5–3 (1999). For example, Georgia includes as grounds for divorce intermarriage between persons within certain kinship relationships, mental incapacity at the time of marriage, impotence at the time of marriage, pregnancy of the wife by another man at the time of marriage (unknown to the husband), and fraud or duress in obtaining the marriage. See *ibid*. The reason for this now outmoded approach was to allow a party to seek alimony or other financial relief that was available in divorce but not annulment.

[62] A special curative provision such as Uniform Marriage and Divorce Act § 207(b) discussed in the text to n 51 above, could validate the marriage after continued cohabitation. Also, in a few jurisdictions a new common law marriage might take place after the removal of the impediment.

Use of the terms 'void' and 'voidable' can be confusing or inconsistent in both statutes and judicial opinions. If a voidable marriage is annulled, the 'relation back' doctrine wipes the marital slate clean; this means that no civil effects were produced except to the extent that an ameliorative statute accords them. Examples of the latter are widespread provisions that children of a void or voidable marriage are legitimate, and that certain property or support rights exist upon annulment. Judicial attitudes have differed about whether alimony scheduled to end on the payee's remarriage is revived by annulment of the payee's second union. It is most common today not to permit such revival, either on the theory that the former spouse/payor was entitled to rely on the subsequent marriage[63] or that 'marriage' for this purpose can be defined as referring to a ceremony regardless of whether it is deemed valid.[64] Increased availability of economic relief in an annulment action also has influenced some courts. It is usual for persons drafting separation and settlement agreements to include language specifically providing that a remarriage, whether valid or not, will permanently end alimony if this is the goal that the parties intend.

As noted previously, in a time of very strict divorce laws, annulment sometimes provided an escape hatch from a marriage which the parties did not wish to continue. With the advent of breakdown divorce through a reasonably non-traumatic procedure, parties who wish to dissolve their unions can do so most states without the need for a highly adversarial proceeding. If state laws entitle persons to seek alimony or property then this eliminates a further basis for distinguishing between divorce and annulment. Thus it is now questionable whether the concept of voidable marriage should be retained in many jurisdictions. The stigma once attached to divorce—another reason given by some for retaining annulment—has greatly diminished, though it still exists in the minds of many and it is perhaps the major obstacle to eliminating the voidable marriage concept.

An action that might be viewed as the flip side of annulment is available in some jurisdictions. Known as affirmation of marriage,[65] it permits a party to a marriage whose validity has come under question to seek to have it declared valid in the courts. It operates in a very similar manner to an action for declaratory judgment.

---

[63] See *McConkey v McConkey*, 215 EE2d 640 (Va 1975).
[64] See *Shank v Shank*, 601 P2d 872 (Nev 1984).
[65] See eg Va Code Ann § 20–90 (Michie 1995).

CONFLICT OF LAWS ISSUES

In a country with as many possible rules regarding eligibility, ceremony, and marriage validity as the number of states, determining the applicable law can be highly important. Application of the Full Faith and Credit clause of the federal constitution comes into play primarily when recognition of a sister state's judicial decree rather than the effect of a marriage ceremony is at issue. However, under a basic conflict of laws doctrine, a marriage valid where celebrated is generally valid elsewhere, subject to the exception in favor of a strong public policy to the contrary in the jurisdiction where recognition is sought. Before anti-miscegenation statutes were invalidated under the federal constitution in the *Loving* case, some states with such laws either refused to recognize miscegenous unions or extended only limited effects to them even if they were valid where celebrated. The same can occur today with restrictions that strongly offend a state's public policy, such as very close kinship and bigamous unions. Some states have enacted specific evasion statutes providing that if one of their domiciliaries leaves the state and marries elsewhere with intent to evade such a restriction and then returns to the state, the domiciliary jurisdiction will treat the union as if it had taken place within its territory. Provisions of this sort, one of which was used by the Virginia courts in the *Loving* case, are of less practical importance today because marriages to which they apply usually are deemed void elsewhere as well. An exception that eventually may occur could be for same-sex marriage if one or more states recognize them in the future. In anticipation of such a development, some jurisdictions have enacted specific statutes declaring that they will not recognize same-sex unions,[66] and in 1996 the US Congress passed the Defense of Marriage Act,[67] which provides that:

No State, territory, possession of the United States, or Indian Tribe, shall be required to give to any public act, record, or judicial proceeding of any other State, territory, possession, or tribe respecting a relationship between persons of the same sex that is treated as a marriage under the laws of such other State, territory, possession, or tribe or claim resulting from such relationship.

With regard to the effect on recognition by individual states, the act seems to do little more than restate the basic conflict of laws rule with specific reference to same-sex marriage. However, its definition of marriage as used in any act of Congress or federal regulation is limited in meaning to 'a legal union between one man and one woman as husband and wife . . . '.[68] Because validity of a marriage often had been determined

---

[66] See eg VA CODE ANN § 20–45.2 (Michie 1999 Supp).
[67] 28 USCA § 1738C.   [68] See *ibid*.

by the state definition in the past, this could accomplish significant change in creating a uniform federal rule in matters ranging from immigration to retirement and even evidentiary rules.

CONFOUNDING THE RULES AND EFFECT OF MARRIAGE

In the last quarter of the twentieth century, numerous suggestions and some actual attempts were made to alter significantly the traditional approach to marriage. In 1971 a Maryland legislator introduced a bill in her state that would provide for 'term marriage' in which the parties would be required periodically to renew their marriage if it were to continue.[69] Suggestions also have been made for establishment of geriatric marriage, which would be more freely dissoluble and allow greater flexibility with regard to inheritance and support rights and duties; theories behind this are that child bearing or child raising would not be part of such a union, and parties could easily assure that their property was transmitted along existing family lines. The ease of dissolution would reflect the fact that time is of the essence for the older participants, who would benefit from the combination of companionship and personal support as well as economies of daily living. In 1966, eminent anthropologist Margaret Meade suggested in a popular magazine[70] that a two-step marriage would give young couples a better chance to succeed at marriage. The first step would carry fewer duties between the parties and would be easier to terminate; it should have the practical effect of allowing the parties to know more about each other and determine whether they felt that a lifelong commitment was appropriate for them. Some likened this step to trial marriage. The second step would carry greater intraspousal rights and duties and would be far more difficult to terminate by divorce; ostensibly this would be the relationship in which children were born and reared. The end result of such an approach would have been a smaller group of traditional marital units whose principal focus would be on child rearing.[71]

While the previous suggestions have met with no formal implementation, another has achieved limited enactment. Known as covenant marriage, it does not alter a state's definition of marriage but rather

---

[69] See WALTER WADLINGTON and RAYMOND F. O'BRIEN, CASES AND MATERIALS ON DOMESTIC RELATIONS 24 (4th edn 1998).

[70] See Margaret Meade, *Marriage in Two Steps*, REDBOOK MAG, July 1966, at 48.

[71] After receiving much mail in response to her first article, Dr Meade wrote a sequel indicating that in her view, neither young people nor their elders wanted to make a change in the traditional marriage. See Margaret Meade, *A Continuing Dialogue on Marriage: Why Just Living Together Won't Work*, REDBOOK MAG, Apr 1958, at 44. For other suggestions from three decades ago about possible or probable changes in marriage, see ALVIN TOFFLER, FUTURE SHOCK, Ch 11 (1970).

permits parties at the time of entering to opt for a limited number of divorce grounds that make dissolution far more difficult.[72] A key problem that remains unsolved is whether anything will preclude a party from moving to another jurisdiction with no covenant marriage provision and obtaining a divorce under that state's divorce grounds.

The preceding approaches would require legislation to implement them. More dramatic incursions on the traditional territory of marriage have come through judicial actions that purportedly do not address marriage at all. One group of these has granted greatly increased freedom for parties privately to order relationships between them that parallel or overlap the traditional institution of marriage. This approach is best typified by the Supreme Court of California's decision in *Marvin v Marvin*.[73] The court's opinion described marriage as 'the most socially promising and individually fulfilling relationship that one can enjoy in the course of a lifetime'[74] and pointed out that 'the structure of society itself largely depends upon the institution of marriage'. It nevertheless concluded that in view of the widespread changes in mores and practices 'the judicial barriers that may stand in the way of a policy based upon the fulfillment of the reasonable expectations of the parties to a non-marital relationship should be removed.'[75] It then held that express or implied agreements for non-marital relationships that do not rest on unlawful 'meretricious' consideration would be enforceable. Some commentators strongly approved of the result because previous reform had centered largely on the form, characteristics, and dissolution of legal marriage whereas *Marvin* was important because of its focus on the unmarried as well.[76] However, the decision has been rejected or its scope limited in some jurisdictions that have faced the basic issues.[77]

A variation of this contractual approach is the somewhat amorphous concept of domestic partnership. It is similar to the provision adopted by the Hawaii legislature in the sense of providing various benefits for unmarried couples.[78] In many cases it has resulted from actions taken by individual employers who wish to deal with same-sex unions among their employees. However, as adopted by the City of San Francisco it can apply to both same-sex and opposite-sex relationships.[79]

---

[72] See eg La Civ Code Ann art. 102 (West 1999).
[73] 557 P2d 106 (Cal 1976).   [74] *ibid* at 122.   [75] *ibid*.
[76] See Herma Kay and Carol Amyx, *Marvin v Marvin, Preserving the Options*, 65 Calif L Rev 937, 976 (1977).
[77] See eg *Hewitt v Hewitt*, 394 NE2d (Ill 1979).
[78] For a broader discussion of domestic partnership, see Raymond F. O'Brien, *Domestic Partnership: Recognition and Responsibility*, 32 San Diego L Rev 163 (1995).
[79] For a copy of the City of San Francisco's Form for Declaration of Domestic Partnership, see Walter Wadlington and Raymond F. O'Brien, Cases and Materials on Domestic Relations 41 (4th edn 1998).

Premarital Contracting

At the time of the *Marvin* decision some parties chose to pursue contractual alternatives to marriage because this offered an opportunity for them to establish their own financial rules both during the existence of their relationship and after its termination. A concern expressed by some after *Marvin* was that recognition of property rights of non-marital partners that differed from those established by the state for married persons would make marriage less attractive. Since then many jurisdictions have clarified the rules and expanded the scope of premarital contracting to allow parties privately to order their economic affairs in anticipation of possible termination of their marriage by divorce as well as by death of a party. A major example of this approach is found in the 1983 Uniform Premarital Agreement Act.[80] Now adopted by some twenty-six jurisdictions, it permits almost unlimited contracting scope for the parties except as to support for children of the marriage. With widespread availability of divorce based on breakdown rather than fault, there is now far less incentive to engage in private ordering outside marriage unless the parties regard this as carrying some special cachet. However, it should be recognized that this also can effect considerable change to the face of traditional marriage by dramatically permitting limitation of the states' regulatory role through private contracts that eliminate previously standard rights and duties between spouses and changes that were established through fixed marital property regimes.

Tinkering with the Definition of Family

Although courts and legislatures have shown reluctance to change laws to redefine (or even define) marriage specifically, they may be doing this tangentially through provisions and decisions based on what constitutes a family. This is distinct from the provisions on premarital agreements, alternative contracting, or domestic partnership.

One example is seen in a New York Court of Appeal decision determining that a same-sex relationship amounted to a family so that the survivor was eligible to continue in a rent controlled apartment.[81] Others, often taking a conflicting tack, have dealt with whether a family under zoning laws can include persons who have no traditional marriage.[82]

---

[80] See 9B ULA (1997 Supp).
[81] See *Braschi v Stahl Associates*, 543 NE 2d 49 (NY 1989).
[82] See eg *Moore v City of East Cleveland*, 431 US 494 (1977); *City of Ladue v Horn*, 720 SW2d 745 (Mo App 1986).

Marriage, Reproduction, and Raising Children

Historically marriage was regarded as the place to bear and raise children. Some of the rules stemming from this included once harsh provisions on the illegitimacy of children born out of wedlock.

Following a series of US Supreme Court cases commencing in 1968,[83] most legal restrictions based on illegitimacy are regarded as unlawfully discriminatory even in states that have not specifically abolished the status. A widely influential 1956 decision by the US Supreme Court in *Griswold v Connecticut*[84] dealt with the constitutionality of state prohibitions against the sale and use of contraceptives for non-medical purposes. The decision by a plurality of the Court is best known for initiating development of the right of privacy, which has had dramatic effect in many areas involving personal autonomy. In striking down the state prohibition, the judges focusing on the right of privacy made clear that it was a right of marital privacy that was at issue. Even so, a short time later the Supreme Court extended the same right to unmarried persons,[85] stating that:

It is true that in *Griswold* the right of privacy inhered in the marital relationship. Yet the marital couple is not an independent entity with a mind and heart of its own, but an association of two individuals each with a separate intellectual and emotional make-up. If the right of privacy means anything, it is the right of the *individual*, married or single, to be free from unwarranted governmental intrusion into matters so fundamentally affecting a person as the decision whether to bear or beget a child.[86]

The Court stated that it saw no rational ground for treating married and unmarried persons differently in the case.

Without commenting on the practicality or social desirability of the extension, it is difficult not to view the decision and its rationale as a further change in the historical view of marriage as the special place for conceiving and raising children.

CONCLUSION

Marriage is now in a period of transition and redefinition. Many state legislatures and courts ostensibly cling to a traditional definition of marriage. At the same time, some courts are expanding the definition of 'family' to embrace relationships that are clearly outside the traditional concept of one man and one woman who achieve a special status through

---

[83] See *Lalli v Lalli*, 439 US 259 (1978); *Gomez v Perez*, 409 US 535 (1973); *Levy v Louisiana*, 391 US 68 (1968).　　[84] 381 US 479.　　[85] See *Eisenstadt v Baird*, 405 US 438 (1972).
[86] *ibid* at 453.

their union. Constitutional challenges to same-sex marriage are being launched, while some states and the US Congress are doing their best to avoid any requirement of recognition of marriages that depart significantly from the traditional definition. Legal recognition to new, marriage-like institutions created by contract or through specific legislation is expanding. After the Supreme Court of Vermont held that its state constitution entitles same-sex couples to equality of benefits with opposite-sex couples having a civil marriage license,[87] the Vermont legislature in April 2000 adopted an Act Relating to Civil Unions. Far broader than any such provisions adopted elsewhere in the United States, the Vermont Act provides for civil unions between parties of the same sex neither of whom is already party to another civil union or a marriage. Restrictions on entering such unions include limitations on kinship and minimum age, and the legal benefits and duties achieved for the parties are remarkably similar to those of marriage. Dissolution of civil unions follows the same procedures and is subject to the same substantive rights and obligations involved in the dissolution of marriage.

The new private ordering means that parties entering marriage are increasingly free to 'make their own deal' about including or rejecting rights and duties that once were superimposed on the parties by the state. Some commentators characterize these developments as a movement from status to contract.[88] The ultimate outlook about whether we will have one broadened definition of marriage or many different types of (and labels for) marriage remains unclear but the current trend seems to be toward recognizing multiple types of relationships that can fall within the general rubric of family.

---

[87] See *Baker v State of Vermont*, 744 A2d 864 (2000).

[88] See Elizabeth S. Scott and Robert E. Scott, *Marriage as Relational Contract*, 84 Va L Rev 1225 (1998). For further contemplative thoughts about contract and marriage as well as marriage as contract, see Sanford N. Katz, *Marriage as Partnership*, 73 Notre Dame L Rev 1251 (1998); Mary Ann Glendon, The Transformation of Family Law (1989).

12

The Constitutionalization of American Family Law: The Case of the Right to Marry

JEROME A. BARRON

THE DUE PROCESS ORIGINS OF THE CONSTITUTIONALIZATION
OF FAMILY LAW

If one is to discuss the extension of constitutional protection in the United States to familial relationships with a British audience, one has to begin with a discussion of the very un-British concept of substantive due process. The due process clause of the Fourteenth Amendment has become the textual home for the slow process of accretion by which the constitutionalization of American family law has proceeded. The Fourteenth Amendment, ratified in 1868 and designed to bring the blessings of liberty to the newly emancipated slaves, provides: 'No State shall . . . deprive any person of life liberty or property without due process of law.'[1] This was not, of course, the first appearance of this clause in the American Constitution; it also appears in the Fifth Amendment where it is directly addressed to the federal government. What has the reference to liberty in the due process clause of the Fourteenth Amendment come to mean? One early issue was whether the due process clause was directed solely to procedural matters or whether it had a substantive content. If the latter, how could the substance of that content be determined? The outcome as well as the contours of this issue were summarized by a comment from Justice Brandeis in 1927: 'Despite arguments to the contrary which had seemed to me persuasive, it is settled that the due process clause of the Fourteenth Amendment applies to matters of substantive law as well as to matters of procedure.'[2]

Brandeis's comment reflects a lack of enthusiasm for substantive due process. The substantive due process with which he was familiar was largely concerned with countering the efforts of the states to regulate business through, for example, minimum wage and maximum hours legislation. None the less, there were substantive due process decisions in his time which involved marital rights, and parental rights—rights

I am grateful to David Barron, Brian Bix, and Sanford Katz for their helpful comments on earlier drafts. I am also grateful to Odin Smith and Paula Zimmerman, Class of 2001 and 2000, respectively, at George Washington University Law School, for their excellent research assistance.
[1] US CONST Amend. XIV, § 1.

[2] *Whitney v California*, 274 US 357 at 373 (1927) (Brandeis J, concurring).

which today we would call civil liberties. These rights, not explicitly mentioned in the constitutional text, acquired constitutional status through a process of judicial interpretation which identified them as components of the liberty which the due process clause of the Fourteenth Amendment protected.

Several cases in the early 1920s dealt with the meaning of liberty in the due process clause in the context of a family law issue—the resolution of conflicts between the state and parents concerning the education of children. *Meyer v Nebraska*[3] dealt with a Nebraska statute which prohibited the teaching in school of any subject in any language but English. Furthermore, the teaching of any foreign language until a child had successfully passed the eighth grade was also forbidden. The statute was a product of the anti-German sentiment which existed during World War I. Indeed, the case which raised the issue involved a German language school run by German Lutherans. Children below the eighth grade were being instructed in a German language book about biblical stories. The statute was justified by the state of Nebraska on the ground that it was essential that the English language be the 'mother tongue' of all children reared in Nebraska.[4] This was said to be necessary to prevent the capture of the young and immature by foreign ideals. The Court held that the statute as applied unreasonably interfered with the liberty of a parent to rear his child— a liberty guaranteed by the Fourteenth Amendment.[5] *Meyer* was an early effort to define the meaning of liberty in the due process clause of the Fourteenth Amendment.[6]

---

[3] 262 US 390 (1923).   [4] *ibid* at 398.

[5] The process of defining the extent to which 'liberty' in the due process clause of the Fourteenth Amendment protects the parental right to rear her child still continues. On Sept 28, 1999 the US Court agreed to review the constitutional validity of a Washington state statute which permitted third parties, including grandparents, to petition for visitation rights. WASHINGTON POST, Sept 29 1999, A3. The Supreme Court of Washington had held that the statute violated the protected liberty interests of parents to raise their children free from the interference of the states: '[P]arents have a fundamental right to autonomy in child rearing decisions.' *Troxel v Granville*, 969 P2d 21, 27 (1998). The petition for certiorari challenged the 'flawed premise' of the state Supreme Court that the fundamental right of a parent to autonomy in child rearing was unassailable and that the state could not act on behalf of a child's welfare without a finding of harm to the child or showing of parental unfitness. See *Troxel v Granville*, Petition for Certiorari, p. 2., Supreme Court of the United States, No 99–138, filed July 6 1999. This challenge was successful. See *Troxel v Granville*, 120 S Ct 2054 (2000).

[6] *ibid* at 399. Justice McReynolds explained: 'Without doubt, it denotes not merely freedom from bodily restraint but also the right of the individual to contract, to engage in any of the common occupations of life, to acquire useful knowledge, to marry, establish a home and bring up children, to worship God according to the dictates of his own conscience, and generally to enjoy those privileges long recognized at common law as essential to the orderly pursuit of happiness by free men.'

Meyer v Nebraska has been an influential case because of the constitutional status it confers on a parent's right to have some control, contrary to the wishes of the state, with respect to the education of her children.[7] *Meyer* was an early harbinger of a powerful theme in American constitutional law: the due process clause placed limitations on state control over the family. In this chapter, I will use the evolution of one of these limitations—the freedom to marry—to illustrate the way the process of constitutionalizing rights in the family law area has proceeded in the United States. *Meyer* is one of the foundation stones of that process. Indeed, *Meyer* specifically recognized that the 'right to marry' is a central component of the liberty protected by the due process clause.

The post-World War II years saw some fundamental changes in the relationship between families and the state. In 1953, President Dwight Eisenhower nominated Earl Warren Chief Justice of the United States. Chief Justice Warren served from 1953 to 1968, and his tenure was a time of tremendous dynamism and growth for American constitutional law. During the Warren era, the Supreme Court gave eloquent recognition to the concept that the family itself, particularly the marital relationship, had constitutional rights. The watershed case was *Griswold v Connecticut*.[8] A Connecticut statute which punished the use of contraceptives or the giving of contraceptive information was held to violate a constitutional right, the marital right of privacy. The Court was deeply divided on the doctrinal basis for this ruling. Justice Douglas for the Court sought to base this right of privacy on the penumbras surrounding various clauses in the Bill of Rights. Others on the Court based it on the traditions and collective conscience of the American people. The critical conclusion was that the liberty protected by the due process clause did not 'allow the police to search sacred precincts of marital bedrooms for telltale signs of contraceptives.'[9] Justice Douglas said he derived this conclusion from a 'right of privacy older than the Bill of Rights, older than our political parties, older than our school system.'[10] Despite Justice Douglas's effort to ascribe a venerable status to the right of privacy which he used to invalidate the Connecticut anti-contraceptives law, the result in the case was hardly preordained.[11]

---

[7] Similarly influential in this regard was *Pierce v Society of Sisters*, which struck down an anti-Catholic measure of the Oregon legislature which required all students to attend the state's public schools, thus placing in jeopardy the Catholic parochial schools. See 268 US at 510 (1925). The text of the federal constitution was silent, then as now, about any right of parents to rear their children free from interference by the state. But it was held that this law was an impermissible interference with the right of parents to rear their children. See *ibid.* at 534–5.   [8] 381 US 479 (1965).

[9] *ibid* at 485.   [10] *ibid* at 486.

[11] In *Rochin v California*, the Court had permitted the police to do precisely what they were prohibited from doing in *Griswold*. See *Rochin*, 342 US 165 (1952); *Griswold*, 381 US at 479. They were permitted to invade the marital bedroom through electronic devices. Even

Conservative Justices, hostile to President Franklin Roosevelt's New Deal economic program designed to deal with the Great Depression, had invalidated major New Deal legislation in the 1930s. Justice Douglas was appointed by President Franklin Roosevelt to the Supreme Court in 1939 in the hope that he would not try, as earlier Justices had, to read his economic philosophy into the Constitution.[12] Indeed, an earlier Court during the so-called *Lochner* era had found freedom of contract to be the bedrock of liberty in the due process clause of the Fourteenth Amendment.[13] Was Douglas in *Griswold* conscripting the due process clause for privacy as previous Justices had done with property and freedom of contract? Justice Black in dissent in *Griswold* certainly thought so. The constitutional scholar Herman Pritchett summarized Black's view: 'For Justice Black this creation of a right of privacy out of general constitutional language was an exact parallel to the Court's earlier creation of property rights out of the due process clause.'[14] Douglas himself revealed in the *Griswold* opinion that he was haunted by the charge he was following in the discredited footsteps of some of his Supreme Court predecessors. He sought to counter the charge by trying to distinguish what he was doing in *Griswold* from what had been done by an earlier Court with respect to property rights. Privacy, unlike economic and property rights, flowed from the very language of the Constitution. A right to privacy flowed from the Bill of Rights itself: '[S]pecific guarantees in the Bill of Rights have penumbras, formed by emanations from those guarantees that help give them life and substance.'[15] But the argument in this regard was attenuated to say the least. Justice Stewart in dissent responded that no provision of the Constitution rendered the Connecticut law at issue in *Griswold* invalid.[16]

though some Justices thought this constituted a violation of due process which shocked the conscience of the Court, the majority felt otherwise.

[12] HERMAN PRITCHETT, THE AMERICAN CONSTITUTION 55 (1968).

[13] In *Lochner v New York*, the Court held, 5–4, that a state law setting a maximum hours law for bakery workers violated the freedom of contract protected by the due process clause of the Fourteenth Amendment. See 198 US 45 (1905). Critics of the decision contended that the Court has enforced its own economic ideas rather than the mandates of the constitution: 'This case is decided upon an economic theory which a large part of this country does not entertain. [A] Constitution is not intended to embody a particular economic theory, whether of paternalism and the organic relation of the citizen to the State or of *laissez faire*.' *ibid* at 75. Legal historian Morton Horwitz stated the historical consensus: 'And while judges and jurists of the *Lochner* era were virtually unanimous in concluding that it was inappropriate to go outside of the Constitution, the charge that they did so nevertheless has been widely shared among constitutional historians.' MORTON HORWITZ, THE TRANSFORMATION OF AMERICAN LAW 1870–1960. THE CRISIS OF LEGAL ORTHODOXY 157 (1992).

[14] PRITCHETT, n 12 above, at 687.   [15] *Griswold*, 381 US at 484.

[16] The fact was, contended Justice Stewart, that there was no 'such general right of privacy in the Bills of Rights, in any other part of the Constitution, or in any case ever before decided by this Court.' *ibid* at 530.

In truth, the substantive due process charge stung. Indeed, it stung so deeply that in *Roe v Wade*, the abortion rights case, Douglas made yet another effort to distinguish what he and his colleagues were doing in *Griswold* and *Roe* from what their predecessors had done vis-à-vis property rights. They were not reviving substantive due process. *Griswold* had not resurrected the idea 'that "liberty" within the meaning of the due process clause of the Fourteenth Amendment was a vessel to be filled with one's personal choices of values.'[17] But the expansion of the privacy right from the protection of a right to receive contraceptive information by the marital couple to the protection of woman's right to terminate her pregnancy indicated that a new constitutional era had begun. The word 'liberty' in the due process clause of the Fourteenth Amendment was proving to be a cup very hospitable to the new wine of marital rights and, ultimately, of individual rights.

The *Griswold* case set in motion an entirely new approach to state control of the marriage relationship. Other infringements on the marital relationship were challenged. A landmark development in the evolving constitutional rights that began to surround the marital relationship was *Loving v Virginia*.[18] The great case of *Brown v Board of Education*[19] held that state-mandated public school segregation violated the equal protection clause of the Fourteenth Amendment. Did this mean that other invidious state-imposed racial classifications such as state law banning interracial marriage were also unconstitutional? This was not a question that the Court in the 1950s and 1960s was anxious to answer. It was not until 1967 that the Supreme Court felt that the time was right to confront the mores of the states of the Old Confederacy. In the aptly named *Loving* case, Chief Justice Warren declared that the Court was ready to resolve a Constitutional issue 'never addressed by this Court.'[20] Did a Virginia statute prohibiting marriages between persons of different races violate the equal protection and due process clauses of the Constitution? The Court's answer to this question was that both clauses of the Constitution were violated.

In the *Loving* case, *Griswold* played no part. Liberty and equality, not privacy, were at the center of the rationale of the Court in the *Loving* case.[21] At the Supreme Court level, Virginia contended that regulation of

---

[17] *Roe v Wade*, 410 US 113 at 213 n 4 (1973).   [18] *Loving v Virginia*, 388 US 1 (1967).

[19] 347 US 483 (1954).   [20] *Loving*, 388 US at 2.

[21] The Supreme Court of Appeals of Virginia in *Naim v Naim* rejected a constitutional attack on the Virginia interracial marriage ban statute a year after *Brown v Board of Ed*. had been decided. See *Naim*, 87 SE 2d 749 (1955); *Brown*, 347 US at 483. The Supreme Court of Appeals, blind to the egalitarian tide swept in by *Brown* in 1954 and the new *Zeitgeist* it created, validated the statute by relying on the state interests supposedly served such as preserving 'racial integrity' and preventing a 'mongrel breed of citizen.' *Loving*, 388 US at 7.

marriage was a state responsibility under the Tenth Amendment. Chief Justice Warren conceded that 'marriage is a social relation subject to the States' police power.'[22] But this did not mean , nor did the state contend, that 'its powers to regulate marriage are unlimited notwithstanding the commands of the Fourteenth Amendment.'[23]

The right to marry could not be limitlessly regulated by the state: 'The Fourteenth Amendment requires that the freedom of choice to marry not be restricted by invidious racial discriminations. Under our Constitution, the freedom to marry, or not marry, a person of another race resides in the individual and cannot be infringed by the State.'[24] Chief Justice Warren protected the marital relationship from state infringement by declaring that the individual had a constitutional right to marry free from invidious racial classifications. The constitutional cloak of protection which the Court extended to the marital relationship had a spillover in the protection of individual rights. A doctrinal bridge from the autonomy and sanctity of the marital relationship to a similar status for individual autonomy and the relationship of unmarried persons was soon constructed.[25]

THE EQUAL PROTECTION CLAUSE AND ITS ROLE IN THE PROTECTION OF UNCONVENTIONAL RELATIONSHIPS IN FAMILY LAW

Griswold protected the rights of the individuals who were parties to the marital union. The state was precluded from extending its scrutiny into the bedroom to ascertain whether or not a married couple were using contraceptives. But what of the right of unmarried individuals? Unmarried persons could not claim the privacy protection which now extended to the marital relationship. Were statutes which limited access to contraceptives for unmarried persons still valid? Exactly such an issue presented itself to the Court in *Eisenstadt v Baird*.[26]

---

[22] The Supreme Court of Appeals at 7.

[23] *ibid*. Relying on *Skinner v Oklahoma*, 316 US 535 (1942) and *Maynard v Hill*, 125 US 190 (1888), Chief Justice Warren stated: 'Marriage is one of the "basic civil rights of man," fundamental to our very existence and its survival.' *Loving*, 388 US at 12. Justice Field in *Maynard* described marriage without attributing to it any constitutional status. Yet he did refer to it as part of the 'fundamental rights of the citizen.' 125 US at 205. This, of course, is written at a time when fundamental rights and constitutional rights were not necessarily co-extensive nor did referring to rights as fundamental rights mean they could not be regulated: 'Marriage, as creating the most important relation in life, as having more to do with the morals and civilization of a people than any other institution, has always been subject to the control of the legislature. That body prescribed the age at which persons may contract to marry, the procedure or form essential to constitute marriage, the duties and obligations it creates, its effects upon the property rights of both, present and prospective, and the acts which may constitute grounds for its dissolution.' *ibid* at 205.

[24] *Loving v Virginia*, 388 US 1 (1967).   [25] See *Eisenstadt v Baird*, 405 US 438 (1972).

[26] *ibid*.

William Baird, a faculty member, exhibited a contraceptive article while giving a lecture on contraception to a group of students at Boston University. He invited the members of the audience to come to the stage and help themselves to the articles. One woman did so and he personally handed her a package of vaginal foam. For these activities he was arrested and indicted for exhibiting contraceptive devices and for giving one such device away.

Establishing a right of unmarried persons to acquire contraceptive information as a part of liberty under the due process clause of the Fourteenth Amendment was not to be easily accomplished. The liberty protected by the due process clause against infringement by the Connecticut legislation in *Griswold* was now understood to extend to the marital relationship. That relationship was protected by the fundamental right of privacy which was a component of liberty. Could unmarried persons claim such a right as part of liberty under the due process clause of the Fourteenth Amendment? Justice Brennan neatly avoided the due process question by deciding the case on equal protection grounds.

The due process clause in *Griswold* was deemed to be infringed by the Connecticut law because it infringed a right of privacy—a component of liberty. But the right of privacy itself was not without limits; it was anchored at least for some of the Justices in the marital relationship. The *Eisenstadt* case therefore was a real challenge. The Court of Appeals below declared that there was a fundamental human right of access to contraceptives and that denial of contraceptives to unmarried persons by the state posed problems of unwanted pregnancy and illegitimacy. The Court of Appeals held that the denial of contraceptives to unmarried persons in Massachusetts was thus beyond the power of the state.[27] However, the Supreme Court did not go so far: '[W]hatever the rights of the individual to access to contraceptives may be, the rights must be the same for the unmarried and the married alike.'[28]

In a critical passage, Justice Brennan said if the distribution of contraceptives to married persons cannot be prohibited, a ban on such distribution to unmarried persons is similarly invalid. Justice Brennan conceded that in *Griswold* the 'right of privacy inhered in the marital relationship.'[29] But he insisted that 'the marital couple is not an independent entity with a mind and heart of its own, but an association of its two individuals each with a separate intellectual and emotional makeup.'[30]

Justice Brennan achieved a *tour de force* in wresting protection against the state for individuals in unconventional sexual relationships on the basis of the protection accorded the marital relationship. Professor Mary Ann

---

[27] *Baird v Eisenstadt* 429 F2d 1398 at 1402.
[28] *Eisenstadt*, 405 US at 453.   [29] *ibid*.   [30] *ibid*.

Glendon, a skeptical observer of the rise of constitutional protection for radical individualisism, observed: 'But if one attends to their outcomes, Lawrence Tribe seems correct in saying that what the Court has characterized as family rights often turn out to be rights for individuals.'[31] *Eisenstadt* extended the frontiers of right of privacy from the marital relationship in *Griswold* to individual freedom with respect to reproductive rights, or, as it has become famously known, the woman's right to choose.[32]

The *dicta* about privacy in *Eisenstadt* helped to create the constitutional climate for the announcement in *Roe v Wade*,[33] only two years later, that a woman had rights, even against the wishes of the state, on whether or not to bear a child. The powerful constitutional dynamic of *Griswold* moved protection of personal relationships from the traditional and conventional marital relationship to protection of less conventionally protected sexual relationships such as those between unmarried persons. The protection of individual freedom even within unconventional family relationships spun off ever new progeny.[34]

The technique employed by Justice Brennan in *Eisenstadt* was ideal for extending constitutional protection to relationships and activities that previously had not been protected as part of liberty under the due process clause: take a limited right which had been recognized under the due process clause and extend it beyond the boundaries set at the time of the recognition of the right by applying the equal protection clause. *Griswold* held that a fundamental right of privacy, flowing from the word 'liberty' in the due process clause of the Fourteenth Amendment, extended to the marital relationship. In *Eisenstadt*, Justice Brennan said that, after all, the basic protection was for the individuals who comprised the marital relationship rather any marital entity. Without therefore specifically extending the fundamental right of privacy to embrace a right of unmarried persons to have access to contraceptive information, the equal protection clause was instead applied to reach that precise result. Was it defensible

---

[31] Mary Ann Glendon, The Transformation of Family Law 103; see also Lawrence Tribe, American Constitutional Law 987 (1978). Professor Glendon stated 'Equality between spouses in a system like the American one tends to be envisioned as existing within a family of independent individuals rather than within a community of life.' Glendon, *ibid* at 103. Yet she notes that even American family law is not entirely individualistic. See Bruce C. Hafen, *The Constitutional Status of Marriage, Kinship and Sexual Privacy—Balancing the Individual and Social Interests*, 81 Mich L Rev 463 (1983). Professor Glendon has also pointed out that protection for problems of 'informal families' has proceeded apace. See Glendon, above at 282–3. Unmarried persons have been given protection particularly with regard to their biological but illegitimate offspring. See *Stanley v Illinois*, 405 US 645 (1972).

[32] 'If the right of privacy means anything, it is the right of the individual, married or single, to be free from unwanted governmental intrusion into matters so fundamentally affecting a person as the decision whether to bear or beget a child.' *Eisenstadt*, 405 US at 453.

[33] *Roe*, 410 US at 113.

[34] *Stanley v Illinois* is illustrative of this protection. See 405 US at 645.

to give a right of access to contraceptive information to married persons and deny it to unmarried persons? Such a distinction or discrimination could not be rationally justified. *Eisenstadt* extended contraceptive freedom from the married couples protected in *Griswold* to the unmarried persons who were left unprotected by that decision.[35]

The key to expansion of constitutional protection for unconventional relationships was to view the due process clause as protecting the liberty of the individual person. A component of that liberty, the right of privacy, was the vehicle for the radical individualism extolled by Brennan in dicta in *Eisenstadt*.[36] In *Eisenstadt*, Chief Justice Burger in dissent argued without success that Justice Brennan's opinion for the Court and Justice White's concurrence revived substantive due process and trespassed on the constitutional prerogatives of the states.[37] *Eisenstadt*, as we have seen, extended a right of contraceptive information to unmarried persons—a right married people had already been accorded.

The equal protection clause itself has been used to protect the freedom to marry from state restraint. A Wisconsin statute imposed criminal sanctions on any person who had child support obligation and who married without approval of a court. The law provided that approval would not

[35] Constitutional protection moved from its moorings within the conventional married relationship to a broader and less conventional range of hitherto unprotected relationships. See *Stanley*, 405 US at 645. In *Stanley*, the Court granted constitutional protection *vis-à-vis* the state to the natural but unmarried father who showed a commitment to his children. See *ibid*. *Moore v City of East Cleveland*, showed that the frontiers for defining the conventional family were becoming ever more porous. See 431 US 494 (1977). *Moore* extended protection against the state beyond the nuclear family to reach grandmothers and nephews. See *ibid*.

[36] In the retreat from *Roe v Wade*, signaled by *Planned Parenthood of Southeastern Pennsylvania v Casey*, the right of privacy had completely vanished from the scene. See *Roe*, 410 US at 113 ; *Casey*, 505 US 833 (1992). No mention was made of it in the plurality opinion for the Court in *Casey*. See 505 US at 833. Similarly, *Michael H. & Victoria D. v Gerald D.*, was extended by Scalia to the unitary family and not to the individual freedom rights of unconventional fathers. See 491 US 110 (1989).

[37] See *Eisenstadt*, 405 US at 465 (Burger, C J, dissenting). Massachusetts had mandated that contraceptives not be distributed by anyone not a physician or a pharmacist. Baird was in neither of these categories and was therefore validly convicted. The legitimacy of the state prosecution of Baird, a person not authorized to distribute contraceptives under Massachusetts law, was before the court, not the right of married persons or unmarried persons to secure contraceptives. The Massachusetts law was valid unless it is irrational. The Court declared that the statute had no legitimate state purpose. Burger in dissent concluded that the law was rationally related to the accomplishment of some legitimate state purpose. It is said, he observed, that the statute was originally enacted as a matter of morality and not health: 'I fail to see why the historical predominance of an unacceptable legislative purpose makes incredible the emergence of a new and valid one.' *ibid* at 467. One is here reminded that at the time of the *Bowers v Hardwick* case the Georgia sodomy statute, since repealed, was originally enacted out of moral disapprobation of sodomy. See 478 US 186 (1986). Some *amici* in *Bowers* argued that the prosecution of homosexual sodomy in *Bowers* could be justified as a way of limiting the spread of AIDS. See *ibid*. If a statute was enacted for an invalid purpose, can it be redeemed by a valid state purpose even though that justification is offered long after the statute's enactment? Burger clearly thought the answer to this was in the affirmative.

be given if support obligations were not met or if the individual involved could not prove that children would not become public charges. In *Zablocki v Redhail*,[38] the Wisconsin law was struck down.[39] The classification infringed the fundamental right to marry. Therefore, it had to be justified by state interests which were sufficiently important to warrant the restriction and further, the law had to be narrowly tailored to accomplish those interests. The Wisconsin law failed this heightened standard of review. To create a classification which limits the right to marry of persons who have support obligations but do not have custody of their children violated the fundamental right to marry.

In striking down the Wisconsin law, Justice Marshall for the Court relied on the interracial marriage case, *Loving v Virginia* above for the fundamental importance of a right to marry. *Griswold* was relied on for its holding that the right to marry was a component of the fundamental right of privacy implicit in the due process clause of the Fourteenth Amendment. The rationale for marriage as a fundamental right offered in *Griswold* contrasts with that offered in *Zablocki*. In Justice Douglas's *Griswold* opinion, the focus is on the intimacy of the marriage relationship. Justice Douglas described the intimacy of the marriage relationship as so intense that it verged on the sacred. Marriage was more than a bilateral relationship; it was a 'bilateral loyalty.'[40]

In *Zablocki*, the marital relationship is looked at through a different lens than it is in *Griswold*; it is described as on the same level as 'procreation, childbirth, child-rearing, and family relationships.'[41] The *Zablocki* opinion stresses that the freedom to marry is a fundamental right. While this does not mean that no regulation of the marriage relationship is possible, *Zablocki* makes it clear that serious scrutiny will be given to state regulation which substantially interferes with the freedom to enter into the marriage relationship. Indeed, in a concurring opinion, Justice Stevens pointed out that there was a world of difference between classifications which are based on marital status and classifications which determine who may enter into the marital relationship. Distinctions based on marital status

[38] 434 US 374 (1978).

[39] In a demonstration of the way protection of one right begets the conferral of protection on others, Justice Marshall for the Court observed: 'It is not surprising that the decision to marry has been placed on the same level of importance as decisions relating to procreation, childbirth, child-rearing, and family relationships. As the facts of the case illustrate, it would make little sense to recognize a right of privacy with respect to other matters of family life and not with respect to the decision to enter the relationship that is the foundation of the family in our society. [I]f appellee's right to procreate means anything at all, it must imply some right to enter the only relationship in which the State of Wisconsin allows sexual relations to legally to take place.' *ibid* at 386.   [40] See *Griswold*, 381 US at 486.

[41] *ibid* at 681. As Justice Marshall puts it: '[I]f the right to procreate means anything at all, it must imply some right to enter the only relationship in which the State of Wisconsin allows sexual relations legally to take place.'

were common in many fields of law—social security regulations, tax laws, and selective service rules. Barriers to marriage itself, however, warranted particular scrutiny.[42] As we shall see subsequently, the serious scrutiny that *Zablocki* brought to state-imposed barriers on entry into marriage have proven influential in contemporary litigation about same-sex marriage.

In *Zablocki* the Court chose to place its decision under the equal protection clause rather than the due process clause of the Fourteenth Amendment.[43] Justice Stewart in a concurring opinion protested that reliance on the equal protection clause was thoroughly mistaken because the problem the case posed was not one of discriminatory classifications but of an unjustified intrusion by the state on a constitutionally protected freedom.[44]

The interplay between the liberty protected by the due process clause and the equal protection clause has been a significant factor in extending constitutional protection to many of the relationships embraced by family law. The extension of contraceptive freedom to unmarried persons from its original moorings in the marital relationship is a case in point. None the less, it must also be pointed out that the use of federal constitutional interpretation by judges to provide new protection to changing family and sexual relationships—whether under the equal protection clause or the due process clause—is looked on with less favor by today's Supreme Court.

The expansive phase of new protection for familial relationships based on substantive due process has come, if not to a close, at least to a halt. Illustrative is *Michael H. & Victoria D.*[45] There a challenge was brought to a California statute which established a presumption based on the English common law, that a child born to a married woman living with her husband is a child of the marriage if the husband is not impotent or sterile.

[42] Of course, not all barriers imposed by government on marriage were impermissible. For example, the state could prohibit marriage to a child, a relative, or a person with venereal disease. But this Wisconsin law made a person's economic status the determinant of the person's eligibility for marriage. By way of illustration, the statute barred poor parents from marriage 'even though their intended spouses are economically independent.' *ibid* at 691.

[43] Justice Marshall declared: 'When a statutory classification significantly interferes with the exercise of a fundamental right, it cannot be upheld unless it is supported by sufficiently important state interests and is closely tailored to effectuate only those interests.' *ibid* at 682.

[44] The constitutionally protected freedom that Stewart was concerned about was not the right to marry. Indeed, he did not think that there was 'a "right to marry" in the constitutional sense.' *Ibid* at 684. But the due process clause of the Fourteenth Amendment protected freedom of personal choice in matters of marriage and family life. Whether the Wisconsin law violated that freedom could only be answered by a subtle and complex inquiry into matters such as the nature of the individual interest affected by the state law and its relationship to the concerns the legislature had for enacting it. Such an inquiry poses a risk to representative democracy. But it is not diminished or disguised by moving from the due process clause to the equal protection clause. Attempting to avoid the charge of reviving the discredited doctrine of substantive due process by taking refuge in the equal protection clause served 'no purpose but obfuscation.' *ibid* at 686.   [45] 491 US 110.

Despite the fact that blood tests performed on the putative natural father indicated a 98.07 per cent probability of paternity, the statute was upheld despite the substantive due process claims of the natural father. The natural father contended that pursuant to *Stanley v Illinois*,[46] he had established a parental relationship with the child. Indeed, he had brought a filiation proceeding to establish paternity and a right to a visitation. In a plurality opinion for the Supreme Court the substantive due process claim of the natural father was rejected. This result was reached on the basis that the natural father had failed to show a liberty interest that merited protection. The states, Justice Scalia said, had never granted recognition to the parental rights claims of the natural father of a child who was conceived and born into an existing marital relationship. Unlike the marital relationship, for example, the traditions of the American people had never granted protection to relationships such as the one the natural father had sought to establish.

A particularly interesting feature of the *Michael H* case was that Justice Scalia argued in a footnote, joined only by Chief Justice Rehnquist, that the inquiry to determine whether a right was fundamental for substantive due process purposes should 'refer to the most specific level at which a relevant tradition protecting or denying protection to the asserted right can be justified.'[47] In Scalia's view, there was such a specific tradition and it 'unqualifiedly' denied protection to the natural father in these circumstances. Justice Brennan in dissent attacked Scalia's restrictive view of substantive due process: the purpose of the due process clause was not to 'confirm the importance of interests already protected by the majority of the states.'[48] The Court has not accepted Justice Scalia's 'specific level' theory to limit the use of substantive due process for the recognition of new constitutional rights in family law.

The substantive due process approach inaugurated by the *Griswold* case is clearly now in a defensive rather than an expansive mode. Yet there is still considerable energy in the process *Griswold* began. For example, the common law constitutionalism described above has proven capable of a parallel dynamic development on the state constitutional level. The movement to establish acceptance of same-sex marriage is illustrative.

STATE CONSTITUTIONS: THE RIGHT TO MARRY—DOES IT INCLUDE
THE RIGHT TO SAME-SEX MARRIAGE?

The Hawaii state constitution, amended in 1978, protects the right of privacy in specific terms. The Hawaiian courts concluded that federal

---

[46] 405 US 645.   [47] *Michael H.*, 491 US at 127.   [48] *ibid* at 141.

constitutional cases such as *Griswold*, *Eisenstadt*, and *Roe* should guide the interpretation of the right of privacy guarantee in the Hawaii constitution.[49] The Hawaii Supreme Court noted pointedly that the United States Supreme Court in *Zablocki v Redhail* had held that the right to marry was part of the fundamental right of privacy implicit in the due process clause. But that did not resolve the matter. The question was not whether the right of privacy under the Hawaiian constitution included the freedom to marry. The question was a different and novel one—does the freedom to marry extend to couples of the same sex? On this question, federal constitutional law could not provide specific guidance. The United States Supreme Court had never passed on the matter. However, the Supreme Court of Hawaii was in no doubt that under United States Supreme Court case law the fundamental right to marry under the federal constitution 'presently contemplates unions between men and women.'[50]

The question for the Supreme Court of Hawaii was whether its interpretation of the right to privacy in its state constitution should go beyond the present reach of that right in federal constitutional law. Should the Supreme Court of Hawaii recognize a new fundamental right—the right to same-sex marriage? In order to answer this question the Hawaii Supreme Court undertook two lines of due process analysis in federal constitutional law. Could a right of same-sex marriage be found in the traditions and collective conscience of our people? Could such a right be found in the concept of ordered liberty? The court concluded on the basis of these inquiries that the same-sex couples who sought to marry in Hawaii contrary to its statutes had no 'fundamental right to same-sex marriage arising out of the right to privacy or otherwise.'[51]

Although the due process route was closed, was there another avenue? What about the equal protection clause of the Hawaiian constitution? The Supreme Court of Hawaii thought that the trial court erred on the equal protection issue. The equal protection clause of the Fourteenth Amendment is a model of brevity. No state shall 'deny to any person within its jurisdiction the equal protection of the laws.' The equal protection component of the Hawaii Constitution in Article I, Section 5, is longer and more detailed: '[n]o person shall . . . be denied the equal protection of the laws, nor be denied the enjoyment of the person's civil rights or be discriminated against in the exercise thereof because of race, religion, sex or ancestry.' The trial court had ruled that homosexuals were not a suspect class under the Hawaiian constitution. The Supreme Court of Hawaii said that it was irrelevant whether homosexuals are a suspect class because the validity of the statute was not dependent on whether they were homosexuals. The refusal of the Hawaiian Department of Health to

---

[49] *Baehr v Lewin*, 852 P2d 44, 55 (1993). [50] *ibid* at 56. [51] *ibid* at 57.

allow same-sex couples to marry deprived them of 'access to a multiplicity of rights and benefits that are contingent upon that status.'[52]

A Hawaii state law[53] restricted the marital relation to a male and a female. The state Supreme Court reasoned that this statute denied same-sex couples access to the rights and benefits which the state bestowed on marital status. This in turn presented an important issue: were same-sex couples denied the equal protection of the law as guaranteed by the state constitution of Hawaii? The State Department of Health said 'No' to this question. Same-sex couples, it was contended, are denied the right to marry not because of impermissible discrimination but because of their biological incapacity to meet the definition of the status they seek to attain. The Hawaii Supreme Court responded that a similar contention had been made and rejected about interracial marriage when the *Loving* case was litigated: 'Constitutional law may mandate, like it or not, that customs change with an evolving social order.'[54] The Supreme Court of Hawaii concluded that the Hawaii constitution 'prohibits state-sanctioned discrimination against any person in the exercise of his or her civil rights on the basis of sex.'[55] The freedom to marry was a fundamental civil right. Denial of that fundamental right on the basis of sex trespassed impermissibly on the equal protection guarantee in the Hawaii constitution.

The Supreme Court of Hawaii vacated the lower court's order and judgment in favor of the state. The matter was remanded to the lower court for trial on the following issue—could the state justify its law denying a marriage license to two members of the same sex under the strict scrutiny standard of review? The demanding strict scrutiny standard had to be used because sex under the Hawaii constitution is a suspect classification. In equal protection law such classifications are valid only if they meet the strict standard of review. This meant that the state had to demonstrate that the law furthered a compelling state interest, and the classification was narrowly drawn to avoid the unnecessary infringement of constitutional rights.

The trial court held that the state failed to show that the adverse consequences of same-sex marriage justified its prohibition.[56] Although the state had the burden of proof, expert witnesses were offered by both sides. A crucial issue was whether same-sex couples could be good parents.[57] An expert witness for the state testified that same-sex relationships do not provide the same type of learning model or experiences as do

---

[52] *Baehr v Lewin*, 852 P2d 58 (1993).   [53] HRS Sec 572–1.   [54] *Lewin*, 852 P2d at 63.
[55] *ibid* at 60.
[56] *Baehr v Miike*, No. 91–1394, 1996 WL 694235 (Haw Cir Ct Dec 3 1996).
[57] One of the editors of this volume, Professor Sanford N. Katz, has pointed out to the author the anomaly that the court here makes the validity of same-sex marriage rest on

male–female relationships. But the same witness also testified that same-sex couples are as capable of good parenting as male–female couples and should be allowed both to adopt children and to provide foster care. The plaintiffs for their part offered expert testimony that there was insufficient data showing that gay fathers or lesbian mothers were any more or less capable of good parenting than heterosexual parents.

The trial court concluded that the state had failed to show that any adverse consequences would flow from invalidating the law limiting marriage to one male and one female. Other than asking the state court to take judicial notice of the federal Defense of Marriage Act,[58] the state had failed to show any adverse impacts which would result from the refusal of other jurisdictions to give effect to recognition of same-sex marriage in Hawaii. The trial court held that the Hawaii law[59] was unconstitutional on its face and as applied under the equal protection clause of the Hawaii Constitution, Art I, Sec 5. The State Department of Health was enjoined from denying an application for a marriage license solely because the applicants were of the same sex. The Hawaii Supreme Court affirmed the lower court decision without opinion.[60]

The Hawaii courts have not yet had the last word on this issue. On July 22 1998, a bill to amend the state constitution passed the Hawaii legislature. The matter was put to a referendum which posed the following question: 'Shall the constitution of the state of Hawaii be amended to specify that the legislature shall have power to reserve marriage to opposite sex couples?' On November 4 1998, nearly 70 per cent of the voters answered, 'Yes.' The Hawaii legislature subsequently granted marital-type benefits to same-sex couples who are unable to legally marry.[61]

---

whether same-sex parents can be 'good' parents. Yet good parenting is not a test for the validity of opposite-sex marriages. Indeed, many such marriages are childless.

[58] 28 USCA § 1738C. The Defense of Marriage Act (DOMA) was signed into law on Sept 2 1996. The statute is designed to free states from being required by the Full Faith and Credit Clause of the US Constitution to recognize same-sex marriages valid in other states. The statute was a congressional reaction to the decision of the Hawaii Supreme Court in *Baehr v Miike*. See 852 P2d at 44. DOMA provides as follows:

'§   1738C. Certain acts, records, and proceedings and the effect thereof.

No State, territory, or possession of the United States, or Indian tribe, shall be required to give effect to any public act, record, or judicial proceeding of any other State, territory, possession, or tribe respecting a relationship between persons of the same sex that is treated as a marriage under the laws of such other State, territory, possession, or tribe, or a right or claim arising from such relationship.'

The Full Faith and Credit Clause of the US Constitution, Art IV, Sec 1 provides: 'Full Faith and Credit shall be given in each State to the public Acts, Records, and judicial Proceedings of every other State. And the Congress may by general Laws prescribe the Manner in which such Acts, Records and Proceedings shall be proved, and the Effect thereof.'

[59] HRS Sec 572–2.   [60] *Miike*, 950 P2d at 1234.

[61] In conjunction with the amendment referendum bill, the Hawaii state legislature passed the 1997 Reciprocal Beneficiaries Law (1997 Hawaii Laws Act 383). The law grants

Other states which have considered the same-sex marriage issue include Vermont and Alaska. In Vermont, three same-sex couples unsuccessfully challenged the state's refusal to authorize same-sex marriage under the common benefits clause of the Vermont constitution.[62] The trial court interpreted that clause under the framework of federal equal protection law. The court declared that although *Zablocki v Redhail* (above) had indeed recognized a fundamental right to marry, the right recognized there linked marriage to procreation. Since procreation would not be possible in same-sex marriages, same-sex couples did not enjoy a fundamental right to marry. Nor did the Vermont marriage laws constitute a suspect classification which discriminated against homosexuals. Unlike race, gender, or alienage, homosexuality was not readily discernible nor were homosexuals as a class politically powerless.

some, but not all, of the rights and obligations of marriage to legally registered 'reciprocal beneficiaries.' A reciprocal beneficiaries relationship is a legal partnership between two persons who are prohibited from marrying each other under Hawaii law, including same-sex couples and immediate family. Reciprocal beneficiaries must be at least 18 years old, unmarried, and cannot already be in a reciprocal beneficiaries relationship. The relationship lasts until one of the parties files to terminate the relationship, or enters into a legal marriage.

The rights and benefits conferred include: inheritance rights and survivorship benefits; health-related rights such as hospital visitation, family and funeral leave, private and public employee prepaid insurance coverage, and motor vehicle insurance coverage; jointly held property rights such as tenancy in the entirety and public land leases; legal standing for wrongful death and crime victim rights; and other benefits related to the use of state facilities and state properties. Rights and benefits not conferred include mutual support, divorce, and child custody. Rights and benefits affecting interstate compacts or federally conferred status, such as joint federal income tax filings, are also not conferred because many states have passed laws prohibiting the recognition of these rights in unmarried persons, as does the federal Defense of Marriage Act.

In 1999, several bills affecting same-sex relationships were introduced in the Hawaii state legislature, but all died in committee. These bills included: HB 884, which would have replaced the Reciprocal Beneficiaries Law with a domestic partnership law conferring all of the rights and benefits of marriage; HB 775, which would have banned same-sex marriage; and HB 717, which would have removed the status of marriage as a legal encumbrance or benefit, but would have allowed both opposite and same-sex 'registered partnerships.'

Hawaii continued to deny civil marriage licenses to same-sex couples. Following the 1998 constitutional amendment, the Hawaii Supreme Court ordered supplemental briefings on how the amendment affected the ongoing case of *Baehr v Anderson*, (formerly *Baehr v Miike*), in which plaintiffs sought to enjoin the State Department of Health from denying marriage licenses to same-sex applicants. The state argued that the amendment validates previous legislation limiting marriage to opposite-sex couples, while the plaintiffs argued that the amendment only gives the legislature a restrictive power it did not previously possess, and which it has not yet exercised. The Hawaii Supreme Court ruled ultimately in favor of the state's position See n 70 below.

[62] *Baker v State of Vermont*, Chittenden (Vt) Superior Court S 1009–97 CnC. Opinion by Chittenden Superior Court Justice Linda Levitt, December 1997. The common benefits clause states in pertinent part: 'That government is, or ought to be, instituted for the common benefit, protection, and security of the people, nation, or community and not for the

In sum, neither the fundamental rights nor the suspect classification branch of federal equal protection law was implicated by Vermont's refusal to permit same-sex marriage; there was no need to subject its marriage laws to a heightened scrutiny standard of review. Similarly, a heightened standard of review was not merited on a theory that the Vermont marriage laws were gender-based.[63] Indeed, Vermont's marriage laws did not treat similarly situated males and females differently. The marriage laws were applied in the same manner to each sex. Finally, the exclusion by the state's marriage laws of same-sex marriage satisfied the rational basis standard of review because it promoted the link between procreation and childrearing. In a surprising development, the Vermont Supreme Court in *Baker v Vermont* reversed the judgment of the lower court and held that the state was constitutionally obliged by the common benefits clause of the Vermont constitution to grant 'to same sex couples the common benefits and protections that flow from marriage under Vermont law.'[64] This constitutional obligation, Chief Justice Amestoy declared, could be enforced by recognition either of same-sex marriage or of a domestic partnership law or some alternative statutory equivalent. The mode of enforcement, however, was the province of the legislature. Indeed, the Vermont legislature responded to this opportunity by enacting trail-blazing legislation, which recognized same-sex unions.

Chief Justice Amestoy described his opinion as providing 'greater recognition of—and protection for—same-sex relationships than had been recognized by any court of final jurisdiction in this country with the instructive exception of the Hawaii Supreme Court.'[65] A remarkable feature of the *Baker* decision is the great effort the court takes to ground both the rationale and holding entirely on the Vermont constitution. The Vermont Supreme Court specifically declared that it did not rely on the equal protection clause of the federal constitution.[66] Instead, it relied on the common benefits clause of the state constitution which has as its chief principle 'the principle of inclusion.'[67] Based on that principle, the court ruled that there was no basis upon which to exclude the same-sex plaintiffs from the 'secular benefits and protection' flowing from marriage and afforded to married persons: 'The extension of the Common Benefits Clause to acknowledge plaintiffs as Vermonters who seek nothing more, nor less, than legal protection and security for their avowed commitment

particular emolument or advantage of any single person, family, or set of persons, who are a part only of that community . . . ' Vt Const, Ch 1, Art 7.

[63] *ibid*. The trial court's analysis on this point is a model of circularity: '[A]ppellants are not being denied entry into the marriage relationship because of their sex; rather, they are being denied entry into the marriage relationship because of the recognized definition of that relationship as one which may be entered into only by two persons who are members of the opposite sex.'   [64] *Baker v State of Vermont*, 744 A2d 864 (Vt 2000).

[65] *Baker*, 744 A2d at 42 (referring to *Baehr*, 826 P 2d 44).   [66] *Baker*, 744 A2d at 8.

[67] *ibid* at 10.

to an intimate and lasting human relationship is simply, when all is said and done, a recognition of our common humanity.'[68]

Finally, Chief Justice Amestoy ruled that the 'appropriate means of enforcing this constitutional mandate' was the prerogative of the legislature.[69] Deferring to the legislature for the crafting of the remedy, Chief Justice Amestoy conceded, might not result in recognition of same-sex marriage but judicial authority was not the only source of wisdom. Insistence on implementation by the legislature of a right 'expounded by this court pursuant to the Vermont Constitution for the common benefit and protection of the Vermont community' was not judicial abdication but compliance with 'constitutional responsibility.'[70]

An effort to establish recognition of same-sex marriage is also under way in Alaska. Two men sought and were denied a license to marry each other by the state of Alaska. An Alaska trial court ruled that this refusal constituted a violation of the fundamental right of privacy guaranteed by the Alaska constitution.[71] Unlike Vermont, the Alaska marriage laws specifically prohibited same-sex marriage. But the Alaska constitution contains a specific provision guaranteeing the right of privacy. Enacted seven years after *Griswold*, and deeply influenced by *Griswold* as was the trial court decision, it provides: 'The right of the people to privacy is recognized and shall not be infringed.'[72] *Griswold* and *Loving* had held that marriage between persons of the opposite sex was a fundamental right. The Alaska trial court acknowledged that the Hawaii Supreme Court had ruled that same-sex marriage was not a fundamental right, because same-sex marriage was not so rooted in the traditions and conscience of our people as to make it a fundamental right. But the Hawaii Supreme Court had asked the wrong question. The question was not whether same-sex marriage was so rooted in our traditions that it was a fundamental right, but whether our traditions protect the choice of life partner: 'It is the decision itself which is fundamental, whether the decision results in a traditional choice or a nontraditional choice.' The trial court held that the choice of life partner was a fundamental right.[73] The prospects for a right

---

[68] *Baker*, 744 A2d at 45.   [69] *ibid* at 39.   [70] *ibid* at 43.
[71] *Brause v Bureau of Vital Statistics*, No 3AN-95–652 CI, 1998 WL 88743 (Alas Super Ct Feb 27 1998).   [72] ALASKA CONST, Art I, Sec 22.
[73] The trial court said it did not need to decide whether the bar to same-sex marriage in Alaska violated the equal protection clause of the Alaska Constitution. The court had already determined that banning same-sex marriage constituted the denial of the fundamental right to choose a life partner based on the state constitutional guarantee of a right to privacy. That right could only be subordinated by a showing by the state of a compelling state interest to justify its ban. However, the court said that if it were required to decide the equal protection issue, it would subject the Alaska prohibition on same-sex marriage to an intermediate level of scrutiny—a higher standard of review than normally applied to constitutional challenges to state legislation.

to same-sex marriage were soon thwarted in Alaska by an amendment to the Alaska constitution in 1999. The amendment states: 'To be valid or recognized in this State, marriage may exist only between one man and one woman.'[74]

If we reflect on the experience gained thus far from the litigation to establish same-sex marriage in Hawaii, Vermont, and Alaska, what emerges is that the chosen terrain for efforts to extend new constitutional protection to these relationships are the state constitutions rather than the federal constitution. The state constitutions have been selected by the litigants because the contemporary United States Supreme Court is not at present in a rights-building mode, and some of the state courts are.[75] One

The state had moved for summary judgment on the ground that the Alaska law did not violate the state constitution. The plaintiff had moved for summary judgment on the ground that the appropriate standard of review for evaluation of the law barring same-sex marriage was strict scrutiny. The trial court granted the plaintiff's motion for summary judgment and denied that of the state. The court ordered the parties to set further hearings on whether a compelling state interest can be demonstrated by the state which would justify the same-sex marriage ban. Review was then sought in the Alaska Supreme Court.

[74] ALASKA CONST. Art 1, § 25 (1999). In response to the Alaska Superior Court ruling in *Brause v Bureau of Vital Statistics*, the state legislature promptly passed the proposed amendment by the required two-thirds vote in each house, and the amendment was passed by the required majority of the voters in the 1998 elections. The actual vote was more than 2–1 in favor of the amendment.

The Alaska Supreme Court ruled in *Bess v Ulmer*, 1999 Alas Lexis 107 (Aug 17 1999) (Nos S-8811/S-8812, No 5167) that the proposed amendment was indeed an amendment, and not a revision of the constitution, and therefore was a proper proposal for the ballot. A revision can only be enacted by constitutional convention.

[75] As we have seen, in Hawaii and Alaska the state courts have taken an expansive view of expansive federal constitutional cases in the family law area. Interestingly, the Texas Supreme Court declined to follow the plurality opinion in a 1989 Supreme Court case, *Michael H v Gerald D*, which took a *narrow* view of the rights of the biological father. See, below, this chapter, for a discussion of *Michael H*, 491 US at 110. In *In the Interest of JWT*, the Supreme Court of Texas held that a state law that denied the putative biological father standing to sue to establish paternity with regard to a child that was born into a marital relationship was unconstitutional under the due course of law guarantee in the Texas Constitution. See 872 SW 2d 189 (1994); see also TEXAS CONST., Article 1, § 19.

The Texas Supreme Court described the analysis of the plurality in *Michael H* as being 'in apparent conflict with recent application of the federal Due Process clause to biological fathers.' *ibid*. The Texas Supreme Court noted that Justice Stevens concurred only in the judgment, and not the opinion, of the plurality in *Michael H*, and only because he found sufficient safeguard in the putative father's right to seek visitation rights under California law, a right not found in the Texas Family Code. *ibid* at 196, nn 20, 22.

In a dissenting opinion, Justice Cornyn made some useful comments on why state supreme courts, interpreting the due process clauses of state constitutions, often rely on United States Supreme Court opinions interpreting the due process clause of the federal constitution:

'First, the United States Supreme Court encounters due process issues far more frequently than does this court, and thus is in a better position to develop a coherent and consistent framework. Second, because federal precedent in this area is more extensive than our state jurisprudence . . . [following federal precedent] promotes certainty in the law and discourages unnecessary or duplicative litigation. Third, the dangers of substantive due process

of the virtues of federalism then is that social change is always possible. More comforting still, the decisions of state courts on state law are insulated from United States Supreme Court review if state court decisions rest solely on state law.[76] Yet it is United States Supreme Court cases such as *Loving, Griswold,* and *Zablocki* which serve as building blocks in the effort to establish a right to same-sex marriage. The state courts confronting these novel issues have, with the exception of the Vermont Supreme Court, done so under the guidance of these cases, cases decided at a time when the United States Supreme Court was in a rights-building mode. But it is not only the US Supreme Court which is not at present in a rights-building mode. As far as same-sex marriage is concerned, the majority of the electorate in Hawaii and Alaska appear to take a similar view. Proponents of same-sex marriage in those states have discovered that reliance on state constitutions is very much a two-edged sword. Adversaries of establishing a right to same-sex marriage in those states have been successful in thwarting state court decisions by securing through referenda amendments to their state constitutions which either defeat the right as in Alaska or make it possible to do so as in Hawaii.

Despite the foregoing, the enduring vitality and rights-generating impact of federal constitutional law cases such as *Griswold* on the effort to expand the concept of a fundamental right to marriage to encompass same-sex marriage as well, is remarkable. The Alaska trial court found a right to same-sex marriage based on its constitutional guaranty of privacy and it did so relying on both *Zablocki* and *Griswold. Griswold* was relied on for the point that the right to privacy recognized that there is a personal zone of intimacy that is protected. The choice of a life partner was personal and intimate and, therefore, merited protection under the state constitutional guaranty of a right of privacy. The Vermont trial court concluded that same-sex marriage was not cognizable under its constitution because, in its view, under *Zablocki,* marriage was a constitutional right only when linked with procreation. The response of the Vermont Supreme Court was

---

going awry are great, and a restrained method minimizes the likelihood that arbitrary decisions will call this court's legitimacy into question. Finally, a restrained method enables our due course jurisprudence to evolve—to the extent it departs from federal cases—with maximum deliberation and care. Simply put, unless differences between the clauses give us a good reason to depart from either the direct holdings of the Supreme Court or its methodology, then we should not do so.' *JWT*, 872 SW 3d at 207–8.

Subsequently, the Texas Legislature amended the Texas Family Code to allow any man alleging himself to be the biological father of a child to contest the paternity of a child born in wedlock. TEX FAM CODE ANN § 160.101(a)(4)(Vernon 1996).

[76] This is called the adequate and independent state ground doctrine. One scholar has described the doctrine with admirable brevity: 'Simply stated, the Supreme Court will not hear a case if the decision of the state's highest court is supported by a state law rationale that is independent of federal law and adequate to sustain the result.' ERWIN CHEMERINSKY, FEDERAL JURISDICTION (2nd edn 1994).

to avoid *Zablocki* and rely entirely on its own constitution. The Alaska trial court saw *Zablocki* quite differently from the Vermont trial court. *Zablocki* indeed protected the decision to marry and raise a child but this did not mean that the choice of a life partner was less worthy. The Alaska trial court saw *Zablocki* not as limiting *Griswold* but rather as yet another illustration that personal choice in intimate and personal decisions was a fundamental right.

The Supreme Court of Hawaii thought that the *Griswold* case did not establish a basis for affording a right to same-sex marriage because such a right was not rooted in the traditions and collective conscience of the American people. Yet the Supreme Court of Hawaii concluded that same-sex marriage was protected under its constitution by relying on the analytical equal protection framework established by the United States Supreme Court. The Supreme Court of Hawaii was able to use that framework to recognize same-sex marriage. It was aided in that effort because the state constitution of Hawaii, unlike the federal constitution, specifically protects against discrimination on the basis of sex.

CONCLUSION

As the case of the right to marry illustrates, the constitutionalization of American family law developed through the judicial creation of rights by means of interpreting the due process clause of the Fourteenth Amendment. The reference to liberty in the due process clause came to be understood as comprehending the sanctity and autonomy of the marriage relationship. The marriage relationship was deemed to be protected by a fundamental right of privacy which demanded strict scrutiny of state regulation substantially interfering with the marriage relationship. The right to marry itself was deemed a fundamental right and exacting review was demanded of state regulation which sought unreasonably to control the freedom essential to the relationship. Through this process of judicial interpretation, limitations were increasingly placed on the power of the states to control family law. The autonomy and privacy rationale for limiting state power to regulate marriage was, in turn, extended by the equal protection clause to protect classes of individuals. The equal protection clause of the Fourteenth Amendment proved to be a powerful tool with which to extend to unmarried individuals generally protections which in a due process context had been limited to the marital relationship.

Case law generated by the United States Supreme Court a generation ago is being used as a contemporary baseline by which state courts interpret—and expand—their own state constitutions in the resolution of novel questions of family law. For example, the Alaska trial court was guided by United States Supreme Court case law when it extended constitutional protection to same-sex marriage under the state constitutional provision guaranteeing a right to privacy. This guarantee of privacy was deemed, as explained in *Griswold* and *Zablocki*, to encompass the right to choose a life partner. Indeed, the right to choose a life partner was held to be a fundamental right. In this way, the constitutionalization of family law continues to reverberate beyond its federal case law beginnings. Indeed, the constitutionalization of family law is enjoying a second life in state constitutional law.

The same-sex marriage cases display in microcosm the nature of the issues that surround the constitutionalization of family and sexual relationships. These cases have their source in the conferral of constitutional status on the marital relationships brought about a generation ago by an activist United States Supreme Court. An inevitable reaction to such activism ushered in a period of retrenchment. But the process of constitutional interpretation proved resilient and moved from federal constitutional terrain to a more hospitable forum and terrain, the state judiciary and the state constitutions. On state terrain, those seeking to broaden the frontiers of the freedom to marry have achieved some initial success. But again these developments have spawned an inevitable reaction. Judicial decisions expanding civil liberties through the process of state constitutional law interpretation have been trumped in Hawaii and Alaska by a majoritarian counter-strike—amendment of the state constitution.[77] But the decisions of the state courts in Hawaii, Vermont, and Alaska nevertheless still have had considerable effect. Once the definitions of liberty and equality are expanded by the courts it is quite difficult to contain their expansion. When these concepts work in tandem as they do in the case of same-sex marriage, it is hard to put the genie back in the bottle. In their conferral of constitutional protection on the marital relationship, *Griswold*, decided in 1965 and *Zablocki* in 1978, continue to affect the legal culture in the United States in a deep and enduring way.

---

[77] In *Baehr v Miike*, the Supreme Court of Hawaii in a summary disposition and order reversed the circuit court (trial court) holding that the Hawaii law, Sec 572–1, denying a marriage license to two members of the same sex violated the equal protection clause of the Hawaii state constitution. See 872 SW 2d at 189. The Supreme Court of Hawaii ruled that 'whether or not in the past' the Hawaii law purporting to limit marriage to opposite-sex couples violated the equal protection clause of the Hawaii state constitution, in the light of the 'marriage amendment,' it no longer does so.

13

Dual Systems of Adoption in the United States

SANFORD N. KATZ

INTRODUCTION

In 1972, the United States Supreme Court set in motion the first fundamental change in American adoption laws in many decades. Ironically, this transformation occurred in a passing reference in a footnote in a dependency case.[1] In that footnote, the Court mentioned that an unwed father should be afforded notice and an opportunity to be heard in his illegitimate children's custody or adoption proceeding. By including adoption in the sentence, it overturned longstanding adoption law, which did not require the consent of a father if his illegitimate child was to be adopted, nor entitle him to notice of the proceeding.

That the United States Supreme Court should have referred to adoption procedure so casually in a case not concerned with adoption was unusual. The Court may not have realized that the immediate effect of a footnote in its opinion could delay adoptions in Illinois, and prompt every state legislature to revise its adoption statute, to provide some kind of notice—personal service or service by publication—to putative fathers who had met certain requirements like registering with a state agency. In addition, it forced every adoption agency to set new policies and procedures regarding their participation in the adoption process where they previously had been invisible or only shadow figures.[2]

---

[1] In *Stanley v Illinois*, 405 US 645 (1972), the United States Supreme Court held that excluding a father from a dependency proceeding that would make state wards of his illegitimate children who lived with him deprived him of the equal protection of the laws guaranteed under the Due Process Clause of the United States Constitution. Footnote 9 read:

'We note in passing that the incremental cost of offering unwed fathers an opportunity for individualized hearings on fitness appears to be minimal. If unwed fathers, in the main, do not care about the disposition of their children, they will not appear to demand hearings. If they do care, under the scheme here held invalid, Illinois would admittedly at some later time have to afford them a properly focused hearing in a custody or *adoption* proceeding.

Extending opportunity for hearing to unwed fathers who desire and claim competence to care for their children creates no constitutional or procedural obstacle to foreclosing those unwed fathers who are not so inclined.' (Emphasis added.) *ibid* at 657.

[2] Professor Jerome A. Barron was the first constitutional law scholar to recognize the difficulties raised by the ambiguities in footnote 9 in *Stanley*. The questions he asked about implementing the Court's comments, for example, whether notice had to be given to all unwed fathers or only those, like Mr Stanley, who had 'sired and raised' his children, are still not completely and clearly answered by state case law and statutes. See Jerome A. Barron, *Notice to the Unwed Father and Termination of Parental Rights: Implementing* Stanley v Illinois, 9 FAM LQ 527 (1975); see also Joan Heifetz Hollinger, *Consent to Adoption* in

The Supreme Court's decision in *Stanley v Illinois* illustrates how modern adoption law has been influenced by the Court's expansion of the protection of individual rights during the civil rights movement of the 1960s and 1970s.[3] Since then, instead of a social issue having an impact on adoption, adoption itself has been used to promote social goals like racial assimilation or integration or even for recognizing the changes in the composition of some American families.[4]

This was not always the case. In mid-century, through placement standards that were designed to match a child's physical characteristics and ethnic background with those of her adopted parents, adoption was meant to create a traditional nuclear family that looked natural. Once adoption was finalized the child's past history was often literally eradicated by changes in the birth certificate. By keeping secret the child's previous life and terminating the child's relationship with her birth parents for almost all purposes, adoption created a legal fiction. Until about 1960, to mention that a person had been adopted was taboo.

During the twentieth century, adoption has been a specialized child welfare service performed by social workers in private and public child welfare agencies. Whether a birth mother relinquishes her infant for adoption voluntarily or whether adoption is the final outcome of a child dependency proceeding, the articulated goal sometimes achieved and sometimes mere rhetoric, is to advance the best interests of the child. In the former case, court involvement occurs as the last judicial act (ordinarily in a judge's chambers) of formally approving the adoption and issuing an adoption decree. In the latter, it is a disposition, often at a separate proceeding, for example, a waiver of consent hearing, following the involuntary termination of parental rights because of parental abuse or neglect.

These two tracks—voluntary relinquishment and involuntary termination of parental rights—resulting in adoption have given rise to dual systems in the past forty years. For the most part, one system—voluntary relinquishment—is consensual and private, involving non-governmental, non-profit or profit-making agencies or individuals;[5] the other system—involuntary termination of parental rights—is non-consensual and

---

1 Adoption Law and Practice §§ 2.1–2.12 (Joan Heifetz Hollinger and Dennis W. Leski eds 1998).

[3] After *Stanley*, the United States Supreme Court decided a number of cases that extended the rights of unwed fathers. See *Quilloin v Walcott*, 434 US 246 (1978), *Caban v Mohammed*, 441 US 380 (1979), and *Lehr v Robertson*, 463 US 248 (1983).

[4] See n 37 below and accompanying text.

[5] Some state social service agencies also include adoption among their services. Some enter into contracts with private child welfare agencies to provide adoption services. Private agencies, some of which have a religious affiliation, receive funds from individual donors, private foundations, community charities, and through fees for services.

public, involving state agencies with major funds provided for foster care and adoption programs by the federal government. Even though the ultimate outcome of adoption for children from either system may be the same in terms of a court establishing the adoptive status, there is a major difference in goals. The goal of the voluntary system may well be to provide a childless couple with an infant so as to continue the adoptive family name. The aim of dependency proceedings resulting in the termination of parental rights is to protect children, and the disposition of adoption is a vehicle for providing a child with a permanent attachment to a family.

A social class distinction tends to exist between the participants in the two systems. Infants voluntarily relinquished by their birth mothers and placed with adoptive parents tend to move into the middle class of which their new parents are a part. Children who are the subject of termination proceedings tend to be the offspring of poor parents from deprived backgrounds who the state claims have neglected[6] or abandoned them, or from parents who have been judicially declared unfit because of abuse, alcoholism, drug addiction, or serious and chronic mental illness. For the most part, couples who adopt these children are their foster parents. In some instances, however, the children are placed with relatives (kinship adoption) or under certain circumstances with middle-class couples or individuals.

Although there have been two major efforts to enact a uniform adoption law, they have been unsuccessful.[7] Perhaps the reason for this

---

[6] The definition of 'neglect' varies greatly, and usually means that the parent has failed to protect her child. See Sanford N. Katz *et al*, *Child Neglect Laws in America*, 9 FAM LQ 1 (1975). There can be social neglect, defined as society's (or a community's) failure to respond to the needs of poor families. Social neglect is not found in state statutes. To what extent there is social responsibility for caring for the poor is, of course, a question that has been around for many decades. In contemporary times it is usually raised during years close to elections both on the state and national level.

The announcement of a policy about homeless people in New York City illustrates how the status of being poor can be used to define 'neglect.' On Dec 4 1999, the *New York Times* reported that the Commissioner of Welfare for the City of New York warned all homeless families that they were subject to having their children removed from their care for neglect if they failed to work or meet shelter and welfare requirements. The Commissioner apparently qualified his threat by saying that there would, of course, be a judicial hearing, presumably after an emergency removal and temporary foster care placement for the children had occurred. See Nina Bernstein, *City May Remove Children from Families in Shelters*, NY TIMES, Dec 4 1999, at A13.

On Dec 9 1999, the *New York Times* reported that on Dec 8, a state court temporarily halted the plan to place the children of homeless parents who refused to work or failed to meet welfare requirements in foster care. See Nina Bernstein, *Work-for-Shelter Requirement is Delayed by New York Judges*, NY TIMES, Dec 9 1999, at A1.

[7] Established in 1892, the National Conference of Commissioners on Uniform State Laws is a non-governmental organization, which promotes uniformity in state law in many legal areas. In 1953, it promulgated the first Uniform Adoption Act. Only one state, Oklahoma,

may be that adoption laws reflect local practice and policies. It also may be an area of family law where it is difficult to reach a consensus because of conflicting interests of the participants in the adoption process.[8] Thus, to understand adoption in the United States, it is important to realize that there are fifty-one adoption laws, one in each American state and the District of Columbia.

This chapter will be divided into two major parts: adoption resulting from the voluntary placement of infants by the birth mother, which I shall label 'voluntary system,' and adoption as the judicial disposition following the termination of parental rights, which I shall call 'involuntary system.' The unifying theme in this chapter will be an examination of the recurring tension between individual autonomy and state regulation in the placement of children for adoption, and how it is reflected in the major developments in adoption in the past half-century.

VOLUNTARY SYSTEM

The Role of Personal Autonomy

In 1851, Massachusetts enacted the first American adoption statute, which required a public judicial process for conferring the status of adoption on a child.[9] Before then, adoption in the United States was created by a contract or deed or in some states by a private statute.[10] By regulating

enacted the Act without revisions. Alaska (1974), Arkansas (1977), Montana (1957), North Dakota (1971), and Ohio (1976) enacted parts of the 1969 Revised Uniform Adoption Act. In 1994, the Uniform Commissioners on Uniform State Laws approved a new Uniform Adoption Act. Two years later, Vermont enacted it, and as of 1999 remains the only state that has done so. The Revised Uniform Adoption Act (1969) can be found in 9 ULA (Part I) 15–78 (1988). The 1994 Uniform Adoption Act can be found in 9 ULA Part I, West Supp 1999).

[8] One illustration of the difficulty of drafting a model state adoption act is evidenced by the actions of the Family Law Section of the American Bar Association, the largest organization of family law lawyers in America. From 1981 to 1985, the Section attempted to reach a consensus among its members so that it could draft an act that would be acceptable to lawyers. One of the major issues of contention was the extent to which adoption agencies would control the placement of children. The model act that was eventually drafted was not enacted in any state. For two views on the Act, see William M. Schur, *The ABA Model State Adoption Act: Observations from an Agency Perspective*, 19 FAM LQ 131 (1985) and David Keene Leavitt, *The Model Adoption Act: Return to a Balanced View of Adoption*, 19 FAM LQ 141 (1985).

[9] See Massachusetts Adoption of Children's Act of 1851, 1851 Mass. Acts, ch 324 (May 24 1851).

[10] Since there was no common law of adoption, a state statute was required to establish the status. The closest analogy to a common law of adoption is 'equitable adoption.' Equitable adoption is a term used in probate proceedings to describe a relationship between an adult and a child who was not formally adopted by the adult but who lived in a de facto parent–child relationship with him or her for an extended period of time. Because the child

adoption, the Massachusetts Act eliminated a parent's unrestricted power to contract away her parental rights or transfer them to others through a deed. It required the consents of the immediate parties to the adoption. In addition, a court had to consider the welfare of the child and the qualifications of the adopters before it approved an adoption and issued an adoption decree.[11] The result was that Massachusetts limited the personal autonomy of birth parents and prevented them from exploiting their children for economic gain.

For nearly one hundred and fifty years, a major question in adoption has been: when a birth mother voluntarily relinquishes her infant, how much decision-making power can she reserve, and at what stage in a state-regulated system of adoption may she exercise it? May she decide herself, or delegate to another, who can adopt her child? Once her consent is given, even though voluntarily, can she revoke it? May she maintain a connection with her child by requiring that she be given post-adoption visitation rights? Years after an adoption decree has been issued, may she have access to adoption records and locate her child? Answers to these questions not only measure the amount of personal autonomy with which the state endows birth parents, but also reflect society's concept of adoption.

Independent and Agency Adoptions

Allowing a birth parent to place a child directly with adoptive parents or to delegate that power to another, such as a lawyer, physician, or clergyman has been called 'independent' or 'private' adoption. Requiring her to relinquish her rights to a public or private child welfare agency for placement has been labeled 'agency adoption.'[12] Most American jurisdictions permit private adoption. Only four restrict placement to agencies in

was neither the biological nor legally adopted child of the adult, the child would not qualify as an heir. In some states, however, where a decedent dies intestate, a probate judge will allow the child to inherit from the de facto parent, but rarely through the parent. This can occur if the judge finds that there is sufficient evidence, usually 'clear and convincing,' to show that the decedent promised to adopt the child or was in the process of adopting the child but never completed all the formalities. For a comprehensive analysis of the history of adoption laws in the United States, see Joan Heifetz Hollinger, *Introduction to Adoption Law and Practice in* 1 ADOPTION LAW AND PRACTICE, n 2 above, at §§ 1.01–1.06; see also 2 ANN M. HARALAMBIE, HANDLING CHILD CUSTODY, ABUSE AND ADOPTION CASES § 14 (1993).

[11] Five years after the Massachusetts Adoption Act was enacted, the Massachusetts Supreme Judicial Court reflected this approach when it wrote that '[adoption] is not a question of mere property, . . . the interests of the minor is the principal thing to be considered.' *Curtis v Curtis*, 71 Mass (5 Gray) 535, 537 (1856).

[12] For a discussion of research that inquired into the risks of independent adoptions, see WILLIAM MEEZAN, *et al*, ADOPTIONS WITHOUT AGENCIES—A STUDY OF INDEPENDENT ADOPTIONS (1978). For an attorney's perspective, see Jed Somit, *Independent Adoptions in California: Dual Representation Allowed in* 1 ADOPTION LAW AND PRACTICE, n 2 above, at § 5.01–04.

non-relative adoptions.[13] Preference for private adoption over agency adoption reveals a general bias toward market mechanisms in American society. It also can be seen as anti-regulation or anti-governmental intervention, even though in all American jurisdictions, adoption must ultimately be state sanctioned by judicial approval. Private adoption can also be viewed purely as a preference for preserving individual autonomy and the state's reluctance to restrict parental choice.

In reality, the forces that have been successful in promoting private adoption are individuals and groups, especially the adoption bar, whose focus is on locating a child for parents rather than finding parents for a child, resulting in a primary concern for birth mothers and adoptive parents.[14] They argue that a birth mother should be free to place her child with whomever she wants, and for whatever reason she chooses.[15] Indeed, such an approach might be similar to the unregulated sale of human organs.[16] In the past thirty years, an adoption industry has devel-

---

[13] As of 1999, these four are: Colorado: Colo Rev Stat §§ 19–5–204(2), 19–5–206 (West 1999); Connecticut: Conn Gen Stat Ann §§ 45–63(3),–69(d) (West 1993); Delaware: Del Code Ann tit 13, § 904 (Michie 1993); and Massachusetts: Mass Ann Laws Ch 210 § 2A (1994). The Massachusetts provision reads:

'No decree of adoption shall be entered for the adoption of a child below the age of fourteen until one of the following conditions has been met:

(A) The child sought to be adopted has been placed with the petitioners for adoption by the department of social services or by an agency authorized by said department for such purpose, . . . '

Massachusetts allows the direct placement of a child with a blood relative, step-parent, or with the petitioner if that person was nominated as a guardian or adoptive parent in the will of the child's deceased birth parent.

[14] Jed Somit has written:

'Various reasons are postulated for the comparative popularity of independent adoption:

- less bureaucratic involvement in the placement process;
- the birth mother's ability to select the adopting parent or parents;
- the expertise developed by attorneys in "networking," "outreach" or otherwise marketing their adoption practice and their clients;
- the perceived relative generosity of support payments made in an independent adoption; and
- the greater freedom to structure the adoption to meet the needs and demands of each particular birth mother.'

* * *

Independent adoption . . . allows the most flexibility in making arrangements (within legal limits) for financial support of the birth mother, for the prospective adoptive parents and the birth mother to form a relationship before the birth of the child, and for the parents to discuss their relationship after the birth. The birth mother's sense of having some control of her child's, and her own destiny may help in her forming a commitment to the adoption, and later in dealing with the loss that is inevitable when placing a child.' Jed Somit, *Independent Adoptions in California: Dual Representation Allowed in* 1 Adoption Law and Practice, n 2 above, at §§ 5.01[1]5–7, 8; [2] 5–9.

[15] It is unclear whether it is a birth mother who is really placing an infant for adoption or the person to whom she has delegated that power, eg a lawyer, physician, or clergyman.

[16] See David E. Jefferies, *The Body as Commodity: The Use of Markets to Cure the Organ Deficit*, 5 Ind J Global Leg Studies 621 (1998); William Boulier, *Sperm, Spleens, and Other Valuables: The Need to Recognize Property Rights in Human Body Parts*, 23 Hofstra L Rev 693 (1995).

oped. The private placement of children has taken on the characteristics of a business, in effect trading in children,[17] even though the sale of children is prohibited, and state statutes limit fees relating to adoption to administrative costs and are often monitored by the courts. Yet questions have been raised about whether such limitations are effective given the broad definition of administrative costs.

Restricting the placement of children to licensed private or public adoption agencies is thought to lessen the risks of flawed placements. Nationally accredited agencies, staffed with experienced and knowledgeable social workers, are able and equipped to screen applicants, and after the completion of a home study, select the most appropriate adoptive couple for the child. It would be unusual for a lawyer, physician, or clergyman to have the same kind of education, skill, and experience as adoption agency social workers who historically have held graduate degrees in social work. Since an agency must be licensed by the state in which it is located, it must conform to state regulations and periodic monitoring. If the monitoring is effective, it would be the vehicle to assure placement decisions advance a child's welfare rather than the special interests of other participants, like the birth mother or the adoptive couple.

The advantages of the involvement of reputable agencies in the adoption process also relate to their administrative structure with a built-in system of accountability and to their delivery of services, both missing in private placements. Agencies keep records. They also have internal procedures whereby placement decisions can be reviewed. Agencies provide social and psychological services to a birth mother (and father if he is identified and involved in the mother's life) in counseling her about her decision to relinquish her child and to prospective adoptive parents in their decisions about undertaking adoption as a way of having a family. They are available for post-adoption services to all the participants, including the child. This aspect of adoption services is particularly important if and when the birth parents and adopted child seek information about each other.

---

[17] 'Making money from adoptive placements, while at odds with the idealized image of adoption as an altruistic service, is not inherently evil. Reputable adoption agencies, attorneys, and psychologists do this daily, with beneficial effects on adoption placements.' Jed Somit, *Independent Adoptions in California: Dual Representation Allowed in* 1 ADOPTION LAW AND PRACTICE, n 2 above, at § 5.02[4]5–17; see also Tamar Frankel and Frances Miller, *The Inapplicability of Market Theory to Adoptions*, 67 BUL REV 99 (1987); Richard A. Posner, *The Regulation of the Market in Adoptions*, 67 BUL REV 59 (1987); RICHARD A. POSNER, ECONOMIC ANALYSIS OF LAW 139–44 (3rd edn 1986); Elizabeth M. Landes and Richard A. Posner, *The Economics of the Baby Shortage*, 7 J LEGAL STUDIES 323 (1978); but see J. Robert S. Prichard, *A Market for Babies*, 34 U TORONTO L J 341 (1984).

However, agencies have been criticized for not being creative in developing strategies to reach minority couples as prospective adoptive parents, for being too rigid in their placement requirements, following only certain theories about child development, or for being less than candid about the social and psychological history of a birth mother or a child. In addition, it has been said that if agencies alone are permitted to place children, a monopoly will be created with the result that they will be overburdened and unable to provide adequate services.[18] Whether an adoption is ultimately more successful if arranged through an agency or privately has not been proven. Success is difficult to define and to measure.

There is also the matter of the legal responsibility for adoption placement. Wrongful adoption is a cause of action first recognized in Ohio in 1986,[19] which extended the common law torts of negligence, fraud, and misrepresentation to adoption. It arises from an agency's failure to fulfill its duty to disclose facts about a child's past history, including genetic information, which would have affected the child's placement. While the tort would also be applicable to a private placement, the likelihood of actually recovering compensatory damages to cover present and future medical bills from a birth mother or a third party compared with a licensed and insured private or public agency would seem remote.

Surrogacy

The complex interplay between private autonomy and regulation was placed in a new perspective in the 1980s with the phenomenon of surrogate motherhood. When *In re Baby M*,[20] the first nationally publicized surrogacy case, was decided in New Jersey in 1988, there was no single legal model to which a court could turn to resolve the conflict resulting from this new method of family formation. Because of the relationship of the three adult parties to each other and to the child in that case and because of the nature of the transaction the parties chose, surrogacy concerned the common law of contracts and statutes relating to adoption,

---

[18] See MEEZAN *et al.*, n 12 above, at 232–3.

[19] See *Burr v Board of County Comm'rs*, 491 NE2d 1101 (Ohio 1986). Breach of contract has also been argued in cases in which adoptive parents have alleged that by not disclosing information about the child, the agency had failed to fulfill its side of the adoption placement agreement. Breach of contract actions brought against agencies have been less successful than tort actions. For a full discussion of the tort of wrongful adoption and other possible remedies for misrepresentation in adoption placement, see D. Marianne Blair, *Liability of Adoption Agencies and Attorneys for Misconduct in the Disclosure of Health-Related Information in* 2 ADOPTION LAW AND PRACTICE § 16.01–08 (Joan Heifetz Hollinger and Dennis W. Leski eds 1998). [20] 537 A 2d 1227 (N J 1988).

paternity, and termination of parental rights. As surrogacy became less of a novelty during the 1990s, the question of whether, like adoption, it should be regulated by the state was raised. States have taken a variety of approaches regarding both the process of entering into a surrogacy arrangement and the enforcement of the surrogacy contract.[21]

In re Baby M was the first surrogacy mother contract case to be decided by an American state supreme court. The issue before the court was the legality and enforceability of a surrogacy contract between a married woman, Mrs Whitehead, and a man, Mr Stern, not her husband (a party to the contract) but married to another woman (not a party to the contract). The terms of the contract included an exchange of promises in which Mr Stern promised to pay Mrs Whitehead $10,000 in exchange for her promising to be artificially inseminated with Mr Stern's semen, conceiving a child, carrying the child to term and after the birth of the child, surrendering her to Mr Stern and his wife. In addition Mrs Whitehead promised to fulfill the legal requirements for the termination of her rights so that Mrs Stern could adopt the child. After the child was born, her birth records indicated that Mrs Whitehead was her mother and, contrary to fact, Mr Whitehead was her father. Following the terms of the contract, Mrs Whitehead gave the newborn infant (referred to by the court as Baby M but named Melissa) to Mr and Mrs Stern.

---

[21] It is difficult to determine how extensively a surrogacy arrangement is used as a substitute for adoption since national statistics are unavailable. Surrogacy laws are in flux. Some state legislatures have declared surrogacy contracts valid if the surrogate is not compensated; some declare them invalid. A few states require the intended mother to be infertile. Two states require judicial approval of a surrogacy agreement in advance of performance. A host of problems have developed from surrogacy agreements, which include determining who the legal parents are. See *R.R. v M.H.*, 426 Mass 501 (1998) for a full discussion of the enforceability of surrogacy contracts in the US and one jurisdiction's guidance for parties entering into these contracts. In that case, the Supreme Judicial Court of Massachusetts held that a surrogacy agreement based on the consideration of $10,000 for services rendered in conceiving a child was unenforceable. The court used the time-frame from the Massachusetts adoption statute concerning consent (Mass Ann Laws Ch 210 § 2 (1994) which reads: '[W]ritten consent shall be executed no sooner than the fourth calendar day after the date of birth of the child to be adopted.'). The court further held that the provision in the surrogacy agreement regarding the mother's promise to surrender her baby before the infant was four days old, was unenforceable. Because a surrogacy agreement concerns the custody of an infant, the enforcement of such an agreement must be determined by the application of best interests of the child test. The court concluded by suggesting that judicial approval of a surrogacy contract before conception would be a wise policy. That requirement is built into the Uniform Status of Children of Assisted Conception Act Alternative A, §§ 5, 6, 9 (a), 9 BULA 201–7 (Master edn Supp 1997). See generally, MARTHA A. FIELD, SURROGATE MOTHERHOOD: THE LEGAL AND HUMAN ISSUES (1990).

Feminist scholars have raised special concerns about surrogacy arrangements and surrogacy contracts. A major question that is discussed in the literature is whether surrogacy is a part of a woman's reproductive rights which should be within her control or whether surrogacy agreements result in the exploitation of women and should not be enforced. See generally, Katharine T. Bartlett, *Feminism and Family Law*, 33 FAM LQ 475, 488–94 (1999).

Four days after she had relinquished Melissa to her new parents, the birth mother asked to have her newborn returned for a week. The Sterns agreed, not fully realizing that Mrs Whitehead had changed her mind. With her baby, Mrs Whitehead fled to Florida and refused to return Melissa to her new parents, thus violating the terms of the surrogacy contract.

Four months later through various legal maneuvers, the Sterns secured possession of Melissa. In New Jersey, Mr Stern sued for the enforcement of his contract with Mrs Whitehead and for the custody of Melissa. He also sought the termination of Mrs Whitehead's parental rights and an order allowing Mrs Stern to adopt the child. The lower court held that the surrogacy contract was valid. It ordered the termination of Mrs Whitehead's parental rights in Melissa, granted custody to Mr Stern, and after a brief hearing allowed the adoption of Melissa by Mrs Stern. Mrs Whitehead appealed.

After invalidating the surrogacy contract (which had provided for the termination of Mrs Whitehead's parental rights by the surrogacy contract), the New Jersey Supreme Court remanded the case to the Superior Court to determine which of the two legal parents—Mrs Whitehead or Mr Stern—should be granted custody. To the New Jersey Supreme Court, the surrogacy contract violated two state statutory provisions: one that barred the payment of money for an adoption, and the other which prevented the enforcement of a pre-birth adoption agreement. The Superior Court held that the best interests of Melissa would be served by her custody being awarded to Mr Stern with visitation rights to Mrs Whitehead. The outcome was a legal anomaly. It had some of the characteristics of a failed adoption as well as of a custodial arrangement after divorce with the husband being awarded physical and legal custody and the wife receiving visitation rights. It was also like a resolution of a conflict between an unmarried couple where the father of the illegitimate child born of that relationship was awarded custody of his daughter.

The case is exceptional in a number of ways. Ordinarily a child born to a married couple is presumed to be the legitimate child of the husband.[22] If that child is relinquished for adoption, the parents must formally consent. Many jurisdictions allow for the revocation of consent within a certain time-frame.[23] In New Jersey, a birth mother can change her mind

---

[22] American law adopted the English common law presumption that a child born in wedlock is the legitimate child of the couple. See *Michael H v Gerald D*, 491 US 110, 124–5 (1989); MICHAEL GROSSBERG, GOVERNING THE HEARTH 201–2 (1985); T. E. James, *The Illegitimate and Deprived Child: Legitimation and Adoption in* R. H. Graveson and F. R. Crane (eds), A CENTURY OF FAMILY LAW 42–3 (1957).

[23] eg Alaska allows birth parents to revoke their consent within ten days after consent has been executed if a court finds it to be in the child's best interest. Revocation is not allowed

within a short period of time after she relinquishes her child to a couple and she has been notified of the adoption proceeding.[24] There is also the inheritance aspect to the case's outcome. Generally, when birth parents' rights are terminated to allow for adoption, the termination is for all purposes including inheritance and succession rights. This was not always the case[25] but occurred over time as adoption became more and more socially acceptable and the adopted child became fully integrated into her new family. There are still some residual effects of the period when adopted children were treated quite differently from children not adopted. For example, at least six state statutes still allow adopted children to inherit from their biological parents.[26] In *In re Baby M* as long as no termination of parental rights had occurred, Melissa would be the statutory heir of Mrs Whitehead and Mr Stern, but not of Mrs Stern nor Mr Whitehead.

If Melissa had been born to Mr and Mrs Whitehead as their legitimate child, and then properly relinquished for adoption to the Sterns, in the

---

after the adoption decree has been issued. See ALASKA STAT § 25.23.070(b) (Lexis 1998). Arkansas allows a consent to be revoked within ten calendar days of the consent having been signed or within ten calendar days of the child's birth. See ARK CODE ANN § 9–9–209 (1998). Maine requires a three-day waiting period after a consent or surrender has been executed before it is valid. See ME REV STAT ANN tit § 1112 (West 1998). Missouri requires written consent to adoption to be reviewed by a judge. The consent can not be obtained before the infant is forty-eight hours old. See MO ANN STAT § 453.030 (West 1997).

[24] In New Jersey, once a birth mother validly surrenders her child to an agency, she can not revoke her consent. In a private placement, she can object to the adoption within twenty days of her receiving notice of the adoption proceeding. See N J STAT ANN § 9: 3–41; 9.3–46 (West 1993); see also Matter of Adoption of Child by D.M.H., 641 A2d 235 (N.J. 1994); Sees v Baber, 377 A2d 628 (NJ 1977).

[25] After reviewing adoption decisions and legislation in the United States, a 1936 Note in the Iowa Law Review concluded with these statements:

'1. The adopted child may inherit from his natural parents and relatives, and from his adoptive parents, but not from his adoptive relatives.

'2. Rights of inheritance from the adopted child are given to adoptive parents and relatives, but not to the natural family; in some states the property is divided according to its source.

'Two unfortunate results are apparent. The adopted child is in a better situation than other children are, for he can inherit from four parents. The framers of the general adoption statutes surely never intended this . . .

'The second injustice is that the adoptive relatives may inherit from him, but he may not inherit from them.' Note, *Legislation and Decisions on Inheritance Rights of Adopted Children*, 22 IOWA L REV 145, 153 (1936).

In sixty-three years, the inheritance rights of adopted children have changed dramatically, reflecting the attitudinal change about fully integrating the adopted child into her adoptive family.

[26] See eg KAN STAT ANN § 59–2118(b) (1994); LA CIV CODE ANN art 214 (West 1993); R I GEN LAWS § 15–7–17 (Michie 1993); TEX PROB CODE ANN art 40 (West Supp. 1999); VT STAT ANN tit 15, § 448 (1993); WYO STAT ANN § 2–4–0107 (Lexis 1999). Wyoming has an unusual provision that allows biological relatives to inherit from the adopted person. See WYO STAT ANN § 2–4–107 (Lexis 1999).

1960s or before, it would have been unusual, but not impossible, for the birth parents to have contact with their child after her adoption. However, from the 1970s into the 1990s, adoption of newborns or infants with visitation rights in the birth parents—called 'open adoption'—has become more and more common but by no means standard practice.

Open Adoption: Visitation Rights for Birth Parents

In non-relative adoptions, the conventional agency practice in mid-century was not to allow a birth mother to have contact with the adoptive family, now referred to as one aspect of 'open adoption.' Adoption agencies followed a theory of child development that the successful integration of an adopted child into the new adoptive family would be complicated if the child's relationship with her birth parents were to continue. It was thought that the child would be confused as to her loyalties and the objects of her affection. To allow a birth mother to conditionally relinquish her child would support her ambivalence toward giving her child up, if she had any, and prevent her acceptance of the finality of adoption. Also, the adoptive parents would have a feeling of being observed and even scrutinized, thus finding it difficult to form a complete and lasting attachment to their adopted child. In a certain sense, open adoption is like some forms of joint custody in divorce without the birth mother and the adoptive couple having had a previous relationship to support the new arrangement.

A birth mother who chose to place her child privately would not be subject to an agency's rules about contact. In the 1990s if she entered into an open adoption agreement as the consideration for relinquishing her child to an adoptive couple, the agreement could be enforced if a state statute specifically allowed visitation rights. Absent a statutory provision a judge, using his discretionary power, could enforce the agreement if it advanced the child's best interests.

Whether a state legislature should modify its adoption statute to allow open adoption or whether a judge should interpret an adoption statute in such a way as to allow it poses a fundamental question: should the model of adoption that has resulted in the complete termination of the birth parents' rights in their child and has been part of American law for many years continue, or should the model be changed? Traditionalists would say that adoption requires termination of parental rights for all purposes. If a birth parent does not want her rights fully terminated, she can agree to relinquish her child to a legal guardian. Guardianship is a flexible status allowing for a variety of ways of dividing responsibilities between the birth parent and the court-appointed guardian. Long-term foster care with visitation may be another alternative if a state or private agency would accept the child and if an appropriate foster family was available. The major drawback of these alternatives is financial. Unless the birth mother has the means to support these alternatives, she might be forced to relinquish her child for adoption.

Open adoption introduces a new model of adoption and an alternative to the traditional family model of one set of parents and their children. It removes the mystery of the birth parents' identity, thus eliminating the need for secrecy in the adoption process and closed adoption records. In some respects allowing open adoption supports personal autonomy by preserving a birth mother's decision-making powers. She can control the terms of the adoption.

Open Adoption: Access to Adoption Rcords

During the 1970s and again in the late 1990s, the issue of whether identifying information from adoption records should be disclosed to adult adopted children and birth parents received national attention in the media.[27] Making adoption records accessible to parties to the adoption is complicated because there might be two sets of records: one in the possession of the placement agency or person who arranged the adoption and the other in the court where the adoption decree was issued. Identifying information including a family and medical history about birth parents and the adopted child would be recorded in a licensed and reputable agency. However, such information might not be available in a private placement unless the lawyer or physician obtained it and safely

---

[27] For a full discussion of open records, see E. WAYNE CARP, FAMILY MATTERS (1998). For the personal stories of adopted adults who searched for their birth parents and the experiences they had, see TIM GREEN, A MAN AND HIS MOTHER—AN ADOPTED SON'S SEARCH (1997); FLORENCE FISHER, THE SEARCH FOR ANNA FISHER (1973).

Mike Leigh's prize-winning 1996 British film, SECRETS AND LIES, examined the issue of a young woman, the illegitimate child of a lower class white mother and black father, who had been adopted by a middle class black family. Following the death of her adopted mother, she began to search for her birth mother, first obtaining information from the agency that placed her and then arranging to meet her mother. She had not known that her mother was white, nor had the mother known the race of her daughter because of events at the child's birth. The film demonstrates in an artistic way the extent to which blood ties are so important to both the adopted child and the birth mother, regardless of the race of either. It also portrayed quite vividly the initial underlying hostility toward race even within a family, and how this lessens and perhaps evaporates once the adopted child becomes better known and integrated into the family.

The act that prompted the young woman's search, the death of her adoptive mother, illustrated an important point made in John Triseliotis's book, IN SEARCH OF ORIGINS (1973) that an adopted person's seeking the identity of her birth parents usually follows some personal loss. That loss, he writes, triggers the person's earliest loss, that of a birth mother. Triseliotis's study has important implications for the law, particularly for the issue of open records and for social work in dealing with adult adopted children and the meaning of their search.

secured it. Court adoption records are impounded and access to them is not a matter of right, but dependent on a judicial determination that the individual seeks the information for a good cause.

Whether adoption records should be open to adult adopted children as a matter of right was raised in 1979 when a group of adult adoptees sued the Director of Vital Records in the City of New York, certain New York judges, and adoption agencies in the federal court in New York.[28] They claimed that the New York statutes that required the sealing of adoption records were a violation of the due process and equal protection clauses of the Fourteenth Amendment to the United States Constitution. In addition, the adoptees argued that the Thirteenth Amendment also applied in that the sealing of adoption records imposed on them an incident of slavery by abolishing the parental relationship. The Federal Court of Appeals affirmed the lower court's decision and held that the New York sealed records statutes did not violate substantive due process in that the state recognized the privacy interests of both birth parents and adopted children. Further, the court held that equal protection was not violated either, because New York had an important state interest in advancing the social policy of protecting the confidentiality afforded birth parents when they place children for adoption. The court rejected the adult adoptees' slavery argument when it held that the sealed records statutes did not divest birth parents of their children. It was the adoption laws which accomplished that, and those laws were not challenged. In the last sentence of the opinion the court basically said that to open adoption records adult adoptees had either to conform to the requirements of the New York statute by obtaining official approval first or seek legislative changes.

Between 1979 and 1999 legislative changes occurred in New York and beyond. At least seven jurisdictions allow identifying information to be released by the court either because of the consent of the adopted child and her birth parents or for good cause. About the same number of jurisdictions allow access to an adopted child's birth certificate when she is an adult, and twenty-four states have statutory provisions that set up mutual consent registries.[29]

In 1997, the 1996 Tennessee statute that allowed adult adoptees to have access to their adoption records was challenged in the federal courts by adoptive parents and birth mothers. They sought to enjoin state officials from enforcing the statute that would have the effect of disclosing confidential information to the adopted child. They argued that the new

---

[28] See *ALMA Society Inc v Mellon*, 601 F2d 1238 (2nd Cir) cert denied, 100 S Ct 531 (1979).
[29] See *Appendix 13–A, State Procedures for Obtaining Identifying Information from Confidential Adoption Records in* 2 ADOPTION LAW AND PRACTICE, n 19 above.

law violated their right of privacy, which they interpreted to encompass family privacy, reproductive privacy, and privacy against disclosure of confidential information under the federal constitution. The Federal District Court denied the injunction, as did the Court of Appeals. To the Court of Appeals, the open adoption records controversy involved competing interests: the interest of a child adopted during her infancy to know the identity of her birth parents and the birth parents' interest in secrecy. The court held that the child's interest outweighed those of the birth parents.

The court added that if the plaintiffs thought that the Tennessee constitution provided them with greater protection, they should sue in the state court.[30] The plaintiffs filed an action in the Tennessee Court of Appeals and were successful in arguing that the statute impaired their vested legal expectations in the adoption statute (before the 1996 amendment), as well as their privacy rights under the state constitution.[31]

The state of Tennessee appealed that decision to the Supreme Court of Tennessee, which upheld the validity of the 1996 amended statute. To the court, the 1996 adoption statute did not violate the parents' privacy rights nor did it impair any vested legal expectations under the former adoption statute.[32]

PLACEMENT

In a jurisdiction that allows private placement, a birth mother who places her child for adoption can choose anyone she likes as adoptive parents. However, if a birth mother relinquishes her infant to an agency, that agency will follow its own regulations regarding placement factors. In certain respects placement factors reflect larger cultural assumptions about parenthood and the family, both of which change in time. They also have been and are used to promote certain values such as religion and ethnic and racial integrity. Whether a placement is arranged privately or through an agency, the placement is subject to judicial approval according to statutory standards.

From the 1950s and into the 1970s agency placements in voluntary relinquishment cases used the nuclear family model as the standard placement for an infant. Agencies tended to prefer married couples of childbearing ages, who were well educated, financially secure, and who could provide a child with all the necessities of life in order for her to

---

[30] See *Doe v Sundquist*, 106 F3d. 702 (6th Cir 1997).
[31] See *Doe v Sundquist*, 1997 WL 354786 (Tenn Cir Ct May 2 1997) (NO 97C-941).
[32] See *Doe v Sundquist*, 2 SW3d 919 (Tenn 1999).

mature into a productive adult. In addition, agencies tried to match the child with the adoptive parents so that the new family would look like it had been created through biology not the law. If a religiously affiliated private agency placed the child, that agency would require the adoptive couple to be a member of its religion or, in certain instances, to promise to raise the child in the religion associated with the agency.

By the 1990s, adoption practice had changed because of a number of factors. They included the decrease in the number of newborns available for adoption because of the availability of abortion and increased social tolerance for unwed mothers and their children.[33] Agency placement criteria also changed, particularly for private religiously affiliated agencies. The reason was that they could no longer choose adoptive placements on a religious basis if they accepted funds from community charities, like the United Way, which conditioned its financial support on non-discrimination policies. In addition, agencies generally recognized the social acceptance of new forms of families such as single-parent and same-sex parents. However, the principle that an adopted child should be loved, wanted, and feel secure in her new family and community has remained constant.

During the 1950s, religion was the factor that was controversial and the subject of litigation. At issue in two widely publicized cases, one in New York[34] and the other in Massachusetts,[35] was the interpretation of adoption statutes that directed the court 'when practicable' to award custody only to persons of the same religious faith as that of the child. The highest court in New York held that 'when practicable' gave the court discretion and included a concern for the best interests of the child, that is whether the current placement with a couple of a different religion from the child was more beneficial than any available alternatives. The Supreme Judicial Court of Massachusetts held that 'when practicable' should be interpreted as a mandate to search for an adoptive couple of the same religion as the child. Thus, to the Massachusetts court placing a child of one religion with a family of a different religion would be approved only if no families of the child's religion could be located.

Forty years later, race replaced religion not so much as a subject of litigation, but as a major concern of African Americans. Basically the question is: under what circumstances should children of one race who are *voluntarily* relinquished for adoption by their birth mothers be placed

---

[33] For this reason, many American couples have sought to adopt foreign children. The whole issue of international adoption is beyond the scope of this chapter.

[34] See *In re Maxwell*, 151 NE2d 484 (NY 1958).

[35] See *In re Goldman*, 121 NE2d 843 (Mass 1954), cert denied, 348 US 942 (1955).

with adoptive parents of another race?[36] Some advocates of transracial placements base their position on the interpretation of the best interests of the child, which they define as advancing the child's psychological need for affection, stimulation, nurturing, safety, and stability. To them such a goal can be achieved regardless of the race of the adoptive parents. Others justify their preference for transracial adoption because of their strong belief in anti-discrimination and their view that racially mixed families provide the first step toward national harmony.[37]

Opponents of transracial adoption (except in unusual circumstances) have suggested that advocates take too narrow a view of the psychological needs of children and fail to understand the extent to which race defines the person in twentieth-century America. They also claim that proponents may be naïve about racial tensions and thus are unrealistic about the abilities of adoptive parents to fully appreciate the difficulties the adopted child raised in a family of a different race will face during its youth and adulthood. Further, it has been said that placing African American children with white adoptive parents robs these children of their heritage, which includes a deep respect for the family and its special educational role for African Americans.[38] There is also the wider issue of the place of the African American family in American life. Transracial adoption may add to the disintegration of that family precisely at a time when its stability is being threatened by social and economic forces.

---

[36] By transracial adoption, I am referring to the placement for adoption of a child clearly identified as having been born of parents of the same race with an individual or a couple of a different race. I am not referring to mixed-race children or mixed-race parents. I am also emphasizing 'voluntary' relinquishments in this discussion. The issue of transracial adoption under the involuntary system is discussed later in this chapter.

[37] Professor Randall Kennedy has written: 'Race matching ought not to be permitted. Eradicating it would have several beneficial consequences. Abolishing race matching would redound to the immediate benefit of children in need of foster care or adoptive homes by removing an impediment that currently slows or prevents child placements when parents of the "correct" race are not on hand. Getting rid of race matching would also have a broader, long-term beneficent consequence by signaling in a vivid way that, in the eyes of the law, monochromatic families are no better than, and certainly entitled to no preference over, racially mixed families . . . People who are persuaded by my approach should insist that administrators and judges *enforce* antidiscrimination norms in the context of family law.' Randall Kennedy, *How are We Doing With* Loving? *Race, Law, and Intermarriage*, 77 BUL REV 815, 821 (1997).

[38] Thirty-two years ago, Andrew Billingsley, who was Assistant Chancellor for Academic Affairs and Associate Professor of Social Welfare at the University of California at Berkeley, wrote in a book that received a great deal of attention at the time:

'For the Negro family, socialization is doubly challenging, for the family must teach its young members not only how to be human, but also how to be black in a white society. The requirements are not the same.

'Negro families must teach their children very early in life, sometimes as early as two years of age, the meaning of being black.' ANDREW BILLINGSLEY, BLACK FAMILIES IN WHITE AMERICA 28 (1968).

Some scholars, questioning the conscious or unconscious motives behind placing African American infants with white adoptive parents, have asked: is transracial adoption another form of racial annihilation? Is transracial adoption a replay of the historical positioning of African Americans in American life, namely of African Americans serving white Americans? These are important questions raising legitimate concerns about how a history of racial oppression affects adoption policies.[39]

Consider the position of the leading American child welfare organization, whose standards were used to accredit adoption agencies in the 1950s, on using religion and race as factors in adoption placement:

A child should ordinarily be placed in a home where the religion of adoptive parents is the same as that of the child, unless the parents have specified that the child should or may be placed with a family of another religion. Every effort (including interagency and interstate referrals) should be made to place the child within his own faith, or that designated by his parents. If however such matching means that placement might never be feasible, or involves a substantial delay in placement or placement in a less suitable home, a child's need for a permanent family of his own requires that consideration should then be given to placing the child in a home of a different religion.[40]

. . . It should not be assumed that difficulties will necessarily arise if adoptive parents and children are of different racial origin. At the present time, however, children placed in adoptive families with similar racial characteristics, such as color, can become more easily integrated into the average family group and community.[41]

The peculiar wording of the race provision in terms of the negative assumption reveals a perspective common for the time. Why is it not assumed that difficulties will necessarily arise if adoptive parents and children are of different religions? Substituting the word 'race' for

---

[39] Professor Linda Gordon has written: '[M]ixed race adoptions, even more than mixed-race couples, occur only in one direction: there is debate about whether whites should adopt children of color, but adoptions of white children by parents of color are so rare they are not even debated. This dimension of racial policy in child welfare suggests something of the degree to which race is about hierarchy, not difference.' Linda Gordon, The Great Arizona Orphan Abduction 309 (1999).

For a full discussion (with extensive references) of the social, historical, and legal context in which transracial adoption has developed and for responses to the empirical research on the subject, see Ruth-Arlene W. Howe, *Transracial Adoption (TRA): Old Prejudices and Discrimination Float Under a New Halo*, 6 BU Pub Int L J 409 (1997); Ruth-Arlene W. Howe, *Redefining the Transracial Adoption Controversy*, 2 Duke J of Gender Law & Policy 131 (1995); see also David S. Rosettenstein, *Transracial Adoption and the Statutory Preference Schemes: Before the 'Best Interests' and After the 'Melting Pot,'* 68 St John's L Rev 137 (1994). For discussion of empirical research supporting the positive aspects of transracial adoption, see generally Rita J. Simon et al, The Case for Transracial Adoption (1994); Rita J. Simon and Howard Alstein, Adoption, Race, and Identity 1–55 (1992).

[40] Child Welfare League of America, Standards for Adoption Services 25 (1958).

[41] *ibid* at 24.

'religion' in the provision on religion is more reflective of the last decade of the twentieth century, when race matters:

A child should ordinarily be placed in a home where the *race* of adoptive parents is the same as that of the child, unless the parents have specified that the child should or may be placed with a family of another race. Every effort (including interagency and interstate referrals) should be made to place the child within his own *race*, or that designated by his parents. If however such matching means that placement might never be feasible, or involves a substantial delay in placement or placement in a less suitable home, a child's need for a permanent family of his own requires that consideration should then be given to placing the child in a home of a different *race*.

Although placement factors have remained fairly consistent in the past forty years, the priority given to individual factors has changed depending on the circumstances of the relinquishment and the availability of adoptive parents. The nuclear family of a man, woman, and child which was thought of as conventional or as an ideal is now one model among others: single parent, unmarried heterosexual parents, unmarried parents of the same sex. The preference given to placement factors used to place infants voluntarily relinquished to adoption agencies differs from those used to place neglected or abused children whose parents' rights have been terminated. The major reason is that unlike the involuntary system where agencies report a shortage of prospective adoptive applicants, the number of married heterosexual couples waiting to adopt healthy white newborns far exceeds the supply of those infants, and therefore agencies give priority to those couples.

Step-parent and Second Parent Adoptions

With serial marriages now more common than in the past, step-parent adoption has become more prevalent. The fact pattern of such adoptions might involve a woman who has divorced her first husband or whose husband has died. Her second husband's seeking to adopt her child usually removes the adoption from the requirements of an agency involvement in those states that mandate agency placements. Judicial approval is still required, although a home study report by a court official or an agency designated to perform the investigation and a waiting period, normally required in adoption, are ordinarily waived. Adoption terminates the child's statutory inheritance rights from and through his birth father.

The conflict that might arise as a result of a step-parent adoption would concern the visitation rights of blood relatives of the divorced or deceased husband over the objection of the child's mother. Since the second husband's adoption of his wife's child would have severed the child's legal relationships with his divorced or deceased father's blood relatives, he would have no legal ties with his paternal grandparents. All American states have grandparent visitation statutes, which were enacted to provide grandparents with standing and the opportunity to maintain a connection with their grandchildren, particularly after the children's parents had divorced. These statutes have been challenged on constitutional grounds as violating parents' right to raise their children without interference from the state, absent abuse or neglect. During the 1990s, four state supreme courts held that grandparent visitation statutes were unconstitutional under their state constitutions.[42] Since the grandparent visitation statutes do not directly relate to adoption, grandparents, technically no longer legally related to their grandchildren, would have to appeal to the judge's discretion or in some states her broad equitable powers to grant them visitation rights. The judge would have to balance the privacy and liberty interests of the parents to raise their children without interference from others with the interests of the grandparents and the child to maintain a connection with each other.

A phenomenon of the past decade is second parent adoption. Two New England cases decided in 1993[43] raised the same issue: whether the state law required the termination of a birth mother's parental rights as a prerequisite to her child being adopted by her partner of the same-sex. In both cases, the state supreme courts held that termination was not required, and that the adoption by the birth mother's partner should be allowed. These cases are important for the courts' statements about a same sex couple as parents. The practical result of a court's approving such an adoption by a birth mother and her female partner is the legal recognition given to them as parents. Since the Hawaii court in a major American case on same-sex marriage[44] spent most of its opinion

---

[42] See *Beagle v Beagle*, 678 So 2d 1271 (Fla 1996); *Brooks v Parkerson*, 454 SE 2d 769 (Ga 1995) cert. denied, 516 US 942 (1995); *Von Eiff v Azicri*, 720 2d 510 (ND 1998); *Hawk v Hawk*, 855 SW 2d 573 (Tenn 1993); For cases holding that grandparent visitation statutes are constitutional, see *King v King*, 828 SW 2d 630 (Ky 1992), cert denied, 506 US 941 (1992); *Herndon v Tuhey*, 857 SW 2d 203 (Mo 1993); see also *Brooks v Parkerson*, 454 SE 2d 769, 775 (dissenting opinion by Justice Bentham). In 2000, the United States Supreme Court held that the Washington statute that permitted any person to petition a court for visitation rights at any time, and which authorized the court to grant such a petition if it served the best interests of the child was an unconstitutional interference with the fundamental rights of parents to raise their children. *Troxel v Granville*, 120 S Ct 2054 (2000).

[43] See *In re Adoption of Tammy*, 619 NE 2d 315 (Mass 1993); *Adoption of B.L.V.B. & E.L.V.B.*, 628 A2d 1271 (Vt 1993).

[44] See *Baehr v Lewin*, 852 P 2d 44 (Haw 1993). On Dec 20 1999, the Supreme Court of Vermont handed down the second major American case on same-sex marriage. In *Baker v State of Vermont*, No 98–032, the court relied on the common benefits clause of the state constitution, and held that there was no basis upon which to exclude same-sex couples from the benefits and protections afforded married couples. The court made passing reference to

discussing whether a same-sex couple could raise a child effectively, implying that parenthood, or at least the potential for it, was a test for marriage, these cases are valuable. They could provide the legal precedent for the proposition that female partners can be parents who will promote the best interests of the birth mother's infant. The Vermont and Massachusetts adoption cases may signal the beginning of social and legal acceptance of unconventional families beyond adoption.[45]

INVOLUNTARY MODEL

The Role of the Federal Government and the Absence of Personal Autonomy

Unlike the infants relinquished for adoption by their birth mothers to agencies or directly to an adoptive couple, children who are freed for adoption after a termination of parental rights proceeding in state courts are or have been in foster care. Because state foster care programs are part of a federally funded child welfare system, the federal government through the United States Department of Health and Human Services, a part of the executive branch of government and the United States Congress, the legislative branch, plays a very important role. The Department of Health and Human Services (formerly called the Department of Health, Education, and Welfare) develops model legislation for states to enact. It provides technical assistance to states, supports research, sets standards, and promulgates regulations for various child welfare programs in the states; the United States Congress enacts legislation authorizing funding for these programs.

---

the rearing of children and its relevance to same-sex marriage, but in no way relied on that issue in reaching its decision to send the matter to the state legislature for its consideration and ultimate determination as to how to implement the court's holding. For an analysis of the case, see Jerome A. Barron, Ch 12 in this volume.

[45] The Supreme Judicial Court of Massachusetts cited *Adoption of Tammy*, n 43 above, when it held that a woman who had established herself as a de facto parent of her female partner's child had visitation rights to that child after the termination of her relationship with the child's mother and over the mother's objection. See *E.N.O. v L.M.M.*, 711 NE 2d 886 (Mass. 1999). Justice Ruth Abrams wrote: 'The recognition of de facto parents is in accord with notions of the modern family. An increasing number of same gender couples, like the plaintiff and the defendant are deciding to have children. It is to be expected that children of nontraditional families, like other children, form parent relationships with both parents, whether those parents are legal or de facto . . . ' *ibid* at 891.

The 1960s and 1970s were decades in which child neglect and abuse began to be recognized as matters for public concern.[46] Major federal initiatives to reform foster care and adoption laws were undertaken to respond to the general problem of child maltreatment. It was during the 1960s that Children's Bureau, a division of the then United States Department of Health, Education, and Welfare, proposed the Model Child Abuse Mandatory Reporting Act.[47] It recommended the Act to the states as a model for a new law, which would put aside traditional concepts of family privacy and professional confidentiality and require certain people to report evidence of abuse or neglect. Within only a decade, all jurisdictions enacted some kind of mandatory child abuse and neglect reporting statute.[48] To provide funding for child abuse programs for states which had enacted child abuse reporting legislation, the US Congress enacted the Child Abuse Prevention and Treatment Act of 1974.

Perhaps not contemplated by policy makers was the effect widespread reporting would have on state foster care systems. By intervening in the family and removing children who were either abused or neglected and placing them in foster care, the state was placing a burden on an already taxed system not only in financial but human terms. During the six-year period from 1964 to 1970, the number of children in foster care rose from 192,300 to 326,700.[49]

By 1975, a child welfare crisis had developed, and the federal government focused on reducing the number of children in foster care as its next major initiative. To this end, policy makers concentrated on twin goals: programs designed to rehabilitate parents so that they could be reunited with their children or if that was not possible, to terminate their parental rights in a procedure that was fair to all the parties, and place the children for adoption. Thus the Model Act to Free Children for Permanent Placement was drafted and recommended to the states for enactment in one form or another.[50] That Act implemented the concept of permanency planning which the Children's Bureau had developed.

As in so many other human endeavors, solving one problem sometimes creates others. In this instance, it was found that a generation of

---

[46] One of the important studies at that time was LEONTINE R. YOUNG'S WEDNESDAY'S CHILDREN: A STUDY OF CHILD NEGLECT AND ABUSE (1964); see also DAVD GIL, VIOLENCE AGAINST CHILDREN (1970); JEANNE M. GIOVANNONI AND ROSINA M. BECRRA, DEFINING CHILD ABUSE (1979); SANFORD N. KATZ, WHEN PARENTS FAIL (1971). An important article that described a new syndrome was C. Henry Kempe, Frederic N. Silverman, Brandt F. Steele, William Droege-Mueller, and Henry K. Silver, *The Battered Child Syndrome*, 181 J AM MED ASSOC 4 (1962).

[47] For the major provisions of the Act, see Katz, n 46 above, at 45, n 13.

[48] See 42 USCA § 5106a(b) (West 1995).

[49] See DAVID FANSHEL and EUGENE B. SHINN, CHILDREN IN FOSTER CARE 29 (1978).

[50] The Act is reproduced in Sanford N. Katz, *Freeing Children for Permanent Placement through a Model Act*, 12 FAM LQ 203 (1978). For a discussion of the development of the Act and the policy underlying it, see Ruth-Arlene W. Howe, *Development of a Model Act to Free Children for Permanent Placement: A Case Study in Law and Social Planning*, 13 FAM LQ 257 (1979).

orphans would be created if adoptive homes could not be found for the children of parents whose parental rights had been terminated. One of the major barriers to adoption was financial. Foster parents who were ready, willing, and able to adopt children in their care learned that adoption would cut off federally funded monthly foster care payments, making adoption unaffordable. The solution to that problem was to create federally funded subsidies that would be attached to foster children who, for whatever reason, were difficult to place for adoption. Thus the concept of subsidized adoption was born, and the Model Subsidized Adoption Act was recommended to the states.[51] To assist states financially that established subsidy programs, the United States Congress passed the Adoption Assistance and Child Welfare Act of 1980.[52] That Act authorized the use of federal funds to support subsidized adoption for 'hard to place children.' In addition, to combat 'foster care drift' (children placed in one foster care facility after another without any planning for the child's permanent home), the Act required states to develop programs to prevent placements outside of the natural family. If a placement in foster care was necessary, the state was mandated to use 'reasonable efforts' to effectuate the child's return to her natural family.

During the 1980s and 1990s, the tension that has historically existed between the preservation of parental rights and termination of those rights for purposes of adoptive placement was played out in federal legislation.[53] In the Adoption and Safe Families Act of 1997[54] the federal government reaffirmed its policy toward protecting parental rights by mandating that state agencies use 'reasonable efforts' to reunite families after an initial intervention has occurred resulting in a child being placed in foster care. In order to further the goal of family preservation, the federal government provides funds to states whose termination of parental rights laws conform to federal requirements. These laws include severing parental ties because of a parent's serious criminal conduct or in cases in which the child has been in the state foster care system for fifteen of the most recent twenty-two months. The Act lists three exceptions to the time-frame limitation: if the child is placed with a relative (kinship placement), if termination would not be in the child's best interests, or if the state agency has not fulfilled its responsibility of using reasonable

---

[51] The Model Subsidized Adoption Act and Regulations is reproduced in Sanford N. Katz, *Subsidized Adoption in America*, 10 FAM LQ 3 (1976).

[52] Adoption Assistance and Child Welfare Act of 1980, Pub L No 96–272, 94 Stat 501, 42 USCA §§ 620–8, 670–9a (West 1994).

[53] This tension is discussed in ELIZABETH BARTHOLET, NOBODY'S CHILDREN: ABUSE AND NEGLECT, FOSTER DRIFT, AND THE ADOPTION ALTERNATIVE (1999).

[54] Adoption and Safe Families Act of 1997, Pub L L105–89, Nov 19 1997, 111 Stat 2115, 42 USCA 1305 (West Supp 1998).

efforts to reunite the child with her natural family. These three exceptions, the second and third of which are essentially vague,[55] suggest that there may be a reluctance of the federal government to promote adoption over termination even though the Act's stated intent is: 'To promote the adoption of children in foster care.'

Placement

The federal government's involvement in adoption placement factors is only relevant in so far as they relate to programs funded by the government. In 1994, Congress enacted the Multiethnic Placement Act of 1994,[56] which permitted a state agency to consider race as a placement factor if, in conjunction with other factors, it was in the best interests of the child. The Act also required state agencies actively to recruit ethnically diverse foster and adoptive parents. The life of the Multiethnic Placement Act was short. Two years after its enactment, it was replaced with provisions in the Small Business and Job Protection Act of 1996.[57] The provision of that law that deals with adoption prohibits any agency or individual involved in adoption or foster care placement who receives federal funds to deny a child's adoptive or foster care placement on the basis of race, color, or national origin.[58]

Transracial adoption is a very relevant issue in the involuntary system of adoption. The reason is that many children in foster care are African American, and they are in the adoption pool.[59] Proponents of transracial adoption claim that African American children must be placed with parents of a different race because of the lack of suitable adoptive parents

[55] Indeed, in *Suter v Artist M*, 503 US 347 (1992), the United States Supreme Court held that the phrase 'reasonable efforts' did not 'unambiguously confer an enforceable right upon the Act's beneficiaries' to confer an enforceable private right under 42 USC § 1983.

[56] See 42 USCA § 5115a (West 1994).

[57] See Pub L 104–88, Title 1 Sub tit H, § 1808, 110 Stat 1755, 1903 (1996) (amending the Social Security Act). The provisions were designed to 'Remove Barriers to Interethnic Adoption.' An interesting aspect to the federal law is that in addition to providing that an agency will lose federal funds if it does not conform to the requirements of the law, it also gives an aggrieved individual a right to sue in the federal court against a state or agency which is in violation of the Act.

[58] Native Americans are exempt from this provision. The adoption of Native American children is governed by the Indian Child Welfare Act of 1978, which limits placement to the child's family, members of the tribe or other Native American families. See 25 USC §§ 1901–63.

[59] Jane Waldfogel wrote, 'In 1980 9.5 of every 1,000 African-American children were in placement, as opposed to 3.1 per 1,000 Caucasians. Ten years later, data from the five states [California, Illinois, Michigan, New York, and Texas] with the largest foster-care population indicated that African-Americans continue to be disproportionately likely to be placed.' JANE WALDFOGEL, THE FUTURE OF CHILD PROTECTION: HOW TO BREAK THE CYCLE OF ABUSE AND NEGLECT 11 (1998).

who share their race. They make the point that if a rigid race-matching requirement were enforced, African American children would have to remain in some kind of foster care setting beyond the federal mandated time-frame.

The argument that African American families are unavailable to adopt children of their own race is difficult to understand in light of the fact that traditionally, African Americans have had a deep-rooted custom of caring for members of their own and extended family as well as friends and neighbors.[60] Indeed, many of the African Americans who migrated from the south to the north lived with relatives or friends. Some have suggested that if major efforts as well as incentives were in place to recruit African American families, the results would be positive.[61]

Because of the need for foster and adoptive families for children in the child welfare system, agencies have chosen individuals and couples to care for these children who may offer different styles of family organizations. Single women and men, couples beyond child-bearing years, and same-sex couples can qualify as foster or adoptive parents of children who are hard to place because they may have a physical disability or emotional problems, may be part of a sibling group, or who are above the age of 5.

Open Adoption

Unless an infant has been removed from her mother at birth, for example because of the mother's drug addiction, children in the involuntary system of adoption may have lived with their parents before their placement in the child welfare system. Thus, the identity of their parents is not an issue. Children may remember their parents and may in fact have had contact with them during their foster care placement.[62] Whereas post-adoption visitation may be the consideration for relinquishing an infant under the voluntary system it occurs most commonly at a different stage in the process. Lawyers for social service agencies or for birth parents use it as a strategy for facilitating a settlement of a termination of parental rights case either before trial or at appeal. Regardless of the adoption

---

[60] See BILLINGSLEY, n 38 above, at 15–26; see also see ROBERT B. HILL, *et al*, RESEARCH ON THE AFRICAN-AMERICAN FAMILY: A HOLISTIC PERSPECTIVE (1993).

[61] Professor Howe presents a forceful argument based on current data supporting her position that if agencies made concerted efforts to recruit African American families for children in need of an adoptive home, they would find success. See Howe, *Transracial Adoption*, n 39 above, at 427–46.

[62] Parental visitation has been regarded as important for a successful foster care placement. See FANSHEL and SHINN, n 49 above, at 110–11.

system, post-adoption visitation agreements need statutory authority and judicial approval based on the best interests of the child standard.

In approving the enforceability of a post-adoption visitation agreement (if it was in the child's best interests) in an involuntary adoption case, Chief Justice Ellen Peters of the Supreme Court of Connecticut linked the new model of adoption—open adoption—with the new family of the late twentieth century:

Case law in other jurisdictions does not persuade us that we should strike down the visitation agreement in this case. To a significant extent, the cases turn on legislative determinations that vary from state to state. We note nonetheless that [a New York case] concluded, as do we, that the statutory creation of an adoptive family does not automatically require complete severance of the child from all further contact with former relatives. Similarly, [a Maryland case] concluded, as do we, that as long as the best interests of the child is the determinative criterion, public policy does not forbid an agreement about visitation rights between a genetic parent and adoptive parents. . . .

Traditional models of the nuclear family have come, in recent years, to be replaced by various configurations of parents, stepparents, adoptive parents and grandparents . . . .We are not prepared to assume that the welfare of children is best served by a narrow definition of those whom we permit to continue to manifest their deep concern for a child's growth and development. . . . '[63]

It remains to be seen whether judicial recognition of this new family will change other aspects of the involuntary model of adoption.

CONCLUSION

During the last half of the twentieth century the institution of adoption has undergone major changes, making it fundamentally different from what it was at the beginning of the century. Throughout the century, but more during the last half, there has been a certain amount of ambivalence about adoption. This attitude may be the result of the common law tradition of using blood ties as determining family membership and ownership of property. In addition, at the beginning of the century, the illegitimate child, the usual subject of adoption, received little protection from the law and was considered a social outcast. The father of the illegitimate child was similarly the object of discrimination. The whole adoption process excluded the father. Illegitimacy with all its negative implications for the mother, father, and child was a status to be concealed. It is little wonder, then, that adoption was clothed in secrecy, and an

---

[63] *Michaud v Wawruck*, 551 A2d 738, 741–2 (Conn 1988).

adopted child's past was hidden from everyone, even the child herself. Adoption was in many ways a state-imposed legal fiction.

The constitutionalization of family law with its emphasis on the protection of individual rights that began in the 1960s and continued into the 1970s had a direct impact on adoption. During that period, putative fathers who showed some interest in their illegitimate children were successful in pressing their claim for recognition and for due process and equal protection rights. Adult adopted children used these same constitutional arguments in their attempt to gain access to their sealed adoption records. At the same time, maintaining that opening adoption records would violate their constitutional right of privacy, birth parents attempted to keep the records closed. Courts seem to be favoring adult adopted children in this constitutional struggle. The wave of the future is in more openness in adoption.

Open adoption with post-adoption visitation presents a paradox. By the end of the twentieth century, in the vast number of states, for purposes of inheritance adopted children no longer are members of their birth families, but have been fully integrated into their adopted families. Yet post-adoption visitation by birth parents continues the relationship that had been legally terminated. If more and more states enact legislation allowing such visitation, two models of adoption will be firmly established in the American adoption laws. One will be open adoption, which will allow post-adoption visitation; the other will be closed adoption.

The central issue at the beginning of the twenty-first century is whether adoption as we have known it, even with the new openness, will continue as the principal alternative to raising one's biological children. If birth and fertility rates drop, and if mothers decide to keep their children and raise them themselves, the voluntary system of adoption may lose its importance. The future of adoption in the involuntary system will be based on the foster care population and the extent to which federal legislation requirements shorten the time children may stay under state supervision. Much depends on the incidence of child abuse and neglect, the major causes for removal of children from their birth parents and their placement in state foster care.

The independent versus agency adoption controversy has raised important issues about state regulation and personal autonomy that are relevant to resolving problems presented by assisted reproduction and surrogacy, perhaps the alternative to traditional adoption in the next century. We have seen the abuses that can occur without regulation: children can become a commodity that can be sold. In the area of reproductive technology, science is ahead of the public's understanding and the law's response to its advancement. Legislatures are the conventional forum in which issues of such social importance are normally resolved. If legislatures fail to act because of lack of will or political consensus, courts will have to respond on a case-by-case basis. In whichever forum these issues are presented for resolution, the century and a half of the legal history of adoption will be an indispensable guide.

14

English Adoption Law: Past, Present, and Future

N. V. LOWE

INTRODUCTION

Adoption was not formally recognized under English law until 1927. In the next forty years, however, the number of orders steadily rose and the concept seems to have been quickly understood and absorbed by the community. In contrast, the last quarter of the twentieth century witnessed a dramatic decline in the number of adoption orders made. Whether this decline is terminal remains to be seen but while a total of 862,629 adoption orders were made in England and Wales in the period 1927–98,[1] at current rates[2] the millionth order will not be made until the 2030s and indeed there must be at least a doubt as to whether this milestone will ever be reached. This chapter discusses the establishment of adoption as a recognized legal order in England, traces the development and changing use of such orders during the twentieth century, and, in the light of that experience, discusses what role, if any, adoption will have in the new century.

GIVING FORMAL RECOGNITION TO ADOPTION

Background

Since at common law[3] parental rights and duties were inalienable,[4] adoption had necessarily to be a statutory creation but, even within the common

---

[1] This figure is calculated by aggregating the number of orders made in each year based on statistics published in Appendix B to the Report of the Departmental Committee on the Adoption of Children (the Houghton Report) 1972 Cmnd 5107 for the years 1927–71, on statistics published in OPCS Monitor, FM3 for the years 1971–4 and on the 1997 Marriage, Divorce and Adoption Statistics (Series FM2, no 25) Table 6.2, for the years 1975–98. Readers are warned, however, that alternative figures based on the Annual Judicial Statistics are less reliable—see further below.

[2] According to the 1997 Marriage, Divorce and Adoption Statistics, 4,387 adoption orders were made in 1998.

[3] Compare Roman Law which had developed the concepts of *adoptio* and *adrogatio*. For a discussion of this and other ancient systems see J. F. Brosnan 'The Law of Adoption' (1922) 22 *Columbia LR* 332. Modern European jurisdictions had tended to develop adoptions law well before England and Wales, see, eg, the Civil Codes of France, Germany, Italy, and Spain (referred to by Brosnan, above, at 334). Scandinavian adoption law also predates (but only just) English adoption law. In Norway, for example, adoption was introduced in 1917.

[4] See *Humphrys v Polak* [1901] 2 KB 385, CA and *Brooks v Brooks* [1923] 1 KB 257.

law world, such legislation came late to the United Kingdom. Thus, while an adoption statute was passed as early as 1851 in the common law State of Massachusetts[5] (an example followed by the rest of the states of the USA by the turn of the century)[6] in 1873 in New Brunswick, Canada,[7] in 1881 in New Zealand,[8] and in 1896 in Western Australia,[9] it was only following the Adoption of Children Act 1926 that formal adoptions became possible in England and Wales, and through the Adoption Act (Northern Ireland) 1929 and the Adoption of Children (Scotland) Act 1930, that such orders could be made respectively in Northern Ireland and Scotland.

Nineteenth-century Attempts to Introduce Adoption Legislation

Attempts to introduce adoption legislation were made in both 1889 and 1890.[10] The object of each Bill was to protect both children and adults involved in so-called 'de facto adoptions' (that is, where children were looked after by relatives or strangers either with the parents' consent or following the latter's abandonment of their children) by preventing parents or guardians from removing their children after they had consented to the 'adoption' unless they could persuade the court that such recovery was for the child's benefit. As the Earl of Meath explained,[11] in such cases it was: 'a common occurrence for children who have been placed in

---

[5] In fact, even before 1851 some states, such as Mississippi, Texas, and Vermont, had adoption statutes but they merely established procedures for recording private adoptions.

[6] See the *Report of the Committee on Child Adoption* (Hopkinson Report), Cmd 1254 (1921) para 5.

[7] See the Adoption Act of that year. Most provinces, however, did not enact adoption legislation until the 1920s, eg the Adoption Act 1920 in British Columbia, followed in Ontario by the Adoption Act 1921—see generally M. Hughes, 'Adoption in Canada' in D. Mendes de Costa (ed), *Studies in Canadian Family Law*, ch 4.

[8] Under the Adoption of Children Act 1881. See B. Inglis, *Family Law*, vol 2 (1970) 422–3.

[9] Namely under the Adoption of Children Act 1896. Tasmania passed legislation in 1920, New South Wales in 1923, and South Australia in 1925. However, adoption legislation in Victoria (1928) and Queensland (1935) postdated the English legislation. See, eg H. Finlay, R. Bailey Harris, and M. Ottowski: *Family Law in Australia* (5th edn 1997) para 8.7. The existence of adoption legislation elsewhere led Sir Henry Slesser to remark during the parliamentary debate on the Adoption of Children Bill 1925 that 'there is scarcely another country in the world either a foreign country or a British Dominion where there is not statutory recognition of the legal relation between the child and the adopted parent' (*House of Lords Debates* (Hansard) (5th Series), vol 182, col 1718). Interestingly, the Earl of Meath made a similar comment in 1889 when introducing the second reading of the ill-fated Adoption of Children Bill, see *House of Lords Debates* (3rd Series), vol 343, at col 1388)—discussed further below.

[10] See respectively, the Adoption of Children Bill (No 101) 1889, which had its first reading on 31 May 1889 (see *Parliamentary Debates* (Hansard) (3rd Series), vol 336, col 1517 but which was withdrawn at its second reading (see *ibid*, vol 338, cols 502–14); and the Adoption of Children Bill (No. 56) 1890, which had its first reading on 17 Apr 1890 (see *Parliamentary Debates* (3rd Series), vol 343, col 665) but which was withdrawn at its second reading (see *ibid*, cols 1385–406). I am indebted to Kazu Niijima for this information.

[11] *Parliamentary Debates* (Hansard) (3rd Series), vol 338 at col 502.

orphanages or adopted to be subsequently removed by their parents for the sole purpose of deriving pecuniary advantage.' Although there was general acknowledgement of the existence of the 'evil' of unscrupulous parents recovering their hitherto deserted children so as to gain advantage of their offspring's earnings, there was overwhelming opposition to what was regarded as a breach of one of 'the cardinal principles of the law of England',[12] namely, the inalienability of parental rights and obligations. Accordingly, both attempts failed.

Developments Leading to the Adoption of Children Act 1926

The Hopkinson Report

Legislative interest in adoption was rekindled in 1920 when a Committee chaired by Sir Alfred Hopkinson was appointed to consider whether it was desirable to make legal provision for the adoption of children. That Committee, which reported in 1921, was 'clearly of the opinion' that provision ought to be made for adoption. It referred to a general concurrence amongst witnesses experienced in social work:[13]

that the number of persons desiring to bring up some child or children, who would be treated in law and generally regarded as occupying the position of natural and lawful children, has very much increased. No doubt this is due to various causes, of which the loss that many families have sustained in the war is one. There is also reason for thinking that the interest in child life and child welfare is growing . . .

Whilst noting some witnesses' apprehension of the possible results of a widespread system of adoption without careful safeguards, the Committee considered that all were agreed that 'some system of regular adoption is desirable'.

As the Committee pointed out,[14] irrespective of whether adoption were to be legally recognized, the practice of de facto adoption would continue, with the attendant dangers of ill-advised agreements being entered into. It referred to other countries, particularly the USA, Australia, and New Zealand, which had had positive experience of adoption and to the evidence that they had heard which showed that in the case of children for whom the natural parents provided no proper home, it was generally better to place them with another family rather than in an institution. In this regard, one committee made the interesting point that it cost considerably less to place a child with a family than in an institution.[15] It

---

[12] See, eg the speeches of the Lord Chancellor (Lord Halsbury) at vols 338, cols 507–10 and 343, cols 1393–6.   [13] Hopkinson Report, n 6 above, para 10.
[14] *ibid*, para 11.   [15] *ibid*, para 15.

noted[16] that a large percentage of foster parents 'desire to retain the care of children, in spite of the trouble and expense to themselves from a genuine love for them and interest in their welfare'. On the other hand, echoing the concerns of the sponsors of the 1889 and 1890 Bills, it highlighted the serious drawbacks of de facto adopters' lack of legal rights over the children and their consequent inability to prevent parents from claiming them back simply in order to take their child's earnings. Indeed, the Committee thought that 'many suitable people are deterred from coming forward to adopt a child by the fear of subsequent claims and the possible necessity, should they wish to retain [the child], of litigation uncertain in its issue'. Notwithstanding this strong recommendation, there followed a lengthy period of legislative inaction, though there were numerous attempts to get adoption onto the statute book.[17] The Government responded by appointing another Committee chaired by Mr Justice Tomlin to investigate the need for adoption legislation. That Committee was set up in 1924 and reported in 1925.[18]

The Tomlin Report

Unlike Hopkinson, the Tomlin Committee was not so enthusiastic about introducing adoption into English law. It doubted, for example, whether persons who were willing to look after other people's children 'have been or would be deterred from [adopting] children by the absence of any recognition by the law of the statutes of adoption'. In any event, it believed the post-war increase in de facto adoptions to have been a transient phenomenon. It acknowledged that the problem of the unwanted child was a serious one but questioned whether an adoption law would do 'much to assist the solution of it'.[19] In the Committee's view, advocates of adoption fell into two groups, namely, those who believed that such a law would diminish the evils of trafficking in children (namely where children are handed from one person to another, with or without payment, advertised for disposal, or even sent out of the country without records being kept);[20] and those who wanted to safeguard the interests of those involved in de facto adoptions and who hoped that by so doing they would encourage 'an increasing number of people ready to adopt children for whom the natural parents are unable or unwilling to provide'.

The Committee was dismissive of the former group, pointing out that those persons whose transactions gave rise to the greatest evils were

[16] Hopkinson Report, para 12.
[17] In fact there were six unsuccessful Bills during 1924–5.
[18] *First Report of the Child Adoption Committee* (Tomlin First Report) Cmd 2401 (1924–5).
[19] Tomlin First Report, n 18 above, para 5.
[20] Hopkinson Report, n 6 above, at para 61. For examples of advertisements, see the *Report of the Departmental Committee on Adoption Societies and Agencies* (the Horsburgh Report) Cmd 9248 (1937) at para 30.

hardly likely to opt for adoption, while a prohibition on all transactions involving the bringing-up of other people's children, unless legalized by adoption, only had to be stated to be dismissed for want of practicality.[21] It was, however, sympathetic to the second group and notwithstanding their view that the claims of insecurity were exaggerated (it commented that the courts had long recognized that the natural parents' right to recovery of their child was to be determined solely by reference to that child's welfare[22]), thought that the case had been made for changing the law so as to enable a parent with proper safeguards 'to transfer to another his parental rights and duties, or some of them'.[23]

Having so concluded, the Report discussed what form and procedure to recommend. In this respect there were important differences between the Tomlin and Hopkinson proposals. A key difference was in relation to succession: whereas Hopkinson recommended that the child should have full rights of succession to the property of his adopted parents (but not of any relative of the adopters) and that the adopters should have full succession rights in respect of the property,[24] Tomlin recommended that there be no succession rights.[25] Tomlin similarly considered that adoption should make no difference to the prohibited degrees of relationship, whereas Hopkinson thought that marriage between adopter and adoptee should be expressly prohibited.[26] Another key difference was whether adoption could subsequently be revoked by a court order: Hopkinson thought it should; Tomlin thought revocation inconsistent with the notion of adoption.[27]

With regard to making an order in the first place, although both Committees recommended a court power to dispense with parental consent, Hopkinson envisaged[28] the dispensing power extending to cases of parental neglect or persistent cruelty and to 'where the child is being brought up in such circumstances as are likely to result in serious detriment to [the child's] moral or physical welfare'. The Tomlin Committee was much less interventionist, confining the power to cases of parental abandonment or desertion of the child, cases where the parent could not be found or was incapable of giving consent or 'being a person unable to contribute to the support of the minor has persistently neglected or refused to contribute to such support'.[29] Further interesting differences

---

[21] Tomlin report, n 18 above, para 7.

[22] This comment was highly questionable at the time, for as S. Cretney and J. Masson, *Principles of Family Law* (6th edn, 1997) at 877 n 28 point out, while the application of the welfare principle did in theory provide security, in practice this was far from certain as the decision in *Re Thain* [1926] Ch 676, illustrates. See Freeman, Ch 20 in this volume.

[23] Tomlin First Report, para 9.   [24] Hopkinson Report, paras 54 and 55.

[25] Tomlin First Report, para 19.

[26] *ibid*, para 20 and Hopkinson Report, para 56.

[27] See respectively paras 57 and 26.   [28] Hopkinson Report, para 34.

[29] Clause 2(3) of the draft Bill prepared by the Tomlin Committee.

include the Hopkinson view that children aged 14 or above should have to consent to their adoption and that in some cases rights of access under agreed conditions might be given to the birth parent notwithstanding the adoption.[30] Neither of these issues were discussed in the Tomlin report but the child's consent was not recommended to be required and was not mentioned in the draft Bill.[31] On the other hand, the Tomlin Committee was against adoption being secret such that the parties should not be known to each other, arguing that such a system 'would be wholly unnecessary and objectionable with a legalised system of adoption'.[32] As will be seen, some of these differences have been the centre of continuing and, indeed, contemporary debate.

The Adoption of Children Act 1926

Although some of the different Hopkinson recommendations subsequently came to be enacted[33] it was the Tomlin recommendations that were immediately acted upon. Shortly after their First Report, the Committee published a Second Report[34] containing a Draft Bill and it was essentially this version that became enacted as the Adoption of Children Act 1926. There are those[35] who say that because s 5(2) expressly refrained from altering succession rights, under the 1926 Act adoption could best be described as creating a special kind of guardianship. Such a view, however, hardly does justice to s 5(1), which provided that under an adoption order:

all rights, duties, obligations and liabilities of the parent or parents, guardian or guardians of the adopted child, in relation to the future custody, maintenance and education of the adopted child, including the rights to appoint a guardian or to consent or give notice of dissent to marriage shall be extinguished, and all such rights, duties, obligations and liabilities shall vest in and be exercisable by and enforceable against the adopter as though the adopted child was a child born to the adopter in lawful wedlock, and in respect of the liability of a child to maintain

[30] Hopkinson Report, paras 32 and 46.
[31] Clause 2(3) of the Draft Bill published as a Second Report (1924–5 Cmd 2469) only required the consent by a person who is parent or guardian.
[32] Tomlin First Report, para 28.
[33] Succession rights, for example, were introduced by the Adoption Act 1949, ss 9 and 10 (and further extended by the Children Act 1975). That Act also expressly (s 11) prohibited marriage between a child and his adoptive or former adoptive parent and, by s 3, widened the grounds for dispensing with consent. The consent of older children (12 or above) has always been required in Scotland (see s 2(3) of the Adoption of Children (Scotland) Act 1930—the requirement is now provided by s 6(2) of the Adoption (Scotland) Act 1978) and is proposed for England and Wales by cl 41(7) of the proposed Adoption Bill. One issue that has not changed, however, is the irrevocability of adoption—see further below.
[34] *Second Report of the Child Adoption Committee*, Cmd 2469 (1924–5).
[35] See *Report of the Departmental Committee on the Adoption of Children* (Hurst Report) Cmd 9248 (1954), para 196.

its parents the adopted children shall stand to the adopter exclusively in the position of a child born to the adopter in lawful wedlock.

In other words, from the outset adoption meant the permanent and
irrevocable transfer of parentage, at any rate for the lifetime of the parties.

It is this permanence and irrevocability that has always distinguished
adoption from all other orders relating to children[36] and not just
guardianship. Even so, given that succession rights were unaffected by
adoption, one could say that all adoption did was sever the legal relationship between child and birth parent prior to death and in that sense
adoption only suspended the parent–child relationship. But once succession rights were altered by adoption, as they were under the Adoption of
Children Act 1949,[37] then *any* argument that adoption was analogous to
guardianship ceased. As will be seen, the changing rules regarding succession were but one of many substantive changes made both to the
nature of adoption itself as well as to its organization. There have also
been important changes in the use made of adoption. It is to these subsequent developments that attention will now be turned.

THE DEVELOPMENT AND CHANGING USE OF ADOPTION

Adoption Statistics

The Overall Numbers

As Figure 14.1 shows, with the exception of the war years and their
immediate aftermath (when there was a significant surge) there was a
steady rise in the number of adoption orders from 1927 to 1968.[38] Since

---

[36] Save for parental orders under s 30 of the Human Fertilisation and Embryology Act
1990, which orders are sometimes referred to as 'fast track adoptions'.

[37] See ss 9 and 10. Although as Cretney has pointed out *total* integration of the child into
the adoptive family for succession purposes was only finally achieved by the Children Act
1975: S. Cretney, 'From Status to Contract?' in B. Rose (ed), *Consensus Ad Idem* (1996) 251 at
266 n 5.

[38] In the following discussion the statistics relied upon are (*a*) for the years 1927–71—
Appendix B of the Houghton Committee Report and (*b*) for the years 1975–98, the 1997 Marriage, Divorce and Adoption statistics. Alternative statistics, particularly the Annual
Judicial Statistics, are generally thought to be less reliable and are at times at considerable
variance with the Marriage, Divorce, and Adoption Statistics. For example, according to the
former, for the years 1996–8 the following number of adoption orders were made, namely,
4936, 4266, and 4675, whereas according to the latter, there were 5,962, 5,306, 4,387 respectively. There is also variance in the early statistics. For example, according to Basil Nield MP,
in 1927 there were 2,967 orders in 1946, 21,280 orders and in 1947, 18,265 orders (*House of
Commons Debates* (Hansard) (5th series) 1948–9, vol 461, col 1479). According to the
Houghton Committee the numbers were respectively 1927: 2,943; 1946: 21,272, and 1947:

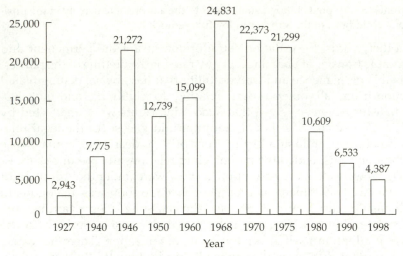

FIGURE 14.1. The total number of adoptions in England and Wales. Source: 1927–71: Houghton Committee Report—Appendix B. 1975–98: 1997 Marriage, Divorce and Adoption Statistics.

1968, however, there has been an almost uninterrupted decline, beginning with a particularly sharp fall in the second half of the 1970s followed by a steady and significant fall ever since.[39] It remains now to discuss the reasons why adoption has waxed and waned in this way.

The Waxing of Adoption—1927–1968

1927–1950

Detailed adoption statistics only became available after 1950, but it is reasonable to suppose that a significant proportion of orders made in the early years were made in favour of 'de facto' adopters. That after all was the *raison d'être* of the Tomlin Committee's recommendation to introduce adoption legislation in the first place and for which special provision was made in the 1926 Act.[40] It seems likely that there would have been a

18,255. According to the *Curtis Report* (Cmd 6922, 1946, para 84) the total number of adoption orders made between 1927 and the end of 1945 was 127,189. According to the Houghton figures the number was 126,987.

[39] England and Wales are not alone in this experience. Similar sharp falls in adoptions have been experienced, for example, in the USA (125,000 in 1970 down to 104,088 in 1986) and Ireland (1,443 in 1975 down to 649 in 1988); W. Duncan, 'Regulating Intercountry Adoption—an International Perspective' in A. Bainham and D. Pearl (eds), *Frontiers of Family Law* (1993) ch 3.

[40] Namely s 10, which provided that in the case of a child brought up, maintained, and educated by any person (regardless of whether the applicant was a male and the child

number of de facto adoptions during World War II, and this, in part, may help to account for the surge of adoptions towards the end of the war and immediately afterwards. It is also reasonable to presume that a substantial number of orders were in respect of babies relinquished by their mothers, usually unmarried mothers, though it seems that a not insignificant number of adoptions were by mothers of their own illegitimate children.[41] It must also have been the case that notwithstanding that the 1926 Act had not contemplated adoption by step-parents (though adoption by relatives had been envisaged) even from early on, such applications were regularly dealt with, even in the early years. Certainly by 1951 such orders were common, constituting just under a third of all legitimate children and just under half of all illegitimate children.[42]

In contrast, so-called public law adoptions, that is, where children are removed from inadequate or incapable parents and, under the aegis of local authorities, placed for adoption, would have been unusual.[43] Indeed, it was felt necessary to include a provision in the 1949 Act (s 7(2)) to make it clear that the local authorities could make and participate in arrangements for the adoption of children. But, even after this Act, and the apparent encouragement of the Curtis Committee, which commented:[44]

[t]he aim of the authority must be to find something better—indeed much better—if it takes the responsibility of providing a substitute home. The methods which should be available may be treated under three main heads of adoption, boarding out and residence in the communities. We have placed these in the order in which, they seem to us, to serve the welfare and happiness of the child,

such orders remained unusual for some time. For example, in 1952, only 453 children were adopted out of local authority care, amounting to but 3.2 per cent of all adoptions for that year and only 1.3 per cent of all discharges from care.[45]

---

female) or two spouses jointly as their own child for two years prior to the commencement of the Act, the court could grant the adoption without requiring parents' or guardians' consent, if satisfied that it was just and equitable and for the child's welfare to do so.

[41] As Basil Nield said when introducing the Adoption of Children Bill in 1949 (HC Debs (5th Series) 1948–9, vol 461 at col 1479): 'It is sometimes said, or implied, that every adopted child is an illegitimate child . . . Of course, many of those who are to be the subject of adoption orders are illegitimate, and I am also told that about one third of such illegitimate children are adopted by their own mothers.'

[42] See J. Masson, D. Norbury, and S. G. Chatterton, *Mine, Yours or Ours?* HMSO (1983), 1–2. It might be noted, however, that s 1(1) of the Adoption of Children Act 1949 made it expressly clear that an illegitimate child could be adopted by the mother or the father either solely *or jointly with a spouse*.

[43] This indeed would seem to reflect the intentions of the Tomlin Committee, see above. Contrast the Hopkinson Committee who were clearly more interventionist.

[44] Curtis Report, n 38 above, at para 447.

[45] I am indebted to Professor Roy Parker for this statistic.

Of even greater rarity would have been contested court applications for adoption. That is not to say that unmarried mothers in particular were not pressurized in some form or other into giving up their babies nor that they were unregretful afterwards,[46] but nevertheless contested adoption hearings of any regularity were a much later phenomenon dating from the 1980s.[47] In this sense the observation by one leading commentator[48] that when adoption was first introduced into English law, it 'was essentially a process whereby under minimal safeguards supervised by the court, a civil contract was registered and recognised', seems apt. What the experience of the first twenty or so years clearly demonstrated was that there was both a need for and growing use made of adoption.

1951–1968

In the foregoing analysis of the patterns of adoption between 1927 and 1950, four principal types were adverted to, namely, de facto adoptions, adoptions of babies, step-parent adoptions, and public law adoptions. As we shall now see, while the first 'type' is no longer of consequence, each of the other three types expanded during what may be described as the golden period of adoption, 1951–68.

Baby Adoptions

In the case of babies, that is children under the age of twelve months at the time of adoption, in 1951 there were 5,101 such orders, which amounted to 36 per cent of all adoptions of that year.[49] By 1968, that number had risen to 12,641, which amounted to 51 per cent of the overall total. Not surprisingly, the vast majority of these babies were illegitimate: 4,704 in 1951, amounting to 92 per cent of all adopted babies of that year; 12,237 in 1968, amounting to 97 per cent.[50] Equally unsurprisingly, but interestingly, baby adoptions accounted for 52 per cent in 1951 and 76 per cent in 1968 of *all* adoptions by non-parents.[51]

[46] Research done by the author together with Professor Mervyn Murch, Margaret Borkowski, and Rosalie Copner for the ESRC, showed, even in the late 1980s, that single mothers could still be subject to family pressure to relinquish their babies.

[47] That is not to say, however, that all applications were granted. Note the concern of the Curtis Committee, n 45 above, at para 457, that adoptive parents who had been refused an order by the court were successful in another.   [48] Cretney, n 38 above, at 252.

[49] These and the following statistics are taken from or based upon those published by R. Leete, 'Adoption Trends and Illegitimate Births 1951–77', (1978) 14 *Populations Trends* 9–16. But note, according to Leete in 1951 there were 14,198 adoptions whereas according to the Houghton Committee (Appendix B) there were 13,850.

[50] But note not all illegitimate children were adopted by strangers. In 1951 62, and in 1968, 194 babies were adopted by one of their own parents either solely or jointly with a new spouse.

[51] If one takes into account adoptions of babies and toddlers under the age of 2, then the respective percentages rise to 63 per cent in 1951 and 93 per cent in 1968.

Small wonder then that in many people's eyes adoption, at any rate by strangers, was all about adopting babies. Analysing adoption statistics according to whether the children were legitimate or illegitimate, Leete observed:[52] 'The annual number of adoptions of illegitimate children started to increase around the mid 1960s, slowly at first and then more rapidly in the 1960s to a peak of some 19,000 in 1968, nearly double the annual figure of the early 1950s.' Leete also points out that there was a close correlation between the rising annual number of illegitimate births in the 1950s and 1960s (the number of illegitimate births in England and Wales nearly doubled between 1958 and 1968)[53] and the number of adoptions by non-parents—there being a steady rate in this period of about twenty non-parental adoptions each year for every 100 illegitimate births. By way of passing, it might also be observed that during this period the overwhelming majority of adoptions by non-parents, 80 per cent in 1951 and 91 per cent in 1968,[54] were of illegitimate children.

Step-parent Adoptions

A key element in the increased number of adoption orders during the period 1951–68 was the rise of step-parent adoptions. Such adoptions are essentially of three types, namely, so-called 'post-divorce' step-parent adoptions, that is, to use the definition of Masson, Norbury, and Chatterton,[55] where the new family comprises a divorced parent, a child of the former marriage, and a step-parent; 'post-death' step-parent adoptions, where the family comprises a widowed parent, a child of the former marriage, and a step-parent; and 'illegitimate' step-parent adoptions, where the family comprises a formerly unmarried parent, an illegitimate child, and a step-parent. However, since the published statistics only contain details of step-parent adoptions according to whether or not the child is legitimate, as Masson *et al* point out, it is not possible to distinguish post-divorce from post-death step-parent adoptions. Nevertheless, it is generally accepted that the vast rise in the number of adoptions of legitimate children by one or both parents is almost entirely accounted for by post-divorce step-parent adoptions and

---

[52] n 49 above at 9. See also P. Selman 'Patterns of Adoption in England and Wales since 1959', (1976) 7 *Social Work Today* 194–7. Note: the apparent difference in the figures quoted by each author is explained by the fact that whereas Leete quotes figures for *all* adoptions, Selman quotes only those for *joint* adoptions. [53] See *ibid* at 195.

[54] The respective numbers were 7,712 out of total 9,639 adoptions by non-parents in 1951 and 14,869 out of 16,314 in 1968.

[55] n 42 above at 1. The authors identified a fourth category which they termed 'mixed', 'where either both parents brought children from former partnerships which had ended in different ways, or one parent brought children from more than one type of former relationship'.

reflects the growing number of divorces during this period.[56] Whereas there were fewer than 1,000 step-parent adoptions of legitimate children in 1950, rising to 1,541 in 1959, by 1968 there were 4,038. Indeed, there was a marked rise during the 1960s and that trend in fact continued to 1975.[57]

In contrast, step-parent adoptions of illegitimate children remained relatively steady throughout the period 1951–68 with 3,606 in 1951, 3,105 in 1959, and 4,479 in 1968.

In terms of the overall proportion, whereas in 1951 step-parent adoptions formed 32 per cent of all adoptions, in 1968 they formed 34 per cent, but as we shall see, although their numbers declined, step-parent adoptions formed an increasing proportion of all adoptions made, peaking in 1975.

Public Law Adoptions

Although on a much smaller scale than either baby adoptions or step-parent adoptions, during the period 1952–68 there was virtually a fivefold increase in the number of children adopted out of local authority care, rising from 453 to 2,168. In terms of percentages, these amounted to 3.2 per cent of all adoptions in 1952, rising to 8.7 per cent in 1968 and as a proportion of discharges from care rose from 1.3 per cent in 1952 to 4.3 per cent in 1968. No doubt a number of the children involved were babies relinquished by their unmarried mothers for, as we shall see, the practice of placing older children out of care for adoption did not really take off until the mid-1970s.

Summary

When adoption numbers were at their peak, one in three were step-parent adoptions and of the remaining two-thirds, 76 per cent comprised the adoption of babies and a further 17 per cent the adoption of toddlers under the age of 2 by non-parents. In other words, where adoption by non-parents was concerned, the vast majority were of babies or toddlers under the age of 2. Indeed, even including step-parent adoption in 1968, just over half of all adopted were aged under 1 and fewer than a quarter were aged 5 or more.[58] As we shall now see, over the next thirty years this overall profile has dramatically changed.

---

[56] As Leete, n 49 above, at 9, points out, the sharp increase of parental adoptions of legitimate children after the Divorce Reform Act 1969 took effect in 1971, reinforces this supposition.

[57] See Masson; *et al*, n 42 above at 12; Leete, n 49 above, at 9; and Selman, n 52 above.

[58] Leete, n 49 above, at 9.

The Waning of Adoption—1969–1998

The Demise of Baby Adoptions

One of the most dramatic changes in adoption patterns over the last thirty years has been the virtual disappearance of baby adoptions. As we have seen, at its peak in 1968, 12,641 babies were adopted, amounting to 51 per cent of all adoptions. That number quickly declined to 8,833 in 1970 (39 per cent of the total), 4,548 in 1975 (21 per cent), 2,599 in 1980 (24 per cent), 969 in 1990 (15 per cent) to just 195 in 1998 (4 per cent).[59] The decline in the number of babies being offered for adoption had been noted in 1972 by the Houghton Committee.[60] That body attributed the reduction to the increasing number of legal abortions (the Abortion Act 1967 came into force on 27 April 1968), more use of contraception, and the changing attitude to illegitimacy, inasmuch as unmarried mothers were becoming less disadvantaged while at the same time there was a 'significant increase in tolerance and understanding towards them and their children'.

Although at one time there was a clear correlation between the number of illegitimate births and adoption numbers,[61] as Leete observed,[62] the decline in adoptions during 1970–7 was steeper than that in illegitimate births. As he pointed out, whereas in the 1950s and 1960s there were about twenty non-parental adoptions for every 100 illegitimate births, by 1977 this figure had fallen to eight. This, he suggested, provided clear evidence of the diminishing proportions of illegitimate children being adopted, and since the vast majority of these were babies,[63] it also accounts for the rapid decline of baby adoptions. Now, with the virtual disappearance of baby adoptions there is no correlation between adoption numbers and the number of children born to unmarried mothers. In fact, as *Social Trends*[64] points out, most of the increase in the number of births outside marriage since the late 1980s has been to cohabiting couples. In 1998, nearly 80 per cent of births outside marriage were jointly registered by both parents and in three-quarters of these the parents were living at the same address.

Although attention has understandably focused on the dramatic decline in baby adoptions, there have also been significant reductions in the number of adoptions in other age groups. Although as we shall see,

---

[59] The 1970 figure was calculated upon the basis of information given in Appendix B, Table 2 to the Houghton Report; the other figures were given by Table 6.2 of the 1977 Marriage, Divorce and Adoption Statistics.   [60] n 1 above, at para 20.

[61] See Leete, n 49 above, fig 2 at 10.

[62] See also Selman's excellent analysis, n 52 above at 196.

[63] 76 per cent in 1968.   [64] 30 *Social Trends* (2000 edn), 43.

in the case of older children this reduction is explained at any rate in part by the diminution of step-parent adoptions, this is less true of the 1–2-year-old group, which declined overall from 3,532 in 1968 to 1,186 in 1977 but especially in the numbers of illegitimate children adopted by non-parents, which fell from 1,736 in 1968 to 532 in 1977.[65] It has been suggested[66] that a possible explanation for this latter decline is that as it became increasingly accepted that unmarried mothers could keep their babies, so there developed a more general culture of families being reluctant to give up their children. Be that as it may, it seems clear from the available statistics (notwithstanding that they do not now break down adoptions into the 1–2-year age group but, instead, provide the numbers of 1–4 year olds, which have declined from 3,002 in 1977 to 1,489 in 1998) that the number of toddlers adopted has continuously declined until the present.

The Decline in Step-parent Adoptions

Unlike adoptions overall, step-parent adoptions continued to rise after 1968. In the case of legitimate children the numbers more than doubled from 4,038 in 1968 to 9,262 in 1975, while in the case of illegitimate children, numbers rose from 4,479 in 1968 to 5,691 in 1974.[67] In the former case the continuing rise can be explained by higher divorce rates and consequential second marriages, but the latter is not so easily explained when set against a background of declining numbers of illegitimate births. One explanation is that given that illegitimate step-parent adoptions tend to be of older children (by 1977 more than half were aged over 5 years old) then the declining birth rate took a longer time to have effect.[68] At any rate, the number of adoptions dropped from its peak figure in 1974 to 3,238 in 1977 and 2,734 in 1979 and presumably has continued to decline since.[69]

The nemesis for post-divorce step-parent adoptions came via legislation. The Houghton Committee[70] expressed concern about the rising number of such adoptions and indeed questioned their desirability, involving as they commonly did, the severing of the link between the child and the non-residential parent. Following the Committee's recommendations, the Children Act 1975 directed[71] the court to dismiss such

---

[65] Leete, n 49 above, Table 1 at 10. Non-parental adoptions of legitimate children dropped from 333 in 1968 to 180 in 1977.

[66] See N. Lowe and G. Douglas, *Bromley's Family Law* (9th edn) at 614.

[67] These figures are drawn from a collection of sources, namely, Leete, n 49 above, figure 1, at 10, Selman, n 52 above, Table 1 at 194 and J. Masson *et al*, n 42 above, 12–14.

[68] See the extensive discussion by Leete, n 50 above, but, cf Masson *et al*, n 43 above, at 19   [69] Detailed figures seem to be unobtainable.

[70] n 1 above, paras 103–10.

[71] Section 10(3), later re-enacted as s 14(3) of the Adoption Act 1976, which provision was subsequently repealed by the Children Act 1989, Sch 15. Not dissimilarly, restrictions were

applications if it considered the matter would be better dealt with by an application to the divorce court for what was then a custody order. This direction, which came into force in 1976, was at first taken to be a clear expression of a policy to discourage adoptions by parents and step-parents,[72] though in point of fact the courts later softened their interpretation.[73] The overall effect,[74] however, of this legislation was dramatic: from a peak figure in 1975, numbers halved to 4,545 by 1977 and virtually halved again to 2,872 in 1983.[75] Detailed breakdown of step-parent adoptions ceased to be available in 1983 but bare figures and percentages have been included since 1992 in the (less reliable) Annual Judicial Statistics, according to which in 1998 there were 2,332 such orders representing 50 per cent of all adoption orders made that year.[76]

Public Law Adoptions

In contrast to baby and step-parent adoptions, public law adoptions have not declined over the last thirty years. Indeed, in terms of overall numbers they have remained relatively steady, fluctuating between a low of about 1,500 in 1977 to a high of 2,700 in 1992.[77] The current indicators show a rising trend both for children adopted after being 'looked after'[78] by local authorities, rising from 1,900 in 1997 to 2,000 in 1998 and to 2,200 in 1999, and for those placed for adoption from 2,400 in 1997 to 2,500 in 1998 and 2,900 in 1999.[79] In terms of the *proportion* of the overall number

contained in the tortuously worded s 37 of the 1975 Act which applied to 'parent death' and 'illegitimate' step-parent adoptions, but these were not brought into force until Dec 1985 and were also repealed by the Children Act 1989.

[72] See Local Authority Circular LAC (76) 22 para 10(ii) and *Re S (Infants) (Adoption by Parent)* [1977] Fam 173, CA.

[73] *Re D (Minors) (Adoption by Step-Parent)* (1980) 2 FLR 102, CA. For a further discussion of step-parent adoptions see N. Lowe and G. Douglas, *Bromley's Family Law* (9th edn) 630–1 and the references there cited.

[74] But, as Masson, *et al*, n 42 above, found, the impact varied from court to court at least at the lower level.

[75] These figures are taken from Table 4 produced by the Inter-Departmental Review of Adoption Law, Discussion Paper No 3, *The Adoption Process* at 9.

[76] But note, the overall number of orders said to have been made, namely, 4,675, is at variance with that cited in the more reliable 1997 Marriage, Divorce and Adoption Statistics, which puts the number at 4,387.

[77] Detailed statistics for the years 1980–90 can be found in Adoption Law Review, Discussion Paper No 3, n 76 above, Table 3. Note that these figures are for England and Wales, whereas the statistics produced in the annual publication *Children Looked after By Local Authorities*, are for England only. The author has also been provided with statistics prepared by Professor Roy Parker.

[78] 'Looked after' children comprise both those subject to a care order and those 'accommodated' by local authorities, see s 22 of the Children Act 1989.

[79] These figures are taken from the 'Looked After' statistics for England, which are calculated by reference to data collected on 31 Mar of each relevant year. The 1999 figure is 14 per cent higher than 1998 but is subject to the caveat that it 'may reflect improvements in recording methods'.

of adoptions, public law adoptions have become much more significant. Whereas in 1968 they accounted for 8.7 per cent of all adoptions, for most of the 1990s they accounted for a third or more of all adoptions.[80]

These bare statistics mask an important change in practice which came about when local authorities began to use adoption to secure the long-term welfare of older children and not just babies. This change of practice sprang from a child care policy which in the 1970s began in the UK to be termed 'permanency planning'.[81] It was stimulated by the work of Goldstein, Freud, and Solnit, *Beyond the Best Interests of the Child*, published in 1973, in which the authors challenged the then prevailing thought that biological and legal parenthood should take precedence over psychological parenthood. Their thesis was intended to reinforce the security of the adoptive, psychological parent–child relationship and they strengthened the view[82] that children from neglectful, disrupted, and severely disordered families might often do much better if placed permanently with loving, secure, more stable families. Other research, particularly Rowe and Lambert's *Children Who Wait*, also published in 1973,[83] which emphasized the need for long-term planning for children in care, together with the report of the inquiry into the death of Maria Colwell[84] (who had been killed by her step-father after having been removed from foster parents), reinforced the view that for certain abused or neglected children, long-term care away from their families was in their best interests and that adoption was a key means of achieving this even where the birth parents were opposed to it.

Although not everyone was swayed by this permanency movement (and in any event it was not infrequently bad social work practice rather than parental failure that had led to many children languishing in care), and indeed there was something of a backlash in the mid- to late 1980s, there were nevertheless lasting significant changes in adoption practice. First, local authorities made and continue to make determined efforts to secure adoption placements for so-called hard to place children. Second, there was a consequential increase in the number of adoptions in which parental agreement was dispensed with.[85] Third, there was an overall rise

---

[80] See, eg *Children Looked after by Local Authorities Year Ending 31 March 1998* (A/F 98 (98/12) 27.

[81] See particularly R. Parker, *Planning for Deprived Children* (National Children's Homes, 1971).

[82] It might be pointed out that the Curtis Report, n 45 above, at para 448 had espoused similar views and even the Hopkinson Report, n 13 above, at para 11 was strongly of the view that adoption was preferable to institutional care.

[83] J. Rowe and L. Lambert, *Children Who Wait*. London: ABAFA (1973).

[84] *Report of the Committee of Inquiry into the Care and Supervision provided in relation to Maria Colwell*, HMSO (1974).

[85] This was noted first by the House of Commons' Second Report on the Children Act 1975, HMSO, 1984, see Table B when 11 per cent of applications involved dispensing with

in the age of children adopted out of care. For example, between 1980 and 1990 the number of children aged between 5 and 9 adopted out of care rose from 348 (21 per cent of all such adoptions) to 739 (28 per cent) and of those between 10 and 15 rose from 140 (9 per cent) to 316 (12 per cent).[86] In a more recent study, *Supporting Adoption*,[87] out of a national sample of 1,525 children placed for adoption by adoption agencies (both local authority and voluntary) in 1993–4, 42 per cent were aged 5 or over. As we shall see, this change of practice is not without significance for the whole future of adoption.

Increasing Regulation

As has already been said, when first introduced, adoption was remarkably unregulated. However, following the recommendations of the Horsburgh Committee,[88] the Adoption of Children (Regulation) Act 1939, s 1, made it an offence for a body of persons other than a registered adoption society or local authority to make any arrangements for the adoption of children. The Act also provided for the local registration of adoption societies. Furthermore, under s 4 the Secretary of State was empowered to make regulations to: (*a*) ensure that parents wishing to place their children for adoption were given written explanation of their legal position; (*b*) prescribe the inquiries to be made and reports to be obtained to ensure the suitability of the child and adopter; and (*c*) secure that no child would be delivered to an adopter until the adopter had been interviewed by a case committee.

In short, the 1939 Act created the rudimentary foundations of what might now be called an adoption service, although at this stage it was only concerned with the placement of children and only controlled the activities of registered adoption societies. Nevertheless, the 1939 Act made express provision for local authorities to arrange adoptions and their role was further clarified by s 7(2) of the Adoption of Children Act 1949, which provided that local authorities had power 'under any

agreement. A later study by M. Murch, N. Lowe, M. Borkowski, R. Copner, and K. Griew, *Pathways to Adoption* (HMSO, 1993) found in a sample of applications made between 1986 and 1988, that 19 per cent involved dispensing with agreement.

[86] Inter-Departmental Review of Adoption Law (Discussion Paper No 3), n 75 above, Table 3 at para 8.

[87] N. Lowe, M. Murch, M. Borkowski, A. Weaver, V. Beckford, and C. Thomas, *Supporting Adoption—Reframing the Approach* (BAAF, 1999). But according to the *Looked After Statistics* for 1998, n 78 above, 27, since 1993/4, the proportion of children aged 5 or more being adopted has been gradually falling.

[88] *Report of the Departmental Committee on Adoption Societies and Agencies* (Horsburgh Report), Cmd 5499 (HMSO, 1937), set up to 'inquire into the methods pursued by adoption societies and other agencies engaged in the arranging for adoption of children'.

enactment relating to children to make and participate in arrangements for the adoption of children'. The local authority role in adoption was further enhanced following the Hurst Committee's recommendation[89] that local authorities be empowered to arrange for the adoption of any child without that child having to be in care.[90] The thinking behind this recommendation was not for local authorities to usurp the function of voluntary adoption societies (which had hitherto done the major work) but to create a more widely available adoption service. This objective also influenced the Houghton Committee's thinking. At the time of its Report in 1972, only 96 of the 172 local authorities in England and Wales acted as adoption agencies. Accordingly, to ensure that a comprehensive service was available to 'all those needing it in any part of the country'[91] the Committee recommended that *all* local authorities should have a statutory duty to provide an adoption service as part of their general child care and family case work provision. However, considering that voluntary adoption societies had a valuable continuing role to play, *inter alia*, to provide a choice of service, the Committee also recommended that local authorities should have a statutory duty 'to ensure, in co-operation with voluntary societies, that a comprehensive adoption service is available throughout their area'. It was recommended that registration of voluntary societies should be national rather than local.[92] These recommendations were eventually implemented in 1988 under what became s 1 of the Adoption Act 1976. Perhaps not surprisingly, given these developments, adoption work undertaken by voluntary societies began to decline, although they continued to deal with the majority of agency adoptions through to the 1970s—in 1966, for example, of adoptions arranged by agencies, 73 per cent were arranged by voluntaries. By 1971 the gap was already closing, with voluntaries dealing with 60 per cent of cases. Now, with the demise of baby adoptions, the majority of agency work is done by the statutory agencies, although exact figures are not available.[93]

Another important development related to restricting further those who could lawfully place a child for adoption. The Hurst Committee was particularly concerned with this stage, which it saw as crucial since, 'Once the child is placed, much harm and unhappiness may result if a change has to be made'. In their view, adoptions arranged by persons of special experi-

---

[89] n 35 above, at para 24. See also I. Goodacre, *Adoption Policy and Practice* (Allen and Unwin, 1966), who advocated that all adoptions by strangers be handled by local authorities.   [90] See Adoption Act 1958, s 28(2).

[91] Houghton Report, n 1 above, at paras 33 and 34 and recommendation 2.

[92] Houghton Report, n 1 above, respectively para 42 and recommendation 3.

[93] N. Lowe 'The Changing Face of Adoption—the Gift/Donation Model versus the Contract Services Model' (1997) 9 *Child & Fam. Law Quarterly* 371 at 374.

ence and training stood a much better chance of success. However, whilst it recommended that social workers employed by societies be fully trained, it stopped short of recommending the prohibition of private or third-party placements. That particular bullet was bitten by the Houghton Committee[94] and, following its recommendation, private placements of children for adoption by non-relatives became an offence with effect from 1982, when s 28 of the Children Act 1975 was brought into force.[95]

It was at this moment that one might say that the process of the 'professionalization of adoption work' was completed, and certainly as far as individuals seeking to adopt a non-relative are concerned, adoption is fully regulated. They must first be approved by an agency, which entails a thorough screening process conducted by what are now known as adoption panels[96] both as to the applicants' commitment to and motive for seeking to adopt, as well as their lifestyle, stability of their relationships, and, of course, their ability to provide a loving and permanent home for any child. Having been approved, applicants must then wait, often for several months, until the agency has found what it considers to be a suitable match. If the subsequent placement is successful, after a minimum period of thirteen weeks, an application can be made to the court for an adoption order. Even applicants (principally step-parents and relatives) for non-agency adoptions cannot escape public scrutiny, for they must give notice to their local authority of their intention to apply for adoption. Upon receipt of such notice the local authority must investigate such issues as the applicant's suitability to adopt, and submit a report to the court.[97]

Some Key Substantive Law Developments

Of the many legislative and judicial changes to adoption law, of particular interest are those which have contributed to what has become a fundamental shift from perceiving adoption as the creation of a new independent family at the expense of the old to considering it primarily to be a means of securing a permanent new home for children without necessarily ending all connection with their birth family and which may still need to be supported by the State. The two areas that will therefore be examined are: preserving adopted children's links with their birth family, and, in the context of public law adoptions, the adoption agency's role after the adoption order has been made.

---

[94] n 1 above, at paras 84–90, and recommendation 13.
[95] See now Adoption Act 1976, s 11. Compare, for the US, Katz, Ch 14 of this volume.
[96] For the constitution of which see the Adoption Agencies Regulations 1983 (SI 1983/1964), reg 5 as substituted by SI 1997/649.
[97] Adoption Act 1976, s 22(1); Adoption Rules 1984, r 22 and Sch 2.

Preserving Adopted Children's Links with their Birth Families

As already discussed, from its inception adoption was said to 'extinguish' previously held parental rights and duties, vesting them instead in the adopters.[98] This was soon interpreted as ending all the child's connections with his birth family. As Vaisey J put it,[99] when deciding upon the property of grandparents applying to adopt their daughter's illegitimate child under the 1926 Act: 'Normally, an adoption presupposes a complete and final separation between the child and its natural parents.' This notion of complete severance was further enhanced when succession rights were also transferred by the adoption order.[100] Practice was also very much predicated upon the notion of severance, being designed to ensure that birth parents would generally have no knowledge of the adopters (and of course no further contact with their child) and adopters would be similarly ignorant of the birth parents' identity.[101] One result of this secrecy was that adopters were encouraged in the belief that the child was 'theirs' and would be commonly reluctant to tell them that they were adopted. Whilst it is not suggested that this practice was officially approved,[102] it made more sense at a time when the vast majority of adoptions by non-parents were of babies or toddlers. At any rate, the legal fiction of a family transplant is clearly more difficult to sustain in the case of older children, the adoption of whom, as we have seen, began to be more common from the 1970s onwards, and it is therefore no surprise that the two major legal developments, permitting adopted children to trace their birth parents and making provision for ongoing contact after adoption, date from this period.

Tracing Parents

Studies in the 1960s and 1970s had demonstrated the harmful effect upon adopted children of not knowing their own identities.[103] The work of Triseliotis in particular on the operation of the Scottish system (which permitted an adopted child's access to birth records at the age of 17) proved influential. It persuaded the Houghton Committee to

---

[98] Adoption of Children Act 1926, s 5(1), discussed above.

[99] *Re DX (An Infant)* [1949] Ch 320 at 321.

[100] As originally provided for by Adoption of Children Act 1949, ss 9 and 10, discussed above.

[101] See J. Triseliotis, *'Open Adoption': The Philosophy and the Practice* (1970) at 19.

[102] It is to be noted, for example, that the Tomlin Committee, n 19 above, at para 28, was against secrecy in adoption from the very start, while the Hurst Committee, n 35 above, at para 150, specifically recommended in 1954 that all adopters should be required to give a formal undertaking to tell the child about his or her adoption.

[103] See A. McWhinnie, *Adopted Children: How They Grow Up: Study of their Adjustments as Adults* (Routledge and Kegan Paul, 1967) and J. Triseliotis, *In Search of Origins: The Experience of Adopted People* (Routledge and Kegan Paul, 1973).

recommend[104] that adopted children should be able to obtain their original birth certificate. This, in time, led to a formal change in the law permitting as from 12 November 1975[105] *adult* adopted children to obtain their original birth certificate, from which they might may be able to trace their birth parents.[106]

Since the introduction of this right, an Adoption Contact Register has been created[107] which 'provides a safe and confidential way for birth parents and other relatives to assure an adopted person that contact would be welcome and to give a contact address'.[108]

Post-adoption Contact

So long as adoption was regarded as *completely* severing the child's connection with his birth family there could be no possibility of making provision for continuing contact. However, in a ground-breaking decision in 1973, *Re J (A Minor) (Adoption Order: Conditions)*,[109] Rees J held that continued contact was not inconsistent with an adoption, adding that 'the general rule which forbids contact between an adopted child and his natural parent may be disregarded in an exceptional case where a court is satisfied that by so doing the welfare of the child may be best promoted'. Accordingly, exercising his power to add conditions to an adoption order,[110] he made provision for continuing contact to avoid lengthy litigation which would otherwise have damaged the child.

Re J was subsequently authoritatively confirmed by *Re C (A Minor) (Adoption Order: Conditions)*,[111] which concerned a child who was in long-term care. The mother refused to agree to her daughter's adoption, arguing that it would weaken the child's relationship with her brother. At first instance, the judge held that the sibling relationship should be preserved and refused to make the order. The applicants appealed and

---

[104] n 1 above, at paras 303 to 306 and recommendation 77.

[105] When s 26 of the Children Act 1975 came into force. Controversially this provision had retrospective effect.

[106] See now Adoption Act 1976, s 51. This right to see the birth certificate is not absolute. See *R v Registrar General, ex p Smith* [1991] 1 FLR 255, where the mother's safety would have been seriously jeopardized.

[107] By Adoption Act 1976, s 51A (added by the Children Act 1989, Sch 10, para 21.

[108] Department of Health: *The Children Act 1989: Guidance and Regulations*, vol 9: *Adoption Issues* (HMSO, 1991) para 3.2. [109] [1973] Fam 106.

[110] Under what is now the Adoption Act 1976, s 12(b). Rees J's approach was affirmed by *Re S (A Minor) (Adoption Order: Access)* [1976] Fam 1, CA. These decisions were criticized by S. Maidment ('Access and Family Adoptions' (1977) 40 *Mod. Law Rev.* 293) who argued that the power to add conditions was *solely* designed to deal with questions of religion. However, notwithstanding that the power to add conditions was included in cl 4 of the proposed Bill recommended in the Tomlin Committee's Second Report, there was *no* discussion of the power in their First Report. It is also worth pointing out that the Hopkinson Committee, n 13 above, at paras 32 and 46 *did* anticipate making provision for continuing contact. [111] [1989] AC 1, HL.

sought a condition attached to the adoption that the brother should have continuing access to his sister. Overruling the Court of Appeal, the House of Lords held that there was power to attach such a condition where it was clearly in the child's interest to do so. Lord Ackner stressed that to safeguard and promote the child's welfare it was important that the court should retain 'the maximum flexibility given to it by the Act'. However, he clearly signalled that the *imposition* of such a condition against the adopters' will would be rarely justified and he also drew a distinction between preserving contact with birth parents and other relatives, the former being harder to justify than the latter if an adoption order is to be made.

Since *Re C*, the Children Act 1989 has simplified the law by allowing the courts to couple an adoption order with a contact order made under s 8 of the 1989 Act, rather than by imposing a condition. Nevertheless, notwithstanding this change of legal regime, courts continue to be reluctant to *impose* contact orders upon unwilling adopters[112] and have also observed that where the parties are all agreed on contact there is no need to make an order.[113] In other words, although the courts are empowered to make provision for continuing contact between an adopted child and the birth family, the preferred option is for the families to work it out for themselves. While this standpoint is not unreasonable, given the well-known difficulty of enforcing contact orders, there remains the lurking suspicion that the courts are still uneasy with the notion of adoptions with continuing contact.[114] If that is so, then it is out of line with current de facto practice in agency adoptions where so-called 'open adoptions' are the norm rather than the exception.[115] Indeed, in a sample of 226 adopters in one recent study, 77 per cent indicated that their adopted children had some form of ongoing contact with a birth relative.[116] Furthermore agencies are not likely to approve would-be adopters who are openly hostile to the idea of there being continuing contact with the birth family.[117]

Although open adoption implies some form of continuing contact, another aspect is to involve birth parents in the process of selecting

---

[112] See *Re H (A Minor) (Freeing Orders)* [1993] FLR 325, CA and *Re P (Minors) (Adoption: Freeing Order)* [1994] 2 FLR 1000.

[113] Per Butler Sloss LJ in *Re T (Adoption: Consent)* [1995] 2 FLR 251 at 257.

[114] See *Re T (Adoption: Contact) ibid* at 257 where Butler-Sloss LJ commented 'the finality of adoption and the importance of letting the new family find its own feet ought not to be threatened in any way by an order [for contact] in this case'. But cf *Re T (Adopted Children: Contact)* [1995] 2 FLR 792, CA in which it was held that where adopters agree to contact they cannot simply resile from it without explanation.

[115] See *inter alia* the review by Ryburn 'In Whose Best Interests?—Post Adoption Contact with the Birth Family' (1998) 10 *Child & Family Law Quarterly* 53.

[116] Lowe and Murch *et al, Supporting Adoption*, n 87 above, at 280 and for their general findings on contact see Ch 15.   [117] *ibid* at 314 ff.

adopters and there are some agencies that actively encourage this. But, perhaps the most extreme form of the mutual involvement of the two families is in so-called 'concurrent planning', which has been pioneered in Seattle and is currently being experimented within England. Concurrent planning involves placing a child with potential adopters whilst still working to rehabilitate the child with his birth family, with the adoption only being able to proceed if rehabilitation fails.

Adoption Agencies' Continuing Post-adoption Role

Consistent with the notion that adoption severs all previous legal relationships was the formerly held view that upon the order being made the work of the adoption agency was completed. Ellison, for example, writing in 1963, said:[118]

Once an adoption is made . . . the infant passes into the family of the adopter. After that, neither the adopter nor the natural mother can revoke what has been done; that is the final step. The work of the adoption agency ends in every case with the granting of the order, although adopters sometimes wish to maintain a friendly contact with an agency, particularly when they intend to follow up a first adoption with a second or a sequence.

Such a view is no longer tenable, for it is now accepted[119] that all local authorities are statutorily obliged either themselves to provide a *post-adoption* service or to secure that such a service is provided by other approved agencies (ie voluntary agencies). This obligation derives from s 1(1) of the Adoption Act 1976 by which *every* local authority has:

to establish and maintain within their area a service to meet the needs in relation to adoption, of

(a)   children *who have been* or may be adopted,
(b)   parents and guardians of such children, and
(c)   persons who *have adopted* or may adopt a child

[Emphasis added]

There is little official guidance on what should be included in a post-adoption service[120] and indeed there is widespread variation in the service provided.[121] Commonly, however, agencies will be concerned to

---

[118]   M. Ellison, *The Deprived Child and Adoption* (Pan, 1963).

[119]   Among the first to mention this were H. Bevan and M. Parry, *The Children Act 1995* (Butterworths, 1979) at 15. Post-adoption support is specifically mentioned (but only for adult adopted children) in the list of services that must be provided by local authorities, see Local Authority Circular *LAC 87 (8), Adoption Act 1976: Implementation and Welsh Office Circular 35(8) Adoption Act 1976: Implementation.* Interestingly, the Houghton Committee, n 1 above, which had recommended the creation of a nation wide adoption service, made no mention of *post*-adoption support.

[120]   See the critique of the *Review of Adoption Law, Discussion Paper 3*, n 75 above, at para 8.

[121]   For a detailed study, see Lowe and Murch *et al, Supporting Adoption*, n 87 above, chs 14 and 15.

facilitate post-adoption contact, to provide counselling and updating information, and to organize support groups. Agencies also have a discretion to pay adoption allowances.

The introduction of the power to pay adoption allowances was controversial. It was first floated by the Houghton Committee[122] and was aimed at finding more adoptive homes for children in need. This suggestion attracted widespread opposition on the twin grounds that it amounted to discriminating against birth parents[123] and in any event was contrary to the notion that the child should be put in the same position as a child born to the adopters. Notwithstanding this opposition, the Houghton Committee persisted with its recommendation.[124] The matter proved equally controversial in Parliament[125] but eventually provision was made permitting agencies to submit schemes for payment of allowances for approval by the Secretary of State.[126] The law has since been amended to empower all agencies to pay adoption allowances subject to the structures of the Adoption Allowances Regulations 1991.[127]

Although this power to pay an allowance is clear recognition by the State of the need to support an adoption even after the order, it is only a limited power. Current guidance[128] states that such allowances should be 'the exception rather than the norm', which limitation has been criticized[129] as penalizing vulnerable and frequently highly damaged children. It is understood that allowances are currently under review.

THE FUTURE—WHAT ROLE WILL THERE BE FOR ADOPTION IN ENGLISH LAW
IN THE TWENTY-FIRST CENTURY?

As we have seen, adoption law and particularly practice has undergone considerable change since its introduction in 1927. What began as a

---

[122] See Working Paper on Adoption of Children (HMSO, 1970) paras 119–22.

[123] As the British Association of Social Workers later put it: 'It would be an intolerable situation if financial resources were made available to subsidize adoption when an allocation of similar resources to the natural parents may have prevented the break up of the family in the first place': *Analysis of the Children Bill* (British Association of Social Workers, 1975), at 22—cited by Bevan and Parry, n 119 above, at para 121.

[124] n 1 above, recommendation 17. The Committee admitted that most witnesses had been against the proposal in their Working Paper.

[125] It was only the chairman's casting vote that saved the provision during its Standing Committee stage—see Standing Committee A (Ninth Sitting), cols 447–80.

[126] Originally by the Children Act 1975, s 32 which was brought into force on 15 Feb 1982. It was later replaced by Adoption Act 1976, 56(4)-(7).

[127] See now Adoption Act 1976, s 57A as added by the Children Act 1989.

[128] Department of Health's *Guidance and Regulations*, vol 9 *Adoption Issues* at para 2.2.

[129] See Lowe and Murch *et al*, n 87 above, at 431. They recommend that there be a national standardized system of eligibility and level of support.

consensual, largely unregulated mechanism for transferring parentage (at any rate for the parties' lives), designed for de facto and baby adoption, has now become a highly regulated procedure dealing with step-parent (and to a lesser extent, other relatives') adoption and public law adoptions, the latter being not infrequently contested and in all cases involving older children (often aged 5 or more) and only rarely babies. The organization of adoption work has also undergone considerable change, with private placements (other than with relatives) now being prohibited and the bulk of the work being done by local authorities (each of whom is *bound* to operate an 'adoption service') rather than by voluntary adoption societies. Even the very notion of adoption has changed, with emphasis shifting from that of completely severing the child from its former family to that of securing a permanent home for the child without necessarily ending all links with the birth family nor ending the state obligation (through adoption agencies) to give continuing support to the adoptive family.

Against this background of change, however, adoption numbers have plummeted to less than 5,000 per year as opposed to 25,000 at their zenith. What then of the future? Will adoptions continue to fall? More fundamentally, for what do we want adoption in the twenty-first century? Is there a case for scrapping it, or if not, for changing its effect and limiting its application? It is proposed to examine the future role of adoption in two ways: first by looking at the likely short-term developments and second, by considering longer-term options.

Likely Short-term Developments

The Immediate Future

Of course it is risky to predict future trends. Nevertheless, there is some reason to think that at any rate in the short term overall adoption numbers will not decline further. Although it is unlikely that there will be a sudden surge of mothers relinquishing babies for adoption (baby adoptions have consistently declined each year from 1975 to 1998), nor is there likely to be a significant rise in step-parent adoptions (numbers of which have declined throughout the 1990s, apart from 1998), there are two areas where adoption numbers are likely to increase, namely public law adoption and intercountry adoptions.

Public Law Adoptions

The Labour Government have taken a strong line on the value of local authorities planning for the adoption of those children whose long-term interests are that they should not be returned to their birth families.

Following concerns about the variable quality of adoption services which emerged from Social Service Inspectorate reports in 1996 and 1997[130] a Local Authority Circular, *Adoption—Achieving the Right Balance*,[131] was issued in August 1998. The circular focused 'attention on adoption as an important and beneficial option in the care of children' and was 'intended to bring adoption back into the mainstream of children's services'. It emphasized that where 'children cannot live with their families, for whatever reason, society has a duty to provide them with a fresh start and where appropriate a permanent alternative home. Adoption is the means of giving children an opportunity to start again; for many children, adoption may be their only chance of experiencing family life.' This positive message about adoption was further underscored by the Quality Protects Programme, one of the aims of which is to 'maximise the contribution that adoption can make to provide permanent families for children in appropriate cases'.[132] Further pressure to increase adoptions has been placed on local authorities by making the number a performance indicator of good practice.[133] The early indications are that this pressure is having effect, with the number of children being looked after by local authorities placed for adoption as at 31 March 1999 increasing by 14 per cent on the previous year. The pressure is clearly set to continue following the publication of the Prime Minister's Review of Adoption Law which concluded that the Government should promote an increase in adoption for children looked after by local authorities.[134]

Intercountry Adoptions

The absence of reference hitherto to so-called intercountry adoptions, that is where applicants seek to adopt children from abroad, commonly developing countries, may occasion surprise to some. However, unlike in many Western European countries, where such adoptions now account for the majority of adoptions,[135] and in the USA, where a substantial number of such orders are made,[136] the number in England and Wales is

---

[130] *For Children's Sake: An SSI Inspection of Local Authority Adoption Services* (Department of Health, 1996) and *For Children's Sake—Part II: An Inspection of Local Authority Adoption Services* (Department of Health, 1997). One suspects that the Government was also influenced by Patricia Morgan's thesis that all children who have been in local authority care for twelve months ought to be adopted, see *Adoption and the Care of Children* (IEA, 1998).

[131] LAC (98) 20. A national survey of implementation of this circular was carried out in 1999.

[132] *The Government's Objectives for Children's Social Services* (Department of Health, 1999), para 1.3.   [133] See Performance Indicator C23, *ibid.* at para 1.3.

[134] A Consultation Report of the Performance and Innovation Unit, *Adoption: Prime Minister's Review*, Department of Health, July 2000, para. 2.

[135] eg France and Sweden.

[136] Annual numbers of intercountry adoptions in the USA are 8–10,000, which is between 40 per cent and 50 per cent of the estimated global number of intercountry adoptions.

remarkably low. Although there are no reliable statistics, before 1990 there were thought to be between fifty and sixty children brought to the UK for adoption through official procedures with a further sixty to seventy a year recorded as arriving without prior entry clearance.[137] In the early 1990s, there were a number of adoptions of Romanian orphans. Indeed, in 1992 the *Adoption Law Review* commented[138] that since March 1990 over 400 children from Romania alone had been brought to the UK for adoption. In 1998, however, the total number of intercountry adoptions through official procedures was 258,[139] amounting to 6 per cent of all adoptions for that year.

It has been speculated[140] that one reason for the low numbers is the absence of any specialist adoption agencies or adoption service for would-be adopters of children from overseas. This in turn has meant would-be adopters having to rely upon their efforts and initiative—with all the expenses and time that that entails. It might also be said that some adoption agencies have been either openly hostile to intercountry adoptions or reluctant to accord them any priority,[141] which will have also had a deterrent effect. Nevertheless, it has never been the case that *no* agency has been prepared to support an intercountry adoption application and indeed during the 1990s agencies were officially encouraged to provide assistance and support. Indeed, the most recent guidance[142] enjoins local authorities to reflect a positive view of intercountry adoption. Even so, beyond being required to provide counselling,[143] at present there is no *statutory* requirement upon local authorities to provide intercountry adoption services. However, this will change when s 9 of the Adoption (Intercountry Aspects) Act 1999 comes into force, for that specifically

---

[137] Adoption Law Review, Discussion Paper 4. *Intercountry Adoption* (1992) para 27. According to findings of Murch and Lowe *et al*, *Pathways to Adoption* study, intercountry adoptions amounted to 3 per cent of their total national sample, but 6 per cent of their London sample.

[138] n 75 above at para 27. For a profile of intercountry adoptions in 1995, see *Focus on Adoption* (BAAF, 1997) ch 6.

[139] M. Brennan *et al*, 'Intercountry Adoption—the Recognition of Foreign Adoptions in the Simple and Full Forms' in the *Report on the Cross Border Movement of Children* (Society for Advanced Legal Studies 1999) Annex C at 121–2, from which it will be seen that a substantial proportion (47 per cent) of these children come from China. In addition, according to the Explanatory Notes to the Adoption (Intercountry Aspects) Act 1999, para 5, there are thought to be approximately another 100 cases each year where people avoid official adoption procedures.

[140] By the Adoption Law Review, Discussion Paper 4, n 139 above. The Review also commented that the *comparatively* low figures may, in part, be accounted for the relatively high number of domestic adoptions and of babies compared with other Western countries. However, with the virtual demise of baby adoptions that now appears a weaker argument.

[141] See *Adoption: The Future* (1993, Cm 2288) para 6.9, and Adoption Law Review, Discussion Paper 4, n 139 above 31.   [142] Local Authority Circular LAC (98) 20, at para 52.

[143] Adoption Act 1976, s 1, Circular LAC (87) 8, Annex 3.

includes intercountry adoptions in the definition of 'adoption service' which all local authorities are obliged to provide.[144] The overall purpose of the 1999 Act is to permit the UK to ratify the Hague Convention on Intercountry Adoption 1993 which is aimed at bringing global control of cross-border adoptions. Once this has been done there is every reason to think that this will be one of the growth areas of adoption.

Organizational Changes

Some changes to the way adoption work is organized seem inevitable, if only because there are too many adoption agencies (160 in 1994)[145] chasing too few children (at current rates about 2,500). One radical suggestion[146] is to remove the adoption function from local authorities altogether and to vest it either in voluntary agencies or in a newly created National Adoption Service. The latter suggestion initially found favour in the Home Office, but was opposed by the Department of Health (which has responsibility for overseeing local authority children's services and all adoption matters).[147] It was perhaps unlikely that such a service would have been created, if only because of the huge expense involved. It also seemed premature to carry out such reform at a time when authorities seem to be responding positively to Local Authority Circular LAC 98(20).[148] In any event this option has now been firmly rejected by the Prime Minister's Review.[149] Less radical suggestions[150] include the systematic development of regional consortia and releasing at least some authorities from the mandatory duty to provide an adoption service. Another quite different suggestion to reduce the local authority workload is to remove the requirement that they prepare a Schedule II Report in the case of step-parent or relatives' adoption applications.[151] Given the court's involvement, there seems no reason to impose this extra check on what is essentially a private law application.

Long-term Options

Having been the one area of child law not to be reviewed in the 1980s, adoption was subjected to a full-scale review during the 1990s. The review,

[144] s 1 of the Adoption Act 1976 will be amended with the addition of s 1(3A).
[145] See Lowe and Murch *et al*, n 87 above, at 448. At that stage there were 116 statutory agencies and 44 voluntary agencies. But since then, following further local government reorganization creating unitary authorities, the number of statutory agencies will have increased.
[146] This is advocated by Morgan, *Adoption and the Care of Children*, but for a balanced argument of the pros and cons see Lowe and Murch *et al*, n 87 above, 438 ff.
[147] See the report in (2000) 10–16 February (Issue 1308) Community Care 17.
[148] See F. Rickford, 'Takeover Bid under Fire'(2000) 3–9 Feb (Issue 1307) Community Care 12.
[149] See n 134 above, recommendation 41.
[150] See Lowe and Murch *et al*, n 87 above, at 440.
[151] See the recommendation by Murch, Lowe *et al*, n 137 above, 248–9.

conducted by an inter-departmental committee under the aegis of the Department of Health, led to the government paper 'Adoption—A Service for Children' which included a proposed Adoption Bill.[152] However, apart from intercountry adoption, no legislative action has been taken and it is now apparent that no further primary legislation can be expected within the lifetime of the current Government. There therefore remains an opportunity to rethink some of the recommendations. One area that might be profitably revisited is the basic assumption throughout the review that there is a continuing need for adoption as it is currently understood and that there should not be a second or 'simple' form.[153] We shall examine this core assumption by asking whether there is a case for (1) restricting the availability of adoption, (2) creating a new concept altogether, or (3) modifying the existing concept of adoption.

Restricting the Availability of Adoption

'In family' adoptions, be they by step-parents or by relatives, lie uneasily with the legal concept of completely severing the child's links with his birth family and might therefore be considered unsuitable adoptions. As we have seen, the Houghton Committee expressed concern about step-parent adoptions but, rather than prohibiting them, recommended discouraging them *inter alia* by providing alternative orders. The Adoption Law Review similarly expressed concern about some step-parent adoption applications appearing 'to be made without full consideration of the needs of the child' but it too felt that it was inappropriate to prohibit them. Instead, it recommended further discouraging inappropriate applications and providing, in those cases where a step-parent adoption was desirable, a new form of order whereby only the step-parent him- or herself actually adopted (it was felt anomalous that, as under the current law, the birth parent should adopt their own child). Among the various changes aimed at discouraging step-parent adoption, the 1992 Consultative Document proposed that it should be revocable where the new marriage ends in divorce or death before the child is 18. It also recommended that it should be possible for step-parents to acquire parental responsibility either by agreement or a court order.[154] In the event, the proposal that a

---

[152] 1996, Department of Health and Welsh Office. Prior to this, the review produced four Discussion Papers (*The Nature and Effect of Adoption* (No 1, 1990), *Agreement and Freeing* (No 2, 1991), *The Adoption Process* (No 3, 1991) and *Intercountry Adoption* (No 4, 1992)) and three Background Papers (*International Perspectives* (No 1, 19990), *Review of Research Relating to Adoption* (No 2, 1990), and *Intercountry Adoption* (No 3, 1992)), and culminated in the publication of *Adoption Law Review: Consultation Document* in 1992. Following this document a government White Paper, *Adoption—the Future* (Cm 2288) was published in 1993. Separate consultation papers 'Placement for Adoption' and 'The Future of Adoption Panels' were published in 1994.   [153] See recommendation 1 of the 1992 Consultation Report.
[154] See para 19.

step-parent adoption could be undone was dropped and the proposed Adoption Bill made provision for a new type of step-parent adoption order (ie by the step-parent) and would amend the Children Act to allow step-parents to acquire parental responsibility by agreement or order.[155]

Although it is tempting to say that step-parent adoptions should be prohibited, it is submitted that both Houghton and the Review were right not to do so, for there are cases where adoption is appropriate; though in case of the death of one of the birth parents, one wonders whether guardianship would be more appropriate. The proposal to extend the power to make parental responsibility agreements and orders is welcome, however, as providing another alternative. In this respect, however, given that step-parent adoptions are made frequently of children aged 10 or over,[156] one wonders whether express provision needs to be made to safeguard their interests, for example by making it mandatory to obtain older children's views or even, as is proposed for adoption,[157] requiring the consent of children aged 12 or more.

The case for prohibiting adoptions by relatives seems weaker than that for step-parents and it is difficult to disagree with the Review declining to do so. The Review envisaged such adoptions being appropriate where the child's parents are dead[158] or living in another country and unlikely ever to be able to make parental decisions in respect of the child's upbringing. It did, however, consider that, as with step-parents, the legislative framework should provide adequate opportunity for applicants to explore other possibilities, particularly residence orders. Perhaps the power to make parental responsibility agreements and orders should be extended to relatives.

Creating a New Concept

Although the 1992 Consultative Document was against the creation of 'a second (or "simple") form of adoption similar in effect to an irrevocable residence order, or the introduction of a basic adoption order with additional features which would be added to it', it did propose that where a court makes a residence order in favour of a person other than a parent or step-parent it should have the further power to appoint that person as the 'child's inter vivos guardian'.[159] This order would automatically last

---

[155] See respectively clauses 45 and 85. This had been one of the recommendations of Murch and Lowe *et al*, n 137 above, at 249.

[156] In Murch and Lowe *et al's* study, n 137 above, for example, 38 per cent of children involved in step-parent adoptions were aged 10 or over (Table 3.10).

[157] See clause 41(7) of the proposed Adoption Bill.

[158] Though query whether in most cases guardianship would be preferable?

[159] *Consultation Document 1992*, n 152 above, at para 6.5 and spelt out further by the White Paper: *Adoption: The Future*, n 152 above, at 5.23 ff. This paper thought that in the case of foster parents who acquired it they would feel that it gave them 'Foster-plus' status.

until the child became 18 and, to emphasize the permanence of the new relationship, court leave would be required to apply to dissolve it. This proposal was embodied in clause 86 of the proposed Adoption Bill, though without the title 'inter vivos guardianship'.

Whether such a proposal would prove popular and reduce the demand for adoption is debatable, but it is tacit recognition that the current law lacks a concept which secures the child's permanent placement without severing the former legal relationships. It also highlights the difficulty of finding an appropriate name for a new order. Taking the latter issue first, perhaps the best name other than adoption and which is widely under-stood, is 'guardianship'. Under English law that term is now reserved for those formally appointed to take the place of a parent upon their death.[160] However, even then it only lasts until the child is 18. Although there is little, if any, legal significance in guardianship lasting beyond the child's majority, it would surely be of important symbolic value for it to last for life. Indeed, the power to make *life-long* so-called inter vivos guardianship orders along the lines envisaged in clause 86 of the proposed Bill would provide a strong alternative to adoption.

Nevertheless, it has to be accepted that so long as adoption exists, any other order is likely to be perceived as a 'second-class adoption'. This would be particularly so if a new form of adoption order, such as a 'sim-ple adoption', were to be introduced. If, therefore, complete severance is thought inappropriate in the light of the current practice of adopting older children, then the remedy is to change the concept of adoption itself rather than to create other types of orders.

Modifying the Existing Concept of Adoption

According to the 1992 Consultation Document:[161]

It is essential that adoption is regarded not as a means of determining with whom the child is to live, but as a way of making a child legally part of a new family and severing any legal relationship with the birth family. It should stand apart from other orders, not in such a way that it is thought of as a superior option but so there are no doubts as to its special features.

While it is undoubtedly important that the irrevocable permanence of adoption should not be undermined, one can take issue with the asser-tion that to maintain this distinction necessarily involves severing any legal relationship with the birth family.[162] Why, for example, should

---

[160] Guardianship is governed by the Children Act 1989, ss 5 and 6.

[161] n 152 above at para 3.6.

[162] In fact, adoption does not end *all* connection or consequence, eg he remains within the prohibited degrees of his birth family. Adoption Act 1976 s 47(1), adoption cannot deprive him of British citizenship: s 47(2). He also continues to have certain rights over pension rights or under certain insurance practices: s 48.

adoptions automatically end the legal relationship between birth siblings or even between children and grandparents? Indeed, might it not
be said that in doing so, our law is in breach of art 8 of the European
Convention on Human Rights, as unjustifiably interfering with family
life? We have previously noted that adoption did not originally alter
succession rights. Is there not a case for preserving the child's succession
rights from his birth parents (though not vice versa), as well as given
child succession rights from his adopted family?[163] In other words it is
by no means obvious that *all* connections should be severed and indeed
with older children being adopted it makes less sense to do so. This
notion of severance should be re-examined and kept to the minimum
necessary to secure the irrevocable permanence of the placement.

Finally, another key area that needs to be investigated is the relationship between local authorities who have previously 'looked after' the
child and the adoptive family. Some clear legislative provision needs to
be made for the continuation of their obligation to support the family. It
needs to be made clear, for example, that a child in need does not ipso
facto cease to be in need because of his adoption. Similarly, adoption
allowances and other support should be regarded as the norm and not
the exception. In turn, this means that the State will have to accept that
while adoption is a good option for many children who cannot live with
their own family, it is not a cheap option.

---

[163] Cf *Re Collins (Dec'd)* [1990] Fam 56 *Watson v Willmott* [1991] 1 QB 140, which might be
thought to illustrate the injustice of not doing so.

C
Regulating and Reorganizing
the Family

15

Divorce in the United States

IRA MARK ELLMAN

The half-century from 1950 to 2000 was a period of great change in divorce law. The story is familiar and oft told. In 1950 proof of marital fault was required everywhere before a court would grant a divorce decree. Divorce by mutual consent, much less unilateral divorce, was not accepted in any state. Whatever people thought about the merits of such a system as a matter of morality or family policy, it clearly did not work on the front lines. At this level the most serious problem was the bar on divorce by mutual consent. Parties who agreed on divorce still had to persuade a court that there were sufficient fault grounds to justify the decree. So every divorce required a proceeding in which one of the spouses was officially labeled guilty of a serious marital offence. Most courts operated under a rule that purported to bar the spouses from co-operating in presenting that evidence. Spouses were supposed to maintain an adversarial posture on the question of whether a marital offence had been committed. Their failure to do so would render them guilty of 'collusion', itself a basis for denying the divorce decree. The doctrine of collusion seemed to follow necessarily from the premise that mutual consent was not a ground for divorce. The entire package of rules encouraged the very sham that the collusion doctrine ineffectually sought to suppress. Most divorces, like most civil actions, were settled, but perjury was the norm in the judicial proceedings that were required to justify the decree that the parties had covertly agreed upon.

Judges and lawyers would welcome reforms that eliminated their participation in this unsavory charade. Elimination of the fault requirement was presented by reformers as the method for achieving this result. It would conform the official law of the books to the law in practice. By recognizing the married couple's right to agree to end their marriage without proof of fault, the law would ratify the practice of mutual consent divorce without requiring the couple to present evidence of marital misconduct by one of them to justify the result. Reviewing this history, Herbert Jacob has concluded that legislators typically understood divorce reform as a technical fix aimed at improving the functioning of the judicial system, rather than as a fundamental change in family policy.[1] Yet the reforms generally went much further than required for that

---

[1] See generally HERBERT JACOB, THE SILENT REVOLUTION (1988).

modest purpose. Overtly recognizing divorce by mutual consent would have ended the sham, but the typical reform, exemplified by the provisions of the Uniform Marriage and Divorce Act, permitted unilateral divorce. Jacob suggests that the reformers were politically astute in packaging their proposals so as to draw attention away from this result. He quotes the language of the original report of the California Governor's Commission that first suggested replacing fault grounds with the requirement that the court find the marriage 'irretrievably broken,' the formulation later adopted by the Uniform Marriage and Divorce Act:

We cannot overemphasize that this standard does not permit divorce by consent, wherein marriage is treated as wholly a private contract terminable at the pleasure of the parties without any effective intervention by society. The standard we propose requires the community to assert its interest in the status of the family, and permits dissolution of the marriage only after it has been subject to a penetrating scrutiny and the judicial process has provided the parties with all of the resources of social science in aid of conciliation.[2]

In fact, the precise impact of the new laws was apparently not as clear at the time as it later became. Dean Herma Kay, who played an important role on the California Governor's Commission and was later Co-Reporter for the Uniform Act, feared that the California legislature's formulation would allow evidence of specific acts of misconduct to show that the marriage was 'irretrievably broken'.[3] At the same time Max Rheinstein observed that if one took the words of the California statute seriously, no marriage could ever be dissolved, for surely one could always argue that there was some possibility, however small, that the marriage was not *irretrievably broken*.[4] Fears like Kay's and Rheinstein's might have been encouraged by an early ruling of the California Supreme Court under the new law. In *McKim v McKim*[5] the spouses had obviously agreed on the dissolution of their marriage. The husband, appearing as a witness for the petitioner-wife (who herself did not appear), testified in conclusory terms that the parties had attempted without success to reconcile and that no further conciliation efforts would succeed. Keeping the collusion doctrine alive, the court held that the new law required the *court*, not the parties, to 'decide whether the evidence . . . supports findings that irreconcilable differences do exist and that the marriage has broken down irremediably and should be dissolved'.[6] Mr McKim's conclusory testimony in

[2] California Governor's Commission, quoted in Jacob, n 1 above, at 55.
[3] Herma Hill Kay, *A Family Court: The California Proposal*, in P. Bohannan (ed), Divorce and After 243, 276–7 (1970).
[4] See Max Rheinstein, Marriage Stability, Divorce and the Law 368 (1970).
[5] 493 P2d 868 (1972).   [6] *ibid* at 890.

support of Mrs McKim's petition was therefore insufficient to allow the marital dissolution they both sought.

But the California Supreme Court's surprising decision in *McKim* proved a poor indicator of the new law's operation, and these early fears were quieted. As the Iowa Supreme Court said, applying a similar new law at about the same time, the spouses' collusion to bring about the marital dissolution would only 'further evidence the fact of the marital breakdown'.[7] Indeed, just one spouse's persistent unilateral demand to end the marriage would show that. And indeed, even if Jacob is right that the legislatures did not appreciate the policy significance of this shift to unilateral divorce, it is clear that many others did. The American Bar Association initially declined approval of the new Uniform Marriage and Divorce Act because of opposition by its Family Law Section to laws that would accept 'divorce on demand'. The eventual compromise required six months' living apart before a unilateral divorce could be granted.[8] Long waiting periods—up to two years was not uncommon—became the most common provision inserted by legislatures with doubts about no-fault reforms. Waiting periods in effect substituted for the therapeutic approach originally urged by the California Governor's Commission. Its report envisioned the creation of an ambitious system of family courts with a staff of professional counselors who would attempt, at least initially, to achieve reconciliation in every case. The abandonment of fault and the easing of the legal requirements for dissolution were thus counterbalanced, in the Commission's plan, with a serious effort to heal rather than dissolve the family. Dissolution would result only after the family court reached the conclusion that such healing was not possible. Budgetary concerns combined with opposition from the bar to defeat the family court proposal in California, and no other state followed that route. The no-fault reform went forward without the therapeutic salve.

Of course, state divorce courts typically do employ counselors today, and conciliation services are typically available to couples who want them. But the main business of court counselors today is the mediation of divorce agreements, not the reconciliation of the parties. The idea that divorce courts should compel parties to embark on a serious course of reconciliation counseling before divorce would be granted never really took hold anywhere, and resistance to funding the required staff was not the only reason. In some ways this is curious. After all, the American no-fault movement was conceived in the California of the 1960s and born

[7] *Marriage of Collins*, 200 NW2d 886, 890 (Iowa 1972).

[8] Actually, the Uniform Act allowed a dissolution before six months if the court found there was 'serious marital discord affecting the attitude of one or both parties toward the marriage.' It appears that this provision 'was little relied upon, however; the alternative requirement of six months' living apart is usually easy enough for most couples to meet.

there ten years later. What more hospitable home could one want for a psychologic approach to divorce, one might think. But that view, one sees in retrospect, would misunderstand that culture. As Carl Schneider has observed, the significance of the rise of the psychologic man in the second half of the twentieth century is its replacement of moral discourse in family relations with psychologic discourse.[9] The question to consider, when dissolution is proposed, became whether the parties find the marriage personally fulfilling, not whether their moral commitments to one another or their children require its continuation. The psychological revolution was a revolution in attitudes more than a revolution in the capacity of marriage counselors to transform unhappy marriages into happy ones. Persevering in an unsatisfactory marriage is not the ideal for which the 1960s and 1970s are known. So one might guess that the proportion of spouses in troubled marriages motivated to work at repairing their relationship was on the decline during the no-fault reform era. In that climate, a therapeutic strategy for improving the marital relationship would have to seem very credible to deter parties otherwise inclined to end it instead. It was surely far easier for the counselor consulted by an unhappy spouse to guide the client through the marriage's dissolution than to work a lasting change in the parties' satisfaction with the marriage.

There is another point as well. Nearly coterminous with the rise of no-fault divorce was an increasing acceptance of a family privacy doctrine in American constitutional law. *Griswold v Connecticut* was decided in 1965, and *Eisenstadt v Baird* in 1971.[10] The long-standing disinclination of the common law to involve itself too deeply in intra-family disputes— a tradition well matched to the pluralist ethic of American democracy— had now found a constitutional footing. The point is not that compelled marital counseling would violate the constitutional rule, but simply that the cultural and social norms of the era that spawned *Eisenstadt* are not entirely compatible with that level of intrusion into the marital relationship.[11] The law was not about to require unwilling parties to have repeated discussions with state-certified strangers about the details of their intimate relationships.

---

[9] See Carl Schneider, *Moral Discourse and the Transformation of American Family Law*, 83 Mich L Rev 1803, 1847 (1985).

[10] See *Griswold v Connecticut*, 381 US 479 (1965); *Eisenstadt v Baird*, 405 US 438 (1971).

[11] But perhaps there is a constitutional argument as well. I am generally not favorably inclined toward changing public policy debates into constitutional questions, and am thus hardly the one to offer such an argument. Post-*Eisenstadt* developments in the constitutional family privacy doctrine clearly established limits on the state's power to condition the availability of divorce and remarriage, however—*Zablocki* made that clear—and perhaps it is not entirely implausible to suggest that at least some forms of compelled counseling might transcend those limits.

But it is no longer the 1960s and 1970s. Recent years have seen an increased willingness to intervene. Such intervention is usually offered for the purpose of ameliorating the divorce process rather than preserving the marriage.[12] Required mediation of custody disputes is the most widespread example. About one-quarter of the states now require such mediation by statute, and many more give the judge the power to require it in a particular case.[13] More recently, some states have begun to require divorcing parents to attend parental education classes meant to help them protect their children from the negative effects of divorce.[14] But the most dramatic evidence of a possible reverse in the pendulum's swing is the recent effort to rehabilitate fault divorce. The effort has been waged in different fronts by different groups—groups one might not always expect to find aligned.

Early on there were feminists who argued that no-fault divorce hurt women economically. Lenore Weitzman was surely the best known of these. There is little dissent today from the proposition that divorce has a disproportionate financial impact on women, though not nearly as large as Weitzman suggested.[15] It is sometimes forgotten, however, that Weitzman herself never favored a return to fault divorce, but rather a reform of the financial remedies that accompanied it. But other writers have now taken that further step.[16] They argue that no-fault divorce is to blame either for an increase in divorce rates or for some other ill, ranging from an unjust allocation of the post-divorce financial burdens to an increase in spousal abuse.[17] The claims are thus not entirely grounded in

[12] Although there have been serious proposals for encouraging premarital counseling, one of which at least has been adopted in Florida. HB 1019, introduced in the Florida legislature in March of 1998, would have required couples to complete a four-hour marriage preparation course as a condition of obtaining a marriage license. As enacted, however, the legislation instead offered a reduction in marriage license fees to those who took such a course. 1998 Fla Sess Law Serv Ch 98–403 (West).

[13] See American Law Institute, PRINCIPLES OF THE LAW OF FAMILY DISSOLUTION, 99–100 (Tentative Draft No 3, Part I) (1998). One could imagine that requiring mediation is no more intrusive than the only alternative—requiring parties who cannot agree to adjudicate their dispute. If mediation is face-to-face, however, it does involve contact and discussion directly between the parties, rather than through lawyer-intermediaries, as in traditional negotiation. The ALI Principles reject mandatory face-to-face mediation. *ibid* at § 2.08(2).

[14] See ELLMAN *et al*, FAMILY LAW: CASES, TEXT, PROBLEMS 244 (3rd edn 1998) (citing several authors who have discussed this issue).

[15] The leading dissenter is perhaps Sanford Braver, whose analysis is set forth in DIVORCED DADS: SHATTERING THE MYTHS (1998). For a summary of the dispute over Weitzman's numbers, which led eventually to her concession that they were flawed, see ELLMAN *et al*, n 14 above, at 373–80.

[16] See eg Barbara Woodhouse's sections of Barbara Bennett Woodhouse and Katharine T. Bartlett, *Sex, Lies and Dissipation: The Discourse of Fault in a No-Fault Era*, 82 GEO L J 2525 (1994).

[17] Brinig has been a persistent proponent of fault. See Margaret F. Brinig and Steven M. Crafton, *Marriage and Opportunism*, 23 J LEG STUD 869 (1994) (arguing fault divorce leads to

the kind of financial analysis Weitzman attempted, and often have a moral tone as well.[18] Their overall theme is that a no-fault system leads to results that are unjust. The sentiments of these American academics found an audience in European politics as well. References to Weitzman were apparently common among the opponents of the initial divorce reform referendum in the Republic of Ireland.[19] One woman politician led the 'vote no' campaign with the memorable slogan that 'a woman voting for divorce is like a turkey voting for Christmas'. [20]

This thread of some feminist writing, that no-fault divorce leads to unjust results, connects with sentiments expressed by another group of writers associated with a communitarian ethic—Schneider, Glendon, Scott, Etzioni, and Galston.[21] Schneider and Glendon do not themselves favor a return to fault divorce—Schneider has said so,[22] explicitly—but they express a kind of nostalgic longing for the time when the governing law contained a more clear moral message.[23] Scott attempts to reconcile those sentiments with a liberal philosophy by resort to a contract rubric[24]—suggesting that spouses commit to one another by enforceable contracts the very making of which, Scott hopes, will alter their behavior and strengthen their marital perseverance.[25] Etzioni and Galston, who are

increased rates of domestic violence); see also Margaret F. Brinig and F. H. Buckley, *No-Fault Divorce and At-Fault People*, 18 INT'L REV L & ECON 325 (1998) (arguing eliminating fault considerations in alimony determinations has the effect of increasing divorce rates). For severe criticisms of Brinig's data and arguments, see Ira Ellman and Sharon Lohr, *Marriage as Contract, Opportunistic Violence, and Other Bad Arguments for Fault Divorce*, 1997 UNIV ILL L REV 718; Ira Ellman and Sharon Lohr, *Dissolving the Relationship between Divorce Laws and Divorce Rates*, 18 INT'L REV L & ECON 341 (1998). Galston, a political scientist normally working in other areas, has received considerable attention for his fault arguments. See William Galston, *Divorce American Style*, 124 THE PUBLIC INTEREST, Summer 1996, at 12. For a comprehensive policy discussion that also replies to Galston's arguments, see Ira Ellman, *The Misguided Movement to Revive Fault Divorce*, 11 INT'L J LAW, POL'Y & FAM 216 (1997).

[18] See eg Woodhouse, n 12 above. I don't mean to suggest that a fondness for fault has become the dominant view of feminist writers. While I claim no good polling data on the topic, there are certainly feminist authors who dissent from any nostalgia for fault divorce. See eg Bartlett's portion of Woodhouse and Bartlett, n 16 above, and especially Jana Singer, *Divorce Reform and Gender Justice*, 67 NCL REV 1103 (1989).

[19] See MICHELE DILLON, DEBATING DIVORCE: MORAL CONFLICT IN IRELAND 71 (1993).

[20] William Duncan, *The Divorce Referendum in the Republic of Ireland: Resisting the Tide*, 2 INT'L J L & FAM 62, 60 (1988) (quoting statement made by Deputy Alice Glenn); see also Dillon, n 19 above, at 77 (citing Glenn's statement as illustrative of a central theme in the Irish anti-divorce discourse, where women were portrayed as victims in need of protection).

[21] See Carl E. Schneider, *Marriage, Morals and the Law: No-Fault Divorce and Moral Discourse*, 1994 UTAH L REV 503; MARY ANN GLENDON, ABORTION AND DIVORCE IN WESTERN LAW (1987); Elizabeth Scott, *Rehabilitating Liberalism in Modern Divorce Law*, 1994 UTAH L REV 687; AMITAI ETZIONI, THE NEW GOLDEN RULE: COMMUNITY AND MORALITY IN A DEMOCRATIC SOCIETY (1996); William Galston, *Divorce American Style*, 124 THE PUBLIC INTEREST (Summer 1996).

[22] See Schneider, n 21 above, at 551.   [23] See Glendon, n 21 above, at 104–11.

[24] See Scott, n 21 above, at 720–5.

[25] *ibid* at 721; see also Elizabeth Scott, *Rational Decisionmaking about Marriage and Divorce*, 76 VA L REV 9, 42–3, 69–70 (1990).

social scientists rather than legal scholars, are also the most willing to embrace a revived fault regime.[26] They urge the enactment of a kind of optional fault divorce, which they label covenant marriage, that newly-weds may choose. That proposal has in turn been picked up at the political level by the family values movement of the Christian right,[27] which succeeded in selling it to the Louisiana legislature,[28] and, in a somewhat softened version, to Arizona.[29] If women's political action groups were to join the family values movement, they would combine in a potent political force behind the revival of fault divorce, as they have in the other arena in which they joined forces, the enforcement of child support obligations.

Is that likely to happen? Probably not. Women initiate most divorces today,[30] and women's groups have generally opposed the abandonment of no-fault divorce. As we shall see below, there is no current increase in divorce rates to give urgency to the movement. Finally, on the merits of the matter, there is little to support the claims of fault proponents that their law will reduce the likelihood of divorce, or improve the lot of divorced women. It is to these last questions that we now turn.

LAW AND DIVORCE: TWO FAULTY ARGUMENTS FOR FAULT DIVORCE

1. It is Needed to Rescue Women from a Financial Disaster Imposed by No-fault

One of Weitzman's most important claims was that no-fault divorce contributed to the relative poverty of divorced women—that women were better off under the predecessor fault system. That conclusion became sufficiently well known to find its way into American legislative debates on divorce reform[31] as well as into the debate over reform of the Irish divorce laws.[32] Weitzman compared the outcomes in a sample of California divorces before and after that state's shift to no-fault grounds

---

[26] See Amitai Etzioni, *Morals Can Work Better than Laws*, WALL ST J, Feb 11 1997, at A21; see also Galston, n 21 above.

[27] See eg *Christian Coalition Revs up Lobbying Effort*, ARIZ REPUBLIC, Feb 21 1998, at R2.

[28] See LA REV STAT ANN § 9–224 *et seq* (West 1990).

[29] See ARIZ REV STAT 25–901 *et seq*.

[30] The question, of course, is not who filed the formal petition, but whether as a factual matter the discussion to end the marriage was the husband's. For some data and a thoughtful examination of the issue, see Braver, Whitley, and Ng, *Who divorced Whom? Methodological and Theoretical Issues*, 20 J DIVORCE AND REMARRIAGE 1 (1993).

[31] See Martha Fineman, *Implementing Equality: Ideology, Contradiction, and Social Change: A Study of Rhetoric and Results in the Regulation of the Consequences of Divorce*, 1983 WIS L REV 789, 801.   [32] See Dillon, n 21 above.

for divorce. How could this change in the *grounds* for divorce make divorced women financially worse off than before the reform? As I noted in an early article, the argument had to do with the bargaining process:

The fault rules gave great bargaining leverage to the spouse who felt no urgency to end the marriage, especially if it would be difficult to prove that spouse guilty of 'fault.' Knowing the difficulty of obtaining a divorce in a truly contested proceeding in which her fault would have to be shown, such an innocent spouse might offer to co-operate with a 'consent' decree only if certain financial demands were met. So, for example, the older married man who abandoned his long-term wife for a younger woman could not obtain his 'freedom' to remarry her without buying it from his first wife. In such a system the laws governing property division and alimony often didn't matter, since in many cases the wife had great [bargaining] leverage regardless of their content. This is not to say that the system necessarily produced equitable results. While it protected the marital investment of an 'innocent' spouse, or one whose 'fault' would be tricky to prove, it failed entirely to protect the 'guilty' spouse who had invested a great deal in her marriage, while giving bargaining leverage to the innocent spouse who had invested very little.

No-fault reform created a sea-change in this legal environment. Although motivated in large part by a desire to end the charade of perjured testimony and falsified residency that permeated consent divorces under the fault system, its effects went considerably further. The no-fault reform effectively recognized unilateral divorce. The man who wants to end his marriage now simply files a petition alleging that it is irretrievably broken; there is no defense against such an allegation. The wife seeking alimony, property division, or child support has no leverage to demand such compensation as the price of her husband's 'freedom', but must rely instead on the substantive law governing these issues. Thus, the law of alimony and property division now count in a way neither did before.[33]

It thus seemed plausible to think that the no-fault reforms adversely affected the financial outcome of divorce for women. Of course, even if one concluded that they did, revision in the law of alimony and property allocation might be a better cure than a return to fault divorce. But no cure is needed if there is no problem, and whether the change to no-fault grounds reduced the average wife's divorce settlement is a testable empirical proposition. Flaws in Weitzman's methods ultimately left claims based on her numbers unpersuasive.[34] And even before her numbers were put in doubt, others concluded that they did not prove the case anyway, that they did not show that women did less well in California after no-fault was adopted.[35]

---

[33] Ira Ellman, *The Theory of Alimony*, 77 CALIF L REV 1, 7–9 (1989).

[34] For a review of the literature generated by Weitzman's critics, see Ellman, Kurtz, and Scott, n 14 above, at 373–6.

[35] Actually, these critics were of two kinds. Some, looking at other data, concluded that

On reflection the theory itself appears less persuasive. There are two problems with it. First, it ignores the possibility that judges might apply new property and alimony provisions in the no-fault laws in a way that gave wives resisting divorce as good a financial outcome as they could achieve with the bargaining leverage they previously had under the old fault system. Early in the no-fault era courts did seem skeptical of wives' claims—as by insisting on transitional assistance only, even for wives with poor employment prospects—but the consensus is that they later adopted more favorable attitudes. One must also note that in focusing on California, Weitzman excluded from her consideration a potentially important change in the common law states that occurred at about the same time as the no-fault reforms: the transition from common law marital property rules to equitable distribution. This development enhanced the property claims at divorce of most wives in common law states.[36] A comparison of two New York Court of Appeals cases provides a convenient and dramatic example of this change. In *Saff v Saff*,[37] decided in 1979, the wife was held to have no interest in the business built up by her husband—with some direct help by her—over the course of their marriage of forty-two years. Under the common law rules that then governed in New York, the titling of the business property in the husband's name was dispositive. Seven years later New York held that its new equitable distribution law even required the court to give the wife a share, as marital property, of the physician-husband's license to practice medicine. There can be no doubt that this enormous shift in marital property law left the average financially dependent spouse in New York better off after divorce than she would have been before the change in the law.[38]

---

no-fault had little impact. See eg Herbert Jacob, *Another Look at No-Fault Divorce and the Post-Divorce Finances of Women*, 23 LAW & SOC REV 95, 112–13 (1989). Others concluded that Weitzman's own published data did not show the effect she claimed, that she had misinterpreted it. See esp Stephen D. Sugarman, *Dividing Financial Interests at Divorce*, in Stephen D. Sugarman and Herma Hill Kay, DIVORCE REFORM AT THE CROSSROADS 130, 132–4 (1990).

[36] I made this point earlier in Ira Ellman, *The Misguided Movement to Revive Fault Divorce*, 11 INT'L J L, POL'Y, & FAM 216, 242 n 45 (1997); see also William Gray, *The Economic Impact of Divorce Law Reform*, 15 POP. RES. & POL'Y REV 275 (1996). Gray concluded that whether no-fault degraded the financial impact of divorce for women depends on their state's marital property rules. Gray assumes that property allocation is more important for most women than alimony or child support, an implausible claim, but not one that is necessary to his evaluation of the effects of no-fault divorce.

[37] 402 NYS 2d 690, *appeal dismissed*, 389 NE 2d 142 (1979).

[38] The shift in New York came very late, in 1980. New York was nearly the last common law state to make this shift. See Ellman, Kurtz, and Scott, n 14 above, at 254. Neighboring New Jersey, for example, did it nearly a decade earlier. See *Painter v Painter*, 320 A2d 484 (NJ 1974).

There is, however, a more pervasive problem with the bargaining lever theory than its failure to consider changes in the common law marital property system. It makes no sense to argue that no-fault would reduce a wife's leverage unless one assumes that men want divorce and women want to avoid it—with no-fault thus removing *from wives* an important bargaining chip (consent to divorce) that they can use to enhance their financial outcome. But if women want out of their marriage as often as men, then no-fault reforms would remove the bargaining chip of consent from men as often as from women, and the reforms would have no effect at all on the average outcome of divorce for women. In fact, available evidence suggests that, at least today, women are almost *twice as likely* as men to be the instigators of their divorce.[39] This fact suggests that the abolition of fault would favor women more often than men, in divorce negotiations.

In sum, despite the theory's initial plausibility, the claim that no-fault divorce hurt women financially is probably wrong. On balance there seems little empirical evidence in its support, and the theoretical arguments for why one would expect that result also weaken under scrutiny. Perhaps most importantly, the case to revive fault divorce is not made even if the theory were true, for the conclusion that removal of the fault lever altered bargaining conditions in a way that systematically burdened women allows more than one response. The perceived injustice might be best corrected by reforming the alimony and property rules to give divorced spouses appropriate claims, rather than by restoring fault grounds (in the hope that the bargaining leverage that fault gives to the spouse resistant to divorce would bring about just results).

The difficulty of designing fault rules that would sensibly distribute such bargaining leverage makes the choice clear. So long as some parties anxious to leave a marriage have good reason to do so, requiring them to prove fault may add injury (financial) to insult (psychological or physical). The cost and delay involved in making the proof of fault—and the risk that the proof will fail—counsels settlement to most divorce plaintiffs in a fault-divorce regime. But settlement negotiations usually lead the party more anxious to end the marriage to concede something in the divorce's financial terms. For example, the spouse who wants out of the marriage to escape from the other spouse's psychological abuse, or persistent alcoholism, may settle for less so as to secure the other spouse's consent and thereby avoid the cost, delay, and risk of litigating fault. Fault restrictions favor the spouse content to delay the divorce, who may or may not be the spouse that third-party observers would identify as

[39] See n 30 above.

blameworthy in the marriage's demise, and so fault rules often exacerbate rather than mitigate any injustice.

2. It is Needed to Staunch Rising Divorce rates

Even if divorce leaves women better off today than it did a generation or two ago, no one would claim that divorce is normally a favorable outcome for family members. One theme in the arguments that reformers offer for revising no-fault is the prevention of divorce. There is a long literature attempting to assess whether no-fault divorce contributed to the divorce rates. The methodological difficulties in making that assessment have defeated most researchers, although only some of them have realized it. But the weight of the evidence is now very strong, and most researchers, including this one, are persuaded that changes in the divorce laws themselves had very little impact on divorce rates.[40] One need not

---

[40] Ellman and Lohr, *Dissolving the Relationship between Divorce Laws and Divorce Rates*, n 17 above. There is one recent article that is both an exception to this general observation and supportive of the claim that there is a relationship between no-fault divorce laws and divorce rates, Friedberg, *Did Unilateral Divorce Raise Divorce Rates?*, 88 AMERICAN ECONOMIC REVIEW 608 (1998). Her work is careful and thoughtful, and obtains results that seem to conflict with those reported by Sharon Lohr and me. The question is how to account for this difference. Friedberg relies on Brinig's compilation of the year in which the states adopted no-fault divorce. In several cases we used different years, believing Brinig to be incorrect, but it is not obvious that this difference would explain the different results. Another possible explanation might be a combined effect of two other differences between her methodology and ours. One competing account of what happened is that no-fault divorce was the result, not the cause, of rising divorce rates, and this account would be consistent with a pattern in which each state's shift to no-fault occurs some years after divorce rates in that state begin to rise steeply. That is in fact the pattern that Lohr and I found. But we looked at the divorce rates between 1960 and 1992, while Friedberg examines that period 1968 to 1988. Her truncated time series excludes for many states a period during the 1960s that preceded any legal change but which included steeply rising divorce rates, and might therefore overestimate the impact of no-fault in the early-adopting states. This possible problem would be exacerbated by her method for correcting for non-legal factors that might affect divorce rates over time. She finds a significant association of divorce rates with no-fault divorce only if she includes in her regression a term that corrects for state-specific trends in divorce laws. But if for each state the rates tend to rise steeply for some years before enactment of no-fault, and level out or decline within a few years after enactment (a pattern we found common), then correcting for each state with state-specific trends has the effect of excluding this real phenomenon from the analysis, effectively biasing the analysis against the competing claim that no-fault was the result rather than the cause of rising divorce rates. None the less, some correction for trends over time is appropriate. We made the correction in a different way. Our assumption was that non-legal factors affecting divorce rates trends, such as social or demographic changes, would be relatively homogenous within regions, so that for each state the average of the other states within its region could provide a basis for the correction that was not affected by the date at which that particular state changed its law. Our method may also have its drawbacks, and we do not claim certainty on the best approach to this problem. I do note, however, that Professor Lohr ran Friedberg's model, including her correction for state-specific effects, using our dates for the year in which each state adopted no-fault rather than Brinig's. She also extended the time series back to 1960 and forward to 1992. The resulting coefficient for no-fault was not significant.

rely on highly sophisticated mathematical models to perceive the import of the data. The basic point is well communicated by pictures showing a careful state-by-state comparison of the temporal relationship between legal changes and divorce rates, for these pictures show little evidence of any long-term effect of the legal change. Sharon Lohr and I have elsewhere provided a comprehensive examination of that kind,[41] which I will not repeat here. Let me instead reprint one figure from that study, showing divorce rates trends in three states of the southern mountain region of the US (Fig 15.1).

Figure 15.1 shows, for the three states for which we have data, that the divorce rate began climbing long before no-fault divorce was adopted. An increase in the divorce rate followed Arizona's adoption of no-fault, but only for a few years, after which the rate declined. A short-term rate increase is precisely what one would expect from a legal reform that made divorce simpler and quicker to obtain, but which had no fundamental impact on the likelihood of divorce: such a reform would speed up divorces already in the pipeline, leading to a transitory one-time increase, followed by a resumption of the basic trends. This pattern is common, and also appears to be what happened after Utah's more recent adoption of no-fault. In Colorado the adoption of no-fault had almost no perceptible impact, not even for the short term. The general pattern shown by these three states is typical—nationally, divorce rates have been stable or declining since 1981—and is very difficult to reconcile with any claim that no-fault caused any important increase in divorce rates.[42]

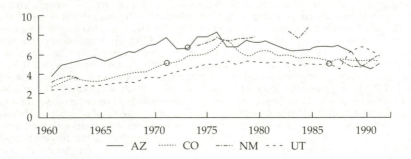

FIGURE 15.1. Divorce rates, in divorces per 1,000 population, for three states, 1960 to 1992 (plus partial data from New Mexico, for which other data is missing). For the three states with complete data, the circle marks the date of enactment of a law which added irremediable breakdown as grounds for divorce and adopted property and alimony rules that excluded consideration of fault.

---

[41] Ellman and Lohr, n 17 above.
[42] Regional influences on divorce rates are very great, as explained in more detail later in this chapter. Because there are also regional patterns in divorce laws, a careful examination

CULTURAL FORCES AND DIVORCE RATES

Law is the product as well as the cause of social change, and my inclination is to believe it more likely that the rising divorce rates of the late 1960s and the 1970s led to no-fault divorce, rather than the other way around. As larger and larger proportions of the population were divorced themselves, or had relatives or close friends who were, the problems with the old fault divorce law became more salient, and the support for reform grew. Changing cultural norms that reduced the stigma of divorce increased both divorce rates, and support for reforms that made divorce easier. Perhaps today cultural norms are changing again, but in the opposite direction, thus explaining both the recent decline in divorce rates and the recent interest in more restrictive divorce laws.

There seem to be many indicators of larger cultural change. Three separate surveys conclude that the proportion of teens who are sexually experienced declined in the 1990s, reversing the increases from earlier decades.[43] In addition, contraceptive use is up among teenagers, especially use of condoms.[44] Teenage birth rates declined from 90 births per thousand in the late 1950s to 50.2 in 1986. While they then climbed back up to a new peak of 62.1 in 1991, they have again declined, reaching 52.9 in 1997.[45] Births to unmarried mothers increased despite the declining birth rate among teenagers, because the age at first marriage has climbed. The most recent available data even shows a decline in the birth rate for unmarried women, from 1994 to 1995, and again from 1995 to 1996.[46] The birth rate for unmarried black women has actually been falling since 1989; the overall increase in the rate from 1989 to 1994 resulted from an increase in the lower unmarried birth rate among whites.[47] Of course crime rates in America have been falling dramatically.

---

of the impact on rates of a state's adoption of no-fault requires some kind of control for these regional effects. One approach is to look at a state's residual changes in divorce rates over time, after removing the average changes of the other states in its region, over the same time period. Examination of the data after such an adjustment confirms the point in the text. See Ellman and Lohr, *Dissolving the Relationship between Divorce Laws and Divorce Rates*, n 17 above.

[43] As cited in nn 14, 15, and 16 of Stephanie Ventura *et al*, *Declines in Teenage Birth Rates, 1991–97: National and State Patterns*, NATIONAL VITAL STATISTICS REPORTS, vol 47, No 12, National Center for Health Statistics, Dec 17 1998.   [44] See *ibid* at nn 14–17.

[45] See *ibid*.

[46] The rate declined from 82.1 births per 1,000 unmarried women in 1994 to 75.9 in 1995 and 74.4 in 1996. CENTER FOR DISEASE CONTROL, NATIONAL CENTER FOR HEALTH STATISTICS, MONTHLY VITAL STATISTICS REPORT, vol 46, No 11, Supplement, June 30 1998, at Table 18.

[47] The birth rate for unmarried black women peaked at 90.7 per 1,000 in 1989; by 1996 it had declined to 74.4 per 1,000. The rate for whites increased from 30.2 in 1989 to 38.3 in 1994, before declining in the next two years, to 37.6. *ibid*.

Rates derived from the National Crime Victimization Survey, conducted by the Justice Department, have now fallen to their lowest levels since the survey was begun in 1973, for both violent crimes and property crimes. The property crime rate is less than half the 1973 rate. Robbery rates fell 32 per cent just between 1991 and 1997, while homicide rates fell 31 per cent.[48] If these data indicate a culture generally on the mend, then the declining divorce rates since the early 1980s fit right into the picture.

None the less, I make this observation with caution. There is a sense in which 'cultural change' is an unpersuasive explanation for any phenomena. What, after all, do we mean by cultural change? If culture is simply a shorthand term for a particular constellation of average group behaviors or preferences, then an explanation of one of them as the product of culture is inherently circular. Nor does the casual observation of several apparently compatible trends show a real relationship. More interesting, perhaps, would be a tighter showing of a relationship between divorce rates and some other, particular, cultural attribute. Let me suggest two such cultural forces.

1. The Relationship of Mobility and Divorce

It has long been observed that divorce rates in the United States vary greatly by region. Divorce rates in the West have been higher than in every other region of the United States since national divorce statistics were first compiled in 1870. Divorce rates in the South, once the lowest in the country, became second highest in 1940 and have remained so since then (Table 15.1).

The regional patterns have misled many who have examined the relationship between the law and divorce rates, since the West was also the first region to adopt no-fault divorce and has in general remained its stronghold. The fact that the West has been the leader in divorce rates since regional statistics have been kept on the matter—in other words, since long before no-fault divorce was imagined—suggests that regional differences other than the law explain the West's higher divorce rates. That suggestion is strengthened by the post-1940 emergence of the South as a high divorce region, since the South has in general been the stronghold of fault divorce. What regional differences can one then examine to explain the differences in divorce rates? There are, of course, demographic differences in the regions, and so one might imagine, for example, that there is a relatively higher proportion of Catholics in the

---

[48] The national data is taken from *Decline of Violent Crimes is Linked to Crack Market*, NY TIMES, Dec 28 1998, at A16.

TABLE 15.1. *Divorces per 1,000 inhabitants, by Region**

Year	Northeast	Midwest	South	West
1870	0.3	0.4	0.2	0.6
1890	0.3	0.7	0.4	1.2
1900	0.4	1.0	0.7	1.4
1916	0.5	1.4	1.1	2.1
1930	0.7	1.9	1.6	2.8
1940	0.9	2.0	2.3	3.7
1950	1.1	2.4	3.2	4.2
1960	0.9	2.1	2.8	3.4
1967	1.1	2.6	3.1	4.1
1978	3.4	4.9	5.7	6.4
1979	3.6	5.0	5.9	6.4
1980	3.5	5.0	6.0	6.3
1981	3.6	4.9	6.1	6.3
1982	3.7	4.6	5.7	6.0
1983	3.6	4.6	5.6	5.8
1984	3.6	4.4	5.5	5.6
1985	3.8	4.5	5.6	5.8
1986	3.6	4.4	5.5	5.6
1987	3.6	4.4	5.4	5.5
1988	3.5	4.5	5.4	5.3

* Rates from 1870 through 1960 taken from Table 9 in *100 Years of Marriage and Divorce Statistics, United States, 1867–1967*, NATIONAL CENTER FOR HEALTH STATISTICS, VITAL AND HEALTH STATISTICS SERIES 21, NO 24, DEPT OF HEALTH, EDUCATION, AND WELFARE PUBLICATION NO (HRA) 74–1902 (1973). Rates from later years taken from the National Center for Health Statistics, *Vital Statistics of the United States, 1987*, Vol III, Marriage and Divorce, DHS Pub No (PHS) 91: 1103, and the equivalent reports issued annually in the preceding years and in 1988. Subsequent to 1988 the NCHS stopped reporting these statistics on a four–region basis. It stopped compiling them altogether in 1990. From that time forward only provisional divorce statistics for each year are available on a state-by-state basis. Divorce statistics are apparently difficult to compile and the NCHS chose to save the costs of improving their collection. See 60 Fed. Reg. 64437–64438 (1995), also available at <http://www.cdc.gov/nchswww/datah/datasite/frnotice.htm>.

Northeast, as compared with the South and West, which might explain its lower divorce rates.[49]

I wish to focus on a difference between the West and other regions that I previously suggested might explain its higher divorce rates: the rate of in-migration: one assumes the West has always had a higher proportion

[49] Although it appears that for Americans born after 1930, Catholic upbringing has no association with the likelihood of divorce, even though it did for Americans born before then. See Sander, *Catholicism and Marriage in the United States*, 30 DEMOGRAPHY 373 (1993). Interfaith marriages remain associated with a higher divorce rate, Lehrer and Chiswick, *Religion as a Determinant of Marital Stability*, 30 DEMOGRAPHY 385 (1993), and perhaps they are more common in the West than in the Northeast—although one would not expect them to be more common in the South than in the Northeast.

of residents who have recently moved to their current home, than do other parts of the country. One also has the sense that immigration into the South, once relatively low, has been much higher in recent decades. Both intuited patterns seem to coincide with divorce trends. One can imagine several possible reasons to expect such an association. Perhaps persons whose temperament makes them more willing to move across the country would also be more willing to leave a marriage. Or perhaps moving is itself associated with other factors, such as employment instability, that contribute to marital instability. A third possibility is that those who move are disproportionately in an age range—from the early twenties to the early thirties—during which persons are also more likely to divorce. I have no data that would tell us if any of these explanations is correct, nor can one assert that mobility is a *cause* of divorce (or vice versa). The data does suggest, however, that there is an association between mobility and divorce, because divorce rates tend to be higher in regions that in preceding years experienced higher net in-migration.

An earlier article by Sharon Lohr and I constructed for each state a ratio of the number of in-migrants into a state between 1970 and 1980, divided by the 1970 population of the state, as an indicator of the proportion of the state's population that (in 1980) consisted of recent in-migrants. The Spearman correlation coefficient between that ratio, and a state's divorce rate (using the average of the annual rates from 1980 through 1985) is .76—a very high correlation for a social science statistic.[50] I offer here some additional evidence that seems to confirm this earlier finding.

Our earlier calculation used data from the decennial census. Another source of mobility data are annual surveys conducted by the Census, but the sample from any one state in any one year is too small to be sufficiently reliable. I therefore looked at data by region. Mobility data by region for five-year periods is available for the periods 1965–70, 1970–5, and 1975–80. These data fortunately overlap with the period of greatest change in American divorce rates. One can calculate a fraction that consists of the number of in-migrants into each of the four regions during each of these five-year periods, divided by the regional population at the beginning of the five-year period.[51] This provides a relative measure, as between regions, of the proportion of the population, for each five-year period in each region, that consists of recent in-migrants as compared

---

[50] We originally reported this statistic in n 25 of Ellman and Lohr, *Dissolving the Relationship between Divorce Rates and Divorce Laws*, n 17 above. Note that for this calculation, as for most calculations reported in that article, we omitted Louisiana and Nevada—the first because its data was incomplete, the second because it is an outlier in divorce statistics, its rates being affected by a large number of divorces granted to *de facto* non-residents.

[51] By 'in-migrant' I mean anyone who moved into the region, most of whom move in from another region, rather than from another country.

with long-term residents. One can then calculate the Pearson correlation coefficient between this proportion for reach region, and that region's average divorce rate over the five following years.[52] The scatterplot is shown in Figure 15.2. One must be cautious about this method. When one examines data that itself consists of averages, artificially high correlations normally result.[53] And the number of data points for each calculation is small. At the same time, the resulting correlations are very high: .98 between the new resident ratio for each region during 1965–70, and the region's average divorce rate for 1971–5, and .94 and .98 for the analogous data calculated for the two subsequent five-year periods.[54] This analysis thus adds some weight to the earlier finding in Ellman and Lohr.[55]

Finally, there are two more bits of confirming data. The first is historical. At one time the federal government calculated the percentage of divorced couples who were married in the state that granted their divorce. If one

[52] For performing these calculations particularly, I wish to thank Lynn Tobin.

[53] This is known as the problem of 'ecological correlations'. See David Freedman, *et al*, Statistics 140–1 and A-7 (2nd edn, 1991).

[54] Five-year migration totals, by region, were obtained from Table A, Interregional Migration: 1965–1970, 1970–1975, and 1975–1980, at page 1 of Bureau of the Census, US Dep't Commerce, Current Population Reports, *Geographical Mobility: 1975 to 1980*, Series P-20, No 368 (1981). The population by region for the relevant years was also taken from Census Bureau reports. Using these figures, I calculated the ratio of in-migrants during each five-year period, over the population in the earliest year of that period, to be as follows:

In-migrants(for the 5-year period) / Population (first year of 5-year period)			
Years	NE	Midwest	South	West
1965–70	0.0268	0.0373	0.0527	0.0717
1970–5	0.0216	0.0306	0.0650	0.0674
1975–80	0.0225	0.0344	0.0604	0.0735

The average divorce rates for the relevant periods can be calculated from the data presented in Table 15.1 in the text, and are as follows:

Average Divorce Rate (per 1,000 population)			
Years	NE	Midwest	South	West
1971–5	2.64	4.04	4.88	6.02
1976–80	3.38	4.86	5.8	6.48
1981–5	3.66	4.6	5.7	5.98

[55] I compare in-migrant rates with subsequent rather than contemporaneous divorce rates because my intuition was not that movers concurrently divorce, but that willingness to migrate may identify persons in the population at a higher risk of divorce over time—because, eg, of their temperament, or employment instability, or level of discontent generally. It has also been observed that people are more likely to move after a divorce, although in most of those cases the divorce decree would be entered in the state from which they move, not the state to which they move, and therefore would not be captured by any of the calculations done here. Some people may move after the *de facto* termination of their marriage, but before any actual decree, and in those cases the decree may be granted by the state to which they move. But here as well, one would see a time lag between the move and the decree. Ideally, I would have investigated time lags of various lengths, and would have thus been able, for example, to compare the divorce rate's correlation to in-migrant rates five years earlier, with correlations to in-migrant rates one, two, three, and four years earlier. But that analysis cannot be done with the available data. *cont. on p. 358*

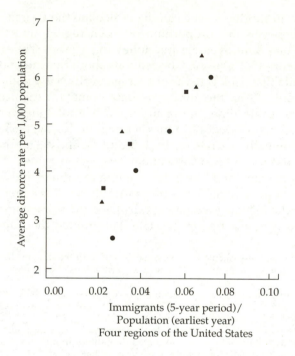

FIGURE 15.2. Immigrant proportions v divorce rates. 1965–70 v 1971–5 in circles (r = .98); 1970–5 v 1976–80 in triangles (r = .94); 1976–80 v 1981–5 in squares (r = .98).

looks at the regional breakdown for each of the five years between 1870 and 1916 for which this calculation was made, two things are clear: the percentage is lowest for the West (ranging from 48.4 to 55.2, and showing no particular trend over time), and highest for the South (ranging from 81.9 to 90.5, but trending consistently downward from 1880 to 1916). During this period, the South also had the lowest overall divorce rates (Table 15.1) and the West, as always, the highest. This statistic is available for only one later year, 1960, by which time the South had the highest divorce rate for any region except the West. And in 1960, the South's percentage of divorces granted to couples married in the state of the divorce had slid to 61.1—the lowest percentage outside the West (which of course continued also to have the highest divorce rates). No other region showed nearly as

A colleague did some calculations and pointed out to me that one does not get similar correlations between divorce rate and in-migrant rate if one examines changes over time, within regions, rather than comparing regions at different times, as I did. However, that alternative analysis is affected by the generally increasing divorce rate everywhere during these particular time periods, a powerful general trend that probably swamps the mobility factor. (I owe this point to Sharon Lohr.)

large a change in either statistic as did the South.[56] Although other explanations are not logically excluded, certainly one plausible explanation for this pattern is that divorce rates are higher among persons who have recently moved into the state, and so as these in-migrants increase in number, they both drive up the overall divorce rate, and drive down the percentage of divorces involving long-term residents.

The second piece of confirming evidence is obtained by relating another census bureau tabulation with divorce rates. The Census reports the percentage of residents of each state who were born in that state, and the states' rank order on this measure.[57] In 1990, 80 per cent of Pennsylvania residents were born in that state, ranking it first among the states on this percentage. Florida ranked last, with only 30.5 per cent of its residents born there. One can also rank the states by their 1990 divorce rate, from the lowest to the highest rate.[58] I did so, and then found the correlation coefficient between these two ranks. It is a positive .26, indicating a tendency for states with the lowest proportion of newcomers to have the lowest divorce rates.[59]

This analysis may also shed light on a transnational phenomena, the relatively high divorce rate for Americans as compared to Western Europeans. One's sense is that Americans are also far more mobile than are Europeans, and Americans are certainly far more recent descendants, on average, of persons willing to move than are Europeans. I leave it to others to test this hypothesis cross-nationally.

2. The Employment of Wives

A second cultural force which most observers believe played an important role in increasing divorce rates is the enormous increase in the participation of married women in the paid labor force. Reviewing the literature, Cherlin concludes that while the evidence that the increase in

---

[56] This data is taken from Table 17, at p 43, of *100 Years of Marriage and Divorce Statistics, United States, 1867–1967*, NATIONAL CENTER FOR HEALTH STATISTICS, VITAL AND HEALTH STATISTICS SERIES 21, NO 24, DEPT OF HEALTH, EDUCATION, AND WELFARE PUBLICATION NO (HRA) 74–1902 (1973). In fairness one must also observe that by 1960 the percentage of divorces issued to couples married in that state had converged, and the South's rate was only very slightly below that of the Midwest. But the shift in the two regions' relative percentages over this time period is still dramatic.

[57] The Census provides this data on the Web. The 1990 data I used here is at <http://www.census.gov/population/socdemo/migration/pob-rank.txt>.

[58] As previously noted, good data on divorce rates began disappearing in the 1990s. For this calculation, I relied upon the *Advance Report of Final Divorce Statistics, 1989 and 1990*, in vol 43, No 9 Supplement, Monthly Vital Statistics Report, Mar 22 1995, published by the National Center for Health Statistics. There is no final report, and this 'advance report' has only incomplete data for Indiana, Louisiana, and New Mexico. I therefore omitted these three states, as well as Nevada (as always) from the calculations I report here.

[59] I thank Sharon Lohr for suggesting this calculation to me.

women's participation in the labor force contributed to the 1960–80 rise in divorce rates is necessarily 'circumstantial, . . . it is stronger and more suggestive than that linking any other concurrent trend with the rise in divorce.'[60] Not mentioned by Cherlin, but supporting his conclusion, is the fact that most divorces today are sought by women.[61] Indeed, the increase in divorce rates between 1950 and 1980 occurred over a period of time during which the proportion of divorces instigated by wives appears to have increased from a minority of the cases to two-thirds of the cases.[62] It thus seems logical to suggest that anyone seeking to explain the increase in divorce rates during this period should look for changes in factors likely to affect the motivation of wives. Their increasing rates of employment is such a factor. Economists suggest simply that such employment, being associated with a decline in marriage role specialization, leads to a decline in the benefits derived by the spouses from their marriage. A more feminist-friendly take on the same phenomenon argues that rising female employment increases the proportion of women who feel financially able to escape a bad marriage. In one version or the other, the argument commands a wide consensus in the social science literature, although methodological difficulties have presented some challenge to those seeking empirical support for it.[63] One can perhaps argue that rising divorce rates encouraged women to seek market labor, or that

---

[60] ANDREW CHERLIN, MARRIAGE, DIVORCE, REMARRIAGE 53 (rev edn 1992).

[61] See Braver, *et al*, n 30 above, at 1.

[62] For the current two-thirds figure. See Braver *et al*, n 61 above. For the older data, see Paula Dewitt, *Breaking Up is Hard to Do*, AMERICAN DEMOGRAPHICS, Oct 1992, at 52.

[63] See Susan Cameron, *A Review of Economic Research into Determinants of Divorce*, 17 BRIT REV ECON ISSUES 1 (1995) for a general review of the literature. He concludes that there is wide consensus on the positive association of divorce with female wage rates and its negative association with male wage rates. A more recent attempt to overcome the methodological challenge, which also contains a more recent if less comprehensive review of the literature, is Steven Ruggles, *The Rise in Divorce and Separation in the United States, 1880–1990*, 34 DEMOGRAPHY 455 (1997). Ruggles looks at census data on marriage and divorce and on male and female employment, by local area, and attempts to prove the theory by showing an association between local areas with a higher percentage of employed women and higher divorce rates. He finds this association for each of the decades he examines between 1880 and 1990. He finds an even stronger relationship over this time period between local divorce rates and male employment, but with a negative sign, also consistent with prevailing theory. But male employment patterns cannot explain the persistent rise in divorce rates over the last 100 years because there has been no corresponding long-term decline in male employment—while of course there has been a corresponding long-term increase in female employment. Male unemployment might thus explain certain short-term changes in divorce rates over particular periods or in particular locales, but not the long-term general trend.

For criticisms of Ruggles, see Anne Preston, *Comment on Steven Ruggles's* The Rise of Divorce and Separation in the United States, 1880–1990, 34 DEMOGRAPHY 473 (1997); Oppenheimer, *Comment on Steven Ruggles's* The Rise of Divorce and Separation in the United States, 1880–1990, 34 DEMOGRAPHY 467 (1997). Preston focuses on the problem of separating the

other phenomena caused changes in both women's economic behavior and their choice to divorce.[64]

SOME CONCLUDING THOUGHTS

Recent interest in fault divorce seems part of a more general cultural trend favoring traditional values, a trend which probably also contributes to the downward movement in divorce rates. This trend is likely to keep the issue alive for some time. One might conclude, however, that the arguments for reviving fault law are simply too weak on merits to prevail in the end. The covenant marriage movement has adopted the politically clever tactic of portraying itself as merely giving prospective spouses a choice, and of relabeling the newly available choice with the appealing term 'covenant' rather than the more accurate term of fault divorce. Even so, it has had a difficult time making headway since its initial adoption in Louisiana. Arizona amended the Louisiana package to permit divorce by mutual consent, and even by unilateral consent with a two-year waiting period, but even this much weakened version passed by the narrowest of margins.[65] Covenant marriage proposals have been defeated in other states.[66]

If one believes that the increasing divorce rates of the 1960s and 1970s led to easier divorce laws, one might argue that today's declining divorce rates forecast a return to restrictive divorce laws. Today's decline is not nearly so steep as that earlier increase. The belief that marriage and divorce are matters for regulation by private commitment rather than legal compulsion also appears to remain strong. The two states adopting covenant marriage have found that their constituents

---

cultural and employment explanations, while Oppenheimer argues from the perspective of one of the few social scientists who does not believe the prevailing theory. Ruggles's response is at 34 DEMOGRAPHY 473 (1997); see also Ian Smith, *Explaining the Growth of Divorce in Great Britain*, 44 SCOTTISH J POL ECON 519 (1997). He compares trends in Scotland with those in England, given that divorce law changed at different times, and concludes the law had little impact on the divorce rate, while the rising real earnings of women did—but not women's rising *relative* earnings (to men).

[64] This point is noted in Preston, n 63 above.

[65] Under the Arizona law, a spouse may petition for divorce with the claim that he or she expects that the parties will live apart for the required two years. The actual divorce decree is then deferred until the two-year period has run, but the court may in the interim issue temporary orders of support. See ARIZ REV STAT § 25–903. These concessions from the language of the original Louisiana statute were required for passage, and even then the law passed by only one vote.

[66] One recent rejection occurred in Colorado. See ARIZONA CAPITOL TIMES, Mar 5 1999 at 13. The defeated Colorado measure was HB 1194.

have little interest in it.[67] If that experience continues, it will be difficult to maintain interest in the proposal, much less in any full-throated return to fault divorce.

[67] The Maricopa County (Phoenix) clerk issued 6,224 marriage licenses between Aug 1 1998 and Jan 31 1999. The new covenant marriage license law took effect on Aug 21 1998, and from that day through Jan 31 1999, thirty-one covenant marriage licenses were issued. These figures actually overstate the proportion of all Maricopa County marriage licenses that are covenant marriages, because justice courts and city clerks in Maricopa County also issue marriage licenses, but not covenant marriage licenses. E-mail from Maureen Ramroth, Maricopa County Clerk's Office, Feb 22 1999. Professor Steven Nock of the University of Virginia found that in the year following adoption of Louisiana's covenant marriage law, only 1.6% of all new marriages in that state were covenant marriages. The percentage remained essentially unchanged during the first six months of the succeeding year. I thank Brian Bix for sharing with me the e-mail he received from Steven Nock containing this data.

16
Divorce in England 1950–2000: A Moral Tale?

CAROL SMART

INTRODUCTION

The fifty years analytically reviewed in this paper constitute a period of considerable change to the law and practice of divorce in England and Wales. Rates of divorce have increased considerably between 1950 and 2000, although the upward trend had started before 1950. Marriage rates also reached a peak in the 1960s but subsequently declined in the 1990s. Statistics also show that across this half-century there have been rises in the numbers of lone-parent families, in step-families, in second divorces, in teenage pregnancies, and in cohabitation. Indeed, it has become almost impossible to talk about family life in late modern societies without reference to a vast array of tables and charts which show trends and changes,[1] all of which apparently attest to the ubiquitous notion that family life is in crisis and that things used to be much better fifty years ago.

> [T]he late twentieth century family appears to be more than creaking. It is falling off its hinges! Increasingly, those activities that the family traditionally co-ordinated take place outside it, and even when it survives as a legal or formal entity, the family appears incapable of providing acceptable levels of care and support. . . . In none of the nation's soap operas is there a single well-established, functioning nuclear family.[2]

It is of course impossible to counter these arguments by reference to statistics collected in the half-century prior to 1950 because they were either too limited in scope, or were of such a dubious nature that they would be quite unreliable as a basis for comparison. In any case, in the field of divorce, comparisons between the pre-war and post-war situation are hardly helpful because before the advent of legal aid in 1949 few could afford to divorce legally even if they could meet the stringent conditions of fault-based divorce at that time.

But arguments about the decline of the family, particularly as a consequence of divorce, are not—and have never been—generated *simply* as a

I am grateful to the ESRC for funding the research on which this paper is based under the Care, Values and Future of Welfare Programme, and to Dr Jennifer Flowerdew for her help in researching some of the background material for this chapter.

[1] D. Morgan, *Family Connections*. Cambridge: Polity Press (1996).

[2] J. Humphries, 'Special Issue on the Family: Introduction', (1999) 23 *Cambridge Journal of Economics*, 515, 516.

result of these statistical trends. Rather the statistics that are collected and analysed have been, and continue to be, generated within a pre-existing politico-moral framework of despair and depression about the declining quality of modern family life. These contemporary statistics provide a modern 'scientific' gloss to what is already a longstanding national obsession with the declining quality of family life in England and Wales. It was asserted, long before there were statistics which might lend credence to it, that family life was on a slippery slope towards indifference, selfishness, lack of discipline, abrogation of duty, immorality, sexual laxity and so on. Indeed, it was on this very note that the history of divorce and family policy in the last half of the twentieth century can be said to have begun.

The large number of marriages which each year are ending in the divorce court is a matter of grave concern.[3] . . . This disturbing situation is attributable to a variety of factors . . . In the first place, marriages today are at risk to a greater extent than formerly. The complexity of modern life multiplies the potential causes of disagreement and the possibilities of friction between husband and wife. . . . It must also be recognised that greater demands are now made of marriage, consequent on the spread of education, higher standards of living and the social and economic emancipation of women. . . . Old restraints, such as social penalties on sexual relations outside marriage, have been weakened . . . [and there is] a tendency to regard the assertion of one's own individuality as a right, and to pursue one's personal satisfaction, reckless of the consequences to others. . . . There is a tendency to take the duties and responsibilities of marriage less seriously than formerly.[4]

This perspective on the declining quality of family life, which has been reiterated throughout the second half of the century has, as a consequence, come to exercise a firm grip on the national imagination. In the 1980s and 1990s this preoccupation became condensed into one indicative and highly symbolic word: *stability*.[5] Above all else it became important in debates and official utterances on marriage and parenthood for the family to be stable, for policies to increase the stability of the family, and for this stability to ensure the wider stability of society. Throughout the second half of the twentieth century politicians and pundits have never

---

[3] Between 1951 and 1955 the average annual number of divorces was 29,500. These numbers had declined from the peak of 40,000 immediately following the war from 1946 to 1950, but were considerably higher than the pre-war figures which were 5,097 between 1931 and 1940. In 1997 there were 147,000 divorces. This is a decline from the peak of 176,000 in 1993. See C. Gibson, *Dissolving Wedlock*, London: Routledge (1994) 133; Office of National Statistics Social Trends 29 (1999) 49.

[4] Royal Commission on Marriage and Divorce (Morton Report), Cmnd 9678 (1956) 7–8.

[5] See for the refrain on stability in M. Phillips, *The Sex-Change Society*. London: The Social Market Foundation (1999).

tired of stating that the family is the cornerstone of society and that, without stable families, there cannot be prosperous and stable societies.

We cannot say we want a strong and secure society when we ignore its very foundation: family life. This is not about preaching to individuals about their private lives. It is addressing a huge social problem. . . . [T]his is a modern crisis. Nearly 100,000 teenage pregnancies every year, elderly parents with whom families cannot cope; children growing up without role models they can respect and learn from, more and deeper poverty; more crime, more truancy . . .[6]

The core element of this desired stability is the monogamous, married couple. Although the Labour Government at the end of the twentieth century did not condemn alternative forms of family life, it—like the Conservative governments before it—plainly stated that marriage is the best foundation for stable families.[7] Within this conceptual framework, it would seem to follow that divorce is not only destabilizing to families but also to society. Divorce is the core of the 'modern crisis' identified by Tony Blair in the late 1990s, just as it had been for the post-war society unfolding before the Royal Commission in the early 1950s. Divorce (and sometimes teenage pregnancy) had become the unit of measurement of failure in modern society by the 1960s.

The problem for governments and policy makers is that, in stressing the centrality of divorce through the emphasis on stability, there inevitably arises a desire to reduce the divorce rate and to stabilize the unstable. Yet, in the UK, family life is regarded as both private and personal, and the idea of too much government intervention *directly* into routine family practices is widely resisted (regardless of whether such interventions might 'work' or not). Family structures, unlike other social institutions such as schools, hospitals, and factories, constitute both a (local) cultural space and a set of relationships which are still largely beyond effective *direct* government regulation. Thus families, especially the idea of unstable families as measured by divorce statistics, are a perpetual problem for government. The statistics routinely give rise to the idea that there is a problem and that this problem, like other measurable social problems, should be amenable to 'cure' once it has been measured. As Rose has argued, 'To problematize drunkenness, idleness or insanity requires it to be counted. Reciprocally, what is counted . . . is what is problematized. To count a problem is to define it and make it amenable to government. To govern a problem requires that it be counted.'[8] Divorce statistics were collected throughout the twentieth

---

[6] Prime Minister's speech, *Guardian* 1 Oct 1997, 8.
[7] Home Office, *Supporting Families: A Consultation Document*. London: The Stationery Office (1998) 4.
[8] N. Rose, *Powers of Freedom*. Cambridge: Cambridge University Press (1999) 221.

century and, because the success of good liberal democracies was increasingly measured in terms of their ability to cure problems calibrated through precisely such statistical techniques, the imperative to find a solution to the problems they had become so adept at defining grew.

I shall return to this issue of how government may now be redefining the cure for family instability, but first I shall explore the recent history of how democratic government has sought to regulate the apparently increasingly unruly family in the last fifty years of the century.

THE ROYAL COMMISSION ON MARRIAGE
AND DIVORCE 1951–1955

I have argued, following Rose, that the inexorable rise of statistical measurement during the twentieth century (although starting in the nineteenth century) created a new aspect to government based on liberal democratic principles. The ability to collect statistics on marriage following Lord Hardwicke's Marriage Act of 1753, followed by the creation of secular divorce in 1857,[9] laid the foundation for the collection of statistics based on clearly established legal statuses. Of course, informal unions and informal separations could not be counted, although illegitimate births could be. All children born to married women were, however, presumed to be legitimate, regardless of their actual paternity, and so even these apparently straightforward statistics concealed certain social practices. The Royal Commission therefore had available to it statistics on marriage and divorce covering almost a century. What was most alarming to the Commission was the sudden escalation in the rate of divorce immediately after World War II.

The Royal Commission (Chaired by Lord Morton of Henryton) had been set up in 1951 as a response to pressure both within and outside Parliament for a change to the laws on divorce which, following the implementation of the Matrimonial Causes Act of 1937, permitted divorce only on the grounds of matrimonial fault evidenced by adultery, cruelty, and desertion for three or more years. The disruptions and social change generated by World War II, combined with changing attitudes towards the nature of marriage in which it was seen increasingly as a companionate union rather than a binding legal duty, led to the demand that marriages should be terminated if relationships 'broke down' rather than as the consequence of a matrimonial offence.[10] Eirene White MP was the champion of the cause of a new kind of divorce which would better reflect the

<hr>

[9] Gibson, n 3 above.   [10] C. Smart, *The Ties That Bind*. London: Routledge (1984).

modern notion of marriage as being a relationship based on love and affection.[11] She advocated that couples be allowed to divorce after having lived apart for seven years and where there was no chance of a reconciliation.

The task of the Royal Commission was to inquire into whether the law should be changed in such a radical way. It had a very wide remit which included not only the issue of the grounds for divorce, but also preparation for marriage, marriage saving, matrimonial proceedings, and matrimonial property and finances. In the end the Commission was hopelessly divided on what should be done, except that all the Commissioners bar one, insisted on retaining fault as the basis of divorce. This consensus was an important indicator of how marriage was perceived and also how a liberal democratic government—which accepted the recommendations for no change—sought to enforce family stability. Embracing fault meant that the Commission and the Government adhered to the definition of marriage as a contract between spouses and the state, rather than simply between spouses. Marriage was therefore an institution, not a relationship. In this context adultery, for example, was an offence against the institution, and harmed the moral and social fabric of society. The response of the state was to 'punish' the wrongdoer and reward the innocent spouse. The Commission's recommendations for no change, and the Government's acceptance of these recommendations, revealed the extent to which the quality of individual marriages was immaterial. Indeed, the Commission made it clear that its concern was with the greater good and that the unhappiness of individuals could not weigh against the benefits that accrued to society of maintaining the state's firm grip on the rate and level of divorce. The Commission actually considered the merits of abolishing divorce altogether and although it did not recommend this, the Commissioners felt that it should be a matter for serious consideration if the divorce rate continued to climb. With the exception of the continuous emphasis on stability, the frame of reference of the Royal Commission in the 1950s could not be more different from the way in which marriage (and divorce) was conceptualized at the end of the 1990s; I propose to analyse the process of transition between the two. But first we need to give further consideration to the social context within which the Commission produced its report.

The Commission relied on high principles and orthodox moral guidelines to formulate its recommendations. It has been much criticized for

---

[11] C. Smart, 'Wishful Thinking and Harmful Tinkering? Sociological Reflection on Family Policy', (1997) 26 *Jnl of Social Policy* 1.

failing to resort to scientific or empirical findings and McGregor,[12] who
mounted a polemical attack on the Commission, saw this as a choice in
favour of ignorance and prejudice, over rationality and objective facts.
From the perspective of the late 1990s McGregor's optimism about the
value and possibility of achieving objective facts to guide policy seems
naïve, but by his own admission his attack on the Commission was a
polemic rather than a sociological analysis. The debate about whether the
Commissioners were prejudiced or ignorant about the lives of ordinary
people is important, but need not be rehearsed again here. Rather I want
to give consideration to the form of governance they were seeking to
sustain and how this needs to be understood in the context of the 1950s.

The Royal Commission expressed—albeit implicitly—a strong sense of
homogeneous nationhood within which only one form of family life
could be seen as morally appropriate. Such an expression of nationhood
could only really be possible in the triumphant post-war moment when,
in addition, Britain still had an empire, or at least colonies. This idea of
the (white) British Nation was, of course, expressed in the Beveridge
Report[13] and was part of the post-war reconstruction of family, nation,
and the British race. It was strongly supported by the Church of England,
which offered a very clear set of prescriptions about the moral boundaries of proper family life. For such an approach, empirical studies on
how ordinary families operated or on ordinary people's attitudes to
public morality were an irrelevance. The approach of the Commission
was not intended to be populist or representative, nor did it mean to
follow current trends. Its aim was to set standards and to reiterate the
moral rules outlined in the law of divorce. The Royal Commission presumed (rightly or wrongly) that it was addressing a homogeneous society, albeit one which appeared to have started down a slippery slope of
moral decline in family matters. The signs were identified in respect of
the growing demand for personal fulfilment in relationships, rather than
satisfaction with the virtuous reward of doing one's duty. This development, which contemporary sociologists now refer to as individualization,[14] was seen in terms of a weakening moral fibre. Although the
Commission did not use contemporary terminology, it is clear that the
members saw signs of a potential shift away from the status of marriage
as an institution, towards marriage as a relationship which could—as a
consequence—be terminated at will rather than after full judicial inquiry
and with the permission of the state. They saw this, however, with a sense

---

[12] O. R. McGregor, *Divorce in England: A Centenary Study*. London: Heinemann (1957).
[13] *Report on Social Insurance and Allied Services*, Cmnd 6404. London: HMSO (1942).
[14] U. Beck and E. Beck Gernsheim, *The Normal Chaos of Love*, Cambridge: Polity Press
(1995); A. Giddens, *The Transformation of Intimacy*, Cambridge: Polity Press (1992).

of dread and foreboding. Not only did this future seem morally unattractive, it seemed likely to undermine the post-war reconstruction of British society. Divorce seemed to be a carry-over of wartime (im)morality and what the Commission wished to regenerate was pre-war decorum and duty: 'We are convinced that the real remedy for the present situation lies in other directions [ie not easier divorce]: in fostering in the individual the will to do his duty by the community; in strengthening his resolution to make marriage a union for life; in inculcating a proper sense of his responsibility towards his children.'[15]

The regulation of marriage was clearly seen as a moral issue and what was required was a form of moral rearmament in which individuals would become bound securely again to the (supposed) values of the pre-war era. This morality was, however, that espoused by the Church of England at that time. It was not a reflexive or negotiated form of morality which could tolerate ambiguity. Rather it was based on a clear set of doctrinal statements derived from the New Testament in which there was little room for doubt and where teachings could be unambiguous,[16] and was fearful of the consequences of freeing people from the old constraints of Christian marriage. At that time the Commission could not envisage alternative forms of regulation of family life, and the pre-war methods of imposing restraint through legislative and religious measures which simply banned and punished incorrect behaviour were still attractive and potentially feasible.

Bauman[17] has discussed the demise of this sort of moral absolutism at length and his analysis is peculiarly fitted to this moment in the 1950s when legislators reached for traditional methods of regulation, unaware that society was becoming increasingly post-traditional. He has argued that there is a tradition in philosophical thinking, especially that arising from Christianity, which equates obedience with 'being good' and free will and choice with 'being morally corrupt'. The Commissioners were not alone therefore in seeing the rise of the 'individual' who asserted his/her free will and desire to choose as symbolizing moral decline. Bauman argues,

This is why modern legislators and modern thinkers alike felt that morality, rather than being a 'natural trait' of human life, is something that needs to be designed and injected into human conduct; and this is why they tried to compose and impose an all-comprehensive, unitary ethics—that is, a cohesive code of moral rules which people could be taught and forced to obey.[18]

---

[15] *Report of the Royal Commission on Marriage and Divorce* (Morton Report), Cmnd 9678 (1956) 14.   [16] Gibson, n 3 above, 102.
[17] Z. Bauman, *Postmodern Ethics*. Oxford: Blackwell (1995).   [18] Bauman, n 17 above, 6.

Bauman acknowledges that by the middle of the twentieth century this cohesive code of moral rules might no longer take the form of unmodified religious dogma but whilst, I suggest, it remained informed by this tradition, it did seem increasingly to take the form of rational teaching based on reason. This is indeed what the Commission recommended:

We consider that the removal of this major source of marital unrest [the tendency to take the duties and responsibilities of marriage less seriously] can be achieved only by the development of a *carefully graded system of education* for young people as they grow up, in order *to fit* them for marriage and family living, and by the provision of specific instruction for those about to enter marriage.[19]

Of course, what the Commission could not see, although McGregor was perhaps unwittingly quite sensitive to it, was that this form of regulation which was a combination of traditional modes of banning behaviour, combined with more modern methods of instruction to ensure obedience, would not simply be unattractive in post-war Britain, but actually irrelevant. What McGregor could identify was the extent to which people's lives were changing in relation to structural changes, not simply as a result of moral laxity. And, although the Commissioners could also identify some of these changes, they still thought it possible to hold fast to a form of marriage which had been consolidated in the nineteenth century. Again, as Bauman so aptly puts it:

It is because modern developments forced men and women into the condition of individuals, who found their lives fragmented, split into many loosely related aims and functions, each to be pursued in a different context and according to a different pragmatics—that an 'all-encompassing' idea promoting a unitary vision of the world was unlikely to serve their tasks well and thus capture their imagination.[20]

As has been well documented elsewhere,[21] the recommendations of the Royal Commission captured no one's imagination. Rather change was stalled and for a further decade and a half, married couples sought to evade the strictures of the divorce law, giving rise to a situation in which the law was seen as thoroughly hypocritical and the stance of the Church was seen as harsh and unyielding. Increasingly the position of the state was itself seen as immoral, as an inversion of 'traditional' values occurred, and those who sought to force people to stay together in miserable marriages (empty shells as they were called) were seen as the ones without compassion and understanding.[22]

---

[19] Morton Report, n 15 above, 93, emphasis added.   [20] Bauman, n 17 above, 6.

[21] Gibson, n 3 above; Smart, n 10 above.

[22] C. Smart, 'Good Wives and Moral Lives: Family and Divorce 1937–51' in C. Gledhill and G. Swanson (eds), *Nationalising Femininity*. Manchester: MUP (1996), 91–105.

SHIFTING FORMS OF GOVERNANCE: THE 1969 DIVORCE REFORM ACT

If the Government had hoped that the recommendations of the Royal Commission would end the social pressure for reform, they were mistaken. In the 1960s there was a growing sense of the injustice of the system. The Church of England began to change. In Bauman's terms it began to move away from the idea that freedom of choice was an invitation to licentiousness, towards the idea that each individual could be trusted to make the right moral decisions without slavishly following rules, but by applying principles in different ways in different circumstances. There was an important shift away from a focus simply on status towards a recognition of the individual occupying the status. In this context it became the quality of a relationship that became the yardstick of its moral worth, not simply the marital status of the parties. A core element in this shift is now recognized to be the scandalous (at the time) book *Honest to God* (1963), written by the Bishop of Woolwich, John Robinson. What Robinson argued was that to tie Christianity to a set of moral dogmas lodged within a pre-scientific age would simply discredit the faith. He called for a 'new morality' which would be more relativistic and which would be guided by 'love'. Robinson promoted a new moral code in which the only intrinsic evil was a lack of love. He argued that love provided an internal moral compass that prevented people from harming others and doing evil. Thus, he suggested that people would still not commit adultery or engage in extramarital sex, but that they would refrain out of a personal sense of obligation based on love, not because they were blindly obedient to a set of rules imposed on them from outside.[23]

Although *Honest to God* caused a huge controversy in the early 1960s, by 1966 the Established Church had withdrawn its support for matrimonial fault as the sole basis for secular divorce and had embraced the idea of irretrievable breakdown.[24] This was a hugely significant shift. It signified that the Church acknowledged that the process of individualization was not necessarily or automatically synonymous with moral decline and that moral relativism was acceptable in a context where the internal quality of relationships—rather than the external structure—was the key to assessing their moral worthiness. The Anglican Church ceased to be an obstacle to divorce reform from this moment and therefore left the state to its own devices to contemplate how to regulate familial relationships. Although the idea of the quality of relationships had began

---

[23] J. A. T. Robinson, *Honest to God*. London: SCM Press (1963).
[24] Archbishop of Canterbury's Group, *Putting Asunder: A Divorce Law for Contemporary Society*. London: SPCK (1966).

to take centre stage in debates about marriage and divorce, none the less, the state was left with what had become defined as the problem of (in)stability. From the perspective of governments at this time, individual cases of divorce might have become more morally acceptable, but divorce *rates* still presented political and practical problems. In particular rising rates gave rise to increasingly visible problems of financial support (especially for women), housing and accommodation problems, and potentially disturbed and delinquent children.

In 1969 the Divorce Reform Act was passed.[25] This Act allowed for divorce on the sole ground of 'irretrievable breakdown' although breakdown was still evidenced by the old matrimonial faults of adultery, desertion, and cruelty (renamed the behaviour ground). In addition divorce was permitted by mutual consent if the parties had lived apart for two or more years, or unilaterally after five years' separation. Arguably, this legislation marked a shift away from the traditional method of controlling family life through restriction and limitation on movement and change, towards regulating it by providing directions for this movement and change. The direction in which individuals were invited to go was away from an unsatisfactory marriage towards a second more satisfactory one. Quite simply, the solution to the divorce problem was seen as (re)marriage. Rose[26] argues that the essence of governance (as opposed to domination) is that the former works with social forces and 'instrumentalize[s] them in order to shape actions, processes and outcomes in desired directions. . . . To govern humans is not to crush their capacity to act, but to acknowledge it and to utilize it for one's own objectives.'

To a large extent this is what the 1969 Divorce Reform Act achieved— although it is not obvious that the Government had a clear set of objectives in mind at the time. Rather, with the benefits of hindsight, we can see that what occurred was the passage of 'permissive' legislation which allowed many more people to divorce with less stigma and pain, but which did so on the clear assumption that people divorced as a step towards remarriage. At that time divorce was—in symbolic terms—the tune according to which the deckchairs on the *Titanic* could be reassembled, it was not seen as the iceberg that might sink the whole thing. In the debates in the House of Commons, MPs spoke of divorce as the process by which individuals could leave miserable relationships in order to start new, legitimate, fulfilling ones. Moreover, although there was concern over the effects of divorce on children at this time, this concern was also

---

[25] Although the Bill was drafted by government lawyers, and the Government allowed time for its passage, the Government remained neutral and the Bill was presented by a private member: see the full account by Stephen Cretney, *Law, Law Reform and the Family*. Oxford: Oxford University Press (1998), ch 2.   [26] n 8 above, 4.

submerged by the faith in the stabilizing power of the reconstituted family. It should of course be remembered that marriage was at this time remarkably popular. As the sociologist Ronald Fletcher (1966) argued, 'The institution of marriage remains firm and stable for the great majority of people, and, what ever the condition of modern marriage may be, more and more people appear to desire it.'[27] This view was echoed in an article in *New Society* in 1968 when Kenneth Johnson wrote: 'Marriage as an institution is not in danger. Unsuccessful marriages could be replaced by successful ones.'[28] The desire for more permissive divorce laws in the 1960s therefore occurred in the context of very high rates of marriage. This is of course very different to the 1990s, when high rates of divorce co-existed with declining rates of marriage, and with increases in cohabitation and in single-occupancy households. But this meant that, in the 1960s at least, divorce was discursively constructed in the popular media, and in much political rhetoric, as a kind of rite of passage towards a more satisfactory state of family affairs.

The only fly in the ointment at that time (besides the traditionalists who held fast to the more orthodox ecclesiastical position) was perceived to be the problem of older women. The solution of remarriage was less obviously going to be a solution for wives of 40 or 50 or more years who were raising teenage children. The plight of these women became the cause of women MPs and Peers who identified the new legislation as highly gendered in its likely effects: benefiting men who could remarry much younger women, rather than older wives who could lose their homes, income, and pensions. Sympathy for these older women did produce some protections for them—albeit more in theory than in practice. But what sympathy there was, quickly evaporated a decade later when they were redefined as alimony drones and as women who were too idle to work. The more powerful argument became the one in favour of the 'clean break', which would allow the divorced to move unfettered from the failed relationship into another. It was generally held that the new relationship (which was by definition the more important in the drive to achieve renewed stability) stood a better chance of survival if the old one was properly buried. The clean break principle was profoundly rooted in the belief that the new marriage was a solution not only to the problems of the first marriage, but to the problems that might otherwise be associated with divorce. Not only did remarriage obviate the need for anyone (husbands and state alike) to pay support to ex-wives, it provided children with fathers at a time when it seems it was

---

[27] R. Fletcher, *The Family and Marriage in Britain*. Harmondsworth: Penguin (1966) 143.
[28] K. Johnson, 'Divorce: The Financial Facts', *New Society*, 14 Mar 1968, 379.

thought that any father would do in the process of providing much needed stability.

Of course, in this modern desire to remarry the adults, the children were trapped in a kind of Victorian time-warp in which they were constituted still as mere property. The emphasis was on the parents' happiness, because it was felt that this provided what children needed, ie stability. But the moral shift that had occurred which allowed the quality of adult relationships to become the guiding principle, was not at that time applied similarly to children. The quality of their relationships was of no real concern; they were not constituted as part of the moral cast of players and so they got what others thought was best for them. In this process we can see the partial democratization of the family.[29] Although men and women were clearly not equal partners in marriage in the 1970s (at least economically speaking), more readily available divorce began to turn marriage into a process of negotiation. If one partner failed to co-operate or persisted with unreasonable behaviour, then divorce was increasingly 'thinkable'. Intimate relationships between men and women could be run on very different grounds which were increasingly akin to democratic relationships.[30] 'There is only one story to tell about the family today, and that is of democracy. The family is becoming democratized, in ways which track processes of public democracy; and such democratization suggests how family life might combine individual choice and social solidarity.'[31] 'But divorce only created a partial democracy, because children were excluded from this process. They had no rights of participation at all[32] and their 'right' to participate or at least to be consulted was still a matter of debate in the late 1990s.[33]

The idea of the clean break was also modelled on an adult's perspective on future happiness rather than a child's. It gave supremacy to the conjugal pair-bond over the triadic parental relationship because it was assumed that children's welfare would be attended to once their parents were decently separated and happily remarried. Of course, what began to emerge was the realization that remarriage and step-parenting were not quite as easy as first-time marriage and parenting.[34] In addition, the state began to realize that for many women with children, remarriage was unlikely, unattractive, or even financially irresponsible. The practice

[29] Giddens, n 14 above.

[30] Giddens, n 14 above; Beck and Beck Gernsheim n 14 above; L. Jamieson, *Intimacy*. Cambridge: Polity Press (1998).

[31] A. Giddens, *The Third Way: The Renewal of Social Democracy*. Cambridge: Polity Press (1998) 93.   [32] J. Holt, *Escape from Childhood*. Harmondsworth: Penguin (1975).

[33] C. Smart, B. Neale, and E. Wade, 'Objects of Concern?: Children and Divorce', (1999) 11 *Child and Family Law Quarterly* 1.

[34] J. Burgoyne and D. Clark, *Making a Go of It*. London: Routledge & Kegan Paul (1984).

of allowing social security to support first wives,[35] which had evolved during the 1970s as a way of facilitating (virtual) clean breaks, began to become very costly because divorced women did not always remarry or, if they did, it became apparent that remarriages were actually less likely to last than first marriages.

By the 1980s there appeared to be yet another crisis surrounding family policy and divorce. The optimism of the 1970s had evaporated. The control of family life through a punitive divorce mechanism had been largely abandoned, but there was no preparation (nor could there be) for what was to follow these reforms. The optimistic scenario in which families happily reconstituted themselves did not materialize. Rather, new patterns emerged and meshed with other cultural and social transformations. Not only did the machinery of statistical production continue its relentless task of (apparently) measuring all aspects of family breakdown, but cultural shifts occurred in which the meanings of motherhood and fatherhood began to change, working practices and patterns of employment were modified, transitions from childhood to adulthood altered, gender relations began to take on new meanings, and parenthood started to become more significant than marital status in matters of policy, employment, and the benefit system.

GOVERNMENT VERSUS GOVERNANCE: THE STRUGGLE OVER THE FAMILY LAW ACT 1996

As I have argued, in the early 1960s there was a conflict between the traditional moralists as exemplified by the Church of England and the 'new' moralists, as exemplified by radicals such as the Bishop of Woolwich. The former stressed the importance of status and duty, the latter stressed the importance of the inherent qualities of relationships and 'love'. The former emphasized the acceptance of the weight of history, the latter had faith in the individual as an independent moral agent who could be free of tradition. Throughout the 1950s and most of the 1960s it was the traditional moralist position that prevailed as far as divorce law was concerned. I have suggested that this conflict dissipated in the late 1960s as the Government and, in particular, the Church of England, moved towards a position of governance rather than government. By this I mean that the English Establishment ceased to think it should control and punish and began to favour guidance, encouragement, and education. In Britain in the 1990s this old conflict surprisingly resurfaced, albeit with different advocates.

---

[35] M. Maclean, 'The Making of the Child Support Act of 1991: Policy Making at the Intersection of Law and Social Policy', (1994) 21 *Jnl of Law and Society* 505.

Those adopting the position equivalent to the established Church in the 1950s were the pro-family right and rhetoricians such as Patricia Morgan[36] (1995) and Melanie Phillips.[37] These writers looked to a more authoritarian approach to family life and decried what they saw as the permissiveness and laxity of moral values of contemporary families. Those positioned as the moral liberals were, in the 1990s, the Bishops of the Church of England.

It was the Conservative Government's proposals for reform to the divorce law embodied in *Looking to the Future: Mediation and the Ground for Divorce*[38] and the subsequent Family Law Bill that provided the catalyst for this renewed intense conflict. As with the debates some decades earlier, the main point of contention in the 1990s was over the best method(s) for the state to deploy in order to facilitate/ensure supportive, stable, and responsible family relationships. One group, led by Baroness Young in the House of Lords, stressed the importance of marriage as the basis of proper family life as well as the need to patrol the boundaries of married life through the imposition of external rules of conduct and state-sanctioned forms of punishment. This group wanted to retain, and indeed enhance, the significance of matrimonial fault in divorce proceedings. The opposing group, led mainly by the Bishops in the House of Lords but also by the Lord Chancellor who introduced the Bill, emphasized that family life was a process of negotiated morality in which blunt notions of matrimonial fault imposed from without by the legal system had no place.

The Family Law Bill proposed to abolish all remnants of matrimonial fault from the divorce process in England and Wales. But this proposal was also intended to be part of a new package in which divorce would be (almost) automatically granted after a nine-month period of reflection (15 if there are children) and compulsory attendance by the iniator at an information meeting (as opposed to hostile fault-finding and emotional blame) and mediation would be encouraged in which reasonable plans for the future could be discussed and put in place (rather than a battle which would leave combatants and their children scarred and unprepared for a new life that would still require co-operation). The core elements of the Bill, namely the information meetings, the period of reflection, and the preference for mediation over litigation, all constituted a prime example of the practice of governance as opposed to government. The theme of the legislation was based on the idea that people need knowledge about

---

[36] P. Morgan, *Farewell to the Family?* London: Institute of Economic Affairs (1995).

[37] M. Phillips, *The Sex-Change Society*. London: The Social Market Foundation (1999).

[38] Lord Chancellor's Department, *Looking to the Future: Mediation and the Ground for Divorce. The Government's Proposals*. London: HMSO, Cm 2799 (1995). See further Maclean at 541 of this volume.

divorce and the financial problems it brings, the difficulties it creates for children, and the need to plan such things as resuming work and pension provision. The period of reflection was proposed as a form of 'time out' in which emotions could settle down in order to allow the divorcing couple to become more rational and more competent citizens, equipped either to manage the transition to divorce, or to change their minds and stay married. Mediation was intended as a way of helping to plan and to resolve any outstanding differences and problems mutually. The modern citizen envisaged by the Family Law Bill was the fact-gathering, rational, caring parent who would make decisions on the basis of knowledge. This citizen could be compared (unfavourably) with the divorced spouse of the former fault-based system who was encouraged to look backwards and cherish resentments and blame, who seized upon children as weapons in the battle, and who—in their emotional haze—failed to make proper financial provision either for themselves or for their former partners and children. The aim of governance would be to produce the former citizen. The aim of government in the latter scenario would be to adjudicate on who should be rewarded and who punished, while admonishing the most guilty for their failure.[39]

The conflict which enveloped the passage of the Family Law Bill was therefore, I suggest, about how the modern state should regulate families (eg government versus governance) rather than about morality *per se*. It was however played out in the rhetoric of morality and fault such that it appeared to be a rerun of some of the 1969 Divorce Reform Bill debates. It is telling to compare the arguments of the main opponents.

Baroness Young led the attack on the Bill: 'It is the no fault provisions that I find to be the least acceptable part of the Bill. . . . The removal of fault undermines individual responsibility. By removing it, the state is actively discouraging any concept of lifelong commitment in marriage, to standards of behaviour, to self-sacrifice, to duty, to any thought for members of the family.'[40] Baroness Young's position was that it is clear that someone is at fault when a marriage breaks down and that the innocent partner should be vindicated and the guilty partner acknowledged as such. She called upon commonsense and the experience of 'wronged' husbands and wives who had been badly treated by callous or immoral spouses in order to present a powerful case for continuing to shame the guilty party. Her argument was not indifferent to children, but it was her case that the retention of fault caused people to hesitate before divorcing and that this meant that more children were spared the trauma of their

---

[39] See J. Eekelaar, 'Family Law: Keeping Us "On Message"', (1999) 11 *Child & Family Law Quarterly* 387.   [40] *House of Commons Debates (Hansard)*, 30 Nov 1995, col 733.

parents' divorce. Hers was an argument in favour of deterrence, punishment, and shame as ways to control family life and to instil commitment.

The opposing argument was put mainly by the Bishops of the Church of England including the Bishops of Oxford, Worcester, Birmingham, and Lord Habgood, the former Archbishop of York. Their argument was that marriage was indeed intended as a lifelong commitment, and that it was clear that some spouses were at fault in marriages, but they maintained that the law of divorce was not the proper instrument to prevent bad behaviour in marriages, nor was it the thing which could make marriages work. They argued that the divorce law should be the process by which the state assists couples to move from one circumstance to another without imposing artificial difficulties which make the transition and its aftermath traumatic for all concerned. As the Lord Bishop of Oxford stated:

My Lords, to state the obvious quickly and get it out of the way, I believe marriage is for life and I find the present high level of divorce dismaying. . . . Sadly, marriages fail, but we do not strengthen the institution of marriage by an unsatisfactory divorce law, which the present law is widely recognized to be. Let us concentrate on the present proposals for their own sake, recognising that marriages break down and that when they do we need the least damaging and most effective procedure possible. Strengthening the institution of marriage is a separate issue. . . . In supporting the Bill, neither I nor my fellow bishops in any way imply that fault is not involved in the breakdown of a marriage. . . . But anyone who knows anything about relationships knows how difficult it is to attribute blame fairly. If we are to have a divorce Bill, let it be one that is *humane and effective.*[41]

To put it briefly, Baroness Young wanted clear rules and deterrence to sustain lifelong marriage, the Bishops wanted education to promote marriage, objective information and reflection to provide the transition out of failed marriages. Both sides claimed to speak from a moral position and thus marriage and divorce was quintessentially reconstructed as a moral matter in these debates. But the issue of morality, which featured most vividly in the tabloid press in the mid-1990s, could really be seen as a subtext to the main issue of how a modern government should regulate family life at the end of the twentieth century.

As with the 1969 Divorce Reform Act, the fierce struggle over the Family Law Bill resulted in compromises. The core of the Bill which would have removed fault and introduced information meetings, the period for reflection and expanded mediation was passed but not enacted. The reason for this was that it was deemed necessary to pilot the information meetings and the new mediation provisions for publicly

---

[41] *House of Commons Debates (Hansard)*, 30 Nov 1995, cols 734–6, emphasis added.

funded applicants to see how effective they would be, before moving to a completely new system. However, the Lord Chancellor announced in 1999 that the implementation of Part 2 of the Act would be delayed, thus leaving divorce reform in limbo at the start of the new millennium.

FAULT AND CHILDREN

The political debate about fault, which was so intense in 1995, continued outside Parliament. Rowthorn,[42] for example, argued in favour of the (proper) reintroduction of fault and its attendant punishments as it would increase the amount of trust that spouses could place in one another because there would be external pressures on marriage partners to keep their vows. This, he argued, would improve the quality of marriage because women would not feel that they had to 'hedge their bets' by staying in the labour market in case their marriages failed. Mothers would feel safe enough to stay out of employment and raise their children secure in the knowledge that if their husbands strayed, they would receive punitive damages as well as the 'custody'[43] of the children. It is part of Rowthorn's argument that it is a mistake to prioritize the welfare of children over and above the issue of justice between spouses. He argued that the children should be 'awarded' to the innocent spouse and not, for example, to a guilty spouse just because the latter might have been the primary carer or because the children might prefer to live with the 'guilty' parent. He argued that the welfare of children-in-general is better served by a system of fault because marriage in general will become more stable for all children. That individual children might suffer should not, in his argument, outweigh the public policy interest of securing stable marriages. In an almost identical vein, Phillips argues,

The unjust disposal[44] of children and assets after divorce, not to mention the imposition of child support upon the victims of such breach of trust, can only be remedied if conduct is returned to centre stage in all divorce settlements. . . .

---

[42] R. Rowthorn, 'Marriage and Trust: Some Lessons from Economics', (1999) 23 *Cambridge Journal of Economics*, 661.

[43] It is interesting that those who argue in favour of fault-based divorce such as Phillips and Rowthorn, still use the terminology of 'custody' and 'access' when referring to children rather than the current terms of residence and contact. It seems that this reflects a particular view of the place of the children of a marriage.

[44] This terminology gives the impression that the 'just disposal of children' would be acceptable to Ms Phillips. Her argument is not against the disposal of children *per se* (as if they were inanimate objects) but simply that they are wrongly disposed of if the guilty spouse has 'custody'.

Only if conduct is re-established in divorce can the custody of children be resolved in their best interests and in the interests of justice.[45]

Both Phillips and Rowthorn identify the shifting emphasis in family law towards the welfare of children as a kind of Trojan horse in the battle to keep the family stable. From their perspective, the child should be returned to the virtual status of a marital asset which is awarded to the innocent spouse. This is an interesting argument because, although the main element of the debate they have revitalized has focused on the matrimonial misdemeanours of parents and ways of curbing these behaviours through state-enforced punishments, their argument rests substantially on the exclusion of children from civil society and/or a form of citizenship within the family. Whilst family policy (combined with social and cultural change) has gradually given rise to more democratic relationships within the family which are on the brink of including children in this newly founded form of private citizenship, Phillips's and Rowthorn's arguments seek discursively to reconstruct children as silent appendages who will concede to (and apparently thrive under) the authority of the innocent parent without the right to utter the slightest objection or preference. In this sense, the return of fault-based divorce would be dependent upon returning children to the sort of status they enjoyed in the first half of the twentieth century. Fault-based divorce would not simply require married couples to submit themselves and the minutiae of their intimate behaviour to the imperfect scrutiny of judicial inquisition for it to be decided who was guilty and who was innocent, it would also render their children as trophies in the adversarial system.

The question is whether the mode of regulation of married life subscribed to by Phillips and Rowthorn (namely authoritarian and rule bound) is in tune with the way in which the state in late twentieth-century Britain has adopted a governmentality that emphasizes the ways in which individuals might govern themselves in tune with favoured 'modern' modes of thinking and conduct. The former approach would lay down clear rules and penalties and would rely on people's sense of self-interest to keep their behaviour within certain fixed boundaries. The latter seeks to persuade people that if their behaviour is changing, they will need to attend to and internalize certain ethical criteria in order that they remain responsible citizens. The essence of this approach is captured in Tony Blair's speech, cited above. In this speech he also stated: 'This is not about preaching to individuals about their private lives. It is addressing a huge social problem. Attitudes have changed. The world has changed, but I am a modern man leading a modern country and this is a

[45] Phillips, n 37 above, 347–8.

modern crisis.' Although the meaning of Blair's speech is somewhat opaque, it does capture the flavour of government policy on family life at the end of the twentieth century if it is read in combination with the Consultation Document *Supporting Families* published by the Home Office in 1998. That document states:

Families do not want to be lectured about their behaviour or what kind of relationship they are in. They do not want to be nannied themselves or to be nagged about how they raise their children. But they do want support: advice on relationships; help with overcoming difficulties; support with parenting; and, should the couple's relationship breakdown irretrievably, a system of divorce which avoids aggravating conflict within the family.[46]

This heavy emphasis on support and advice, along with the creation of a National Family and Parenting Institute, was prefigured in the Royal Commission on Marriage and Divorce of the 1950s, and even the Denning Committee[47] of the mid-1940s. However, the renewed emphasis on it in the 1990s carries a different significance because of the extent to which the divorce laws have changed and because of the increased normalization of divorce itself. Although high rates of divorce are regretted in the Consultation Document,[48] the emphasis is on supporting marriage when people opt for it, but also on 'normalizing' other forms of family arrangement: 'It is not for the state to decide whether people marry or stay together. There are strong and mutually supportive families and relationships outside marriage and many unmarried couples remain together throughout their children's upbringing and raise their children every bit as successfully as married parents.'[49] It is particularly interesting that the Consultation Document should state that 'it is not for the state to decide whether people marry or stay together' because in the middle of the twentieth century this was seen as very much the province of the state. But by the end of that century the state appears to have relinquished its responsibility for regulating the movement into and exit from the institution of marriage. Marriage is defined as significant only in as much as it appears (from the statistics) to create a more stable form of parenting. It is therefore parenthood that seems to have become the focus of government policy at the end of the twentieth century, rather than marriage and divorce.

---

[46] Home Office, *Supporting Families: A Consultation Document*. London: The Stationery Office (1998) 30.

[47] *Second Interim Report of the Committee on Procedure in Matrimonial Causes*, Cd 6945. London: HMSO (1946).

[48] This is evidenced by the heavy praise heaped on marriage and the stated desire to strengthen marriage.   [49] Home Office, n 46 above, 30.

This shift in emphasis reflects trends in divorce laws and judicial pronouncements in England and Wales since the reforms in 1969, which have moved much closer to an emphasis on contextual ethics and a diminishing emphasis on contractual status. As Dame Brenda Hale[50] has argued, family law has moved away from equating the family with marriage and is therefore less preoccupied with regulating spousal relationships. The growing emphasis on the welfare of children has instead given further impetus to the shift, initially apparent in the 1970s, towards a greater attention to the quality of relationships, including parental relationships. This shift has given rise to new mechanisms of governmentality which are constructed around an intensified interest in children rather than spouses.

CONCLUSION: FOR THE SAKE OF THE CHILDREN

Throughout the second half of the twentieth century divorce has been equated with harming children.[51] However, this concern reached a climax in the late 1980s and 1990s as social scientific evidence appeared to give weight to the idea that divorce harmed children in a range of ways including affecting their health, educational achievement, and marriage prospects.[52] We can think of the concept of 'harming the children' as a discursive device which has been used in different ways at different times. For example, the idea of staying together for the sake of the children was a powerful rhetorical device in the 1950s and 1960s. However, it gave way (partially) to the idea that children were harmed by conflict more than by divorce—at least if the divorce resolved the conflict within the family. As divorce lost its moral stigma, the guilt associated with matrimonial fault and failure gave way to a new guilt over the harm caused to children. This, in turn, gave way to a different focus on new forms of parental obligation[53] generated in part by the ethos embraced by the Children Act 1989. This new ethos was based on the idea that divorce might sever spousal relationships, but that it did not and should not impede parental relationships and obligations. A new form of parental conduct began to be formulated which envisaged shared parenting across households or, at the very least, a more substantial role

---

[50] B. Hale, 'Private Lives and Public Duties: What is Family Law For?' (1998) 20 *Jnl of Social Welfare and Family Law* 125.

[51] C. Smart and S. Sevenhuijsen (eds), *Child Custody and the Politics of Gender*. London: Routledge (1989).

[52] See L. Burghes, *Lone Parenthood and Family Disruption*, London: Family Policy Studies Centre (1994) for a full appraisal of research in this field.

[53] M. Maclean and J. Eekelaar, *The Parental Obligation*. Oxford: Hart (1997).

for fathers in post-divorce parenting than had seemed desirable or feasible in the 1970s and 1980s. While mothers had been the focus of the divorce debates in the 1950s and 1960s, in the 1970s and 1980s attention shifted to fathers, firstly as economic providers and latterly as potential carers. This focus on shared parenting, or the new conduct of post-divorce parenthood, was also embedded in the idea that (nuclear) families were no longer restricted to co-residence or shared domicile. Divorce no longer had to mean family breakdown; it could simply mean marital breakdown, because the family could continue to survive (even thrive) across households.

The rise of mediation, the demise of emphasis on fault, and the proposed information meetings outlined in the 1996 Family Law Act all produced a mode of governance of marriage based on the reduction of conflict and the maximization of information and (desirable) options for the organization of post-divorce family life. Whereas in the 1950s adulterous wives were demonized, and in the 1980s deadbeat dads were vilified, by the end of the century the main villain became conflict. Divorce was being transformed into a process designed to minimize conflict—for the sake of the children.

Perhaps one of the most significant differences between the management of divorce in the 1950s and at the end of the twentieth century is the centrality of a new set of ideas about childhood and parent–child relationships. We can trace how notions of the welfare of the child have changed in content over this fifty years but, more importantly, by the end of the 1990s the child emerges as a social actor whose wishes and feelings should be ascertained, not simply as a minor whose welfare is safeguarded by his/her elders and betters.[54] From the standpoint of governmentality, the child becomes the key to encouraging certain forms of parental behaviour which are more socially acceptable. The vile hostilities and hypocrisies of fault-based divorce, the wildly optimistic ideals of the 'clean break', and the very idea of awarding the 'custody' of children to one parent, all seem to be practices which are only possible in a legal culture based on the centrality of marriage and adult relationships rather than reciprocal, caring relationships within diverse family forms.

In this context, the private law provisions of the Children Act 1989 are a good example of the shift towards governmentality away from domination and restraint. This Act promoted clear notions of 'good' post-divorce parenting by presenting the positive ideal of shared parenting while also relying on the already created impetus towards fathers'

---

[54] C. Sawyer, 'Ascertaining the Child's Wishes and Feelings', (2000) 30 *Family Law* 170; C. Smart and B. Neale '"It's My Life Too"—Children's Perspectives on Post-Divorce Parenting', (2000) 30 *Family Law* 163.

participation generated by the fathers' rights movement and rhetoric. It also harnessed the nascent idea of the voice of the child to give validity to the idea of the importance of continued shared parenting, while also pointing to the damage caused to children by parental conflict. The legislation sought to find ways of reducing conflict in order that its positive principles could start to flourish and change the ethos of post-divorce family life. The Children Act 1989 was perhaps the first legislative measure to address itself to the idea that there could be a family after divorce and that this family could be subject to (indirect) regulation just as the married or remarried family could be. The very advent of the term 'post-divorce' family—ugly as it may be—is indicative of a shifting conception of the relationship between family, marriage, and divorce at the start of the new millennium. It also indicates the existence of a new site for legislative, social, or cultural intervention, as well as recognition of a new set of relationships which can give rise to new forms of social agency and cultural practices. Thus, for example, divorced couples may start to opt to live near each other; step-parents may cease to be parents at all, becoming family friends instead; children may inhabit several households and networks of relationships; children may even start to choose which parent they co-reside with. These practices may in turn have effects on employment practices, on housing provision, on mobility patterns, on remarriage, and on relationships across the generations.

The twentieth-century obsession with the institution of marriage has not evaporated with the arrival of the twenty-first century, however. The Consultation Document *Supporting Families* (1998) is a clear example of how family policy in England and Wales attempts to look backwards and forwards at the same time. In this document marriage is celebrated as the best basis for family life, yet other forms of families are recognized as legitimate (as long as they are stable). Schools are instructed to teach children the value of heterosexual marriage as the basis of family life, yet the ban on representing to schoolchildren the idea that homosexual relationships can constitute proper families is proposed to be lifted.[55] These are clearly contradictory policies and they reveal the extent to which the state can no longer presume that it addresses and/or regulates a homogeneous national culture. This must surely be one of the most significant transformations to have taken place since the 1950s. There are now several moral constituencies for the state to govern, each of which seems to demand different modes of governmentality.[56] Those who cleave to marriage form

---

[55] *Guardian*, 28 Jan 2000. The government's attempts to do this failed in the House of Lords. It has, however, been lifted in Scotland.

[56] The most extreme example of parallel universes of governmentality seems to be demonstrated in the Louisiana experiment of 'covenant' marriage. See Wadlington, Ch 11 of this volume.

a strong constituency which cannot be ignored, yet those who practise diversity are equally significant and may even be in the ascendant. A middle ground seems inconceivable and so family policy embraces two different forms of regulation. It will of course be of considerable sociological interest to see how these competing tendencies unfold in the twenty-first century.

17

The Financial Incidents of Family Dissolution

GRACE GANZ BLUMBERG

The intact family routinely redistributes wealth from parents to children, and from one spouse to the other. For the most part, redistribution is a largely unavoidable aspect of joint and shared household consumption.[1] Wealth redistribution in the intact household is so commonplace (and requires so little legal regulation) that the critical role of the family in adjusting economic inequality often goes unnoticed. The topic of this chapter is wealth redistribution when family members no longer share a common household. The chapter traces the history of wealth redistribution at family breakdown in the United States during the second half of the twentieth century. For expository purposes, the chapter follows the American pattern of distinguishing three forms of wealth distribution: property division, spousal support, and child support. Although the parties may consider the three forms fungible, American law has conceptualized and regulated each according to different principles.

Mid-century began with a relatively long-established formal law of divorce, which corresponded to a well-established social model of the ideal family. John Demos describes this model, which initially appeared in the nineteenth century and persisted well past World War II, as one in which the husband and wife occupied separate spheres.[2] The husband's place was in the world, and he was entirely responsible for the economic support of the family. The wife's place was in the home, where she was responsible for the material and spiritual comfort of all family members. Separation of the spheres was enforced by legal rules and social norms that severely limited the labor force participation of women, particularly married women.

---

[1] Housing, consumer durables, and food are either shared (such as housing and automobiles) or consumed together (such as food). Expenditures for consumption intended for one family member alone, such as clothing and education, represent only a minor portion of total family expenditure. Ninety per cent of household expenditure is for shared goods or for privately consumed goods, such as food, that are not readily attributable to a given family member. LEWIN/ICF, ESTIMATES AND EXPENDITURES ON CHILDREN AND CHILD SUPPORT GUIDELINES 2–3 (1990).

[2] See John Demos, *Images of the American Family, Then and Now, in* Virginia Tufte and Barbara Myerhoff (eds), CHANGING IMAGES OF THE FAMILY 43, 49 (1979), reprinted in JOHN DEMOS, PAST, PRESENT, AND PERSONAL: THE FAMILY AND LIFE COURSE IN AMERICAN HISTORY (1986). In his three-part model of American family history, Professor Demos describes this second model as the 'the Family as Refuge,' and contrasts it with the earlier 'settlement' model of 'the Family as Community.' For discussion of the third model, see n 7 below, and accompanying text. Of course these models cannot be chronologically cabined, and elements of all of them cumulate in current notions of the family. Demos at 59.

Understanding this version of the family as timeless and immutable, the United States Supreme Court constitutionalized it in decisions upholding legislative restrictions on female labor force participation.[3]

The American law of divorce reflected this model of the family and was, at least in principle,[4] protective of the interests of the home-bound wife and children. Divorce was nominally available only for grievous fault, and a blameless wife was in theory entitled to support for life, or until the burden of support was assumed by a new husband. Aside from the eight Spanish-law community property states, the concept of property distribution at divorce was largely or entirely undeveloped. Because spousal fault was not legally monitored, divorce was in fact freely available if parties were willing to negotiate the conclusion of their marriage. Given limitations on female labor force participation, most divorces were initiated by husbands, who obtained their freedom with property settlements (even in the absence of any marital property regime) and continuing support obligations.[5] Although this system occasionally engendered egregious unfairness, it often produced rough justice, and results were in any event not remarkably different than under the successor regime.[6]

[3] See Justice Bradley's concurrence in *Bradwell v State*, 83 US (16 Wall.) 130, 141–2 (1872) (sustaining exclusion of an otherwise qualified woman from the Illinois Bar): 'The paramount destiny and mission of women are to fulfil the noble and benign offices of wife and mother. This is the law of the Creator. And the rules of civil society must be adapted to the general constitution of things, and cannot be based upon exceptional cases.' See also *Muller v Oregon*, 208 US 412 (1908) (sustaining legislative limitations on the employment of women for more than ten hours a day); *Goesaert v Cleary*, 335 US 464 (1948) (sustaining state statute allowing women to serve as waitresses in taverns, but barring them from the more lucrative job of bartender).

[4] Any discussion of law 'on the books' risks overstating the impact of the law and of any particular formal legal change on outcomes in actual cases. This is particularly true in divorce law, where trial courts have historically exercised almost unbridled discretion, where the various elements of economic reordering are generally fungible, and where the law has generally been far more redistributive in principle than in result. For example, although a blameless wife was traditionally entitled to life support from the husband she divorced for fault, alimony was in fact rarely awarded. See eg Leon Carroll Marshall and Geoffry May, The Divorce Court (1933) (surveying Maryland and Ohio divorce judgments in 1932 and 1933 and finding alimony was granted in only 6% of cases). Surveying national divorce data from 1887 and comparing the incidence of California alimony awards before and after the 1969 adoption of no-fault divorce, Lenore Weitzman concludes that 'the promise of alimony has always been a myth.' Lenore Weitzman, *The Economics of Divorce*, 28 UCLA L Rev 1181, 1221 n 142 (1981). Professor Weitzman's *The Divorce Revolution* may be read to imply that no-fault divorce reduced the incidence and duration of alimony. See generally Lenore Weitzman, The Divorce Revolution (1985). However, a careful reading of her data shows little change in awards from 1968 to 1977. See Stephen D. Sugarman, *Dividing Financial Interests on Divorce, in* Steven D. Sugarman and Herma Hill Kay (eds), Divorce Reform at the Crossroads 133 (1990); see also sources cited in Principles of the Law of Family Dissolution § 5.05 cmt a (Proposed Final Draft 1997).

[5] See William J. Goode, After Divorce 133–6, 144 (1956) (classic study of a generally representative 1948 sample of metropolitan Detroit divorces).

[6] See Marsha Garrison, *Good Intentions Gone Awry: The Impact of New York's Equitable Distribution Law on Divorce Outcomes*, 57 Brook L Rev 621 (1991); see also n 4 above.

As the role-differentiated ideal family of the 1950s gave way to the increasingly egalitarian ideal family of the 1960s and 1970s,[7] family law effectively became the ideological handmaiden of the movement to eliminate sex discrimination in the labor market. Title 7 of the Civil Rights Act of 1964,[8] intended to achieve equality of employment opportunity, was interpreted to prohibit employers from taking traditional sex roles into account in hiring, or other employment decisions. In *Phillips v Martin Marietta Corp*,[9] the first Title 7 case to reach the United States Supreme Court, the employer had persuaded two lower courts that its refusal to hire mothers (but not fathers) of pre-school children was not unlawful sex discrimination because it was not based on sex alone, but rather on 'sex plus,' that is, the conjunction of sex and a gender-neutral characteristic, parentage of young children. The Supreme Court rejected the 'sex-plus' defense, concluding that generalizations about sex roles in the family could not justify refusal to hire individual job applicants.

It was not a large conceptual step from refusal to generalize about sex roles in the family for purposes of equal employment opportunity, to refusal to generalize about (or even consider) sex roles in thinking about the law of continuing economic obligations at family dissolution. Proponents of equal employment opportunity for women were prone to deny or minimize the disproportionate demands that family life made on the time and energy of married women, as compared to their husbands.[10] Divorcing husbands and disingenuous trial judges were quick to invoke women's new economic opportunities as a justification for ungenerous awards at divorce.[11] United States Supreme Court Justice Brennan, presented with a wealthy husband's equal protection challenge to a state law allowing alimony for women only, seemed unable to give any coherent account of alimony as he examined it through the lens of a decade of equal employment opportunity law.[12]

---

[7] Demos, n 2 above, describes the third (c 1979) model as 'the Family as Encounter Group.' By contrast with the prior model ('the Family as Refuge'), the third model eschews role differentiation and 'advocate[s] an opposite principle, which exalts the diffusion and mixing of roles.' Of course, any particular marriage and marriages generally may share attributes of all three ideal forms. Moreover, the models themselves tend to cumulate. See Demos, n 2 above, at 59.

[8] 42 USC § 2000e (2000). Title 7 prohibits sex discrimination in hiring, and in the terms and conditions of employment. [9] 400 US 542 (1971).

[10] See Martha Albertson Fineman, The Illusion of Equality: The Rhetoric and Reality of Divorce Reform 24–5 (1991).

[11] See Herma Hill Kay, *Beyond No-Fault: New Directions in Law Reform*, in Divorce Reform at the Crossroads, n 4 above, at 19.

[12] In *Orr v Orr*, 440 US 268 (1979), Justice Brennan, writing for the Court, struck down the Alabama alimony statute, which allowed alimony for wives only, as violative of the equal protection clause of the Fourteenth Amendment. *Orr* is interesting not for the equal protection holding, which was a foregone conclusion by 1979, but for the Court's hostile and uncomprehending discussion of the rationales and purposes of alimony. As Justice Bradley

As new legal norms of gender equality transformed husbands and wives into degendered spouses, and mothers and fathers into parents, continuing support obligations were pared down accordingly. This was evident not only in family law itself,[13] but also in constitutional jurisprudence of the era.[14]

In the United States, divorce is primarily regulated by state law. Wide variation in state law and the broad discretion traditionally exercised by divorce courts make it difficult to generalize about the content of state law. To etch sharper images than would otherwise emerge from a survey of state law, and to consider where the law may be heading in the twenty-first century as well as to describe its content during the second half of the twentieth century, this chapter examines and compares two national law reform documents. Each may be understood to reflect prevailing views of prominent actors, including judges, law professors, legal practitioners, and other family law experts. The Uniform Marriage and Divorce Act,[15] approved by the National Conference of Commissioners on Uniform State Laws in 1970, is a model act proposed for adoption by individual states. The American Law Institute's Principles of the Law of Family Dissolution,[16] drafted during the final decade of the century, is intended to guide legislatures and courts in the twenty-first century. In some respects the Principles follow the Act; in others the Principles depart sharply. The differences between the Act and the Principles are at least partly explainable in terms of intervening developments and new ways of thinking about the family and family dissolution.[17]

The Act, drafted in the late 1960s and twice amended in the early 1970s,[18] covers all aspects of marriage and divorce. It states general principles, but is neither detailed nor exhaustive in its treatment of particular topics. The Act was path-breaking in its adoption of a single no-fault ground for divorce. Like California legislation enacted at the same time,

---

constitutionalized an earlier model of the ideal family in *Bradwell v State*, 83 US (16 Wall) 130, 141–2 (1872), Justice Brennan similarly constitutionalized the later egalitarian model in *Orr*. See nn 3, 7 above.

[13] See nn 18–29 below, and accompanying text.

[14] Cf *Orr*, 440 US at 268 with *Kahn v Shevin*, 416 US 351 (1974), in which Justice Douglas, writing for the majority, sustained a state law property tax exemption for widows, but not widowers. *Orr* and *Kahn* are difficult to reconcile. *Orr* may reasonably be understood to overrule *Kahn*.

[15] Unif Marriage and Divorce Act, 9A ULA 159–688 and 9B ULA (1998). The Act has been adopted, in whole or in part, by eight states: Arizona, Colorado, Illinois, Kentucky, Minnesota, Missouri, Montana, and Washington. 9A ULA 159 (1998).

[16] The American Law Institute, a non-governmental organization of judges, attorneys, and legal scholars, is best known for its Restatements of the Law. Occasionally, the Institute undertakes the more ambitious project of entirely rethinking a particular area of law. To signal such a choice, the Institute uses the term *Principles*, rather than *Restatement*.

[17] See nn 30–51, 75–79 below and accompanying text.   [18] See 9A ULA 169 (1998).

the Act requires only that the marriage be 'irretrievably broken.'[19] The Act's rejection of fault is pervasive; it may not be taken into account for purposes of property distribution[20] or support.[21] Consistent with developing constitutional and statutory sensitivity to sex discrimination, the Act eschews the gendered terminology of prior law. Mothers and fathers are ungendered 'parents,' while husbands and wives are 'spouses.'[22]

Analogizing divorce to the dissolution of a business partnership,[23] the Act prescribes an equitable distribution of the parties' property.[24] The Act introduces a new principle to common law states: in apportioning property, the court should take into account, *inter alia*, the 'contribution of a spouse as a homemaker, or to the family unit.'[25] The Act's quid pro quo for property redistribution is contraction of alimony, or spousal support.[26]

---

[19] See Unif Marriage and Divorce Act §§ 302–5, 9A ULA 200–42 (1998). California adopted no-fault divorce grounds in The Family Law Act of 1969. See Cal Fam Code §§ 2310–11 (West 2000). Herma Hill Kay, a reporter of the Act, was also a member of the California Governor's Commission on the Family, which recommended the adoption of no-fault divorce. Professor Kay attributes the innovation to California: 'Following California's lead, the National Conference of Commissioners on Uniform State Laws adopted a dissolution standard for the Uniform Marriage and Divorce Act . . .' Herma Hill Kay, *An Appraisal of California's No-Fault Divorce Law*, 75 Cal L Rev. 291, 292 (1987).

[20] See Unif Marriage and Divorce Act § 307, 9A ULA 288 (1998) ('the court, without regard to marital conduct, shall . . . finally equitably apportion between the parties the property and assets belonging to either or both').

[21] See *ibid* at § 308(b) ('The maintenance order shall be in amounts and for periods of time the court deems just, without regard to marital conduct . . . ').

[22] Although this linguistic strategy worked well enough with nouns, pronouns proved troublesome. Following the then standard practice of using 'his' as a universal possessive adjective, the Act uses constructions that defy social reality. See eg nn 26–7 below, and accompanying text.

[23] The Prefatory Note explains: 'The Act's elimination of fault notions extends to its treatment of maintenance [spousal support] and property division. The distribution of property upon the termination of a marriage should be treated, as nearly as possible, like the distribution of assets incident to the dissolution of a partnership.'

[24] See Unif Marriage and Divorce Act § 307, 9A ULA 288–9 (1998). The Act proposes two alternatives. Alternative A, intended for common law states, empowers the divorce court to distribute all property of either or both parties 'however and whenever acquired.' This 'hotchpot' inclusion is a minority variant common in Midwestern states. Alternative B, intended for community property states, preserves their distinction between property earned by either spouse during marriage (community property) and all other property (separate property). (By the end of the century the community property distinction had been adopted by a majority of the common law states.)

[25] *ibid* at § 307, 9A ULA 288–9 (1998). The principle was not, of course, new to the community property states, in whose marital property systems it is embedded. See Susan Westerberg Prager, *Sharing Principles and the Future of Marital Property Law*, 25 UCLA L Rev 1 (1977).

[26] The Prefatory Note explains that the Act authorizes property distribution as the primary means of providing for the future financial needs of the spouses. Where the marital property is insufficient for this purpose, an award of maintenance may be available. 'But, because of its property division provisions, the Act does not continue the traditional reliance upon maintenance as the primary means of support for divorced spouses.' 9A ULA 161 (1998).

Tellingly recharacterized as 'maintenance,' it is available only when a spouse lacks sufficient property 'to provide for his reasonable needs' and 'is unable to support himself through appropriate employment or is the custodian of a child whose condition or circumstances make it appropriate that the custodian not be required to seek employment outside the home.'[27] Neither the prior standard of living of the family nor the wealth of the potential obligor is a factor in determining eligibility for maintenance.[28] Even when a divorcing spouse satisfies the eligibility threshold, the Act contemplates a transitional award. In determining the amount and duration of a maintenance award, the Act instructs the court to consider 'the time necessary to acquire sufficient education or training to enable the party seeking maintenance to find appropriate employment.'[29] The Act does not explicitly advocate the desirability of a 'clean break' to justify the substitution of an immediate property distribution for a continuing duty of spousal support. However, offering no other strong rationale for the choice, the Act's preference for property distribution may implicitly be understood as a cautious and guarded adoption of a clean break, or fresh start, principle.

The Act's treatment of child support broke little new ground. As is typical in American law, the measure of child support refers only to the child and not to the parent who cares for the child. As was typical when the Act was promulgated, the amount of support payable by the non-custodial parent, if any, is left to the judge's relatively unbounded discretion. Finally, given the constriction of maintenance and the definition of child support as 'an amount reasonable or necessary for [the child's] support,' the Act's direction to the court to consider, *inter alia*, 'the standard of living the child would have enjoyed had the marriage not been dissolved' seems, in the typical case, to defy the economic fact that the child and the custodial parent share not only a household, but also a

---

[27] *ibid* at § 308(a), 9A ULA 446 (1998). The child custodian provision was not understood to open a wide door to maintenance claims. In the United States, divorced custodial parents have long been expected to pursue gainful employment and have had a high rate of labor force participation. The provision thus should be understood to contemplate, at most, the care of pre-school children and older children with special needs. Of course, labor force participation data do not measure the extent to which custodial parents tailor and subordinate their market labor (and hence their earnings) to the needs of their children. For a general survey of the literature, see IRA MARK ELLMAN, *et al*, FAMILY LAW 40–52 (1998).

[28] However, once threshold eligibility is established, these factors are taken into account in determining the amount and duration of maintenance. Under the Act, an award of maintenance requires a two-step determination: eligibility and, if eligibility is found, determination of the duration and amount, if any, under § 308(b). See UNIF MARRIAGE AND DIVORCE ACT §§ 308(a)–(b).

[29] *ibid* at § 308(b)(2). This type of award is frequently characterized as 'rehabilitative alimony.'

standard of living. The disjunction between the law's lofty aspiration for the child and the readily predictable consequences of application of the law is typical of legislation and case law of the era. However, it is unusual for the Act, which otherwise speaks plainly and realistically about what it intends to accomplish.

Following promulgation of the Act, no-fault divorce was universally legislated, and property distribution flowered. Some states adopted the single 'irretrievable breakdown' ground proposed by the Act, while others added a no-fault ground, often requiring proof of separation for a specified period of time, to their pre-existing fault grounds. Both no-fault formulations found support in the text of the Act.[30]

Although community property principles were well established in the handful of states influenced by Spanish law,[31] when the Act was promulgated most states still followed common law title principles. Many prominent eastern states, including New York, Pennsylvania, and Virginia, did not allow their courts to distribute the parties' property at divorce. Some Mid-western states had authorized their courts to distribute property equitably at divorce, but the practice was not routine and was generally reserved for unusual cases.[32] Following promulgation of the Act, the law of property distribution developed in three distinct ways.[33] First, it was adopted by every jurisdiction. Second, it progressed from relatively ungenerous redistribution to a still-developing norm of presumptive 50–50 distribution.[34] Third, the definition of 'property' subject to distribution grew to include virtually all tangible assets and some intangibles as well.[35]

---

[30] Section 3.02 of the Act provides that the court shall order a decree of divorce if it 'finds that the marriage is irretrievably broken, if the finding is supported by evidence that (i) the parties have lived separate and apart for a period of more than 180 days . . . or (ii) there is serious marital discord affecting the attitude of one or both parties toward the marriage.' See 9A ULA 200–1 (1998). For an exhaustive survey of state no-fault provisions, see Herman Hill Kay, *Equality and Difference: A Perspective on No-Fault Divorce and Its Aftermath*, 56 U Cin L Rev 1, 4–6 (1987).

[31] Moving geographically from northwest to southeast, they are: Washington, Idaho, Nevada, California, Arizona, New Mexico, Texas, and Louisiana. After the Uniform Marital Property Act was promulgated in 1983, Wisconsin, the only state to adopt it, also became a community property state. See 9A ULA 103 (1998).

[32] See eg *Anderson v Anderson*, 68 NW2d 849 (ND 1955) ($2,000 equitable distribution award to wife reversed because she had contributed no extraordinary services, that is, no services beyond those of an ordinary housewife).

[33] The extent to which the Act caused this development, or merely presaged it, is difficult to determine. But see Robert J. Levy, *A Reminiscence About the Uniform Marriage and Divorce Act*, 1991 BYU L Rev 43, 44 (1991).

[34] See Grace Ganz Blumberg, *Marital Property Treatment of Pensions, Disability Pay, Workers' Compensation, and Other Wage Substitutes: An Insurance, or Replacement, Analysis*, 33 UCLA L Rev 1250, 1251 n 4 (1986).

[35] See Grace Ganz Blumberg, *Intangible Assets: Recognition and Valuation*, in 2 Valuation and Distribution of Marital Property §§ 23.01–23.08 (John P. McCahey ed, 1995).

As the doctrine of property distribution expanded and the doctrine of spousal support contracted, there was increasing pressure on property distribution to include the present value of assets that would otherwise have been treated as streams of future income for purposes of spousal support. Pensions were soon included, first vested pensions and then unvested pensions.[36] The goodwill of businesses and professional practices was next recognized as an asset subject to distribution at divorce. In some states, even unmarketable goodwill may be recognized and valued in terms of its worth in the hands of the spouse who created it.[37] Celebrity goodwill has been similarly treated by several states.[38] Most courts have drawn the line at professional education and credentials earned during marriage.[39] However, the New York Court of Appeals[40] and several Michigan intermediate appellate courts[41] treat professional education and credentials earned during marriage as distributable assets, which are valued in terms of the present value of future earnings attributable to their acquisition.[42]

Even such a robust law of property distribution could not fulfill the task that the Act prescribed for it, for in the United States most divorcing couples either have no significant assets, or none that suffice as an effective substitute for spousal support. From a comparative perspective, the savings rate in the United States is extremely low, at times even negative.[43] The two most frequent spousal assets are pensions and the family home. A pension that is not yet mature[44] is unreachable as a source

---

[36] For comprehensive treatment of divorce distribution of pensions, see *ibid* at § 23.02.

[37] See *ibid* § 23.05; see also Grace Ganz Blumberg, *Identifying and Valuing Goodwill at Divorce*, 56 Law and Contemporary Probs 217 (1993) (also published as chapter 25 in Valuation and Distribution of Marital Property, n 35 above).

[38] See *Piscopo v Piscopo*, 555 A2d 1190, 1192 (NJ Sup Ct Ch Div 1988), *aff'd*, 557 A2d 1040 (NJ Super Ct App Div), *cert. denied*, 564 A2d 875 (NJ 1989); *Elkus v Elkus*, 572 NYS 2d 901, 904 (NY App Div 1991), *appeal dismissed*, 588 NE 2d 99 (NY 1992); see also sources cited n 37 above, at 269–70.   [39] See Blumberg, n 35 above, at § 23.06.

[40] See *O'Brien v O'Brien*, 489 NE 2d 712 (NY 1985).

[41] See eg *Lewis v Lewis*, 448 NW 2d 735 (Mich Ct App 1989) (husband's MBA is a marital asset and wife is entitled to one-half the present value of the degree); *Woodworth v Woodworth*, 337 NW 2d 332 (Mich Ct App 1983) (accord); but see *Postema v Postema*, 471 NW 2d 912 (Mich Ct App 1991); *Olah v Olah*, 354 NW 2d 359 (Mich Ct App 1984).

[42] That is, the distributable value of the professional degree or credential is the present value of the difference between what the degree holder will earn with the degree and what he would earn without it.

[43] The personal savings rate in the United States fell from 3.5% in 1995 to 0.2% in the second half of 1998. *OECD Economic Surveys—United States November 1, 1999*. In August 1999, the savings rate fell to a record low of negative 1.5%. *The Markets*, NY Times, Oct 2 1999, at C3. In terms of divorce law, the low savings rate may be illusory in so far as it reflects confidence in self-investment, often characterized as human capital, to yield an ever increasing stream of future earnings. To the extent that growth in human capital does replace traditional savings, the law of property distribution may appropriately take a harder look at the various forms of human capital acquisition. See nn 36–42 above, and accompanying text.

[44] A pension matures when the pension plan participant becomes eligible to start collecting benefits. At that point, the pension is (or can be) a source of current income. Until then,

of current income. The equity of the family home is reachable only if it is sold, which may not be desirable when one spouse is otherwise unable to generate adequate income because, for example, of the need to care for young children.

In the years following promulgation of the Act, legislators, courts, and commentators expressed two areas of dissatisfaction with the maintenance provision of the Act.[45] It often ruled out the possibility of spousal support in long marriages where the parties had assumed traditional roles and the wife had contributed to the husband's career success, even when the husband could well afford to share some of his post-divorce income with his former spouse.[46] This perceived lacuna prompted some adopting states to modify and soften the Act's maintenance provision.[47] The other dissatisfaction concerned support for parents caring for young children. It arose not so much from the eligibility provision, which allowed spousal support for the child carer under certain circumstances, but rather from the Act's general disapproval of the notion that one spouse should have a continuing support obligation to the other and the Act's scaling down of the content and duration of maintenance, even when it was appropriately awarded.

The law of child support languished in the 1960s and 1970s, perhaps because 'Great Society' welfare benefits were sufficient, at least in some northern states, for single parents and children to survive without contribution from an absent parent. With subsequent curtailment of the welfare state, the federal government became interested in child support as a means of reducing federal welfare expenditure. In the 1980s, the federal

---

even a vested pension is only a non-alienable right, often contingent upon survival, to collect benefits at some future time.

[45] For a survey of alimony case law during this period, see Joan M. Krauskopf, *Rehabilitative Alimony: Uses and Abuses of Limited Discretion Alimony*, 21 Fam L Q 573 (1988).

[46] See eg *Otis v Otis*, 299 NW 2d 114 (Minn 1980) (applying newly adopted Uniform Marriage and Divorce Act, Minnesota Supreme Court finds no abuse of discretion in divorce decree awarding modest maintenance scheduled to decline and terminate entirely within four years, after a marriage of twenty-four years in which 45-year-old wife abandoned significant employment to give birth to the parties' child and assist husband in furthering his career, at which he was earning more than $120,000 a year).

[47] See eg Ariz Rev Stat Ann § 25–319 (West 1999); Minn Stat Ann § 518.552 (West 1999). The Minnesota statute was amended in 1985, five years after Otis. See 299 NW 2d at 114; see also n 46 above, and accompanying text. Legislation authorizing more generous spousal support was also enacted in states that had not adopted the Act, but whose spousal support statutes had either been influenced by the Act or whose judges, who may have been influenced by the Act, were not awarding alimony where the governing statute would seem to warrant it. See eg 1986 NY Dom Rel Law, ch 884, § 4, amending NY Dom Rel Law § 236, Part B(6)(a),(c) (McKinney's 1999) (emphasizing the divorce court may award permanent maintenance, and replacing 'reasonable needs' with the 'standard of living of the parties established during the marriage' as the basis for an award). To similar effect, see Cal Fam Code § 4320 (West 2000).

government required that each state adopt a presumptively applicable child support formula.[48] Although initially resisted, child support formulas became well accepted and gave rise, in the 1990s, to interest in the development of spousal support formulas.[49]

The last two decades of the century evidence two dominant developments. The first is the movement from indeterminate rules to highly determinate rules.[50] Judicial discretion has not been eliminated, but it is increasingly subject to constraints. The second is the development of new and relatively robust rationales for wealth redistribution at family dissolution. These two developments are closely related, for the wealth redistribution contemplated by the new rationales is suitably accomplished by determinate rules. Thus the movement to determinate rules expresses not only concern for uniformity of result and efficient mass administration of justice, but also reflects the view that substantively superior results may be obtained from the application of carefully designed formulas than from the ad hoc decisions of judges.[51] The most coherent expression of these two developments is the American Law Institute's Principles of the Law of Family Dissolution, but they are also evidenced in the evolving law of the more than fifty jurisdictions that formulate family law in the United States.

In scope, the ALI Principles are both narrower and broader than the Act. The Act regulates all aspects of marriage and divorce. The Principles treat only the financial and custodial incidents of family breakdown, but include non-marital as well as marital families. The operative provisions of the Act are fairly general and, with respect to the economic incidents of divorce, merely suggestive of the direction that courts should take, given the discretion that courts traditionally exercised and were expected to exercise under the Act. By contrast, the operative provisions of the Principles are highly detailed and judges are, by and large, given discretion to deviate from them only to avoid a 'substantial injustice.'[52] In

---

[48] See generally Irwin Garfinkel and Marygold S. Melli, *The Use of Normative Standards in Family Law Decisions: Developing Mathematical Standards for Child Support*, 24 FAM LQ 157 (1990).

[49] See PRINCIPLES OF THE LAW OF FAMILY DISSOLUTION § 5.02 cmt e, Reporter's Notes (Proposed Final Draft 1997); Ira Mark Ellman, *The Maturing Law of Divorce Finances: Toward Rules and Guidelines*, 33 FAM L Q 801 (1999).

[50] This theme is universally expressed in child support formulas, often called 'guidelines.' In property division, it is evidenced in growing acceptance of presumptive rules of 50–50 distribution. In spousal support, the movement to determinate rules is least developed, but there is some motion in this direction.

[51] See Ira Mark Ellman, *Inventing Family Law*, 32 UC DAVIS L REV 855 (1999).

[52] See eg PRINCIPLES OF THE LAW OF FAMILY DISSOLUTION: ANALYSIS AND RECOMMENDATIONS § 5.05 (Proposed Final Draft 1997) (presumption that the value of compensatory payments award, determined by state's formula, is correct; presumption may be overcome only by trial court findings that application of the formula in the particular case would yield a substantial

contrast to the Act, which offers spare commentary for its operative provisions, the Principles accompany their exhaustive 'black letter' rules with elaborate commentary. The Principles observe that all families are not alike, and propose decisional rubrics that respond to their differing economic and child-rearing arrangements.[53]

Chapter 4 of the Principles treats property division at divorce. In many ways chapter 4 confirms the developments of the preceding decades; in others it advances or limits them. Reflecting widespread acceptance of the partnership view of marriage propounded by the Act, the Principles ordinarily require equal division of the marital property, defined as property acquired by the labor of either spouse during marriage. In the 1970 Act, property distribution was proposed as a need-based substitute for continuing spousal support.[54] A quarter of a century later, the Principles' division of property more closely resembles community property recognition of vested property rights. Property earned by either spouse during marriage is divided equally because, as marital partners, the parties have equal ownership claims to that property. Reconciling the conflict between the substantial minority of American states that allow the divorce court to redistribute all the spouses' property whenever and however acquired (the 'hotchpot' states), and the majority that allow the divorce court to redistribute only property earned during marriage, the Principles introduce the concept of *transmutation over time*. In long marriages, unless a party elects otherwise, property that would otherwise be the separate property of one of the spouses (because acquired before marriage, or acquired during marriage by gift) becomes, over time, marital property. Transmutation over time is intended to reflect the gradual merging of economic identity and the expectations of spouses in long marriages.[55]

The Principles exhaustively classify problematic assets that have troubled state courts,[56] and set limits on the tendency of state courts to

---

injustice). Comparing the Act and the Principles in terms of discretion accorded the divorce court, the innovation of the Act is that it constrains the court's discretion to redistribute future income (and then allows the court discretion to order, or not order, maintenance within those constraints), while the innovation of the Principles is that they limit the court's discretion not to redistribute future income when redistribution is generally deemed appropriate.

[53] This perspective is implicit in the financial provisions and is explicitly developed in the child custody chapter. See *ibid* ch 1 (Introductory Discussion to Principles Governing the Allocation of Custodial and Decisionmaking Responsibility for Children), at 10–11 (Tentative Draft No. 3, 1998). [54] See nn 26–9 above, and accompanying text.

[55] See PRINCIPLES OF THE LAW OF FAMILY DISSOLUTION §§ 4.15, 4.18 (Proposed Final Draft 1997).

[56] eg personal injury (tort) recoveries, certain forms of wage replacement arguably earned during marriage but intended to replace wages that would otherwise have been earned after divorce, such as retirement pensions, disability pay, workers' compensation, severance pay, and term life insurance proceeds.

reify human capital acquisition and distribute it as property at divorce. The Principles understand that this tendency was prompted by the absence of any other mechanism to reach the higher-income spouse's income at divorce. However, the application of principles of property distribution to uncertain streams of future income generates other problems and injustices.[57] Instead, the Principles respond to future-income claims under the chapter 5 rubric of 'compensatory payments,' which replaces traditional spousal support. The Principles observe that family dissolution may impose financial losses on one or both parties and, because of the circumstances of family life, those losses may fall disproportionately on one party. The compensatory payments rubric determines both when and the extent to which those losses should be shared by the parties at dissolution. The Principles draw their substance from the equitable concerns long expressed by courts and commentators, and formulate a framework that systematically responds to those concerns. In terms of its equitable foundation, chapter 5 may be understood as a restatement of the law; in terms of its systematic reformulation, chapter 5 is an innovation.

The Principles observe that spousal support cannot ethically be justified by the needs of the obligee alone. The mere fact of marriage does not warrant an obligation, lifetime or otherwise, to support another person. A continuing obligation to transfer income to another must be based on other considerations.[58] Two types of marriages are prominent in the American case law of spousal support: those that endure a long time and those in which one spouse primarily cares for the children. In such marriages, dissolution is likely to impose disproportionate losses that should equitably be shared by the parties. The Principles contemplate and implicitly approve the 'clean break' approach for most short marriages.[59] However, when there would otherwise be significant income disparity after dissolu-

---

[57] They include the speculativeness of valuation and the finality and unalterability of property distribution in the event that anticipated income does not materialize, or the economic circumstances of the payee improve with, for example, remarriage. By contrast, treatment of future income as spousal support, or some other variety of equitable income-sharing, allows for modification or termination of the award.

[58] With respect to the rationale for income redistribution at dissolution, ch 5 rejects *relief of need* in favor of *compensation for loss*. See PRINCIPLES OF THE LAW OF FAMILY DISSOLUTION § 5.02 cmt a (Proposed Final Draft 1997). Ch 5 can also be rationalized in more traditional terms. In divorce law, need has been expansively defined as post-dissolution decline in standard of living. The Principles' loss is also measurable in terms of decline of standard of living. The Principles require loss sharing only when certain equitable factors are present. Similarly, the amount and duration of need-based alimony have been subject to those same equitable considerations. On the malleability of rationales for property and income redistribution, see Grace Ganz Blumberg, *Fineman's* The Illusion of Equality: *A Review-Essay*, 2 UCLA WOMEN'S L J 309, 323 (1992).

[59] But see the relatively rare exceptions described in n 60 below.

tion and the marriage has been long or the lower-income spouse has disproportionately cared for the children, the Principles ordinarily require that the higher-income spouse share some of the other spouse's loss by paying a percentage of the difference in incomes as 'compensatory payments' for a set period of time. The percentage payable and the duration of payments are functions of the length of the marriage and the period of time during marriage that the lower-income spouse disproportionately provided care for the children of one or both parties. Sharing is never full; that is, the parties' incomes are never fully equalized. The earner always has a greater claim to the fruits of his labor.[60]

While chapter 5 (compensatory payments) may be understood as a new rubric to encompass a set of persistent equitable concerns, the challenge faced by chapter 3 (child support) was quite different. In terms of rubric, federal law requires a presumptively applicable child support formula. The states responded accordingly and, with a few exceptions,[61] similarly. On close inspection, what was notably missing was any coherent and accurate conception, implicit or explicit, of the legal principles expressed by the child support formula.[62] The states, for the most part, adopted what the Principles characterize as a 'marginal expenditure' measure of child support. The 'cost' of a child may appropriately be measured in terms of the additional expenditure required to keep the family standard of living constant when a child is added to the household. This marginal expenditure measure may be expressed as a percentage of family expenditure, or family income. The percentage of family income spent on a child (or children, as the case may be) in two-parent households is the basis of most state child support formulas. The non-custodial parent is required to contribute, as child support, the percentage of income he would contribute to the support of the child if he were sharing a home with the child and the child's custodial parent. The marginal expenditure measure of child support has been variously misunderstood to ensure that the child will not suffer at all, or will suffer no more than any other family member.[63]

---

[60] Planned revisions to the commentary suggest that the rule maker might reasonably set the upper limit of compensatory payments, for the very longest marriages, at 40% of the difference between the parties' incomes. In shorter marriages, the percentage would be significantly lower. See PRINCIPLES OF THE LAW OF FAMILY DISSOLUTION 173 (Council Draft No. 6, 1999). Ch 5 also addresses less frequently presented equitable claims, such as unusual career sacrifices in relatively short marriages and career threshold divorces in marriages that have largely been devoted to the professional education of one of the spouses. *ibid* at §§ 5.12–5.16 (Proposed Final Draft, 1997).   [61] See n 65 below.

[62] For an excellent examination of the conceptual issues in American child support formulas, see David Betson *et al*, *Trade-Offs Implicit in Child Support Guidelines*, 11 J POL'Y ANALYSIS & MGMT 1 (1992).

[63] See Grace Ganz Blumberg, *Balancing the Interests: The American Law Institute's Treatment of Child Support*, 33 FAM LQ 39, 67–8 and n 65 (1999). Essentially, marginal expenditure child support mistakes an economic truism for a legal principle.

However, it guarantees neither, for with marginal expenditure child support, the child's standard of living is largely a function of the independent income of the parent with whom the child shares a home.[64]

The Principles observe that marginal expenditure child support does reach appropriate results when the child's parents have equal incomes before the payment of child support. Then the payment of a marginal expenditure amount will tend to ensure that no family member suffers disproportionately owing to family breakdown or the allocation of responsibility for the parties' child, which is clearly a just result when the parties otherwise have equal incomes. However, when the pre-transfer incomes of the child's parents are substantially unequal, as is usually the case, marginal expenditure child support often produces results that are patently unjust. The amount of child support is often too high when the payor is the lower-income parent, for it may cause the payor to suffer greatly without achieving any commensurate benefit for anyone else. The amount of child support is often too low when the payor is the higher-income parent, for it may leave the child in poverty when the payor is comfortably off and well able to afford higher payments. The results in such cases cannot be understood to serve any coherent set of legal principles.

Chapter 3's search for legal principles begins with a close analysis of the often competing interests of the child, state, custodial parent, and non-custodial (payor) parent. It recognizes some of those interests as cognizable, but concludes that others should not be taken into account by the law of child support. Chapter 3 next weighs and balances the cognizable competing interests, and derives a set of objectives that a child support formula should seek to achieve. Addressed primarily to the state rule maker, chapter 3 sets out a methodology for developing a child support formula. It constructs tests to determine whether a contemplated formula meets its objectives across a broad variety of fact patterns. Finally, it proposes a formula designed to achieve chapter 3 objectives, and tested to ensure that it does. Essentially, the ALI formula begins with a marginal expenditure measure of child support, expressed as a percentage of obligor income, and augments or diminishes that percentage in relation to the absolute and relative pre-transfer incomes of the child's parents.[65] The 'adjustment mechanism' of the formula is mathe-

---

[64] For a history and critique of the marginal expenditure model of child support, see PRINCIPLES OF THE LAW OF FAMILY DISSOLUTION app § 3.05A cmt (Tentative Draft No. 3, 1998); see also Blumberg, n 63 above, at 67–8 and n 65, 93–5 and nn 124–7.

[65] *ibid* at § 3.05 (Tentative Draft No 3, 1998). The ALI formula was inspired by a variant approach to child support developed by Massachusetts and later adopted by the District of Columbia. See Commonwealth of Massachusetts Administrative Office of the Trial Court, Child Support Guidelines, effective Jan 1 1998; see also DC CODE ANN § 316–916.1. The ALI

matically calibrated to achieve appropriate results at any ratio of parent income inequality.

American law makes no distinction between child support obligations to marital and non-marital children.[66] However, with some notable exceptions,[67] most American jurisdictions sharply distinguish, for purposes of property distribution and spousal support, between the dissolution of marital and non-marital relationships. The former are regulated by family law; since the 1970s, the latter have been regulated by contract law in most jurisdictions.[68] The judicial application of contract law to the dissolution claims of non-marital cohabitants was welcomed as a liberal reform, but did not prove satisfactory in theory or practice.[69] The subject of non-marital relationships arose again in the 1990s as same-sex couples sought access to the incidents of marriage[70] and to the status of marriage itself, either directly or through the parallel institution of 'domestic partnership.' Following the lead of several states[71] and Canadian provinces,[72] the Principles adopt a status approach to non-marital cohabitation. Under chapter 6 of the Principles, '[d]omestic partners are two persons of the same or opposite sex, not married to one another, who for

child support formula uses the net (after tax) income of each parent, taking into account all other transfers required under the Principles and state support law. Thus for purposes of child support, compensatory payments are treated as income to the payee and are deducted from the income of the payor. *ibid* § 3.12.

[66] This is generally believed to be constitutionally compelled by the equal protection clause of the Fourteenth Amendment. *ibid* at § 3.01, Reporter's Notes.

[67] There are two varieties of exception. The twelve jurisdictions that still recognize common law marriage, generally by evidence of habit and reputation, effectively apply the law of marriage to informal cohabitation. See Ellman *et al*, n 27 above, at 60–9. Additionally, the states of Washington, Oregon, and Mississippi apply some or all of their marital property distribution law to non-marital relationships that socially resemble marriages. For case citations, see *ibid* at 963–7. The state of Washington has the most developed law. See *Connell v Francisco*, 898 P 2d 831 (Wash 1995).

[68] *Marvin v Marvin* is the leading case. See 557 P 2d 106 (Cal 1976). For a survey of state law treatment, *see* Ellman *et al*, n 27 above, at 929–6; see also Principles of the Law of Family Dissolution § 6.03 cmt b (Council Draft No 6, 1999).

[69] See *ibid* at § 6.03 cmt b and Reporter's Notes (Council Draft No 6, 1999); Grace Ganz Blumberg, *Cohabitation Without Marriage: A Different Perspective*, 28 UCLA L Rev 1125 (1981); Richard E. Denner, *Nonmarital Cohabitation after Marvin: In Search of a Standard*, 2 Cal Fam L Monthly 229 (1986) (California trial judge reflects on failure of *Marvin* to meet its promise).

[70] In the US, health care, old age provision, and other forms of social insurance are generally incidents of employment compensation. Ordinarily, an employee's family members are derivatively covered, often with little or no additional contribution. Traditionally, derivative coverage has been available only to an employee's 'lawful spouse' and minor children.   [71] See n 67 above.

[72] Ontario includes non-marital cohabitants in its statutory definition of 'spouse' for purposes of spousal support obligations. A 'spouse' includes: 'either of a man or a woman who are not married to each other and have cohabited, (a) continuously for a period of not less than three years, or (b) in a relationship of some permanence if they are the natural or adoptive parents of a child.' Ontario Family Law Reform Act of 1986, §§ 29 and 30, codified at RSO 1990, c F3, s 29 and s 30.

a significant period of time share a primary residence and a life together as a couple.'[73] The Principles treat domestic partners, for most purposes, as they do marital partners.

In the United States, the financial incidents of divorce may generally be varied, or waived entirely, by agreement. Thus, the legal principles regulating the dissolution of marital and non-marital relationships may be understood as default rules, which apply in the absence of the parties' agreement to the contrary. Although divorce courts have generally subjected premarital agreements to greater scrutiny than ordinary business contracts, from a comparative perspective[74] American law accords unusual deference to the parties' contractual autonomy. The Principles continue this general deference, limited only by measures intended to avoid egregious injustice at dissolution.[75]

This chapter has traced the law regulating the financial incidents of family breakdown during the second half of the twentieth century. Some developments, such as the movement from relatively unfettered judicial discretion to presumptively applicable or binding legal rules,

In *M and H*, a same-sex cohabitant challenged the Ontario statutory definition ('either of a man or a woman who are not married to each other and have cohabited') as violative of the equal protection guarantee of the Canadian Charter. The Supreme Court of Canada concluded that the exclusion of same-sex cohabitants is not rationally connected to the legislative objective of assuring adequate economic provision for cohabitants at the termination of their relationship. 1999 Can Sup Ct LEXIS 28.

See also Family Relations Act of British Columbia [RSBC 1996, as amended Oct 1 1998], ch 128, § 1 (for purposes of spousal support, a 'spouse' includes a person who 'lived with another person in a marriage-like relationship for a period of at least 2 years . . . and, for purposes of this Act, the marriage-like relationship may be between persons of the same gender').

[73] PRINCIPLES OF THE LAW OF FAMILY DISSOLUTION § 6.03(1), (Council Draft No 6, 1999).

[74] With American law, compare § 24 of the English Matrimonial Causes Act of 1973, which allows the divorce court to make 'an order varying for the benefit of the parties to the marriage and of the children of the family or either or any of them any ante-nuptial or post-nuptial settlement . . . notwithstanding that there are no children of the family.' British Columbia allows 'judicial reapportionment on the basis of fairness' when 'the provisions for division of property between the spouses under their marriage [including premarital] agreement . . . would be unfair having regard to' a broad variety of equitable factors. Family Relations Act of British Columbia [RSBC 1996], ch 128, § 65.

[75] PRINCIPLES OF THE LAW OF FAMILY DISSOLUTION ch 7 (Council Draft No 6, 1999). Section 7.05 sets entry requirements designed to ensure that the party or parties giving up rights had adequate knowledge of those rights and adequate time to make a reasoned choice. Section 7.07 requires that the divorce court take a 'second look' to ensure that a premarital or marital agreement does not work a 'substantial justice' (as defined by that section) when: (i) the marriage has been a long marriage (as defined by a rule of uniform application); (ii) a child has been born to, or adopted by, the parties; and (iii) when the circumstances of the parties have unforeseeably changed in ways that are significant to the agreement. In these three cases, a 'second look' at divorce is justified on both contractual and policy grounds. They involve circumstances the implications of which could not fully be appreciated when the contract was entered, and they are also the three cases about which the law of economic reordering at divorce is specially concerned. *ibid* at § 7.02 cmt.

may be understood as reactive and relatively disjunctive. Other developments appear to proceed logically, at least in retrospect, from earlier innovations and their internal tensions. For example, the Act's embrace of marital property distribution was intended as an egalitarian 'clean break' replacement for continuing spousal support. However, in rationalizing the measure in terms of the parties' 'partnership' and dividing property according to a host of equitable factors, with particular emphasis upon differentiated roles in marriage,[76] the Act paved the way for the Principles' treatment of property division and compensatory payments. The Principles' equal division of marital property takes the partnership metaphor to its logical conclusion, recognizing a species of equal ownership claim. Contradistinctively, the Principles' compensatory payments build upon the equitable factors identified by the Act for the guidance of the court in property distribution. Although family law's initial repudiation of sex-role stereotyping was accompanied by a contraction of spousal support, family law later recognized that spouses may nevertheless occupy different and complementary roles with respect to the family and labor force. This recognition was facilitated by a newly developing area of economics, the economics of the family,[77] which informed much of the literature and the law reform during the last quarter of the century. This branch of economics points out that role specialization in the family is often efficient, and economic efficiency (as opposed to sexual oppression) often explains why the earning power of the spouse who enters the marriage with greater earning power generally increases at the expense of the spouse who enters the marriage with lesser earning power.[78] In other words, even absent sex discrimination, the economics of the family create and explain spousal income inequalities, and those inequalities, because they are generated or exacerbated by family life, require equitable adjustment at dissolution. Thus the Principles end the century with a law of divorce that allows the parties free exit from marriage, but that may require one of them to accept continuing economic responsibility for the sequelae of the defunct marriage. In the quarter-century following the introduction of no-fault divorce, American law gradually came to recognize that no-fault need

---

[76] See nn 24–6 above and accompanying text.

[77] See Theodore Schultz (ed), ECONOMICS OF THE FAMILY: MARRIAGE, CHILDREN, AND HUMAN CAPITAL (1974); see also GARY BECKER, A TREATISE ON THE FAMILY (1981).

[78] The work of Becker, n 77 above, has been criticized because it may be read to assume a traditional worker–homemaker couple. See eg June Carbone and Margaret F. Brinig, *Rethinking Marriage: Feminist Ideology, Economic Change, and Divorce Reform*, 63 TUL L REV 953 (1991). However, Becker's analysis also explains the market and family behavior of spouses in two-earner marriages. See sources cited and discussed by ELLMAN *et al*, n 27 above, at 40–52.

Grace Ganz Blumberg

not imply 'no continuing economic responsibility,' and that the end of sex discrimination as a legal principle, and even as a factual matter, need not mean that full role equality in the family is possible or even, for many, desirable.[79] The Principles may be read to embody such an understanding.

[79] For an early articulation of this view, see Prager, n 25 above.

18

Post-divorce Financial Obligations

JOHN EEKELAAR

FAMILY, STATE, AND EMPLOYMENT

Surveying the evolution of Western European family law from the early nineteenth century, Harry Willekens[1] maintains that, despite surface national variations, there has been universal movement away from the pivotal role of legitimacy in determining parent–child relationships; from the marital and parental authority of husbands; from highly restrictive divorce; and from legal hostility to domestic cohabitation outside marriage. He finds an explanation in the evolution of the socio-economic structure of Western societies. Traditional family laws operated in societies where successful production depended on efficient family enterprises, centred on a secure marriage bond. But as income acquisition through employment spread, the economic incentives for the bonding of family groups through (almost) indissoluble marriage, legitimate status of children and paternal authority weakened. The logical result of this 'defamiliasation of capitalism' would be 'complete individualisation' (ie the absence of distinctive family obligations) were it not for 'the immaturity of the human infant, whose care to an extent binds at least one adult to him'. This has left the family with a residual 'social security' role: 'there would be no social *security* if a *full* and rapid exit from the relationship were possible and each partner could simply take his assets with him.'[2]

This analysis must be seen alongside that of Mary Ann Glendon,[3] who also remarks on 'attenuation' of the 'ties that support' in European and American families during the twentieth century, especially during the 1970s. The circle of family members owing each other support obligations narrowed; the former presumption that interspousal support obligations survive divorce was reversed; and, though child support obligations were retained after separation, their enforcement was feeble.[4] Glendon then contrasted those events with the *contemporaneous* increase in security provided by employment, noting the growing importance of benefits (in

---

[1] H. Willekens, 'Long Term Developments in Family Law in Western Europe: An Explanation', in John Eekelaar and Thandabantu Nhlapo (eds), *The Changing Family: International Perspectives on the Family and Family Law*. Hart Publishing (1998), ch 3.

[2] Willekens, n 1 above, 61, 65.

[3] M. A. Glendon, *The New Family and the New Property*. Toronto: Butterworths (1981) 11–13, 31.   [4] Glendon, n 3 above, 47.

particular, pensions) attached to specific employments. Individuals seemed to be becoming more bonded with their employment than with their marital partners. But Glendon did not see these new bonds as providing stable alternatives to those of the family.[5]

Glendon was right to be cautious, even sceptical, of the potential for government and employment-related benefits to *replace* family-based security. The emergence of a new economic order following policies associated with President Reagan and Prime Minister Thatcher, maintained up to the end of the century by Democrat and 'new' Labour administrations respectively, has diminished the social security role of the state and seen a change in the nature of employment. In the United States, 'roughly one in five workers saw his or her job disappear permanently during the 1980s'. Duration of unemployment spells grew. Increasing use was made of part-time, temporary, and contract employment.[6] Thus, although women's job tenure improved during this period as employment law improved safeguards to their jobs during pregnancy and maternity, the employment market into which they were entering was becoming increasingly harder to characterize as a form of 'bonding' between employer and employee. In view of this weakening of the relationship between individuals and the state, and between individuals and their employers, one might expect a corresponding movement towards reinforcing familial support obligations. A closer examination of the detailed evolution of the law, however, shows a more complex story.

It will be observed that the above discussion assumes that the relevant family support obligations are grounded in marriage. Until the last quarter of the century few, if any, would have imagined that, outside parent–child relationships (dealt with elsewhere), they could arise in any other way. It still remains the case at century-end that the occasion at which legal intervention has the most significant impact on support obligations between adults is on disssolution (or, rarely, annulment) of marriage. This, then, will be the focus of this chapter. However, it will be seen that, though the parties' marriage remains an important precondition for conferring jurisdiction to exercise legal powers, the underlying basis for the exercise of these powers has little do to with the marriage in itself.

---

[5] Glendon, n 3 above, 198. See also M. A. Glendon, *The Transformation of Family Law*. University of Chicago Press (1989) 29.
[6] Peter Capelli *et al*, *Change at Work*. New York: Oxford University Press (1997) chs 2 and 6.

THE POST-DIVORCE SUPPORT OBLIGATION: THE SEARCH FOR A RATIONALE

Mavis Maclean and I have argued[7] that the functional family operates to distribute resources between its members through a network of 'social' obligations which family members believe they 'ought to' comply with.[8] Parents' obligations to support their children were seen as being moral rather than legal. Whenever the weakening of these obligations has been perceived to threaten wider community interests, the state has intervened to strengthen their legal effect. Thus just as the disruption of agrarian working class family life during the sixteenth century pushed the Tudor state to attempt to reinforce these obligations by casting them in legal form through the poor laws,[9] so the increase in lone-parent families in the late twentieth century impelled the enactment of more rigorous child support laws.[10] Protection of individuals seemed less urgent. While a husband's obligation to support his wife has long been recognized by law, it was not capable of direct[11] enforcement by the wife until late in the nineteenth century, and then only in limited circumstances,[12] and even now the support obligation between married people who are still living together is seldom invoked. If a married couple separated, any support which an ecclesiastical court may have ordered in favour of the wife was not legally enforceable before 1813, and thereafter the remedies remained very weak, as they still are.[13] When judicial divorce was first introduced in England and Wales in 1858, its economic consequences for divorced women (and their children) and the community were not perceived to constitute a serious threat to the community, and the powers of the new divorce courts were initially very restricted. They could not make a direct order for maintenance out of the husband's income until 1866,[14] and could not attack his property at all (other than as security for income maintenance) until 1971. The basis for a post-divorce support obligation could no longer be the marital duty, because

---

[7] J. Eekelaar and M. Maclean, *Maintenance after Divorce*. Oxford: Oxford University Press (1986). J. Eekelaar and M. Maclean, 'The Evolution of Private Law Maintenance Obligations: the Common Law' in M. T. Meulders-Klein and J. Eekelaar (eds), *Family, State and Individual Economic Security*. Brussels: Story Scientia (1988), vol 1, ch 6.

[8] The importance of the interaction between social and legal obligations is developed in John Eekelaar, 'Uncovering Social Obligations: Family Law and the Responsible Citizen', in Mavis Maclean (ed), *Making Law for Families*. Oxford: Hart Publishing (2000).

[9] The Poor Law Act 1601 consolidated these measures.

[10] See p 206 above and p 544 above.

[11] *Indirect* enforcement was possible through the agency of necessity, but even this rested more on principles of agency than on the marital relationship.

[12] Matrimonial Causes Act 1878 (applicable only if wife assaulted by husband).

[13] For a full discussion, see J. Eekelaar, 'Family Solidarity in English Law', in D. Schwab and D. Henrich (eds), *Familiäre Solidarität*. Bielefeld: Gieseking (1997) 64–6.

[14] Matrimonial Causes Act 1866.

the parties were no longer spouses. Nor were there clearly discernible social obligations between formerly married spouses on which the judiciary could easily draw. Parliament provided no guidance, simply directing the court 'if it shall think fit' to make whatever order 'having regard to (the husband's) Fortune (if any), to the Ability of the Husband, and to the Conduct of the Parties it shall deem reasonable'.[15] However, three bases for making orders emerged. One was to provide some (seldom complete) recompense to a former wife whose personal property had (as the law then stood) passed to the husband on marriage. Two others looked to communal interests: to deter some men from abandoning their marital vows;[16] and to attempt to avert the risk of the former wife resorting to prostitution. If the former wife could look after herself, she could expect nothing.[17] The communal interest of supporting marriage was reflected in another feature of what became known as the 'ancillary' jurisdiction, namely, that, although financial agreements reached in the context of separation were valid,[18] it was dangerous to make them because their presence raised suspicions that the divorce was consensual, which could lead to a dismissal of the suit.

The courts did not therefore simply project the 'marital support' obligation beyond the termination of the marriage. In some early cases the courts adopted an approach occasionally used by ecclesiastical courts in judicial separation cases awarding a wife one-third of the joint income of the couple prior to separation, but this was later 'quietly abandoned' in favour of a broad discretion.[19] The debates around divorce in the first half of the twentieth century centred on the grounds for divorce, not its economic effects. The Report of the 1956 Royal Commission on Marriage and Divorce made no serious investigation of the post-divorce circumstances of women and children, merely quoting 'a number of witnesses' who 'suggested that the effect of the present law is to encourage a (former) wife to live in idleness for the rest of her life on the maintenance paid by her husband or former husband'.[20] The debates

---

[15] Divorce and Matrimonial Causes Act 1857, s 32.

[16] See Lord Penzance in *Sidney v Sidney* (1865) 4 Sw & Tr 178: 'Those for whom shame has no dread, honourable vows no tie, and violence to the weak no sense of degradation, may still be held in check by their love of money.'

[17] *Robertson v Robertson* (1883) 8 P & D 94.   [18] *Hunt v Hunt* (1862) 4 De G F & J 221.

[19] See the classic account by J. L. Barton, 'The Enforcement of Financial Provisions', in R. H. Graveson and F. R. Crane (eds), *A Century of Family Law*. London: Sweet & Maxwell (1957) ch 14. But although not prominent in judgments, the one-third rule may have been widely used in practice, and was still used by some practitioners at the end of the century as a general guide to eligibility for spousal support: see Stephen Cretney, 'Trusting the Judges: Money after Divorce', in M. D. A. Freeman (ed), *Current Legal Problems 1999*. Oxford: Oxford University Press (1999), 286, at 288.

[20] See *Report of the Royal Commission on Marriage and Divorce 1951–55* (Chairman: Lord Morton: London, HMSO, Cmd 9678, 1956), para 485.

leading to the enactment of the Divorce Reform Act 1969 concentrated on the issues of fault and the sanctity of marriage, although some concern was expressed that the new no-fault ground of divorce after five years' separation might lead husbands to abandon their wives without adequate provision.[21] The Act allowed a court to refuse to dissolve a marriage on that ground if doing so would result in 'grave financial or other hardship to him and that it would in all the circumstances be wrong to dissolve the marriage'.[22] These worries raised for the first time the perception that post-divorce life for women might entail economic hardship, and highlighted the clash between the growing acceptance of freedom to divorce and its impact on family support obligations. Nevertheless, the belief that it might be possible to ensure compliance with those obligations by denying divorce for a broken marriage (thus maintaining the fiction of a functioning economic unit) was disappointed and there is no evidence that the power to withhold a decree had any effect on the general economic position of divorced women, although it might have given some wives an additional bargaining counter in a very few cases.[23]

Until the Divorce Reform Act 1969 came into effect on 1 January 1971, the powers of the courts to deal with finance and property on divorce, and the principles on which they exercised those powers, had been virtually unchanged since the nineteenth century. The duty to provide *income* support fell on the husband, not the wife; the court could attack the *property* of a guilty wife (settling it in favour of the husband or children) but could make no order against the husband's property. Although since 1859 courts could vary an ante- or post-nuptial settlement made in favour of either the husband or wife, the purpose was largely to allow courts access to property which would normally have been settled on the wife at marriage. In 1963 the courts acquired the additional power to order lump sum payments, but this was seen as providing an alternative, or supplement, to income support, and not a means of redistributing property between former spouses. The introduction of the new divorce law in 1971 provided an occasion for reform, and recommendations by the Law Commission[24] were enacted in the Matrimonial Proceedings and Property Act 1970. There were three major strands in the reforms. First, the law was henceforth to be expressed in gender-neutral terms. Second, the previously unguided

---

[21] These concerns were expressed particularly by Lady Summerskill. See B. H. Lee, *Divorce Reform in England*. London: Peter Owen (1974) 201.

[22] Divorce Reform Act 1969, s 4(2).

[23] An example is *K v K (financial relief: widow's pension)* [1997] 1 FLR 35.

[24] Law Commission, *Family Law: Report on Financial Provision in Matrimonial Proceedings*, Law Com No 25. London: HM Stationery Office (1969).

discretion was given a statutory objective that, having taken into account a range of factors, the court should 'place the parties, so far as is practicable and, having regard to their conduct, just to do so, in the financial position in which they would have been if the marriage had not broken down and each had properly discharged his or her financial obligations and responsibilities towards the other' (sometimes called the 'minimal loss' principle). The third conferred on courts general powers to order the transfer of property from one former spouse the to other.[25]

The first strand coincided with the ideology of gender equality emerging in the 1960s. The second seems to have been thought to be no more than an encapsulation of the then current law, though this was probably a mistake.[26] It can be seen as a continuation of the perception that this part of the law should continue to serve the wider social goal of discouraging divorce, for if no-fault divorce now removed this function from the divorce law itself, the notion that married people should nevertheless be held to their contractual obligations *of support* could be seen as an alternative way of upholding the obligations of marriage. This is supported by the fact that the Commissioners considered that entitlement should be related to an evaluation of marital conduct.[27] The courts at first tried to do this.[28] But, in what was perceived as a change in policy in 1973, the Court of Appeal laid down that conduct should be relevant only if 'obvious and gross'.[29] As time went on, courts refused to allow 'matrimonial' misconduct, except of the most extreme kind, to be raised in the settlement of financial and property issues, and practitioners strongly discouraged it.[30] Without this qualification, the 'minimal loss' principle came under increasing strain during the 1970s and by the early 1980s was seen as being impractical to achieve, inconsistent with the 'right' to divorce, and unfair on husbands. It was seldom applied in practice.

Thus during the 1970s the law of post-divorce financial obligations began to lose whatever was left of its role in attempting to influence marital behaviour and to assume a strongly pragmatic character, designed to 'make the best' of the circumstances that had arisen for all the parties. Of great practical significance in this process was the acquisition of judicial power to redistribute property. The Commission seemed unaware of its potential impact, but during the 1970s it became clear that

---

[25] Another reform was that maintenance orders for former spouses were to cease automatically on the remarriage of that spouse. Previously this was achieved by variation.

[26] Eekelaar and Maclean (1986), n 7 above, 11–12.

[27] See the discussion by S. M. Cretney, 'The Maintenance Quagmire', (1970) 33 *Modern Law Review* 662, 667–8.   [28] *Ackerman v Ackerman* [1972] Fam 225.

[29] *Wachtel v Wachtel* [1973] Fam 72.

[30] See John Eekelaar, *Regulating Divorce*, Oxford: Clarendon Press (1991) 87: 'The registrars, almost with one voice, proclaimed that arguments about misconduct were a thing of the past. Many were unable to think of any instances.'

the ability of the court to transfer a husband's interest in the matrimonial home to the wife, either absolutely or for a limited period (for example, while the children were still at school, or until she remarried[31]), would transform the bargaining power of women on divorce. Women have generally been more inclined to initiate divorce proceedings than men because it is normally they who require the protection of the law or the capacity to recover economic security through remarriage, but during the 1970s this tendency vastly increased.[32] This may partly be explained by their growing participation in the work-force,[33] but the effect of this factor must have been diminished by the fact that in the last third of the century only about half of *divorced* women with dependent children have been in paid employment,[34] and then with generally low wages. But consider the effect of the new power to transfer property. In 1952 a leading divorce judge stated that, on divorce, the wife would 'inevitably have to leave the home'.[35] By 1977 a registrar (the judicial officer who most commonly dealt with these matters, later called a District Judge) said with respect to the objectives of post-divorce settlement: 'the main criterion should be that the children should remain in the home and this can be managed in most cases.'[36] This period also saw a sharp rise in owner-occupation, from 52 per cent of homes in 1971 to 67 per cent in 1994,[37] so it became much more common for a mother to remain in the home with the children.[38] If the mother were unemployed, her security was assisted by the willingness of the Department of Social Security to meet the interest of mortgage

---

[31] *Mesher v Mesher* [1980] 1 All ER 126 (case decided in 1973); *Martin v Martin* [1978] Fam 12; *Clutton v Clutton* [1991] 1 All ER 340.

[32] Total divorce petitions increased by 83% between 1969 and 1971; those by husbands by 96.6% and those by wives by 74.9%. Between 1971 and 1981, the total number of petitions increased by 53.6%; those by husbands by 5.5% and those by wives by 85.5%. Calculations based on *Civil Judicial Statistics* and *Judicial Statistics* in relevant years.

[33] Women constituted 34% of the workforce in Britain in 1966 and 43% in 1991. Between 1961 and 1991 the proportion of *married* women in work or seeking it rose from 30 to 53%. See Rosemary Crompton, *Women and Work in Modern Britain*. Oxford: Oxford University Press (1997) 25–7. See also Ellman, Ch 15 of this volume.

[34] There may have been an increase in unemployment of divorced lone mothers towards the end of the century: compare Eekelaar and Maclean (1986), n 7 above, 89 (44% of divorced lone mothers unemployed); Maclean and Eekelaar, *The Parental Obligation*. Oxford: Hart Publishing (1997)114: (56% non-repartnered formerly married mothers unemployed). The differences may however reflect different sampling frames.

[35] *Murcutt v Murcutt* [1952] P 266 at 271.

[36] J. Eekelaar and E. Clive, with S. Raikes, *The Matrimonial Jurisdiction of Registrars*. Oxford: SSRC Centre for Socio-Legal Studies, Wolfson College, Oxford (1977) 37.

[37] L. Fox Harding, *Family, State and Social Policy*. London: Macmillan (1994) 148.

[38] Data from the 1970s revealed that former wives in owner-occupation stayed in the home after divorce in 26% of cases: J. Eekelaar and M. Maclean, 'Financial Provision on Divorce: A Reappraisal', in Michael D. A. Freeman (ed), *State, Law and Family: Critical Perspectives*. London: Tavistock Publications and Sweet & Maxwell (1984) 214. In the 1990s the proportion had increased to 48%: Maclean and Eekelaar, n 8 above, 112. The proportions in rented accommodation who stayed remained about the same (around 80%).

payments and of mortgage lenders to accept this arrangement. However, the benefits of owner-occupation declined during the early 1990s. The steep fall in the housing market resulted in the resale value of many houses falling below the debt owed to the mortgage lender. But the effect of this may have been to some women's advantage, for, instead of selling the home at a loss, it was better for all concerned for her to remain in it, at least until the housing market improved.[39] However, in 1995 social security payments of mortgage interest were severely restricted, causing divorced women to look to the former husband to service the mortgage.[40]

As the divorce rate rose during the 1970s,[41] divorce increasingly resulted in the loss by men of the occupation of their homes.[42] The new pragmatic, non-judgmental, stance of the law appeared to divorced men and their second families to be operating against their interests, and this sense of injustice found expression in 1978 in the creation of the Campaign for Justice in Divorce. In 1980, its call for reform was met by a Discussion Paper from the Law Commission,[43] which generated extensive public debate. In 1981 the Law Commission made recommendations. It was persuaded that the 'minimal loss' objective should be formally removed. However, it forcefully stated that to remove it without doing more would 'involve an abdication of responsibility by Parliament in favour of the judiciary. Individual judges would be left to achieve whatever they subjectively regarded as "just" without any guidance as to the principles by which the justice of the case should be determined.'[44] It proposed that guidance should be provided in the following manner: first, the provision of adequate financial support for children should be an 'overriding priority'; and, second, increased weight should be given to 'the desirability of the parties becoming self-sufficient', which should be 'formulated as a positive principle'.[45] In 1984 the Matrimonial and Family Proceedings Act removed the 'minimal loss' objective. However, instead of enacting that the provision of financial support for children should be an 'overriding priority', the Act simply stated that the courts were to give

---

[39] There is evidence that fewer owner-occupied houses were sold on divorce in the 1990s than twenty years earlier: 37% as against 46%. See Maclean and Eekelaar, n 34 above, 112 (divorcing couples with children only).

[40] Nick Wikeley, 'Income Support and Mortgage Interest Revisited', (1999) 29 *Family Law* 702.

[41] In 1969, 54,151 divorce decrees nisi were granted; in 1980, there were 150,385.

[42] It has been found that many formerly married fathers whose former wives stayed in the owner-occupied sector 'fared worse than the mothers and children' and 'take considerable time to return to that sector': Maclean and Eekelaar, n 34 above, 112–13.

[43] Law Commission, *Family Law: The Financial Consequences of Divorce: The Basic Policy—A Discussion Paper*, Law Com No. 103. London: HM Stationery Office (1980).

[44] Law Commission, *Family Law: The Financial Consequences of Divorce*, Law Com No 103. London: HM Stationery Office (1981), para 18.

[45] Law Commission, n 44 above, paras 24, 27, 46.

'first consideration' to the 'welfare while a minor of any child of the family who has not attained the age of eighteen'.[46] Nor was self-sufficiency proclaimed as a 'positive principle'. The courts were simply put under a duty to 'consider' whether it would be 'appropriate', when exercising their powers, 'so to exercise those powers that the financial obligations of each party towards the other will be terminated as soon after the grant of the decree as the court considers just and reasonable'.[47] Parliament in effect threw the matter to the discretion of the courts. But the prevailing ethos suggested the advent of a new dispensation: post-divorce dependence by former wives on their erstwhile husbands was to be replaced by the values of self-sufficiency and self-determination. The new pragmatism was not only to operate to protect the children in the family home, but also to require their mothers to make the best of job opportunities in the employment market. This might have marked a decisive step in the transition foreseen by Glendon from family-based support to reliance on the employment market. However, the events seem more complex.

THE 'CLEAN BREAK': THE LIGHT THAT FAILED?

The 'new dispensation' which received statutory recognition in the Matrimonial and Family Proceedings Act 1984 was often summarized in the expression: the 'clean break'. This had received the approval of the House of Lords in 1979, where Lord Scarman said:

'There are two principles which inform the modern legislation. One is the public interest that spouses, to the extent that their means permit, should provide for themselves and their children. But the other, of equal importance, is the principle of the 'clean break'. The law now encourages spouses to avoid bitterness after family breakdown and to settle their money and property problems. An object of the modern law is to encourage the parties to put the past behind them and to begin a new life which is not overshadowed by the relationship which has broken down.[48]

The idea of the 'clean break' incorporates three elements: self-determination, self-sufficiency, and finality. The issue of finality is relevant to each of the first two elements, which will be considered separately.

---

[46] Now Matrimonial Causes Act 1973, s 25(1). The Court of Appeal ruled that 'first consideration' does not require giving those interests priority: *Suter v Suter & Jones* [1987] 2 All ER 336.   [47] Matrimonial Causes Act 1973, s 25A(1); see also s 25A(2).
[48] *Minton v Minton* [1979] AC 593 at 608.

Self-determination

The idea that it is preferable for the parties, rather than an external agency, to determine their post-divorce obligations is one of the most profound revolutions of late twentieth-century family law. It has already been remarked[49] that the earlier legislative goal of supporting marriage deterred consensual agreements over post-divorce issues. It probably explains the longstanding practice of settling financial and property matters *after* the divorce is granted.[50] However, after the 1971 reform allowed consensual divorce, the objection to collusion disappeared and the practice grew of presenting draft agreements to the court for approval before the divorce was granted, to be incorporated in Consent Orders made on or after that event. The advantages of agreements being incorporated in court orders were that they became enforceable as court orders rather than as private contracts, and finality was more assured. From the 1970s, then, there has been a rapid rise in the number of court orders made 'ancillary' to divorce proceedings, most of them by consent,[51] generating official alarm at the growing 'costs' of divorce.

Consistent with the general diminution of state supervision over domestic arrangements, the history of the last quarter of the century has been of progressive withdrawal of the courts from supervision over the contents of financial and property agreements. During the 1970s it was assumed that judges would 'investigate' claims made in applications for financial and property orders (even where made by consent),[52] and in 1984 the House of Lords made a similar assumption.[53] But the 1984 Act allowed the courts to form a conclusion on the basis of submitted documents alone, and in 1987 Lord Oliver stated that the primary duty for ensuring the genuineness of the agreement 'must lie on those concerned with the negotiation and drafting of the terms of the order'.[54] The Family Law Act 1996 is premised on this approach. In a clear break from tradition, the new divorce scheme set out in that Act permits the parties to obtain any necessary financial and property order *before* the divorce is granted and generally prevents courts from pronouncing

---

[49] See above at p 408.

[50] For fuller accounts see Richard Ingleby, 'Rhetoric and Reality: Regulation of Out-of-Court Activity in Matrimonial Proceedings', (1989) 9 *Oxford Journal of Legal Studies* 230; J. Eekelaar, 'A Jurisdiction in Search of a Mission: Family Proceedings in England and Wales', (1994) 57 *Modern Law Review* 839.

[51] In 1974 the ratio of 'ancillary orders' to divorce decrees was 1 : 3. In 1981 it was 1 : 1.5: Legal Aid Advisory Committee, *Thirty-second Annual Report* (Lord Chancellor's Department, 1982) HC 189. [52] See Matrimonial Proceedings Rules 1977, Rule 77(5).

[53] *Livesey v Jenkins* [1985] 1 All ER 106.

[54] *Dinch v Dinch* [1987] 1 All ER 818 at 821, asserting a position criticized in *Livesey v Jenkins*, n 49 above.

the divorce unless these issues have been settled. But little effort is made to ensure judicial supervision over the content of such settlements. To obtain a divorce order, the parties need only *produce* a Consent Order, a negotiated agreement, a declaration that 'they have made their financial arrangements', or even a declaration that they have no significant assets and that 'there are therefore no financial arrangements to be made'.[55] The scheme had not, however, been introduced by 2000, and it is unclear whether a party will be permitted to reopen issues apparently settled in these ways after the divorce is granted. During the late 1970s and early 1980s Lord Justice Ormrod favoured retaining 'maximum flexibility' which would allow courts to overturn agreements or orders when these turned out to be disadvantageous to a vulnerable party.[56] But other judges were less sympathetic[57] and in 1996 the Court of Appeal laid down very stringent conditions for overturning a Consent Order.[58] Little else than non-disclosure of material matters would permit a review. Similarly, although agreements reached in the course of negotiation prior to settling on the terms of a Consent Order have been held not to be contractually binding,[59] in order to prevent unnecessary costs, courts will be reluctant to allow parties to depart from terms they have apparently settled.[60]

However, despite its apparent ascendancy, the self-determination principle is subject to a significant qualification. It is well settled that parties cannot oust the jurisdiction of the court in matters of child support, so where the interests of children are involved, it is usually possible to reopen agreed settlements.[61] Furthermore, the scope for self-determination is limited by the Child Support Acts 1991–5 which settle the amount of child support payable by a formula details of which are given by Maclean in Chapter 24 of this volume. Nevertheless, unless one of the parties is receiving social security benefits, it is not obligatory to use the child support scheme, and many divorcing parties incorporate provisions for child maintenance in a Consent Order.

Self-sufficiency

As stated earlier, during the 1970s the perception grew that divorced men were unfairly treated, and, in particular, that divorced wives were

[55] Family Law Act 1996, s 9.
[56] *Dipper v Dipper* [1981] Fam 31; *Camm v Camm* (1982) 4 FLR 577.
[57] See eg *Edgar v Edgar* [1980] 3 All ER 887.
[58] *Harris v Manahan* [1996] 4 All ER 456. It would be easier to vary an order which was still running, for example, by extending a time limit.
[59] See criticisms by Hoffmann LJ in *Pounds v Pounds* [1994] 4 All ER 777 at 792.
[60] *Xydhias v Xydhias* [1999] 2 All ER 386.
[61] *Minton v Minton* [1979] 1 All ER 79 at 87; *Crozier v Crozier* [1994] Fam 114; *N v N (Consent Order: Variation)* [1993] 2 FLR 868 at 884.

continuing to rely on the resources of their former husbands rather than support themselves in the labour market. The Matrimonial and Family Proceedings Act 1984 therefore required courts to consider the appropriateness of terminating financial obligations between the parties as soon after the divorce as reasonable, and whether to put a time limit on maintenance orders, with a power to exclude subsequent review. Whereas it had previously only been possible to bar later attempts to review an order if this was agreed,[62] finality could now be imposed *whether or not this was agreeable to both parties*. But empirical research, first published in 1984, demonstrated that the perception was misplaced. It was shown that maintenance was rarely ordered for divorced women, and that when it was, it was almost always confined to women who were, or had been, looking after children (that is, they were divorced *mothers*) and that, as most of them were receiving social security benefits, any maintenance paid mostly went directly to the state. Far from being a substitute for earned income and a deterrent to employment, maintenance payments were invariably of benefit to the recipient only if she was in employment, when they could provide a modest supplement to low earnings (thus possibly providing some *incentive* to work).[63] So it appeared that the preoccupation of the instigators of the 1984 Act with the self-sufficiency of former wives overlooked facts about the economic position of children and their carers after parental divorce.

In fact, judicial practice showed an appreciation of those realities. Cases reported in the 1970s indicated that the courts attempted first to ensure adequate accommodation for the children of the marriage, and then that the needs of each spouse be met as far as possible. The needs were those arising from caring for children, from having to adapt to the labour market after a lengthy stay at home or from being too old, at marriage breakdown, to become fully self-supporting.[64] Much the same picture was revealed in cases after the 1984 Act was passed, and the desire among registrars (District Judges) to keep the home for the children appeared to be even stronger.[65] The view that women whose children were old enough should seek employment had, however, strengthened, but judges remained unwilling to make an order preventing a young mother who was caring for children or middle-aged mother who had completed that role from returning to the court for a review if

---

[62] *Dipper v Dipper* [1981] Fam 31.

[63] Eekelaar and Maclean (1986), n 7 above. The publication of these findings coincided with similar findings in the US: Lenore Weitzman, *The Divorce Revolution: The Unexpected Social and Economic Consequences for Women and Children in America*. New York: The Free Press (1985).

[64] J. Eekelaar, 'Some Principles of Financial and Property Adjustment on Divorce', (1979) 95 *Law Quarterly Review* 253. 					[65] Eekelaar, n 30 above, 71.

circumstances changed.[66] Appreciative of the persistent nature of the consequences of divorce, courts were reluctant to finalize matters too hastily.

However, the number of spousal maintenance orders made on divorce dropped from 29,617 in 1985 to 17,193 in 1994 (over this period the number of divorces dropped from 157,491 to 154,873). The number of property orders rose slightly (from 27,216 to 30,996).[67] It is evident that spousal maintenance orders, always relatively rare, are made in only a very few divorce cases. But this is not inconsistent with the policy stated above since nearly half of divorces do not involve children under 16, and many divorces are of second marriages. Still, capital awards are becoming more common. To these we now turn.

ASSET REDISTRIBUTION

From 1882 husbands and wives have held all their property independently of one another. Since land and other capital assets have tended to be owned by husbands rather than wives, the consequence was a serious imbalance in economic power between spouses. Deech[68] has pointed out that, while the marriage remained legally intact, wives were protected in their occupation of the home because they could not be expelled by their husbands. But they stayed very much on his terms. They would lose the protection if they 'misbehaved'[69] and during World War II it was judicially stated that a wife was bound to follow her husband to a home of his choosing.[70] She had no protection if he sold the house to a third party without her knowledge, and the third party sought to evict her.[71] Nor could she prevent the husband putting the home at risk by securing a charge on it; she might know nothing of the transaction. The position has been transformed over the last quarter of the century. First, in *Williams & Glyn's Bank v Boland*,[72] the House of Lords held that if a person with a beneficial interest in a house that was registered in the name of another is in 'actual occupation' at the time a third party acquires an interest in it, the third party takes subject to that interest. Since it is often difficult to know whether an occupier has a beneficial interest, it has become standard conveyancing practice to obtain from the person in

---

[66] For examples, see *Clutton v Clutton* [1991] 1 All ER 340; *M v M* [1987] 2 FLR 1; *Waterman v Waterman* [1989] 1 FLR 380; *Flavell v Flavell* [1997] 1 FLR 353 at 358.

[67] Figures from *Judicial Statistics* in relevant years.

[68] Ruth Deech 'Matrimonial Property and Divorce: Century of Progress?', in Michael D. A. Freeman (ed), *State, Law and Family: Critical Perspectives*. London: Tavistock (1984) ch 15.

[69] *Gurasz v Gurasz* [1970] P 11.   [70] *King v King* [1942] P. 1 at 8.

[71] *National Provincial Bank v Ainsworth* [1965] AC 1175.   [72] [1981] AC 487.

occupation a waiver of any rights they may have. So any cohabitant will now invariably have knowledge of such an attempted transaction[73] and can prevent it by refusing to co-operate.[74] But these measures protect occupation; they do not confer rights to capital value. In the first two decades after the end of World War II the courts tried to respond to the gradual increase in home ownership by manipulating the law of trusts in such a way as to allow some wives to acquire a proprietary interest in the capital value of the house.[75] But this involved difficult questions of proving financial contributions or something equivalent, and these efforts became irrelevant when the courts acquired their wide powers to reallocate property between divorced spouses in 1971.

In exercising those powers, courts are expressly required to have regard to (amongst other things) 'the contributions which each of the parties has made or is likely in the foreseeable future to make to the welfare of the family, including any contribution by looking after the home and caring for the family'.[76] The permission to include domestic contributions certainly assisted courts to transfer the ownership of the matrimonial home from husbands to wives,[77] or to order sale of the home and share the proceeds between the divorcing parties.[78] But courts have been very reluctant to allocate former wives a share in their husband's *business* assets unless they had been actively engaged in the enterprise.[79] So the approach was very far from one of liquidating a general partnership with equality as a starting point.[80] The decisions are dominated by references to 'needs', although this was given an 'elastic' interpretation deriving from Lord Justice Ormrod in the sense of 'requirements'.[81] This allowed account to be taken of the applicant's accustomed standard of

---

[73] The occupying spouse was also given a right to register 'occupation rights' by the Matrimonial Homes Act 1967, which would bind third parties. But such registrations are unusual, and the *Boland* case gives better protection in practice, which extends to the unmarried.

[74] However, it has been empirically shown that women characteristically find it very difficult to oppose their partners in such deals, even if they believe them improvident, and even if the partner requires the woman to offer *her own* interest in the home as security: see Belinda Fehlberg, *Sexually Transmitted Debt: Surety Experience and English Law*. Oxford: Clarendon Press (1997).

[75] The cases stretch from *Re Roger's Question* [1948] 1 All ER 328 to *Gissing v Gissing* [1971] AC 886.   [76] Matrimonial Causes Act 1973, s 25 (2)(f).

[77] See *Wachtel v Wachtel* [1973] Fam 72.

[78] The power to order sale was acquired in 1981: Matrimonial Homes and Property Act 1981, s 7; later Matrimonial Causes Act 1973, s 24A.

[79] *Trippas v Trippas* [1973] 2 All ER 1 at 4–5; *Page v Page* (1981) 2 FLR 198; *Preston v Preston* [1982] 1 All ER 41 at 47.

[80] See *W v W* [1995] 2 FLR 259 (although the relationship lasted fifty-five years, because the wife did not contribute directly to the build-up of assets, equality was not an appropriate starting point for division).   [81] *O'D v O'D* [1976] Fam 83.

living.[82] In truth, once the primary needs of the children and their carer were dealt with, the basis upon which surplus assets might be carved up was very unclear. Courts would attempt to give restitution if a former spouse had contributed materially to building them up, but beyond that the fluid notion of 'contributions' allowed courts to throw into the decision-making 'pot' anything from the length of the relationship to the moral qualities of the parties.[83] There was vacillation as to whether to use one-third, two-thirds, or equality as a 'starting point', or whether any starting point was appropriate at all. So in *Dart v Dart*[84] a wife (after fourteen years marriage) obtained £9 million from a totality of £400 million, it being thought that this sum would have catered adequately for her 'reasonable requirements'. (It was believed she would have been awarded £100 million had the case been determined by a Michigan court.) The court appeared to ignore her 'domestic' contributions, though four years earlier Purchas LJ rejected any distinction between wives who contributed directly to their husbands' business and those who supplied the 'infrastructure and support in the context of which the husband is able to work hard, prosper and accumulate his wealth'.[85] While the principles, and indeed outcomes, of this discretionary system had stabilized well before the 1990s with respect to the vast number of divorces in a manner which permitted fine tuning by negotiation to stretch resources to cover, as far as they could, the essential needs of the children and their carer and also of the other party (usually the former husband), a significant minority of cases in which there were additional assets appeared to have no stable basis for decision.

CLARIFICATION OF THE NEW DISPENSATION AND RE-EMERGENCE OF OLD WORRIES

A number of apparently disparate issues appeared to converge as the century drew to its close. Ministerial agitation over costs of divorce settlements, especially in financial and property matters, has been discussed elsewhere in this volume.[86] These worries were partly based upon a belief that the discretionary system encouraged litigation, or, at least, excessive negotiation, although this has not been empirically proved. Nevertheless, it led to governmental suggestions that parties

---

[82] *F v F* [1995] 2 FLR 45.   [83] *Boylan v Boylan* [1988] 1 FLR 282; *A v A* [1998] 2 FLR 180.
[84] [1996] 2 FLR 286; [1997] 1 FLR 21.
[85] *Vicary v Vicary* [1992] 2 FLR 271. Although this was approved in *Conran v Conran* [1997] 2 FLR 615, where the wife was awarded £10.4 million, leaving her husband with £75 million, despite having made a substantial direct contribution to the husband's fortunes.
[86] See Mavis Maclean, Ch 24 of this volume.

should be enabled to predetermine these issues by binding ante-nuptial contracts and, failing that, that there should be presumptive equal property division. These ideas seemed over-simplistic, and were eventually presented with heavy modifications. Antenuptial agreements would not be binding in any cases where there were minor children of the marriage, and equal property division would occur only after provision had been made for the accommodation of the parties and their children.[87] If enacted, the law of post-divorce settlements would take on an interesting shape. Where there were no children, the parties would be free (subject to various safeguards) to control the outcome in advance. Since the safeguards proposed are fairly extensive, it would seem likely that this would only be used by couples quite resolutely set against having children. Cases involving children would be governed by the default rules, including the equal sharing of marital property once accommodation had been secured. Since the evolution of the law described above shows the centrality of child rearing to the content of the orders made by courts, this development carries the policy further by recognizing the joint upbringing of children as being sufficient in itself to warrant a claim to a share (indeed, an equal share) in the totality of family assets. Although set out in the context of marriage, the underlying logic is inescapable: it is the presence of children, rather than the fact of marriage, which grounds the claim.[88] This avoids perceiving the post-divorce obligation as representing a conflict between female dependency and self-sufficiency, a perception which dominated earlier debates,[89] by now grounding obligation on entitlement earned by work expended on a common project. The approach was well expressed by Hale J late in 1999 when awarding ongoing maintenance to a former wife of a marriage of twenty-nine years which had produced four children: 'It was a classic example of the sort of case where the wife . . . gave up her place in the world of work to concentrate upon her husband, her home and her family. That must have been a mutual decision from which they both benefited . . . Over the many years of that marriage she *must have built up an entitlement to some compensation for that.*'[90]

The move towards a property-sharing approach was anticipated in discussions about pension rights. Since these vested only on retirement,

---

[87] *Supporting Families: A Consultation Document* (the Stationery Office, October 1998), paras 4.20–3 and 4.44–9.

[88] Hence similar orders may be made between unmarried parents, though there the property must revert to its original owner when the children have grown up: *J. v C. (child: financial provision)* [1999] 1 FLR 152.

[89] R. Deech, 'The Principles of Maintenance', (1977) 7 *Family Law* 229; K. O'Donovan, 'Legal Recognition of the Value of Housework', (1978) 8 *Family Law* 215; C. Smart, 'Regulating Families or Legitimating Patriarchy? Family Law in Britain', (1982) 10 *International Journal of the Sociology of Law* 129.

[90] *SRJ v DWJ* [1999] 2 FLR 176 at 182 (emphasis supplied).

the courts could not reallocate them if divorce preceded that event. In so far as they were considered at all, practitioners might award a divorcing wife a larger share of the capital assets to make up for her lost prospects of sharing in her husband's pension. The Pensions Act 1995 gave courts the power, on divorce, to order a portion of a pension to be 'earmarked' for payment to a former spouse, but this payment was contingent on the pensioner reaching retirement age, and (his) circumstances at that time.[91] After considerable pressure, the Conservative Government accepted the principle of pension-splitting, which allows the payment of the accrued value of a pension at the time of divorce, and the Labour Government empowered courts to order payment of the money equivalent of the accrued value of pension entitlements on divorce, though this will occur within the discretionary framework discussed above.[92] There is no automatic equal division.

As the turn of the century approached, there were renewed worries about the health of the institution of marriage and there was some suggestion that the law on post-divorce financial provision might again be used to strengthen it. For example, a provision (which has been implemented) of the Family Law Act 1996[93] could be interpreted as requiring courts to place greater weight on matrimonial misconduct when making post-divorce financial awards, although there is no evidence this is having any effect in practice. However, most of the measures contemplated are administrative, such as the encouragement of mediation and the proposal to introduce information meetings for parties contemplating divorce.[94] As far as the law on financial provision is concerned, the disjuncture between the formal basis of the law (dissolution of marriage) and its underlying substance (sharing of resources acquired during a failed common enterprise—specifically the task of beginning to bring up a child) seems to be becoming more visible. The extension of the substance in due course to unmarried cohabitants who also have children seems irresistible. The basis of this new dispensation seems to be that the law of post-divorce obligations should not be used to pursue the goals of upholding marital relationships. Rather, the law should first look to securing the circumstances of children when any relationship breaks down, then to making sure (if possible) that the role of the children's carer is properly recognized, and that includes characterizing that role as one which generates entitlements to capital or, in some cases, to ongoing support. Beyond that, parties will be given wide freedom to determine their own interests.

---

[91] These uncertainties are a considerable deterrent against making such orders: *T v T (financial relief: pensions)* [1998] 2 FCR 364

[92] Welfare Reform and Pensions Act 1999, Parts III, IV and Sch 3.

[93] Family Law Act 1996. Sch 8, cl 9.   [94] See Smart, Ch 16 in this volume.

19

The Status of Children:
A Story of Emerging Rights

BARBARA BENNETT WOODHOUSE

INTRODUCTION

'A prime part of the history of our Constitution,' according to United States Supreme Court Justice Ruth Bader Ginsburg, 'is the story of the extension of constitutional rights and protections to people once ignored or excluded.'[1] This chapter of *Cross Currents* tells a small part of this story, the gradual extension of rights to children and young people, and envisions its continuing development in the years to come. One source of emerging rights is the United States Constitution, with its Bill of Rights and especially its Fourteenth Amendment.[2] It influences children's status indirectly, by placing limits on the powers of state legislatures and courts to invade the privacy and autonomy of the family. But the Constitution does not tell the whole story. As central as the Constitution may be to American law, no one source of law provides a comprehensive picture of children's status in America. In fact, laws on custody, emancipation, and family life are the province of state courts and legislatures, rather than the federal Congress or federal courts. Regional variations are the norm, so that children's law defies easy synthesis. One standardizing influence on the development of children's law is federal spending to 'promote the general welfare.'[3] Federal programs on child welfare, child support, health care, and adoption, to name a few of the many state activities supported by federal dollars, often condition eligibility for funds on changes in state laws and policies. Another standardizing force is the work of organizations that create and disseminate model laws, including the National Commission on Uniform State Laws, the American Law Institute and the American Bar Association. Children's changing status in American family law can only be understood by examining this complex interplay between state laws and model acts (operating at the local level), federal funding initiatives which promote uniform standards, and constitutional principles which define boundaries on state intervention in the family and establish the constitutional rights of individuals within the family.

---

[1] *US v Virginia*, 518 US 515, 557 and n 21 (1996).
[2] See US CONST Amend I–XI, XIV.
[3] See US CONST art I, § 8.

In order to provide historical context for examination of the post-war period, let me sketch in broad strokes the status of children at the beginning of the twentieth century.[4] Children were traditionally conceptualized as subordinate members of the marital family unit, lacking any articulated political rights and dependent on adults to vindicate their interests. To the extent that children were perceived as having 'rights', these rights were simply the mirror image of their parent's duties. Children's fortunes were dictated by the marital status of their mother. The law protected the child born to a married mother, by presuming that the child was the offspring of her husband and thus 'legitimate.'[5] The law imposed on married fathers (and to some extent on mothers) the duty to shelter, nurture, educate, and discipline their children in a manner fitting the parent's station in life. The marital child could thus lay claim to specific 'rights' to a father's as well as a mother's care. In exchange, children owed a duty of filial obedience, enforceable with the rod. The child's labor belonged to the father and fathers controlled the custody and training of their children, subject to minimal state intervention.[6]

Many unlucky children fell outside this paradigm, because of either poverty, illegitimacy, or racial oppression. Children whose fathers and mothers were too poor or 'shiftless' to provide basic care or exercise socially appropriate control could be seized by government authorities and placed in involuntary indentures to earn their keep. Children of color were especially vulnerable to involuntary placement in state custody. Children of all colors whose fathers had not married their mothers, even if they eluded state custody, were stigmatized as bastards and excluded from many of the benefits of family relationship.[7]

The twentieth century was heralded by reformers as the 'Century of the Child.'[8] Those who coined this phrase focused not on children's autonomy rights but on their rights to protection from exploitation and on their rights to enjoy a sheltered and nurturing childhood.[9] The first half of the twentieth century, beginning with Theodore Roosevelt's progressive reforms and culminating in Franklin D. Roosevelt's New Deal, witnessed increasing regulation at the federal, state, and local levels of matters formerly within fathers' zone of exclusive authority. State laws

---

[4] For a comprehensive discussion of changes in children's status during the past two hundred years, see MARY ANN MASON, FROM FATHER'S PROPERTY TO CHILDREN'S RIGHTS: THE HISTORY OF CHILD CUSTODY IN THE UNITED STATES (1994).

[5] See Barbara Bennett Woodhouse, *Hatching the Egg: A Child-Centered Perspective on Parents' Rights*, 14 CARDOZO L REV 1746, 1775 and n 105 (1993) (describing the presumption of paternity).

[6] See Barbara Bennett Woodhouse, *'Who Owns the Child?:* Meyer & Pierce & the Child as Property*, 33 WM and MARY L REV 995, 1041–6 (describing parental rights in children).

[7] MASON, n 4 above, at 24–36.   [8] See ELLEN KEY, THE CENTURY OF THE CHILD (1909).

[9] See Woodhouse, *Who Owns the Child*, n 6 above, at 1050–8.

requiring all children to receive primary education, imposing vaccination and other public health requirements, and restricting child labor began to limit the power of the parent unilaterally to dictate the terms of childhood.[10] The Supreme Court occasionally struck down state initiatives as unconstitutional burdens on parents' liberty, and cases like *Meyer v Nebraska* and *Pierce v Society of Sisters* preserved a realm of parental autonomy.[11] But by the end of World War II, cases construing the powers of government to regulate child labor, health, and safety had firmly established the principle that government has a compelling interest in assuring children's well-being which justifies regulation and even direct intervention in the 'private' family.[12]

As divorce became increasingly common, fathers' authority was further eroded by court decisions increasing the powers of mothers.[13] By the mid-twentieth century, family court judges had enthusiastically embraced a 'tender years presumption' that allocated custody of young children to their mothers.[14] This rule was based on a belief that women were better fitted to provide care and nurture. These changes were partially driven by early feminists' claims for equal rights, but also evidenced an increasing understanding of the emotional and psychological needs of the developing child. Child development, reflected in the adoption of the 'best interest of the child' standard for resolving custody disputes, had become a central focus of children's law across the states by the midpoint of the twentieth century.[15] In the second half of the twentieth century, children's status has undergone another major paradigm shift. On the first stage of their journey to personhood, the dominant legal images of children had evolved from fathers' valuable property to fragile creatures entrusted to mothers' tender care. During the later twentieth century, children and youths began to figure as agents rather than objects of law, and emerged as legal persons with rights and interests of their own.

In this chapter I will trace how children's status has changed over the past fifty years, discussing laws on legitimacy, custody, and majority. I will also highlight the role played by the United States Constitution and the United States Supreme Court in recognizing children as constitutional

---

[10] See *ibid* at 1059–68 (outlining clash between reformers and conservatives).

[11] *Meyer v Nebraska* struck down a Nebraska law prohibiting parents from providing German language schooling for their children and announced a zone of parental autonomy surrounding child rearing. See 262 US 390 (1923). *Pierce v Society of Sisters* invalidated an Oregon law forcing all parents to send their children to public schools. See 268 US 510 (1925).   [12] See *Prince v Commonwealth of Massachusetts*, 321 US 158 (1944).

[13] For a comprehensive overview of the courts' gradual displacement of patriarchal authority, see MICHAEL GROSSBERG, GOVERNING THE HEARTH: LAW AND THE FAMILY IN NINETEENTH-CENTURY AMERICA (1985).

[14] Barbara Bennett Woodhouse, *Child Custody in the Age of Children's Rights: The Search for a Just and Workable Standard*, 33 FAM LQ 815, 818 (1999).

[15] See MASON, n 4 above, at 122.

persons. The Court's focus on tradition as the touchstone of rights, and on the individual as the entity in which rights are vested, tends to cast children's emerging rights as a contest between children and parents. Our individualist model of rights, I will argue, makes it difficult to recognize children's rights while still protecting children's relationships within family systems.

CHILDREN'S CHANGING STATUS UNDER THE CONSTITUTION

Emerging rights must always contend with entrenched tradition and with opposition from competing interests of other rights bearers. A review of the past fifty years confirms that battles for children's rights have been hard fought and marked by prolonged struggle. The recognition of new rights always involves a dialogue between culture and law. It is often hard to tell whether cultural change is pushing the law, or the law is pushing changes in the culture of the family. In America, conservatives claim that activist judges have misinterpreted the Constitution in order to intrude on states' rights and to undermine traditional family structures and parental authority. Liberals respond that traditional family laws and state statutes classifying people according to their race, legitimacy, and sex, or subordinating the rights of some to the authority of others, must meet the tests established by the equal protection and due process clauses for equality of treatment and fundamental fairness. Whichever view one adopts, the Supreme Court's responses to emerging claims of children's rights can only be understood in the context of a surrounding culture that was itself in rapid transition.

Attacking Race-based Discrimination Against Children

Cross Currents takes up the story of children's status as World War II ends and Americans seek a return to normalcy. During this post-war period, children provided powerful unifying images. These years saw an intense refocusing on family and child rearing, as soldiers returned home, started new families, and replaced women who had been drawn into the labor market by wartime necessity. A surge in births commonly called 'the baby boom' was the most tangible evidence of this return to hearth and home.[16] The decade of the 'fifties' is often viewed through a mist of nostalgia as a time of backyard barbecues and burgeoning suburban communities of stay-at-home moms and dads in gray flannel suits. While

---

[16] See Stephanie Coontz, The Way We Never Were: American Families and the Nostalgia Trap 24–5 (1992).

these images may fail to capture the complex realities, it is clear that Americans' hopes for their children seemed to unite them as they put the disruptions and the sacrifices of the war years behind them and looked to a more secure future for their children.

Meanwhile, children were playing another, very important role, in the political and legal life of the nation. America's rejection of the Nazis' racist policies drew pointed attention to racism at home. In many southern states, de jure segregation based on race forced African-Americans and other citizens of color to accept second-class citizenship in every aspect of civil life, from schools and hotels, to marriage and employment, to voting and jury service. Segregation in residential zones, commerce, and schooling, was the de facto norm in the North as well.[17] Civil rights advocates, seeking to dismantle American apartheid, understood the power of the child as a unifying symbol and used this as a wedge to expose race-based discrimination. They brought a series of test cases in Kansas, South Carolina, Virginia, and Delaware. In 1954, the United States Supreme Court decided these cases in its landmark opinion *Brown v Board of Education*,[18] holding that the principle of 'separate but equal' as applied to the education of children in public schools, was indefensible. The Court examined the emotional impact of segregation, with its message of inferiority, on Black children's psychological development. The Court held that the stigma of separatism, even assuming school facilities were of equal quality, deprived Black children of the equal protection of the laws guaranteed to all persons under the Fourteenth Amendment. This case is widely recognized as the most important American civil rights case of the twentieth century. It is no accident that children, given their centrality to the American dream of equal opportunity, played a pivotal role. *Brown v Board* confirmed children's 'status' as constitutional persons, protected from state discrimination, and also illustrated a new willingness to take children and their experiences seriously in applying principles of constitutional law. However, the aftermath of *Brown* also illustrates the tenacity of race bias. School desegregation efforts moved with glacial speed, often followed by residential resegregation: the promise of *Brown* has never been fully realized.

Race discrimination, in education and in cultural life, figured in other Supreme Court opinions concerning children. In 1982, in *Plyler v Doe*,[19] the Court struck down a Texas law that excluded the children of illegal

---

[17] For a compelling account of one child's experience of racism in the 1950s, see GREGORY HOWARD WILLIAMS, LIFE ON THE COLOR LINE: THE TRUE STORY OF A WHITE BOY WHO DISCOVERED HE WAS BLACK (1995).   [18] 347 US (1954).
[19] 457 US 202 (1982).

aliens, primarily Mexicans, from the public schools. The Court distinguished between adults who bore responsibility for entering the country illegally and their blameless children, and refused to allow the state to punish the children for a characteristic beyond their control.[20] In 1984, the Court in *Palmore v Sidoti*,[21] extended the equal protection clause's prohibitions of race-based discrimination to adjudications of custody disputes. Theoretically, a race-based classification might survive strict scrutiny if the state could show it was narrowly tailored to serve a compelling state interest. The Court rejected the argument that the adverse effects of racial bias on the child provided a legitimate basis for denying custody to a mother who had remarried a man of a different race. *Palmore* suggests that the Constitution protects children from custody decisions that are merely reactive or symptomatic of societal prejudice against their parents, rather than being based in an examination of the parent–child relationship. In some jurisdictions, the theory behind *Palmore* has been applied to cases involving children of gay and lesbian parents.[22]

Attacking Discrimination Against Illegitimate Children

Differential treatment of children based on the parents' marital status had long been a pillar of family law and policy. However, in the post-war period advocates for children invoked the equal protection clause to challenge laws that gave lesser protection to children born out of wedlock. In today's open climate, it is difficult to imagine the shock value of these claims. In most segments of American post-war society, unwed mothers were hidden from public view and their children were placed for adoption at birth, in a climate of deepest secrecy. But in 1968, in *Levy v Louisiana*,[23] the Court struck down a wrongful death statute that excluded illegitimates as beneficiaries. In 1971, however, it seemed to back away from *Levy*, suggesting in *Labine v Vincent* that states had wide latitude to create classifications based on legitimacy.[24] Then, in *Weber v Aetna Casualty & Surety Co*, a 1972 challenge, it changed course again, rejecting a law that excluded illegitimate children from workmen's compensation. In a key passage, the Court dismissed a central justification for such laws— that they served to discourage illicit relationships. '[V]isiting this condemnation on the head of an infant is illogical and unjust.'[25]

The notion that illegitimate children possess protected fundamental rights in the parent–child relationship produced a strong dissent from

---

[20] See *ibid* at 220.   [21] 466 US 429 (1984).
[22] *SNE v RLB*, 699 P2d 875 (Alaska 1985).   [23] 391 US 68 (1968).
[24] *Labine v Vincent*, 401 US 532 (1971) (upholding statute denying equal treatment to acknowledged illegitimate children).   [25] 406 US 164, 175 (1972).

now Chief Justice Rehnquist. He questioned the existence of such a right, given the long history of treating legitimate and illegitimate births differently, and urged application of the highly deferential standard of 'minimal scrutiny' generally applied to non-racial classifications. 'The Equal Protection Clause of the Fourteenth Amendment requires neither that state enactments be "logical" nor does it require that they be "just" in the common meaning of those terms. It requires only that there be some conceivable set of facts that may justify the classification involved.'

During the 1970s, the Court continued to 'see saw' in its decisions about illegitimates. The 1977 case of *Trimble v Gordon* built on the foundation laid in *Weber*, holding that laws burdening illegitimates violated equal protection guarantees, unless the state could show the differential treatment was 'substantially related to permissible state interests.'[26] The Illinois intestate succession statute in *Trimble* foreclosed children born out of wedlock who had not been legitimated by their parents' subsequent marriage from inheriting from their fathers. The Court examined the practical rationale offered in defense of the rule—to avoid evidentiary difficulties in proving paternity—and held that the categorical exclusion even of children who could prove the fact of paternity through other means was not sufficiently closely tailored to a permissible state interest. A year later, in *Lalli v Lalli*, the Court again applied heightened scrutiny to a New York law requiring a certain form of proof of paternity for an illegitimate child to inherit by intestate succession. This time, however, a majority of the Court believed the statute passed muster and it was upheld. Justice Blackmun, concurring in the judgment, urged the Court to overrule *Trimble* and return to its pre-*Levy* posture of extreme deference to state laws on legitimacy. This view did not prevail. In *Clark v Jeter*, and subsequent cases, the Court has made clear that the same 'intermediate scrutiny' applies to legitimacy classifications as to gender classifications. Such classifications will survive constitutional challenge only if 'substantially related to an important governmental objective.'[27] Of course, the technological revolution has played a large role in these changes. Blood analysis and DNA testing now provide reliable methods for determining the biological paternity of a child, and diminish the importance of marriage and formal legitimation in establishing the identity of the male parent.[28]

[26] *Trimble v Gordon*, 430 US 672 (1977).

[27] See *Mills v Habluetzel*, 456 US 91 (1982); *Clark v Jeter*, 486 US 456 (1988) (striking down time limits within which a minor born to an unmarried mother must sue to establish paternity).

[28] See US DEPT OF HHS, OFFICE OF CHILD SUPPORT ENFORCEMENT, ESSENTIALS FOR ATTORNEYS IN CHILD SUPPORT ENFORCEMENT 370 (1986)(describing various tests for establishing paternity).

Another case from the 1970s, *Stanley v Illinois*,[29] was instrumental in establishing the illegitimate child's right to protection of an established relationship with his or her father. Peter Stanley had never married the mother of his children, but he had lived with and supported his family for many years. When the mother died, the children were placed in foster care without a hearing on Stanley's fitness. Under Illinois law, an unmarried father was treated as a legal stranger to his children, with no special claim to custody. The Supreme Court held that the law violated Stanley's rights to equal protection. While its decision rested on the father's rights, and did not mention the rights of the children, its effect was to require a hearing before removing a child from the custody of his or her parent or denying contact with a parent.

In one set of cases, however, the marital status of the child's parents may continue to determine the child's relational and legal rights. In *Michael H v Gerald D*,[30] a married woman conceived a child in an extra-marital affair. The Supreme Court upheld a California law allowing the mother and her husband to block the biological father from asserting parental rights. Rejecting the notion that the child might have her own independent right to a relationship, the Court held that the state may justifiably decide to protect the marital family from claims by an 'adulterous unwed father.' This case illustrates the effects of the Court's historic focus on the rights of parents to custody, rather than on reciprocal rights in intimate family relationships shared by both parent and child. Justice Scalia, over a strong dissent, dismissed the child's constitutional claim as no more than a mirror image of the biological father's. Since *Michael H* could point to no deeply rooted tradition protecting adulterous unwed fathers' rights, his daughter Victoria's claim collapsed as well. In refusing to analyze the child's rights as distinct from her competing fathers' claims, the Court failed to honor the principle, articulated in earlier cases, that illegitimate children should not be punished for the sins of their fathers.

Michael H remains an anomaly in a general trend towards treating children equally regardless of their parents' marital status. As the Court's conservatives who opposed this trend understood, heightened scrutiny of classifications based on illegitimacy would soon spell the death knell of large numbers of traditional rules stigmatizing non-marital procreation. Recognition of children as persons with rights to family relationships meant that government could no longer use innocent children as a means of punishing non-marital sex between adults. Over the past thirty years, this remarkable revolution in social policy has thoroughly permeated American popular culture and has transformed both state and federal

---

[29] 405 US 645 (1972).   [30] 491 US 110 (1989).

law. Statutes on child support, intestate succession, tort law, insurance benefits, and social insurance eligibility, which once drew stark lines between the 'bastard' and the 'legitimate' child, now routinely treat children equally.

Challenging Gender Discrimination as it Affects Children

Gender stereotyping in our treatment of young children is so entrenched as to seem benign and natural. All children experience *de facto* classification by gender virtually from birth, and even before, now that we can identify the sex of babies *in utero*. Until recently, children were routinely subject to *de jure* gender discrimination as well. The most obvious such laws treated male and female children differently in inheritance rights and support rights, or established different ages of majority for males and females and different ages at which males and females could marry, or set lower ages for girls' consumption of alcohol than for boys. Less obviously discriminatory were statutory rape laws that criminalized sex with under-age girls, but not boys. These gender-based classifications were challenged by the same advocates who challenged discrimination against adult women. In 1975, the Court in *Stanton v Stanton*[31] struck down a Utah law establishing differential age-of-majority criteria for girls and boys. This statutory scheme left girls without post-divorce support from their non-custodial parent after age 18, while boys were entitled to support until age 21. The state, defending its laws, relied on its interest in fostering readiness for family life, arguing that girls were destined for domestication and motherhood while boys must prepare for work in the labor economy. With only one dissenting voice, the Court flatly rejected this pretext as merely perpetuating outdated stereotypes.

If a specified age of minority is required for the boy in order to assure him parental support while he attains his education and training, so, too, is it for the girl. To distinguish between the two on educational grounds is to be self-serving: if the female is not to be supported so long as the male, she hardly can be expected to attend school as long as he does, and bringing her education to an end earlier coincides with the role-typing society has long imposed.

Where laws appeared to favor girls over boys, or provide females with greater protection, the Court has often seemed ambivalent. In *Craig v Boren*, the Supreme Court struck down a state law that allowed the sale of 3.2 per cent beer to females 18 and older but prohibited sale of the same beer to males under 21.[32] In 1981, however, the Court upheld a statutory rape law that defined as unlawful consensual sexual intercourse with a

---

[31] 421 US 75 (1975).   [32] See 429 US 190 (1976).

female (but not a male) under 18.[33] The feminist movement affected children's law in other, less direct ways. As noted earlier, by mid-century, the tender years presumption favoring awarding custody of young children to their mothers had replaced the common law presumption treating the father as presumptive custodian. In the wake of decisions like *Stanton v Stanton*, state courts interpreted the constitutional prohibitions on gender stereotyping as extending to custody as well as other areas of family law.[34] Custody adjudications, cut loose from these gender-based presumptions, refocused on a case-by-case examination of the individual child's 'best interest,' stressing the importance of maintaining important parent–child attachments and promoting the child's healthy psychological development.

Separation of the sexes in schools has proved far harder to challenge than other forms of segregation. At first, males seemed to be the primary beneficiaries of gender equality, as the Court's decisions such as *Hogan v Mississippi University School of Nursing* opened formerly female professions like nursing to males. Finally, in 1995, almost half a century after its decision in *Brown v Board*, the Court rejected the notion of separate but equal schools for males and females in the context of élite education for leadership. In *United States v Virginia*,[35] the Court held that the State of Virginia could not deny girls admission to Virginia Military Academy, its prestigious post-secondary school, despite its claim that a separate but equal program was available to females. These decisions, in reshaping the legal and cultural images of young males and females in the home, in schools, and in the economy, have also shaped the lives of boys and girls who may now aspire to a wide range of careers with far less fear of stigmatization and exclusion.

As this section has shown, children's emerging rights played a central role in the post-war development of constitutional law. Indeed, the latter half of the twentieth century was bracketed by powerful images of young people seeking equality of opportunity through education. In the early years of the 1950s, we saw African-American children braving the anger of the mob in order to integrate the public schools. As the century closed, we saw the determined young women who had sought entry into élite male schools such as Virginia Military Academy, risking taunts and hazing to assert their hard-won equality. While these Supreme Court decisions have been viewed largely as victories for racial minorities and for women, they were also victories for children, establishing children as key players in the quest for equal rights.

---

[33] *Michael M v Superior Court of Sonoma County*, 450 US 464 (1981).
[34] See *Devine v Devine*, 398 So 2d 686 (Ala 1981); *Pusey v Pusey*, 728 P 2d 117 (Utah 1986).
[35] 515 US 518 (1995).

Custody Law: The Emerging Right to a Fair and Child-centered Adjudication

Children and their advocates began to assert claims not only to equal treatment with other children but also to fair treatment at the hands of courts, schools, and other authorities. The Fourteenth Amendment, in addition to guaranteeing equal protection of the laws, provides that the state shall not deprive any person of 'life, liberty or property without due process of law.' Many cases seeking to change or establish rules of law or procedure are not styled or described as asserting constitutional rights, but nevertheless are grounded in notions of fundamental fairness embodied in the Fourteenth Amendment's due process clause. This clause has both a procedural and a substantive component. Its procedural component protects individuals against unfair rules or procedures in actions by public entities, including the court system. The substantive component draws a protective circle around basic 'liberties', including the rights to home and family, and requires the state to justify intrusions on such liberties by showing that they are necessary to protect compelling state interests. This form of 'strict scrutiny' has similar effects to the equal protection clause strict scrutiny tests discussed above. When applied to children, due process rights take an interesting twist—children are often too immature to assert their own autonomy, so others must act on their behalf to protect their vital interests in fundamental liberties such as bodily integrity, privacy, and protection of family bonds.

Family law grew up around this framework, which entrusted the protection of children to caring adults, preferably their parents. Traditionally, while adults were described as having 'rights' deserving of protection by the courts, children were more often described as having 'interests' which adults and the state were obligated to protect. The notion that, in family law and especially in child custody and adoption, the child's welfare comes first was firmly established (although not always respected) by mid-century. The statement found in countless family law statutes and cases that 'the child's best interest is paramount' reflected a sense that exertions of power over children ought to be justified as advancing the child's welfare and not merely serving the adult's selfish ends.

Best Interest of the Child: A Standard Under Fire

The best interest standard remains the dominant rule in custody determinations across the United States. However, despite its near universal acceptance, it is harshly criticized by scholars of every description. According to its early critics, the best interest standard failed to control the trial judge's discretion and allowed the judge to impose her own value systems on child-rearing decisions within the post-divorce family. Some believed that the standard was inherently indeterminate, and that courts lacked the capacity to discern which custodial placement was in a child's 'best interest.'[36] Others, primarily feminists, charged that it favored fathers by applying a double standard that discounted women's contributions to child rearing and overvalued men's more sporadic and peripheral role in children's care and nurture.[37] Advocates for fathers countercharged that the vague standard provided cover for continuing discrimination in favor of women as the preferred parent. Critics also questioned the expansive role of so-called 'experts' from the 'helping professions.' They claimed it displaced traditional rules protecting the authority of the primary custodian with a therapeutic approach that uncritically favored involvement of both parents in post-divorce childrearing. Frequent visitation and shared legal decision-making authority severely limited the custodial parent's autonomy.[38] Finally, some questioned why custody law should elevate the interest of one family member, the child, over those of other family members. Instead, critics claimed, custody determinations should focus on shared relationships and interconnectedness.[39] Finally, many family scholars who are concerned about harm to children from judicial or legal discrimination against non-traditional families, have stressed the importance of focusing on family function rather than family form. In evaluating the child's attachments to parenting figures and in determining which custodial setting will serve the child's best interest, courts should ask whether the party seeking custody or continued contact has acted like a parent and not whether he or she fits the traditional model of the nuclear marital family.[40]

The Shift from Presumptions to Intermediary Norms

Despite its many critics, the best interest standard has won a vast following among judges. Instead of rejecting it outright, state courts and

[36] See Robert Mnookin, *Child-Custody Adjudication: Judicial Functions in the Face of Indeterminacy*, 39 LAW & CONTEMP PROBS 226 (1975).

[37] See Karen Czapanskiy, *Volunteers and Draftees: The Struggle for Parental Equality*, 38 UCLA L REV 1415 (1991).

[38] See MARTHA ALBERTSON FINEMAN, THE ILLUSION OF EQUALITY: THE RHETORIC AND REALITY OF DIVORCE REFORM 149 (1991).

[39] See Katherine T. Bartlett, *Re-expressing Parenthood*, 98 YALE L J 293 (1988).

[40] See Nancy D. Polikoff, *This Child Does Have Two Mothers: Redefining Parenthood to Meet the Needs of Children in Lesbian-Mother and Other Nontraditional Families*, 78 GEO LJ 459 (1990); Barbara Bennett Woodhouse, *'It All Depends on What You Mean by Home:' Towards a Communitarian Theory of the Nontraditional Family*, 1996 UTAH L REV 569.

legislatures have struggled to bring predictability, consistency, and theoretical validity to the open-ended best interest standard. One method of providing consistency is the creation, by judges and by legislatures, of guiding 'presumptions' about what placements generally serve children's best interests. One such presumption is the presumption that a child's mother and father are the persons best able to meet his needs and most concerned with his welfare. This basic presumption undergirds parental 'rights' in contests between the biological parent and a third party, and protects the powerful interests of all children in minimizing destabilizing interventions in their families of origin.

The paternal presumption and the maternal presumption provide two other historical examples, no longer viable. In contemporary custody disputes between two fit parents, some advocate replacing the tender years presumption with a gender-neutral rule favoring the parent who had assumed primary responsibility for child care during the marriage. Only one jurisdiction has adopted a true primary caretaker presumption, but many state statutes or cases count the primary caretaker role as a positive factor suggesting a deeper and more stable attachment.[41] Even more influential in the last decades of the twentieth century has been the presumption in favor of joint or shared custody.[42] Studies suggest that California's shared custody presumption may actually have reshaped the way fathers relate to their children.[43] These presumptions, however, have flaws of their own. The more powerful the presumption, the more likely it is to overbalance other more subtle values. In addition, these presumptions are hardly value-neutral nor are they neutral in operation. While the primary caretaker presumption tends to favor women, the shared custody presumption tends to favor men.

Most states have opted in favor of retaining the best interest standard as the overarching rule, while providing the decision-maker with guidance in the form of case law or statutory criteria detailing crucial factors that should be examined by the court. These intermediary norms put flesh on the bones of the best interest standard. A list of such principles has evolved, based on the shared belief that certain factors—for example, avoiding disruption of important attachment relationships, maintaining stability in home and school settings, preserving contact with siblings and both parents—are likely to promote the best interest of the child. Obviously, two factors may pull in opposite directions. For example, continuity of schooling or sibling relationships may entail separation from a parent or other attachment figure. In such cases, courts

---

[41] See *Garska v McCoy*, 278 SE 2d 357 (W Va 1981).

[42] See Woodhouse, *Custody Law*, n 14 above, at 822–5.

[43] See ELEANOR E. MACCOBY and ROBERT H. MNOOKIN, DIVIDING THE CHILD: SOCIAL AND LEGAL DILEMMAS OF CUSTODY (1992).

must consider all of the factors and weight them according to their importance in the specific family context. Finally, certain factors have been singled out as highly damaging to children—above all, exposure to domestic violence. Other factors which used to play a dispositive role— such as a parent's sex life, choice of work or companions, or consumption of alcohol—have been relegated to the sidelines, and can only be considered if a nexus exists between the parental conduct and the welfare of the child.[44]

All in all, child custody law has evolved to reflect the child's emerging status as a person. While judges and legislatures continue to shy away from the rhetoric of 'children's rights,' it is clear that the interests of the child now occupy the foreground of custody law. The child is seen as the person most centrally concerned and the person whose rights and liberties are most in play.

Children's Voices in the Courtroom

Another radical change in the status of children is their increasing access to the justice system. It is now mandatory in many jurisdictions for judges to consult the child and take her preference into account in deciding custody cases. The 'children's attorney' is a common sight in modern family courts and most judges now have the authority to appoint a lawyer to represent the child in complex cases where it appears that a child's rights are at risk or that parents cannot sufficiently represent the child's interests. A personal anecdote illustrates the rapidity of this change. In 1989, when I had just begun law teaching and was designing a course on lawyering for children, a colleague scoffed at the very idea, noting that a child's attorney could hardly be expected to take direction from a child client. When I begged to differ, he exclaimed, 'Why, that's not just ridiculous; that's malpractice!' In 1996, an entire symposium issue of a major law journal was dedicated to 'Ethical Issues in the Legal Representation of Children.'[45]

Court practices have changed in ways both large and small to accommodate the needs of children. The United States Supreme Court played a major role in bringing children's voices into the courtroom. In a series of cases decided in the last decade of the twentieth century, the justices analyzed how far courts might go in relaxing rules against hearsay and the rules favoring live testimony to accommodate the needs of child victims of sexual abuse. These rules traditionally served not only to advance the truth-finding function, but also to protect the Sixth Amend-

---

[44] See Woodhouse, *Custody Law*, n 14 above, at 826, 829.
[45] See generally 64 Fordham L Rev 1279–2132 (1996).

ment rights of the defendant in criminal cases 'to be confronted with the witnesses against him.'[46] In *Maryland v Craig*,[47] the Court permitted the use of television monitors to allow a young child who would have been too terrified to speak in the defendant's presence to testify without being visually and physically confronted by the defendant. In *White v Illinois*,[48] the Court held that a child's hearsay statements to a third party, provided the context in which they were made supplied sufficient indicia of reliability, could be introduced without requiring that the child also be made available or forced to testify. In discussing these accommodations, the Court viewed the reliability of children's statements and the ability of children to withstand cross examination through a consciously developmental lens, acknowledging that children, despite their differences from adults, have much to contribute to the judicial process and a right to be heard. These cases illustrate the contrast between children's former exclusion from court proceedings, as either unreliable or incapable of understanding the 'oath,' and the current policies of inclusion.

FORECASTING FUTURE DIRECTIONS

The task of reviewing past trends leads naturally to forecasting their likely trajectories. In the area of custody law, the next phase will surely be influenced by a project now in its final stage of completion. The American Law Institute is about to complete its work in drafting a set of *Principles of the Law of Family Dissolution*. These principles, compiled by a group of eminent lawyers, judges, and professors, provide a strong indication of future directions. While identifying the primary objective of custody law as 'to serve the child's best interest,' the ALI has adopted a series of intermediary principles to promote this norm. These include common sense policies, such as a policy of allocating custodial responsibility in proportion to each parent's past care-taking activities. The Principles also identity six values that advance children's best interest: (1) parental planning and agreement about the child's custodial arrangements; (2) continuity of existing parent–child attachments; (3) meaningful contact between the child and each parent; (4) caretaking relationships by adults who love the child, know how to provide for the child's needs, and place a high priority on doing so; (5) security from exposure to physical and emotional harm; and (6) expeditious, predictable decision-making and the avoidance of prolonged uncertainty.[49] If the rest of the country follows

---

[46] US Const Amend VI.   [47] 497 US 836 (1990).   [48] 112 S Ct 736 (1992).
[49] See Principles of the Law of Family Dissolution, Tentative Draft No 3, Part I, section 2.02 (Mar 20 1998).

the ALI's lead, child custody law will continue to develop around the core principle of children's best interest. However, courts will have better guidance in providing individualized yet consistent custody decisions.

The Supreme Court will continue to play a large role in shaping the direction of children's law, as it deals with new cases posing new questions about family-based rights. One such case is *Troxel v Granville*,[50] the last family law case of the old millennium and the first of the new to appear on the high court's docket. Filed in October of 1999, it presented the question whether state laws protecting relationships between children and important figures in their lives (grandparents, stepparents, *de facto* kin, and extended family) impermissibly intrude on the rights of parents to control their children's upbringing. While the statute at issue in *Troxel* was extraordinarily broad, 'allowing any person at any time' to seek visitation, the majority of states had passed similar statutes allowing courts to order visitation with children's extended family members in certain circumstances. These visitation statutes, often characterized as protecting 'grandparents' rights,' were also based on respect for children's rights. They represented an attempt by state legislatures, based on new appreciation of children's developmental needs, to redraw the balance between parental autonomy and children's right to protection of their intimate family relationships. The Court's decision, rendered on 5 June 2000, found the Washington statute unconstitutional 'as applied'. Consisting of six separate opinions, this fractured plurality illustrates the difficulties of reaching consensus in an area of change and ferment. A majority of the justices agreed that the Constitution required 'some deference' to parents' choices about access to grandparents, but a majority also agreed that this liberty 'swapped'. As it has before, the Court must continue to tread a cautious path, honoring established rights while allowing space in which the constitutional story of new rights can unfold.

I will close with one last prediction. My discussion of children's status has involved a mix of constitutional law and ordinary family law principles. I believe that the child-centered adjudication I have described, and the inclusion of children's voices in the adjudicatory process, will ultimately be recognized as not just good policies and enlightened ideas, but as constitutional rights of the child under the Fourteenth Amendment's due process clause. The awesome powers that the law confers on adults to control the lives of children demands a child-centered justification. Children, like adults, should be entitled to a hearing before being coercively removed from their homes. And children, like adults, should have a right to participate in decisions regarding their custody, education,

---

[50] See *Troxel v Granville*, 120 S. Ct. 2054 (2000).

and bodily integrity, even if they lack full capacity to make their own decisions.

The twentieth-century shift that defines parental powers not as rights in and of themselves, but as a means to advancing children's welfare, is consistent with the human rights revolution generally, and with the children's rights revolution taking place around the globe. At the time of writing, the United States is virtually alone in having failed to ratify the 1989 United Nations Convention on the Rights of the Child.[51] Whether Americans like it or not, children's human rights are becoming firmly entrenched in international law. Can the extension of constitutional rights to American children, the last class of excluded persons, be far behind?

---

[51] See Art 3, Nov 20 1989, 28 ILM 1448. See Woodhouse, *Protecting Children's Relationships with Extended Family: The Impact of Troxel v Granville*, 19 ABA Child Law Practice 65 (July 2000).

20

Disputing Children

MICHAEL FREEMAN

Fifty years ago there were disputes over children—many fewer than there are now because there were many fewer divorces and we were a less rights-conscious society—but their character was very different from those of today. Society in 1950 was more stable and less questioning. A consensus had been forged, initially perhaps by the deprivations of war and subsequently by a reforming Labour Government. Marriage was the bedrock of the family. People knew their place and did what they were told. Feminism had not (re)emerged and, though the world had focused on children in the aftermath of World War I,[1] there was no talk of children's rights.[2] There were few reported cases relating to children and these often related to issue of legitimacy.[3] Cases did not need to go to court: the divorcing couple bargained in the shadow of legal and psychological truths—by the 1950s the former undoubtedly a reflection of the latter—and this was encapsulated in the writings of John Bowlby.[4]

In 1945 the leading case on children was *Re Thain*.[5] This had decided in 1926 that the parental right of an unimpeachable parent should take priority over considerations of a child's welfare. A father, unable to cope after the death of the mother, had handed his eight-month-old daughter to his brother-in-law and wife and had sought six years later her return. Eve J, ordering the delivery up of the child, remarked:

It is said that the little girl will be greatly distressed and upset at parting from Mr and Mrs J. I can quite understand it may be so, but, at her tender age, one knows from experience how mercifully transient are the effects of partings and other sorrows, and how soon the novelty of fresh surroundings and new associations effaces the recollection of former days and kind friends, and I cannot attach weight to this aspect of the case.

Whether *Re Thain* would have been decided the same way if a mother had handed her child to relatives in similar circumstances may be doubted: she would have been expected to put caring for her child before her career. But mothers who surrendered children for adoption and then changed their minds were held to be acting unreasonably only where they

---

[1] Reflected in the Declaration of Geneva of 1924.
[2] Writers like Kate Douglas Wiggin, Janusz Korzcak, and Ellen Key had no impact on policy makers.   [3] And, in effect, to questions of property transmission.
[4] Originally a WHO publication in 1951, it was popularized as J. Bowlby, *Child Care and the Growth of Love*. Harmondsworth: Penguin Press (1953).   [5] [1926] Ch 676.

could be said to be callous or culpable in some way.[6] The law prioritized parental rights over children's interests and welfare. As late as 1966 the ideology of *Re Thain* was being upheld.[7] It was the end of that decade before welfare was held to prevail over the right of an unimpeachable parent. The child's welfare is 'the first consideration because it is of first importance and paramount because it determines the course to be followed', proclaimed Lord MacDermott.[8] And this interpretation was held to apply to disputes between parents and non-parents as well as to those between parents themselves. Stephen Cretney has convincingly shown that the House of Lords misinterpreted the legislation,[9] but it was undoubtedly a construction consonant with an emergent image of children.

In 1945 disputes about children were about rights. It was the mid-1970s before the right of the so-called 'unimpeachable' parent was finally scotched There were several cases[10] of which the most important were *Re K*[11] and *S(BD) v S(DJ)*.[12] Only fifteen years before, in *Re L*,[13] the Court of Appeal had denied a mother who had left her husband for another man, care and control of the daughters. As Lord Denning MR reasoned, in an outburst of moral fundamentalism:

It would be an exceedingly bad example if it were thought that a mother could go off with another man and then claim as of right to say: 'Oh well, they are my two little girls and I am entitled to take them with me. I can not only leave my home and break it up and leave their father, but I can take the children with me and the law will not say me nay'. It seems to me that a mother must realise that if she leaves and breaks up her home in this way she cannot as of right demand to take the children from the father.

It may well be that the father had been wronged, but, it will be observed, there is no reference in Lord Denning's peroration to the children's best interests. It is significant that twice in his judgment he used the expression 'as of right', and he went on to refer to the case as 'a matter of simple justice' between mother and father. 'The claims of justice', he insisted, 'cannot be overlooked.' But, with the legislation interpreted so that 'first and paramount'[14] meant 'only', the effect of *J v C*,[15] there could be no space for 'justice', and in *S(BD) v S(DJ)* Ormrod LJ retorted that the question was not what the 'essential justice of the case' requires but 'what the best interests of the children' demand.[16] In 1977, the date of this judgment, 'best interests' was essen-

---

[6] This remained the law until *Re W* [1971] 2 All ER 49 (an earlier attempt was Lord Denning MR's judgment in *Re L* (1962) 106 Sol Jo 611).
[7] *Re C (MA)* [1966] 1 All ER 838.   [8] In *J v C* [1970] AC 668, 710.
[9] Stephen Cretney, *Law, Law Reform and The Family*. Oxford: Clarendon Press (1998), ch 7.
[10] See also cases reported as news items in *The Times*, 11 Nov 1975 and 18 Nov 1975.
[11] [1977] 1 All ER 647.   [12] [1977] 1 All ER 656.   [13] [1962] 1 WLR 886.
[14] Guardianship of Minors Act 1971 s 1.   [15] n 8 above.   [16] n 12 above.

tially a brocard with little normative content, but its emphasis was significant in providing a focus: it was the child's interests which counted, and no one else's.

The *Gillick* decision did not emerge out of thin air[17] and, as Eekelaar showed shortly after the House of Lords' decision,[18] it was consistent with principle. But it shocked and it also offended.[19] Popular opinion supported parental rights, and *Gillick* undercut them. The issue in *Gillick* concerned the lawfulness of a notice issued by the Department of Health and Social Security which enabled a doctor to give contraceptive counselling and treatment to children under 16 without consulting a parent. At first instance, Woolf J held the notice to be lawful. The Court of Appeal reversed, unanimously, though the three judges concerned used different arguments (none of which, it may be said, was convincing).[20] The House of Lords, by 3–2, upheld the lawfulness of the notice.[21]

The decision accepted that growing up is a process. As Lord Scarman put it:

The law relating to parent and child is concerned with the problems of growth and maturity of the human personality. If the law should impose upon the process of 'growing up' fixed limits where nature only knows a continuous process, the price would be artificiality and a lack of realism in an area where the law must be sensitive to human development and social change.

The majority of the Lords thus rejected a status test in favour of one which looks to capacity. For them Gillick competence, as it has come to be called, hinged on understanding and intelligence. Thus, for Lord Scarman, 'parental right yields to the child's right to make his own decisions when he reaches a sufficient understanding and intelligence to be capable of making up his own mind on the matter requiring decision'. Elsewhere in his judgment he referred to a competent child as one who 'achieves a

---

[17] Earlier indications are *Hewer v Bryant* [1970] 1 QB 357, and *R v D* [1984] AC 778.

[18] J. Eekelaar, 'The Emergence of Children's Rights', (1986) 6 *Oxford Journal of Legal Studies* 161.

[19] A national campaign 'to protect the family from interference from officialdom' was established. See *The Times*, 28 May 1985. The concerns (pre-Gillick) were voiced by the 'right' in such texts as F. Mount, *The Subversive Family*. London: Jonathan Cape (1982).

[20] [1985] 2 WLR 413. For Eveleigh LJ the notice contravened a parental right which pertained to the upbringing of a child. For Parker LJ a child's consent was a nullity so that presumably an intelligent 15-year-old could not have a sore throat examined without a parent's consent. [21] [1986] AC 112.

sufficient understanding and intelligence to enable him or her to understand fully what is proposed', and also (and this is often overlooked by
commentators on the case) has 'sufficient discretion to enable him or her
to make a wise choice in his or her own interests'.[22] In these terms, competence combines understanding and knowledge with wisdom and experience. There are dangers in conflating knowledge and wisdom, but this
is commonly done. Few adults are Gillick competent if competence is to
hinge upon abilities fully to understand what is involved in a decision.
But many children, far below the age with which Gillick competence is
conventionally associated, are competent within the test articulated by
Lord Scarman if 'wise choice' is genuinely situated within the child's
personal, experiential knowledge of his or her own interests. Alderson
and Goodwin have noted that we tend to value highly 'professional,
textbook knowledge',[23] whilst discounting the importance of personal
experiential knowledge. And, once such 'wisdom' is devalued, the child
can be assumed to be ignorant, except in so far as he or she can recount
medical or other professional information.

That *Gillick* is a watershed decision cannot be denied, but from the
perspective of 2000 it begins to look like a false dawn. Writing shortly
after the decision, Eekelaar predicted that its effect was to overturn
parental authority once an adolescent had acquired competence;[24] and
not just parental authority but logically also that of a wardship court,
the jurisdiction of which was based both in history and on principle in
its acting as *parens patriae*. Children now had, Eekelaar claimed, 'that
most dangerous but most precious of rights: the right to make their
own mistakes'. Yet, when the opportunity presented itself for the
courts to test the implications of this they flinched. In *Re R*[25] and *Re W*[26]
(and subsequently in other cases,[27] most recently the heart transplant
case of *Re M*[28]), they held that, although a Gillick competent child
could consent to medical treatment on her own behalf, she could not
refuse to consent to treatment. As a result, as Brazier and Bridge
observe, 'the right to be wrong applies only where minors say yes to
treatment'.[29]

But, both here and elsewhere,[30] the courts have raised the level of
Gillick competence beyond that which is required to consent to treat-

---

[22] At 188.

[23] P. Alderson and M. Goodwin, 'Contradictions within Concepts of Children's Competence', (1993) 1 *International Journal of Children's Rights* 303, 305.   [24] n 18 above, at 181.

[25] [1992] Fam 11.   [26] [1993] Fam 64.

[27] *Re E* [1993] 1 FLR 386; *Re S* [1994] 2 FLR 1065.   [28] [1999] 2 FLR 1097.

[29] M. Brazier and C. Bridge, 'Coercion or Caring: Analysing Adolescent Autonomy',
(1996) 16 *Legal Studies* 84, 88 ; see also C. Smith, 'Children's Rights: Judicial Ambivalence
and Social Resistance', (1997) 11 *International Journal of Law, Policy and the Family* 103.

[30] eg *Re E*, n 27 above; *Re K, W and H* [1993] 1 FLR 854.

ment. Indeed, the more far-reaching the effects of refusal, the higher the level of competence is raised. In *Re R*,[31] where the evidence was that without treatment the girl would lapse into a dangerously psychotic state, Lord Donaldson MR said that what was required was not merely an ability to understand the nature of the proposed treatment, but a full understanding and appreciation of the consequences both of the treatment in terms of intended and possible side effects and, equally important, the anticipated consequences of a failure to treat. This goes way beyond what was envisaged in *Gillick* and is also more stringent than the test laid down for mentally disordered adults.[32] That test (first formulated in *Re C* by Thorpe J)[33] has been used by courts to test the competence of 16–18-year-olds,[34] but not to supplant that articulated in *Re R* for children under 16. Lord Donaldson MR's test in *Re R* demands more of children than is required of adults in another respect too. Lord Donaldson himself accepts that an adult's capacity to decide about treatment has to be assessed at the time the decision is made.[35] But in *Re R* he required a permanent state of competence: where this fluctuates, as it did in *Re R*, the adolescent cannot be judged by her capacity on her 'good days'.[36]

Despite *Gillick* and in the face of legislation (both the Family Law Reform Act 1969 and the Children Act 1989),[37] the courts evince reluctance to give rein to a child's autonomy. Where the child is under 16 they do this by concluding that the child is not Gillick competent. This is well illustrated by two Jehovah's Witnesses' 'blood transfusion' cases. In *Re E*[38] a boy of 15¾, though of sufficient intelligence to be able to take decisions about his own well-being, was not, it was held, Gillick competent because there was a range of decisions confronting him which lay outside his full comprehension. Said Ward J: 'He may have some concept of the fact that he will die, but as to the manner of his death and the extent of his and his family's suffering I find he has not the ability to turn his mind to it nor the will to do so[39].' In *Re S*,[40] a girl of 15½ who had suffered from thalassaemia virtually since birth became a Jehovah's Witness and decided to cease having blood transfusions. Forcing them on her was, as she described it, 'like rape'.[41] To Johnson J: 'There are those who are children

---

[31] n 25 above. [32] In *Re C* [1994] 1 FLR 31.

[33] In *Re C*, n 32 above: applied in *Re JT* [1998] 1 FLR 48 to a 25-year-old learning-disabled adult held competent to refuse life-saving renal dialysis.

[34] *A Metropolitan Borough Council v DB* [1997] 1 FLR 767, 773 *per* Cazalet J and *Re C* [1997] 2 FLR 180, 195 *per* Wall J.   [35] *Re T* [1992] 2 FLR 458, 470.

[36] n 25 above at 26. And see J. Montgomery, 'Parents and Children in Dispute: Who Has the Final Word?' (1992) 4 *Journal of Child Law* 85.

[37] See sections 38(6), 43(8), 44(7). However, note the courts' interpretation in *South Glamorgan County Council v W and B* [1993] 1 FLR 574.   [38] n 27 above.

[39] *Re E* at 391.   [40] n 27 above.   [41] *Re S* at 1072.

and there are those who are adults and those who are in-between'.[42] He did not see S as in-between. She was 'a child' with the 'integrity and commitment of a child and not of somebody who was competent to make the decision that she tells me she has made. She hopes still for a miracle. My conclusion is, therefore, that she is not "*Gillick*-competent"'. Her capacity, he concluded, was not 'commensurate with the gravity of the decision which she has made'. She needed greater understanding of the manner of the death, the pain, and the distress. In *Re E* the boy died shortly after his eighteenth birthday—when treatment could no longer be imposed upon him.[43] It is possible that the same fate befell the girl in *Re S*. Both cases were decided upon what courts deemed to be in the child's best interests, but whether either of the children involved would have seen it that way or, had they lived, would have come to see it in that way, may be doubted.

When the child is over 16 Gillick competence is not the issue. It was thought that legislation[44] had made the law clear: at 16 a child could take his or her own decisions in relation to medical care.[45] But in *Re W*[46] the Court of Appeal decided we laboured under a misapprehension, and, even though the girl was 16, the local authority was granted leave to make an application for the exercise by the court of the inherent jurisdiction of the High Court. An anorexic, with sufficient understanding to make an informed choice, could be force-fed.[47]

THE CHILDREN ACT 1989

Of children's legislation passed since the end of World War II,[48] only the 1989 Act addresses the status of children. The Act has a number of sources, of which *Gillick* is one and Cleveland[49] another, and is the product of a number of value positions. For Fox Harding[50] dominant are paternalism and defence of the birth family: in my view the non-interventionist strand in the Act is overarching.[51] To Cleveland's assertion

---

[42] *Re S* at 1076.   [43] This fact was revealed in *Re S*, n 27 above, 1075.
[44] Family Law Reform Act 1969 s 8(1).
[45] But s 8(3) was ambiguous, thus leaving open the possibility that someone else could consent on behalf of a child of 16 or 17.   [46] n 26 above.
[47] See also *A Metropolitan Borough Council v DB*, n 34 above; *Re C*, n 34 above.
[48] Other Acts of importance are/were Children Act 1948, Children and Young Persons Act 1963, Children and Young Persons Act 1969, and Children Act 1975.
[49] *Report of Inquiry into Child Abuse in Cleveland*. London: HMSO Cm 62 (1988); below p 584.
[50] L. Fox Harding, 'The Children Act 1989 in Context: Four Perspectives in Child Care Law and Policy', (1991) *Journal of Social Welfare and Family Law* 179 and 285.
[51] M. Freeman, 'In the Child's Best Interests: Reading the Children Act Critically', (1992) 45 *Current Legal Problems—Annual Review* 173.

that 'the child is a person and not an object of concern', the Act responds with a package of children's rights measures, but it does so within a framework which emphasizes family autonomy[52] and within a network of practices which prioritizes family support over child protection.[53] Perhaps, therefore, it is not surprising that there should have been the retreat from *Gillick* just described, or that those provisions in the Act which emphasize the participatory powers of children should have been interpreted so restrictively.[54]

It would be wrong to conclude that the Act empowered children, as some commentators believed.[55] But it certainly gives children a number of powers which they lacked previously. For example, the power to initiate court actions. Thus, a child may challenge an emergency protection order,[56] seek contact when in care,[57] ask for a care order to be discharged[58] and, most importantly in the context of this chapter, seek the court's leave to obtain a s 8 order making decisions where s/he is to live or with whom have contact, or deciding a specific issue relating to his or her upbringing or prohibiting a parent from exercising parental responsibility in a particular way.[59]

The ability to seek leave to apply for a residence order led to suggestions (and criticisms) that this offered a facility for children to divorce their parents.[60] The image arrived neatly packaged from the United States[61] and what threatened for a short time to be a moral panic erupted. Gym-slipped folk-devils—that as many of them were boys as girls was conveniently ignored—were destroying the family. The reality is that there were very few cases and the courts kept a tight rein (indeed, an over-tight) on them. To apply for a residence order, the child, and no age is specified, requires leave to make the application, and the court must be satisfied that s/he has 'sufficient understanding'.[62] This in itself may be difficult enough to establish, but in *Re SC*[63] Booth J ruled that a court has discretion whether to grant leave even if it has been established that the child has sufficient understanding to make the application. The likely success of the substantive application is also to be considered. It has also been suggested (by Johnson J in *Re C*[64]) that the welfare principle

---

[52] See in particular s 1(5).

[53] M. Freeman, 'The End of the Century of the Child?' (2000) 53 *Current Legal Problems* (forthcoming).   [54] See below pp 449–52.

[55] D. Hodgson, 'Power to the Child', *Social Work Today* 12 July (1990) 16.

[56] Children Act 1989, s 45(8).   [57] *ibid* s 34(2).   [58] *ibid* s 39(1).   [59] *ibid* s 10(8).

[60] And see M. Freeman, 'Can Children Divorce Their Parents?' in M. Freeman (ed), *Divorce: Where Next?* Aldershot: Dartmouth (1996) 159.

[61] After publicity surrounding the Gregory Kingsley case: *Kingsley v Kingsley* 623 So 2d 780 (1993).   [62] Children Act 1989 s 10(8).

[63] [1994] 1 FLR 96, 98.

[64] [1994] 1 FLR 26, 28. Neither Booth J in *Re SC*, n 63 above, nor Stuart Smith J in *Re C* [1995] 1 FLR 927 agree.

should operate at the stage of the leave process. But this cannot be right, for at the filter stage it must be the child's wishes that are in issue.[65] Best interests would then come into play at the trial of the substantive issue.

The Act also emphasizes the importance of a child's wishes and feelings.[66] But a concern remains that children are not able to put their views to a court as readily as should be the case. Their views will often reach the court only through the filter of a welfare officer's report and may not, as a result, coincide with the child's views, particularly where these are not consistent with what the welfare officer believes to be in the child's best interests.[67] The case of *Re M*[68] graphically illustrates these difficulties. M was 12½ and deemed by the court to be able, intelligent, articulate, and having an attractive personality. She wanted to live with her father who had been denied a residence order. But she was not allowed to swear an affidavit supporting her father's appeal. On one level this is understandable: the welfare officer's report had already conveyed to the court what M's views were. But, since the welfare recommendation went against these views, it undermined the participatory rights of the person most affected by the decision. Butler-Sloss LJ was clearly concerned to prevent children becoming entangled in their parents' litigation, and alarmed that a child might be manipulated by a parent. But the end result—the silencing of an intelligent adolescent—sends out the wrong messages about the status of children.

On several occasions since the Children Act judges have positively discouraged children from participating in proceedings which related directly to them. In *Re C*,[69] where the views of a 13-year-old girl were discounted (she was, it was said, 'too young to carry the burden of decisions about her own future, and too young to have to bear the weight of responsibility for a parent who lacks authority and plays on her feelings of protectiveness'), the judge commented that 'to sit for hours, or it may even be days, listening to lawyers debating one's future is not an experience that should in normal circumstances be wished upon any child as young as this'. In *Re W*,[70] the liberty of a boy of 10 was at stake. The local authority was applying for a secure accommodation order. For the child it was contended that this was the equivalent of a custodial order in a criminal court, and that natural justice dictates that he should be allowed

---

[65] I expressed the opposite view in Freeman, n 60 above, at 169, but now concede that I was wrong to do so. See further M. Hayes and C. Williams, *Family Law: Principles, Policy and Practice*. London: Butterworths (1999) 101–4.

[66] Children Act 1989 s 1(3)(a). These must be considered in the light of the child's age and understanding.

[67] See, further, M. Freeman, 'The Next Children's Act?' (1998) 28 *Family Law* 341 and A. L. James and A. James, 'Pump up the Volume: Listening to Children in Separation and Divorce', (1999) 6 *Childhood* 189.   [68] [1995] 2 FLR 100.

[69] [1993] 1 FLR 832.   [70] [1994] 2 FLR 1092.

to be in court before an order is made which will have that effect. But the judge could not see 'any analogy between orders made in [the Family] Division and orders made by the criminal court'. And he added, in what may be thought a give-away line, 'the purpose of the criminal court is to deal with criminal offences committed *by people or children*' (my emphasis). By contrast, this jurisdiction is 'a benign jurisdiction'. That is how lawyers see it, but it is doubtful whether most adults, let alone most children, would so perceive it.

The judiciary has been hardly more receptive to allowing children to communicate their views in private. Back in 1981, Ormrod LJ said that whether a judge should see a child in private was a personal matter for himself to determine.[71] Earlier still, in 1974, Megaw LJ commented that it was 'of course most desirable . . . that the judge hearing the case should see the children and should see the children otherwise than in open court'.[72] But, despite the Children Act and the United Nations Convention (in particular Article 12), there is now an ambivalence, with a greater willingness to see children in public law proceedings than in private law cases. Thus, in *Re M*,[73] Wall J suggested that an 'intelligent and articulate 12 year old who had an excellent grasp of the issues and who had discussed the matter fully was entitled to see the judge who was to decide his future'. But the same judge, in *B* v *B*,[74] detected an inherent contradiction in seeing children to ascertain their wishes whilst being obliged to report to their parents anything material they said. The ambivalence also appears when the judiciary allow themselves the jurisdiction to see children in private but deny this to magistrates, who hear the bulk of the cases. Booth J thus thought it was only in 'rare and exceptional cases'[75] that magistrates were entitled to see children privately.

A striking difference between contemporary child litigation and that even a generation ago is the understanding of the importance of the child being independently represented. But how much autonomy should the child be given? In *Re S*[76] the then Master of the Rolls, Sir Thomas Bingham, addressed two considerations:

First . . . the principle that children are human beings in their own right with individual minds and wills, views and emotions, which should command serious attention. A child's wishes are not to be discounted or dismissed simply because he is a child. He should be free to express them and decision-makers should listen. Second is the fact that a child is, after all, a child. The reason why the law is particularly solicitous in protecting the interests of children is that they are liable to be vulnerable and impressionable, lacking the

---

[71] *D v D* [1981] 2 FLR 74.   [72] *H v H* [1974] 1 All ER 1145, 1147.
[73] [1994] 1 FLR 749, 755.   [74] [1994] 2 FLR 489.   [75] *Re M* [1993] 2 FLR 706, 709.
[76] [1993] 2 FLR 437.

maturity to weigh the longer term against the shorter, lacking the insight to know how they will react and the imagination to know how others will react in certain situations, lacking the experience to match the probable against the possible.

The case concerned a boy of 11. An application had been made by his father for residence and contact orders. He was made a party to the proceedings, and the Official Solicitor was appointed to act as his guardian ad litem.[77] The Official Solicitor recommended that V should continue to live with his mother (he had done so since he was 5), and should see his father less frequently. It was the father's contention, which S supported, that S should live with him in the United States. S contended from the outset of the proceedings that the Official Solicitor would not represent him, and that he should be able to act independently through a solicitor. The Court Rules allow this but they stipulate that the child must have 'understanding'. In line with the reasoning in *Gillick*, Sir Thomas Bingham MR emphasized understanding rather than age, and he accepted that this increased with the passage of time. He noted that 'different children have differing levels of understanding at the same age. And understanding is not an absolute. It has to be assessed relatively to the issues in the proceedings.'[78] But he concluded that 'where any sound judgment on these issues call for insight and imagination which only maturity and experience can bring both the court and the solicitor will be slow to conclude that the child's understanding is sufficient'. The boy's application was rejected. He may have been influenced, even over-influenced, by his father, and he may have been impressionable. But the Rules provide for children to be able to make such decisions and these decisions do not belong to the category of decisions where a mistake might harm them severely or irreparably.

A similar conclusion could have been reached in *Re H*,[79] but it was not. A 15-year-old boy was warded by his parents after the man with whom he was living was charged with sexual offences against another boy. He had been left in England when his parents moved to France. He now wished to stay in England, and ran away each time he was taken to France. It was his view that the Official Solicitor was not representing his views. He wished him to be removed and to be able to continue to defend the proceedings without the Official Solicitor acting as his guardian ad litem. There was a difference of psychiatric opinion. The psychiatrist instructed by the Official Solicitor considered that H lacked sufficient understanding to participate in the proceedings because he did not appreciate the dangers posed by a suspected sex offender. The psychia-

---

[77] On the role of which see D. Venables, 'The Official Solicitor', (1990) 20 *Family Law* 53.
[78] n 76 above, 444.   [79] [1993] 2 FLR 552.

trist treating H considered that the views expressed were those of H, and that having his own representative would assist him to feel that justice was being done, and so would ease his acceptance and compliance with the provisions made for him and reduce the risk of rash and unwise decisions. It was the latter opinion which Booth J preferred. She held that H had the understanding necessary to instruct his own legal advisor without the services of the Official Solicitor. This is a liberal conclusion, the more so since, if anything, one might have supposed that H was in greater need of protection than S. She also adopted a broader approach to competence than Sir Thomas Bingham MR did in *Re S*. She noted:

The court must be satisfied that H . . . has sufficient understanding to participate as a party . . . without a guardian ad litem. [This] . . . means much more than instructing a solicitor as to his own views. The child enters the arena among other adult parties. He may give evidence and he may be cross-examined. He will hear other parties, including in this case his parents, give evidence and be cross-examined. He must be able to give instructions on many different matters as the case goes through its stages and to make decisions as need arises. Thus a child is exposed and not protected in these procedures.

Of course, many adults do not have these abilities.

FROM RIGHTS TO RESPONSIBILITY

The second half of the twentieth century also saw a shift in the way parent–child relations were characterized, though the change can be exaggerated. The language and the symbolism altered, but there was not all that much substance to the change. The most significant change was effected by the Children Act 1989, some fifteen years after it was first recommended in a *Justice* report.[80] Parent–child relations were now to be characterized in terms of parental responsibility rather than parental rights. The 1980s, the dismal years of Thatcher, were a period in which we were supposed to believe that there was no such thing as society, only individuals. This is not an environment in which an emphasis on responsibility could be expected to emerge. That it did may say something for the relative autonomy of the law-making process. It may also explain why the change was more apparent than real. The new 'politics of the common good',[81] with responsibility as one of its key features, does not seem to have been a major influence.

[80] *Parental Rights and Duties and Custody Suits*. London: Stevens (1975).
[81] M. Sandel, 'Morality and the Liberal Ideal', *New Republic* (7 May 1984) 15.

The shift from parental rights to parental responsibilities was generally welcomed. It also led to a questioning of where rights, and to a lesser extent, responsibilities came from. That the debate emerged at all may partly be explained by the reproduction revolution.[82] The fact that the 'private'[83] (and hence the family) was being opened up to theoretical analysis was equally, if not more, significant.[84] Rights are redolent of property, whereas responsibility conjures up an image of trusteeship.[85] By emphasizing parental responsibility rather than rights, the 1989 Act conveyed three messages. First, that responsibility is more important than rights. Even where parents have rights they may have responsibilities not to exercise them.[86] The courts have long stressed the importance of parental responsibilities: parental rights being justified because they enabled a parent to perform duties towards the child.[87] Second, that it is parents, and not therefore children, who are the decision-makers. This and the *Gillick* decision send out conflicting messages. Interestingly, the Lord Chancellor responsible for the Children Act 1989 gave assurances that the new emphasis on parental responsibility did not overturn the *Gillick* principle.[88] The retreat from *Gillick*, discussed above, suggests the courts may think otherwise. Third, the emphasis on parental responsibility conveys the all-important message that it is parents, and not the state, who have responsibility for children. The consequences of this are that parents have responsibility in a normative sense even when they act with complete disregard for that responsibility.[89] Thus, English law now only allows a parent to be divested of parental responsibility when the child is transplanted into another family by adoption.[90] The grossly abusive parent retains parental responsibility even where the child is subject to a care order and is removed from parents.[91]

Who has parental responsibility? Mothers always do, but as far as fathers are concerned, English law has moved little in the last fifty years. Indeed, with births outside marriage now more than a third of all births

---

[82] J. L. Hill,'What Does it Mean to be a "Parent"? The Claims of Biology as the Basis for Parental Rights', (1991) 66 *New York University Law Review* 353.

[83] N. Rose, 'Beyond the Public/Private Divide: Law, Power and the Family', (1987) 14 *Journal of Law and Society* 61.

[84] K. Bartlett, 'Re-expressing Parenthood', (1988) 98 *Yale Law Journal* 293.

[85] And see C. Beck, G. Glavis, M. Barnes Jenkins, and R. Nardi, 'The Rights of Children: A Trust Model', (1978) 46 *Fordham Law Review* 669. Also see C. Barton and G. Douglas, *Law and Parenthood*. London: Butterworths (1995) 22–8.

[86] M. Brazier, 'Liberty, Responsibility, Maternity', (1999) 52 *Current Legal Problems* 359.

[87] eg Lord Scarman in *Gillick*, n 21 above.

[88] *House of Lords Debates (Hansard)*, vol 502, col 1351.

[89] J. Eekelaar, 'Parental Responsibility: State of Nature or Nature of the State?', (1991) *Journal of Social Welfare and Family Law* 37.

[90] Or after surrogacy (see Human Fertilisation and Embryology Act 1990 s 30).

[91] Children Act 1989 s 33(3)(b), (4).

(though most of these take place in stable cohabitations),[92] a higher percentage of men today do not require parental responsibility than had parental rights vested in them in 1945. In the period in between, illegitimacy ceased to have the legal significance or social stigma that it once had. Legislation in 1987[93] has meant that the fact of marriage between parents is irrelevant unless statute expressly provides to the contrary. An example is the British Nationality Act 1981 under which a person born in the United Kingdom shall be a British citizen if at the time of his birth, his father or mother is a British citizen or is settled in the United Kingdom.[94] But 'the relationship of father and child shall be taken to exist only between a man and any legitimate child born to him'.[95] Gay men cannot inter-marry and thus can never pass on citizenship to any child. This problem arose in acute form at the beginning of 2000, when a child was born by a surrogacy arrangement in California and was denied entry to the United Kingdom even though the homosexual couple involved were both British citizens.[96] But, short of amending legislation, it is likely to happen again and again.

Fathers are only ascribed parental responsibility when at the date of the child's birth they are married to the mothers.[97] Whether married or not, they come within the definition of 'parent' in the Children Act. This means that they are in the same position as all other parents for the purposes of succession.[98] An unmarried father without parental responsibility has an obligation to maintain.[99] There is a presumption of reasonable contact in his favour.[100] He has the right to be consulted by a local authority about decisions taken in relation to his child where the local authority is providing accommodation for the child.[101] He can apply without leave for a s 8 order.[102] On the other hand, his agreement is not required for adoption.[103]

Thus, English law emphasizes the importance of parental responsibility but withholds it from more than one-third of fathers. And it may be supposed that most of these men live in stable cohabitations and remain blissfully unaware that they are denied responsibility.[104] Only where there is a dispute (about education or medical treatment, for example) or when the relationship breaks down is the significance of their defective status likely to bite. The justifications offered for discriminating against unmarried

---

[92] Three-quarters of births to unmarried women are jointly registered and three-quarters of these registrations are by couples at the same address.

[93] Family Law Reform Act 1987 s 1(1). [94] s 1(1). [95] s 50(a)(b).

[96] See *The Independent*, 12 Jan 2000. [97] Children Act 1989 s 2(2)(b).

[98] Famly Law Reform Act 1987 s 1(1). [99] Under the Child Support Act 1991.

[100] Children Act 1989 s 34(1)(a). [101] *ibid* s 22(4). [102] *ibid* s 10(4)(a).

[103] See *Re C* [1993] 2 FLR 260.

[104] As also the mothers: see S. McRae, *Cohabiting Mothers: Changing Marriage Parenthood*. London: Policy Studies Institute (1993).

fathers in this way are weak,[105] were countered by the Scottish Law Commission in 1992,[106] and are no longer seriously advanced.[107] Most hyped was the thin end of the wedge argument that to confer rights on all fathers would amount to a 'rapists' charter'. But, as Barton and Douglas conclude, the rapist is a 'phantom figure'.[108] English law is likely to change early in the millennium, very possibly to ascribe parental responsibility to all fathers whose names appear on the register of births.[109] Until it does, the law offers fathers a number of ways of acquiring parental responsibility. This (since the Children Act 1989) can be done by private agreement[110] (although there are formalities, these are of an administrative rather than judicial nature and so scrutinize neither whether the man is indeed the father nor whether the sharing of parental responsibility will be in the child's best interests). If the mother is unwilling to share responsibility voluntarily, the father may apply to the court for a parental responsibility order[111] (or, if he wishes to take over the physical care of the child, for a residence order[112]). There are few reported cases where parental responsibility orders have been refused.[113] The overriding consideration is the child's welfare: so, for example, acrimony between the parents is not, it has been held, a good reason to refuse an order.[114] And an order can be made where a contact order is refused.[115] The courts are clear what the father needs to satisfy to be granted an order (commitment, attachment, and good reasons for applying[116]) but are not so clear as to what orders are for. They will eventually disappear with emerging reforms, leaving us with greater scope for parental disputes to be decided by specific issue and prohibited steps orders.

English law is also rather poor at defining parental responsibility. It does not even lay down the standards of care which children can expect

---

[105] A. Bainham, 'When is a Parent not a Parent? Reflections on the Unmarried Father and His Child in English Law', (1989) 3 *International Journal of Law and the Family* 208. But for a contrary view see R. Deech, 'The Unmarried Father and Human Rights', (1992) 4 *Journal of Child Law* 3.

[106] Scottish Law Commission, *Report on Family Law*. Edinburgh: HMSO (1992) paras 2.36–2.51.

[107] The views of Ruth Deech, n 105 above, are isolated and dated.   [108] n 85 above, 93.

[109] Lord Chancellor's Department, *The Law on Parental Responsibility for Unmarried Fathers*. London: HMSO (1998).

[110] Children Act 1989 s 4(1)(b). In 1996 there were 3,590 agreements registered, a ludicrously low figure, suggesting that the facility is not known about.

[111] Children Act 1989 s 4(1)(a).   [112] *ibid* s 12(1).

[113] Examples of refusals are *Re P* [1997] 2 FLR 722 (where the father had a long term of imprisonment); *Re H* [1998] 1 FLR 855 (where he had injured the child in a sadistic manner); and *Re P* [1998] 2 FLR 96 (father's motivation inappropriate). Contrast *Re S* [1995] 2 FLR 648 (order despite possession of obscene literature and failure to pay child maintenance).

[114] *Re P* [1994] 1 FLR 578.   [115] *Re H* [1993] 1 FLR 484.   [116] *Re H* [1991] 1 FLR 214.

from parents,[117] which puts it in breach of the United Nations Convention which requires States Parties to 'render appropriate assistance to parents and legal guardians in the performance of their child-rearing responsibilities'.[118] The Children Act simply defines parental responsibility as 'the rights, duties, powers, responsibilities and authority which by law a parent has in relation to the child and his property'.[119] This, of course, begs the question and leaves the courts to provide content in the context of disputes. Perhaps no other solution was practicable. Certainly a comprehensive list would be difficult.[120] But there remains the feeling that English law has sacrificed principle to pragmatism. Scottish law, by contrast, at least attempts to formulate some parental responsibilities.[121] This incoherence is well illustrated also by the vast amount of recent litigation testing the rights of mothers to change children's surnames. The Children Act 1989, short of a residence order, would seem to have enabled one parent to change the child's surname without the other's consent.[122] But that surely cannot have been intended and so Holman J held in *Re PC*,[123] where any suggestion that a parent with parental responsibility could unilaterally change his or her child's surname was criticized as 'little short of bizarre'.[124] This would put the unmarried mother into a stronger position than her married counterpart. Only she can register the child's surname[125] and she can change it by deed poll without the father's consent (only the consent of those with parental responsibility is required). Or so we thought.[126] But the House of Lords recently held that the Court of Appeal was right to conclude that:

the registration or change of a child's surname is a profound and not a merely formal issue, whatever the age of the child. Any dispute on such an issue must be referred to the court for determination whether or not there is a residence order in force and whoever has or has not parental responsibility. No disputed registration or change should be made unilaterally.[127]

There is, accordingly, 'a heavy responsibility on those who seek to effect the change, first, as a matter of prudence if not of direct law to take the issue of dispute for the resolution of the judge and to appreciate that

---

[117] C. Lyon, 'The Definition of, and Legal and Management Responses to, Child Abuse in England and Wales', in M. Freeman (ed), *Overcoming Child Abuse: A Window on a World Problem*. Aldershot: Ashgate (2000) 95.   [118] Article 18(2).

[119] Children Act 1989 s 3(1) and see N. Lowe, 'The Meaning and Allocation of Parental Responsibility—A Common Lawyer's Perspective', (1997) 11 *International Journal of Law, Policy and the Family* 192.

[120] In the past attempts were made to define parental rights: the best was J. Eekelaar, 'What are Parental Rights?' (1973) 89 *Law Quarterly Review* 210.

[121] Children (Scotland) Act 1995 s 1(1). Parental rights are defined in s 2(1).

[122] By s 2(7).   [123] [1997] 2 FLR 730.   [124] At 736.

[125] Births and Deaths Registration Act 1953 s 10(1).

[126] This was the view of the textbook writers; indeed, it passed barely noticed and certainly as uncontentious.   [127] *Dawson v Wearmouth* [1999] 2 All ER 353 at 358.

good reasons have to be shown before the judge will allow such a change'. On one level this is understandable, for what it does is to circumscribe the exercise of parental responsibility to the promotion of a child's welfare. But on another level all that it achieves is to prevent the mother from changing the child's surname where the father contests the change. It may seem odd to ordinary people that someone with parental responsibility cannot do what someone without it can seek to stop. The cases confirm how unclear the concepts are and, most importantly, the way children's welfare has continued to eclipse parental responsibility.

DISPUTES ABOUT CHILDREN

In the period under consideration there have been enormous changes in the ways adults have disputed about children The language has changed. No longer are children regarded as packages or pieces of property to be moved about.[128] The concepts have changed.[129] In 1945 one sought the custody of a child (this has a broader and narrower meaning, though this was rarely recognized[130]). There must have been disputes over access (as it was then called[131]) but there is no evidence in the law reports that this was a live issue. Wardship had only just emerged as an institution to protect a child's welfare,[132] rather than family property, but for a quarter of a century thereafter was used primarily to target elopement.[133] The law operated with presumptions: young children should be placed in the custody of their mothers;[134] older children, especially boys, should be brought up by their fathers.[135] Whether the law favoured mothers, as is often claimed, or whether decisions to give custody to the mother reflected an understandable desire to protect the residential status quo— it being commonly the case that it is fathers who leave when a marriage breaks down—it was (and still is) mothers who usually got/continued to care for children after divorce.[136] This was what nature had 'ordained', as Stamp LJ put it in 1978. And he added: 'however good a man may be, he cannot perform the functions which a mother performs by nature in relation to her own little girl.'[137]

---

[128] *Re B* [1992] 2 FLR 1, 5 *per* Butler-Sloss LJ.
[129] Since the Children Act 1989 concepts like 'custody' and 'access' have been replaced by 'residence' and 'contact'.　　　　　[130] It was in *Dipper v Dipper* [1980] 2 All ER 722.
[131] Since the Children Act the word 'contact' has been used.
[132] See N. V. Lowe and R. A. H. White, *Wards of Court*. London: Barry Rose (1986) ch 1.
[133] See G. Cross, 'Wards of Court', (1967) 83 *Law Quarterly Review* 200.
[134] *Re B* [1962] 1 All ER 872; *Re S* [1958] 1 All ER 783; *Re O* [1971] ch 748 (the more so when she did not work: see at 752).　　　　　[135] *Re C (A)* [1970] 1 All ER 309.
[136] J. A. Priest and J. C. Whybrow, *Custody Law in Practice in the Divorce and Domestic Courts*. London: HMSO (1986).　　　　　[137] *M v M* [1978] 1 FLR 77.

The presumptions have gone, replaced by 'considerations'. Thus, Butler-Sloss LJ in *Re S* could still talk, in 1991, of its being 'natural' for young children to be with their mothers, but, she added, 'where it is in dispute, it is a consideration . . . not a presumption'.[138] She explained this further in *Re A*.[139]

In cases where the child has remained throughout with the mother and is young, particularly when a baby or a toddler, the unbroken relationship of the mother and child is one which it would be very difficult to displace, unless the mother was unsuitable to care for the child. But where the mother and child have been separated, and the mother seeks the return of the child, other considerations apply, and there is no starting-point that the mother should be preferred to the father . . .

And she stressed again that there is no presumption which requires the mother, 'as mother', to be considered as the primary caretaker in preference to the father. Even so, it is rare for the father to be preferred to the mother where the child is young. When this happened in 1998 in *Re K*[140] the case attracted considerable media attention.[141] The child had been with his mother for 'a good deal of his life, but not the whole of it, and had never been in the exclusive care of his father'. In the United States the tender years presumption may have been displaced because of feminist demands that men and women be treated equally.[142] There is no evidence that the attenuation of the doctrine in England—for that is what the replacement of presumptions by considerations amounts to—can be similarly explained.

Throughout the period under consideration the courts have purported to decide disputes about children guided by their best interests. The governing legislation in 1945 was the Guardianship of Infants Act 1925. This was passed to inject some equality into the rights of parents.[143] It certainly was not passed to make the child's best interests the only consideration, nor was it intended to apply to disputes between parents and third parties (foster parents, relatives). But the House of Lords in *J v C* in 1969 put both these constructions on the legislation.[144] Legislation in 1969[145] did not change the test and the child's welfare remained 'first and paramount' until the Children Act 1989 replaced this by 'paramount',

---

[138] [1991] 2 FLR 388, 390.   [139] [1991] 2 FLR 394.   [140] [1999] 1 FLR 583.

[141] Thus 'Mother's Day Has Gone, says Custody Judge' said *The Times*, 27 Nov 1998. It noted that twice as many men were looking after their children compared with 1993.

[142] M. A. Mason, *The Custody Wars*. New York: Basic Books (1999) ch 1.

[143] J. Brophy, 'Parental Rights and Children's Welfare: Some Problems of Feminists' Strategy in the 1920s', (1982) 10 *International Journal of the Sociology of Law* 149; I. Théry, ' "The Interest of the Child" and the Regulation of the Post-Divorce Family' in C. Smart and S. Sevenhuijsen (eds), *Child Custody and the Politics of Gender* (1989) 78–99; See also S. Cretney, n 9 above.   [144] [1970] AC 668.

[145] Guardianship of Minors Act 1969.

thus endorsing the Lords' construction of twenty years earlier.[146] Section 1 of the 1989 provides that:

When a court determines any question with respect to
(a) the upbringing of a child; or
(b) the administration of the child's property or the application of any income arising from it,
the child's welfare shall be the court's paramount consideration.

The courts have construed 'upbringing' narrowly. For example, where what is in issue is the child's paternity, this only indirectly concerns a child's upbringing and so falls outside the paramountcy test.[147] So, it has been held, do applications to restrict the publication of a book that might be harmful to a child:[148] the courts apparently still think that free speech is more important than the protection of a child's interests. Although the paramountcy principle has come under attack in recent years, in particular for allowing other policies and principles to 'smuggle themselves' into children's cases,[149] it has been extended in the latest divorce legislation to guide courts into refusing to make a divorce order.[150] The paramountcy principle is, of course, an indeterminate notion. Without the injection of normative content it is exposed to the criticism that decisions will be atomistic, or worse, idiosyncratic.[151] English law accordingly made a major advance in 1989 (a practice followed in the 1996 Act too[152]) when it structured the discretion of the courts by laying down a checklist of factors to be considered before making a decision about a child.[153] This checklist requires a court to have regard in particular to such matters as a child's wishes and feelings; needs; the likely effect of any change of circumstances; age, sex, and background; any harm suffered or risk of harm; the capability of his parents (and any other relevant person) of meeting his needs; and the range of powers open to the court. The list can be said

---

[146] It is generally acknowledged that the removal of the words 'first and', leaving the child's welfare as the 'paramount consideration' merely confirmed the *J v C* interpretation of the previous language.   [147] *S v Mc (formerly S)* [1972] AC 24.

[148] *Re Z* [1997] Fam 1. See generally J. Moriarty, 'Children, Privacy and the Press', (1997) 9 *Child and Family Law Quarterly* 217.

[149] H. Reece, 'The Paramountcy Principle: Consensus or Construct?' (1996) 49 *Current Legal Problems* 267, 268.   [150] Family Law Act 1996 s 11(3).

[151] On indeterminacy see R. Mnookin, 'Child Custody Adjudication: Judicial Functions in the Face of Indeterminacy', (1975) 29 *Law and Contemporary Problems* 226; S. Parker, 'The Best Interests of the Child—Principles and Problems' in P. Alston (ed), *The Best Interests of the Child*. Oxford: Clarendon Press (1994).   [152] Family Law Act 1996 s 11(4).

[153] Children Act 1989 s 1(3). 'Best interests' is applied in areas of medical law as well (eg to decisions about sterilization of the learning disabled: *Re B* [1988] AC 199; *Re F* [1990] 2 AC 1) but without a structuring or an injection of normative content, each case is decided on its merits as individual judges see it. This is criticized by I. Kennedy, *Treat Me Right: Essays in Medical Law and Ethics*. Oxford: Oxford University Press (1992).

to reflect a broad-based consensus of both professional and popular opinion. It is child-centred: there is thus no reference to parental conduct, sexual orientation, or new relationships. In many cases those factors which
are relevant may all point in the same direction. But obviously there are
cases where different items in the guidelines will suggest different conclusions. The legislation does not prioritize any factor, though many will
take comfort from its placing of the ascertainable wishes and feelings of
the child as first in the list.

Inevitably, areas of controversy still exist, and however constrained the
discretion there will remain an irreducible element of value judgment. A
good example is the case where the judge made a residence order in
favour of the father because he disapproved of the attitude of the mother
and her new partner to nudity and communal bathing. The Court of
Appeal, not surprisingly, allowed the mother's appeal.[154] A high profile
area of controversy in recent years—and one where values necessarily
intrude—concerns a parent's sexual orientation.[155] In one case[156] Balcombe
LJ advised that it was necessary to apply the moral standards of the
community. He continued:

> It is still the norm that children are brought up in a home with a father, mother
> and siblings (if any) and, other things being equal, such an upbringing is most
> likely to be conducive to their welfare. If, because the parents are divorced, such
> an upbringing is no longer possible, then a very material factor in considering
> where the child's welfare lies is which of the competing parents can offer the
> nearest approach to the norm.

It was, he said 'clearly the father' since the mother was living in a lesbian
relationship. The father would offer 'a normal home by the standards of
our society'. The court was concerned with both the stigma a child would
suffer if brought up in a lesbian relationship and the effect this would
have on the child's own sexuality.[157]

It has come to be accepted that an important consideration in a dispute
over where the child shall live is which of the parents will be best able to
encourage a continuing relationship between the child and the absent
parent and the wider family.[158] But shared parenting lacks the profile that
it has in the United States. There is no evidence that the early Wallerstein
and Kelly research *Surviving the Break-up* had any impact in Britain.[159] In

---

[154] *Re W* [1999] FLR 869.

[155] And see K. Standley, 'Children and Lesbian Mothers', (1992) 4 *Journal of Child Law* 134;
H. Reece, n 149 above.   [156] *C v C* [1991] 1 FLR 223.

[157] Cf *B v B* [1991] 1 FLR 402. Curiously, the courts take a much more liberal attitude to
homosexuality in the context of adoption: *Re W* [1997] 2 FLR 406.

[158] See J. Pryor and F. Seymour, 'Making Decisions about Children after Parental Separation', (1996) 8 *Child and Family Law Quarterly* 229.

[159] But see M. Freeman, 'How Children Cope With Divorce—New Evidence on an Old
Problem', (1981) 11 *Family Law* 105.

1945, and for most of the period under consideration, shared parenting was not even discussed in Britain. In 1986 the Court of Appeal decided that it was not open to a court to make what was then called a joint care and control order.[160] The 1989 Act, however, does allow for such orders to be made.[161] Few are. Initially, the view taken was that such orders were to be made only in 'exceptional circumstances'.[162] The Court of Appeal later ruled that they may be made in 'unusual' circumstances'.[163] It is a way of conferring parental responsibility on a step-parent and this, it has been held,[164] is an example of such an unusual circumstance (though the reality is that such reconstituted families are very common). The Court of Appeal has given guidance on when a shared residence order is not appropriate: this would be when there are concrete issues still to be resolved, such as the type and amount of contact and education questions.[165] The probability is that shared parenting works best where the parties do not need to go to court for any order.[166]

It is recognized now—it certainly wasn't in 1945—that parents, with or without help,[167] can make post-separation child arrangements themselves. This has led to what is perhaps the greatest change in the English approach to disputes about children. Before the Children Act 1989 court orders were sought and made in almost all divorce cases involving children.[168] But, following the view of the Government that 'families should generally be left to sort out matters for themselves unless it is shown that without an order the child's welfare will suffer',[169] section 1(5) of the Children Act provides: 'Where a court is considering whether or not to make one or more orders under this Act with respect to a child, it shall not make the order or any of the orders unless it considers that doing so would be better for the child than making no order at all.' Orders are accordingly only to be made where they resolve disputes or in some other way benefit a child, for example to facilitate the grant of public housing and thus ensure the child is properly housed. Also, if the child is to be looked after by someone who would not otherwise have parental responsibility (a grandparent, for example), then making an order (a residence order in favour of the grandparent which would confer parental responsibility on her) may well benefit the child, since

---

[160] *Riley v Riley* [1986] 2 FLR 429.
[161] s 11(4).   [162] *Re H* [1994] 1 FLR 717.   [163] *A v A* [1994] 1 FLR 669.
[164] *Re H* [1995] 2 FLR 883.   [165] n 163 above, at 677.
[166] So that where they seek an order, it probably should not be made (it will not be better for the child than making no order).
[167] Counselling, conciliation, and mediation. See *Practice Direction: Conciliation—Children* [1992] 1 FLR 228. See also G. Davis, *Partisans and Mediators: The Resolution of Divorce Disputes*. Oxford: Clarendon Press (1988).
[168] See J. A. Priest and J. C. Whybrow, n 136 above, 222.
[169] Lord Mackay, 'The Joseph Jackson Memorial Lecture', (1989) 139 *New Law Journal* 505.

the person with whom he is now living will be able to take decisions about his upbringing.[170]

Some of the most hotly contested disputes about children concern contact. Disputes arise about frequency and about venue[171] and also over the quality of the contact (for example, whether staying contact is to be allowed). Until the Children Act came into operation the normal practice was to order reasonable access (as it was then called) and leave it to the parties to agree on what was reasonable. With the adoption of the minimal intervention principle in s 1(5), the reasonable contact order has fallen into desuetude. In 1962 the Court of Appeal was clear that access was a non-custodial parent's right.[172] By 1973 it was being viewed as the right of the child, so that no court was to deprive a child of access to a parent unless wholly satisfied that it was in the child's interest that there should be none.[173] This was the earliest judicial pronouncement on children's rights, and it has been repeated many times.[174] The importance of contact is reflected in the development of contact centres, and in the encouragement of indirect contact (letters, presents, telephone calls) where direct contact is impracticable or undesirable.[175] Also, courts have imposed obligations on the residential parent to send photographs, school reports, and the like, and to read the non-residential parent's letters to the child.[176] The courts have also increasingly recognized the importance to a child of retaining or regaining contact with persons other than parents. In one recent case,[177] the court ordered contact to resume between a man (a father figure) and his former stepson, whilst at the same time denying him contact to his own son.

There is a perception that disputes over contact (and probably over residence as well) have intensified in the 1990s.[178] This may be explained in a number of ways. First, with almost no divorces being defended and with the growth of mediation, divorce has become much more a private affair, less visible and less controlled.[179] Second, whether or not men are taking on more child care responsibilities, many now think differently about their role as fathers and their relationship with their children, which, not surprisingly, they wish to survive their

---

[170] *B v B* [1992] 2 FLR 327.
[171] Hence the development of contact centres, on which see E. Halliday, 'The Role and Function of Child Contact Centres', (1997) 19 *Journal of Social Welfare and Family Law* 53.
[172] *S v S and P* [1962] 2 All ER 1, 3 *per* Willmer J.
[173] *M v M* [1973] 2 All ER 81, 85 *per* Wrangham J.   [174] eg in *Re R* [1993] 2 FLR 762.
[175] As in *Re M* [1994] 1 FLR 272. See also *Re P* [1999] 2 FLR 893.
[176] *Re O* [1995] 2 FLR 124.   [177] *Re C and V* [1998] 1 FLR 392.
[178] R. Bailey-Harris, G. Davis, G. J. Barron, and J. Pearce, *Monitoring Private Law Applications under the Children Act 1989*. Bristol: University of Bristol (1998).
[179] See J. Roche, 'Children and Divorce: A Private Affair?' in S. D. Sclater and C. Piper (eds), *Undercurrents of Divorce*. Aldershot: Ashgate (1999) 55–75.

divorce.[180] Third, we have become much more aware of domestic violence:[181] this only re-emerged as a social problem in the 1970s and may
now feature in a quarter of the marriages which end in divorce.[182]
Domestic violence has also come to be accepted as a form of child
abuse.[183] Fourth (and ironically) as mediation and counselling grow to
take the heat out of divorce, they may also fuel or rekindle anger as
couples relive the past even as they disentangle themselves.[184] Whatever the explanation, we have seen the emergence of the 'implacably
hostile' parent (invariably the mother), of a growth of allegations of
sexual abuse,[185] and of domestic violence being raised in the context of
contact.

The courts do not react favourably to implacable hostility. Thus, in *Re
O*,[186] Sir Thomas Bingham MR said: 'Neither parent should be encouraged or permitted to think that the more intransigent, the more unreasonable, the more obdurate and the more unco-operative they are, the more
likely they are to get their own way.' In *Re P*[187] this reluctance to allow
implacable hostility to prevail led the Court of Appeal to order supervised contact to a father with a history of psychiatric illness, alcohol and
drug abuse and who had Nazi sympathies,[188] despite the fact that contact
was thought likely to cause the mother stress and anxiety which would
communicate itself to the children whose welfare would as a result suffer
detriment. But, in another case where a court welfare officer concluded
that it would not be in a 10-year-old boy's best interests to be forced into
a situation which for him was 'fraught with anxiety and insecurity',[189] the
judge allowed the mother's implacable hostility to prevail. Balcombe LJ
acknowledged that the father might feel he is suffering injustice. He was,

---

[180] See B. Lupton and L. Barclay, *Constructing Fatherhood Discourses and Experiences*.
London: Sage (1997).

[181] See M. Kaye, 'Domestic Violence, Residence and Contact', (1996) 8 *Child and Family
Law Quarterly* 285.

[182] The Law Commission in 1998 said 22% (*Facing The Future*, Law Com. No. 170,
Appendix C), L. Anderson, 'Contact between Children and Violent Fathers—In Whose Best
Interests?' *Rights of Women Bulletin* (Summer Issue, 1997) reports nearly one-third of cases
involve violence *after* proceedings commenced. See also R. Ingleby, *Solicitors and Divorce*.
Oxford: Clarendon Press (1992).

[183] A. Mullender and R. Morley (eds), *Children Living with Domestic Violence: Putting Men's
Abuse of Women on the Child Care Agenda*. London: Whiting and Birch (1994).

[184] See C. Piper, *The Responsible Parent*. Hemel Hempstead: Harvester Wheatsheaf (1993).

[185] On which see N. Thoennes and P. G. Tjaden, 'The Extent, Nature and Validity of
Sexual Abuse Allegations in Custody/Visitation Disputes', (1990) 14 *Child Abuse and Neglect*
151. C-A. Hooper, *Mothers Surviving Child Sexual Abuse*, London: Routledge (1992) refers to
the suggestion that allegations are false as a 'new myth' (at 18).   [186] [1995] 2 FLR 124.

[187] [1996] 2 FLR 314.

[188] Rather disappointingly the judge held that a father who is a racist cannot be denied
contact to his children on that ground alone (see at 320). Given that he dressed his sons
(aged 5 and 8) in Nazi regalia this is a quite unacceptable conclusion.

[189] See *Re J* [1994] 1 FLR 729, 732.

but 'this is yet another example where the welfare of the child requires the court to inflict injustice upon a parent with whom the child is not resident'.[190]

Because there are so many allegations of implacable hostility there is a danger that opposition to contact by a mother will attract this label even where she has genuine and rationally held fears for her child or herself. The two situations must be distinguished.[191] In *Re D*, where there had been domestic violence, the Court of Appeal agreed with the judge that the mother's fears of the father were genuine and that contact should not be restored in the immediate future.[192] The child was of mixed parentage (Ghanaian father, Canadian mother): unfortunately, the court addressed only the negative features of this (since the child thought his father 'nasty', he might accept racial stereotyping), and not the positive (denying the child contact would deprive him of cultural heritage and identity). The courts have been reluctant to refuse contact because of domestic violence. In an early case[193] in which it was refused, the mother had left the father before the child was born (because of his violence) and the father had not seen the child since his birth. In *Re A*[194] there were assaults on a child of 3 (for which there had been police cautions) and domestic violence. In *Re K*[195] there had not only been violence but a particularly brutal kidnap of the child before his second birthday. Indirect contact only was allowed. It may be that the court paid insufficient attention to the fact that the child (now nearly 6) actually enjoyed contact.[196] Most recently has come the firmest denunciation of domestic violence in a contact case. In *Re M*[197] Wall J said:

Often in these cases where domestic violence has been found, too little weight . . . is given to the need for the father to change. It is often said that, notwithstanding the violence, the mother must nonetheless bring up the children with full knowledge and a positive image of their natural father and arrange for the children to be available for contact. Too often . . . the courts neglect the other side of the equation, which is that a father . . . must demonstrate that he is a fit person to exercise contact; that he is not going to destabilise the family, that he is not going to upset the children and harm them emotionally.

---

[190] At 736. Balcombe LJ may have been over-sympathetic to a man who had used violence against his son and who was a pimp.

[191] See to this effect Hale J in *Re D* [1997] 2 FLR 48, 53.

[192] It was envisaged that the father might reapply for contact in three to four years, when it might succeed since he was becoming 'gentle, considerate and caring'.

[193] *Re D* [1993] 2 FLR 1. For cases involving domestic violence and contact, 1993 must be regarded as 'early'. [194] [1998] 2 FLR 171.

[195] [1999] 2 FLR 703.

[196] The child's confusions were expressed in guilt feelings: it was clear to him that contact distressed the mother. [197] [1999] 2 FLR 321.

RELIGION AND RACE

Neither religion nor race is specifically referred to in the welfare checklist to which reference has already been made, but both are clearly embraced by 'background'.[198] In the past, religion has assumed what to us today is a disproportionate and disruptive influence on decisions about a child's upbringing.[199] Until recently, questions of race (and concomitantly of culture and colour) were not issues. But one of the main differences between the England of 1945 and today is that it is now a multicultural society with nearly 6 per cent of the population belonging to non-white ethnic minorities. There is also considerable religious diversity. One result is that both religion and race issues have thrown up some of the most difficult, and certainly some of the most controversial, questions in relation to children.

The courts have consistently declined to discriminate between one faith and another.[200] Nor have they throughout the period under consideration been prepared to favour a religion over none at all.[201] They have occasionally taken the view that a particular form of religious upbringing is intrinsically harmful to the child, because it isolates him socially and educationally.[202] Even stronger opposition was taken in one case[203] to the cult of scientology, and it was held that its harmful effects necessitated transferring the care of the children from the father to the mother (a scientology court having given the father custody), even though they had lived with him for five-and-a-half years in a stable relationship.[204] But in general the view prevailing is that it is not for the court to pass any judgment on the beliefs of a parent where they are socially acceptable and consistent with a decent and respectable life.[205] Where the residential parent has a religious practice which could potentially harm a child (for example, a Jehovah's Witness who will not countenance blood transfusions), courts have imposed undertakings. Courts have sometimes required persons looking after a child to bring him up in his religion even where it is not theirs. This happened in the leading

---

[198] Children Act 1989 s 1(3)(d). In *Re P* [1999] 2 FLR 573, Ward LJ said that 'Religious beliefs must not be devalued' (at 596). Religion also comes within 'educational needs', see s 1(3)(b) and *Re J* [1999] 2 FLR 678, 685 *per* Wall J.

[199] See eg *Hawksworth v Hawksworth* (1871) 6 Ch App 539, where reference was made to the need to have 'sacred regard to the religion of the father'.   [200] *Re Carroll* [1931] 1 KB 317.

[201] They once showed antipathy to atheism: *Shelley v Westbrooke* (1817) Jac 66n; *Re Besant* (1879) 11 Ch D 508.

[202] This view was taken of the Exclusive Brethren in *Hewitson v Hewitson* (1977) 7 *Fam Law* 207.

[203] *Re B and G* [1985] FLR 134 (Latey J). He was affirmed by the Court of Appeal: see [1985] FLR 493.

[204] Latey J described scientology as immoral, socially obnoxious, corrupt, sinister, and dangerous.   [205] *Re T* [1981] 2 FLR 239; *Re R* [1993] 2 FLR 163.

case of *J v C*:[206] English foster parents who were Anglicans were ordered to continue to bring up the son of Roman Catholic Spanish parents as a Roman Catholic and were not allowed to send him to an Anglican choir school.[207] But now it has been said that only in unusual circumstances would a court require that a child be brought up in a religion which was not that of the parent with whom the child was residing.[208]

Such circumstances occurred in the most graphic recent example of religious conflict about a child's upbringing to challenge an English court. In *Re J*,[209] a Turkish Muslim father sought specific issue orders from the court in relation to his 5-year-old son, one requiring the nominally Christian mother to raise the child as a Muslim, and another requiring her to have the boy circumcised. The mother and the guardian ad litem opposed both applications. The father was not a devout Muslim. The court refused to make either order. As far as upbringing was concerned it was 'not practical to make an order that a child whose home is with a mother who is a non-practising Christian should be brought up as a Muslim'. The judge saw this as an application of the minimal intervention principle.[210] He held that male[211] circumcision was lawful—the first authority to this effect in England—but that to circumcise a son was not a decision that a parent could take alone, despite legislation[212] which provides that each person with parental responsibility 'may act alone and without the other (or others) in meeting that responsibility'. This judicial inroad on a clear legislative provision was justified by the judge because circumcision is 'an irrevocable step'.[213] The only other issue relating to parental responsibility which divided the parents concerned the eating of pork, a matter, thought the judge, for compromise and agreement. But, whatever, it was not 'in J's welfare interests . . . to make a specific order in relation to it':[214] that is, presumably, it was not better for J that an order be made. If the circumstances had been such that an order was appropriate, the court would have had to decide whether the eating of pork was in this child's best interests. The boundaries of justiciability are fast being approached!

The imperatives of religion were tested also recently in the heart-rending case of *Re P*.[215] The case has echoes of *Re Thain*, with the added complications of a handicapped (Down's Syndrome) child and religion—

---

[206] [1970] AC 668.
[207] See also *Re E* [1963] 3 All ER 874 (Jewish couple required to bring up ward as Roman Catholic). [208] *Re J* [1999] 2 FLR 678.
[209] n 208 above. [210] In s 1(5) of the Children Act 1989, discussed above.
[211] Female circumcision is prohibited by the Prohibition of Female Circumcision Act 1985. Unlike in France, there have not been any prosecutions for breaking this law.
[212] Children Act 1989 s 2(7). [213] n 208 above at 702.
[214] n 208 above, at 687; upheld by the Court of Appeal: [2000] 1 FLR 571.
[215] [1999] 2 FLR 573.

and it has a different conclusion. The case records the end of a battle by orthodox Jewish parents to recover their 8-year-old from Roman Catholic foster parents with whom the child had lived for seven years and with whom she had clearly bonded, though contact had not been lost with her family of origin. The child had been placed with the particular foster parents when the biological parents could not cope and attempts to find a suitable Jewish family had failed. The court accepted that the final loss of their daughter was tragic, but the conclusion was inevitable. There couldn't be a clearer case of foster parents having become psychological parents. The evidence was plain that a move back now would bewilder and distress the child who might see it as 'punishment'. What a contrast with the reasoning of Eve J in *Re Thain*! Butler-Sloss LJ thought the residential *status quo* argument was 'sometimes over-emphasised' but had no doubt that it had 'real validity in this case'. Religion was a 'relevant' consideration: here it was an 'important factor' since 'no one would wish to deprive a Jewish child of her right to her Jewish heritage'.[216] But— and here there was a nod in the direction of European jurisprudence,[217] 'in the jurisprudence of human rights, the right to practise one's religion is subservient to the need in a democratic society to put welfare first'.[218]

At the end of a century which has seen religion decline—at least the religion which purports to be *the* religion in Britain—it continues to exercise the court's careful judgment. Only in the final decades of the century did issues of race assume the same (or greater) importance. The Children Act 1989 is the first children's legislation to be alert to the issue.[219] Two years before, the courts were saying—rather as they have now done with religion—that they would not prioritize it over other aspects of a child's welfare.[220] The child, a Nigerian girl of 9 who had been with white foster parents for five-and-a-half years was 'adamant' that she wished to remain with her foster parents. But this was not what tilted the balance: 'one must, of course, approach the statements of young children with a degree of caution' said Swinton Thomas J.[221] The decision that the child should remain with her foster parents was dictated by paramountcy considerations. And significantly it was in striking contrast to the somewhat over-ideologized expert evidence to the effect that 'any child of West African background, regardless of the length of time that a child has been in an alternative family, must be placed back with a West

---

[216] n 215 above at 585.   [217] *Hoffmann v Austria* [1994] 17 EHRR 293.
[218] n 215 above at 598 *per* Ward LJ.
[219] See in particular s 22(5)(c) and Sch 2, para 11 (discussion of which falls outside the remit of this chapter).   [220] *Re A* [1987] 2 FLR 429.
[221] n 220 above, at 436. Children cannot dictate decisions relating to their welfare, he added.

African family'. This expert had 'not met or spoken' with either the foster parents or the child.[222]

Another illustration of the conflict is *Re N*,[223] a case which contains a trenchant condemnation of the domination of social services departments by political correctness. The case related to a Nigerian child of 4½ ('a person in her own right and not just an appendage of her parents') who had lived with white foster parents since she was three weeks old. They wished to adopt: the father (by birth Nigerian but now a naturalized American living in the USA) wanted care and control (the child had been warded). Bush J, after commenting that he had been 'bombarded by a host of theories and opinions by experts who derive their being (*sic*) from the political approach to race relations in America in the 1960s and 1970s', concluded that to separate the child from her foster parents would cause serious psychological damage both at present and in the future. The compromise—which seems to have given greater weight to the father's interests than the child's—was to reject adoption. This is not an institution known in Nigerian culture and to the father it was redolent of 'slavery'. The foster parents were given care and control (which left the court, in whom were vested major decisions, and the mother, who played no part in the child's life, as the only persons with parental rights).[224]

These two cases are evidence of a judicial commitment to welfare over colour. And there are other instances.[225] But there are also cases which have gone the opposite way. One,[226] which was particularly controversial, had the Court of Appeal refusing to interfere[227] with a trial judge's decision to remove a child of mixed race aged sixteen months from a white foster mother with whom he had been since he was five days old. The Court of Appeal held the judge had been entitled to conclude that the advantages of bringing up a child of mixed race in a black family— one of Jamaican origin had been found—outweighed the importance of maintaining the *status quo* for the child who was thriving in a stable home. The most recent case suggests that this emphasis on colour or culture—the two are not clearly distinguished and Bush J in *Re N* ridiculed this—has assumed new importance since the Children Act 1989. In *Re M*,[228] a Zulu boy of 10 was being brought up by an Afrikaans foster mother in London (he had been in London for four years). She wished to adopt or at least keep him in England by obtaining a residence

---

[222] It remains an article of faith (or political correctness) that transracial placements are intrinsically bad for children. A good critique is P. Hayes, 'The Ideological Attack on Transracial Adoption in the USA and Britain', (1995) 9 *International Journal of Law and the Family* 1. [223] [1990] 1 FLR 58.
[224] Today, a residence order in favour of the foster parents would be made.
[225] For example, *Re JK* [1991] 2 FLR 340. [226] *Re P* [1990] 1 FLR 96.
[227] See *G v G* [1985] 2 All ER 225. [228] [1996] 2 FLR 441.

order. She was undoubtedly his psychological parent (or at least one of them, for his mother could also be so characterized[229]). The Court of Appeal was impressed by the trial judge's view that the boy's development 'must be, in the last resort and profoundly, Zulu development and not Afrikaans or English development'. There was expert evidence to the effect that a swift return to South Africa would cause him severe trauma. Astonishingly, the views of the boy were not sought. The court, following a passage in Waite LJ's judgment in *Re K*,[230] saw the immediate return of the child as one of his rights as part of his welfare: 'to have the ties of nature maintained wherever possible with the parents who gave [him] life'. The boy certainly did not see it this way. He had to be removed forcibly, and subsequently returned to England. It is an interesting reflection on our times that where once the courts would have justified their decision in terms of the sacred rights of parents a generation ago in terms of the pseudo-scientific 'blood tie', now they invoke the rights of the child.

WHERE NEXT?

Disputes about children have been, and will continue to be, controversial. They will also continue to be bitter. The tensions that currently exist, for example between determinate rules and individualized decision-making, each having its advantages and drawbacks, will persist. Domestic violence will not disappear and in more and more cases it will be an issue. So will sexual abuse. Conflict over contact could get more intense: there is no sign that the implacably hostile mother will go away or that courts will find better ways of dealing with her congruent with promoting the child's best interests.[231] The courts will be forced into paying more attention to the wishes and feelings of (at least) the maturer child. The backlash against *Gillick* is temporary.

The checklist (in section 1(3) has been invaluable, but disputes still arise as to the weight to be attached to different factors, to the balancing exercise, and to evaluation. Does the future lie in trying to find a better way of determining what is best for, what one writer called, these 'children of Armageddon'?[232] If, as I suspect, children will emerge best where arrangements for their caretaking can be reinforced rather than

---

[229] *Per* Thorpe J, quoted at 452.   [230] [1990] 2 FLR 64, 70.

[231] See Julie Wallbank,'Castigating Mothers: The Judicial Response To "Wilful" Women in Disputes over Paternal Contact in English Law', (1998) 20 *Journal of Social Welfare and Family Law* 357.

[232] A. Watson, 'The Children of Armageddon: Problems of Custody Following Divorce', (1980) 21 *Syracuse Law Review* 55.

disrupted, then the need to identify paramountcy with caretaking (rather than residential) *status quo* becomes critical. Nor should it be difficult to form an opinion as to who the caregiver is. It will not necessarily be a parent, but it usually will be—and this will usually mean the mother. This is not a retreat to the maternal presumption. Nor will it work to the detriment of fathers (it is possible that more men will be awarded their children under such a standard). And there will need to be important exceptions to cater for domestic violence and sexual abuse, to take account of the views and preferences of maturer children, to tackle the obstructive or obdurate parent who wishes (without justification) to cut the other parent out of the child's life. It may be objected that this is to look to the past, but on such matters as parenting competence, emotional ties, and commitment to the child's welfare, the past is as good guide as any to what will happen in the future. There is a model for the standard suggested here: the state of Washington's Parenting Act gives first priority to 'the strength, nature, and stability of the child's relationship with each parent (including which parent has taken more responsibility for daily care)'.[233]

Washington and Montana in addition require a parenting plan.[234] There has been as yet no call for this to be introduced in England. This is a surprising omission given the presumption against an order unless it can be shown that the requested order is better for the child than not making an order,[235] and given the development of the care plan where a local authority is seeking a care order. It may be predicted that the parenting plan will be mandated in England—and sooner rather than later. The value of the plan is that it makes parents focus on their plans for their children for the future. As such it is consonant with the new divorce model—the implementation of which has been postponed—which requires divorcing couples to look to the future.[236] It may be assumed that the ideal plan will be jointly submitted. Where this is impossible and separate proposed plans are designed, it will give the court more information upon which to base its decision than is often the case now. Plans will, of course, need to be both flexible and dynamic, to cope with change both foreseen and unpredicted. The relationship of plans to counselling and to mediation, for there will be an inevitable link, will need to be worked out. It may be predicted also that the parenting order, introduced in England in 1998 in a different context[237]—as a way of assisting parents

---

[233] See J. Ellis,'The Washington State Parenting Act in the Courts: Reconciling Discretion and Justice in Reconciling Parenting Plan Disputes', (1994) 69 *Washington Law Review* 679.

[234] A number of other states in the US require such plans as a condition of a joint custody order. [235] Children Act 1989 s 1(5).

[236] The Family Law Act 1996. This will not come into force until after the next General Election (if at all). [237] Crime and Disorder Act 1998 s 8(1)(a).

to prevent their children offending—will find its way into the legal structure for the post-divorce family. Parenting classes loom on the near horizon. At a certain point there will be resistance. The refusal by the Labour Government even to contemplate making corporal punishment by parents unlawful is in part a recognition that even the 'nanny state' has some limits.[238] But we have long accepted that its tentacles can intrude further into the deviant and the dysfunctional, and governments may push on despite resistance.

[238] Department of Health, *Protecting Children, Supporting Parents. A Consultation Document on the Physical Punishment of Children* (2000).

21

The Law and Violence Against Women in the Family at Century's End: The US Experience

ELIZABETH M. SCHNEIDER

INTRODUCTION

Cross Currents examines changes in family life and law in both the United States and England in the last half of the twentieth century. The beating of wives or girlfriends is a long-hidden aspect of family life that has existed over time and throughout cultures. Although this problem was largely invisible at the beginning of the historical period which we cover, there has been dramatic change in both public and legal recognition at the end of the century that has resulted from the work of a social movement: feminism. Although many aspects of family law have been influenced by the struggle for gender equality, legal transformation on domestic violence has been spearheaded by the women's rights movement. This chapter examines some of the crucial aspects of this process and the legal reforms which have resulted.

In the late 1960s a movement of feminist activists and lawyers began to bring the problem of woman abuse to public attention. At that time, there was no legal recognition of a harm of violence against women by intimates—what has been known as 'domestic violence'—it simply didn't exist in the legal vocabulary.[1] Since then there has been substantial change. In 1992, the United States Supreme Court recognized the pervasiveness and severity of intimate violence for the first time in *Planned Parenthood v Casey*, and in 1994 Congress passed the Violence Against Women Act. And, on a global level, violence against women has been condemned as a violation of women's international human rights.

Planned Parenthood v Casey is widely known as the decision in which the Supreme Court narrowly upheld constitutional protection for women's right to reproductive choice. But the restrictive Pennsylvania abortion statute challenged in this case included a mandatory 'spousal notification' provision. Battered women's advocacy organizations argued that this provision would mean that women who faced intimate violence and who could not safely tell their partner that they were pregnant without fear of

I am grateful to Catherine Paszkowska for invaluable research assistance. This chapter is adapted from BATTERED WOMEN AND FEMINIST LAWMAKING (Yale University Press, forthcoming 2000).

[1] I use different terms interchangeably in this essay, such as 'intimate violence,' 'violence against women,' 'domestic violence,' 'woman-abuse,' and 'battered women.' As I explain in the text, n 35 below, each of these terms conveys a different meaning.

harm, would be unable freely to exercise their reproductive choice. The Court struck down this provision as unconstitutional on these grounds.

In its decision, the Court recounted the seriousness and the pervasiveness of the problem of domestic violence, drawing on a startling statistical picture:

- In an average 12–month period in this country, approximately two million women are the victims of severe assaults by their male partners. In a 1985 survey, women reported that nearly one of every eight husbands had assaulted their wives during the past year. The [American Medical Association] views these figures as 'marked underestimates,' because the nature of these incidents discourages women from reporting them, and because surveys typically exclude the very poor, those who do not speak English well, and women who are homeless or in institutions or hospitals when the survey is conducted. According to the AMA, 'researchers on family violence agree that the true incidence of partner violence is probably *double* the above estimates; or four million severely assaulted women per year.'
- Studies on prevalence suggest that from one-fifth to one-third of all women will be physically assaulted by a partner or ex-partner during their lifetime. . . . Thus on an average day in the United States, nearly 11,000 women are severely assaulted by their male partners. Many of these incidents involve sexual assault. . . . In families where wife-beating takes place, moreover, child abuse is often present as well.
- Other studies fill in the rest of this troubling picture. Physical violence is only the most visible form of abuse. Psychological abuse, particularly forced social and economic isolation of women, is also common.
- Many victims of domestic violence remain with their abusers, perhaps because they perceive no superior alternative. . . . Many abused women who find temporary refuge in shelters return to their husbands, in large part because they have no other source of income. . . . Returning to one's abuser can be dangerous. Recent Federal Bureau of Investigation statistics disclose that 8.8 per cent of all homicide victims in the United States are killed by their spouses. . . . Thirty per cent of female homicide victims are killed by their male partners.[2]

While the statistics that the Court recited speak for themselves, they were not new. Feminists in this country had argued for more than two centuries that women's legally sanctioned subordination within the family denies them equality and citizenship. They saw intimate violence as an important vehicle of this subordination, for, as Wendy Williams has put it, it involves the 'ultimatum: do as I say, . . . subordinate yourself to

---

[2] *Planned Parenthood v Casey*, 505 US 833, 891–2 (1992).

me, or you will be injured.'³ Feminists claimed that domestic violence not only threatens women's right to physical integrity and perhaps even life itself, but women's liberty, autonomy, and equality. Yet it is only in the last thirty years that any aspect of this link between violence and equality has been reflected in law and culture.

The development of a battered women's movement has been one of the most important contributions of the women's rights struggle in this country over these years. This movement created the theoretical concept of battering, and the issue has now moved from social invisibility as a 'private problem' to an important 'public' concern. There is hardly a day when a story on some aspect of domestic violence does not appear in the newspapers, television, or other media. The O. J. Simpson case, with its subtext of femicide, consumed public attention for several years. There has been an explosion of activist and advocacy efforts in both state and federal legislative arenas, and there is a federal Violence Against Women office in the United States Department of Justice. Organizations have founded shelters or networks of 'safe homes,' set up telephone hotlines, challenged police practices that fail to intervene effectively to assist battered women, drafted new legislation to protect women through civil orders of protection as well as criminal and tort remedies, and developed programs to work with battering men. Lawsuits and legislation have produced improved police and court practices. Advocates have developed teen-dating violence programs, and special law school, social work, and medical school courses. Government reports, legal and social-science literature, and media coverage have proliferated. Advocates and scholars continue to formulate new legal approaches to violence against women. Nevertheless, this many-faceted barrage of activity has not prevented intimate violence for women, nor has it remedied the problem of violence; instead, there has been complex change, partial inroads, and deep resistance.

THE SOCIAL AND HISTORICAL CONTEXT OF VIOLENCE

Anglo-American common law originally provided that a husband, as master of his household, could subject his wife to corporal punishment or 'chastisement' so long as he did not inflict permanent damage upon her.⁴ During the nineteenth century, an era of feminist organizing for reform of

---

³ WENDY WEBSTER WILLIAMS, FIXING LOCKE: LIBERAL ORTHODOXIES AND THE FEMINIST CHALLENGE TO INTIMATE VIOLENCE (unpublished manuscript 1998).
⁴ For historical sources, see generally, *Bradley v State*, 1 Walk (Miss) 156 (1824); *State v Black*, 60 NC 262 (1864).

marriage law, authorities in England and the United States declared that a husband no longer had the right to chastise his wife. Yet for a century after courts repudiated the right of chastisement, the American legal system continued to treat what was then called wife-beating differently from other cases of assault and battery. While authorities denied that a husband had the right to beat his wife, they rarely intervened. Men who assaulted their wives were often granted formal and informal immunities from prosecution, in order to protect the privacy of the family and to promote 'domestic harmony.'[5] In the 1960s, with the rebirth of an active women's movement in the United States, feminists contested the concept of family privacy that shielded wife abuse.[6]

Elizabeth Pleck observes that 'there was virtually no public discussion of wife beating from the turn of the century until the mid-1970's.'[7]

Wifebeating was called 'domestic disturbance' by the police, 'family maladjustment' by marriage counselors and social caseworkers. Psychiatry, under the influence of Helene Deutsch, regarded the battered woman as a masochist who provoked her husband into beating her. In the *Journal of Marriage and the Family*, the major scholarly journal in family sociology, no article on family violence appeared from its founding in 1939 until 1969.

Very few modern novels contained scenes of marital violence . . . Newspapers did not begin to report on abuse of wives until 1974. The next year, however, women activists organized conferences in several cities to establish shelters for battered women, demand arrest of wife beaters by the police, and draft new legislation. In 1977, the *New York Times* carried forty-four articles on wife beating, ranging from stories about hotlines and shelters to the trials of women who had murdered their assaultive husbands.[8]

It took the rebirth of feminism in the 1960s to 'rediscover' battering.[9] With a new spotlight on intimate violence and the ensuing development of a battered women's movement that has raised public consciousness about battering, many reforms designed to protect women from marital violence have been secured.[10] In both the United States and England, the focus of feminist consciousness-raising about domestic violence was on intimate violence in the context of heterosexual relationships. The term which was first used to describe the problem was 'wife-abuse,' which revealed that it was viewed primarily through the lens of a marital relationship. Domestic

---

[5] Reva B. Siegel, *The Rule of Love: Wife Beating as Prerogative and Privacy*, 105 YALE L J 2117, 2118 (1996).

[6] See *ibid*.

[7] ELIZABETH PLECK, DOMESTIC TYRANNY: THE MAKING OF SOCIAL POLICY AGAINST FAMILY VIOLENCE FROM COLONIAL TIMES TO PRESENT 182 (1987).

[8] PLECK, n 7 above, at 182.

[9] *ibid* at 183.

[10] See *ibid* at 183. For an account of the first English refuge at Chiswick, see ERIN PIZZEY, SCREAM QUIETLY OR THE NEIGHBOURS WILL HEAR (1974).

violence was viewed as part of the larger problem of gender inequality, as an aspect of patriarchy within the marital relationship.

Feminist activism around issues of domestic violence was highly diffuse and took many different forms. One primary focus was the development of battered women's 'refuges,' 'shelters', or 'safe houses.' These houses, women-run, and women-centered, were established as places for battered women to go when they left a violent home, and to provide safety for them and their children. The idea of temporary residences for battered women was devised by a group of women in London who established a neighborhood center at Chiswick in London which offered child care and a refuge for homeless women; many of those who needed the help of the center were women who had been abused. Police, social workers, social service agencies, and doctors wouldn't help them, and Chiswick admitted any woman who wanted to stay. Soon, women began to arrive from all over, and the center received wide publicity. Other shelters were set up around the country.

During those shelters' first years, many Americans visited them. In the United States, however, the only available models were safe houses for the wives of alcoholics.[11] One of the first American shelters for battered women was Women's Advocates in St Paul, Minnesota, founded in 1974 by Women's Advocates, a consciousness-raising group that had previously written a divorce rights handbook and organized a legal information phone service for women. When battered women called the group's telephone hotline for assistance, they were housed at first in the staff's own apartments. Eventually, a twenty-four-hour crisis telephone operated from the house, which could accommodate twelve women and their children at any one time. There was a paid staff, as well as volunteers, but Advocates operated as a collective and divided administrative responsibilities; they opposed hiring professionally credentialed staff.[12]

Battered women's organizations were important sites of political activism and coordination—in communities, college campuses, and national women's rights organizations. As state-wide task forces and national coalitions were formed, the battered women's movement began to shape public debate. The theoretical approach to battering that developed from the battered women's movement was 'political.' Its dimensions were not made explicit; they were never listed anywhere as part of a social program, but functioned as precepts of activist literature and work. First, 'battered women' were set forth as a definable group or category, with battering regarded within the larger context of 'power and control'; physical abuse was a particular 'moment' in a larger continuum of 'doing power,' which might include emotional abuse, sexual abuse and

[11] See PLECK, n 7 above, at 189.   [12] *ibid*.

rape, and other maneuvers to control, isolate, threaten, intimidate, or stalk. Battering, and the problem of power and control, were understood within a systemic framework of gender subordination which included gender role socialization, social and economic discrimination in education, workplace, and home, and lack of access to child care. Battered women and battered women's experiences were the focal point of strategies for change; battered women were viewed as 'sisters,' actors, participants in a larger struggle. Their needs for safety, protection, refuge, and social and economic resources drove the movement.

Today, some of this has changed. In the United States, the trend within battered women's organizations has been towards a service orientation and away from explicitly feminist organizing. Although many groups that began as feminist organizations are still actively involved in battered women's work, many newer groups that have organized around battering see themselves primarily as service providers. They do social service work, and perceive battered women as 'clients,' not 'sisters,' as persons to be helped, not participants in a larger struggle.

THE CHALLENGE TO FEMINIST PERSPECTIVES

The battered women's movement defined battering within the larger framework of gender subordination. Domestic violence was linked to women's inferior position within the family, discrimination within the workplace, wage inequity, lack of educational opportunities, the absence of social supports for mothering, and the lack of child care. But traditionally, intimate violence had been viewed within a psychological perspective. This approach, which predated the feminist analysis of the 1960s, had been concerned with how violence is linked to specific pathology in individual personality traits and psychological disorders. Significantly, this psychological perspective has not focused primarily on the pathology of male batterers. Although it is a common social response that violent men are 'sick' or 'emotionally disturbed,' in the public mind this perspective of pathology focuses largely on the woman who is battered. Those who are battered, and 'stay' in battering relationships are regarded as more pathological, more deeply troubled, than the men who batter them. Some psychiatrists attributed domestic violence to the victim's inherent sexual and biological problems, or regarded battering as related to women's masochism, a construct within which women are seen first to provoke battering and then to remain in battering relationships.

More recently, this psychological perspective has been stoked by public perception of 'battered woman syndrome,' a term originally intended as a clinical description of certain psychological effects of battering on women.[13] Paradoxically, 'battered woman syndrome' is now used as a catch-all phrase by the media and in courtrooms to describe a great range of issues, including a woman's prior responses to violence and the context in which those responses occurred, and the dynamics of the abusive relationship; it may also be used to refer to a subcategory of post-traumatic stress disorder, or as shorthand for woman abuse as a larger social problem.[14] Employing 'battered woman syndrome' as an explanatory framework shifts the focus of the violent act to the woman, and the use of 'syndrome' suggests that it is she who is emotionally or mentally impaired.

A second perspective, a sociological approach, rests on the premiss that social structures affect people and their behaviors, and focuses on the problem of family violence—the way that the institution of the family is set up to allow and even encourage violence among family members. This view looks at violence as a result of family dysfunction, and examines the way in which all participants in the family may be involved in perpetuating the violence. Both psychological and sociological perspectives have done much to shape the context of research and the nature of public views of violence. Evan Stark has observed:

For fifty years or more, the realities have been concealed behind images that alternately 'pathologize' family violence or else 'normalize' it, making it seem the inevitable byproduct of some combination of predisposition—because the abuser was mistreated as a child, for example—and environmental 'stress.' The use of violence is abstracted from its political context in gender and generational struggles, and its varied meanings in different cultures and classes are simply glossed over. Static conceptions posit aggression as inherent in (male) human nature or as inevitable given poverty, 'violence prone' cultures or personalities, and inter-generational transmission.[15]

Advocates of psychological and sociological perspectives recognize the significance of the 'alternate' perspective and acknowledge that both psychological and social factors are significant variables. Yet both of these approaches minimize the role and the impact of gender and are grounded in gender-neutral explanations.[16]

The notion of 'family violence' exploded as a focus of research on battering in the early 1980s. The impact of this research was to further deflect

---

[13] See generally Lenore E. Walker, The Battered Woman (1979); see also Lenore E. Walker, Terrifying Love 35–7 (1989). Walker's work has now been criticized by other psychologists who have worked with battered women. See Mary Ann Dutton, *Understanding Women's Responses to Domestic Violence: A Redefinition of Battered Woman Syndrome*, 21 Hofstra L. Rev 1191 (1993); Evan Stark, *Re-presenting Woman Battering: From Battered Woman Syndrome to Coercive Control*, 58 Albany L Rev 973 (1995).

[14] See Dutton, n 13 above, at 1195. See also Walker, n 13 above, at 48; Stark, n 13 above, at 974.

[15] Evan Stark, *Heroes and Victims: Constructing Family Violence*, 19 Socialist Rev 137, 139 (Jan–Mar 1989).   [16] See Stark, n 15 above.

attention from the crucial link to gender, and to focus on research tools which deeply challenged feminist approaches. In a review of the 'family violence' literature in 1983, Wini Breines and Linda Gordon insightfully perceived the dangers in this approach:

First, all violence must be seen in the context of wider power relations; violence is not necessarily deviant or fundamentally different from other means of exerting power over another person. Thus, violence cannot be accurately viewed as a set of isolated events but must be placed in an entire social context. Second, the social contexts of family violence have gender and generational inequalities at their heart. There are patterns to violence between intimates which only an analysis of gender and its centrality to the family can illuminate.[17]

One of the consequences of this shift to 'family violence' theory has been the move to gender-neutral explanations, highlighting the long-standing and continuing debate surrounding the question of whether women are as violent as men. Some researchers, notably Murray Straus and Richard Gelles, have resuscitated the view that violence against husbands is as prevalent as violence against wives.[18] Spousal violence has been said to be symmetrical in its extent, severity, intentions, motivational contexts, and even its consequences.[19] Prominent violence researchers R. Emerson Dobash and Russell Dobash, along with many others, have argued that this is a 'myth,' maintaining that women use violence primarily in self-defense, and have rebutted these arguments.[20]

Despite these rebuttals, the 'women are as violent as men' perspective has had considerable impact on public consciousness through the news media, as well as on academic and clinical thinking. Claire Renzetti, an expert in the field, observes that 'there is an important battle being waged over the nature of women's behavior and its role in woman abuse.'[21] Right-wing organizations such as the Independent Women's Forum have challenged feminist interpretations of battering, placing op-ed pieces and editorials in prominent newspapers and magazines around the country, and filing *amicus curiae* briefs in litigation. Renzetti concludes that 'this is a battle whose outcome has serious consequences for battered women, especially in terms of our society's institutionalized responses to their behavior.'[22]

---

[17] Wini Breines and Linda Gordon, *The New Scholarship on Family Violence*, 8 SIGNS 490 (1983).

[18] See Martin Schwartz and Walter S. DeKeseredy, *The Return of the 'Battered Husband Syndrome' Through the Typification of Women as Violent*, 20 CRIME, LAW AND SOCIAL CHANGE 249–65 (1993).

[19] See Russell P. Dobash, *et al*, *The Myth of Sexual Symmetry in Marital Violence*, 39 SOCIAL PROBLEMS 71–90 (Feb 1992). [20] See Dobash *et al*, n 19 above.

[21] Renzetti, *On Dancing with a Bear: Reflections on Some of the Current Debates Among Domestic Violence Theorists*, 9 VIOLENCE AND VICTIMS 195, 197–8 (1994); see also Dobash *et al*, n 19 above. [22] Renzetti, n 21 above, at 197–8.

NEW DEVELOPMENTS

At the same time, there have been important new developments in activist and legal work on battering. There has been increased sensitivity to issues of race and culture, and to differing experiences of women across racial, ethnic, and cultural boundaries who are battered.[23] There has been greater attention to the problems of immigrant women.[24] Related issues of same-sex violence and elder abuse have also been addressed.[25]

New attention has focused on the particular experiences of battered women as mothers and the impact of violence on the children of battered women.[26] Finally, activists and lawyers have begun to document the impact of intimate violence on women's lives—on reproductive choice as in *Casey*; on divorce, custody, visitation, child support, and child care; and on welfare, employment, insurance, and housing.

---

[23] For essays on the diverse experiences of battered women, see generally, Beverly Hors-burgh, *Domestic Violence in the Jewish Community*, 18 HARV WOMEN'S LJ 171 (1995); Linda L. Ammons, *Mules, Madonnas, Babies, Bathwater, Racial Imagery and Stereotypes: The African-American Woman and the Battered Woman Syndrome*, 1995 WISCONSIN LAW REVIEW 1003 (1995); Jenny Rivera, *Domestic Violence against Latinas by Latino Males: Analysis of Race, National Origin, and Gender Differentials*, 14 BC THIRD WORLD LJ 231 (1994); Sharon A. Allard, *Rethinking Battered Woman Syndrome: A Black Feminist Perspective*, 1 UCLA WOMEN'S LJ 191 (1991); Nilda Rimonte, *A Question of Culture: Cultural Approval of Violence against Women in the Pacific-Asian Community and the Cultural Defense*, 43 STAN L REV 1311 (1991); Kimberle Cren-shaw, *Mapping the Margins: Intersectionality, Identity Politics, and Violence Against Women of Color*, 43 STAN L REV 1241 (1991).

[24] For the impact of domestic violence on battered immigrant women, see Linda Kelly, *Stories from the Front: Seeking Refuge for Battered Immigrants in the Violence Against Women Act*, 92 NW U L REV 665 (1998); note, *Trapped in Domestic Violence: The Impact of United States Immigration Laws on Battered Immigrant Women*, 6 BU PUB INT LJ 589 (1997). Under the Violence Against Women Act of 1994, a battered woman can self-petition for immigration status. 8 USC § 1154 (a) (1) (A) (iii) (I). A battered woman who is undocumented and in danger of being deported can apply for 'cancellation of removal', asking to stay in this country because deportation would cause her 'extreme hardship'. Violent Crime Control and Law Enforcement Act, Pub L No 103–322, 108 Stat 1796 (2000); 8 USC § 1254(a)(3).

[25] For same-sex violence, see generally, Nancy J. Knauer, *Same-Sex Domestic Violence: Claiming a Domestic Violence Sphere While Risking Negative Stereotypes*, 8 TEMP POL & CIV RTS L REV 325 (1999); Kathleen Finley Duthu, *Why Doesn't Anyone Talk About Gay and Lesbian Domestic Violence*, 18 THOMAS JEFFERSON L REV 23 (1996); Phyllis Goldfarb, *Describing Without Circumscribing: Questioning the Construction of Gender in the Discourse of Intimate Violence*, 64 GEO WASH L REV 582 (1996).

For a discussion of elder abuse, see Seymour Moskowitz, *Saving Granny from the Wolf: Elder Abuse and Neglect—The Legal Framework*, 31 CONN L REV 77 (1998).

[26] For the impact of domestic violence on children, see Audrey E. Stone and Rebecca J. Fialk, *Criminalizing the Exposure of Children to Family Violence: Breaking the Cycle of Abuse*, 20 HARV WOMEN'S LJ 205 (1997); Howard A. Davidson, *Child Abuse and Domestic Violence: Legal Connections and Controversies*, 29 FAM LQ 357, Part II (1995).

THE LAW

From the beginning of the battered women's movement in the 1960s, legal work played an important role in activist efforts on battering. Activists saw the law as a necessary and important tool in obtaining safety and protection for battered women. Many local legal groups and national organizations were formed to do legal work and advocacy on issues of violence against women, including the National Center on Women and Family Law in New York and the Center for Women's Policy Studies in Washington, DC. The focus of much of this work was the development or expansion of legal remedies to protect women and stop the abuse and to assert battered women's rights to be free from violence.

One of the first and most important legal issues that came to the fore was the failure of police to protect battered women from assault. In the early 1970s, class-action lawsuits were filed in Oakland, California and New York which challenged police failure to arrest batterers. This litigation raised the dramatic notion that domestic violence was a criminal, sanctionable activity that was a harm against the 'public,' the state, not just an individual woman, and should be treated the same as an assault against a stranger. The New York case, *Bruno v Codd*, was the focus of much national attention.[27] Developing injunctive remedies to keep the batterer away, known as civil protective or restraining orders, was also an important area of innovative work. These orders were first sought in the late 1960s, and during the late 1960s and early 1970s many states passed statutes to provide for civil protective remedies.

Since that time, domestic violence has been the focus of an extraordinary degree of legal activity in the context of both law reform and litigation. New state statutes have required mandatory arrest by the police,[28] developed complex civil protection order provisions,[29] required mandatory reporting by certain helping professionals,[30] and governed the disposition of custody upon divorce where there is evidence of domestic violence.[31] New legislation, the Violence Against Women Act of 1994, asserts federal power to remedy violence.[32] Feminist legal

[27] See Laurie Woods, *Litigation on Behalf of Battered Women*, 5 WOMEN'S RTS L REP 7 (1978).
[28] See discussion of mandatory arrest nn 62–9, and accompanying text.
[29] See Catherine F. Klein and Leslye E. Orloff, *Providing Legal Protection for Battered Women: An Analysis of State Statutes and Case Law*, 21 HOFSTRA L REV 801, 950 (1993).
[30] See Ariella Hyman and Dean Schillinger, *Laws Mandating Reporting of Domestic Violence: Do They Promote Patient Well-Being?*, 273 JAMA 1781 (1995).
[31] See Jack M. Dalgleish, Jr, Annotation, *Construction and Effect of Statutes Mandating Consideration of, or Creating Presumptions Regarding, Domestic Violence in Awarding Custody of Children*, 51 ALR 5th 241 (2000).
[32] See eg Violence Against Women Act of 1994, Ch 42, §13981(c) [1994], USC (authorizing a cause of action for crime of violence motivated by gender and providing for compensatory and punitive damages and injunctive and declaratory relief).

advocates have recently begun to draw important interconnections between battering and economic discrimination and poverty, linking issues of homelessness, insurance, workplace violence, and welfare to battering, proposing new federal and state legislative initiatives, and working to protect battered women's interests in recent welfare 'reform' legislation.[33] Much of this law reform activity and litigation has been premised on the link between gender discrimination and violence.

As Carol Smart suggests, struggles over meaning in law are important sites of definition and resistance.[34] Descriptions of legal process and legal images of battered women are discourses that convey particular political meanings. Feminists have long struggled over the characterization of the problem as 'domestic violence,' 'family violence,' 'spouse abuse,' and 'woman-abuse,' and recognized that each of these terms is limited, problematic, and provides only a partial description.[35]

The procedural remedies for woman-abuse that have been developed over the last thirty years reflect a range of meanings. While orders of protection—injunctive orders that a woman who is battered can get from a court to stop a man from beating her or restrict his activity—are now available in all states, they are only 'pieces of paper' and may be rendered ineffective by lack of police enforcement and by the lack of assigned counsel.[36] Criminal statutes now provide for arrest of batterers, either for a violation of protective orders or for felonies generally.[37] Tort remedies have been made possible by the abolition of interspousal immunity.[38] More private and informal processes such as mediation are being used on family law issues, despite criticism by advocates who believe that they hurt battered women who are disadvantaged with respect to power, money, and resources, and signal that battering is an individual woman's

---

[33] A major expansion of the 1994 Violence Against Women Act, VAWA II as it is dubbed, has been introduced in Congress. The new legislation addresses the problems of battered women at work. For example, VAWA II contains provisions that prohibit employment discrimination and allow for payment of unemployment compensation to domestic violence survivors, encourage employers to establish programs to assist survivors, and encourage employers to provide time off for survivors to attend court hearings.

[34] See CAROL SMART, LAW, CRIME AND SEXUALITY: ESSAYS IN FEMINISM (1995).

[35] See eg Liz Kelly, *How Women Define Their Experiences of Violence*, in Kersti Yllo and Michele Bograd (eds), FEMINIST PERSPECTIVES ON WIFE ABUSE (1988) 130 (stressing importance of language in defining and shaping our conceptions of violent acts); Christine Littleton, *Women's Experience and the Problem of Transition: Perspectives on Male Battering of Women*, 1989 U CHIC LEGAL F 23, 27 n 18 (1989) (observing that denial of sexism has replaced terms but has not solved problem); Woods, n 27 above, at 8 (discussing terminology problem).

[36] See Catherine Klein and Leslye Orloff, n 29 above.

[37] See discussion of mandatory arrest, nn 62–9 below, and accompanying text.

[38] For domestic violence and torts, see Clare Dalton, *Domestic Violence, Domestic Torts and Divorce: Constraints and Possibilities*, 31 NEW ENGL L REV 319 (1997).

private problem.[39] More recently, violence against women has been defined as a more explicitly 'public' harm, as a civil rights violation and as an international human rights violation. New anti-stalking laws have expanded the definition of the harm of battering by criminalizing threats of violence and harassment.[40] The law has an impact on battered women in many other areas as well. Many cases involving battered women who have killed their assailants and are now criminal defendants have raised important and challenging issues concerning the characterization of their actions and experiences as self-defense.[41] There have been several successful efforts in a number of states to get clemency for battered women on the ground that evidence concerning their battering was not admitted at trial or that they were not effectively represented.[42]

But neither of the two major legal vehicles to prevent and sanction violence, protective orders and arrest, have been widely viewed as effective. Although police training on violence exists in virtually all states, there are still serious problems of police failure to intervene.[43] At the same time, controversial programs to treat battering men in order to stop the violence have developed.

By 1998, forty states and the District of Columbia either had established or facilitated the promulgation of guidelines for batterers' treatment programs or were in the process of doing so.[44] Batterers' treatment programs are not the same in all jurisdictions. Some programs are ordered by and managed by the court and part of sentencing procedures for criminal violators or protective order violations, some are 'self-help' programs, and others are run by social services or private agencies. Most of the programs focus on the connection between power and control and the men's use of violence, and they stress victim safety as an overriding concern.[45]

---

[39] For discussion on domestic violence and mediation, see generally, Karla Fischer *et al*, *The Culture of Battering and the Role of Mediation in Domestic Violence Cases*, 46 Smu L Rev 2117 (1993).

[40] All fifty states and the District of Columbia have stalking statutes. *Stalking and Domestic Violence: The Third Annual Report to Congress Under the Violence Against Women Act*, US Department of Justice, Violence Against Women Office, www.ojp.usdoj.gov/vawo/statistics.htm (visited Jan 25 2000).

[41] See generally Elizabeth M. Schneider, *Resistance to Equality*, 57 U Pitt L Rev 477 (1996).

[42] For a discussion of the availability of clemency for battered women, see Cookie Ridolfi, *Courtroom, Code and Clemency: Reform in Self-Defense Jurisprudence for Battered Women*, 23 Golden Gate U L Rev 829, 833 (1994); Linda L. Ammons, *Discretionary Justice: A Legal and Policy Analysis of a Governor's Use of the Clemency Power in the Cases of Incarcerated Battered Women*, 3 J L & Pol'y 1 (1994).

[43] Under the Violence Against Women Act of 1994, states or local governments can apply for grants for police departments to design mandatory arrest or pro-arrest programs, train police to track cases, and co-ordinate law enforcement responsibility for cases involving domestic violence. 42 USC § 3796hh (b) (2000); 42 USC § 13992 (2000).

[44] See Jeffrey Fagan, *The Criminalization of Domestic Violence: Promises and Limits*, National Institute of Justice Research Report 1 (1996).   [45] See Fagan, n 44 above.

An approach used by many states is modeled after the Domestic Abuse Intervention Project in Duluth, Minnesota. This program focuses on educating and counseling the batterers, instead of teaching them just to control their anger, with the goal of exposing and eliminating the men's need to dominate their partners. Data about the effectiveness of batterers treatment programs is inconclusive. Some research does show that the programs may lead to a decrease in physical abuse, but they also do not stop the violence entirely or prevent other forms of abuse.[46]

One of the most recent and important developments in lawmaking has been the co-ordinated community response. Co-ordinated community responses to domestic violence were developed by activists who saw that individual legal remedies were not effective. A co-ordinated response brings together police, probation officers, judges, prosecutors, advocates, and counselors to devise and use policies and guidelines to prevent domestic violence. There are three main examples of co-ordination: community intervention projects, criminal justice projects, and co-ordinating councils.[47]

The community intervention projects are traditional non-profit organizations that work on advocacy for battered women and are usually connected to the battered women's movement. The Duluth Domestic Abuse Intervention Project, a model community intervention project, has focused on several components: enhancing victim safety, tracking system responses, and creating treatment programs for batterers.[48] Projects developed in the criminal justice system include pro-arrest policies, no-drop prosecution, probation and batterers' treatment programs, prosecution of violations of orders of protection, vertical prosecution, and specialized victim advocacy units in the district attorney's offices and police departments.[49] Co-ordinating councils include task forces

---

[46] See Cheryl Hanna, *The Paradox of Hope: The Crime and Punishment of Domestic Violence*, 39 WM & MARY L REV 1532 (1998). Statistics range between 53 and 85% for participants in treatment who stopped being physically abusive. See Jeffrey L. Edleson, *Do Batterers' Programs Work?*, www.mincava.umn.edu (visited May 8 2000). Other statistics show that men who are treated keep abusing their partners at the same rate as men who were never treated, and that six months after treatment, the rate of recidivism is as high as 54%. Hanna, above, at 1533. Other findings in a study of four treatment programs included: between 32 and 39% of participants reassaulted their partners; 59% of those who reassaulted did so more than one time; and the participants' partners reported that 70% of the men were verbally abusive, 45% were controlling, and 16% stalked them. See Edward W. Gondolf, *Multi-Site Evaluation of Batterer Intervention Systems: Summary of 15-Month Follow-up*, www.mincava.umn.edu (visited May 8 2000). See generally Edward W. Gondolf and Robert J. White, *'Consumer' Recommendations for Batterers Programs*, 6 VIOLENCE AGAINST WOMEN ISSUE 2, 9 (2000).

[47] See *Evaluating Co-ordinated Community Responses to Domestic Violence*, NATIONAL INSTITUTE OF JUSTICE, www.mincavumn.edu (visited May 8, 2000).   [48] See n 47 above, at 2.

[49] See n 47 above, at 2; see also Kristin Littel *et al*, *Assessing the Justice System Response to Violence Against Women*, PROMISING PRACTICES INITIATIVE OF THE STOP VIOLENCE AGAINST WOMEN GRANTS TECHNICAL ASSISTANCE PROJECT, www.vaw.umn.edu (visited May 8 2000).

and committees on domestic violence. A model one, the Santa Clara County Domestic Violence Council, has held several conferences, promulgated protocols for medical and probation employees, written a domestic violence death review report, and given abuse victims emergency systems to alert the police.[50] Studies of community intervention projects show that they increase the rates of arrests, prosecutions, and convictions, and the number of batterers who are court-mandated to undergo counseling.[51]

NEW DIRECTIONS IN LEGAL REFORM: MANDATORY ARREST AND THE VIOLENCE AGAINST WOMEN ACT

Legislative work has been a major aspect of feminist legal reform efforts with respect to domestic violence. State domestic violence coalitions have formed, lobbied for, and helped to pass state legislation on issues ranging from mandatory arrest and child custody to insurance. On the federal level, a coalition of women's and civil rights organizations spearheaded the passage of the Violence Against Women Act of 1994 (VAWA) and have continued to develop and lobby for Congressional efforts on a variety of issues. In conception, vision, and purpose, much of this legislation has been ground-breaking. Recent innovative legal reform efforts focused on intimate violence, such as state mandatory arrest policies and the federal Violence Against Women Act of 1994, 'VAWA I,' underscore the complex issues presented when feminists 'engage with the state'[52] on issues of violence. Feminist efforts to use state or federal governmental mechanisms for law reform on intimate violence present serious theoretical and practical contradictions.

The development of mandatory arrest legislation, which made domestic violence a crime, came after years of debate within the battered women's movement concerning the degree to which criminalization of

---

[50] See n 47 above, at 4.

[51] See n 47 above, at 5; see also Rose Thelen, *Advocacy in Co-ordinated Community Response: Overview and Highlights of Three Programs*, GENDER VIOLENCE INSTITUTE www.vaw.umn.edu (visited May 8 2000).

[52] Nickie Charles, *Feminist Politics, Domestic Violence and the State*, 43 THE SOCIOLOGICAL REV 617 (1995) (exploring the question of how feminists ought to 'engage with the state' on the issue of domestic violence); Claire Reinelt, *Moving onto the Terrain of the State: The Battered Women's Movement and the Politics of Engagement*, in Myra Marx Ferree and Patricia Yancey Martin (eds), FEMINIST ORGANIZATIONS: HARVEST OF THE NEW WOMEN'S MOVEMENT, (1995) 84 (describing a 'politics of engagement' that involves autonomous feminist institutions working with mainstream institutions). As Deborah Rhode has observed, there are many dimensions to the term, 'the state.' See Deborah L. Rhode, *Feminism and the State*, 107 HARV L REV 1181, 1182 (1994). Here, I use the term in the conventional sense of federal and state government.

battering was an appropriate response in light of historic feminist ambivalence about state power. Despite extensive efforts to train police, police continue to resist arresting battering men, and frequently arrest both battering men and the women they batter. Many women who are battered are reluctant to charge their batterers with a crime, and many prosecutor's offices have developed controversial 'no-drop' policies which can force women to face criminal charges if they refuse to testify against their assailant. In addition, VAWA I's civil rights remedy is controversial because it explicitly links violence with gender, and because it is premised on federalizing offenses of intimate violence, which have historically been in the province of the state. Here too, enforcement is plagued by longstanding tensions, the historic public–private dichotomy that labels intimate violence as a 'private' matter so that it should not be litigated in the federal courts, and resistance to the connection between violence and gender.

Historically, the role of the state was one of the most vexing issues that the battered women's movement has faced.[53] The battered women's movement was an outsider movement, a grass-roots movement that developed from the civil rights and feminist movements in the 1960s.[54] Many feminists saw battering as the product of patriarchy, as male control over women. Many in this movement were skeptical of an affirmative role for the state; they saw the state as maintaining, enforcing, and legitimizing male violence against women, not remedying it; they rejected the idea that battered women activists ought to trust the state, expect much from the state, or engage with the state in any way.[55] The movement developed shelters, safe houses, and alternative institutions. Groups rejected governmental funding for battered women's services and programs. The legal remedies supported by the movement also reflected a fundamental ambivalence about engagement with the state: many feminist activists initially rejected criminalization as an appropriate remedy or strategy to redress domestic violence because battered women 'did not necessarily want their partners jailed, they wanted the violence condemned and stopped.'[56]

Yet, as the movement developed, engagement with the state became more inevitable. Susan Schechter, an activist in, and historian of the

[53] Susan Schechter, Women and Male Violence: The Visions and Struggles of the Battered Women's Movement, 94, 201 (1982). Schechter identifies the role of the state as an important issue for the battered women's movement and examines the movement's ambivalence toward the state in a number of different ways.

[54] See Reinelt, n 52 above, at 91; Schechter, n 53 above, at 53–81.

[55] See Schechter, n 53 above, at 29–79.

[56] *ibid* at 26. In this section, I am simplifying a far more complex story of different approaches within the battered women's movement that Susan Schechter describes in great detail.

movement, has detailed the contradictions of state involvement in the movement. Schechter describes the resistance of some grass-roots organizations in the battered women's movement to accept Law Enforcement Assistance Agency funding in the late 1970s. Some groups feared that acceptance of governmental aid would result in the relinquishment of control and principles surrounding feminist ideological views of the movement as a separate and independent force in combating violence against women. She observes that funding from the government operated as a mixed blessing for the shelter movement:[57] although it helped to legitimize the movement, it also served to undermine shelter philosophy and organizational structure, requiring the employment of credentialed shelter staff, transforming grass-roots shelters into social service agencies serving clients instead of empowering battered women. She also discusses the way in which government support of the battered women's movement redefined feminist political analysis of violence. Government-produced pamphlets and educational material on 'spouse abuse' and other generic categorizations of domestic violence obscured the feminist grass-roots history and politics of the movement.[58] We have witnessed a cyclical development of the issue of state engagement. Advocates are actively involved in legislative reform efforts and the issue of intimate violence is now on the legislative agenda of every state and the federal government. As this issue has moved from one raised on the margins to one that has now been appropriated by government, feminist liberatory discourse challenging patriarchy and female dependency, which shaped this work, has been replaced by discourse emphasizing crime control.[59] Many battered women's activists have moved from a view that rejected state engagement to support state and federal legislative reform as well as both the pro-criminalization stance of VAWA I, and mandatory arrest. This, in turn, has led to considerable debate and critique within the battered women's movement and among legal advocates, particularly among communities of color, who do not see the state as benevolent.[60] But the impact of state and federal involvement continues to be complex, as money provided by states and by VAWA I grants now supports many important and innovative battered

[57] See SCHECHTER, n 53 above, at 185–9; see also Merle H. Weiner, *From Dollars to Sense: A Critique of Government Funding for the Battered Women's Shelter Movement*, 9 L & INEQUALITY J 185, 277 (1991) (arguing that government funding ensures existing male control over women and 'results in autonomy loss, permits a band-aid approach by the government to violence against women . . . undercut[ing] the movement's revolutionary potential'). Weiner at 187 above. [58] See SCHECHTER, n 53 above, at 201.

[59] See Kathleen J. Ferraro, *The Dance of Dependency: A Genealogy of Domestic Violence Discourse*, 11 HYPATIA 77, 89 (Fall 1996).

[60] See Sheila James Keuhl, *Introduction to Forum: Mandatory Prosecution in Domestic Violence Cases*, 7 UCLA WOMEN'S L J 169 (1997).

women's organizations, and educational and legal projects around the country.[61]

Mandatory arrest and 'no-drop' policies have garnered a great deal of public attention. A 'mandatory arrest' law requires police to arrest a suspect if there is probable cause to believe that domestic violence has occurred, removes the decision to press charges from the victim, and generally limits or eliminates police discretion. A 'no-drop policy' denies the victim of domestic violence the option of withdrawing a complaint at her discretion once formal charges have been filed, and limits prosecutors' discretion to drop a case based only on the fact that the victim is unwilling to co-operate or participate. Historically, criminalizing domestic violence has been a strategy dogged by controversy. Because the state has been deficient in protecting women from abuse in the past, feminists have been wary of using state mechanisms to intervene on behalf of battered women. Although studies in the 1980s claiming that arrest and prosecution were the most effective legal remedies led to the implementation of criminalization on the state level, and although VAWA reflects a strong pro-criminalization position, many feminist advocates continue to be critical.[62] Feminist advocates are deeply divided because of the equally compelling, yet competing concerns as to whether mandatory arrest, prosecution, and no-drop prosecution, may be a better policy choice than the courts' current practice of dismissing cases when the battered woman refuses to participate. For a host of reasons, women who are battered routinely refuse to prosecute complaints after they have been filed. They may be afraid of retribution, guilt-ridden about prosecuting a loved one, torn between conflicting emotions, afraid of losing economic support or taking a father away from children, or weakened by violence. It is widely recognized that mandatory arrest, prosecution, and no-drop rules are, at best, imperfect solutions to domestic violence because of the extreme risk involved regarding women's autonomy. Studies regarding the effectiveness of mandatory prosecution are inconclusive; indeed, both those in favor of and opposed to it cite studies to bolster their respective positions.[63]

Four major areas of arguments favor mandatory prosecution and no-drop. Proponents of these measures argue that they best effectuate the state and prosecutors' roles regarding domestic violence, compensate for

---

[61] For the range of VAWA Office of Justice Program grants, see www.ojp.usdoj.gov/vawgo/htm(visited June 11 1999).

[62] See Linda G. Mills, *Intuition and Insight: A New Job Description for the Battered Woman's Prosecutor and Other More Modest Proposals*, 7 UCLA WOMEN'S L J 183 (1997).

[63] See eg Marion Wanless, *Mandatory Arrest*, 1996 U ILL L REV 533, 554–7; Joan Zorza, *Mandatory Arrest for Domestic Violence, Why it May Prove the Best First Step in Curbing Repeat Abuse*, 10 FALL CRIM JUST 2 (Fall 1995).

problems associated with victims of domestic violence, wrest control away from batterers, and send a strong message regarding the 'public' wrong of domestic violence.[64] Those who support mandatory prosecution and no-drop view them as effectuating the proper roles of the state and prosecutor in domestic violence cases. A prosecutor's 'client' is the state, not the victim. Moreover, it is the role of the prosecutor to represent the people of the state; the decision whether to prosecute a crime should not rest with victims but with the state. Because domestic violence affects society as a whole, and not just the victim of abuse, it concerns public safety and the protection of children. Thus, the state cannot ignore human tragedies caused by domestic violence, just as it cannot ignore tragedies caused by other crimes.[65] Supporters of mandatory arrest and no-drop maintain that these measures place the state in a better position to move forward with domestic violence prosecutions. Proponents also maintain that this approach protects victims because it relieves them from pressure exerted by a batterer to drop the case; it relieves the victims of making this decision and puts it on the shoulders of the state, where it belongs. Because victims may be unable to trust that criminal intervention can assist in the shared goal of ending the violence, this approach shows victims that criminal intervention works. Even though forcing a victim to participate in a trial violates her autonomy, those who support mandatory prosecution and no-drop argue that this loss of autonomy cannot be equated with the loss of autonomy and harm which results from battering and violence. Another major argument advanced to support mandatory prosecution and no-drop is the effect they have on the batterer himself. These policies tell the batterer that violent conduct and abuse is criminal and unacceptable, and that incarceration is a legitimate way to persuade him to reconsider before resorting to violence against his intimate. Shifting the decision to prosecute from victim to the state also disempowers batterers and prevents them from further manipulating justice and endangering their victims' lives. In short, mandatory prosecution and no-drop take control of the justice system out of the hands of batterers.

Building on this control issue is the broader reason favoring mandatory prosecution and no-drop: that they send a message that domestic violence shall not be treated as a less serious crime than violence between strangers, and thus transform the private nature of domestic violence into a public matter. Otherwise, by refusing to intervene under a rationale that

---

[64] For a comprehensive analysis of the current debate surrounding no-drop policies and mandatory prosecution, see Cheryl Hanna, *No Right to Choose: Mandated Victim Participation in Domestic Violence Prosecutions*, 109 HARV L REV (1996), at 1849. For a pro-aggressive prosecution stand, see Donna Wills, *Domestic Violence: The Case for Aggressive Prosecution*, 7 UCLA WOMEN'S L J 173 (1997).   [65] See Wills, n 64 above, at 173.

domestic violence is a private family matter, the state not only condones battering, but in fact promotes it. Once the presence of mandatory prosecution policies is common knowledge, proponents maintain, battered women will be more likely to co-operate and batterers will be less likely to intimidate women throughout the prosecution process.[66]

Critics argue that a number of overarching problems with mandatory prosecution and no-drop policies must be realistically considered. Four major criticisms of these policies are: they are paternalistic and essentialize women's experiences by presuming that society knows what is right for all women; they re-victimize women by subjecting them to further coercion at the hands of the state; they increase the risk of retaliation against the victim by the batterer; and, finally, they disempower women by taking their autonomy away from them. According to these arguments, the opportunity to make a choice for herself regarding violence in her life is power that a battered woman needs. Deciding whether to prosecute an intimate may well be the first opportunity that a battered woman has to take an affirmative step in a generally powerless relationship. Mandatory prosecution and no-drop thus disempower battered women by robbing them of their voice in the decision to prosecute. Not only are battered women powerless in their ability to control their relationship, but they become powerless to prevent the government from interfering in their lives. This hurts battered women by reinforcing the notion that they are incapable of making rational decisions, and by increasing the chance that they will be blamed for being reluctant to take action about their battering.

Critics maintain that additional state interference into a battered woman's life can hardly be described as liberating. If arrests lead to automatic prosecution, women will be less likely to call police for help. Indeed, these policies may reinforce battered women's distrust of police and the justice system. In addition, the effect of forcing prosecution may well be that the battered woman becomes aligned with her batterer in order to protect him, thereby further entrenching her in the abusive relationship. At the extreme, these policies even lead to jailing and punishing battered victims who refuse to co-operate—an ironic result indeed for policies that purport to protect battered women.[67]

---

[66] For a general discussion on the negative aspects of mandatory prosecution and no-drop policies, see Linda G. Mills, *Intuition and Insight: A New Job Description for the Battered Woman's Prosecutor and Other More Modest Proposals*, 7 UCLA Women's L J 183 (1997); Donna M. Welch, *Mandatory Arrest of Domestic Abusers: Panacea or Perpetuation of the Problem of Abuse?*, 43 DePaul L Rev 1133 (1994); Miriam H. Ruttenberg, *A Feminist Critique of Mandatory Arrest: An Analysis of Race and Gender in Domestic Violence Policy*, 2 Am UJ Gender & L 171 (1994).

[67] See eg Art Golab, *'No-Drop' Rule on Abuse Puts Woman in Jail*, Chi Sun-Times, 1 (Dec 6 1996); John Johnson, *Tougher Abuse Laws Bite on the Bitten; Mandatory Arrest For Domestic*

For these reasons, feminist advocates have recently argued more vigorously against criminalization. For example, Linda Mills has suggested that a more flexible and individualized approach to domestic violence is necessary than the rigidity and harshness of criminal prosecution.[68] She argues that criminal justice intervention requires a severance of relationship that is too rigid for many women, who say they want the relationship to continue but the battering to stop. Mills notes that each woman's situation with and experience of abuse demands some type of specialized or tailored response, so lawyers need to be flexible enough to exercise judgment and apply 'intuition and insight' in representing and strategizing with the woman, rather than demand a rigid formula.

VAWA is the first federal legislation that addresses the problem of violence against women. It resulted from the work of an extraordinary coalition of women and civil rights groups, over several years.[69] It is a comprehensive legislative effort to address the problem of violence against women through a variety of different mechanisms, including substantial federal funding for women's shelters and other programs,[70] a national domestic abuse hotline,[71] rape education and prevention programs,[72] and training for federal and state judges.[73] It provides for the reform of remedies available for battered immigrant women[74] and a number of other reforms, including criminal enforcement of interstate orders of protection[75] and the development of an innovative civil rights remedy for gender violence.[76]

While the articulation of the civil rights provision has been significant on a symbolic level, the passage of this provision has been plagued by controversy. Questions had been raised as to whether federal jurisdiction is appropriate for 'domestic' matters, and on the particular meaning of the phrase 'motivated by gender.'[77] After several years of litigation, in May

---

Violence is Putting More Women in Jail, But the Evidence is Controversial, Guardian (London) 11 (Apr 30 1996).

[68] See Linda Mills, *On the Other Side of Silence: Affective Lawyering for Intimate Abuse*, 81 Cornell L Rev 1225, 1250 (1996).

[69] See Sally Goldfarb, *The Civil Rights Remedy of the Violence Against Women Act: Legislative History, Policy Implications & Litigation Strategy*, 4 J L & Pol'y 391 (1996).

[70] See 8 USC § 1154(a)(1994).   [71] See 42 USC § 10416(3)(2)(E) (1994).

[72] See 42 USC § 10418 (1994).   [73] See eg 42 USC §§ 13701, 13991, 13992, 14036 (1994).

[74] See eg 8 USC § 1154(a) (providing self-petition by immigrant women for legally recognized status).

[75] For example, criminal sanctions will be imposed if a person crosses state lines with an intent to violate a protective order, or for causing injury to a spouse or intimate partner in the process of forcing that person to cross state lines by use of force, coercion, duress, or fraud. 18 USC § 2262(a) (1994). Punishment ranges from five years' imprisonment for violations that do not result in physical injury to life imprisonment in cases where the violation results in death. 18 USC § 2262(b). Fines may also be imposed. *ibid*.

[76] See 43 USC § 13981 (1994).

[77] Few cases under the civil rights remedy had interpreted gender-motivation on the merits in the context of domestic violence. The legislative history of the civil rights remedy

2000, the Supreme Court held that the provision was unconstitutional. In *United States v Morrison*,[78] the Supreme Court by a vote of 5–4 invalidated the civil rights remedy of VAWA, holding that Congress had exceeded its authority under the commerce clause and the Fourteenth Amendment in enacting this provision. The Court's decision focused on federalism and Congressional power rather than on violence against women. However, the majority recognized the devastating impact that gender-motivated violence has on victims and others. The majority specifically noted that Congress had found that victims of gender-motivated violence are often discriminated against in their state justice systems.

Congress received evidence that many participants in state justice systems are perpetuating an array of erroneous stereotypes and assumptions. Congress concluded that these discriminatory stereotypes often result in insufficient investigation and prosecution of gender-motivated crime, inappropriate focus on the behavior and credibility of the victims of that crime, and unacceptably lenient punishments for those who are actually convicted of gender-motivated violence.

The effect of *Morrison* is to wipe out the civil rights remedy and to nullify any existing lawsuits under the statute. However, the decision does not have an impact on the rest of VAWA. For example, one provision of the Act makes it a federal crime to cross state lines to commit an act of domestic violence.[79] The Supreme Court declined to hear a challenge to that part of VAWA in 1999.[80] Attorney-General Janet Reno had made it clear that she thinks that this provision and all other provisions of the Act are still constitutional after *Morrison*. *Morrison* does not affect any programs that were funded under VAWA and does not prohibit Congress from reauthorizing funding for those programs under proposed VAWA II. In fact, in response to the Supreme Court decision, many political figures pledged to reauthorize VAWA funding and pass new domestic violence legislation contained in VAWA II. President Clinton, after expressing his 'disappointment' in the *Morrison* decision, stated that he has 'made reauthorization and strengthening of VAWA a top legislative goal for [2000].'[81]

This redefinition of a woman's right to be free from gender-motivated violence as a federally protected civil right has had considerable theoretical potential in shaping public consciousness and transforming our concept of violence. For the first time, there was a law which explicitly links

---

sets out a 'totality of the circumstances' standard. However, the cases that had been decided suggest the difficulty that many judges have in seeing domestic violence within a framework of equality.

[78] 120 S Ct 1740 (2000)   [79] 18 USC § 2261(a)(1)

[80] *US v Gluzman*, 154 F 3d 49 (2nd Cir 1998), cert denied, 526 US 1010 (1999); see Linda Greenhouse, 'Women Lose Right to Sue Attackers in Federal Court', *New York Times*, May 16 2000, A1.   [81] Statement of the President, Presswire May 16 2000.

violence with equality. The legislative history of the Act includes substantial showing of the impact that gender violence has on the economy,
commerce, and travel by virtue of its effect on women's freedom and
autonomy to work, travel, live freely, and make choices about their own
lives. It equates and connects the national with the individual, the public
with the private. Congress made this connection explicit in enacting the
civil rights remedy. But the civil rights remedy was not the only part
of the Violence Against Women Act of 1994 that reflected Congress's
recognition of a link between equality and violence. The legislative history of the Act suggests that the connection between violence and equality played an important role in Congress's formulation of other
provisions of VAWA. The Senate report accompanying the VAWA Bill
stated that 'there are also some crimes, including rape and family violence, that disproportionately burden women . . . Both our resolve and
our laws must change if women are to lead free and equal lives.'[82] The
Senate also found that the criminal and civil justice systems were not protecting women and were in fact often discriminating against women.
'From the initial report to the police through prosecution, trial, and sentencing, crimes against women are often treated differently and less seriously than other crimes . . . The Nation's misconception that crimes
against women are second-class crimes needs to change.' The House also
noted similar findings in its report. It recognized that the US legal system
'historically failed to address violence against women with appropriate
seriousness, and has even accepted it as legitimate.' It found that the system in some ways has continued to legitimate the violence, by police officers responding differently to domestic violence assaults than to other
assaults; by prosecutors refusing to bring cases against batterers; and by
judges and juries viewing domestic violence victims as less credible than
other victims of crimes.[83]

Both mandatory arrest and VAWA are examples of recent shifts in
ascription of state responsibility on both state and federal level. Far more
important and more challenging is the need for provision of state and
state-supported resources to deal with the real problems that battered
women face—child care, shelters, welfare, work, and workplace violence—to make it possible for women to have the economic and social
independence that is a prerequisite to women's freedom from abuse.
Indeed, the coalition of activist groups that organized VAWA I have recognized this in the organizing work that they have done for VAWA II; the
proposed VAWA II[84] now pending in Congress focuses on the interrela-

---

[82] S Rep No 103–38 (1993).
[83] HR Rep No 103–395 (1993) and HR Conf Rep No 103–711 (1994).
[84] HR 357, 106th Cong (1999).

tionship between violence, employment,[85] insurance,[86] and economic and social service resources, placing domestic violence within a broader framework of gender discrimination. For example, a provision of VAWA II, the Domestic Violence and Sexual Assault Victims' Housing Act, amends the McKinney Homeless Assistance Act to provide available funding for housing services for domestic violence victims, including rental assistance;[87] The Workplace Violence Against Women Prevention Tax Credit Act implements tax credits to businesses providing workplace safety programs to combat violence against women.[88] These provisions are an important antidote to the criminalization emphasis in VAWA I, and represent a different form of state involvement and assistance.

This leads to the third and most significant facet of state involvement in domestic violence issues, the need for an explicit gender-equality framework for state and federal law reform efforts respecting intimate violence. The civil rights remedy of VAWA I, which explicitly identifies 'gender-motivated' violence[89] as a harm and requires proof of 'gender animus,'[90] is an example of this important approach. The identification of intimate violence, sexual abuse, and rape as gendered, impacting on women's freedom, citizenship, and autonomy, and fundamental to women's equality, revives the core precept of the battered women's movement that generated the last thirty years of important legal work around battering.[91]

However, this context of gender equality has been lost in both public and legal discourse around domestic violence. While our highest governmental officials, like President Clinton and Attorney-General Janet Reno, talk about domestic violence and legitimate it as an important topic of public discourse, this discourse does not link violence to larger issues of gender.[92] Indeed, the fact that President Clinton could simultaneously eliminate welfare payments to battered women and proclaim an end to domestic violence is significant. But the good news is that in response, advocates on domestic violence and welfare have now forged important connections that have had significant legislative consequences, and have made some difference in the lives of battered women on welfare.[93]

---

[85] The Battered Women's Employment Protection Act provides unemployment insurance for victims of domestic violence who are forced to leave their jobs as a result of domestic violence, and entitles employed victims of domestic violence to take reasonable leave under the FMLA of 1993 to seek medical help, legal assistance, counseling, and safety planning and assistance without penalty from their employers, HR 357, 106th Cong § 743 (1999).

[86] The Victims of Abuse Insurance Protection Act provides that victims of domestic violence are protected against insurance discrimination, HR 357, 106th Cong §423 (1999).

[87] HR 357, 106th Cong § 404 (1999).   [88] HR 357, 106th Cong § 732 (1999).

[89] 42 USC § 13981(c).   [90] 42 USC § 13981(d)(1).

[91] See n 6 above, and accompanying text.

[92] The focus, instead, has been on criminalization.

[93] As a result of the efforts of both violence and welfare advocates working together, the Personal Responsibility and Work Opportunity Reconciliation Act of 1996 allows states to

The identification of a concept of gender violence as in VAWA I is a critical theoretical move; the important work of building connections between welfare and violence documents the crucial relationship between gender-equality and the economic impact of violence on women's lives.[97] However, the work that needs to be done to build more explicit connections between violence and gender equality is just beginning. An explicit gender-equality framework, which makes the link between battering and power and control, battering and attitudes of disrespect, battering and verbal abuse, battering and economic coercion, battering and the workplace, battering and housing, battering and welfare, and battering and child care, is necessary to the possibility of meaningful legal reform.

In sum, the last half-century has seen a sea-change in public education and legal reform on domestic violence. But there has been much continuity as well: the realities of women's lives within the family are still shaped by violence. In order to make the promise of these reforms meaningful, violence must be understood within the broader framework of gender equality.

adopt the 'Family Violence Option' which would allow them to exempt a family from the Act's sixty-month cap on state benefits 'if the family includes an individual who has been battered or subjected to extreme cruelty.' 42 USC § 608(a)(7)(C)(i) (1996). Implementation of the Family Violence Option also allows states to waive time limits when a member of a family has been a victim of domestic violence or is at risk of domestic violence. See *ibid* § 602(a)(7)(A)(iii). See Jody Raphael *The Family Violence Option*, 5 VIOLENCE AGAINST WOMEN 449, 455–6, 465 (1999) (concluding that although the FVO is implemented in most states, it is unclear whether the main objective of the FVO to provide battered women with extra time and services in obtaining employment is truly effective in assisting these women in making the transition from welfare to work).

[94] See Lucie White, *No Exit: Rethinking 'Welfare Dependency' from a Different Ground*, 81 GEO L J 1961 (1993).

22
Violence Against Women in the Family

REBECCA DOBASH AND RUSSELL DOBASH

The beating and killing of wives by husbands is perhaps as old as time, and social and legal responses to it appear throughout recorded history. Over time and across cultures, there are elements both of continuity and of change in the nature of the violence itself, in beliefs about its acceptability, and in legal and community responses to perpetrators and those who are victimized. A broad understanding of these continuities and changes provides an important context from which to consider the role and effectiveness of legal responses to violence against women in the home. For the most part, a broad world view reveals continuities in the phenomenon of this violence while local examinations provide the best vantage point to examine changes in specific responses, policies, programmes, interventions, and legislation. The nature of the violence, the frequency of its occurrence, the general orientation to this problem within a given society, and the predicaments of those who are abused as well as the abusers are all subject to continuities and changes within different social and cultural contexts that more or less condone or condemn the violence and provide social and material conditions in support of these positions. The examination of the legal response to violence against women in Britain and the USA contained within this volume provides insight into the conditions of continuity and change within the family and in these two societies at a period of relatively rapid change at the end of the twentieth century and at the start of the next century. Here, we shall concentrate on Britain and consider continuities and changes in legal responses to violence against women in the home with respect to both victims and perpetrators.

The terms used to describe this particular form of violence changed from the nineteenth-century term of wife beating, to late twentieth-century terms of violence between intimate partners, violence against women, woman abuse, spouse abuse, family violence and, most commonly, 'domestic violence'. The changes in terminology were meant to reflect changes in social and domestic relations away from earlier and more rigid conceptions of 'husbands', 'wives', marriage and family with all that these terms traditionally implied to more contemporary conceptions of men and

The Rockefeller Foundation, the Harry Guggenheim Foundation, and the Scottish Office and Home Office provided important support for the research reported in this chapter. The authors would like to thank Nicole Harwin of Women's Aid Federation England.

women living in intimate relationships that may or may not be sanctioned by marriage. Despite changes in the terminology used to describe the phenomenon, the implicit understanding of the problem has generally remained constant, referring to severe and repeated violence by a man against a woman partner living in some form of marital-like relationship. Historical and contemporary evidence supports this conception; wives and ex-wives, lovers and ex-lovers, girlfriends and ex-girlfriends form the main group of those beaten and killed by intimate partners.[1] While some men have been the recipients of violence from a woman partner, most evidence about assaults and homicides from around the world clearly points to *asymmetry* in 'domestic' violence with men as the most usual perpetrators and women as the most usual victims. This conception reflects one of the main continuities in the phenomenon worldwide, that, for the most part, the problem of 'domestic violence' is, in fact, one of men's violence against a woman partner.

THE VIOLENCE

A brief statement of the general characteristics of the phenomenon is presented in order to provide an essential backdrop to the examination of changes in social and legal responses, but by virtue of its brevity this can only stand as a characterization rather than a detailed examination, which is provided elsewhere.[2] Evidence from numerous countries confirms the widespread and serious nature of this form of violence in intimate relationships. The most recent and valid national surveys from Britain, USA, and Canada show that about one-quarter of women have experienced at least one incident of violence from an intimate partner or ex-partner during their lifetime (Britain: 23 per cent, USA: 22 per cent, and Canada: 29 per cent).[3] The British Crime Survey reveals that a quarter of all violence incidents were domestic violence and women were the

---

[1] R. P. Dobash, R. E. Dobash, M. Wilson, and M. Daly, 'The Myth of Sexual Symmetry in Marital Violence', (1992) 39 *Social Problems* 71; R. E. Dobash and R. P. Dobash, *Women, Violence and Social Change*. London and New York: Routledge (1992).

[2] R. E. Dobash and R. P. Dobash, *Rethinking Violence against Women*, (Thousand Oaks, Calif: Sage (1998); R. E. Dobash, R. P. Dobash, K. Cavanagh, and R. Lewis, *Changing Violent Men*, Thousand Oaks, Calif: Sage (2000).

[3] C. Mirrlees-Black, *Domestic Violence: Findings from a New British Crime Survey Self-Completion Questionnaire*. A Research, Development and Statistics Directorate Report, London: Home Office (1999); H. Johnson and V. F. Sacco, 'Researching Violence against Women: Statistics Canada's National Survey' (1995) 37 *Canadian Journal of Criminology* 281; P. Tajeda and N. Thoennes, *Prevalence, Incidence, and Consequences of Violence against Women: Findings from the National Violence Against Women Survey*. Research in Brief. National Institute of Justice, Centers for Disease Control Prevention. Washington, DC: US Department of Justice (1998).

victims in two-thirds of the cases.[4] In addition, survey research and find-ings from more intensive investigations reveal that some women experi-ence forced sexual relations and rape from intimate partners and this is especially the case for women suffering persistent physical assaults.[5] For most women, violence from an intimate partner is serious and repetitive and often results in physical injuries and emotional problems. Intimate relationships are also the most likely context for the killing of women. Evidence from a wide variety of societies indicates that when women are killed, it is most likely to be by a husband, common-law partner, or ex-partner. In England and Wales, for example, about 40 per cent of the women who are killed every year are killed by an intimate male partner or ex-partner.[6]

These acts of physical violence are usually linked with other coercive and intimidating behaviour as men attempt to control, dominate, and iso-late women partners.[7] Elsewhere we have delineated this phenomenon and described it as the 'constellation of violence'.[8] Research reveals that certain socio-demographic characteristics appear to be risk factors for this constellation of violence. Both lethal and non-lethal violence against women is more likely to occur among couples who are young and eco-nomically disadvantaged, and among those in non-state sanctioned rela-tionships. Women who are separated or are attempting to leave a violent relationship also experience an elevated risk of lethal and non-lethal vio-lence from partners and ex-partners.[9]

Some of the main features of this phenomenon relevant to legal inter-vention are: 1, it is gender-based in nature and largely perpetrated by men against women in a context in which men are privileged over women and attempt to dominate and control them; 2, definitions of the levels of violence that are deemed 'acceptable' within society and within the law vary across time and cultures and are largely driven by public

[4] C. Mirrlees-Black, P. Mayhew, and A. Percy, *The 1996 British Crime Survey: England and Wales* (Home Office Statistical Bulletin 19/96). London: Research and Statistic Directorate (1996); Mirrlees-Black, n 3 above, 8.

[5] K. Painter and D. Farrington, 'Marital Violence in Great Britain and its Relationship to Marital and Non-Marital Rape', (1998) *International Review of Victimology*, 5; C. Mirrlees-Black, *Domestic Violence: Findings from a New British Crime Survey Self-Completion Question-naire*. A Research, Development and Statistics Directorate Report. London: Home Office (1999); J. C. Campbell, 'Forced Sex and Intimate Partner Violence', (1999) 5 *Violence Against Women* 1017; R. E. Dobash *et al*, n 2 above, 92.

[6] Home Office, *Criminal Statistics England and Wales, 1997*. London: Research, Develop-ment and Statistics Directorate (1998) 76.

[7] R. E. Dobash and R. P. Dobash, *Violence against Wives*. New York: The Free Press (1979); M. Wilson, H. Johnson, and D. Daly, n 7 above; Dobash *et al*, n 2 above.

[8] Dobash *et al*, n 2 above, 76–81.

[9] M. Wilson and M. Daly, 'Lethal and Nonlethal Violence against Wives and the Evolu-tionary Psychology of Male Sexual Proprietariness', in R. E. Dobash and R. P. Dobash (eds), *Rethinking Violence Against Women*. Thousand Oaks, Calif: Sage (1998) 199–230.

pressure and protest and generally move toward increasing intolerance of violence and expansion of the definitions of what constitutes such violence; 3, there is a tendency for the definition of what constitutes violence to expand beyond physical violence to include sexual violence as well as various forms of intimidation and intention to cause fear.

THE ROLE OF LAW AND LAW ENFORCEMENT

In the past, there was widespread acceptance or tolerance of this violence, representing continuity across many different social and legal systems. Now, there is enormous variation in the level of its legal and social acceptance or rejection which represents change in some locations and continuity in others. Changes in the 'acceptability' or tolerance of this violence are one of the main starting points of changes in law and law enforcement as well as in other state and community responses. This raises the important issue of the nature and role of the law and law enforcement and its response to this violence. Law and its enforcement play both a symbolic and a 'real' role concerning this violence. In a symbolic sense, legal responses reflect cultural standards regarding the relative significance of this problem in a given society at a particular point in time. Crimes against property and crimes against the person are sometimes deemed to be of greater or lesser importance, and various crimes against the person vary in terms of their perceived importance as measured by the voracity of responses to them. In a general sense, the justice system is commonly believed to reflect what is deemed 'right' or 'wrong' and what will or will not be 'tolerated' by the agency of the state charged with the responsibility for adjudicating such matters. Whether it is deemed worse to steal money or to beat one's partner is, in some notional sense, gauged by what happens to offenders brought to the attention of the police and the courts.

In this case there are numerous witnesses to the 'messages' of justice: the men who perpetrate the violence and weigh the cost to themselves of subsequent acts of violence; the women who are the victims of violence and measure the utility of seeking relief through legal avenues; the children who learn through direct experience the costs and rewards of using violence; and the community who witness the relative placing of this problem within the justice system and within the wider society . Thus, the response of the justice system contains important 'symbolic' messages for all. Just as condemnation of this violence provides a message for all, so too does its toleration. The message is made all the more powerful when delivered by the agency of the state charged with public protection and the adjudication of 'right and wrong'. In this sense, the symbolic becomes real.

There is also a concrete or 'material' dimension contained within the responses of the justice system, particularly for those directly involved either as perpetrators or as victims. For women who are abused, the police are often the only twenty-four-hour service from which they may seek assistance and protection. For the abusers, legal response may constitute the only barrier to repeat victimization. Thus, what happens when the police are called or an abuser goes to court has very real consequences concerning the specific event called to their attention and subsequent events that may occur.

With regard to the 'symbolic' and the 'real' or 'material' effects of law and law enforcement upon the individuals directly concerned and upon the community and society at large, there are three wider 'transformative' projects in which they play a vital role: the attempt to transform institutional and societal 'acceptance' or toleration of this form of violence to its rejection; the attempt to change the violent person to a non-violent one by responding effectively to the offender and the offending behaviour; and, finally, the attempt to provide appropriate assistance and support for those who have been victimized. The law and legal institutions play a part in all of these transformative projects and cannot be exempted from them although, at the same time, law is not wholly responsible for any of these transformations. The community and other institutions of the state must also play vitally important parts in this overall process.

RELEVANCE OF LAW TO VIOLENCE AGAINST WOMEN

It must be asked, however, if law and law enforcement can actually do anything that might help deter perpetrators and/or assist victims, much less help transform wider social beliefs and practices. Various positions have been taken with respect to this question as it relates to various forms of violence against women including woman abuse, rape, sexual harassment, and stalking. Some say 'yes', some say 'no', and others say 'maybe'. Some believe in the effectiveness of the responses of the justice system as presently constituted; others maintain that the system can never have any meaningful effect upon such violence and violations; many adopt varying reformist positions seeking relevant changes and withholding judgment until evidence of their effectiveness is available.[10]

Feminists, abolitionists, and abstentionists maintain that as the justice system was constructed upon a patriarchal foundation, it can never be altered to serve effectively the needs of women, particularly when they

---

[10] See Dobash and Dobash, n 1 above, chs 5 and 6 for a fuller discussion.

are in conflict with those of men. Therefore, the law cannot be effectively used to address this problem. Abolitionists of other persuasions maintain that activists seeking reforms for victims, including abused women, play into the hands of a reactionary justice system that would, in the name of protecting women, use this to further 'punish' men, particularly the poor and members of ethnic groups, by over-enforcement of the law, including excessive arrests and incarceration. Such abolitionists see the role of the justice system as restricted only to 'punishment' and see no place for the transformative project of personal reform within it. Other commentators propose a very strong position for the place of law provided it can be altered to make it truly work for women. For them, the difficulty is one of creating the desired legal reforms, but once they have been achieved the law can then take its pre-eminent place among responses to violations against women. By contrast, sceptical feminist reformers adopt the position that legal reforms are necessary in order more effectively to address the problem of violence against women in the home and that reforms can be achieved albeit not without considerable difficulty and setbacks. For them, the primary goal is the pragmatic support of abused women. For some sceptical reformers, the goal also includes the 'personal transformation' of violent men. For them, the goal is to effect an end to the violence that can be sustained over time and this, they argue, necessitates the use of the justice system in order to bring these men within the orbit of change.

THE LAW

All over the world, changes in the social acceptance of the abuse of women have brought increasing pressure on legal systems to respond in ways that depart from long-legal legacies of 'acceptance' of this form of violence in all but its most extreme forms. For the most part, these changes have been initiated outside the legal system rather than within it and have usually been spearheaded by advocates of the victims of abuse seeking to provide some form of relief or escape from abuse rather than from legal, social, political, or religious institutions.

Historically, English Common Law supported a husband's right to chastise his wife; Blackstone's *Commentaries on the Laws of England* (1765) endorsed a husband's right to apply 'moderate' chastisement in order to correct his wife for whom he was responsible. Clear support for the patriarchal privileges of men was widely endorsed throughout the eighteenth century and serious challenges did not occur until the mid-nineteenth century when early feminists sought greater protection for abused women.[11] In 1853, the Aggravated Assault Act was introduced in order to provide better protection for women and children. A successful prosecution under the Act allowed for a maximum fine of £20 or six months' imprisonment. In 1861, the provisions of the Act were incorporated into a section of the Offences Against the Person Act which provides the foundation for most cases of assault in Britain today. The result of the two Acts was to recognize violent assaults against women as crimes but, at the same time, to relegate them to the lower magistrates' courts. Very few successful prosecutions were brought, and following strong criticisms of the system from early feminists such as Francis Power Cobbe, the Matrimonial Causes Act was introduced in 1878 which allowed a woman to seek a separation and financial support if her husband was convicted of an 'aggravated assault' against her. Again, very few women benefited from this Act because the assault and cruelty had to be both persistent and severe, and was thus difficult to prove in a court of law. While these legal developments were theoretically innovative for their time, the evidence suggests that, in practice, they provided little or no relief to the vast majority of women experiencing violence in the home. Attempts by suffragists to improve legal provisions in the early part of the twentieth century were unsuccessful, the problem was all but forgotten, and the legal situation remained virtually unchanged until the 1970s.

At that time, and in the context of a strong women's movement in Britain and the United States, the problem of 'battered women' was rediscovered. The personal accounts of abused women revealed an almost wholesale failure of social and legal institutions to provide either support or protection. Women's Aid (now Women's Aid Federation England, WAFE) and the National Coalition Against Domestic Violence in the USA began to provide direct and tangible assistance through the creation of refuges, shelters, and help lines which grew at an astonishing rate. Within this context, abused women revealed that both criminal and civil law had failed to provide meaningful protection and support and women activists began to campaign for changes in both law and law enforcement.

As a result of this public pressure, Parliament appointed a Select Committee in 1974 to consider the problem of domestic violence and make recommendations.[12] Testimony from abused women, Women's Aid representatives, and legal advocates recounted numerous examples of inadequate police responses and the ineffectiveness of the provisions of civil

---

[11] Dobash and Dobash, n 7, above 31–76; E. Pleck, *Domestic Tyranny*. Oxford: Oxford University Press (1987).

[12] See *Report from the Select Committee on Violence in Marriage*, Session 1974–5, Vol 1, HC 553–I (1975) and Vol 2 (Evidence) HC 329–2; R. E. Dobash and R. P. Dobash, *Women, Violence and Social Change*. London and New York: Routledge (1992).

remedies. Despite this evidence, police and judicial representatives were opposed to changes in the law and law enforcement, maintaining that police powers of arrest were adequate and that new laws and sanctions were unnecessary. The Select Committee did not agree. As a result of the recommendations of the Committee and continued pressure from Women's Aid, two acts were introduced: the Domestic Violence and Matrimonial Proceedings Act 1978 and the Domestic Proceedings and Magistrates' Courts Act 1976. Through this legislation, women were able to seek an injunction without first having to file for separation or divorce and, for the first time, a power of arrest could be attached to orders excluding someone from the home should they be breached. However, the legislation was confusing (with different courts having different powers) and narrowly interpreted. Powers of arrest were rarely used and arrests uncommon. Subsequently the Family Law Act 1996 streamlined the legislation and provided that powers of arrest must be attached to orders of protection if violence had been used or threatened to an applicant or child unless the court was satisfied that they were adequately protected without it. As a result, such attachments doubled in 1998 from their previous level.[13] Nevertheless, although the provisions were intended to simplify the law, they make complicated distinctions depending on whether one or both of the people involved have a legal interest in the dwelling, whether they are married to each other or not, and whether or not the relationship is heterosexual.[14] A potentially more far-reaching and straightforward provision was the Protection from Harassment Act 1997, dealt with below.

LAW ENFORCEMENT

By the mid-1980s, research by the police and independent researchers revealed that police policies and practices regarding domestic violence were not given serious attention at all levels and it was still judged to be a problem best dealt with by civil law and social solutions rather than through police action and arrest.[15] By this time, however, there were some differences between police forces in terms of the importance attributed to this problem and public pressure for change continued.

---

[13] Briefing Note, 'Civil Law Remedies', *Reducing Domestic Violence: What Works?* Home Office Crime Reduction Research Series, 1999. M. Hester, C. Pearson, and N. Harwin, *Making an Impact: A Reader on Children and Domestic Violence*. London: Jessica Kingsley (1999).

[14] J. Murphy, 'Domestic Violence: The New Law', (1996) 59 *Modern Law Rev* 845.

[15] Dobash and Dobash, n 12 above; S. M. Edwards, *Is Change Possible?* London: Community Safety Unit and Domestic Violence Forum (1998).

Response to Victims of Violence

In England and Wales, changes in law enforcement generally occur through administrative directives from the Home Office, similar to the US Dept of Justice, rather than through new legislation as in the USA. In 1985, against the backdrop of continuing public pressure and research findings, the Home Office issued an official Circular to all Chief Constables in England and Wales to clarify police practice and training in this area. The Circular emphasized the need to ensure the safety of victims and children and noted that opportunities for arrest were limited. Training advice to new recruits stressed that 'usually no criminal offence' is involved and 'good policing involves restoring the peace'. In 1990, a second Home Office Circular proposed a rather more interventionist strategy for domestic violence. Police forces were urged to establish registers of victims at risk, to create units of specially trained officers, and to place greater emphasis on arresting and charging offenders. This Circular was a watershed in police policy as it endorsed the possibility of an arrest without warrant and indicated that it was not necessary for an officer to witness the violence in order for an arrest to occur. For the first time, the police were being urged to create special provisions for domestic violence and to view it as a problem warranting both civil and criminal intervention rather than simply as a social issue for intervention by other institutions. It should be noted that Home Office Circulars are merely advisory and Chief Constables are not required to alter policy or practice on the basis of them.

Despite this, changes in police practice have occurred and one of the most widespread developments was the introduction of specialized Domestic Violence or Family Protection Units within police forces during the 1990s.[16] A national survey of all Women's Aid refuges in England and Wales conducted at the beginning of the 1990s assessed changes in police policy and practice. Of the 102 refuges reporting, 65 per cent indicated that their local police force had changed their policy, 58 per cent reported changes in practice, and about half indicated that a Domestic Violence Unit had been established by their local police force.[17] By the end of the 1990s, all English and Welsh police forces were operating such units. Findings from Home Office research and from the 1996 British Crime Survey show an improved evaluation of police response among abused women who seek their assistance. The BCS shows that when chronically abused women seek help they usually approach family and friends.

[16] S. Grace, *Policing Domestic Violence in the 1990s*, Home Office Research Study No 139. London: HMSO (1995).

[17] G. Hague and E. Malos, *Domestic Violence: Action for Change*. Cheltenham: New Clarion Press (1993).

However, when approaching agencies, they were most likely to go to the police, followed by medical professionals including doctors and nurses.[18] Of these women, 68 per cent said the police offered advice and support and 58 per cent found them either 'very' or 'fairly' helpful, although greater proportions of these women found other sources of assistance more helpful. Home Office findings based on reports from women seeking police assistance further suggest that Domestic Violence Units provide meaningful support for women and children and are often an important source of referral to other agencies.[19] Overall, these findings seem to suggest an improvement in women's assessment of help from the police in the 1990s in contrast to their evaluations of police performance in the 1970s and 1980s.

In addition to the positive benefits, Home Office research also shows that Domestic Violence Units, usually staffed by women police officers, often ghettoize both the officers and the problem itself. They often focus on violence against children and rape from 'strangers' rather than on physical and sexual assaults against women by intimate partners. They may perpetuate the notion that the problem should only be dealt with by 'special' police officers and ignored by other officers.[20] These units may also contribute to the idea that domestic violence is not a problem of criminal law which would, of necessity, include a focus on the perpetrator of the violence and the use of arrest and prosecution.

Despite these limitations, Domestic Violence Units have provided an important form of assistance for abused women and are a useful part of the overall compliment of responses of the system of justice. However, it would be curious indeed if the responses of the justice system to acts of violence did not also focus upon the violent act itself and the perpetrator of the violence and attempt to develop equally innovative approaches to them. To ignore them would be particularly curious since the primary purpose of the justice system is to focus upon offences, offenders, and offending behaviour. This raises the issues of arrest, prosecution, and effective sanctions and, of course, brings criminal law more clearly into play. Here, the issue becomes what to do about the violence itself and about the men who perpetrate violence. While many police policies and practices (particularly those relating to the treatment of victims) have changed, others (particularly those relating to the perpetrators) remain relatively untouched.

---

[18] C. Mirrlees-Black, *Domestic Violence: Findings from a New British Crime Survey Self-Completion Questionnaire*. A Research, Development and Statistics Directorate Report, London: Home Office (1999) 80–1   [19] Grace, n 16 above
[20] *ibid*.

Response to Perpetrators of Violence

The criminal law relating to domestic violence is the 1861 Offences Against the Persons Act. Its provisions allow for charges ranging from simple assault to grievous bodily harm, although this is rarely used, and offenders are usually charged with criminal damage and breach of the peace under other statutes, the most usual sanctions being official warnings, fines, and suspended sentences. While the 1990 Home Office Circular to Chief Constables stressed the importance of using arrest and prosecution to deal with domestic violence, evidence from that time echoed earlier findings from the 1970s and 1980s and suggested that arrest and prosecution were still very unlikely outcomes of police contacts with cases of domestic violence. However, this continuity of response may have begun to change by the mid-1990s as arrests appeared to be increasing in some police jurisdictions.[21] The Criminal Justice Act 1998[22] allows prosecutions to proceed on the basis of written testimony only to protect fearful witnesses, but this has been little used in domestic violence cases, where the Crown Prosecution Service has been criticized for not pressing prosecutions even when the evidence was sufficient. Several police forces have been developing new ways of 'enhanced evidence gathering' at the scene (such as the use of photographs) in order to improve the chances of successful prosecution in the absence of the victim. It has been found that the practice also induces guilty pleas and assists victims towards supporting the prosecution.[23]

In 1997 the English courts were provided with a new law that may be used in a small number of cases of domestic violence. Although intended to deal with cases of 'stalking', the Protection from Harassment Act 1997 is wide enough to cover cases of intimidation within the domestic context. It links criminal and civil law, creating two criminal offences. One covers 'harassment' and the other covers causing fear of violence. The former is also a civil wrong, which gives rise to a damages claim and may be restrained by civil injunction, but breach of which is a criminal offence. In its first six months 518 persons were prosecuted under the Act (mostly for the former offence), and 5,788 in the next twelve months. However, it is not yet possible to know how many of these prosecutions arose from 'domestic' situations.[24]

---

[21] S. Wright, 'The Role of the Police in Combatting Domestic Violence', in R. Emerson Dobash, R. P. Dobash, and L. Noaks, *Gender and Crime*. Cardiff: University of Cardiff Press (1995) 410–29; Edwards, n 15 above, 6–7.   [22] Section 23(3)(b)

[23] Briefing Note, 'Use of the Criminal Law', *Reducing Domestic Violence: What Works?* Home Office, Crime Reduction Research Series, 1999.

[24] Briefing Note, 'Use of the Criminal Law', *Reducing Domestic Violence: What Works?* Home Office Crime Reduction Research Series, 1999.

Overall, there has been very little change concerning the criminal law, and prosecution continues to be an infrequent outcome of police response. Despite the legislation, it is important that all members of the justice system receive adequate training in this area, and in this respect the police are more advanced than other branches of the system. The training of prosecutors, magistrates, and judges is important because the outcomes of their deliberations are highly public and thus contain symbolic messages to the entire community about the relative importance of this problem, and because their decisions have a real effect upon the lives of those who suffer from this violence.[25] Yet, by the late 1990s, only ad hoc training was available to English magistrates and judges.

RESPONDING TO THE OFFENDER

Responding to any offence of violence requires a response to those who commit such acts. For the victims of violence, efficient, informative, and supportive responses should be an essential part of effective policing of violent events, and effective processing through the courts requires attention to witnesses who may be intimidated or made vulnerable to further attack because of using the justice system. In Britain, most of the initial innovations in policies and practices attempted to provide relief for victims of violence. This is essential and must continue. However, while proper attention to those victimized is an essential part of the overall response of the justice system, this cannot stand as a substitute for responding to the act of violence itself, and this requires a response to the perpetrator. If the goal is to end violence, this is not possible unless the perpetrators are engaged. Unless men cease to be violent to women partners, there can be no end to this abuse, and civil and criminal law and law enforcement have essential roles to play in this process.

Engaging Men who use Violence

How might violent men be engaged, and what part can be played by the justice system? In answering these questions it is essential to consider some of the main components of the phenomenon and beliefs associated with its perpetration.[26] Basically, men use violence against women partners in ways that are functional and purposeful. Violence is used to main-

[25] J. Ptacek, *Battered Women in the Courtroom: The Power of Judicial Responses*. Boston: Northeastern University Press (1999).

[26] See R. E. Dobash and R. P. Dobash, 'Violent Men and Violent Contexts', in R. E. Dobash and R. P. Dobash (eds), *Rethinking Violence Against Women*. Thousand Oaks, Calif: Sage (1998), 141–68.

tain power and control over the partner, to obtain domestic and sexual services, and to punish perceived wrongdoing. This is seen through the lens of what has traditionally been deemed to be the appropriate behaviour of husbands and wives, men and women. The violence is not usually deemed to be wrong or consequential by the men who use it, and they believe that no one has a right to intervene in their 'private' life. Many become habituated in the use of violence and expect that no one will intervene either to stop their violence or to assist their partner. Since abusers do not see themselves as having a problem and do not view the violence as important or severe, they rarely seek assistance to end this behaviour unless they are 'mandated' to do so either by the woman who threatens to leave or by a justice system which threatens sanctions unless the violence ceases. Both of these possibilities often represent a strong punctuation point for the man who does not see his behaviour as wrong, and they may also constitute a crisis point in terms of presenting him with costs to himself should he persist. Here, the justice system not only has a vital role to play in terms of the 'symbolic' statement relative to the importance and unacceptable nature of the violence, but it also has a concrete role in terms of a focused and positive intervention relative to the cessation of violence by those specifically involved. What is needed are interventions that demand the man's engagement in the positive process of eliminating his violence. Through court-mandated abuser programmes, the justice system has been involved in this process since the 1980s in the USA and Canada and the 1990s in Britain. This new sanction offers the opportunity to deal more effectively with these violent offenders.

The first British court-mandated abuser programmes, CHANGE and the Lothian Domestic Violence Probation Project, began in Scotland in 1990.[27] They were undertaken on an experimental basis and since then the probation services in England have issued a position paper on domestic violence stressing the need for such programmes; a number of departments now operate various forms of abuser programmes.[28] The initial experimental programmes were themselves based on model programmes from the USA and have themselves become models for Britain. Both were based on a cognitive behavioural approach and the philosophy of the model programme from Duluth, Minnesota and modified to meet local conditions. In the British court-mandated programmes, men found guilty of an offence involving some form of physical violence to an intimate partner are sentenced to probation with a condition that they attend the

---

[27] D. Morran and M. Wilson, *Men Who are Violent to Women: A Group Work Practice Manual*. Lyme Regis, Dorset: Russell House (1997).

[28] NAPO (National Association of Probation Officers), *Domestic Violence. Draft Guidelines on Domestic Violence* (1997); J. B. Scourfield and R. P. Dobash, Programmes for Violent Men: Recent Developments in the UK, (1999) 38 *The Howard Journal* 128.

programme for a period of several months. This usually involves weekly attendance at group meetings in which they work through a systematic programme focused on the violence and associated beliefs and attitudes. Issues of alcohol and drugs are dealt with elsewhere should that be required. The conditions of probation stipulate that they must attend and participate in the programme and remain violence-free. Failure to do so constitutes a breach of the conditions of probation and may result in a return to court. The approach is primarily educational rather than psycho-dynamic, and woman abuse is deemed to be an issue involving power and control which is learned in various personal and social contexts. An alternative model is presented which is non-violent and more egalitarian and men work through and examine the negative consequences of the violence for the woman who is beaten, for the children who often witness such violence, and for themselves as its perpetrators. Learning new ideas and new behaviours and practising concrete practical skills form the core of the work.[29]

Overall, the justice system, through its *symbolic* role as adjudicator of 'right and wrong', may serve to help shift the man's conception that the violence is generally acceptable not only to himself but also to this relevant agency of the state. In its concrete, 'real' or material role, it provides surveillance, control, and potential costs to men who persist in using violence. Through arrest and prosecution, the justice system provides the necessary elements of initial engagement of men who see no reason to engage about behaviour they deem unproblematic. Through probation and abuser programmes, that engagement is then sustained for a period of time during which men focus specifically on changing their offending behaviour and related beliefs. Rather than ignoring or diminishing the importance of the problem by diverting it to other services, or by simply using traditional punishments such as fines and suspended sentences, court-mandated abuser programmes provide a sanction that departs from past practice by clearly focusing on the offence, the offending behaviour, and the need for the man to change.

The effectiveness of this approach was examined in research designed to compare court-mandated abuser programmes with other sanctions traditionally used by the courts.[30] In the *Violent Men Study*, the constellation of violence (violence, injuries, and controlling behaviour) was examined at three points in time over a one-year period after a criminal justice intervention in order to compare the relative effects of abuser programmes

---

[29] R. P. Dobash and R. E. Dobash, 'Criminal Justice Programmes for Men Who Assault their Partners', in C. R. Hollin (ed), *Handbook of Offender Assessment and Treatment*. Chichester: John Wiley and Sons (in press).

[30] R. E. Dobash, R. P. Dobash, K. Cavanagh, and R. Lewis, *Changing Violent Men*. Thousand Oaks, Calif: Sage (2000).

with other types of criminal justice sanctions (eg fines). The reports of women partners were used as the most stringent measure of changes in men's behaviour. Based on the reports of women partners, the findings show that: (1) all forms of criminal justice intervention had some effect, particularly in the first three months after intervention; (2) men who participated on abuser programmes were more likely to eliminate violence and reduce controlling behaviour than were men who received other sanctions; (3) changes in both violence and controlling behaviour were more likely to be sustained over the one-year period among men who had successfully completed the abuser programme than those receiving other sanctions; (4) violence and controlling behaviours (including intimidation) rise and fall together, with a reduction in one associated with a reduction in the other; and (5) participation on the programme was associated with an improvement in the quality of life for both women victims and male abusers.[31] Similar findings have emerged from research conducted on court-mandated abuser programmes in the USA and Canada.[32]

REPOSITIONING LAW AND LAW ENFORCEMENT FOR THE TWENTY-FIRST CENTURY — FROM ISOLATED REACTION TO INTEGRATED RESPONSE

During the last quarter of the twentieth century, there have been numerous changes in public recognition and social and legal responses to the issue of domestic violence. There has been considerable continuity with respect to civil law, particularly in the continued use of injunctions intended to protect victims of abuse by deterring men from committing subsequent acts of violence against them. The significant departure from the past has been the possibility of excluding men from the home for acts of violence and the use of the criminal law to sanction men for breaches of injunctions or exclusion orders. In the area of criminal justice, there has been a departure from almost total inaction to a greater acceptance of the need to respond effectively to this problem. The creation of special Domestic Violence Units within many police forces, and improved understanding of this problem throughout the police, have led to greater support and safety of women victims and have generally met with approval from them. The violence and the offender have come into focus as arrest, prosecution, and new sanctions have been used more frequently.

---

[31] Dobash *et al*, n 30 above.
[32] E. W. Gondolf, 'Batterer Programs: What We Know and What We Need to Know', (1997) 6 *Journal of Interpersonal Violence* 337.

It is essential to bear in mind the general patterns of domestic violence if explanation and understanding are to continue to develop and if we are to understand better how legal and social responses affect it. It is here that the task should begin and here that it should end. It is not possible to construct effective remedies for this problem unless the components of each intervention are carefully designed to address the basic elements of the problem itself. Whether based on civil or criminal law, effective approaches need to contain responses to both the victims and the perpetrators of this violence within an overall set of responses from other agencies and the community. All innovative policies and practices need to be monitored as they are introduced and evaluated for their effectiveness in terms of supporting victims of abuse and eliminating subsequent acts of violence by perpetrators. While practices still fall short of the visions of new policy and legislation there has, none the less, been a sea-change in the overall response to this problem throughout society, with the legal system increasingly playing its role in this process.

D
The Family and Governmental Agencies

23

A Forum for Every Fuss: The Growth of Court Services and ADR Treatments for Family Law Cases in the United States

JESSICA PEARSON

THE GROWTH OF DOMESTIC RELATION CASES

Demographic and Economic Trends

Domestic relations cases are the largest and fastest growing of state court civil caseloads, comprising an estimated 25[1] to 50[2] per cent of all civil actions (and increasing 77 per cent between 1985 and 1997). Between 1988 and 1995, divorces registered an 8 per cent increase, while custody cases increased 43 per cent, domestic violence cases grew by 99 per cent, and paternity cases increased by 48 per cent.[3] Domestic relations cases are defined as those involving divorce, child support, custody, domestic violence, paternity, adoption, visitation, and interstate child custody. Although many dismiss these cases as having little legal significance, others regard them as the most complex and challenging: 'When considered in terms of the disputes presented and the impact of their resolution upon the litigants and others, the family court is the most powerful branch of the judiciary.'[4]

The surge in domestic relations filings is a product of rising rates of divorce and out-of-wedlock births. There was a 67 per cent increase in the divorce rate between 1970 and 1990; it more than doubled from 10.6 per 1,000 in 1965 to 22.8 in 1979. Although the rate has stabilized and even declined slightly since then, it still remains at very high levels, and each year more than 1.5 million children experience a parental separation or divorce.[5]

Simultaneously, the rate of out-of-wedlock births increased from 6.9 per cent in 1964 to 30.5 per cent in 1992.[6] Between 1970 and 1991, unwed births went from 5.5 per cent to 22 per cent for white women and from 38 per cent

[1] See Brian Ostrom and Neal Kauder, Examining the Work of State Courts, 1995 (1998).
[2] See Jana Singer, *The Privatization of Family Law*, 34 Wisc L Rev 1443 (1992).
[3] See Brian Ostrom and Neal Kauder, Examining the Work of State Courts, 1995: A National Perspective from the Court Statistics Project (1996).
[4] Ted Rubin and Geoff Gallas, *Child and Family Legal Proceedings: Court Structure, Statutes and Rules*, in Meredith Hofford (ed), Families in Court, 25 (1989).
[5] See National Center for Health Statistics, Monthly Vital Statistics Report (1991).
[6] See US Commission on Child and Family Welfare, Parenting our Children: in the Best Interest of the Nation: A Report to the President and Congress (1996).

to 68 per cent for black women. As a result of these demographic trends, the percentage of children not living with both biological parents increased from 33 per cent in 1981 to 43 per cent in 1993[7] and it is estimated that over 50 per cent of US children born in the early 1990s will spend some part of their childhood living apart from at least one of their parents.[8] Many will grow up in poverty. Half of all children living in mother-only households have incomes below the poverty line, and another quarter have incomes that are only marginally higher. Among the hardest hit are young children, below the age of 6, who are almost ten times as likely to be very poor if they live with single mothers rather than married parents.[9]

This chapter describes how American courts have responded to the surge in domestic relations filings in families increasingly characterized by poverty and its attendant risks and dysfunctions.

Legal, Political, and Representation Factors

The Trend Toward Joint Custody and Access

A number of legal, political, and representation factors affect how courts have responded to the deluge of domestic relations cases. With the enactment of no-fault divorce statutes beginning in 1969, divorce began to be viewed as a private matter subject to 'individual ordering.' Maternal presumptions governing custody awards gave way to gender-neutral custody criteria stressing the best interests of a child as well as those favoring joint custody and continued contact with both parents. Since the first joint custody statute was passed in North Carolina in 1957 and California passed the first statute requiring that the courts grant joint custody on a presumptive basis in 1980, forty-five states have codified joint custody statutes of various types.[10]

Psychological research findings and clinical accounts stressed the negative effects of conflict on child adjustment to divorce and the importance of maintaining regular contact with both parents.[11] Disputes about custody and denied access and visitation became more common in the wake of the burgeoning fathers' rights movement which emphasized the

[7] See Nicholas Zill and Christine Nord, Running in Place: How American Families are Faring in a Changing Economy and an Individualistic Society (1994).

[8] See Gregory J. Duncan and W.L. Rodgers, *Has Children's Poverty Become More Persistent?* 56 Amer Soc Rev (1991).

[9] See National Center for Children in Poverty, Young Children in Poverty: A Statistical Update (1998).

[10] See Gerald Hardcastle, *Joint-Custody: A Family Court Judge's Perspective*, 32 Fam LQ 201 (1998).

[11] See Joan Kelly, *Current Research on Children's Post-Divorce Adjustment: No Simple Answers*, 31 Fam & Concil Cts Rev 29 (1993).

benefits of joint custody, the problems of denied visitation, and the inequities of a judicial system committed to the enforcement of child support orders without parallel emphasis on access and visitation. As a further complication, many family disputes became more contentious and fraught with issues that were not easily addressed by legal rules and adversarial procedures. Thus, increasing proportions of family court matters came to involve non-traditional relationships as well as allegations of domestic violence, child abuse, substance abuse, and other forms of serious parental misconduct.[12]

The Aggressive Enforcement of Child Support

Another trend that contributed to the rise in domestic relations filings and their contentiousness was the development of child support programs in every state and the adoption of aggressive legislation aimed at establishing and enforcing child support orders.[13] In lieu of individual judicial determinations about child support, every state was required to adopt presumptive child support guidelines based on an income-sharing perspective. Child support order levels increased and were imposed in a more consistent and uniform manner. Court-based procedures for establishing paternity for children born outside of marriage were replaced with voluntary hospital acknowledgements and/or administrative processes based on presumptive genetic testing results (there are an estimated 200,000 DNA paternity tests a year).[14] As a result, thousands of men became legal fathers with attendant rights and child support responsibilities. In a similar vein, case-by-case procedures for seizing and attaching the income and assets of delinquent non-residential parents were replaced with streamlined, automatic, administrative and computer-driven processes. Owing to a series of federal laws passed in 1984, 1988, and 1996,[15] state child support programs acquired a vast array of enforcement remedies that included universal monitoring of child support payments, universal wage withholding, the revocations of driver's and occupational licenses, the attachment of income tax refunds, bank accounts, property and other assets, mandatory reporting of new employees, and automatic matches between required directories of new

[12] See Gary B. Melton, *Children, Families and the Court in the Twenty-First Century*, 66 S CAL L REV 1993 (1993).

[13] See Irwin Garfinkel, D. Meyer, and Sarah McLanahan, *A Brief History of Child Support Policies in the United Sates*, in Irwin Garfinkel *et al* (eds), FATHERS UNDER FIRE: THE REVOLUTION IN CHILD SUPPORT ENFORCEMENT (1998).

[14] See Linda Elrod and Robert Spector, *A Review of the Year in Family Law: A Search for Definitions and Policy*, 31 FAM LQ 613, 615 (1998).

[15] See Paul Legler, *The Coming Revolution in Child Support Policy: Implications of the 1996 Welfare Act*, 30 FAM LQ 519 (1996).

hires and child support orders for the purpose of keeping track of employment changes.

Although the precise impact of aggressive paternity and child support policies on requests for custody and/or visitation is not known, it is believed to be substantial. For example, a mediator with Chicago's Marriage and Family Counseling Service (MFCS), which offers court-mandated mediation to parents with custody and/or visitation disputes, reports that almost 30 per cent of the 2,300 families seen at MFCS in 1995 were never married to each other and were referred by the child support court.[16] Studies show increasing conflict over visitation levels as a means of reducing child support obligations or to retaliate for aggressive enforcement actions.[17] And in a complete reversal of past policy, during 1997–9, the federal Office of Child Support Enforcement (OCSE) made annual grants of $10 million to states to support access and visitation projects and some child support agencies are starting to provide dispute resolution services to clients with parenting disputes.[18]

The Trend Toward Self-representation

Changing patterns of representation also affect how the growing volume of family law cases is felt in the courts. Although America provided some legal services for the poor with family law problems as part of the federally funded Office of Economic Opportunity beginning in 1965 and the Legal Services Corporation in 1974, federal appropriations for these programs were slashed by 25 per cent in 1982[19] and 30.5 per cent in 1996.[20] It is estimated that government-funded legal services plus private and pro bono services satisfy only about 20.5 per cent of the total legal needs of Americans whose income falls below poverty.[21] Cost factors also affect the use of legal services for the population with incomes above the poverty line. Nationally representative surveys of the adult population in 1974 and 1989 show that the proportion of divorcing persons seeking legal services declined from 81 per cent to 75 per cent, with only 41 per cent reporting that both divorcing parties were represented by counsel in

[16] See Joan Raisner, *Family Mediation and Never-Married Parents*, 35 FAM & CONCIL CTS REV 90 (1997).

[17] See *generally* Jessica Pearson and Jean Anhalt, *When Parents Complain about Visitation*, 11 MEDIATION Q (1993).

[18] See Laurie Coltri and Joan Hunt, *A Model for Telephone Mediation*, 36 FAM & CONCIL CTS REV 179 (1998).

[19] See LINDA PERLE and ALAN HOUSEMAN, THE LEGAL SERVICES CORPORATION ITS FUNCTIONS AND HISTORY (1993).

[20] See LEGAL SERVICES CORPORATION, 1998 FACT BOOK AND PROGRAM INFORMATION.

[21] See Richard Spangenberg *et al*, *Report of the Civil Legal Needs of the Poor*, in ABA CONSORTIUM ON LEGAL SERVICES AND THE PUBLIC, TWO NATIONAL SURVEYS: 1989 PILOT ASSESSMENT OF THE UNMET NEEDS OF THE POOR AND THE PUBLIC GENERALLY (1989) [hereinafter ABA CONSORTIUM].

1989.[22] Local studies of legal utilization show even more extreme patterns of non-representation. Indeed, the most rigorous study of representation in divorce cases in Maricopa County (Phoenix, Arizona) showed that self-representation in divorce rose from 24 per cent in 1980 to 88 per cent in 1990.[23] These patterns stand in sharp contrast to the earliest study of self-representation in two Connecticut courts in 1974–6, when only 2.7 per cent of domestic relations cases involved a self-represented litigant.[24] High rates of self-representation place new burdens on crowded and stressed court systems that are forced to assist pro se litigants in completing forms and following court procedures without giving 'legal advice.'

THE RESPONSE OF COURTS: ALTERNATIVE DISPUTE RESOLUTION

Divorce Mediation

To deal with overburdened dockets, protect children from the harmful effects of adversarial proceedings, and accommodate the rising tide of allegations of dysfunction and the declining use of lawyers in family law cases, courts turned to alternative dispute resolution generally and mediation in particular. Growing out of reconciliation counseling and begun as an experimental program to resolve amicably divorce disputes in the Los Angeles Conciliation Court in 1973 and a private mediation center in Atlanta, Georgia in 1974,[25] divorce mediation evolved into an established area of practice in both the private and public sectors[26] and became a standard feature of many domestic relations courts. There are rules of practice for divorce mediators, professional journals, and professional organizations.

Although we don't know the precise number of family mediation programs in the US, it is estimated that there was a fourfold increase in dispute resolution programs during the 1980s following the enactment of the first mandatory mediation statute in California in 1981. In the early 1990s, the National Center for State Courts reported that there were approximately 205 programs offering court-based or court-annexed

[22] Barbara Curran, *Survey of the Public's Use of Legal Services*, in ABA CONSORTIUM, n 21 above.

[23] See Bruce Sales *et al*, *Self-Representation in Divorce Cases*, Report prepared for THE AMERICAN BAR ASSOCIATION, STANDING COMMITTEE ON THE DELIVERY OF LEGAL SERVICES, Nov 1992.

[24] Sue Alexander and Kristena LaMar, *From Self-Service to Unbundling: The Continuum of Legal Services*, paper presented at the FAMILY DISPUTE RESOLUTION CONTINUUM, SOUTHEAST REGIONAL CONFERENCE AND BOARD OF DIRECTORS MEETING, Orlando, Fla Oct 29–31 1998.

[25] See Daniel Brown, *Divorce and Family Mediation: History, Review, Future Directions*, 20 FAM & CONCIL CTS REV (1982).

[26] See Bruce McKinney, *et al*, *A Nationwide Survey of Mediation Centers*, 14 MEDIATION Q 155 (1996).

services for divorce disputes (at pre- and post-dissolution stages) with half focusing on custody and visitation disputes and the other half including child support, spousal support, and property division as well. A 1998 survey of 3,118 US counties and independent cities led to the identification of divorce mediation programs in 402 counties.[27] In 1998, all but six states had statutes that explicitly mentioned family mediation of some type:[28] twelve states mandate its use for custody or visitation disputes, while one state (Arizona) relies on court rules to do the same; another nineteen states have discretionary mediation statutes. The model rules of professional conduct for lawyers require them to advise their clients about mediation.[29] Despite this widespread level of acceptance among policy makers and professionals, public knowledge remains low, with only 20 per cent of respondents to a national survey of low-and-moderate income households reporting awareness of mediation.[30]

The conclusion of two decades of research on divorce mediation is that it is an extremely useful adjunct to family courts.[31] Across the studies, mediation settlement rates stand in the 50–85 per cent range. These patterns hold for divorcing couples as well as never-married parents[32] and in programs that use less traditional techniques like telephone mediation,[33] as well as face-to-face formats. Mediation leads to the production of agreements that are perceived to be satisfactory and fair, even among non-custodians and others who may be viewed to have lost. Mediation clients appreciate the ability to communicate with each other in a controlled setting and consistently report higher satisfaction than those who use adversarial procedures. In most studies, there are no gender differences in satisfaction with mediation in contrast to the adversarial process in which men are significantly more dissatisfied than women. In addition to it often being the only form of assistance available to a growing *pro se* population, one California study found that clients with less education, and lower income, and ethnic minorities, rated mediation as more helpful.[34]

---

[27] See Margie Geasler and Karen Blaisure, *A Review of Divorce Education Program Materials*, 47 FAMILY RELATIONS 23 (1998).

[28] See Nancy Rogers and Craig McEwen, MEDIATION: LAW, POLICY, PRACTICE (2nd edn Cum Supp 1998).

[29] See Alison Gerenscer, *Family Mediation: Screening for Domestic Abuse*, 23 FLA ST UL REV 43 (1995).

[30] See AMERICAN BAR ASSOCIATION, LEGAL NEEDS AND CIVIL JUSTICE: A SURVEY OF AMERICANS (1994).

[31] See Jessica Pearson, *Family Mediation*, in Susan Keilitz (ed), NATIONAL SYMPOSIUM ON COURT-CONNECTED DISPUTE RESOLUTION RESEARCH: A REPORT ON CURRENT RESEARCH FINDINGS— IMPLICATIONS FOR COURTS AND FUTURE RESEARCH NEEDS (1994); Joan B. Kelly, *A Decade of Divorce Mediation Research: Some Answers and Questions*, 34 FAM & CONCIL CTS REV (1996) (for comprehensive summaries of the literature on divorce mediation).

[32] See Raisner, n 16 above.   [33] See Coltri and Hunt, n 18 above.

[34] See Charlene Depner, *et al*, *Client Evaluations of Mediation Services: The Impact of Case Characteristics and Mediation Service Models*, 32 FAM & CONCIL CTS REV 306 (1994).

Although mediation does not eliminate conflict between divorcing parents, it is typically viewed as less damaging than adversarial interventions and less costly to parents. And while mediation has failed to achieve some of the claims and hopes made by the proponents, the research does not lend empirical support to the more extreme fears of unfairness and imbalance voiced by the critics. Thus, while mediation produces short-term improvements in co-operation and compliance, it does not lead to long-term improvements in these areas or generate agreements that break down at greater rates than those produced in other forums.

Mediated agreements tend to resemble non-mediated ones, but typically contain more language about joint custody, more detail about visitation arrangements, and more discussion about payments for 'extras' and college expenses. Of course, the quality of the mediation makes a difference. Outcomes appear to be more durable and appreciated when mediation involves more communicative and problem-solving approaches rather than those that are narrowly focused on producing agreements. This is particularly true for high-conflict couples who are able to produce agreements, but need lengthier and more costly mediation interventions with more highly skilled and better trained mediators. Most outcome patterns are essentially comparable for programs employing mandatory versus voluntary formats; those stressing confidentiality versus those in which mediators report to the judiciary; those that deal with custody and visitation issues versus those that also deal with financial matters; those that use volunteer or staff mediators versus those that contract with private mediators; and programs that utilize orientations versus those that do not. Given the fact that a variety of mediation formats appear to work equally well, programs should be shaped to fit the needs and capacities of the communities in which they are situated rather than a preconceived model. The impact of divorce mediation on case backlogs and delays in the courts is hard to quantify, since domestic relations filings continue to rise and efficient case processing is affected by many other factors. Nevertheless, it is relevant to note that in California, which mandates mediation in contested custody and access disputes and has court-based mediation services in every judicial district which are funded by earmarked filing fees, the number of filed cases resolved by adjudication has dropped from an estimated 10 per cent[35] to fewer than 2 per cent.[36]

---

[35] See Andre Derdeyn and Elizabeth Scott, *Joint Custody: A Critical Analysis and Appraisal*, 54 AMER J OF ORTHO (1984).

[36] See ELEANOR MACCOBY and ROBERT MNOOKIN, DIVIDING THE CHILD: SOCIAL AND LEGAL DILEMMAS OF CUSTODY (1992).

Other Court Responses

Parent Education

A more recent and even more dramatic development in court services is the growth of education programs for separated and divorced parents. Begun in 1978 in Johnson County, Kansas, parent education programs are brief didactic interventions that attempt to prevent conflict by focusing on the post-divorce needs of children, the consequences of parental conflict, and the divorce adjustment process.[37] A 1994 survey identified programs in 541 counties;[38] by 1998, the number had increased by 180 per cent with 1,516 counties or cities reporting such a program.[39] Many states have enacted legislation (twenty-five) or local court and administrative rules (nineteen) authorizing or mandating attendance by divorcing parents with minor children or those who contest custody or visitation.[40] Program variants have been developed for violent[41] and high conflict families,[42] as well as stepparents, never-married parents, and ethnic minorities.[43] Clearly, parent education programs have quickly become an attractive way for US courts to provide assistance to a substantial population at a relatively low cost.

Parents seem to share the court's enthusiasm. Without exception, evaluations show high rates of user satisfaction,[44] with most attending parents favoring a mandatory attendance policy and crediting the pro-

[37] See Karen Blaisure and Margie Geasler, *Results of a Survey of Court-Connected Parent Education Programs in US Counties*, 34 FAM & CONCIL CTS REV 23 (1996); Sanford Braver, *et al*, *The Content of Divorce Education Programs: Results of a Survey*, 32 FAM & CONCIL CTS REV 41 (1996); Margie Geasler and Karen Blaisure, n 27 above (for descriptions of content and teaching strategies).

[38] See Karen Blaisure and Margie Geasler, n 37 above.

[39] See Margie Geasler and Karen Blaisure, *1998 Nationwide Survey of Court-Connected Divorce Education Programs*, 37 FAM & CONCIL CTS REV 36 (1999).

[40] See Debra Clement, *1998 Nationwide Survey of the Legal Status of Parent Education*, 37 FAM & CONCIL CTS REV 219 (1999).

[41] See Geri Fuhrmann, *et al*, *Parent Education's Second Generation: Integrating Violence Sensitivity*, 37 FAM & CONCIL CTS REV 24 (1999).

[42] Hugh McIsaac and Charlotte Finn, *Parents Beyond Conflict: A Cognitive Restructuring Model for High-Conflict Families in Divorce*, 37 FAM & CONCIL CTS REV 74 (1999); Janet Johnston, Developing and Testing a Group Intervention for Families at Impasse (1998) (unpublished report) (on file at Center for Families in Transition).

[43] See ASSOCIATION OF FAMILY AND CONCILIATION COURTS, PROCEEDINGS FROM THE THIRD INTERNATIONAL CONGRESS ON PARENT EDUCATION PROGRAMS, Breckenridge, Colorado (1997).

[44] See CAROLINE LOVERIDGE, STATEWIDE MANDATORY DIVORCE EDUCATION PROGRAM EVALUATION RESULTS (1995); Jack Arbuthnot and Donald Gordon, *Does Mandatory Divorce Education for Parents Work? A Six-Month Outcome Evaluation*, 34 FAM & CONCIL CTS REV 60 (1996); Stephanie Deluse *et al*, *Who Volunteers for Programs to Help Their Children: A Test of a Recruitment Method and a Theoretical Extension*, paper presented at the SOCIETY FOR COMMUNITY RESEARCH AND ACTION BIENNIAL CONFERENCE, Chicago (1995); Jack Arbuthnot, *et al*, *Patterns of*

grams with helping to sensitize them to their children's needs and make visitation more successful and enjoyable even six months later. Not surprisingly, perhaps, education programs do not revolutionize relationships between parents, with attending and non-attending parents[45] reporting comparable levels of conflict over child custody and access six months after filing for divorce or attending education classes, and litigating at identical rates over a four-year period of time. Valuable as they are, parent education programs do not obviate the need to develop more intensive services for high-conflict families or help parents navigate through the court system.

Supervised Visitation

Providing third-party supervision of contact between a child and a parent is a service for high-conflict families that has evolved in the last two decades of the twentieth century.[46] A 1995 survey identified ninety-four programs in the United States and Canada.[47] An officer of the Supervised Visitation Network, an international membership association created in 1992, estimates that there are 112–68 programs in operation in nearly a dozen countries.[48] Families are ordered by the court to use supervised visitation services in separation and divorce cases marked by high levels of conflict, particularly when there is a history of or allegations of domestic violence, child sexual abuse, visitation denial and other forms of parental misconduct and/or safety concerns. Supervised visitation is also viewed as a way of teaching inexperienced, non-marital parents how to care for their children and/or introducing them into the lives of their children.

Although it is used by a tiny fraction of the population for a short period of time, multi-program evaluations in both Canada[49] and the US[50] show that supervised visitation is valued by parents, lawyers, and judges. It allows parents to maintain contact with their children when there are

---

Relitigation Following Divorce Education, 35 FAM & CONCIL CTS REV 269 (1997); Nancy Thoennes and Jessica Pearson, *Parent Education in the Domestic Relations Court: A Multisite Assessment*, 37 FAM & CONCIL CTS REV 195 (1999a).

[45] See Nancy Thoennes and Jessica Pearson, n 44 above.

[46] See Robert Straus, *Supervised Visitation and Family Violence*, 29 FAM LQ 229 (1995).

[47] See Jessica Pearson and Nancy Thoennes, *Supervised Visitation: The Families and Their Experiences*, FAM & CONCIL CTS REV (forthcoming Jan 2000); Nancy Thoennes and Jessica Pearson, *Supervised Visitation: A Profile of Providers*, 37 FAM & CONCIL Cts REV 460 (1999b).

[48] See Robert Straus, *et al*, *Standards and Guidelines for Supervised Visitation Network Practice: Introductory Discussion*, 36 FAM & CONCIL CTS REV 96 (1998).

[49] See Norman Park, *et al*, *An Evaluation of Supervised Access I: Organizational Issues*, 35 FAM & CONCIL CTS REV 37 (1997); Jennifer Jenkins, *et al*, *An Evaluation of Supervised Access II: Perspective of Parents and Children*, 35 FAM & CONCIL CTS REV 51 (1997); Michelle Peterson-Badali, *et al*, *An Evaluation of Supervised Access III: Perspectives from the Legal System*, 35 FAM & CONCIL CTS REV 66 (1997).

[50] See Jessica Pearson and Nancy Thoennes, n 47 above.

safety concerns; the records of visits maintained by visitation supervisors are often used to refute various allegations of misconduct; judges use written reports of supervisors to help them make decisions about the children. The evaluations also point up some serious problems. Many US programs struggle with financial survival, a problem which is compounded by the fact that they serve low-income families and rely on user fees. Another problem is that many families simply stop coming to the program and are never heard from again, especially those who fail to receive court evaluations, assessments, or review hearings. In the US evaluation, only 36 per cent of families received any evaluations or assessments about their alleged misconduct prior to or during their participation in supervised visitation.

Supervised visitation programs clearly work best when they complement other therapeutic interventions and when the court plays an aggressive oversight role and orders families into the program, refers them for evaluations and treatments, and schedules timely reviews to ensure that case progress is being monitored and that the families are receiving needed services. This finding is consistent with court trends to improve case management and recommendations that courts improve the delivery of needed services to court populations both within the courts and in the community.[51]

Other Services for High-conflict Families

Courts have struggled to develop appropriate ways to enforce visitation rights, respond to allegations of parental misconduct, and address relitigation. Since the research on visitation problems[52] shows that they typically involve a lack of clarity about the visitation schedule, long-standing relationship problems, and/or allegations about safety, courts have turned to non-adversarial techniques to enforce visitation orders rather than punitive approaches like contempt proceedings, changes of custody and fines which may have damaging consequences for children.[53] In addition to the previously noted interventions dealing with education, mediation, and supervised visitation, courts may use counseling and monitoring interventions. For example, when a parent in Maricopa County (Phoenix, Arizona) complains to the court that his visitation is

---

[51] See Pamela Casey, *Court Populations in Need of Services: Defining the Court's Behavioral Role*, 6 BEHAVIORAL SCI & THE LAW 157–67 (1998); CAROL FLANGO, *et al*, HOW ARE COURTS CO-ORDINATING FAMILY CASES? (1999).

[52] See Jessica Pearson and Jean Anhalt, n 17 above; JESSICA PEARSON, *et al*, EVALUATION OF THE CHILD ACCESS AND DEMONSTRATION PROJECTS: FINAL WAVE II REPORT (1996); Jessica Pearson and Nancy Thoennes, *Programs to Increase Fathers' Access to their Children*, in Irwin Garfinkel, *et al* (eds), FATHERS UNDER FIRE (1998).

[53] See Robert Horowitz and Diane Dodson, *Child Support, Custody, and Visitation*, in IMPROVING CHILD SUPPORT PRACTICE, VOL 2 (1985).

being denied, court staff meet with the parents to review their visitation order and monitor visitation for six months by placing telephone calls with each parent following scheduled visits.[54]

Other court interventions for high-conflict families include: custody evaluations by mental health professionals for couples unable to reach agreements in mediation, resulting in recommendations to the court; special masters and arbitrators who assess issues and make binding decisions in disputes that involve children; hybrids of evaluation and mediation where mediators, mental health professionals, and/or judges work together both to facilitate parental agreement and make binding recommendations; and more intensive therapeutic/legal inverventions that combine mediation with counseling, evaluation and longer-term therapy.[55]

How well the programs work depends on the types of families being served. While mediation, counseling, and education work best with families with newer disputes and lower levels of conflict, it is harder and more expensive to assist parents in high-conflict relationships fraught with anger, distrust, and extreme communication deficiencies.[56] For example, one recent intervention for high-conflict couples in Alameda County, California, that was determined to be effective involved eight families meeting simultaneously in ninety-minute sessions for a total of eight sessions, which translated into 16.5 counselor hours with each family.[57] The most serious disputes require traditional custody evaluation by mental health professionals, assessments that result in recommendations to the court that are almost always followed, but are extremely time-consuming and costly. It will clearly take more experimentation to develop some affordable and effective interventions for families who come to the court with serious allegations and high levels of conflict.

Pro Se Assistance

Courts have grappled with ways of assisting pro se litigants in domestic relations cases.[58] These efforts have ranged from simplifying legal forms and instruction sheets to creating self-help centers using sophisticated

---

[54] See JESSICA PEARSON, *et al*, n 52 above.

[55] See ASSOCIATION OF FAMILY AND CONCILIATION COURTS, THE FAMILY DISPUTE RESOLUTION CONTINUUM SOUTHEAST REGIONAL CONFERENCE, Orlando, Florida (1998); Robert Zibbell, *The Mental Health Professional as Arbitrator in Post–Divorce Child Oriented Conflict*, 33 FAM & CONCIL CTS REV 462 (1995); Linda Cantelon, *Manitoba's Access Assistance Project New Directions for 'Old' Problems of Access*, 30 FAM & CONCIL CTS REV 26 (1992).

[56] See JESSICA PEARSON *et al*, n 52 above; Jessica Pearson and Nancy Thoennes, n 56 above.

[57] See Janet Johnston, n 42 above.

[58] See John Greacen, *'No Legal Advice From Court Personnel' What Does That Mean?*, Winter JUDGES' JOURNAL 10 (1995).

video and computer technologies both at the court and in shopping centers and other off-site settings. Internet-based forms of legal assistance have also been developed for victims of domestic violence.[59] Some courts conduct clinics for *pro se* litigants, others offer volunteer legal assistance programs in conjunction with local Bar associations and law schools. King County (Washington State) uses paid paralegals as 'courthouse facilitators' to help litigants file their domestic relations actions.[60] In addition to these forms of *pro se* assistance, legal services programs and attorneys are both debating about and experimenting with providing limited or 'unbundled' legal assistance to clients for discrete tasks that are too complicated for them to pursue on their own.[61] Following unbundled models, lawyers may provide one or more services such as brief advice, research, drafting, negotiation, document review or court appearance rather than the full package that they have traditionally provided to clients.[62]

Unified Family Courts

The elements of co-ordination and resource development needed in family law cases are perhaps best articulated in the unified family court model.[63] Although it was pioneered in Cincinnati, Ohio in the first half of the twentieth century (1914), the first statewide systems did not emerge until the second half following the enactment of the Standard Family Court Act in 1959 and the creation of the unified family court in Rhode Island in 1961. Eleven states currently have courts that they label unified family courts, with pilot courts operating in at least one jurisdiction in twenty-three states and the District of Columbia. Although they take different forms when they are implemented, they embody several common features, including: intake processes designed to provide an assessment of needed services; support staff; integrated, comprehensive services including legal representation, substance abuse counseling and, referral to emergency services; the use of Alternative Dispute Resolution (ADR); speedy resolution of cases;

---

[59] See Zorza and Klemperer, The Internet-Based Domestic Violence Court Preparation Project, NY (unpublished) (1998).

[60] See Linda Ridge, *The Courthouse Facilitator Program: King County's Experience*, Summer The Court Manager 12 (1995).

[61] See Michael Millemann, *et al*, *Rethinking the Full-Service Legal Representational Model: A Maryland Experiment*, Mar–Apr Clearinghouse Rev 1178 (1997).

[62] See Forrest Mosten, *The Unbundling of Legal Services in Family Law Practice*, 28 Fam LQ 421 (1994); Forrest Mosten, *Emerging Roles of the Family Lawyer A Challenge for the Courts*, 33 Fam LQ 213 (1995).

[63] See Barbara Babb, *Where We Stand: An Analysis of America's Family Law Adjudicatory Systems and the Mandate to Establish Unified Family Courts*, 32 Fam LQ 33 (1998); C Ross, *The Failure of Fragmentation: The Promise of a System of Unified Family Courts*, 32 Fam LQ (1998); Jeffrey Kuhn, *A Seven-Year Lesson on Unified Family Courts: What We Have Learned Since the 1990 National Family Court Symposium*, 32 Fam LQ 67 (1998).

case monitoring and tracking; and interdisciplinary training for judges and court personnel. As one scholar puts it:

[A unified family court] is a single court system with comprehensive jurisdiction over all cases involving children and relating to the family. One specially trained and interested judge addresses the legal and accompanying emotional and social issues challenging each family. Then under the auspices of the family court judicial action, informal court processes and social services agencies and resources are co-ordinated to produce a comprehensive resolution tailored to the individual family's legal, personal, emotional, and social needs. The result is a one family-one judge system that is more efficient and more compassionate for families in crisis.[64]

Despite professional enthusiasm for the unified family court and the fact that the American Bar Association has recommended the establishment of unified family courts in all jurisdictions,[65] it has been resisted in most states, with seventeen providing no specialized or separate system for family law cases, nine offering only family court pilot projects in a single jurisdiction, and fourteen offering only rudimentary separation of family law cases within a family division.[66] Cost considerations, large case volumes, the low status of family law cases, and the opposition of matrimonial lawyers are some of the reasons why unified family courts have not spread further and faster. Another reason is the objection of advocates for victims of domestic violence who fear that unified family courts foster a variety of goals that are inappropriate for victims of domestic violence.[67] In their view, the objectives of developing co-operative relationships between separating parents, parental access to children, non-adversarial approaches to dispute resolution and the identification and preservation of the best interests of the family unit are inappropriate when 'domestic violence is in the picture.' Rather, the role of the courts in cases of domestic violence is to focus on helping victims, punishing abusers, and participating in community-wide prevention efforts.

---

[64] Paul A Williams, *A Unified Family Court for Missouri*, 63 UMKC L REV 383, 384 (1995): 384, (cited in Babb n 63 above).

[65] See American Bar Association, Working Groups on the Unmet Legal Needs of Children and Their Families, AMERICA'S CHILDREN AT RISK: A NATIONAL AGENDA FOR LEGAL ACTION (1993).

[66] See Barbara Babb, n 63 above.

[67] See Billie Lee Dunford-Jackson *et al*, *Unified Family Courts: How Will They Serve Victims of Domestic Violence?*, 32 FAM LQ 131 (1998).

CLASSIFYING AND SERVING FAMILY LAW CASES

Conflict Pyramids

At the end of the twentieth century, there is growing recognition that families with legal problems are extremely different and need a variety of dispute resolution forums. This is true for families with and without domestic violence, for it is impossible to prescribe the legal/court interventions that would best serve all battered women given the different profiles of domestic violence offenders, victims and episodes of abuse.[68] Disputes between and among family members involve complicated relationships; courts and criminal justice agencies are learning that they must 'customize' their responses. Legal interventions, punitive sanctions and rational dispute resolution processes have limited effectiveness with people with serious dysfunctions and financial or emotional problems. As the authors of a recent report on court co-ordination in family cases observe: 'In many instances courts are the service co-ordinators of last resort for dysfunctional families, matching the needs of individuals to the services available in the community.'[69]

Minimally, courts must be able to inform families about their dispute resolution options and sort between those requiring different types of treatments. Borrowing from Maccoby and Mnookin,[70] we can depict divorcing families as a conflict pyramid. Fortunately, most divorcing parents (51 per cent) fall at the base and have no disagreement about custodial arrangements, while another 24 per cent have only mild levels of conflict that are readily resolved. The remaining 25 per cent includes those with serious problems, some of whom respond well to brief interventions like parent education, mediation, and short-term counseling, and others who engage in more protracted legal conflict. They typically have lengthier disputes, intense levels of parental hostility, serious allegations of parental misconduct, and higher levels of dysfunction and communication problems. These families may need lengthier and more therapeutic interventions, such as impasse-directed mediation,[71] and other types of intensive treatments and forms of supervision.[72] Estimates of the number of these 'obsessive parent litigants' range from 5 to 10 per cent of the total population of divorcing and

---

[68] See Eve Buzawa, *et al*, *The Response to Dometic Violence in a Model Court: Some Initial Findings and Implications*, 16 BEHAV SCI & THE LAW 185 (1998).

[69] CAROL FLANGO, *et al*, n 51 above.

[70] See Eleanor Maccoby and Robert Mnookin, n 36 above.

[71] See Janet R. Johnston and Linda E. G. Campbell, IMPASSES OF DIVORCE: THE DYNAMICS AND RESOLUTION OF FAMILY CONFLICT (1988).

[72] See Janet Johnston, n 42 above; Linda Cantelon, n 55 above.

separating parents,[73] although California researchers find that only 2 per cent actually go to trial in a setting with mandatory mediation.[74]

The Conflict Continuum

The conflict continuum is another image that has been invoked to characterize different families and the types of court interventions that they need. As one writer puts it:

Contrary to popular belief in the legal community, all divorcing and separating parents are not locked in perpetual mortal combat. Rather, empirical research establishes that such parents are neither completely co-operative nor hopelessly conflicted; they fall along a complex conflict continuum, and their place on the continuum changes as their family reorganizes and their emotional reactions subside.[75]

Likening family conflict to a disease, Schepard argues for courts to adopt a public health approach aimed at the prevention and minimization of conflict. This includes the adoption of 'primary, secondary and tertiary prevention programs,' which aim to address conflict through community and court-based preventive education programs. Targeted at school-age populations, separating and divorcing parents, and chronic litigants, respectively, these programs seek either to prevent or to contain conflict and its attendant negative consequences for children, litigants themselves, and the court system as a whole.

A Forum for Every Fuss

Judicial Case Management

The continuum is a useful image to guide court reform as well as identify the range of legal, court, and community services that may be provided to litigants. Like the concept of a multi-door courthouse[76] (or more parochially, 'a forum for every fuss'), continuums imply that litigants have different capacities and needs and that courts should establish consumer-friendly intake systems to give consumers options to solve their problems. For low-conflict and low-stakes cases, simplification and reduced attorney and court involvement make sense. For example, Justice Donald B. King[77]

---

[73] See PEARSON, *et al*, n 52 above.

[74] See Eleanor Maccoby and Robert Mnookin, n 36 above.

[75] Andrew Schepard, *Parental Conflict Prevention Programs and the Unified Family Court: A Public Health Perspective*, 32 FAM LQ 105 (1998).

[76] See Frank Sander, *Varieties of Dispute Processing*, in A. Leo Levin, *et al* (eds), THE POUND CONFERENCE: PERSPECTIVES ON JUSTICE IN THE FUTURE (1979).

[77] See Donald King, *Is Justice Served by More People Representing Themselves in Court?* 33 FAM & CONCIL CTS REV 163 (1995).

proposes statutory changes for smaller cases with marital assets under $400,000 in order to eliminate unnecessary legal work, reduce the expense of divorce, and permit parents successfully to represent themselves. Based on King's principles, Hennepin County, Minnesota implemented a judicial case management program known as Divorce With Dignity (DWD).[78] It involves informal discovery, negotiated settlement, prior court approval of all motions, and the use of one independent neutral if experts are needed. Following the implementation of DWD, the trial rate in Hennepin County dropped from 1.8 per cent to 0.6 per cent.

Administrative Divorce

Another more radical model for simplification comes from the Danish method of administratively processing applications for divorce and separation where the parties are in agreement on all relevant matters.[79] Approximately 94 per cent of all Danish divorces and separations are dealt with through a free, administrative process that involves a meeting with a civil servant who explains the process, advises the parties on the tax and social services implications of their proposed arrangements, and acts as a mediator between the parties. Following this approach, dissolution might be treated like a marriage certificate and simply filed with the Clerk and Recorder without any presentation of a parenting plan or a division of property. The courts would only be used for conflicts between divorcing couples that they could not resolve themselves.

Covenant Marriage

Of course, the opposite trend is also in effect as seen in the 1997 enactment of the Covenant Marriage Act by the Louisiana legislature and subsequently in Arizona. Covenant marriage aims to restrict divorce by reintroducing fault-based divorce law and requiring pre-divorce counseling before a divorce may be decreed.[80] Covenant marriage is being considered in at least eight other state legislatures, including Colorado, where it was recently defeated but earned a 69 per cent public approval rating in a poll conducted by the Rocky Mountain Family Council.[81] The effort to end unilateral divorce reflects the believe that no-fault divorce is responsible for the high divorce rate and for other societal problems that

---

[78] See Minnesota State Court Administrator, Divorce with Dignity Report (1996).

[79] See Henrik Andrup and Jean Graham Hall, *Mediation and Divorce: The Danish Contribution*, 33 Fam & Concil Cts Rev 194 (1995).

[80] See Heather McShain, *For Better or for Worse? A Closer Look at Two Implications of Covenant Marriage*, 32 Fam LQ 629 (1998).

[81] See Richard Crouch, *Divorce Reform Legislation News*, Americans for Divorce Reform (1999).

are correlated with divorce and single-parent homes. It remains to be seen whether covenant marriages gain momentum in other legislatures.

Comprehensive Services

If dramatic simplifications are introduced to advantage at the low end of the conflict continuum, specialized service, case co-ordination, and more intensive interventions are needed at the high end. The Oregon Task Force on Family Law has perhaps gone the furthest in developing a comprehensive proposal for families undergoing divorce.[82] In addition to recommending preventive interventions like early conflict education and preparation for marriage, the Task Force endorses the creation of community dispute resolution and family resource centers, ready access to counseling on relationship 'options,' education seminars for those going through separation and divorce, assessment by court personnel resulting in a menu of dispute resolution options, and recommendations for the appropriate avenue for the family in question. The options to be provided include: mediation, custody evaluation when mediation fails, settlement conferences for all cases not resolved by mediation or evaluation, arbitration, and the creation of a ritual to commemorate the closure of family relationships through dissolution.

If trends in court services continue, judges and courts will be intimately involved in meeting the service needs of families in the twenty-first century. As one judge put it, 'Courts are the portal to the service delivery system.'[83] A survey of courts shows that judges try to meet the service needs of family court populations by establishing in-house services or linking with community service agencies.[84] Judges also act at the systemic level by serving on advisory boards to create and support needed services. In their oversight role, they help to assure service quality. Finally, judges adopt policies and procedures that encourage or even compel family participation in service interventions. Clearly, the next generation of judges will have to become even more adept at working with human service agencies and co-ordinating service delivery.[85] As Judge King of California observes, 'The judge of the future is not going to be primarily a trial or a settlement judge, but a case manager.'[86]

---

[82] See William Howe and Maureen McKnight, *Oregon Task Force on Family Law: A New System to Resolve Family Law Conflicts*, 33 FAM & CONCIL CTS REV 173 (1995).

[83] See RICHARD FITZGERALD, JEFFERSON FAMILY COURT (1998) (as cited in CAROL FLANGO, *et al*, n 51 above).

[84] See Pamela Casey, n 51 above.   [85] See CAROL FLANGO, *et al*, n 51 above.

[86] See Donald King, *Accentuate the Positive—Eliminate the Negative*, 31 FAM & CONCIL CTS REV 9 (1993).

FAMILY, COURT, AND COMMUNITY RESOURCES

Of course, the bottom line in the implementation of these 'therapeutic jurisprudence principles' is the availability and quality of services to address the underlying problems that some families that come to the court face. Many of the nation's 2,400 domestic relations courts lack mediation and/or an array of dispute resolution options. Where public sector programs exist, they often face rising caseloads and shrinking or non-existent court appropriations. Like overburdened judges, mediators handle heavier dockets by according less time to each case; they burn out and leave, even though research shows that angrier, entrenched disputants require lengthier interventions by more highly skilled staff. Outside the courthouse, supervised visitation programs lack the money to hire supervisors during peak weekend and evening hours, substance abuse treatment programs have long wait lists, legal services programs will not accept family law matters unless there has been serious domestic abuse, and free or low cost counseling or mental health treatment is virtually non-existent.

Courts and communities need an array of relevant dispute resolution, education, investigation, counseling, drug treatment, and support services to which parents may be referred without excessive wait lists, fees, or other entry obstacles. These need to be quality services rather than perfunctory. These are tall orders for court systems that face shrinking financial resources and communities that are charged by taxpayers to cut rather than expand the publicly funded service sector. And to the extent that unemployment, job instability, and other financial factors contribute to non-visitation, non-payment of child support, and other 'family law matters,' the long-term solution to many so-called legal problems may be more basic economic reform.

It remains to be seen whether America's welfare reform initiative, the Personal Responsibility and Work Opportunity Reform Act of 1996,[87] with its work requirements and time-limited benefits, serves to enhance or weaken the financial fabric of poor families. While the number of families receiving cash assistance between 1994 and 1998 has declined nationally by more than 50 per cent, the impact of these declines on families appears to be mixed. While some states report increased job placement rates and higher percentages of families participating in welfare-to-work programs,[88] studies find that welfare leavers often wind up in jobs that pay wages which still leave them below the poverty level and offer no

---

[87] PL 104–193, 110 Stat 2105.
[88] See GENERAL ACCOUNTING OFFICE, WELFARE REFORM: INFORMATION ON FORMER RECIPIENTS' STATUS (1999).

health coverage or other benefits.[89] These patterns track with extremely strong economic patterns in the States and the departure of perhaps the 'easiest' welfare clients. Under weaker economic conditions and/or when recipients with multiple barriers to employment begin to approach the end of their benefits, the outcome patterns for families are likely to be even less favorable.

Welfare reform has the potential to have a great impact on American families and courts in the twenty-first century. If it translates into better economic opportunities for America's poor families, then many will be a lot closer to experiencing justice than any court reform can provide. And if it is shown to have serious, negative consequences for families, the courts will experience further increases in caseload, non-representation, and family dysfunction that they will be unable to address satisfactorily.

[89] See Pamela Loprest, How Families that Leave Welfare are Doing: A National Picture (1999); GAO, n 88 above.

24

Access to Justice in Family Matters in Post-War Britain

MAVIS MACLEAN

INTRODUCTION

In 1948 T. H. Marshall gave the seminal lecture in Cambridge entitled 'Citizenship and Social Class'[1] in which he argued that the acceptance of state funding for legal services was a necessary condition for the full and equal exercise of civil rights which legitimizes our democratic form of government. To make rights effective they must be accessible to all. The pressing need for help with divorce following the social stress of World War II provided the stimulus for a new system of access to justice not only in family matters but also in a far wider range of civil disputes. Family justice was to underpin a wider movement towards social equality and individual well-being, because the divorce lawyers played a key part in the setting-up of the Legal Aid Scheme, a publicly funded legal service.

In the immediate post-war period collectivist welfare provision was at its height. But as we move towards an individually oriented society in which the high aspirations associated with marriage lead to high rates of divorce and the resolution of private quarrels at public expense, the high costs associated with demand-led provision of legal aid have been questioned. No government is now willing to go on providing one of the most expensive access to justice systems in the world. In 1990 according to the French Conseil d'Etat,[2] England and Wales were spending £9.80 per head of population on legal aid compared with £3 in Germany and 70 pence in France. The story of access to justice in family matters over the last fifty years can well be told as a tale of containing public expenditure in the face of rising demand.

This chapter will describe access to the different forms of professional intervention in family matters which have developed over the last fifty years, and point up the move away from courts and lawyers as the preferred mode of intervention for those in need of public subsidy. Instead

---

[1] T. H. Marshall, 'Citizenship and Social Class', in *Sociology at the Crossroads and Other Essays* (Routledge, 1963).

[2] Conseil d'Etat, *L'Aide juridique: pour un meilleur accès au droit et à la jústice*, Section du Rapport et des Études, cited in A. A. Paterson and T. Goriely (eds), *A Reader on Resourcing Civil Justice* (Oxford University Press, 1996) 13.

we have seen the adoption of a combination of administrative procedures for dealing with child support and encouragement to try alternative forms of dispute resolution on divorce for those seeking access to family justice.

POST-WAR CRISIS MANAGEMENT : DIVORCE LAWYERS AND THE RISE AND
FALL OF LEGAL AID

As early as 1912 the Gorell Commission[3] had highlighted the number of poor but honest artisans whose marriages had broken down and whose only hope of respectability, in order to avoid the social stigma of adultery, bigamy, or bastardy was divorce. The only remedies available to them lay in the limited jurisdiction of the magistrates' courts to make financial orders between separated spouses. The Commission had suggested offering cheap divorce in the county courts, but the Church and the Bar had vigorously opposed this. Instead a poor persons' procedure had been set up by the Bar to help the very poor to obtain a High Court divorce. When this procedure became unable to cope with the growing demand resulting from wartime conditions, it was replaced by temporary legal aid sections run by the services, and a service divorce department staffed by one salaried solicitor for the Law Society. By 1947 there were twenty-seven salaried units run by the Law Society in nine areas, handling both service and civilian cases. At this time the divorce rate was ten times what it had been immediately before the war (0.45 per thousand couples in 1935 had divorced compared with 5.6 per thousand in 1947).

When the legal aid scheme was established in 1950 on the recommendation of the Rushcliffe Committee[4] it constituted a part of post-war reconstruction. Tamara Goriely[5] places the development squarely within the creation of the welfare state, at a time of hope and social solidarity. The aim was not to provide minimum benefits to the poor, but to offer equal benefits to all. The Rushcliffe Committee did not envisage that legal aid would be confined to 'those normally classed as poor'. But when the Law Society expressed anxiety about potential encroachment by the scheme into work for private paying clients, a compromise was reached. A means test would remain but the eligibility criteria would be generous, embracing almost 80 per cent of the population.

At a time of confidence in public service following the wartime period during which eight million people had joined the armed services and

---

[3] *Report of the Royal Commission on Divorce and Matrimonial Causes,* Cd 6478 (1912), para 51.
[4] *Report of the Committee on Legal Aid and Legal Advice in England and Wales,* Cmd 664, 1945.
[5] T. Goriely, 'Rushcliffe Fifty Years On: The Changing Role of Civil Legal Aid within the Welfare State', (1994) *Journal of Law and Society* 545.

almost three-quarters of a million had become civil servants, there was an acceptance and appreciation of state control and the effectiveness of working together in a number of spheres. The Cabinet was discussing grouping doctors in health centres run by local authorities, where they would be paid a salary rather than a capitation fee. In 1948, however, as Goriely points out, Aneurin Bevan, the creator of the National Health Service, was critical of the Lord Chancellor for giving in to the Law Society and allowing a greater role for the legal profession in the running of legal services than that secured by the medical profession in health services. Rushcliffe had proposed a salaried divorce department, which would be expected to use almost half of the legal aid budget (44 per cent). Careful lobbying by the Law Society however had resulted in the continuation of access to solicitors by clients in the normal way, the only difference being that the state would contribute towards the bill on a fee for service basis.

However, the divorce system, inherited from the introduction of judicial divorce in 1858, proved unable to cope with the course of events which unfolded in the twenty-five years following the establishment of the legal aid system. Divorce was thought to be such a serious matter that only the High Court should be empowered to grant a decree of divorce.[6] The Denning Report (1946–7)[7] on Procedure in Matrimonial Causes had stated that 'the gravity of divorce . . . affecting . . . the family life, the status of the parties, the interests of their children, and the interests of the State in the social and moral well being of its citizens' required that it be determined at the highest level of the judicial hierarchy. However, the demand for divorce was such that it threatened to overwhelm the judges of the Probate, Divorce and Admiralty Division of the High Court. A great deal of the judicial work associated with divorce was therefore delegated to county court judges and barristers sitting as Commissioners in divorce. The role of the lawyer was central in what was still a divorce trial, where 'the central tenet of the divorce law was punishment and reward'.[8] A matrimonial offence had to be established before a decree could be granted, though the practice of exercising discretion concerning the adultery of a petitioner was gradually increasing. The court more and more often found itself in the position of pronouncing a decree against a guilty respondent at the request of a guilty petitioner. The flavour was well captured by a contemporary divorce barrister:

[6] For a full discussion, see Gwynn Davis, Stephen Cretney, and Joan Collins, *Simple Quarrels* (Clarendon Press, Oxford, 1994) at 10.

[7] *Second Interim Report of the Committee on Procedure in Matrimonial Causes*, Cmd 6945, 1946.

[8] Finer Report, *Report of the Committee on One Parent Families*, Vol 1 Cmnd 5629 (1974). at 77.

Large incomes can be made at the Bar out of practices which consist almost entirely of undefended divorces. The hearing of an undefended suit commonly takes between ten and fifteen minutes, though much higher speeds are possible. Counsel are paid at an approximate rate of 12s. 6d per minute for asking a string of leading questions. The paperwork involved in settling documents, advising on evidence, and the like can be done by an experienced practitioner almost in his sleep. Some of it indeed can be mass produced; before the war one of the busiest members of the Probate and Divorce Bar used to settle a divorce petition simply by filling in half a dozen blanks in a mimeographed form from the stock which he carried in his chambers, Undefended divorces also provide useful initial training in court work for young men who are just starting at the Bar.[9]

In 1953 the House of Lords enunciated five considerations which the court should have in mind when exercising its discretion. These included the interest of the children of the marriage, the interests of the petitioner and his partner and their possible future marriage and ability to live respectably, the possibility of reconciliation, and the interests of the community at large 'which make it contrary to public policy to insist on the maintenance of a union which has utterly broken down'.[10] It is clear that the courts were by that time attaching great significance to the fact of breakdown. As the Finer Committee said, 'the reality was that thousands passing through the divorce courts were obtaining consensual decrees under a system under which they were theoretically prohibited'. The new legal aid system, established originally to help servicemen whose marriages had broken down in wartime, enabled many more petitioners to achieve access to the courts. But in the Finer Committee's view it also helped to push forward the move towards divorce reform, and away from the divorce trial, by promoting a reluctance among the judiciary to preside over expenditure of large sums of public money in heavily contested cases in which three or more parties, depending on the number of co-respondents, might all be legally aided, although the outcome might be plain almost from the start.[11] Even in undefended cases, the system involved heavy expense for what seemed to be increasingly little public benefit.

The legal aid scheme was thus set up in response to what was regarded in the post-war period as a divorce crisis. Its main purpose was to deal with marriage breakdown, and this is the task it has so far performed. Yet neither the Law Society nor the Lord Chancellor's Department wished to dwell on this aspect. Instead reference was made more broadly to the need to be able to prosecute a just and reasonable claim or defend a legal

---

[9] C. P. Harvey, 'On the State of the Divorce Market', (1953) 16 *Modern Law Review* 129.
[10] *Blunt v Blunt* [1953] AC 517.
[11] See eg Professor L. C. B. Gower's evidence to the *Royal Commission on Marriage and Divorce*, Cmd 9678 (1956), First Day, 16–26.

right.[12] As the War Office told the Department in 1942, 'we do not want to give the impression that the morale of the whole army will suffer if there is no machinery for easy and cheap divorce'.[13] Despite owing its existence largely to the need for legal help in divorce, civil legal aid soon came under pressure from the growing number of divorce petitioners, especially during the 1970s,[14] as the population which was formerly restricted to the inferior remedies of the magistrates' courts acquired access to the remedy they really required: judicial divorce. The importance of the magistrates' jurisdiction accordingly declined. It is clear that family work has remained dominant within the legal aid budget to a remarkable degree. In 1995–6 family work accounted for a third of all legal aid expenditure, and formed the largest single category of work, even though legal aid was now specifically designed to cover only those living at or close to benefit levels, and not the 80 per cent of the population originally within its eligibility criteria. Family work for the Legal Aid Fund was not highly paid but there was so much of it that consideration of this part of the total legal aid budget began to have a disproportionate impact on legal policy making. The political need for the Lord Chancellor to control legal aid expenditure, and not to be seen as being manipulated by the profession as in 1948, remained a strong factor in the development of family law throughout the period under review.

The first serious step in reducing legal aid expenditure in family matters was the introduction, in a limited way in 1973, and then on a universal basis in 1977, of the 'special procedure' which removed the court hearing from the granting of undefended divorces, simultaneously removing the provision of legal aid from this essentially administrative process. But this failed to stem the rise in legal aid expenditure in family matters as court work shifted from granting divorce decrees to making orders, usually by consent, in 'ancillary' proceedings (finance, property, children).[15] Various experiments on court-centred 'mediation' were developed in the 1980s, but in the 1990s the legal aid system itself came in for radical review.

In 1996 the Conservative Lord Chancellor, Lord Mackay, announced a thorough review of the legal aid scheme, the central part of which involved the provision of public funding through contracts between the Legal Aid Board and 'providers in the private and voluntary sectors'.[16]

---

[12] See Lord Chancellor's Department, *Legal Aid and Advice Bill 1948, a summary of the proposed new service*, Cmd 7563 (1948).

[13] Letter from P. J. Grigg to Sir Claud Schuster dated 9 Feb 1942 (PRO file LCO2/2845), quoted by Goriely, n 5 above.   [14] Gibson, Ch 2 of this volume.

[15] For a full discussion, see John Eekelaar, *Regulating Divorce* (Clarendon Press, Oxford 1991) ch 3.

[16] *Striking the balance: the future of legal aid in England and Wales*, Cm 3305 (1996).

The same policies were pursued by the New Labour Government, which replaced the Legal Aid Board with the Legal Services Commission.[17] For the first time, through contracting, the state will contribute to purchasing legal services from non-lawyers as well as lawyers. There is likely to be more diversification among the legal profession, with specialists, salaried lawyers, multi-disciplinary partnerships and so on, and also closer co-operation between lawyers and non-lawyers in providing legal services. However, there is also expected to be a contraction of the availability of publicly funded legal advisers, as such legal provision is confined to licensed contractors. It is also unclear, as the system begins in 2000, whether the provision of these services will appear attractive enough to the profession to maintain an acceptable level of provision.

MARRIAGE SAVING, RECONCILIATION, AND CONCILIATION (MEDIATION)

Any family justice system would prefer to be unnecessary. The promotion of reconciliation has long played a primary part in family law policy discussion, and continues to do so. In 1947 Lord Merriman, then President of the Probate, Divorce and Admiralty Division, proposed to the Denning Committee a tribunal to deal with undefended divorces, and this was to be responsible to a Commission of Conciliation and Enquiry. Each tribunal would begin by considering the possibility of reconciliation. The proposal was rejected by the Committee on the grounds that it introduced the principle of reconciliation so late into the divorce process that it would diminish the chance of success, and that this would be exacerbated by the association of the concept of reconciliation with the authority of such an august tribunal. The report of the Denning Committee placed great emphasis on preserving the marriage tie and attempting reconciliation in every case where there was a prospect of success. It concluded that there should be a Marriage Welfare Service 'to afford help and guidance in preparation for marriage and also in difficulties after marriage. It should be sponsored by the State but should not be a state institution. It should evolve gradually from the existing services and societies just as the probation system evolved from the Court Missionaries and the Child Guidance Service from the children's clinics.'[18] In the Finer Committee's words, this part of the report 'fell by the wayside',[19] but it did foreshadow the role of the court welfare officers, first appointed in

---

[17] *Modernising Justice*, Cm 4155 (1998).
[18] *Final Report of the Committee on Procedure in Matrimonial Causes*, Cmd 7024 (1947) para 28(iii).   [19] Finer Report, n 8 above, para 4.290.

1950, in investigating and reporting on the welfare of children in divorce proceedings.

Section 3 of the Divorce Reform Act 1969 (subsequently section 6 of the Matrimonial Causes Act 1973) empowered the court to adjourn proceedings for divorce for such periods as it thought fit to enable attempts to be made to effect reconciliation, and provided that rules should be made to require the solicitor to certify whether he had discussed the possibility of reconciliation with the petitioner and given him or her the names and addresses of persons qualified to help effect a reconciliation between the parties to a marriage who had become estranged. However, the provisions about adjournment became almost immediately redundant after the introduction of the 'special procedure'.[20] Any attempt, it seemed, to use the process as a means for saving marriages had been abandoned.

By the late 1970s the Marriage Guidance movement had moved away from concentration upon saving marriages, to smoothing the transition from one status to another. As the Home Office put it in 1979: 'Methods of casework were developed designed to enable the client to understand more of himself and his problems, and, in understanding, help himself. Out of this grew "marriage counseling" rather than "marriage guidance" . . . the outcome may be a marriage ended, with less hurt, perhaps less insult to the emotional and spiritual relationship than otherwise there may have been.'[21] So we begin to see the marriage savers moving away from reconciliation towards conciliation, partly as a result of the appreciation by the judiciary that by the time a matter reached court the chances of marriage saving were remote. However, late in the century, under the pressures of what Grossberg[22] refers to as 'reactions' to the divorce revolution, attention reverted to the possibility of using the divorce process to save savable marriages. The 'period of reflection and consideration' proposed by the Family Law Act 1996 and the compulsory attendance by the initiator of the process at an information meeting were seen as mechanisms which might make the parties pause before going through with the divorce.[23] The scheme had not been brought into effect by the end of the century, and its prospects of success as a marriage-saving venture are extremely speculative.

The Finer Committee is often identified as the source of key innovative ideas on family law in this period. But the beginnings of the move from reconciliation to conciliation predate the Committee. In 1972 the

[20] See above, at 537.
[21] Home Office Working Party, *Marriage Matters* (1979), paras 1.15–16. For a full discussion, see Robert Dingwall and John Eekelaar (eds), *Divorce, Mediation and the Legal Process* (Clarendon Press, Oxford, 1988) ch 1. [22] Ch 1 of this volume.
[23] See John Eekelaar, 'Family Law: Keeping Us "On Message"' (1999) 11 *Child and Family Law Quarterly* 387.

President of the Family Division directed that courts should refer cases to probation officers for conciliation, an activity which was distinguished from either reconciliation or inquiry leading to an investigative report. According to Dingwall and Eekelaar[24] this was the Family Division's response to section 3 of the Divorce Reform Act of 1969 which permitted the courts to adjourn cases for attempts at reconciliation. But the direction widened the scope of that provision to allow adjournment where conciliation might assist the parties to resolve their dispute or any part of it by agreement. It is doubtful whether this direction had any immediate effect, but it bridged the gap between the tradition of reconciliation and the new concept of conciliation. It was made all the easier by the disappearance of 'collusion' as a bar to granting divorces with the reform of 1971. Some argued that such a development would contribute to the welfare of the children, the couple, and the institution of marriage.[25] This was later developed by the conciliation (now more commonly termed mediation) movement of the 1990s which sees its role as improving communication between the parties rather than always achieving a specific outcome.[26]

During the period when the marriage guidance services were ambivalent about extending their work to the unsavable marriage, the cause of mediation was taken forward primarily by the out-of-court or independent conciliation services first established in Bristol in 1975, rather than by the court welfare service. Financial support for this service in Bristol remained temporary and unpredictable, but the service has been regarded as being in the vanguard of mediation services in the United Kingdom. It was provided predominantly as a freely available social service rather than as a commercial, market-based activity as in the United States. The co-ordinator of the Bristol service, Lisa Parkinson, went on to occupy the key role of training officer for the National Family Conciliation Council. She stresses in her writing the value of the process to the parties in increasing their capacity for self-determination, and encouraging people to 'take control of their own affairs and to work out their own solutions'. In addition mediation is now believed to offer benefits to children by mitigating the emotional impact of divorce and enabling divorcing parents to develop the necessary skills to remain in co-operative contact as co-parents of the children of the marriage. By 1986 the not-for-profit mediation services were dealing with 2–3,000 cases per year. This must be put alongside a totality of some 150,000 divorces a year during that period.

[24] See n 21 above.
[25] A. H. Manchester and J. M. Whetton, 'Marital Conciliation in England and Wales' (1974) 23 *International and Comparative Law Quarterly* 339.
[26] Jane Lewis, *The Role of Mediation in Family Disputes in Scotland* (Scottish Office, 1999).

However, in the closing decade of the century, the mediation movement became caught up in a different agenda. Concern over legal aid expenditure had continued to grow, and now governmental sources saw mediation as a means of reducing these costs. The Law Commission's proposal in 1990[27] to replace the divorce scheme of the Divorce Reform Act 1969 with a single waiting period became, in the Government's hands, an instrument for promoting mediation over lawyer-based negotiation.[28] The early consultation paper of the Conservative administration placed mediation centre-stage,[29] and the succeeding Labour Government maintained the same policy. Most significantly, all clients seeking public funding for legal help (save in exceptional situations, for example, where violence is present) will now need to meet a mediator in the first instance. If the mediator considers the case to be suitable for mediation, funding for the use of a lawyer is unlikely to be granted. This policy[30] has been introduced in stages to allow monitoring of its efficacy. It will take a couple of years before the outcome will be known, but it is safe to say that the future of mediation as a major part of the process of dealing with family disputes in England and Wales turns on the extent to which it develops alongside the publicly funded legal services.

THE FAMILY COURT MOVEMENT

The key role played by the Finer Committee in the development of family justice lies not only in the development of the interest in conciliation but also in the concern about the wisdom of maintaining a dual system of family law, divided between the summary jurisdiction of the magistrates and the High Court and county courts. In 1980, Mervyn Murch[31] stressed the need not only for information but also for counselling for those involved in disputes related to their divorce. But for all disputed matters which cannot be settled by negotiation or conciliation he supported the concept of a family court, suggesting that the institution should be supported by a body to deal with preliminary hearings. This would be known as the family tribunal and would have four tasks: first, to sift evidence and evaluate interests, and take over all the administrative tasks

---

[27] Law Commission, *Family Law: the Ground for Divorce*, Law Com No 192 (1990).
[28] For a full discussion of these issues, see John Eekelaar, Mavis Maclean, and Sarah Beinart, *Family Lawyers: The Divorce Work of Solicitors* (Hart Publishing, 2000).
[29] *Looking to the Future: Mediation and the Ground for Divorce: A Consultation Paper*, Cm 2424 (1993); followed by the White Paper of the same title, Cm 2799 (1995).
[30] Enacted in the Family Law Act 1996, s 29.
[31] Mervyn Murch, *Justice and Welfare in Divorce* (Sweet & Maxwell, 1980).

then undertaken by the county court registrars and the magistrates' clerk's office. Second, it would investigate those matters where there was insufficient documentary evidence to justify making the orders sought. The chairman would have powers to call parties in to discuss, for example, questions of satisfaction with arrangements concerning children. Third, the tribunal could grant orders where there was no dispute, or where the state's interests were satisfied on the strength of the evidence before the tribunal. And fourth, the tribunal would promote the settlement of family disputes by a process of negotiation and conciliation. Parties and their representatives could be called together for pre-trial review, and to sit at the table with minimal formality to try to reach a settlement. Only when these avenues had been exhausted would the case be set down for a contested hearing. Using the experience of the social security tribunals, Murch suggested that the chairman of such a tribunal could sit with specialists in family finance and child welfare dedicated to reaching settlement. The procedure would leave the way open to return to trial and to have legal representation and could not be thought to impinge on the legal rights of the parties. But 'it is clearly more satisfactory for the parties, their children and society as a whole if both parties emerge in an amicable frame of mind'.[32]

Murch argued for conciliators and welfare officers to form two branches of a single family court welfare service, as although both need a similar range of knowledge their tasks are different. He saw this system as gradually taking on responsibility for most juvenile matters, especially care and protection of children and matters relating to the Education Acts, and to deal with adoption. The emphasis is different from that of the Finer Committee, which was mainly concerned to overcome the inadvisability of having two jurisdictions dealing with similar matters in rather different ways.[33] These arguments were supported by developments in other fields of social policy akin to family justice. The Finer proposals in the section of the report entitled 'One remedy One court' followed on from the ideas contained in the Seebohm Report on the organization of local authority social services, which advocated a generic social service.[34]

This movement towards a simplified, comprehensible, and efficient service, which was implemented, though not without criticism, in social work, was not followed through for family justice, for a number of reasons. I have referred to the cost of such a radical change, but there was also a structural issue, and that concerned the place of juvenile crime within the system. Although it was part of the Labour Government's

---

[32] Murch, n 31 above, at 263.
[33] Finer Report, n 8 above, vol 1, at 189.
[34] See Masson, Ch 26 of this volume.

policies in the 1960s to view delinquency in the context of family prob-lems,[35] the family court policy was not brought into being in England and Wales before the conservative reaction in the 1970s.[36] However, while Murch's ideal of a unified family court combining a judicial and welfare role was never realized, some of the more limited objectives of the Finer Committee were achieved. The Children Act 1989 restyled magistrates' courts which dealt with family matters 'Family Proceedings Courts' and conferred on them a jurisdiction parallel to that of the higher courts in both child protection and private law matters concerning children. At the end of the century proposals to unify the Family Court Welfare Service (which deals primarily with children in private law cases) with Guardians ad litem (who are involved in public law cases concerning children) will bring a unified service closer. In another respect, a proce-dure which started in the divorce courts in London, but which will be applied throughout England and Wales during 2000, envisages close judi-cial management over private law family disputes which reach the courts. Part of the process will include an appointment before a judge to clarify issues and accelerate preparatory steps, followed by a Financial Dispute Resolution hearing (before a different judge) which it is hoped will assist parties in reaching agreement. These steps are intended to reduce delay and the cost of the legal process, whether publicly or pri-vately funded, but the extent to which they will successfully do so is unproved.[37]

THE FLIGHT FROM COURT: THE CHILD SUPPORT SCHEME

Professional intervention in family matters during the post-war period is characterized by the development of expertise in dealing with chil-dren deprived of a normal home life, and a growing acceptance of the notion of children's best interests interspersed with discussion of chil-dren's rights The responsibility of the state to provide access to a lawyer through legal aid is under threat, though at a period when there is growing family disruption and awareness of its adverse consequences. Hence the Government has turned to alternatives. We have discussed the emergence of mediation as a favoured option for publicly funded service provision in such cases. But the most dramatic manifestation of the flight from the courts has been the child support scheme.

---

[35] See Home Office, *The Child, the Family and the Young Offender*, Cmnd 2742 (1965).

[36] Unlike in Scotland, where the children's hearings system currently operated dates from that period: see Christine Hallett, 'Ahead of the Game or Behind the Times? The Scottish Children's Hearings System in International Context', (2000) 14 *International Journal of Law, Policy & the Family* 31.   [37] See Eekelaar, Maclean, and Beinart, n 28 above.

During the Thatcher administration the cost to the social security budget of serial partnerships resulting in one-parent families at a time of stringent cuts in public spending became an urgent problem. The child support schemes adopted first in Wisconsin and later in Australia whereby a child was deemed to have a right to a share in the income of the parents, rather than a claim through the parent with care, were attractive. The existing court-based mechanisms for recovering child support payments were deemed ineffective, especially where these payments were made directly to the state in return for state support of the family the debtor had left.[38] Thus a formula was developed to ensure that the 'absent parent' should make a contribution which would as far as possible recompense the state for its support of that family: this was termed the 'social security bill'. Furthermore, this was to be implemented through an administrative agency, with minimal discretion.[39] The scheme reversed overnight the previous policy that when a man with limited income resources formed a second family, and his first family required state support, the state should be lenient in permitting him to retain resources necessary to support his second family. Now the first family was to be seen as having a prior claim on his resources, with very limited recognition afforded to his new dependants.[40] This change in itself gave rise to great public concern, and this was exacerbated by the complexity of the scheme. In order to provide an acceptable substitute for court-based decisions, the Child Support Agency was required to replicate the level of detailed information collected by courts when dealing with individual claims. But the Agency was located within the social security system, which is accustomed to allocating welfare payments to applicants when criteria are met, and not to dealing with two-party disputes which require information from families whose circumstances are often changeable and difficult to verify. The hybrid nature of the organization led to delay in assessment, heavy bills for arrears, and public disquiet both among the men who were being asked to pay more and also the women on welfare, whose benefits were reduced pound for pound when support payments were made. There was little evidence of any benefit to the children.[41] With limited exceptions, anyone claiming

---

[38] See *Children Come First: The Government's proposals on the maintenance of children*, Cm 1263 (London, HMSO, 1990).   [39] Child Support Act 1991.

[40] For detailed discussions, see M. Maclean and J. Eekelaar, 'Child Support: The British Solution' (1993) 7 *Int Journal of Law & the Family* 205; M. Maclean and A. Warman, 'A Comparative Approach to Child Support Systems: Legal Rules and Social Policies'; and J. Eekelaar, 'Child Support as Distributive and Commutative Justice: The United Kingdom Experience', in J. Thomas Oldham (ed), *Child Support: The Next Frontier* (University of Michigan Press, Ann Arbor, 2000).

[41] For a detailed critique, see Gwynn Davis, Nick Wikely, and Richard Young, *Child Support in Action* (Hart Publishing, 1998).

state support for children where the other parent had left the home was obliged to activate the machinery. Courts lost most of their jurisdiction to order child maintenance, except when the order incorporated a prior written agreement about it between the parents.

The Conservative administration responded to criticisms by allowing departure from the formula in strictly defined circumstances, which only added to the scheme's complexity.[42] The Labour administration, however, instituted a major simplification of the formula. Liability would now be assessed to a straight percentage slice of net income: 15 per cent for one child, 20 per cent for two-children, and 25 per cent for three or more children.[43] It was hoped that this simplicity would enable the Agency both to benefit more children and to increase the proportion of non-resident parents paying their full due amount, which was only 40 per cent. As before, any lone parent claiming social security benefit would be required to use the scheme, but on receiving child support would now receive a £10 allowance before benefit was reduced. Parents who wished to make their own arrangements through the courts would be able to do so, but the option of returning to the Agency remained.[44] Whether these changes will improve what has been generally accepted as a disappointing service remains to be seen.

CONCLUSIONS

This chapter began with T. H. Marshall's account of the importance of access to legal services in order to ensure access to justice for all citizens. But as the new century begins, access to justice appears to have been redefined by those who make legal policy as being no longer dependent on the services of lawyers and the courts. If we look to a justice system to provide resolution of disputes, in the context of divorce we see a strong emphasis on mediation as an alternative to the legal process. If we look to courts to provide enforcement of rightful claims, then again we see an alternative provided through clear formulation of rights which can then be implemented by an administrative body, such as the Child Support Agency. The common strategy is the avoidance of courts and the common aim is to distinguish between the needs of adults and children, by encouraging private agreement between adults who wish to alter their living arrangements, combined with public acknowledgment of the indisputable obligation of parents to children which can be ascertained and enforced without the need for lawyers and courts.

[42] Child Support Act 1995.
[43] Department of Social Security, *A new contract for welfare: Children's Rights and Parents' Responsibilities*, Cm 4349 (July, 1999).
[44] Child Support, Pensions and Social Security Bill 2000.

25

Child Welfare Policy and Practice in the United States 1950–2000

MARTIN GUGGENHEIM

A VERY BRIEF PRE-1950 HISTORY

For most of the first 160 years after the creation of the United States, government played a very minor role in protecting children from harm suffered because of the abuse or neglect of their parents. American society and its laws regarded children as the business of families; a child's well-being was considered beyond the regulatory power of the state. This perception, in turn, was undoubtedly influenced by a shared understanding that children were better off being raised by their parents and that very few, if any, children were actually harmed in serious ways by their parents.

An important exception to this description involves the children of the poor. For much of the nineteenth century, and particularly after 1860 when the United States was engaged in its Civil War, children of the poor, especially those found wandering on the streets begging for sustenance, were routinely rounded up and placed in almshouses and reformatories, or apprenticed out to people working in industry or agriculture, often to farmers in the middle western portion of the country.[1] Except when children were publicly neglected in this way, however, neither American law nor practice focused much attention on the adequacy of conditions in a child's home.

Although there has been a foster care system in place in the United States for well over 150 years, for much of that period—up to the 1970s—most children in foster care had been placed there by parents who were temporarily unable to care for them. Very few foster care placements resulted from formal charges of unfitness brought against parents in civil legal proceedings. Instead, formal coercive state intervention to protect children from harm was left largely to the criminal legal system through prosecution for such criminal acts as homicide, assault, and endangering the welfare of a minor.

Beginning in the 1830s, almshouses were built for the poor, the insane, and orphans. By the middle of the nineteenth century, children were approximately 40 per cent of the almshouse population; at roughly the

---

[1] See Douglas R. Rendleman, *Parens Patriae: From Chancery to the Juvenile Court*, 23 SCL REV 205, 223–36 (1971); STEVEN SCHLOSSMAN, LOVE AND THE AMERICAN DELINQUENT (1977).

same time, public sentiment towards the use of almshouses turned negative. As a consequence, New York's legislature recommended the
'removal of children from poorhouses and their placement in orphanages
and similar institutions for special care.'[2] Throughout the 1860s and
1870s, towns and counties began contracting with private orphanages to
receive and provide for children with public money. This system of placing children in state-subsidized private agencies became the settled practice within a very few years.

The few entities paying attention to children's well-being in the United
States were private associations, which were commonly affiliated with
religious organizations. In 1877, New York was the site of the formation
of the country's first Society for the Prevention of Cruelty to Children.
Once such organizations were formed, states passed laws to protect children by giving the organizations the legal authority to place children on
farms and away from their parents. It was only in the twentieth century
that specialized juvenile courts were formed in the United States.[3] With
these courts, legal authority to remove children from homes was transferred from the private organizations to the courts.

Outside of child labor protections, the federal government's first venture into the child welfare arena was the passage of the Social Security
Act of 1935.[4] That law established the Aid to Dependent Children program, which offered cash assistance to enable poor, single mothers to care
for their children.[5]

FROM 1950 TO 2000

Around 1950, no significant child protection scheme existed in any
jurisdiction. Neither lawmakers nor policy makers perceived families as
dangerous or harmful to children's well-being. As a result, there were

---

[2] *Wilder v Sugarman*, 385 F Supp 1013, 1019–20 (SDNY 1974) (citing FENERSTOCK, HISTORY OF
NEW YORK SOCIAL WELFARE LEGISLATION, INTRODUCTION, NY SOC WELFARE LAW, 52A, ix, xxiii
(McKinney 1966).   [3] The first, in 1899, was Chicago's Juvenile Court.
[4] See Social Security Act § 521, Pub L No 74–271, 49 Stat 620, 633 (1935). Child Welfare
Services Program, Title I-B of the Social Security Act (1935) provides grants to states to support preventive and protective services to vulnerable children and their families. Initially,
most funds went to foster care payments; since 1980, federal law has encouraged prevention of out-of-home placement.
[5] Foster care payments under the Aid to Dependent Children program, Title IV-A of the
Social Security Act (1961) provided federal funds to help states make maintenance payments for children who are eligible for cash assistance and who live in foster care. Such payments go to foster parents to cover the costs of children's food, shelter, clothing,
supervision, travel home for visits, and the like. In 1980, this program was transferred to a
new Title IV-E of the Social Security Act. A lesser-known part of that legislation (Title IV-B,
Child Welfare Services) provided limited federal funding to encourage states to develop
preventive and protective services for vulnerable children.

no special mechanisms to investigate officially allegations of child abuse. Neither child abuse nor child neglect, at least as these terms have come to be understood in the United States, were regarded as serious social issues requiring public attention.

The core of child welfare policy in 1950 revolved around federal monetary programs established in the 1930s, as part of President Franklin Roosevelt's New Deal, to provide cash benefits to needy families through programs such as Social Security and Aid to Dependent Children. The Social Security Act was amended in the 1960s and 1970s to add federal support for payments to families of children in foster care and for additional social services.[6] Policy makers believed they had taken sufficient action to protect children by creating schemes to distribute income, food stamps, and publicly financed medicine to poor families and to families with single mothers.

Underpinning this strong preference for the *laissez-faire* policy of child rearing were two important conceptions about families in the United States. First, that the rights to raise children and to live within a family unit free from government oversight and regulation numbered among the core freedoms of Americans. This conception has formed the nucleus of bedrock constitutional doctrine in the United States for most of the twentieth century. The state's power to regulate the lawful prerogatives of parents over their children or to intrude into the realm of family life is limited by the Constitution. The general understanding of the relationship between the family and the state is perhaps best summarized by language from a number of vitally important Supreme Court decisions issued between 1922 and 1972. The primacy of parental rights has remained fairly constant since the Supreme Court first considered the issue in the 1920s, although the Court has relied upon an amalgam of rights that, in combination, constitute 'parental rights.'

In 1923, for example, the Supreme Court struck down a Nebraska law that prohibited the teaching of a foreign language in state-run schools because 'the right of parents . . . to instruct their children' is protected by the due process clause of the Fourteenth Amendment to the Constitution.[7] In a 1944 opinion in a case involving a clash between state regulation of child labor and a parent's right to train a child religiously, the Court wrote: 'It is cardinal with us that the custody, care and nurture of the child reside first in the parents, whose primary function and freedom include preparation for obligations the State can neither supply nor

---

[6] See Social Security Act Amendments, Pub L No 87–31, §§ 2–7, 75 Stat 75, 76–8 (1961). These funds were eventually consolidated in Title XX of the Social Security Act, which became the Social Services Block Grant in 1981. See Omnibus Budget Reconciliation Act, Pub L No 97–35, 95 Stat 357, 511–19 (1981).

[7] See *Meyer v Nebraska*, 262 US 390, 400 (1923).

hinder.'[8] In 1972, in a challenge to a compulsory education requirement, the Court reaffirmed the primacy of parental prerogatives to rear children by stating: 'The history and culture of Western civilization reflect a strong tradition of parental concern for the nurture and upbringing of tl.eir children. This primary role of the parents in the upbringing of their children is now established beyond debate as an enduring American tradition.'[9]

Family rights, grounded in the constitutional guarantees of privacy and liberty, are sometimes known as rights of 'family integrity.' The Supreme Court has determined that, although there is no specific textual reference to it, the right of family integrity exists among the 'penumbra' of other rights protected by the Constitution. On several occasions, the Supreme Court has made clear that family rights are specially protected rights, superior even to other rights explicitly recognized by the Constitution. To cite only two of many illustrations: in 1953, the Supreme Court said that the custody rights of parents are 'far more precious ... than property rights;'[10] and, in 1972, the Court stated: 'It is plain that the interest of a parent in the companionship, care, custody, and management of his or her children "come[s] to this Court with a momentum for respect lacking when appeal is made to liberties which derive merely from shifting economic arrangements."'[11]

The right of privacy, located in the Fourteenth Amendment's due process clause, was first secured in a 1965 case involving a challenge to a Connecticut statute prohibiting the sale of birth-control devices, even to married persons. The Court found the law unconstitutional and held that a state may not interfere with marital privacy by prohibiting couples from using contraceptives. In a concurring opinion, Justice Goldberg wrote:

The home derives its pre-eminence as the seat of family life. And the integrity of that life is something so fundamental that it has been found to draw to its protection the principles of more than one explicitly granted Constitutional right . . . . The entire fabric of the Constitution and the purposes that clearly underlie its specific guarantees demonstrate that the rights to marital privacy and to marry and raise a family are of similar order and magnitude as the fundamental rights specifically protected.[12]

---

[8] *Prince v Massachusetts*, 321 US 158, 166 (1944).
[9] *Wisconsin v Yoder*, 406 US 205, 232 (1972).
[10] *May v Anderson*, 345 US 528, 533 (1953).
[11] *Stanley v Illinois*, 405 US 645, 651 (1972) (quoting *Kovacs v Cooper*, 336 US 77, 95 (1949) (Frankfurter, J, concurring)).
[12] *Griswold v Connecticut*, 381 US 479, 495 (1965) (quoting *Poe v Ullman*, 367 US 497, 551–2 (1961) (Harlan, J, dissenting).

The second conception that supported America's *laissez-faire* policy in the child welfare area was the general sense that all was well within these families and that there was no need to oversee child rearing practices aggressively. Although today the constitutional principles supporting familial privacy remain quite vibrant in American law and culture, a dramatic change has occurred with respect to society's sense of a child's safety in his or her own home. This perception began to change in the 1960s; in that decade, medical professionals focused public attention on evidence that many physical injuries to children were apparently inflicted by parents. The medical profession labeled the pattern of unexplained physical injuries, such as multiple burns or broken bones, which were inflicted on children by their caregivers, as 'battered child syndrome.' Doctors explained to the public the possibility that parents were capable both of injuring their children and of falsely explaining these injuries as accidents in the home.[13] As concern for this condition increased, so did policy makers' sensitivity that children may be at risk of serious harm at the hands of family members. For the first time, child abuse became an issue of national significance.

Also during this time, the burgeoning children's rights movement—which was partly an effect of the 1960s Civil Rights Movement in general and partly a consequence of the 'discovery' that children could be at risk living with their parents—encouraged policy makers to focus on the separate human rights of children to be raised in safety, even if that meant separating them from their birth families. In 1967, the Supreme Court stated for the first time that 'neither the Fourteenth Amendment nor the Bill of Rights is for adults alone.'[14] Two years later, the Court declared that children are 'persons' within the meaning of the Fourteenth Amendment.[15] As a consequence, it was less likely that children would continue to be regarded under the law as mere appendages of their parents or as parental property.[16] Instead, there was a growing societal consensus that children were independent persons with rights of their own, even when enforcement of those rights came at the expense of their parents.[17]

As a result, by the early 1970s, vast changes had been made to individual states' civil legal structures that were designed to protect children from abuse or neglect.[18] During the same time period, Congress began to play a prominent role, one which it continued to play for the remainder

---

[13] See C. Henry Kempe *et al*, *The Battered Child Syndrome*, 181 JAMA 17 (1962).

[14] In *re Gault*, 387 US 1, 13 (1967).

[15] See *Tinker v Des Moines Indep Community Sch Dist*, 393 US 503, 511 (1969).

[16] See Barbara Bennett Woodhouse, *Who Owns the Child?: Meyer and Pierce and the Child as Property*, 33 Wm & Mary L Rev 995, 998 (1992).

[17] See *Bellotti v Baird*, 443 US 622, 633–5 (1979).

[18] See eg NY Fam Ct Act § 311 *et seq* (McKinney 1970).

of the century, in 'federalizing' child protection law and practice. Fortunately, this development—the federalization of child protection law—makes the task of describing American law in this field much tidier. Before federal intervention, child protection policy was a hodgepodge of various practices across the fifty states. Beginning in the 1970s and accelerating in the 1980s and 1990s, federal law became the dominant influence as Congress attached conditions to the receipt of considerable federal dollars that paid for the out-of-home placement of children. No state proved willing to remain in conflict with federal legislation because it could not afford the loss of federal revenue that typically paid for 50 per cent of all foster care-related costs. Thus, it is sufficient to describe federal law and requirements in this area to know the practices in the country.

Although there is no single reason that can fully explain the extraordinary bi-partisan interest in the seemingly newly discovered social problem of child protection, it is useful to consider the political forces at work during the 1970s, the crucial period of congressional attention to child welfare. During the Great Depression in the 1930s, Congress was able to pass, for the first time in American history, a significant public welfare program that ensured both the financial security of the elderly through the landmark Social Security Act of 1935 and public support through welfare payments to needy families through the Aid to Dependent Children Act (ADC). In the 1940s, the American economy substantially rebounded, largely as a result of World War II. Beginning in 1945, when World War II ended, the United States began an era of steady economic growth, supplied in significant part by government loans to war veterans, which allowed them to purchase homes and to assist in the development of suburban growth. As economic growth moved from rural to urban areas, a huge demographic shift took place as African Americans, in search of jobs in manufacturing, moved from the rural south to populate large cities in the north, including New York, Chicago, Detroit, and Philadelphia.

In the 1960s, the Civil Rights Movement promoted the enactment of federal laws prohibiting discrimination in housing, employment, and other areas on the basis of race. Many Americans saw the decade as an opportunity to invoke the power of government to redistribute wealth and ameliorate the effects of poverty. President Lyndon Johnson, riding the wave of the Civil Rights Movement, declared a war on poverty as part of his 'Great Society' crusade.

This period in American history proved remarkably short. By the end of the 1960s, particularly after the election of Richard Nixon as President in 1968, liberals feared that their influence in national politics was on the wane as the country seemed poised to reject poverty programs. The largest program used in the 1960s to provide money for poor families was the Aid to Families with Dependent Children program (AFDC). Its expansion in the 1960s was largely attributable to the increase in the percentage of non-white recipients of the program. As poverty programs were viewed increasingly as providing tax money for poor African Americans and other minorities, public support for such programs eroded.[19] By this point, conservatives were able to suggest in public debate that liberal anti-poverty legislation had exacerbated the problems of the poor.[20] Policy makers who wanted to use the power of government to redistribute wealth and ameliorate conditions of poverty needed a new strategy.

In the early 1970s, liberals interested in the well-being of children fixed upon a new device for drawing federal money by recasting poverty concerns in a medical rather than an economic model. This deliberate transformation occurred in 1974, in the process of enacting what may reasonably be considered the most important child protection legislation passed in the second half of the twentieth century: the federal Child Abuse Prevention and Treatment Act of 1974 ('CAPTA').[21] As part of a conscious plan to prevent the legislation from being classified as a disguised poverty program, its principal sponsor, Senator Walter Mondale, chose to emphasize that child abuse is a 'national' problem, not a 'poverty problem.'[22] Mondale's purpose was to avoid controversy by stressing the classlessness of the issue.[23] Sponsoring a Bill that was designed to help children across class and race lines won widespread support from politicians who could line up on the side of helping *all* children.[24]

CAPTA created the structure for government investigation of child abuse cases for the entire country. In particular, all states were encouraged to pass laws creating a child abuse registry, refurbishing the child abuse investigatory system, and mandating—under penalty of criminal sanction—that professionals report any suspicion of child neglect or abuse to a civil abuse investigatory unit.[25] Spurred by this legislation, by the mid-1970s, all of the states had passed mandatory child abuse

---

[19] See WILLIAM JULIUS WILSON, THE TRULY DISADVANTAGED 119–31 (1987).

[20] See MICHAEL B. KATZ, THE UNDESERVING POOR: FROM THE WAR ON POVERTY TO THE WAR ON WELFARE (1989).

[21] See Child Abuse Prevention and Treatment Act of 1974 (CAPTA), 42 USC §§ 5101–19 (1994 and Supp II 1996).

[22] BARBARA NELSON, MAKING A CASE OUT OF CHILD ABUSE 135 (1984).

[23] See *ibid* at 105–6.

[24] See *ibid* at 93–4.

[25] CAPTA provides limited funding to states to prevent, identify, and treat child abuse and neglect. It created the National Center on Child Abuse and Neglect, developed standards for receiving and responding to reports of child maltreatment, and established a clearing house on the prevention and treatment of abuse and neglect. Changes in 1996 reinforced the Act's emphasis on child safety. See 42 USC § 5105 (1994 and Supp II 1996).

reporting laws and set up procedures for investigating suspected cases of child abuse and neglect. A new government entity came into being— child protective services. Today, every state has laws that create a mechanism for people to report their suspicions of child abuse and neglect. These laws are designed to bring cases of possible wrongdoing to the attention of public authorities who are in a position to help children and provide assistance to neglectful parents. Most state laws require reporting from professionals who deal with children and may detect certain telltale signs of child abuse and neglect. These professionals often include doctors, nurses, police officers, welfare workers, and teachers. Persons not required to report suspected abuse or neglect are encouraged to do so.

These reports are used in two ways. First, they become the starting point for most investigations to determine whether coercive action will be necessary to protect a child. In addition, these reports are placed in a computerized statewide central register.[26] In most states, these records are used exclusively to aid authorities in the detection of abuse.

Most states have screening procedures for receiving a report. In these states, the person receiving the report will make an initial determination about whether there is sufficient cause even to undertake an investigation. This determination is based on many factors, which include how the reporter obtained the information and the seriousness and currency of the allegation. All states have laws that authorize police officers, doctors, or social-welfare agents to remove children from their home (or to keep them in hospitals) even when the parents object, if the person authorized by law believes that the child would otherwise die or be seriously injured.

Congress's major role in the shaping of child protection policy and practice continued with the passage of the Adoption Assistance and Child Welfare Act of 1980.[27] In the face of widespread evidence that children were being needlessly separated from their families by child care agencies and courts pursuant to child protection proceedings in the 1970s, Congress concluded that there was a need for federal action to effect change in local practices. Congress was particularly concerned about the ease with which children were separated from their parents through entry into the foster care system and the excessive amount of time they spent there. It acted to correct these evils by providing federal money for foster care and conditioning the receipt of that money upon compliance with federal rules.

---

[26] See eg NY Soc Serv Law § 422 (McKinney 1992).
[27] See 42 USC § 602(a)(20)(E); 42 USC §§ 671(a)(15), 672(a)(1) (1994).

In the 1980 legislation, Congress mandated that states receiving federal money comply with specifications designed to prevent unnecessary separation of children from their parents; assure a careful monitoring of children who are separated; and provide an infusion of services into the family to speed the ultimate return of children to their parents. Before receiving reimbursements for foster care maintenance payments, states were required to make 'reasonable efforts . . . to prevent or eliminate the need for removal of the child from his home, and . . . to make it possible for the child to return to his home.'[28] In addition, states had to maintain individualized 'case plans' for all children in their care to assure appropriate placement and services.[29] Finally, states had to set up a 'case review system' that, among other things, guaranteed court or administrative reviews at least every six months and required a judicial 'dispositional hearing' no more than eighteen months after entry into care.[30]

State statutes vary regarding the circumstances under which a child may be summarily removed from the custody of his or her parents. The statutes commonly apply to situations in which there are grounds to believe that a child is endangered in his or her present surroundings and that immediate removal is necessary for his or her protection. Some statutes, by declining to specify the situations in which removal is warranted, are extremely vague. For example, Oklahoma permits an immediate seizure of a child '[b]y a peace officer or employee of the court, without a court order, if the child's surroundings are such as to endanger the welfare of the child.'[31] By contrast, Texas allows an *ex parte* temporary order only when there is an affidavit stating that '(1) there is an immediate danger to the physical health or safety of the child or the child has been a victim of sexual abuse and continuation in the home would be contrary to the child's welfare; and (2) there is no time, consistent with the physical health or safety of the child, for an adversary hearing or to make reasonable efforts to prevent or eliminate the need for the removal of the child.'[32]

Specialized juvenile and family courts hear the allegations of abuse and neglect brought against families by police and child protective services agencies. Although it is common for children to be temporarily removed from their families without judicial authorization on an emergency basis, courts ultimately must approve these removals and are responsible for final decisions concerning the propriety of coercive separation of children from their families. Formally, the test used to determine whether removal

---

[28] 42 USC §§ 671(a)(15); 672(a)(1) (1994).   [29] See *ibid* at § 675(1).
[30] See *ibid* §§ 671(a)(16), 675(1), 675(5)(B)–(C).
[31] Okla Stat Ann tit 10, § 7003–2.1(A)(1) (West 1995).
[32] Tex Fam Code Ann § 262.101 (West 1999).

is warranted asks whether there is an imminent risk of harm to the child if removal is not ordered.[33] In addition, in accordance with federal mandates since 1980, courts deciding whether to remove or to ratify the removal of a child pending the completion of the court case alleging neglect or abuse are to determine whether there are less drastic alternatives or, in particular, whether services can be provided to eliminate the need for removal. These alternatives—known as 'preventive services'—have been required as a matter of sound policy because they are less disruptive to the lives of children and their families and are less expensive than the costs associated with placement in foster care.

However, there is significant evidence to suggest that courts 'rubber stamp' agency recommendations to remove children from their parents, even in circumstances that would not constitute true emergencies.[34] This is one area of child welfare practice that is not especially uniform throughout the United States. Some states take seriously formal rules limiting removals to cases in which children are at serious risk of injury, while other states appear to use far more flexible standards depending on the policy of local child welfare officials (which can change dramatically from one administration to another). New York City, as one prominent example, has seen its foster care population soar in the aftermath of notorious and highly publicized cases of child abuse. In the three-year period from 1995 to 1998, the number of new child abuse and neglect petitions filed in court rose 55 per cent, from 6,658 to 10,398. Even more significantly, the number of children removed from their families and placed in foster care over parental objection rose by nearly 50 per cent between 1995 and 1997.[35] New York City's foster care population of nearly 47,000 represents approximately 10 per cent of the foster care population of the United States. This striking rise in prosecution suggests more of a change in the philosophy of the prosecutors than in the conditions in a child's home.

No two states have laws that define child abuse in exactly the same language, but there are common aspects among them all. Virtually every state law equates the infliction of serious physical injury or sexual abuse upon a child by a parent or custodian with child abuse. Many state child abuse laws are written broadly to permit child protection agencies to charge abuse when a parent creates a risk of serious physical injury or inflicts psychological abuse. Still others consider the infliction of any injury to be abusive, whether 'serious' or not. A typical definition of child abuse is found in the California law:

[33] See eg NY Fam Ct Act § 1028 (McKinney 1999).
[34] See National Council of Juvenile and Family Court Judges *et al*, Making Reasonable Efforts: Steps for Keeping Families Together 8 (New York: Edna McConnell Clark Foundation, 1987).
[35] Removals rose from 8,000 in 1995 to 11,958 in 1997. See 4 Child Welfare Watch 4 (1999).

'[C]hild abuse' means a physical injury which is inflicted by other than accidental means on a child by another person. 'Child abuse' also means the sexual abuse of a child or any act or omission . . . [of] (willful cruelty or unjustifiable punishment of a child) or . . . (unlawful corporal punishment or injury). 'Child abuse' also means the neglect of a child or abuse in out-of-home care, as defined in this article.[36]

If parents have placed their children at serious risk, sufficient evidence exists to find them guilty of child abuse. If parents have permitted their children to be harmed or failed to take reasonable steps to protect them, parents may be found guilty of abuse even when it is undisputed that the parent did not inflict the harm directly. However, parents are not automatically liable for injuries suffered by their children. A showing must be made that the parents have not fallen below the minimum level of care they owe their children.

A frequent basis for neglect charges is a parent's failure to provide needed medical care for their children. In many cases of medical neglect, parents have refused, often on religious grounds, to consent to an operation for their child that was recommended by the treating physician. The right of a parent to practice religion does not include the liberty to expose the child to ill health or death.[37] There are many examples of cases in which courts have authorized medical care over a parental objection, even when the treatment was not required to save the child's life.[38] In virtually all cases in which court intervention is sought solely to order a particular treatment to which the parents are opposed, courts will issue a temporary order transferring authority to consent to the authorized medical procedure to some person other than the parents (often the treating physician), but otherwise will not interfere with parental authority.

In most jurisdictions, a trial is supposed to occur within sixty to ninety days of the first court appearance to determine whether the child was abused or neglected. However, relatively few trials are actually conducted because the vast majority of cases are resolved by an admission of some kind of wrongdoing by the parent. Once a court makes a formal determination of neglect or abuse (whether by admission or after a contested hearing), a dispositional hearing will be held to establish custody. This hearing will determine not only with whom the child will reside (placement in foster care or placement in the parents' home are the most common options), but will also establish the longer plan for the family, which includes such details as the terms and conditions for reunification services. If the child remains in out-of-home care, periodic review hearings are held to ensure that efforts are being made to reunify the family or to give the child a new permanent home.

[36] CAL PENAL CODE § 11165.6 (West 1992).
[37] See eg *People ex rel Wallace v Labrenz*, 104 NE 2d 769, *cert denied*, 344 US 824 (1952).
[38] See eg In *re Seiferth*, 127 NE 2d 820 (1955).

Generally, when a court declares a child neglected or abused, it may order placement of that child in foster care for a specified period of time, usually a year at the start. Depending on the severity of the case, courts may prefer to place parents on probation for a period of time, during which they will be supervised and may be required to engage in a specific rehabilitative or educational program while the child remains with them in their home. When children are removed from parental care, the parents will be expected to take steps to correct whatever problems led to the removal. If parents fail to take these steps, the temporary removal may lead to permanent termination of parental rights. Unfortunately, many children spend years in foster care, unable to return to their birth families and yet still legally tied to them and thus unable to find a new, permanent family through adoption.

Children in foster care live away from their parents in a variety of settings, which include individual foster homes and group facilities. In some states, foster care is operated directly by the state government; in others, a state agency provides some form of supervision, regulation, or standard-setting. Counties, which are semi-autonomous subdivisions of the state, run the programs with varying degrees of state control.

Foster parents enter into a contract with the agency to obtain permission to take foster children into their homes. These contracts typically provide that the foster care agency retains the authority to make virtually all important childcare decisions, including the number of visits to be scheduled between the child, parents, and siblings; the length of time the child remains in care; and the ultimate decision whether to return the child to the biological family or to place the child with an adoptive family. Agencies also retain the contractual authority to visit and inspect the foster home to monitor the well-being of the child.

The foster parent–child relationship, viewed as temporary, is designed to provide the child with the benefits of living in a family setting (instead of institutionalized care) when residence outside of the child's original home is necessary. The theoretical goal is for the child to remain in foster care for a maximum of one to two years. While the child is in foster care, the state generally provides a variety of social services to the biological parent(s), such as parenting education, homemaker services, rehabilitation programs, job training, and respite care. These services are intended to alleviate the problems that necessitated the child's entry into foster care in the first place and facilitate the child's reunification with the birth family.

Many states have statutes that express a preference for children being placed first with extended family members, if possible,[39] or in foster families instead of group facilities.

---

[39] See eg CAL WELF & INST CODE § 16501.1(c) (West 1994); COLO REV STAT § 19-5-104(2) (1994); MO REV STAT § 210.565(1) (West 1994).

In an arrangement called 'kinship care,'[40] some children in foster care live with members of their extended family who become licensed foster parents under at least nominal supervision by the state child welfare agency.

In addition, some states have laws that either express a statutory preference for, or require matching children with, foster families of the same religious background as the child.[41] In interpreting New York's statute, a federal court ruled that religious matching was permissible only if it was not mandatory, took each child's interests into account, and did not result in discrimination.[42] In 1994, Congress passed the Multi-Ethnic Placement Act (MEPA) with the goal of eliminating the racial barriers that stood in the way of placing black children in foster and adoptive homes. The statute was amended in 1996 to prevent federally funded agencies from delaying or denying the placement of a child for adoption or into foster care on the basis of race, color, or national origin.[43]

Many children who enter the foster care system cannot return to their parents, for a variety of reasons. Sometimes the parents' problems are too severe to be alleviated, even with services; sometimes services are not provided or the parents refuse to accept them; and sometimes the parents have abandoned the children. When reunification is not a realistic possibility, an alternative goal is to find a new, permanent family for the child. In these cases, the child's caseworker may decide that adoption is the appropriate goal to pursue for a child, often because the parent is not likely to be able to resume custody within a reasonable period of time. Commonly, caseworkers will attempt to persuade parents to surrender parental rights voluntarily, or, failing that, seek to have legal proceedings brought to sever parental rights.

Children cannot be adopted without the consent of the living parent(s) unless there is a court order severing parental rights. Severance is accomplished through formal court proceedings seeking termination of parental rights—the permanent ending of the parent–child relationship. The principal purpose for seeking termination is to free the child to be adopted into a new family. After termination, the parent has no legal relation to or rights and responsibilities for the child. The vast majority of terminations are effected voluntarily, usually when parents relinquish a child to a child care agency or place a child with an individual or couple chosen by the parents for adoption; an ever increasing number, however,

---

[40] See *Miller v Youakim*, 440 US 125 (1979).
[41] See eg NY Soc Serv Law § 373 (McKinney 1992).
[42] See *Wilder v Bernstein*, 848 F2d 1338 (2nd Cir 1988).
[43] See Howard M. Metzenbaum Multi-Ethnic Placement Act of 1994 (MEPA) §§ 551–555, 42 USC 5115a (1994), as amended by the Small Business Job Protection Act of 1996 (SBJPA), 42 USC §§ 671, 1996B, Pub L 104–88, § 1808(a)(3), 110. Stat 1755, 1903 (1986).

are involuntarily imposed when statutory grounds for termination are proven by clear and convincing evidence[44] or, in certain cases, by proof beyond a reasonable doubt.[45]

In some cases, termination is sought because the child is believed to have bonded psychologically with the adult(s) with whom he or she has been living, so that the child's best interests are perceived to be advanced by terminating parental rights to enable eventual adoption by the 'psychological parent.'[46] In other cases, termination is sought simply on the remoteness of reunification, without regard to the actual prospects of the child's adoption.

Involuntary termination of parental rights usually requires proof of gross or longstanding neglect, which includes abandonment of parental obligations, repeated neglect or abuse, or parental inability to care for children. Many states add mental illness, conviction of a crime affecting the fitness of a parent, and lack of financial support as conditions justifying termination. Often, these laws are rather complex, so that the state agency must prove not only that the parents have been inadequate, but that the agency's efforts to correct deficiencies in the home were unsuccessful. In New York, for example, the agency must prove that, despite its 'diligent efforts to encourage and strengthen the parental relationship,' a parent failed to 'maintain contact with or plan for the future of the child' for at least one year.[47] Many states, like New York, have passed laws that require proof that agencies have done everything in their power to assist the family before termination is permitted.[48] A few state courts have ruled that agencies must comply with all federal rules governing foster care before a termination of parental rights may be effected.[49]

Where a parent has failed to assume any responsibility for a child's care and support, the Supreme Court has ruled that a parent's right to the child's custody may be terminated. This commonly arises in connection with the rights of fathers. Although fathers have both a constitutional due process and an equal protection right to the care and custody of their children, 'the mere existence of a biological link' between a biological parent and his child is not entitled to constitutional protection, in the absence of evidence that the parent had 'grasp[ed] that opportunity' to 'develop a

---

[44] See *Santosky v Kramer*, 455 US 745 (1982).

[45] See Indian Child Welfare Act of 1978, 25 USC § 1912(f) (1994).

[46] See generally JOSEPH GOLDSTEIN *et al*, BEYOND THE BEST INTERESTS OF THE CHILD (1973).

[47] See NY FAM CT ACT § 614 (McKinney 1992); NY SOC SERV LAW § 384–b(7)(a) (McKinney 1992).

[48] See eg CONN GEN STAT ANN § 45a–717 (West 1993); NY SOC SERV LAW §§ 384–b(7)(a), (8)(a)(ii), (8)(b)(ii) (McKinney 1992); RI GEN LAWS § 15-7-7 (1996).

[49] See eg *In the Matter of Burns*, 519 A2d 638 (Del 1986).

relationship with his offspring' and to 'accept[] some measure of responsibility for the child's future.'[50]

Despite Congress's efforts in passing the Adoption Assistance and Child Welfare Act to reduce out-of-home care as a prominent child welfare practice, foster care populations soared in the 1980s.[51] Once huge numbers of children were separated from their families and placed in foster care, the most pressing problems of child protection in the 1980s and 1990s were seen as the ancillary costs associated with long-term foster care placements, including 'foster care drift,' and indeterminacy or lack of permanency. The median stay in foster care increased on a national level to over two years and more children than ever appeared to have experienced multiple placements in foster care.[52]

The solution to those problems was identified by Congress in 1997 as being more, and speedier, adoptions. In that year, Congress enacted the Adoption and Safe Families Act (ASFA),[53] which excuses states from directing reasonable efforts toward reunification when parents have been convicted of certain crimes against children.[54] States are not required to make reasonable efforts if the parent has committed specified violent crimes against any of his or her children.[55] Nor are reasonable efforts required if a court determines that the parent has subjected a particular child to certain 'aggravating circumstances' defined by state law.[56] Together, these provisions aim to prevent the dangerous reunification efforts that Congress perceived were occurring.

ASFA explicitly discourages states from making 'reasonable efforts' to return foster children to dangerous households. The Act also speeds up and modifies permanency hearings. Permanency hearings must now be held every twelve months; can no longer produce temporary foster care

---

[50] *Lehr v Robertson*, 463 US 248, 261–2 (1983).

[51] See Toshio Tatara, *The Recent Rise in the US Child Substitute Care Population: An Analysis of National Child Substitute Care Flow Data*, in 1 Child Welfare Res. Rev. 126, 130 tbl 6.1 (Richard P. Barth *et al.* eds, 1994) (showing the foster care population increased from 273,000 at the beginning of fiscal year 1986 to 429,000 at the end of fiscal year 1991).

[52] See Robert M. Gordon, *Drifting through Byzantium: The Promise and Failure of the Adoption and Safe Families Act of 1997 (ASFA)*, 83 Minn L Rev 637, 648 and n 64 (1999) (citing California study showing that '[46%] of infants living in nonkinship care will have four or more homes in six years').

[53] Pub L No 105–89, 111 Stat 2115 (codified as amended in scattered sections of 42 USCA (West Supp. 1999).

[54] See Kathleen Haggard, Note, *Treating Prior Terminations of Parental Rights as Grounds for Present Terminations*, 73 Wash L Rev 1051, 1057–8 (1998) (discussing relevant ASFA provisions).

[55] These crimes are murder, voluntary manslaughter, attempted murder, manslaughter, or felony assault resulting in serious bodily harm. See ASFA, Pub L No 105–89, 111 Stat at 2118 (codified as amended at 42 USCA § 675(5)(E) (West Supp 1999)). Additionally, ASFA suggests that reasonable efforts to return the child home shall not be required when the State has terminated parental rights to a sibling, but does not treat prior terminations as sole grounds to file immediately for termination. *ibid* (codified as amended at 42 USCA §671(a)(15)(D)(IV) (West Supp. 1999)).   [56] *ibid*.

as a formal disposition; and can now only result in long-term foster care based on a 'compelling reason,' not 'special needs or circumstances.'[57] To reduce delays in placements following unexpected shifts in parental conduct, ASFA formally endorses the practice of 'concurrent planning,' or efforts to find an alternative placement while also attempting reunification prior to the permanency hearing.[58] In addition, the law was designed to increase the number of children moving from foster care to adoption. Although the law increases the funds for family support and family presentation programs, it substantially shortens the time parents are given to regain custody of their children before the state is authorized to initiate proceedings to terminate their parental rights. Adoption is now promoted as a solution for children who are not safe at home.

The Act further mandates that after a child has spent fifteen of twenty-two months in foster care, the state must file a termination of parental rights petition unless one of three exceptions applies: (1) the child is in the care of a relative; (2) there is a 'compelling reason' to maintain parental rights based on the interests of the child; or (3) the state has failed to provide mandatory 'reasonable efforts.'[59]

Finally, ASFA created an incentive program designed to increase adoptions of foster children. Under the program, states receive an additional $4,000 per child for the increase in the number of foster children adopted per year over the average number prior to the passage of the Act, and an additional $6,000 per additional foster child with special needs.[60] Congress authorized $30 million in expenditures for this program for 1998–2000.[61]

As we look back on the history of child protection in the United States in the twentieth century, some important observations may be made. First, 'child abuse and neglect' in the United States, particularly since the 1970s, have come to be seen and defined—especially by public policy makers, such as legislators—as individual problems caused by faulty parents.[62] The evidence suggesting a correlation between both abuse and neglect, on

---

[57] *ibid* (codified as amended at 42 USCA § 675(5)(C) (West Supp 1999)).

[58] See *ibid* (codified as amended at 42 USCA § 671(a)(15)(F) (West Supp 1999)).

[59] *ibid* (codified as amended at 42 USCA § 675(5)(E) (West Supp 1999)).

[60] See *ibid* (codified as amended at 42 USCA § 673b(d)(1)(A)-(B) (West 1999)).

[61] See *ibid* (codified as amended at 42 USCA § 673(i)(4) (West 1999)).

[62] Child welfare services are by their nature residual, serving only those children suffering or at great risk of suffering the gravest mistreatment, rather than the whole population of families in which children experience serious deprivation. Many scholars argue that the residual approach is doomed to fail absent vast new investments in anti-poverty programs. See MARK E. COURTNEY, THE FOSTER CARE CRISIS 16 (1994); DUNCAN LINDSEY, THE WELFARE OF CHILDREN 4–5 (1994); LEROY H. PELTON, FOR REASONS OF POVERTY: A CRITICAL ANALYSIS OF THE PUBLIC CHILD WELFARE SYSTEM IN THE UNITED STATES (1989).

the one hand, and poverty, on the other[63] has been ignored or understated in many of the public debates. Indeed, a remarkable characteristic of the growth of support for child protection in the United States was the calculated claim that child protection legislation and policy was needed for middle-class and upper-class children as well as for poor children.

The consequences of this strategy are profound. Since the 1970s, the subject of child protection in the United States has come to be seen primarily as a defect in a family, with limited or virtually no broader societal implications. Indeed, the subject matter commonly is discussed using medical terminology, with parents seen as 'pathological' and 'in need of treatment'; problems are resolved by removing children from their care. This, in turn, encourages the removal of very large numbers of children from their families into state-supervised foster care.

Maintaining the claim that child maltreatment is classless and all-pervasive has allowed child protection policy to be built on the medical model that looks for individual deficiencies in the caregiver and seeks to correct them. Thus, 'child welfare' in the United States has become, for most of the latter half of the twentieth century, an individualized, case-by-case problem. The opportunity to examine root causes of neglect and abuse, which may be explainable by factors outside of any deficiency in the immediate family, has been lost.

In addition, the children's rights movement influenced child protection policy and practice in less obvious ways. Publicly, the movement contributed to an accelerated focus on child protection, partly leading to the major federal legislation enacted in 1974 and 1980. In addition, once children came to be seen as independent of their parents and as having rights that may conflict with those of their parents, law and practice came to require that children be represented by independent lawyers or guardians ad litem in child protective proceedings.[64] More subtly perhaps, in the 1980s, the foster care population in the United States soared from 280,000 to more than 460,000 in a five-year period.[65] Although most commentators attribute this growth to the popularity of crack cocaine use among low-income mothers, other forces contributed to the sharp rise in the number of children in foster care. A new breed of children's rights advocates took

---

[63] See Leroy H. Pelton, *Resolving the Crisis in Child Welfare: Simply Expanding the System is Not Enough*, 48 Public Welfare 19, 23 (1990); Leroy H. Pelton, *Child Abuse and Neglect: The Myth of Classlessness*, 48 Amer J Orthopsychiatry 608, 609 (1978). Recent studies reach the same conclusion. See eg Peter J. Pecora *et al*, The Child Welfare Challenge: Policy Practice and Research 66–7 (1992).

[64] In 1974, Congress enacted the Child Abuse and Prevention Treatment Act of 1974, which was later amended to create the first nationwide incentive for appointing representatives for children in all child protective proceedings. See n 25 above, and accompanying text; see also Jean Koh Peters, Representing Children in Child Protective Proceedings: Ethical and Practical Dimensions (1997).   [65] See n 51 above, and accompanying text.

center stage, demanding the treatment of children as independent persons with their own set of rights.[66] These children's advocates clashed with more traditional advocates of children's rights, who argued that because children are inherently dependent beings, their rights were generally best advanced by helping their parents and families provide the best home possible.[67] This conflict between different kinds of children's rights advocates may be said to define the subtext for much of the dispute in child welfare from the 1980s to the end of the century (often argued in terms of those in favor of, or opposed to, 'family preservation' programs).[68]

Thus, at the end of the twentieth century, American child welfare policy contains important ingredients that are reminiscent of central issues in the debates in the nineteenth century. At that time, many children's advocates encouraged sending children far from their families to live in new environments and learn trades from families that needed child labor. An important underlying belief was that children deserved the right to be raised by people other than their parents. An explicit, related belief was that their parents were unworthy people who would contaminate their children if they raised them. Although the underlying reasoning may have changed, American child welfare policy today is closer than it has been in a hundred years to encouraging the permanent banishment of biological parents from their children's lives.

Although one could imagine a society regarding government-sponsored adoptions of children by non-relatives when the children's parents are alive and willing to care for them as an evil to be avoided, a remarkable feature of the Adoption and Safe Families Act of 1997 is its celebration of adoption as a solution to the plight of children born into inadequate homes. That is the tale of child protection in the United States at the close of the twentieth century. It remains to be seen whether future generations will regard the period from 1950 to 2000 as one of enlightened child protection policy in the United States or as a series of lost opportunities to create a society more friendly to needy families living in poverty, who are trying their best to raise children in conditions that most Americans are no longer obliged to endure.

[66] See eg ELIZABETH BARTHOLET, NOBODY'S CHILDREN: ABUSE AND NEGLECT: FOSTER DRIFT, AND THE ADOPTION ALTERNATIVE (1999).

[67] See eg Peggy Cooper Davis, *The Good Mother: A New Look at Psychological Parent Theory*, 22 NYU REV L & SOC CHANGE 347, 348–9 (1996).

[68] See eg Ira M. Schwartz *et al*, *Family Preservation Services as an Alternative to Out-of-Home Placement of Adolescents*, *in* K. WELLS and D. E. BIEGEL, (eds), FAMILY PRESERVATION SERVICES: RESEARCH AND EVALUATION 33–46 (1991).

26

From Curtis to Waterhouse: State Care and Child Protection in the UK 1945–2000

JUDITH MASSON

INTRODUCTION

Many of the current concerns about the care system, set out in parliamentary papers and government reports, consultation documents and circulars, mirror the concerns of the Curtis Committee which surveyed the provision for 'children deprived of a normal home life'[1] at the birth of the welfare state. Both in the mid-1940s and at the end of the 1990s alarm was expressed about the quality of care provided to children looked after in public care.[2] In 1946, the recognition of the problems of the dismal care provided to children in barrack-like institutions, cut off from the community, was framed in optimism—simplifying and unifying the exercise of public responsibility would bring improvements; but by the end of the century there was dismay. 'The extent to which the outcomes of looked-after children fall short of their peers is very worrying . . . the system itself is under-performing. In the field of education the failure to provide adequate opportunities and support . . . is scandalous.'[3] 'Widespread sexual abuse of boys occurred in children's residential establishments in [North Wales] between 1974 and 1990 . . . [M]any of the aspirations of policy makers . . . in relation to children's services were not realized.'[4]

The responses to poor state care were also similar. After care by the child's own family, adoption was seen as 'the most completely satisfactory method of providing a substitute home'.[5] It was 'not an option of last resort', so the decision to place a child with a permanent substitute family

---

[1] *Report of the Care of Children Committee* (1946 Cmnd 6922) (1946). Hereafter referred to as 'the Curtis Report'; J. Packman, *The Child's Generation*, Oxford: Basil Blackwell (1975); J. Heywood, *Children in Care*, London: Routledge (1959); S. Cretney, 'The State as Parent: The Children Act 1948 in Retrospect', (1998) 114 *Law Quarterly Review* 419.

[2] Select Committee on Health, Second Report of the Select Committee on Health session 1997–8 *Children Looked after by Local Authorities*, HC 247 (1998); W. Utting, *People Like Us* London: TSO (1997); Department of Health, *Response to the Children's Safeguards Review*, London: TSO (1998); Department of Health, *Quality Protects*, Circular LAC (98)28 (1998).

[3] Select Committee on Health, n 2 above, paras 50, 118.

[4] *Report of the Tribunal of Inquiry into the Abuse of Children in Care in the Former County Council Areas of Gwynedd and Clwyd since 1974*, HC 201 London (2000), hereafter referred to as the Waterhouse Report, paras 55.10(1), and 55.11.

[5] Curtis Report, n 1 above, para 448.

should be 'a matter of priority'.[6] The development of foster care was crucial.[7] Children seemed to flourish, in marked contrast with their starvation of affection in residential care.[8] But by 1998, years of neglect had produced a 'crisis in foster care' which could trigger the collapse of the entire system.[9] For those brought up in care, aftercare support was essential so that young people could 'establish themselves successfully in the world of work' or 'to ensure their social inclusion and active engagement in society'.[10]

A deeper understanding of the processes of substitute care and its dangers—instability, emotional neglect, and, particularly, abuse has brought new concerns. Children's homes were not just deprived environments with harsh regimes and impersonal care but centres of 'serious and systematic abuse'.[11] There was also greater awareness of the severe risks that some families pose to their children. This rediscovery of child abuse provided further, graphic examples of the failings of state services through public inquiries into the deaths of children supposedly under state protection.[12] The view that children should be rescued from unsatisfactory homes has been tempered by loss of confidence in the state's ability to do better than poor parents. Policy makers have sought to reset the balance between the state and the family and to refocus on the state's role in family support.

The Curtis Committee was directly concerned with the welfare of 125,000 children living away from home in institutions or with foster carers, but less than half of these came into the public care system established by the Children Act 1948.[13] Others remained in the care of religious and charitable organizations (voluntary organizations), hospitals, residential schools run by local education authorities, establishments for delinquents (approved schools), or with private individuals paid by their

---

[6] Department of Health Circular LAC 98(20) paras 4, 8.

[7] Curtis Report, n 1 above, para 46; D. Robbins, *Mapping Quality in Children's Services: An Evaluation of Local Responses to the Quality Protects Programme*, London: Department of Health (1999), para 2.6.

[8] Curtis Report, n 1 above, para 370, but note there were concerns about children who had a succession of placements, and foster carers were thought to be opposed to 'interference' by parents: paras 461 and 463(ii).

[9] Select Committee on Health, n 2 above, para 50, rec 22.

[10] Curtis Report, n 1 above, para 502; Department of Health, *Me, Survive out There?* London: Department of Health (1999) para 1.5.

[11] Utting, n 2 above, para 1.2.

[12] P. Reder, S. Duncan, and M. Gray, *Beyond Blame*, London: Routledge (1993); Department of Health and Social Security, *Child Abuse: A Study of Inquiry Reports 1973–1981*, London: HMSO (1982); Department of Health, *Children Act Regulations and Guidance*, vol 3, London: HMSO (1991).

[13] Figures for this section are drawn from the Curtis Report, n 1 above, Table IV; J. Packman, *Child Care Needs and Numbers*, London: Allen and Unwin (1966); DoH *A/F/12*, published annually. Department of Health statistics relate to England.

parents to care for them. Public care grew steadily, with the numbers of children looked after rising to a peak of over 100,000 in the late 1970s and the rate per 1,000 population under 18 years rising from 5.6 in 1952 to 7.8 in 1980. This reflected development of public care and a decline in care by voluntary organizations rather than increased intervention by the state. Since 1982, the numbers and rates of children in public care have generally declined; 53,000 children (a rate of 4.7) were looked after at the end of March 1998 and another 11,000 children, mostly those with disabilities, spent short periods in respite care. However, wide variations in the rates of children looked after, which do not simply reflect different levels of deprivation or need in different counties, suggest that there is no single interpretation of how the state should act. Over the last decade, admissions to the system have remained fairly constant but the duration of care and the age of leaving have declined, reflecting policies aimed at rehabilitation, adoption, and early (premature) independence.[14]

England and Wales at the end of the twentieth century provide a very different context for state care provision. Illegitimacy which was so stigmatized that it precipitated adoption or the entry to residential care for thousands of children in the 1950s and 1960s now accounts for over a third of all births. Britain is a multi-ethnic society with sizeable Black minority communities originating from the Caribbean and South Asia. If services are to be responsive to families, diverse cultures, languages, and religious beliefs must all be accommodated. The transracial placement of Black children remains a sensitive issue[15] and ethnic monitoring is not generally undertaken. However, a widely quoted research study established that 'a mixed race child was two-and-a-half times more likely to enter care as a white child',[16] raising issues about discrimination in the provision of care and alternative support.

Contrary to the aspirations of the architects of the welfare state, want, disease, squalor, ignorance, and idleness have not been banished.[17] Access to health care improved markedly with the introduction of the National Health Service but health inequality, linked to poverty, remains.[18] Housing shortages continue and many of the high-rise buildings of the 1960s were poorly constructed, damp, and provide unhealthy housing. Homelessness continued to be a reason why children entered

---

[14] Department of Health, *Me, Survive out There?* London: Department of Health (1999) para 2.1.

[15] J. Thoburn, *Review of Research Relating to Adoption*, Interdepartmental Review of Adoption, background paper 2, London: Department of Health (1990).

[16] A. Bebbington and J. Miles, 'The Background of Children Who Enter Local Authority Care', (1989) 19 *Brit J Soc Wk* 349, 356.

[17] The impact on neglected children is painfully recounted in Charles Causley's poem *Timothy Winters*. C. Causley, *Collected Poems*. London: Macmillan (1975).

[18] Department of Health, *Our Healthier Nation: A Contract for Health* Cm 3852 (1998).

public care but priority given to homeless families in the Housing (Homeless Persons) Act 1977 attempted to ensure that families were not broken up for this reason alone.[19] De-industrialization in the 1980s brought high levels of unemployment and removed much semi-skilled factory work, ending opportunities of employment in many communities, particularly in the North and in South Wales. Unemployment and relationship breakdown have left over 2.5 million children dependent on (inadequate) social security benefits. Whilst poverty no longer justifies substitute care, it remains a major factor for families whose children come to the attention of social services. Other problems have come to the fore; children entering public care come from socially isolated families (often lone parents), with problems of ill health, substance abuse, and domestic violence.[20]

THE ORGANIZATION OF PUBLIC CARE FOR CHILDREN

This section outlines the key organizations involved in the public care of children and outlines their changing roles, responsibilities, and interrelationships.

Local Government

The Children Act 1948 created children's departments to take over responsibilities for child care from the various departments which had dealt with it. Children's departments, headed by a Children's Officer and directed through a Children's Committee, looked after children whose parents were unable to provide proper care and those in need of care and protection, who had been committed by the courts. The Committee had the power to remove rights from parents whose children were looked after; administrative removal of parental rights was not abolished until 1991, despite the recommendations made in 1946.[21]

By the late 1960s the organization of personal social services was viewed as inadequate. Services were not sufficiently adaptable or responsive; the services to different client groups were poorly co-ordinated, precluding a holistic approach to families in difficulty and the understanding of their

---

[19] The plight of homeless families, graphically portrayed in the BBC television play *Cathy Come Home* (1967), helped to create a climate for reform. The Housing Act 1996 limited the local authority's obligations but additional responsibilities are owed under the Children Act 1989, pt III (see below).
[20] J. Packman and C. Hall, *From Care to Accommodation*, London: TSO (1998) 134–5; Dartington Research Unit, *Child Protection: Messages from Research*, London: HMSO (1995).
[21] Curtis Report, n 1 above, para 425.

problems in their wider context.[22] Inspired by a belief in the capacity of the state to provide social services to all, the Seebohm Committee recommended the creation of a single local department to take over the work of the children's departments, educational welfare, and welfare services to pregnant women, nursing mothers, the elderly, and those with mental illness, in order to provide a community-based, family-oriented service for all.[23] The Local Authority Social Services Act 1970 established social services departments under Directors of Social Services and staffed by generic social workers. The specialism of the children's departments was lost, although by the 1990s social services departments had reorganized, often more than once, and children's teams had been re-created with specialists in child protection, fostering, and adoption. The marketization of social services has brought further re-ordering, with some departments organizing on the basis of a purchaser–provider split. Social workers identifying a need have to make a case for its provision and then commission it, from a provider in their agency, or from the voluntary or private sectors. This process is far removed from the personal work envisaged for children's departments but, unlike adult services, most provision for children still comes from within the local authority.

There has been steady growth in the responsibilities local authorities have had towards children. The Children and Young Persons (Amendment) Act 1952 required them to 'cause enquiries to be made' where there was information 'suggesting' that a child was in need of care and protection.[24] This was the beginning of an involvement which would come to dominate children's social services by the 1990s, absorbing resources, preventing the development of family support services,[25] skewing social services' response to individual families, and adversely effecting relationships between social workers and the public.

Although the Curtis Committee recognized that 'every effort should be made to keep the child in its home' its terms of reference did not include considering how this would be done. Central government encouraged local authorities to develop preventive services and it is clear that some local authorities and voluntary agencies made strenuous efforts in this direction.[26] The Ingelby Committee which was chiefly concerned with juvenile delinquency was also given the task of considering whether local authorities should be given new duties 'to prevent or forestall the suffering

---

[22] *The Report of the Committee on Local Authority and Allied Personal Social Services*, Cmnd 3703 (1968), ch 5 (hereafter referred to as the Seebohm Report).

[23] Cretney, n 1 above, 456.   [24] s 2; see now Children Act 1989, s 47.

[25] Audit Commission, *Seen but Not Heard*, London: HMSO (1994) 23–5; Dartington Research Unit, n 20 above.

[26] J. Packman, *The Child's Generation*, Oxford: Basil Blackwell (1975) 54; J. Heywood, n 1 above, 177; J. Stroud, *The Shorn Lamb*, London: Longmans (1960) 242–3.

of children'.[27] Following its recommendations, Children Act 1948, s 1 was amended to allow local authorities to provide services (and exceptionally cash) aimed at keeping children out of care. Allocating 'section 1 payments' became a major activity for social workers; small payments to stop disconnection of electricity or pay fares to sort out welfare benefit claims were a mainstay for poor families.[28]

The new responsibilities drastically altered the balance of work within the child care service; within a short time those being looked after were vastly outnumbered by those receiving services in their families.[29] A further consequence was the neglect of care services. Resources expended on casework with families were not available for substitute care; the 'duty to prevent' relegated care to second best, a service to be used if prevention failed. However, the strategy of prevention did not look successful; the numbers of children looked after continued to rise and the parliamentary Social Services Committee noted in 1984 'a lack of any organizational commitment to prevention'.[30] These limitations ultimately provided the foundation for replacing the notion of prevention with the broad duty to provide family support, in the Children Act 1989, Part III. This requires local authorities 'to safeguard and promote the welfare' of 'children in need' in their area by providing a range and level of services, including accommodation.[31] Services are intended to promote care by children's own families, prevent neglect, abuse, and the need to bring court proceedings, and minimize the effects of disability.[32] Local authority responsibility is limited; they are not expected to meet all need.[33] Families do not have rights to services, and their redress, if services are refused, is generally limited to an internal complaint.[34] Despite the emphasis in the Department of Health's implementation programme for the Act, family support has yet to revolutionize children's services.

Until the 1970s, adoption was largely a service for unmarried mothers and childless families, transferring babies to new homes. Approximately half the local authorities acted as adoption agencies but many adoptions were arranged through voluntary adoption societies, often linked to a

---

[27] *Report of the Committee on Children and Young Persons* Cmnd 1191 (1960), hereafter referred to as the Ingelby Report.

[28] B. Jordan, *Poor Parents*, London: Routledge & Kegan Paul (1974) 86–93; T. Murray, 'Section 1: A View from the Field', (1980) 3 *J Soc Welf Law* 96.

[29] J. Packman, n 26 above, 135.

[30] *Second Report from the Social Services Committee Session 1983–4 Children in Care* HC 360 (1984), hereafter referred to as the Short Report.

[31] Children Act 1989, s 17   [32] Children Act 1989, Sch 2.

[33] Department of Health, *Children Act Regulations and Guidance*, vol 2. London: HMSO (1991) para 2.11.

[34] *R. v Kingston upon Thames RBC, ex parte T.* [1994] 1 FLR 798: *R. v Birmingham City Council, ex parte A.* [1997] 2 FLR 841.

particular religious denomination. Changing patterns of adoption, particularly its use to secure homes for older children, and greater emphasis on the needs of children in adoption, led to a new duty on local authorities to provide a comprehensive adoption service.[35]

Local authorities now provide a wide range of services for children and families, and have a myriad of child welfare functions. They run family centres and residential homes; arrange foster and adoption placements; investigate allegations of abuse, bring protection proceedings, and look after children. In addition, they have regulatory functions, inspecting and registering child minders, day care, private foster carers, some residential homes and boarding schools. However, it looks as if the continual adding to social services departments' responsibilities is over. The Government has proposed replacing local authority regulation of residential services with Regional Commissions for Care Standards.[36] To prevent concerns about children's services being obscured by the needs of the much larger volume of adult's services there are to be regional children's rights officers.[37]

Reorganization within local government has also occurred throughout the last fifty years. Social services functions are now undertaken by London Boroughs, the councils of large cities such as Birmingham and Manchester, large counties such as Cornwall, Norfolk, and Lancashire, and much smaller, unitary authorities, with responsibility for housing which counties do not have. In some places, this has brought services closer to the people and facilitated a corporate response to the problems of homeless families or children leaving care but has left some areas without experienced officers and too small to provide a range of specialist services for children.[38]

In theory, organizing personal services within local authorities under the control of a committee of local politicians ensures accountability to the community and responsiveness to local needs. In practice, services for poor families and the care of sometimes-difficult children have tended to attract public interest only when things have gone seriously awry. Containment of problems, children, and expenditure have had higher political priority than evaluation of the quality or effectiveness of services.[39] These matters have been left to professional officers who have often been too overburdened with the problems of providing services to focus

---

[35] Children Act 1975, s 1 (now Adoption Act 1976, s 1) a recommendation of the Houghton Report: *Report of the Departmental Committee on Adoption of Children*, Cmnd 5107 (1972). See Lowe, Ch 14 of this volume.

[36] Care Standards Bill 1999.

[37] Department of Health, *Modernising Social Services*, Cm 4167 (1998), paras 4.07–18, 4.41.

[38] G. Craig and J. Manthorpe, *Unfinished Business? Local Government Reorganization and Social Services*, Bristol: Policy Press (1999); Waterhouse Report, n 4 above.

[39] A. Levy and B. Kahan, *The Pindown Experience and the Protection of Children, the Report of the Staffordshire Child Care Inquiry 1990*, Staffordshire County Council (1991).

sufficiently on planning and managing them. The emphasis has been on rationing rather than service development, with social workers acting as gatekeepers of scarce resources. And lack of information about needs and services has been a barrier to provision for the community.[40]

Central Government

Before the 1948 Act central government responsibility for the public care of children was distributed between four government departments—the Home Office, the Ministry of Health, the Ministry of Education, and the Ministry of Pensions. The ending of the Poor Law necessitated reform and precipitated a spat between the Home Office and the Ministry of Health as to which should take responsibility for children deprived of a normal home life. The Home Office triumphed by a combination of their experience of providing well-regarded residential schools with political machinations.[41] However in 1971, child care functions were transferred to the Department of Health and Social Security (DHSS) and remained with the Department of Health when the DHSS was divided.

This centralization never brought all issues relating to children's care and welfare within the purview of a single department. Recognition that children's well-being is dependent on that of their families raises questions about housing and income but the departments responsible for these issues have had almost no involvement with child welfare matters. However, as the courts became increasingly involved in committing children to care, the Lord Chancellor's Department was drawn in. Consequently, the review[42] which preceded the Children Act 1989 involved officials from the DHSS, the Home Office, and the Lord Chancellor's Department and the implementation programme for the Act drew in the Department for Education. Turf wars claiming (or more usually seeking to offload) responsibility, have continued. The Department of Health and the Home Office are passing their responsibilities for services which provide welfare reports to an agency under the Lord Chancellor's Department.

Central government plays a major role in resourcing social services. Initially children's departments received grants of up to half their expenditure; later, the costs of children's services were taken into account in cal-

---

[40] Audit Commission, n 25 above, 19; *First Report to Parliament on the Children Act 1989*, Cm 2144 (1992); D. Robbins, n 7 above.

[41] S. Cretney, n 1 above, 443–9; R. Parker, 'The Gestation of Reform: The Children Act 1948', in P. Bean and S. Macpherson (eds), *Approaches to Welfare*, London: Routledge & Kegan Paul (1983) 196.

[42] Department of Health and Social Security, *Review of Child Care Law*. London: HMSO (1985).

culating rate support grants. These grants could be spent on any local authority function, social services, education, or even leisure facilities; within any local authority children's services might win or lose through these arrangements. Until the 1980s local government could set its own level of local property taxes (rates) to raise its desired income but the Thatcher governments of the 1980s capped rates to force down expenditure. When evidence emerged of wide-scale failure in the child protection services, local government, blaming central government, identified financial constraints as the cause. Central government rejected this, indicating that local management was at fault.[43] Local authorities shifted their obligations to maintain children over 16 onto the Department of Social Security by discharging them from care, a response curtailed by the removal of young people's rights to benefits.[44] Central government also used specific grants, for training, to direct the development of services, and sometimes when new functions were imposed. At the end of the century, grants attached to the *Quality Protects* programme are forcing local authorities to develop Management Action Plans to improve outcomes in social services for children, measured against the Government's targets.[45]

Apart from financial support, central government has three essential functions to perform in relation to social services: to make policy and ensure that local authorities implement it; to set and ensure minimum levels of service; and to collect and disseminate relevant information.[46] From the beginning, the Home Office sought to influence the work of children's departments through issuing Circulars. These not only explained statutory duties but also the policies, such as developing preventive services, to be followed. The Local Authority Social Services Act 1970, s 7 required local authorities to exercise their social services functions under the guidance of the Secretary of State but this did not provide control nor produce a coherent set of policies.[47] A large volume of such

---

[43] Health Committee, Second Report Session 1990–91: *Public Expenditure on Personal Social Services: Child Protection Services*, HC 570 (1991) para 58. The Committee considered both equally responsible and criticized the DoH for not ensuring that local authorities could fulfil their statutory obligations.

[44] Unlike most people under the age of 18, those estranged from their families could continue to claim Income Support after 1992. The Department of Health viewed early discharge of care as inappropriate: Department of Health, n 10 above, paras 3.4–6; 3.27–31. The Children (Leaving Care) Bill 1999 increases local authorities obligations to children in public care on their sixteenth birthday.

[45] D. Robbins, n 7 above; Department of Health (1998), *Adoption—Achieving the Right Balance*, Circular LAC(98)20 DoH (1998).

[46] Seebohm Report, n 22 above, para 646.

[47] A. Webb and G.Wistow, *Social Work, Social Care and Social Planning: The Personal Social Services since Seebohm*, Harlow: Longman (1987) 130; J. Harris, 'Scientific Management, Bureau-Professionalism, New Managerialism: The Labour Process of State Social Work', (1998) 28 *Brit J Soc Wk* 839.

direction has been issued including *Working Together*,[48] which sets out the social services obligations in relation to child protection, and ten volumes on the operation of the Children Act 1989.

The Social Work Advisory Service of the DHSS provided a two-way channel for information and consultation between central and local government but did not allow for central control. Through its replacement, the Social Services Inspectorate, the Department of Health became more active in setting and monitoring standards across the whole range of children's services. SSI reports have played a major part in identifying shortcomings in child protection, residential care, adoption, foster care, and the provision of services for children in need.[49]

In the late 1970s the DHSS began to commission research into social work with children. The Children Act 1975, s 105 required the Secretary of State to report on its operation; a series of studies was commissioned to this end and, with the Social Science Research Council, a further programme looking more broadly at decision-making in child care. The findings of this programme were widely disseminated together with specific practice messages through publication, in 1985, of the 'pink book'. This exercise was repeated; research became an important tool for changing social services policy and social work practice.[50] The *refocusing debate*, which seeks to emphasize family support over child protection investigation, resulted from research findings of the early 1990s, and the *Looking after Children* system, which is used to improve the making and recording of decisions about individual children, was initially designed for research rather than practice.[51]

Through these mechanisms central government has come to dominate child care policy whilst leaving the responsibility for practice, and blame when things go wrong, with local authorities. Through research, guidance, and the work of the Social Services Inspectorate, the Department of Health has been able to claim superiority in knowledge and understanding and to exert much closer control than legislation alone would have allowed.

[48] Department of Health and Social Security, *Working Together*, London: HMSO (1988); Department of Health, *Working Together under the Children Act 1989*, London: HMSO (1991); Department of Health, *Working Together to Safeguard Children*, London: Department of Health (2000).

[49] See eg W. Utting, n 2 above; SSI, *Someone Else's Children*, London: Department of Health SSI (1997); Annual reports of the Chief Inspector, Social Services Inspectorate.

[50] The first 'pink book': Department of Health and Social Security, *Social Work Decisions in Child Care*, London: HMSO (1985); the second 'pink book': Department of Health, *Patterns and Outcomes in Child Care*, London: HMSO (1990); Dartington Research Unit. N 20 above.

[51] H. Ward, *Looking after Children: Research into Practice*, London: HMSO (1995); S. Jackson, 'Better Outcomes from Residential and Foster Care: The "Looking after Children" programme' in Colton *et al*, *The Art and Science of Child Care*, Aldershot: Arena (1995).

Voluntary Organizations and the For Profit Sector

In 1946 voluntary organizations such as Dr Barnardo's Homes, the Church of England Children's Society (formerly the Waifs' and Strays' Society), and the National Children's Home provided homes for 40,000 children. In the following fifty years, financial concerns, changing demands, and different approaches to meeting need have changed their character completely, but they remain important service providers and have considerable influence with central government. No longer running large children's homes, their work focuses on children in need and specialist provision, frequently under contracts with social services departments, for example, home-finding for children with severe disabilities and working with mothers with HIV or AIDS. Financial relationships rather than inspection have brought these organizations under closer control of local authorities but they retain some independence to determine the services they provide.

The National Society for the Prevention of Cruelty to Children also changed its character from a uniformed force investigating (and even prosecuting) cases of child neglect to an organization focusing on education and research in child protection. It also undertakes specialist work with abused children, their carers, and abusers, and investigates abuse in local authority establishments.[52] Although the NSPCC successfully campaigned to retain its power to bring child protection proceedings, it stopped this work shortly after the Children Act 1989 was passed.

In the late 1970s, new voluntary organizations such as the Family Rights Group and the National Association for Young People in Care, were established to advise people caught up in the care system, to advocate consumers' views, and to lobby for reform. Although small and poorly funded, they played a major role in the consultation exercises leading to the Children Act 1989, and in developing training for its implementation. By the end of the century, involving users had become an essential element in ensuring service quality.

The marketization of social services, problems running residential homes, and finding foster placements have lead to the development of child care as a business. Private fostering, the care of individual children, for reward, by direct arrangement with their parents has a long history but only in the last decade have commercial organizations become involved in looking after children in state care. The Children Act 1989 encouraged this development by requiring local authorities to facilitate provision by others and by failing to regulate fostering agencies and

---

[52] B. Joel-Esam, 'The NSPCC in the Nineties', in A. Levy (ed), *Refocus on Child Abuse*. London: Hawksmere (1994) 158.

small children's homes. Local authorities have found it difficult to retain foster carers who could receive better pay and support from private agencies, and convenient to place the most troublesome young people in private residential homes outside their area.

The Courts

In 1946, juvenile courts with lay magistrates were the only courts that could determine whether a child should be removed from his or her family. Children could be committed to the care of a fit person (the Children's Department) if specific offences had been committed against them or if their parents were not exercising proper care and they were being harmed.[53] Juvenile courts also dealt with juvenile offenders and this was reflected in the nature of the proceedings; parents were not parties and could only appear to rebut allegations made against them. Changes in the grounds and terminology in the Children and Young Persons Act 1969 retained this basic structure; local authorities, the police, and the NSPCC could seek care orders, and parents could require the local authority to seek an order where their child was beyond control.

Care proceedings were brief affairs 'legitimizing if not actually rubber stamping' local authority action.[54] Although it was asserted that these were not adversarial proceedings magistrates relied exclusively on the parties for information. Parents were not parties to the proceedings but, before 1981 when the Law Society advised against this practice, usually instructed the lawyer representing the child. Guardians ad litem, independent social workers with responsibility for investigating the case and ensuring the child's representation, could be appointed from 1976 but only in unopposed applications to discharge a care order.[55] The guardian ad litem service was extended in 1984, but only after the Children Act 1989 were appointments expected in all 'specified' cases.[56] In 1988, parents were given rights of representation with access to legal aid but only gained party status with the implementation of the Children Act in 1991. The quality of representation and the focus on the grounds limit the ability of the magistrates' court to make local authorities accountable.

---

[53] Children and Young Persons Act 1933, s 61, later amended by the Children and Young Persons (Amendment) Act 1952, s 1.

[54] Short Report, n 30 above, para 66.

[55] Children Act 1975, ss 64, 65. These were the circumstances which had preceded the death of Maria Colwell, the subject of a highly influential public inquiry.

[56] Children Act 1989, s 41; J. Masson and M. Shaw, 'The Work of Guardians ad litem' (1988) 10 *J Soc Welf Law* 165; J. Masson and M. Winn Oakley, *Out of Hearing*, Chichester: Wiley (1999).

Concern for the welfare of children in divorce proceedings lead to the county courts being given jurisdiction to commit children to the care of the local authority in exceptional circumstances;[57] these orders were generally made at the request of the local authority when other grounds could not be proved and could be made by a judge without an application. During the 1980s the High Court's power of wardship was increasingly used to commit children to care; the welfare-based grounds, relaxed rules of evidence, party status and representation for parents, and a professional judge made this the preferred route for many local authorities. The higher courts' relationship with local authorities was theoretically very different from that of the magistrates' court; judges could control how the child was to be cared for through directions, and if a child was made a ward, all major decisions had to be referred to the court. In practice, courts rarely issued directions and social workers, often ignorant of the law or the child's status, did not seek permission for decisions which required court ratification, other than adoption.[58]

Contact between parents and children, which is crucial to rehabilitation and thus the discharge of care orders was not regulated through the courts. In *A. v Liverpool City Council*[59] the House of Lords upheld a decision not to allow a mother to challenge the local authority's refusal of contact with her child through the inherent jurisdiction, on the basis that Parliament had intended day-to-day decisions to be under local authority control. Judicial review was only available where the local authority had acted improperly. However, litigation before the European Court of Human Rights held that termination of contact without court review breached articles 6 and 8 of the Convention.[60] Amending legislation was introduced which enabled parents to challenge termination of contact.[61] Court review was extended in the Children Act 1989; courts had to consider contact when making care orders and had jurisdiction over all disputes about contact.[62] Nevertheless, the courts remained reluctant to exercise their powers in ways which might undermine a local authority's plan for a child.[63]

---

[57] Matrimonial Proceedings (Children) Act 1958; subsequently this power was included in custody and wardship proceedings; it applied in all levels of court, see S. Maidment, 'The Fragmentation of Parental Contact and Children in Care' [1981] *J Soc Welf Law* 21.

[58] J. Masson and S. Morton, 'The Use of Wardship by Local Authorities', (1989) 52 *Mod Law Rev* 762.

[59] [1982] AC 363.   [60] *W., R., O., B. and H. v UK* [1998] 2 FLR 445.

[61] Health and Social Services and Social Security Adjudications Act 1983 introducing Child Care Act 1980, ss 12A–12G; S. Millham *et al*, *Access Decisions in Child Care*, Aldershot: Gower (1989).   [62] s 34.

[63] J. Masson, 'Thinking about Contact: A Social or a Legal Problem', (2000) 12 *Child and Family Law Quarterly* 1; S. Jolly, 'Cutting the Ties—The Termination of Contact in Care', (1994) 16 *J Soc Welf and Fam Law* 299.

The proliferation of routes into care, the differing standards applied, and the general complexity of the law were major reasons for establishing the *Review of Child Care Law* which led, somewhat tortuously, to the Children Act 1989. The courts could not be better than the laws under which they operated and child care law needed to be comprehensible to social workers and families.[64] A clear division between the roles of courts and local authorities and a system for ensuring accountability of the latter were essential. The 1989 Act introduced the 'significant harm test'[65] to replace all other tests for committal to care. It divided duties between local authorities and the courts, making the former responsible for the decision to seek a care order and for day-to-day care of the child. Care cases should be heard in the level of court which reflected their complexity; magistrates retain jurisdiction but cases can be transferred to higher courts to be heard by specialist judges. The court's role is to decide whether an order should be made on the basis of the evidence, including assessments it orders the local authority to arrange,[66] and the local authority's plan for the child. The welfare and 'no order' principles apply; the court can only make an order if this is better for the child than making no order.[67] Although initially the Act appeared to check the growth in the use of compulsion, the number of care orders is again increasing. Approximately 4,500 care orders are made each year and 60 per cent of children in state care are the subject of care orders, compared with 70 per cent in 1991.

The process of obtaining a care order has become far more substantial. Parents and children have party status, legal representation, and legal aid. Proceedings generally last more than six months and involve investigations by a guardian ad litem and assessments by experts from child and family mental health services. Although there are cases with long, contested hearings, the majority are uncontested at final hearing stage, reflecting the emphasis on negotiation and the inevitability of a care order where alternative solutions have not been identified during the proceedings.[68] Despite the centrality of the significant harm test to the legal framework its application has rarely been an issue in court. Care plans have become the focus of litigation but concerns remain about local

---

[64] Short Report, n 30 above, paras 114–19.
[65] s 31(2) 'A court may only make a care order . . . if it is satisfied—
(a) that the child concerned is suffering, or likely to suffer significant harm; and
(b) that the harm, or likelihood of harm, is attributable to—
    (i) the care given to the child . . . not being what it would be reasonable to expect a parent to give him; or
    (ii) the child's being beyond parental control.'
[66] Children Act 1989, s 38: *Re C. (interim care order: residential assessment)* [1997] 1 FLR 1.
[67] Children Act 1989, s 1(3),(5).
[68] J. Brophy, C. Wale, and P. Bates, *Myths and Practices*, London: BAAF (1999); J. Hunt and A. Macleod, *The Last Resort*, London: TSO (1998).

authority accountability because there is no court review of the plan after the order has been made.[69]

The public care of children is now recognized as having a rights dimension for both parents and children. The provisions of the European Convention on Human Rights were taken into account when the 1989 Act was drafted. The courts have become more important in terms of the numbers and proportions of children they commit to care and the issues over which they have jurisdiction. Issues relating to the care of children and parents' rights are no longer relegated to the lowest courts and representation is provided. The Children Act 1989 brought greater procedural rights and involved the courts in a thorough investigation of the local authority's initial plan for each child committed to care. However, the extent to which care services and local authority decision-making are controlled by the courts remains unclear.

Emphasis on the quality of care is leading to the development of a new strand of litigation by children, people brought up in care, and others seeking compensation from local authorities for negligence. In *F v Wirral Metropolitan Borough Council*[70] the Court of Appeal held that a parent could not sue a local authority for infringement of their parental rights. Subsequent decisions have related to children harmed because the local authority removed them, failed to remove them from their parents, or provided inadequate care. In *X v Bedfordshire County Council*,[71] the House of Lords held that a local authority had immunity from liability in negligence in relation to its involvement in the child protection system. However, following a decision in the European Court of Human Rights relating to police liability in negligence[72] it is clear that immunity can only be granted after an analysis of each individual case. Consequently, in *Barrett v Enfield London Borough Council*[73] the court refused to dismiss a claim by a young man who alleged he had been harmed by the negligent care he had received from the state. In addition, local authorities and their insurers face substantial numbers of compensation claims by young people abused in the care system. There is a possibility that compensation proceedings will hold local authorities accountable for the care they provide and systems to ensure adequate care will be imposed by insurers to minimize the risk of future claims.

---

[69] J. Dewar, 'The Courts and Local Authority Autonomy', (1995) 7 *Child and Family Law Quarterly* 15; M. Hayes, 'The Proper Role of the Courts in Child Care Cases', (1996) 8 *Child and Family Law Quarterly* 20; M. Thorpe and E. Cooke, *Divided Duties*, Bristol: Family Law (1998). A care order can only be discharged during childhood by a court.

[70] [1991] Fam 69.

[71] [1995] 2 AC 633. The European Commission on Human Rights concluded that articles 3 and 6 had been breached: *Z and others v UK* application No 29392/95 (1999).

[72] *Osman v UK* [1999] 1 FLR 193 ECHR.

[73] [1999] 3 All ER 193 HL; see also *S v Gloucestershire CC* [2000] 3 All ER 346.

DRIVERS OF CHANGE AND PROCESSES OF REFORM

A combination of internal change and external influence has produced the current care system. This is not a linear process but one of constant readjustment where different agencies respond at different rates, producing practices across the country that are quite diverse. This section identifies key factors which have helped to shape the organizations involved and the law and policies they operate.

Ideology

The relationship between the family and the state lies at the heart of child care policy. Although governments have repeatedly reaffirmed the importance of the family generally and to individual children, this rhetoric has frequently been disapplied to questions of provision for deprived or abused children. Fox Harding[74] identified four distinct perspectives—*laissez-faire* and patriarchy; state paternalism and child protection; the defence of birth parents' rights; and children's rights and child liberation—which combined in different measures, have shaped law and practice. The process of reform in the 1980s, involving as it did debate between local authorities, voluntary organizations, academics, lawyers and civil servants with widely different experiences and perspectives, made it possible to develop legislation based on realism and a broad consensus rather than the narrow political agenda and expediency which had marked the 1948 and 1975 Acts.[75]

The growth of state welfare services after 1945 reflects both state paternalism, the belief that the state could provide better care for children rescued from neglectful parents, and parents' rights to state support for their care. For much of this period state paternalism predominated; professionalization and the development of child care science strengthened the position of social workers and local authorities. The Children Act 1975 which facilitated the termination of parents' rights and adoption represents its high point. Subsequently, failings in the child protection and child care systems, identified through research and inquiries, undermined belief in state care, and the recognition that parental failure was often the result of deprivation reset the balance in favour of parents' rights.

Although the Thatcher Government of the 1980s marked the ascendancy of the New Right and generally presided over a withdrawal of state involvement in welfare, social services provision for children was

---

[74] L. Fox Harding, *Perspectives in Child Care Policy*. London: Longmans (1991) 10.
[75] N. Parton, *Governing the Family*. London: Macmillan (1991).

not subject directly to these policies. Changes in the economy and in local government financing put pressure on both families and local authorities but there were no arguments that the care system should be dismantled. Rather, there were suggestions that more concerted state action could promote adoption and reduce the need for further state intervention. The Children Act 1989 did not include adoption reform; adoption continued uneasily alongside new provisions whereby parents retained parental responsibility even though their child's removal had been sanctioned by the courts.[76] Under the Act, reducing state intervention meant discouraging court orders[77] and less coercive state action, rather than a reduction in state involvement in family life.

The notion that each child should have individual care had been stressed by the Curtis report, but thinking did not extend to involving children in decisions about their care. The focus of the care system was *child welfare*, defined by professionals, or parents' rights, not *children's rights;* it was considered damaging to involve children in decisions about their care. Although the drafting of the UN Convention on the Rights of the Child was roughly contemporaneous with the development of the Children Act 1989, little explicit attention was given in England to the rights set out in the Convention.[78] However, the decision of the House of Lords in *Gillick*[79] had forced both parents and local authorities to accept that competent children had some rights to make decisions about their own lives. The drafting of the Children Act 1989 made specific provision for mature children to refuse medical examinations ordered by the court in child protection proceedings but also removed the right of competent young people to request state care before the age of 16 years.[80]

Overall the Children Act sought to set a 'new balance'[81] between parents and the state based on the notion that the primary responsibility for children lies with their parents and the state's role is to support families. Services should be arranged for children 'in partnership' with their parents, even where they are necessary for the child's protection.[82] As partners (or consumers) parents have rights to participate in decisions about their child's care[83] and to complain about services provided (or not

---

[76] Children Act 1989, s 33(3)(4).   [77] Children Act 1989, s 1(5).

[78] Nevertheless the British Government claimed that the Act met many of the main obligations of the Convention: *First Report to Parliament on the Children Act 1989,* Cm 2144 (1992) para 1.13.

[79] *Gillick v W. Norfolk and Wisbech AHA* [1986] AC 112.

[80] Children Act 1989, s 38(6), 20(11).

[81] Department of Health, *An Introduction to the Children Act 1989.* London: HMSO (1989) iii.

[82] Department of Heath, *Child Abuse a Study of Inquiry Reports 1980–1989.* London: HMSO (1991) para 2.10–12; Department of Health, *The Challenge of Partnership.* London: HMSO (1995).

[83] Children Act 1989, s 22(4)(5).

provided).[84] However, implementing these ideals has not been easy; social workers continue to regard families as the problem rather than the solution[85] and focus on child protection rather than family support.

Professionalism

Professionalism in social work has had a major impact. Claims to know better than parents or courts have rested on the development of a qualified workforce. Although the majority of field social workers have qualifications, basic qualifications have increasingly been seen as inadequate for specialist work in child care. High proportions of residential care staff remain unqualified.[86] Successive governments have rejected proposals to raise standards by extending the length of social work training even though lack of knowledge and understanding has been a contributory factor in many of the failures of the child protection system and the low standards in residential care. Another consequence has been a growing emphasis by the courts on expert witnesses and deference to the views of guardians ad litem in preference to those of social workers. In order to raise standards, the Government proposed in 1998 to establish a General Social Care Council with the power to register individuals as social workers and to take responsibility for the regulation of social work training.[87] Such an organization would give social work the mark of a profession[88] but it is far from clear that it would raise either standards or public confidence.

The Rediscovery of Child Abuse

The failure of parental care had been recognized in the nineteenth century but it was not until the identification[89] of the 'battered baby' syndrome[90] in the 1960s that social workers began to focus on child abuse. The death of Maria Colwell in 1971 raised public awareness and increased expectations that social workers would help abused

---

[84] Children Act 1989, s 26(3).

[85] J. Masson and C. Harrison, 'Rebuilding Partnerships with Parents of Looked-After Children', in J. Masson *et al* (eds), *Lost and Found*. Aldershot: Arena (1999).

[86] W. Utting, *Children in the Public Care*, London: HMSO (1991); Utting, n 2 above, 12.7–25.

[87] Department of Health, *Modernising Social Services*, Cm 4167 (1998) ch 5; Care Standards Bill 1999. In July 2000 the Government announced its acceptance of the extension of social work training to three years.

[88] P. Barclay, *Social Workers Their Role and Tasks*. London: Bedford Square Press (1982) 178.

[89] E. Farmer and M. Owen, *Child Protection Practice: Private Risks and Public Remedies*. London: HMSO (1995) 12; N. Parton, *The Politics of Child Abuse*, Basingstoke: Macmillan (1985).

[90] C. H. Kempe *et al*, 'The Battered-Child Syndrome', (1962) 181 *J Am Med Assoc* 17; D. Griffiths and F. Moynihan, 'Multiple Epiphysial Injuries in Babies ("Battered Baby Syndrome")', (1963) *British Med JMJ* 1558.

children. However, child abuse was not always easy to identify; co-operation between all the relevant agencies was essential. In 1974, the DHSS inaugurated a system for local authority management of child abuse.[91] Local authorities began holding 'case conferences' where all professionals with contact with a family could share their concerns about cases of suspected abuse, and established 'child protection registers' so that children at risk could be monitored. Initially the focus was physical abuse but later this was extended to neglect, emotional and sexual abuse. Social work involvement with sexual abuse developed in the mid-1980s following similar developments in the USA. However, the rapid diagnosis of a large number of cases by paediatricians in Cleveland in 1987 overwhelmed social services and other agencies, precipitating a crisis and an inquiry.[92]

The local authority response to abuse was coercive action. During the 1970s and 1980s social services departments made increased use of their powers to remove children to a place of safety, to remove parental rights administratively, and to obtain court orders to protect children.[93] Criminal prosecution was also used, although in cases of sexual abuse the rules relating to children's evidence often precluded this.[94] In the 1990s, evidence law was amended and court procedures changed[95] in order to make it easier for child victims to obtain justice and abusers to be controlled.[96] However, the majority of those who offend against children are not prosecuted.

The large numbers of children at risk coming to local authority attention and the nature of the procedures to be followed have absorbed a high percentage of social services' resources, effectively limiting family support for children in need and the development of fostering and residential care. Each year, over 150,000 child protection inquiries are held and 40,000 children are the subject of a child protection conference.[97] Despite the Children Act 1989, identifying children as 'at risk' rather than as 'in need' remains a way of accessing services, but many families who are subject to child protection investigations receive no services. Changing

---

[91] Parton, n 75 above, 118.

[92] *Report of the Enquiry into Child Abuse in Cleveland in 1987*, Cm 412 (1988), hereafter referred to as the Butler-Sloss Report.

[93] Parton, n 89 above.

[94] J. Spencer and R. Flin, *The Evidence of Children: The Law and the Psychology* (2nd edn). London: Blackstone Press (1993).

[95] S. Cretney and J. Masson, J, *The Principles of Family Law*, London: Sweet & Maxwell (1997) 835–42; Youth Justice and Criminal Evidence Act 1999.

[96] Those convicted of specific offences are barred from working with children: Protection of Children Act 1999; sexual offenders are required to register with the police: Sex Offenders Act 1997.

[97] Dartington Research Unit, n 20 above, 28.

this, whilst remaining vigilant in child protection, is the aim of the Department of Health's attempt to refocus children's services.

Scandals and Inquiries

The history of child care has been marked by scandals and moral panics to which government, local or central, has found it expedient to respond by establishing inquiries. In 1946, the death of Dennis O'Neill, following ill treatment by his foster father[98] contributed to the reforming tone of the Curtis report. Almost thirty years passed before another such inquiry but over fifty such inquiries were conducted in the 1970s and 1980s.[99] Whilst these generally focused on the failure to take action to protect a child, the Cleveland Inquiry in 1987[100] examined the decisions to remove over a hundred children from their parents because of allegations or diagnoses of sexual abuse. There was also a series of inquiries into abuse of children in residential care[101] that served to identify major, long-term failings in the way residential homes had been managed and general indifference within social services departments to the way young people were looked after. Containment and control rather than care and support characterized the care provided to those in residential care throughout the period.

Inquiries have contributed to a general lowering of confidence in social workers and the decisions of social services departments. Inquiries generally identified inadequacy in local authority staff or procedures justifying greater direction from central government. The police and the Health Service were also criticized for their failure to co-operate over child protection. By raising public awareness, inquiries have contributed to a climate where something had to be done and resources, civil servants, and parliamentary time had to be committed to child care issues. As a response the Department of Health issued guidance on interagency co-operation and the organization of child protection.[102] Most findings of inquiries received no direct legislative or policy response but the establishment of the guardian ad litem system,

---

[98] *Report by Sir Walter Monckton on the Circumstances which Led to the Boarding out of Dennis and Terence O'Neill*, Cmd 6636 (1945); S. Cretney, n 41 above; R. Parker, n 41 above.

[99] See P. Reder, S. Duncan, and M. Gray, n 12 above; Department of Health and Social Security, *Child Abuse: A Study of Inquiry Reports 1973–1981*, London: HMSO (1982); Department of Health, *Children Act Regulations and Guidance*, vol 3, London: HMSO (1991).

[100] Butler-Sloss Report, n 92 above.

[101] A. Levy and B. Kahan, n 39 above; A. Kirkwood, *The Leicestershire Inquiry 1992*, Leicestershire County Council (1993); Waterhouse Report, n 4 above.

[102] Department of Health and Social Security, *Working Together*, London: HMSO (1988); Department of Health, *Working Together under the Children Act 1989*, London: HMSO (1991); Department of Health *et al*, *Working Together to Safeguard Children*, London: TSO (2000).

stricter controls on orders to remove children at risk, and the formalization of the child protection system resulted partly from inquiries.

Although local authorities are still required to undertake a review when a child subject to the child protection system dies,[103] public inquiries are rare. Acceptance that the child protection system cannot prevent all deaths and of the limited usefulness of inquiries has combined with media-weariness to keep such deaths in the shadows. The massive scale of the Waterhouse Inquiry is likely to have a similar effect on further inquiries into residential care.[104] The Government will not be keen to show that its controlling approach produces flawed care. Consequently, the twenty-first century can be expected to start without repeated public exposure of failure by social services.

Permanency Planning

The publication of the research report *Children Who Wait*[105] in 1973 highlighted the plight of 7,000 children in care who needed a permanent family. Increasing and using local authority powers was seen to be the solution; minimal parental involvement should not stand in the way of the child's adoption once adoption had been seen to be suitable for older children as well as babies.[106] The Children Act 1975 increased local authorities powers to remove parental rights, the Association of British Adoption Agencies encouraged local authorities to plan permanent care and to terminate parents' contact in order to facilitate this.[107] However, this more coercive action was challenged in the courts and a formal process was established for ending parental contact.[108]

A broader approach to permanency in the 1980s recognized that there were many ways of providing a stable home for children in care, including rehabilitation with their families.[109] Research by Millham and colleagues also emphasized the importance of family contact and swift social work action if children were to return to their families.[110] Despite recognition of the importance of security for children and powers to ensure it, at the turn of the century local authorities are still not providing this for many of the children they look after. The Department of

---

[103] Department of Health, n 102 above, Pt 8.

[104] The Inquiry sat for 201 days, heard 264 witnesses, received 311 written statements, and read 12,000 documents; its report is over 900 pages long.

[105] J. Rowe and L. Lambert, *Children Who Wait*. London: ABAFA (1973).

[106] B. Tizard, *Adoption: A Second Chance*. London: Open Books (1977).

[107] Association of British Adoption and Fostering Agencies, *Terminating Parental Contact*, London: ABAFA (1979); [now called British Agencies for Adoption and Fostering (BAAF)].

[108] See nn 59–63 above.

[109] J. Thoburn, 'What Kind of Permanence?' (1985) 9 *Adoption and Fostering* 29.

[110] S. Millham *et al*, *Lost in Care*. Aldershot: Gower (1986).

Health is trying to address this through its *Quality Protects* programme and guidance on adoption.[111]

CONCLUSION: CHILD CARE IN THE NEW CENTURY

At the end of the century far more is known about the problems which prevent families from providing adequate care and which face those trying to provide substitute care, but there has been less progress in developing solutions in terms of both policy and practice. Particularly, there is an awareness that the consequences of past policies return to haunt future generations. The Select Committee on Health identified one legacy of the late twentieth-century care system—thousands of socially isolated young people whose upbringing has not equipped them to cope with the demands of life, particularly parenthood. Social services departments will have continued involvement with some of these people, supporting them or caring for their children. Another legacy is likely to be large numbers of compensation claims.

Lawyers and the courts have become far more important in the child care process but the majority of children and families who become involved with social services do so by agreement, without legal questions being raised. Government acceptance that local authorities must be able to control their resources means that the division of responsibilities between courts and local authorities, established in the 1989 Act, is unlikely to be substantially altered. The courts' prime role is assessing whether children should be committed to care for their protection. Closer definition of plans[112] or even the approval of major changes in care may marginally strengthen the courts' powers, but day-to-day care will remain a matter for local authorities, challengeable through complaints processes rather than courts.

Lord Mackay, then the Lord Chancellor, stated that the Children Act 1989 was the 'most comprehensive and far reaching reform of child law which has come before Parliament in living memory'.[113] Although the incorporation of the European Convention on Human Rights will raise the profile of rights issues, it is unlikely that there will be further major legislation for a considerable time. The flow of regulations and guidance from the Department of Health will continue with the aim of refocusing services and raising practice standards. The framework for children's ser-

---

[111] Department of Health, *Quality Protects*, Circular LAC (98)28 (1998); Department of Health, *Adoption—Achieving the Right Balance*, Circular LAC (98)20 (1998).
[112] Department of Health, *Care Plans and Care Proceedings under the Children Act 1989*, LAC (99)29 (1999).
[113] 502 *House of Lords Debates (Hansard)* (5th series) col 488.

vices in the Children Act seeks to safeguard children's welfare through supporting their families, or where coercive action is necessary, supervising or replacing the family's care. The Act's balance between support and control, set through the court proceedings applying the 'significant harm test', will not stop the pendulum swinging between the contrasting ideologies of state paternalism and the defence of birth parents' rights. This remains a contested area with continual claims of over- and under-intervention by the state. The notion of significant harm allows for different interpretations, and local authority support for children in need will not resolve chronic problems of family stress generated through economic and social decay. Adoption is unlikely to provide families for many more children than at present. Parents, children, and some social workers will continue to resist the cutting of old ties which it represents and it will remain difficult to recruit adopters for older children who cannot return to their families. Legal reform is unlikely to make adoption much easier; indeed the emphasis on the European Convention on Human Rights may make it more difficult to retain law which permits adoption without parental consent.

It remains unclear whether the new emphasis on central control and managerialism from the Department of Health will produce either higher standards or standardization in the care system. The use of national guidance has not produced a uniform approach. Any gains achieved through short-term initiatives such as *Quality Protects* will need to be sustained if they are to form a foundation for improvements. In the face of accumulated evidence from the last fifty years, only the most confirmed optimist would believe that in the twenty-first century corporate parenting will achieve for children in the care system the standards of ordinary families. However, there is no suggestion that either central or local government will give up on the project of trying to provide better state care, at least whilst this issue remains one of public concern. Social services departments will continually have to adapt to changing demands and expectations; there will never be sufficient resources to respond to all need.

27

The Hague Children's Conventions: The Internationalization of Child Law

LINDA SILBERMAN

INTRODUCTION

The theme of this chapter is the internationalization of 'child law,' a trend which can be expected to continue into the twenty-first century. Family law matters more generally have been the subject of a number of international conventions throughout the last century, but the emphasis on children has been a late twentieth-century development. During the course of the last century, the Hague Conference on Private International Law, which concentrates largely on issues of choice of law and jurisdiction rather than substantive provisions, developed conventions on marriage, divorce, support, adoption, protection of children, and matrimonial property.[1] However, with the exception of the Conventions on support, these Conventions did not have widespread adoptions and as a result were not particularly successful. The jurisdiction and choice of law model used for other Hague Conference Conventions seemed too theoretical and abstract to address successfully important issues of family law; at the same time, obtaining agreement on 'substantive' provisions among countries with very different cultural and legal traditions seemed even less likely to achieve success. Despite these odds, the three recent 'Children's Conventions', concluded by the Hague Conference on Private International Law in the last two decades, managed to find significant areas of commonality and to create a framework for establishing international standards on issues relating to children. In addition to the jurisdictional and procedural provisions usually found in Hague Conventions, the Conventions introduced various structures for intercountry administrative and judicial co-operation on matters involving children. The three Conventions are:

© 2000 Linda Silberman. This chapter is drawn from my more extensive manuscript *Co-operative Efforts in Private International Law on Behalf of Children* delivered for Summer 1999 Hague Academy Lectures, to be published in Recueil Des Cours (forthcoming). My research assistants, Karin Wolfe and Michael Jordan, students at New York University School of Law, provided valuable research help on that project, and thus their contributions are acknowledged here as well. My secretary, Richard Kelsey, assured that computer compatibility and stylistic requirements were met, and all his efforts in preparing this article are greatly appreciated.

[1] See generally Adair Dyer, *The Internationalization of Family Law*, 30 UC Davis L Rev 625 (1997).

(1) the 1980 Convention on the Civil Aspects of International Child Abduction, (2) the 1996 Convention on Jurisdiction, Applicable Law, Recognition, Enforcement, and Co-operation in Respect of Parental Responsibility and Measures for the Protection of Children, and (3) the 1993 Convention on Protection of Children and Co-operation in Respect of Intercountry Adoption. The three Conventions have an 'operational' focus, ie they provide specific rules and institute particular mechanisms for achieving their objectives. In contrast, the United Nations Convention on the Rights of the Child is aspirational in character. Like the Hague Conventions, it signifies the globalization of child law, but the general and open-ended nature of its provisions are less likely to have a direct impact on day-to-day cross-border issues relating to children. This essay offers an overview of the three Hague Conventions; it describes each Convention's solution for achieving its objective: deterring international child abductions (the Abduction Convention), recognizing measures and enforcing international custody decrees across transnational borders (the Protection Convention), and facilitating intercountry adoptions (the Adoption Convention). The essay concludes with observations about the internationalization of children's issues as the new millennium begins.

THE HAGUE CONVENTION ON THE CIVIL ASPECTS OF INTERNATIONAL CHILD ABDUCTION

Background

The Hague Convention on the Civil Aspects of Child Abduction was adopted in 1980;[2] over sixty countries have now ratified or acceded to the Convention.[3] Notwithstanding the reference to abduction in its title, the Convention covers violations of custody rights more generally, encompassing

---

[2] Convention on the Civil Aspects of International Child Abduction, Oct 25 1980, 19 ILM 1501 [hereinafter Abduction Convention].

[3] Countries that were members of the Hague Conference at the time of the adoption of the Convention ratify the Convention; other countries may accede to the Convention, but their accession must be accepted by other states. As of September 2000 the countries that have ratified the Convention are : Argentina, Australia, Austria, Belgium, Bosnia and Herzegovina, Canada, Croatia, Czech Republic, Denmark, Finland, Former Yugoslav Republic of Macedonia, France, Germany, Greece, Hong Kong Special Administrative Region, Ireland, Israel, Italy, Luxembourg, Macau Special Administrative Region, Netherlands, Norway, Portugal, Spain, Sweden, Switzerland, Turkey, United Kingdom of Great Britain and Northern Ireland (including the Isle of Man, Cayman Island, Falkland Islands, Montserrat, and Bermuda), United States of America, and Venezuela. As a result of accession, the Convention is in force in Bahamas, Belarus, Belize, Brazil, Burkina Faso, Chile, Colombia, Costa Rica, Cyprus, Ecuador, Fiji, Georgia, Honduras, Hungary, Iceland, Malta, Mauritius, Mexico, Republic of Moldova, Monaco, New Zealand, Panama, Paraguay, Poland, Romania, Saint Kitts

wrongful removals or wrongful retentions of children.[4] If a child (up to the age of 16) habitually resident in a signatory country is wrongfully taken to or retained in another signatory country, the authorities of that country to which the child is taken are required to return the child back to the country of its habitual residence.

The Convention remedy is a very particular and specialized remedy: it does not confer jurisdiction on a country to hear a custody case; it does not require enforcement of a custody order; and most importantly, it does not involve any determination of the merits of custody. Rather, the Convention remedy can almost be thought of as a fast-track extradition-type remedy: countries adhering to the treaty agree to return children wrongfully removed or retained in their country back to the country of the child's habitual residence where further proceedings on the merits of custody will take place. In this sense, the Convention operates only as a provisional remedy by returning children so that further action can be taken.

The widespread adoption of the Convention reflects a growing international consensus about issues surrounding international custody disputes. First, it recognizes that authorities in the state of the child's habitual residence are the appropriate authorities to make decisions about the long-term custody arrangements between disputing parents. In general, the country of habitual residence presumptively has the strongest interest in making provisions for the child and its parents, and the authorities in the state of habitual residence are best situated with relevant information to determine the ultimate merits of what custodial arrangement is in the child's best interests. Second, there is a growing intolerance for unilateral behavior by one parent in taking action as to where their children should live and for attempting to exploit local biases and cultural differences as part of the custody decision-making process. Finally, the emotional and psychological trauma of wrongful removals and retentions upon children has been fully recognized, and the Convention is understood as the international instrument that can deter these wrongful takings.

---

and Nevis, Slovenia, South Africa, Trinidad and Tobago, Turkmenistan, Uruguay, Uzbekistan, and Zimbabwe. See Hague Conference on Private International Law, *Status Sheet Convention #28* <http://www.hcch.net/e/status/abdshte.html>.

[4] I have described the operation of the Convention elsewhere. See Linda Silberman, *The Hague Convention on International Child Abduction*, in Anne-Marie Trahan (ed), A NEW VISION FOR A NON-VIOLENT WORLD: JUSTICE FOR EACH CHILD (PROCEEDINGS OF THE 4TH BIENNIAL INTERNATIONAL CONFERENCE OF THE INTERNATIONAL ASSOCIATION OF WOMEN JUDGES 21–39 (1999). For more extensive treatment of the issues, see Linda Silberman, *Hague Convention on International Child Abduction: A Brief Overview and Case Law Analysis*, 28 FAM LQ 9 (1994); Linda Silberman, *Hague International Child Abduction Convention: A Progress Report*, 57 LAW & CONTEMP PROBS 209 (1994).

Operation of the Convention

The Convention's formal mechanisms have two aspects. The first is the structure of formal co-operation for assisting foreign applicants in locating children who have been wrongfully removed or retained. The second is the creation of a judicial remedy to achieve the return of a child if more informal or voluntary returns cannot be achieved.

The Central Authority Mechanism

With respect to the first, each country is required to create a Central Authority, which undertakes a series of obligations to achieve return of the child, including helping to locate the child, to prevent harm to the child, and to facilitate the exchange of information between authorities in both states.[5] The Central Authorities assist in both 'outgoing cases'—when a child has been taken from a country—and in 'incoming cases' when a child has wrongfully been brought to or retained in a country. More specifically, the Central Authority in the state from which the child has been removed responds to 'outgoing requests' by helping an applicant prepare and process a case, providing information about the options in the foreign state, and contacting the relevant Central Authority in the state to which the child has been taken. The Central Authority of a state to which a child is taken responds to 'incoming requests' for return of the child, and by providing information about how to proceed to applicants and to the Central Authority in the state from where the child was taken as well as facilitating access to legal assistance and advice. In some countries, the Central Authority itself may initiate proceedings to secure the return of the child. A party may submit an application for return either to the Central Authority in the state of the child's habitual residence or to the Central Authority of the state where the child has been taken, if that is known.

The Judicial Remedy

In addition to the use of Central Authorities (which an applicant may bypass altogether), the Convention creates a judicial remedy for an applicant seeking return of a child. An application for return of a child is filed (under local procedures) in the country to which the child has been taken. The court's role in that country is limited and circumscribed. The court's obligation is to decide whether there has been a 'wrongful removal or retention' as defined in Article 3 of the Convention, and if so, to order

---

[5] The role of Central Authorities is discussed in depth in Carol S. Bruch, *The Central Authority's Role under the Hague Child Abduction Convention: A Friend in Deed*, 28 Fam LQ 36 (1994).

return as provided in Article 12. The merits of the custody dispute are not the province of the Hague application; the determination of custody is for the court in the home country once the child is returned.

The issues on a Hague application are relatively straightforward. The threshold inquiry of a wrongful removal or retention under Article 3 of the Convention depends on whether there has been a 'breach of rights of custody' under the law of the state in which the child was habitually resident immediately before the removal or retention. Thus, the requested state makes an inquiry to determine whether there has been a violation of custody rights under the law of the habitual residence. The concept of 'custody rights' is a term of art within the Convention and only if 'custody rights' are violated is there an obligation of return. In defining 'custody rights', the Convention distinguishes between concepts of 'visitation and access'[6]—which are not 'custody rights'—and other types of custody arrangements, such as joint custody'—which have been interpreted under the Convention as 'custody rights'. The definition appears in Article 5 of the Convention, defining custody rights as 'rights relating to the care of the person of the child and, in particular, the right to determine the child's place of residence'. Such definition, along with the Pérez-Vera Report accompanying the Convention,[7] goes a long way toward creating an autonomous treaty definition—one separate from domestic law understandings of custody or custody rights—of when there has been a breach of custody rights warranting return under the Convention.

Another important feature of the 'custody rights' of the Abduction Convention is that a violation of 'custody rights' can occur whether or not there is an existing custody order or agreement. As a result, the Convention applies to pre-decree disputes that occur between parents and prior to any resolution of the parties' rights by an agreement or a decree. Thus, unilateral action by one parent in taking a child to another country or failing to return to the country of habitual residence will be found to be a breach of custody rights under the Convention. In this area particularly, the Convention has filled a gap by providing a remedy in the absence of a custody order.

The Abduction Convention's innovative remedy is the order for return of the child as provided for in Article 12. Article 12 states that when proceedings are brought within one year of the child's wrongful removal or retention in the contracting state where the child is now physically present, the authorities within that state 'shall order the return of the child

---

[6] A separate article of the Convention—Article 21—authorizes Central Authorities to facilitate and secure rights of access, but the Convention's key remedy of return is not triggered.

[7] See Elisa Pérez-Vera, *Explanatory Report*, in HAGUE CONFERENCE ON PRIVATE INTERNATIONAL LAW, ACTS AND DOCUMENTS OF THE FOURTEENTH SESSION, CHILD ABDUCTION 426 (1982).

forthwith'.[8] When proceedings are brought after the expiration of the one-year period, the authorities 'shall also order the return of the child, unless it is demonstrated that the child is settled in its new environment.'[9] In such a case, the court has discretion about whether or not to order return.

A party resisting a Hague application for return of a child has a limited number of defenses. First, under Article 13a, if custody rights were not being exercised, or if there was consent to the removal or retention, or subsequent consent or acquiescence—in effect when there has been a *de facto* agreement about a move—no return is required. Second, and the defense that has created the most dangerous loophole in the Convention, is the provision in Article 13b, which permits the authorities to refuse return of the child if 'there is a grave risk that his or her return would expose the child to physical or psychological harm or otherwise place the child in an intolerable situation'.[10] An additional paragraph in Article 13 also authorizes a refusal of return if the authorities find that the child objects to being returned and the child has attained an age and degree of maturity at which it is appropriate to take account of those views. Finally, Article 20 offers a defense sounding in 'human rights' terms: return may be refused if fundamental principles of the requested state relating to the protection of human rights and fundamental freedoms would not permit the return.[11]

A Brief Assessment of the Convention

After two decades of usage worldwide and over a decade within the United States, the Convention must be applauded as having made real headway in securing co-operation in returning children removed or retained across national borders.[12] In addition to orders of return secured under the Convention, many disputes have been resolved without court action through voluntary returns. There is also reason to believe that the Convention has had an impact in deterring wrongful removals and has encouraged parties to seek resolution in the court of the state of habitual residence rather than resort to self-help.

---

[8] Abduction Convention, n 2 above, at art 12.   [9] *ibid.*   [10] *ibid*, art 13b.

[11] Interestingly, neither Finland nor the United Kingdom included this final discretionary exception in its implementing legislation, apparently because it was thought redundant to Article 13(b)'s grave risk of harm or otherwise intolerable situation. See PAUL R. BEAUMONT and PETER E. MCELEAVY, THE HAGUE CONVENTION ON INTERNATIONAL CHILD ABDUCTION 172–6 (Oxford University Press 1999) [hereinafter INTERNATIONAL CHILD ABDUCTION].

[12] An excellent compendium of the case law experience worldwide under the Abduction Convention is found in INTERNATIONAL CHILD ABDUCTION, n 11 above.

Unfortunately, a changing political climate has altered some attitudes about the Abduction Convention. When the Convention was originally drafted in 1980, the perception (and to some extent the prediction) was that most abductors were (and would be) non-custodial fathers. In recent years, the 'abductors' have largely been mothers—indeed mothers who are 'custodial' parents wishing to return to their home country after living abroad in a marriage that has broken down. Often, concerns by the mother that she will not be permitted to leave the country of habitual residence with the child—particularly at a time when restrictions on relocation are common—may lead the mother to take unilateral action to remove the child. But the Convention cannot withstand a double standard based on gender; unlawful unilateral removals as well as real abductions are harmful to children, whether the parent who removes is a mother or a father. And if the Convention is not adhered to in all cases, its force and efficacy will be undermined.[13]

The Convention has suffered from other 'growing pains'. Although Article 11 of the Convention requires states to act expeditiously in return proceedings and even provides an applicant with the right to request a statement of reasons for delay if no decision has been reached within six weeks from the date of commencement, proceedings are conducted according to local procedures. Thus, depending upon the particular country, the length and nature of proceedings varies, including the process for appeal.[14]

Foreign applicants have often had difficulty obtaining counsel to pursue an application under the Convention. The Convention provides that

---

[13] Not surprisingly, no 'formal' double standard is advocated, ie no one suggests that there should be one rule for abducting mothers and another for abducting fathers. Rather, the 'gender issues' are more subtle and affect how the Convention is to be understood and interpreted. For example, if a parent has the right to control relocation of the child, most courts have viewed the right as one to determine the residence of the child and a conferral of 'custody rights' within the meaning of the Convention. See eg *C v C* [1989] 2 All ER 465 (Eng CA Dec 14 1988); *David S v Zamira*, 574 NYS 2d 429 (Fam Ct.), *aff'd sub nom. In re Schnier*, 17 *Fam L Rep* 1237 (NY App Div, Feb 27 1991). However, two Supreme Court of Canada decisions have offered more restrictive interpretations, see *Thomson v Thomson*, [1994] 2 SC R 551 and *DS v VW* [1996] 134 DLR 4th 481, in the interest of protecting the mobility rights of custodial parents, primarily mothers. For a more extensive discussion of this issue, see Linda Silberman, *Custody Orders under the Hague Abduction Convention*, in A NEW VISION FOR A NON-VIOLENT WORLD: JUSTICE FOR EACH CHILD, n 4 above, at 234–6; Martha Bailey, *The Right of a Non-custodial Parent to an Order for Return of a Child Under the Hague Convention*, 13 CAN J FAM L 287, 299–300 (1996).

[14] For example, one leading case in the United States, *Friedrich v Friedrich*, 983 F2d 1396 (6th Cir 1993) and 78 F3d 1060 (6th Cir 1996) required two separate rulings by an appellate court to reach a favorable and correct decision ordering return of the child; the proceedings took almost four years through two trial decisions and two appeals. By contrast, return proceedings in England have been conducted in summary fashion with affidavit evidence. See Nigel Lowe, *International Child Abduction—The English Experience*, 48 INT & COMP LQ 127 (1999).

an applicant is not required to pay for the costs and expenses of proceedings, including those arising from the participation of legal counsel. However, Article 42 permits a country to take a reservation from this clause when such costs are not covered by the general system of legal aid. Thus, in some countries, including the United States, which made the reservation, foreign applicants often find it difficult to obtain legal representation.

Enforcement of orders of return is also uneven, depending on the particular Convention country. There is speculation that as many as a quarter of all return orders are not enforced. In the United States, contempt remedies offer some threat of compliance, but many countries do not have effective enforcement mechanisms.

The most serious danger to the success of the Convention has been an increasingly expanded use of the defenses to the Convention, particularly the 13(b) 'grave risk' defense as well as the role given to the objections of a child, even a very young one. On these and other issues, courts have allowed too many of the aspects of a traditional custody hearing—concerns for harm to the child, the wishes of the child, individual case assessments of 'best interests', and procedural protections for the child—to become part of a Hague proceeding.[15] This criticism should not be regarded as an attack on the best interests of the child standard, but rather understood as insistence upon differentiating a Hague application from a plenary custody proceeding. The Convention is directed to protecting the 'best interests' of a child by creating a structure and framework for having children returned. The ultimate determination of custody—to be made by the authorities in the country of habitual residence—will, of course, focus on an individual child's best interests, including a full inquiry into the child's background and lifestyle, relationships with parents, allegations of harm or abuse, as well as the wishes of the child. But none of these trappings should be imposed on a Hague proceeding—because it is not a custody case.

---

[15] Although a number of important decisions in Convention countries have construed the art 13b defense narrowly, both substantively and procedurally, see eg *Thomson*, 2 SCR at 551; *Friedrich*, 78 F3d at 1060, more recent decisions suggest a different trend. See eg *Blondin v Dubois*, 78 F Supp 2d 283 (SDNY 2000). In *Blondin*, the appeals court vacated the district judge's non-return ruling and ordered the judge to consider whether options were available that would protect the children and still allow them to be returned to France as the Convention required. 189 F 3d 240, 242 (2nd Cir 1999). Rather than focusing on the means of protecting the children on return, the district judge interviewed the children in chambers and held a three-day evidentiary replete with testimony from a mental health expert, who had examined the children; the district judge reaffirmed the decision not to return the children to France. The case is on appeal, as this article went to print.

THE 1996 CONVENTION ON JURISDICTION, APPLICABLE LAW, RECOGNITION, ENFORCEMENT AND CO-OPERATION IN RESPECT OF PARENTAL RESPONSIBILITY AND MEASURES FOR THE PROTECTION OF CHILDREN

Background

The latest effort of the Hague Conference—the 1996 Convention on Jurisdiction, Applicable Law, Recognition, Enforcement and Co-operation in Respect of Parental Responsibility and Measures for the Protection of Children—was successfully concluded at The Hague on October 19 1996.[16] The 1996 Convention—often referred to as the Protection of Children Convention to avoid repeating its very long title—builds on the success of the 1980 Abduction Convention. As the elements of its formal title suggest, it has a much broader scope and encompasses a wide range of cross-frontier problems and issues affecting children.[17] The 1996 Convention has been promoted largely as a jurisdiction and recognition of judgments convention for custody-type orders, but its day-to-day impact may turn more on its other expansive provisions for recognition and co-operation with respect to routine types of measures.[18]

The very simple task of assuring that measures taken with respect to the protection of a child or an order attributing parental responsibility to a particular adult in one country are honored in another country is encompassed by the Convention. For example, if an order entitles someone to act for a child with respect to a social, education, or medical situation, the Convention requires recognition of that order.[19] In addition, the Convention permits a party given such authority to request a certificate from the authorities that granted the measure of protection indicating the capacity in which that person is entitled to act and the powers conferred. Thus, in many situations the 1996 Convention makes possible the recognition of single and straightforward measures taken in one country without necessitating additional action in a second country.

[16] Convention on Jurisdiction, Applicable Law, Recognition, Enforcement and Co-operation in Respect of Parental Responsibility and Measures for the Protection of Children, Oct 19 1996, 35 ILM 1391 [hereinafter Protection Convention].

[17] See generally Eric Clive, *The Role of the New Protection of Children Convention*, in Sharon Detrick and Paul Vlaardlingerbroek (eds), GLOBALIZATION OF CHILD LAW (1999); Linda Silberman, *The 1996 Convention on Jurisdiction, Applicable Law, Recognition, Enforcement and Co-operation in Respect of Parental Responsibility and Measures for the Protection of Children: A Perspective from the United States*, in PRIVATE LAW IN THE INTERNATIONAL ARENA: FROM NATIONAL CONFLICT RULES TOWARDS HARMONIZATION AND UNIFICATION, LIBER AMICORUM KURT SIEHR 559 (TMC Asser Press 2000)(forthcoming) [hereinafter FESTSCHRIFT].

[18] The Convention also relates to measures with respect to the property of the child, but this essay focuses only on measures relating to the protection of the child.

[19] See Protection Convention, n 16 above, at art 23.

As of August 2000, the 1996 Convention has been ratified only by Monaco and the Czech Republic and as a result the Convention is not yet in force.[20] Therefore, it is hard to project how it will actually operate in practice. Moreover, some of its provisions are complex—some might even say labyrinthian—and it may take some time for countries fully to understand all of the implications and be willing to join the Convention. Still, the Convention's provisions on co-operation between states should prove extremely useful in an era in which goods, services, and families move freely and easily across transnational borders.

Like the 1980 Abduction Convention and the 1993 Adoption Convention, the 1996 Protection of Children Convention provides for the establishment of a Central Authority to facilitate communication and exchanges of information between contracting states. However, the role for Central Authorities in this Convention is much more amorphous than in the other Conventions. In part, that is because the responsibilities under the 1996 Convention fall to a variety of different local authorities and institutions, and they are difficult to centralize.

Allocation and Conflicts of Jurisdiction

The primary objective of the 1996 Convention was to resolve conflicts of jurisdiction—that is, when more than one state claims authority to act with respect to a child.[21] Conflicts among states with respect to custody orders can be particularly difficult in the international context.[22] The 1996 Convention gives the authorities of the state of habitual residence jurisdiction over the child to the exclusion of the authorities of the state of nationality.[23] As explained to the Preparatory Report on this Convention, the authorities of the state of habitual residence were thought to be in the

---

[20] Five countries—Monaco, Morocco, the Netherlands, the Czech Republic, and Slovakia—have signed the Convention. See Hague Conference on Private International Law, *Status Sheet Convention #34* <http://www.hcch.net/e/status/proshte.html>.

[21] An earlier Convention, the 1961 Protection of Minors Convention, had failed to resolve conflicts of jurisdiction between the state of nationality and the state of habitual residence.

[22] These issues also arise domestically. In the United States, the UNIFORM CHILD CUSTODY JURISDICTION ACT, 9 (Part 1A) ULA 271 *et seq* (1999) ('UCCJA') and more recently its 1997 revision, the UNIFORM CHILD CUSTODY JURISDICTION AND ENFORCEMENT ACT, 9 (Part 1A) ULA 657 *et seq* (1999) ('UCCJEA') established a set of rules within the United States to allocate jurisdiction and require enforcement of judgments in custody cases. In addition, an obligation to enforce sister state custody decrees, consistent with these standards, as a matter of federal law, was implemented in the Parental Kidnapping Prevention Act, 28 USC § 1738A (1980).

[23] See Protection Convention, n 16 above, at art 5; see also Peter H. Pfund, *The Developing Jurisprudence of the Rights of the Child—Contributions of the Hague Conference on Private International Law*, 3 ILSA J INT'L & COMP L, 665, 672–4 (1997).

best position to ascertain the needs of protection for minor children.[24] The authorities in the state of habitual residence are also directed to apply their own law, although they are permitted to take into consideration the law of another state with which the situation has a substantial connection.[25]

The Convention's adoption of 'habitual residence' reinforces a key concept in private international family law.[26] However, significant problems of interpretation persist because a formal definition of 'habitual residence' has been resisted by the Hague Conference.[27] Moreover, how to deal with a change in the child's habitual residence—both when it occurs as the result of an agreed family move and when it is created by a wrongful removal or retention—were controversial issues during the drafting of the Convention; and the resolution of the issue by the Convention has left some confusion.[28]

The 1996 Convention does not ignore the potential role of authorities in the state of nationality as well as other states in the protection of children; but any exercise of jurisdiction by such authorities is in a subsidiary capacity. To that end, the 1996 Convention introduced an innovative mechanism, familiar to common law countries[29] but less well known in civil law jurisdictions—the concept of a transfer of jurisdiction. If authorities in the state of habitual residence believe that another state— either the state of nationality, the state in which property of the child is located, the state where a divorce, separation, or annulment action is being heard, or the state with which the child has a substantial connection—is in a better position to assess the best interests of the child, it may transfer jurisdiction to that other contracting state.[30] Concomitantly, authorities in any of those states are permitted to make a request to authorities in the state of habitual residence that they be permitted to

---

[24] See Adair Dyer, *Report on the Revision of the 1961 Hague Convention on Protection of Minors —Part One, Preliminary Document No. 1, in* HAGUE CONFERENCE ON PRIVATE INTERNATIONAL LAW, PROCEEDINGS OF THE EIGHTEENTH SESSION, PROTECTION OF CHILDREN 13 (1994).

[25] See Protection Convention, n 16 above, at art 15.

[26] 'Habitual residence' is also an important aspect of the 1980 Abduction Convention.

[27] In certain categories of cases the 1996 Convention provides greater direction. For 'refugee children and those children who due to disturbances in their country, are internationally displaced' the 1996 Convention equates presence in the territory with habitual residence. See Protection Convention, n 16 above, at art 6(1). For a comprehensive article on the concept of habitual residence as used in multilateral conventions, see E. M. CLIVE, THE CONCEPT OF HABITUAL RESIDENCE, 1997, PART 3 JURIDICAL REVIEW 137.

[28] See nn 38–43 below, and accompanying text.

[29] The doctrine of *forum non conveniens*—permitting a forum to refuse to exercise its jurisdiction when an alternative forum is more appropriate—is a feature of many common law countries. More particularly, the interstate allocation of child custody jurisdiction in the United States under the Uniform Child Custody Jurisdiction Act § 7 (and the revised Uniform Child Custody Jurisdiction and Enforcement Act, § 207) provides for a declination of jurisdiction if a court in another state is a more appropriate forum.

[30] See Protection Convention, n 16 above, at art 8(2).

exercise jurisdiction or to invite the parties to make such a request of the authorities in the state of habitual residence.[31]

The Convention also provides for concurrent jurisdiction in limited circumstances. In situations of urgency,[32] or when certain provisional or temporary measures of a territorial nature may be necessary,[33] the Contracting state where the child is present may act to take measures. Limitations in both provisions are designed to prevent any serious conflict of jurisdiction with the state of habitual residence. The measures taken lapse as soon as the appropriate authority of the Contracting state with jurisdiction has taken measures or recognizes measures taken by the authorities of another state.

An additional ground of concurrent jurisdiction is permitted in a contracting state that has jurisdiction over a divorce, separation, or annulment; this 'divorce' jurisdiction is subject to certain conditions,[34] including a requirement that the parents have agreed that measures of protection be taken by that court.[35] This non-exclusive basis of jurisdiction was thought necessary because of the concurrent negotiations of the Brussels II Convention (since concluded)[36] which establishes principles for jurisdiction and recognition of judgments in matrimonial matters within the European Union, and includes a 'divorce' jurisdiction.

The 1996 Convention avoids the conflicts of jurisdiction in this and other situations by adopting a mechanism in the manner of *lis pendens*. A state is directed to abstain from exercising jurisdiction if corresponding measures have been requested from authorities in another contracting state which has jurisdiction, and that request is still under consideration.[37]

The Issue of Continuing Jurisdiction and the Special Problem of Child Abduction

A frequent concern during the negotiations of the Protection Convention was the interrelationship between the 1996 Convention and the 1980 Abduction Convention; there was an overriding concern to ensure that the 1996 Convention did not in any way undermine the Abduction Convention. Although an express provision in the 1996 Convention purports

---

[31] See Protection Convention, n 16 above, at art 9.   [32] See *ibid*, at art 11.
[33] See *ibid*, at art 12.   [34] See *ibid*, at art 10.
[35] This jurisdiction is likely to be exercised in cases where the parties have agreed on the appropriate custodial arrangements for the child and where the court's function is primarily that of reviewing and approving the agreement of the parties.
[36] See Convention on Jurisdiction and Enforcement of Judgments in Matrimonial Matters (Brussels II), May 28 1998, 41 C221 Official Journal of the European Communities 10 (July 16 1998).
[37] See Protection Convention, n 16 above, at art 13.

to keep the two Conventions separate,[38] there are several points of potential friction.

A basic problem relates to the issue of the allocation of authority to take or modify measures when there has been a change of habitual residence. Even in the non-abduction context, there is a strong argument that a state that has taken protective measures should continue to exercise jurisdiction in order to ensure stability and avoid modification of measures in a second state by authorities who may lack a historical context in which to assess the dispute. Such a rule of continuing jurisdiction has been adopted in the United States for its interstate and international rules of custody jurisdiction.[39] On the other hand, in the international context, where the change of habitual residence involves a relocation to another country, often at a substantial distance from the former habitual residence, an absolute rule of 'continuing jurisdiction' may be impractical. Even a more modest continuing jurisdiction with a limited time-frame was rejected by the Convention negotiators; thus, the Convention provides that in the 'case of a change of the child's habitual residence to another contracting state, the authorities of the state of the new habitual residence have jurisdiction.'[40] Other provisions of the Convention—those requiring recognition and enforcement of measures and a *lis pendens* provision—should none the less operate to limit changes in prior measures that are under consideration or have been taken in another contracting state.[41]

Whatever the consequences of a change in habitual residence are for the normal case, a more difficult tension is created in the case of a wrongful removal or retention. In order to avoid such a wrongful removal or retention from automatically creating a basis of jurisdiction as the new state of habitual residence, the 1996 Convention establishes a special rule for such cases. Article 7 of the 1996 Convention provides that in case of wrongful removal or retention, the state with jurisdiction

---

[38] Art 50 of the Protection Convention provides that the 1996 Convention 'shall not affect the application of the [Abduction Convention], as between Parties to both Conventions.' It continues: 'Nothing, however, precludes provisions of the Convention from being invoked for the purposes of obtaining the return of a child who has been wrongfully removed or retained or of organizing access rights'. See Protection Convention, n 16 above.

[39] See UNIFORM CHILD CUSTODY JURISDICTION ACT § 14. The principle of exclusive continuing jurisdiction was made more explicit in the recently revised Uniform Child Custody Jurisdiction and Enforcement Act § 202. See Robert G. Spector, *Uniform Child-Custody Jurisdiction and Enforcement Act (with Prefatory Note and Comments)*, 32 FAM LQ 303, 339–44 (1998); Patricia M. Hoff, *The ABC's of the UCCJEA: Interstate Child-Custody Practice Under the New Act*, 32 FAM LQ 267, 308–9 (1998).

[40] See Protection Convention, n 16 above, at art 5(2).

[41] The concept of continuing jurisdiction was rejected at least in part because it was widely accepted that the new state would not act to modify an order absent a change in circumstances.

at the time of removal or retention retains jurisdiction until the child acquires a new habitual residence and *either* of two situations occurs: (1) there has been acquiescence in the removal or retention by the person possessing a right of custody *or* (2) the child has resided in the new state for at least a year after the person with a right of custody had knowledge of the whereabouts of the child, there is no request for return still pending, and the child is settled in its new environment. Article 7 attempts to mesh the 1996 Convention and provisions in the 1980 Abduction Convention, which itself does not deal with jurisdiction at all but is effectively a provisional remedy limited to the restoration of the status quo ante. Most importantly, the 1996 Convention underscores the fact that non-return of a child (under the 1980 Abduction Convention or otherwise) does not create jurisdiction in a state merely because return of the child is refused.

Unfortunately, however, the failure to provide for an exclusive continuing jurisdiction in the original habitual residence means that an abduction can mature into a basis of jurisdiction once an order refusing return has been made. If a Hague application filed in the abducted-to state for return of a child is successfully resisted on the basis of one of the Article 13 defenses—'grave risk' or the 'child's objections'—a new 'habitual residence' jurisdiction may then be found in the abducted-to state.[42] Once again, the *lis pendens* provision of Article 13 should prevent the new state of habitual residence from immediately acting if proceedings have been initiated and are not resolved in the original state of habitual residence. But even though the new state of habitual residence will have to recognize and enforce initial measures taken by the original habitual residence state under the provisions of Article 23, the new state of habitual residence will none the less have jurisdiction to modify and/or impose other measures once those proceedings have finished.

The Issue of Applicable Law

The 1996 Convention addresses issues of applicable law, but for the most part the formal choice of law rules should not be very important in the

---

[42] No petition for return would be pending, and the other conditions of art 7—the elapse of the one-year period and the child's acclimatization in the new environment—would most likely be satisfied given the length of return proceedings. However, an alternative interpretation of the language in art 7 could prevent a change of habitual residence in some situations. The condition that no request for return still be pending could be understood as including a request for return of the child in the original state of habitual residence. If such an application for return is made in the abducted-from state of habitual residence and is not dismissed until the child is returned, the formal conditions of art 7(1)(b) would not be met; and jurisdiction could not be assumed by the new state of habitual residence to which the child had been removed.

operation of this Convention.[43] One provision, however, is worth mentioning, and that is the rule on the attribution/extinction of parental responsibility through operation of law. The imposition of parental responsibility continues under the Convention if it is authorized by an original state of habitual residence of the child; a move to a new habitual residence does not alter such responsibilities. The primary focus of this provision was to continue in effect the attribution of parental rights of unmarried fathers. In addition, a new habitual residence state can accord additional rights of parental responsibility by operation of law when the new residence is more 'generous' than that of the original habitual residence. Such expanded obligations of parental responsibility are not extinguished by a later change of residence of the child, even if the child moves back to the original state which did not accord such rights. In this instance, stability (at least in a certain direction) gives way to a substantive judgment in favor of equal parental rights. However, several limitations mitigate the potentially harsh effect of attributing rights of parental responsibility when they did not exist initially. The authorities in the child's current habitual residence can apply their own laws to 'the *exercise*' of parental responsibility,[44] and may if necessary take measures under their own laws to modify or terminate parental responsibility which has arisen by operation of law or by agreement.[45]

Recognition and Enforcement of Measures

Measures taken consistent with the jurisdiction provisions of the 1996 Convention are entitled to recognition under the Convention.[46] The primary exception[47] is the familiar one of public policy, but it can be invoked only where recognition would be 'manifestly contrary to public policy, taking into account the best interests of the child'.[48] A more controversial provision, reflecting the influence of the United Nations Convention on the Rights of the Child, permits recognition to be refused where measures of protection (except in the case of urgency) have been taken 'without the child being given an opportunity to be heard, in violation of fundamental principles of procedure of the requested state.'[49] The exception could

---

[43] The choice of law rules are found in arts 15 through 22 of the Convention. The provisions are all subject to art 22, which provides that 'the application of the law designated by the provisions of this Chapter can be refused only if this application would be manifestly contrary to public policy, taking into account the best interests of the child.' For a more extensive discussion of these provisions, see Linda Silberman, Festschrift, n 17 above.

[44] Protection Convention, n 16 above, at art 17.   [45] See *ibid*, at art 18.

[46] See *ibid*, at art 23 (1)(2)(a).

[47] The exceptions are set forth in arts 23(2)(a through f).

[48] See Protection Convention, n 16 above, at art 23(2)(d).

[49] *ibid*, at art 23(2)(b).

prove to be an expansive one because the procedures of many countries do not provide for an across-the-board right of a child to be heard in proceedings; often the right to be heard is contingent on context as well as the age of the child. However, any attempt to construe the 1996 Convention to impose uniformity of procedural practice on state parties to the Convention would be inconsistent with the drafters' understanding of this provision; the Lagarde Explanatory Report accompanying the Treaty disavows any such intent and emphasizes a narrower scope for the exception.[50]

Another important feature of the 1996 Convention is the mechanism for having measures taken in one contracting state enforced in another.[51] However, because of the wide divergence in the protective measures that may be applied in different countries and the difficulty in giving effect to measures for which there is no equivalent in domestic law, the Convention adds a proviso that enforcement shall take place 'in accordance with the law of the requested state to the extent provided by such law, taking into consideration the best interests of the child.'[52] Although intended only to accommodate the law of the requested state, such language could be construed to superimpose a 'best interests' test at the enforcement stage. No such broad review was contemplated, although the flexibility sought to be maintained in permitting internal law to control could none the less interfere with effective enforcement under the Convention.[53]

Co-operation and Mutual Assistance

The Special Problem of Access Rights

One specific article on co-operation addresses the particular problem of access (visitation) rights in a custody dispute.[54] The 1980 Abduction Convention, which contains a provision requiring a state to assist in organizing access to the child but establishes no specific procedures,[55] has been disappointing as a means of ensuring and enforcing access rights. The 1996 Protection Convention has tried to fill that gap by authorizing a parent residing in a state other than that of the child's habitual residence to request that state to gather information and evidence and to make a preliminary ruling on the suitability of that parent to exercise access and the

---

[50] See Paul Lagarde, *Explanatory Report*, in HAGUE CONFERENCE ON PRIVATE INTERNATIONAL LAW, PROCEEDINGS OF THE EIGHTEENTH SESSION, PROTECTION OF CHILDREN 538 (1996) at para 123 at 585 [hereinafter Lagarde Report].
[51] See Protection Convention, n 16 above, at art 26.   [52] *ibid*, at art 28.
[53] For examples, see Lagarde Report, n 50 above, at para 134 at 589.
[54] See Protection Convention, n 16 above, at art 35(2)(3)(4).
[55] See 1980 Abduction Convention, n 2 above, at art 21.

conditions appropriate to the exercise of that access. That preliminary ruling can be transmitted to the authorities exercising jurisdiction over a dispute on access (usually a court in the state of the child's habitual
residence), who must admit and consider that information before reaching any decision. This approach allows a non-custodial parent, living in a
different country from the child, to establish fitness for access in a place
where much of the relevant evidence is likely to be located; and at the
same time, it keeps authority for the final determination in the state of
habitual residence, where the child and parent are living.

Other Provisions on Co-operation

The obligations with respect to co-operation and mutual assistance are
designed to fit with the various mechanisms in the 1996 Convention. As
noted earlier, the role for the Central Authorities is primarily one of
superintendence and channeling of information on the laws and child
protection services in their respective states. The Convention envisions
the exchange of information between the courts or child protection agencies involved in a particular case as well as the aid of non-governmental
organizations in offering co-operative help in a more general fashion.[56]
Among the areas of co-operation mentioned in the Convention are assistance in locating a missing child,[57] notification that a child in serious danger is in another state,[58] facilitation through mediation or other means of
possible solutions to disputes,[59] and consultation when authorities in one
state take steps to place a child in care in another state.[60] In certain situations, such as possible transfers of jurisdiction between contracting states
or in cases of urgency, direct communication between the authorities in
the contracting states is authorized,[61] including the furnishing of reports
and other information.[62]

Final Observations

The 1996 Convention on the Protection of Children is an ambitious effort
to foster co-operation between public authorities with respect to measures of protection and to have these measures recognized, as well as to
provide a formal system of jurisdiction and enforcement of judgments for
private law disputes concerning children. Whether uniform principles of
jurisdiction can serve such a wide range of jurisdictional authority
remains to be seen. The detail and complexity of the Convention could

---

[56] There was a concern that a Convention provision that imposed heavy burdens or costs
on the Central Authority would be unacceptable to many countries.
[57] See Protection Convention, n 16 above, at art 31(c).   [58] See *ibid*, at art 36.
[59] See *ibid*, at art 31(b).   [60] See *ibid*, at art 33.   [61] See *ibid*, at art 31(a).
[62] See *ibid*, at arts 32, 33, 34, 36.

present difficult issues of interpretation, and the possibility of its interference with the Abduction Convention may dampen enthusiasm for its
ratification. None the less, it symbolizes an important international effort
in achieving co-operation among the countries of the world to better protect the interests of children everywhere, and, it is hoped will be widely
adopted and used to that end.[63]

THE HAGUE CONVENTION ON PROTECTION OF CHILDREN AND CO-OPERATION IN RESPECT OF INTERCOUNTRY ADOPTION

Background

The Hague Convention on Intercountry Adoption addresses another
important aspect of the law relating to children.[64] General concerns as
well as a series of specific incidents about the trafficking of children and
illegal buying of babies lie behind this Convention. Perhaps nothing crys-
tallized the issue more than the Baby-Bazaar in Romania after the fall of
the Ceausescu regime in 1989. Many individuals in the US and other
countries were affected by the reports of children living in wretched conditions in Romanian orphanages and moved to adopt these children.
Apparently, however, not all of the children adopted came from the
orphanages, and, to some extent lack of controls led to a situation in
which some prospective adoptive parents, or their representatives,
walked the streets of Romania offering cash and other inducements to
parents in exchange for their babies. The Adoption Convention, by establishing certain minimum safeguards and promoting co-operation and
communication between countries, is designed to expose and eliminate
such abuses.

---

[63] For additional commentary on the 1996 Convention, see Andreas Bucher, *La Dix-
huitième Session de la Conférence de la Haye de droit international privé (the Eighteenth Session of
the Hague Conference on Private International Law)*, SWISS REVIEW OF INTERNATIONAL AND EURO-
PEAN LAW, Vol 7 No 1 (1997) at 67; KURT SIEHR, DIE RECHTSLAGE DER MINDERJÄHRIGEN IM INTER-
NATIONALEN RECHT UND DIE ENTWICKLUNG IN DIESEM BEREICH: ZUR REVISION DES HAAGER
MINDERJÄHRIGENSCHUTZABKOMMENS', ZEITSCHRIFT FÜR DAS GESAMTE FAMILIENRECHT, Vol 43, No 17
(1996) at 1047.

[64] See 1993 International Co-operation and Protection of Children in Respect of Intercountry Adoption, May 29 1993, 32 ILM 1134 (1993) [hereinafter Adoption Convention]. For
a discussion of events leading to the desire for an international convention, see J. H. A. Van
Loon, *International Co-operation and Protection of Children with Regard to Intercountry Adoption*,
244 RECUEIL DES COURS 203, 233 (1993).

But regulation is only one aspect of the intercountry adoption picture. The other side of the adoption crisis is the tragic condition of unwanted children and the failure of any system to handle adoptions in a way that facilitates their placement. While critics of intercountry adoption view transnational and transracial placement of children as forms of imperialism and genocide, others argue that intercountry adoption offers the only viable opportunity for many of these children.[65]

Without formal mechanisms of co-operation in place, intercountry adoption was plagued by an overly cumbersome process, in which prospective adoptive parents, as well as biological parents wishing to give up a child, were forced to undergo a series of duplicative, and sometimes conflicting determinations and processes. By allocating responsibilities between the 'sending' state and the 'receiving' states and instituting formal mechanisms for co-operation, the Adoption Convention seeks to avoid duplication and conflict.

The Structure of the Adoption Convention

Basic Premises

One important premiss of the Adoption Convention is its favorable view of intercountry adoption. Consistent with the UN Convention on the Rights of the Child 'subsidiarity principle' of intercountry adoption,[66] the Preamble to the Adoption Convention states that as a matter of first priority each state should take appropriate measures to ensure that a child remains in the care of his or her family of origin. However, the Convention deviates from the UN Convention's second priority of preferring that a child remain in the country of origin—even in institutionalized care—and provides that 'intercountry adoption may offer the advantage of a permanent family to a child for whom a suitable family cannot be found in the state of origin.'[67]

---

[65] See Anthony D'Amato, *Cross-Country Adoption: A Call to Action*, 73 Notre Dame L Rev 1239 (1998); Elizabeth Bartholet, *International Adoption: Propriety, Prospect and Pragmatics*, 13 J Am Acad Matrim L 181 (1996).

[66] United Nations Convention on the Rights of the Child, Nov 20 1989, 28 ILM 1448 (1989), corrections at 29 ILM 1340 (1990) [hereinafter UN Convention]. Art 21 of the UN Convention states that 'intercountry adoption may be considered as an alternative means of a child's care, if the child cannot be placed in a foster or an adoptive family or cannot *in any suitable manner* be cared for in the child's country of origin'.

[67] The Parra-Aranguren Explanatory Report to the Convention makes this clear: 'the placement of a child in a family, including in intercountry adoption, is the best option among all forms of alternative care, in particular to be preferred over institutionalization'. See Gonzalo Parra-Aranguren, *Explanatory Report*, in Hague Conference on Private International Law, Proceedings of the Seventeenth Session, Adoption—Co-operation 543 at para 46 at 553 (1993) [hereinafter Parra-Aranguren Report].

The goals of the Adoption Convention are set forth in its first article: (1) providing a system of co-operation among contracting states, thereby deterring the abduction, sale of, and trafficking in children; (2) establishing minimum safeguards to ensure that an intercountry adoption is in the best interests of the child; and (3) securing the recognition of adoptions made in accordance with the Convention.

The Convention applies whenever a child habitually resident in one contracting state (the state of origin) has been, is being, or is to be moved to another contracting state (the 'receiving' state) either after adoption in the state of origin or for the purpose of such an adoption in the receiving state or in the state of origin.[68] The Convention thus applies regardless of whether the adoption takes place in the state of origin or the receiving state,[69] and, in fact, regardless of whether the adoption takes place at all; the Convention does not apply, however, unless the prospective adoptive parent(s) and the child are habitually resident in different contracting states.

The Adoption Convention applies not only to 'full adoptions' but also to 'simple adoptions', ie adoptions in which the pre-existing legal relationship between the child and family of origin is not completely severed. Given the widespread use of 'simple' adoptions in some countries, it was thought desirable to extend the Convention in this way.[70]

Allocation of Functions

The Convention avoids many of the conflict of laws and jurisdiction problems that have plagued intercountry adoption by allocating responsibilities between 'sending' and 'receiving' states. But rather than adopting a formal conflict of laws approach to adoption as a whole, the Convention subdivides the adoption decision into discrete determinations and then allocates authority for certain issues between the two states. The Convention then gives each state a 'veto power' in Article 17(c),[71] thus requiring both states to co-operate in and ultimately take joint responsibility for the adoption decision as a whole, regardless of where the final adoption takes place. Article 17(c) thus becomes the linchpin of the Convention.

---

[68] See Adoption Convention, n 64 above, at art 2.

[69] The Convention does not specify where the adoption is to take place; however, the state of origin can require that the adoption of a child habitually resident in that state take place in that state. See Adoption Convention, n 64 above, at art 28.

[70] However, other foster and guardian relationships that do not create a permanent parent–child relationship—such as the Islamic kafala—are not covered by the Convention. Art 2(2) of the Convention is explicit: 'The Convention covers only adoptions which create a permanent parent–child relationship.'

[71] Under art 17(c), a child can be entrusted to prospective adopting parents only if the Central Authorities of both states have agreed that the adoption may proceed.

Article 4 of the Convention is directed to the primary responsibilities undertaken by the state of origin. Before an adoption can be granted in any contracting state, the 'competent authorities'[72] in the state of origin must determine that the child is adoptable; that an intercountry adoption is within the child's best interests, after possibilities for placement of the child within the state of origin have been given 'due consideration'; and that the relevant consents, including the child's if required, have been granted. The state of origin thus controls the issue of adoptability,[73] although the receiving state will have a veto over that determination before any adoption may proceed.

Apart from allocating functions, the Convention also establishes minimum conditions that must be met[74] in each state regardless of where the adoption takes place. One example of how the Convention imposes such standards is in the area of consents surrounding adoption. The applicable law in the state of origin will determine who must consent to an adoption, but the Convention provides that those persons are to be counseled and must be informed of the effects of their consents. The Convention also requires that the consent be given 'freely, in the required legal form, and expressed or evidenced in writing.'[75]

Article 5 of the Convention addresses the responsibilities of the receiving state in regard to the adopting parents; once again, the Convention mandates certain minimum conditions that must be met, this time with respect to the qualifications of the adoptive parents. The receiving state determines, in accordance with its law, the eligibility and suitability of the adoptive parents; it also must ensure the adoptive parents have been counseled; and that the child is or will be authorized to enter and reside permanently in the state. While the receiving state will have primary responsibility for determining the eligibility of the adoptive parents, the sending state may withhold its agreement for the adoption under Article 17(c).

---

[72] The Convention leaves the term 'competent authorities' undefined. The Parra-Aranguren Report specifies that the contracting state is at liberty to determine which are the competent authorities, 'either administrative, judicial, or even the Central Authority.' Parra-Aranguren Report, n 67 above, at para 176 at 575. In most states, it is likely that the judiciary will serve this role. See J. H. A. Van Loon, n 64 above, at 340.

[73] Typically, states will use their own law in making the determination, but the Convention does not specify the applicable law.

[74] It should be stressed that any of the minimum standards established in the Convention are just that, 'minimum' standards. The contracting states are fully entitled to adopt more exacting standards. See Parra-Aranguren Report, n 64 above, at para 108 at 565.

[75] In the hope of creating a uniform application of the consent requirement under art 4(c), a model form for these consents was developed by a Special Commission convened in 1994. The model form is recommended, but not required.

The Role of Central Authorities and Other Bodies

A system of co-operation is established through the mechanism of a Central Authority;[76] many of the responsibilities of the Central Authority can be performed by public authorities or accredited bodies.[77] The 'accredited bodies' will normally be approved adoption agencies, which must under the Convention be non-profit agencies.[78] The duties performed by public authorities and accredited bodies will include carrying out the duties with respect to a particular adoption, such as determining that the child is adoptable, that consents have been properly given and executed, and that the adoptive parents are eligible and suited to adopt and have been counseled as necessary.[79]

Whether other persons, such as lawyers or for-profit agencies, could also perform functions under a Convention regime was an issue of some controversy during the negotiation of the Convention. To deny such a role for such intermediaries would, of course, have prohibited independent adoptions. Independent adoptions are adoptions in which persons or groups—other than accredited agencies—act as intermediaries for the placement of the child; or where the prospective adoptive parents act directly on their own behalf. In the United States, independent adoptions have long been a common practice in order to avoid the bureaucracy of adopting through accredited adoption agencies.[80] Many countries,

[76] Central Authorities are directed to co-operate with other Central Authorities and to take all appropriate measures to provide information on their adoption laws and other information and to keep other Central Authorities informed about the operation of the Convention. See Adoption Convention, n 64 above, at art 7. Under the proposed United States implementing legislation, the Department of State would function as the Central Authority. See Intercountry Adoption Act of 2000, H.R. 2909, 106th Cong (2000). The legislation passed in both Houses of Congress and is awaiting signature by the President.

[77] Art 22(1) of the Adoption Convention provides that the functions of a Central Authority in carrying out the obligations of the Convention may be performed by public authorities or by accredited bodies, to the extent permitted by the law of its state.

[78] Art 11 of the Adoption Convention establishes certain requirements for an 'accredited body'. It shall (a) pursue only non-profit objectives; (b) be directed and staffed by personnel qualified in the field of intercountry adoption; and (c) be subject to supervision by competent authorities of the state as to its composition, operation, and financial situation.

[79] In addition, art 9 provides that Central Authorities shall take measures, directly or through public authorities or other accredited bodies, to (1) collect and exchange of information about the situation of the child and the prospective adoptive parents in order to complete the adoption, (2) facilitate and expedite proceedings, (3) promote the development of adoption counseling and post-adoptive services, (4) provide and exchange evaluation reports about the experience with intercountry adoption, and (5) reply in so far as permitted under national law to requests with respect to a particular adoption situation.

[80] For the debate about the merits of independent adoptions versus agency adoptions, compare L. Jean Emery, *Agency Versus Independent Adoption: The Case for Agency Adoption*, 3 FUTURE OF CHILDREN 139 (1993), with Mark T. McDermott, *Agency Versus Independent Adoption: The Case for Independent Adoption*, 3 FUTURE OF CHILDREN 146 (1993).

perceiving abuse in independent adoptions, objected to including them within the scope of the Convention; but other countries, including the United States, insisted that a failure to permit independent adoptions would jeopardize ratification in their states.[81]

A compromise was reached, permitting non-accredited bodies or persons to perform some of the functions of Central Authorities under certain conditions.[82] The non-accredited body or person must be authorized by the state to perform the relevant functions and must be supervised by competent authorities in that state. Moreover, the contracting state must declare its intention to authorize independent adoptions when it deposits its instrument of ratification; however, any other contracting state has the option of declaring that it will not accept independent adoptions with respect to any child habitually resident within its territory.

A related issue was the extent of contact the prospective adoptive parents should have with the child and the biological parents prior to the adoption. Contact between the prospective adoptive parents and the child's parents is allowed at any time if the adoption takes place within the family, or if the contact is in compliance with the conditions established by the competent authority in the state of origin.[83]

Proceeding with an Intercountry Adoption Under the Convention

It may be useful to consider how an intercountry adoption would proceed under the Convention. A person wishing to adopt goes to the appropriate authority in the state of habitual residence. That 'authority', which in the United States is likely to be an accredited adoption agency, will determine the eligibility and suitability of the applicant and provide information about the applicant for a report which will be issued and transmitted to the relevant authority in the state which has a child available for adoption. Authorities in the 'sending' state prepare a report on any child who may benefit from an intercountry adoption, even if there is no particular request for the child.

Once a 'sending' country receives the report on an applicant wishing to adopt, it makes a preliminary determination that a particular placement is in the best interests of the adoptable child, giving due consideration to the child's ethnic, religious, and cultural background.[84] It then transmits to the receiving state the report on the child as well as proof that the necessary consents have been obtained, and the reasons for its determination that the envisaged placement is in the child's best interests. In some states

---

[81] See William Duncan, *The Hague Convention on the Protection of Children and Co-operation in Respect of Intercountry Adoption 1993*, in Eleizer D. Jaffe (ed), INTERCOUNTRY ADOPTIONS: LAWS AND PERSPECTIVES OF SENDING COUNTRIES 217, 225 (1995).

[82] See Adoption Convention, n 64, at art 22(2).   [83] See *ibid*, at art 29.

[84] See *ibid*, at art 16(1).

of origin, the identity of the mother (and possibly the father) are not to be disclosed, and thus care must be taken not to reveal those identities.[85]

The final steps in the adoption process involve the 'entrustment'[86] of the child to the prospective adoptive parents and the transfer of the child to the receiving state. Article 17 of the Convention places primary responsibility on the state of origin for the entrustment decision; it is the state of origin that must ensure that the adopting parent agrees to the placement. No approval of the placement by the receiving state is necessary, unless either the receiving or sending state imposes such a requirement.[87] However, authorities in both the sending and receiving states must agree that the adoption may proceed.[88] Thus, any decision to go ahead with the adoption is made jointly, and either state is fully empowered—indeed obligated—to stop an adoption from going forward and withhold approval of the adoption if it appears that there is a legal bar to the adoption or its recognition in either state. Finally, the state of origin must verify that the prospective adoptive parents are eligible and suitable to adopt and that the child is or will be authorized to enter and reside permanently in the receiving state.[89]

Both states involved in the intercountry adoption are required to 'take all necessary steps to obtain permission for the child to leave the state of origin and to enter and reside permanently in the receiving state'.[90] Transfer of a child is authorized once all conditions have been satisfied; there is a preference to have the transfer take place in the company of the adoptive or prospective adoptive parents.[91]

The issue of whether there should be a probationary period prior to adoption was again resolved by a Convention compromise. A receiving state may require that a child serve a post-placement probationary period with the prospective adoptive parents before a final adoption order is issued;[92] but the state of origin can avoid such a probationary period by

---

[85] See Adoption Convention at art 16(2).

[86] The Convention uses the term 'entrust' rather than 'place' because the latter term is ambiguous in French. In English the basic meanings are seen as interchangeable. Entrustment simply means that the child is physically placed with the (prospective) adoptive parents. See Van Loon, n 64 above, at 361 n 383.

[87] This condition represents a compromise, in that some receiving states, particularly the United States, prefer to remain uninvolved in a placement decision if the adoption order is to be effectuated in the state of origin. Other states, however, believed that both states should be involved in the matching process. See Parra-Aranguren Report, n 67 above, at paras 332–5 at 601.

[88] The decision that the adoption may proceed is viewed as more significant than the decision to entrust or transfer the child; note, however, that approval of the final grant of the adoption is not required. See Parra-Aranguren Report, n 67 above, at para 335 at 601.

[89] See Adoption Convention, n 64, above at art 17 (d). These determinations are to be made by the receiving state; the state of origin need only verify that they have been made.

[90] Adoption Convention, n 64 above, at art 18.   [91] See *ibid*, at art 19.

[92] See *ibid*, at art 20.

insisting that an adoption order be granted prior to the placement or transfer of a child habitually resident in that state.[93]

The final order of adoption can be made in either the sending or the receiving state. An adoption certified as having been made in accordance with the Convention must be recognized not only by the sending and receiving states but also by all other contracting states.[94] Recognition may be withheld only if the adoption is 'manifestly contrary to [its] public policy', taking into account the best interests of the child.[95] Of course, since both the receiving and sending states had the opportunity under Article 17(c) of the Convention to withhold agreement for the adoption to proceed prior to the formal adoption, neither state is likely to invoke the exception.[96] As to other contracting states, the Parra-Aranguren Report specifies that the public policy provision is to be read restrictively.[97]

Under the Convention, all adoptions result in the establishment of a permanent parent–child relationship between the child and the adoptive parents, with the adoptive parents assuming parental responsibility for the child.[98] The status of the child with respect to pre-adoption parental relationships depends upon the effect of the adoption in the state where the adoption took place.[99] For example, if the state of origin grants a full adoption—which terminates any pre-existing legal parent–child relationship—the receiving state must give the same effect to the adoption.[100] However, in the situation where the state of origin grants only a simple adoption—an adoption which does not involve a complete severing of the legal ties between the adopted child and the birth family—the Convention permits the receiving state to convert the simple adoption into a full adoption if the law of the receiving state so permits and if the consents to the adoption were not limited.[101] Thus, the receiving state does not have to obtain permission from the state of origin to convert the adoption; but the state of origin can withhold its agreement for the

---

[93] See *ibid*, at art 28.   [94] See *ibid*, at art 23.   [95] *ibid*, at art 24.

[96] Since both states are given the opportunity to object at an early stage in the process and indeed both must affirmatively agree to proceed with the adoption prior to the grant of any adoption, there should be little room for either state to object once the adoption has been effected. See Van Loon, n 64 above, at 366.

[97] The Parra-Aranguren Report specifically states that a contracting state may not refuse recognition of a particular adoption solely because it does not recognize the institution of adoption, or a particular form of adoption in general. See Parra-Aranguren Report, n 67 above, at para 428 at 617.

[98] See Adoption Convention, n 64 above, at art 26.   [99] See *ibid*, at art 26(1)(c).

[100] Of course, the receiving state could have refused to proceed with the adoption under Article 17(c) if it disapproved of this eventual result.

[101] See Adoption Convention, n 64 above, at art 27. The situation is more problematic when it is the receiving state which issues the adoption order. In those circumstances, a full adoption may be granted in the receiving state even though the consents obtained under art 4 in the state of origin were only for a simple adoption. Once again, however, the state of origin could invoke art 17(c) to prevent the adoption.

adoption to proceed under Article 17(c) if it wishes to prevent the conversion of a simple adoption into a full adoption.

The Convention leaves rules on confidentiality up to individual contracting states. It does require the preservation of information concerning the child's origin and in particular, the identity of the child's parents.[102] However, access to that information is governed by the law of that state.[103]

Enforcement issues are also within the province of individual states. The Convention requires only that competent authorities report any provision of the Convention that has not been respected, and that Central Authorities ensure that appropriate measures are taken.[104] Party states, including the United States, are likely to impose some type of penalty on parties in violation of the Convention—suspension or revocation of accreditation, civil fines, and possibly imprisonment.[105]

Final Observations on the Adoption Convention

The Adoption Convention has been praised for raising the standards for intercountry adoptions and yet avoiding many difficult conflict of laws issues that in the past have complicated intercountry adoptions. At the same time, the Convention has not actually provided much of a solution to those conflicts; indeed, it may simply have ignored the conflicts in the hope that they would go away. The Convention allocates primary responsibility over certain determinations to each state, but it does not confer exclusive responsibility. A contracting state which does not have primary responsibility over a particular issue may none the less revisit a determination by the other state, and if it disapproves of the determination made by the state with primary responsibility, it may withhold agreement to proceed with the adoption under Article 17(c). In attempting to put everything back together again, Article 17(c) provides a way for either a receiving or sending state to prevent an intercountry adoption if it disapproves of one of the conditions imposed by the other state, eg age or consent requirements, revocability, probationary periods, etc, or if it disapproves of one of the effects to be granted to the adoption by the other state, eg, simple versus full adoption. Rather than eliminating duplicative processes in the respective states, the Convention may have

---

[102] See Adoption Convention, n 64 above, at art 30(1).

[103] See *ibid*, at art 30(2). The access to information issue will often be addressed in implementing legislation. In the United States, the issue also has federalism implications since access issues are generally governed by individual state law. For example, the Uniform Adoption Act contains a general provision in favor of sealed records. See UNIFORM ADOPTION ACT (1994) § 6–102, 9 (Part 1A) ULA 6, 119 (1999).

[104] See Adoption Convention, n 64 above, at art 33.

[105] Such penalties are included as part of the US implementing legislation. See Intercountry Adoption Act 2000, 106th Cong (2000). HR 2909 (§ 404).

substituted a *de facto* cumulative rule: adoptions will only take place between two states if the more restrictive standard is satisfied. The end result could be fewer intercountry adoptions.

A more optimistic view of the Convention envisions a co-operative system whereby a contracting state defers to the judgment of another contracting state with primary responsibility. The imposition of minimum safeguards in the Convention itself may encourage contracting states to trust the determinations made in other contracting states.[106]

In the end, the Convention is very much a 'framework document'.[107] Perhaps more than the other Hague 'Children' Conventions, it represents an accommodation of differing legal traditions and perspectives by finding areas of compromise between 'sending' and 'receiving' countries. It is also unusual in that it imposes basic fundamental uniform principles relating to intercountry adoption. At the same time, the Adoption Convention leaves significant autonomy to regulate intercountry adoptions in the respective contracting states through implementing legislation. But the success of this Convention will ultimately rest on co-operation between the respective states in working through intercountry adoptions.[108]

THE GLOBALIZATION OF CHILD LAW: A CODA

Together, the three Hague 'Children's Conventions' signify an internationalization of 'child law' through the development of international

---

[106] Many of the problems that have plagued intercountry adoptions pertain to the failure of the country of origin to assure that proper consents have been obtained from the biological parents. See eg *Hao Thi Popp v Lucas*, 182 Conn 545, 438 A2d 755 (1980)(requiring return of child to biological mother because consents were issued under duress as part of 'operation baby lift'). With minimum standards for consent in place, such situations may be avoided. Unfortunately, however, many states of origin still lack sufficient resources to assure that the standards will be met. See William Duncan, *Regulating Intercountry Adoption—An International Perspective*, in Andrew Bainham and David S. Pearl (eds), FRONTIERS OF FAMILY LAW, 46, 60 (1993).

[107] See William Duncan, the Hague Intercountry Adoption Convention, talk delivered at International Family Law Conference, London, Feb 5 1998 at p 5 [on file with the author].

[108] The Adoption Convention has had an extremely favorable reception. As of August 2000, forty states had ratified or acceded to the Adoption Convention. The United States signed the Adoption Convention in 1994, but has not yet ratified. States that were members of the Hague Conference at the time the Convention was adopted and other states that participated in the session are eligible to ratify; other states may accede. The following states have ratified the Convention: Australia, Austria, Brazil, Burkina Faso, Canada, Chile, Colombia, Costa Rica, Cyprus, Czech Republic, Denmark, Ecuador, El Salvador, Finland, France, Israel, Italy, Mexico, Netherlands, Norway, Panama, Peru, Philippines, Poland, Romania, Spain, Sri Lanka, Sweden, and Venezuela. These states have acceded: Andorra, Burundi, Georgia, Iceland, Lithuania, Mauritius, Moldova, Monaco, Mongolia, New Zealand, and Paraguay. See Hague Conference on Private International Law, *Status Sheet Convention #33* <http: //www.hcch.net/e/status/adoshte.html>.

norms to resolve child-centered disputes.[109] While the UN Convention on the Rights of the Child represents a major international legal reference point for the protection of children's rights,[110] the Hague Conventions put the aspirational goals of that Convention into operation. A number of international norms emerge from the Hague treaties. They include (1) the allocation of primary decision-making authority with respect to children to the state of the child's habitual residence; (2) the acceptance of broad protective measures that may be taken with respect to children; (3) a commitment to deter and remedy international child abduction and the introduction of an innovative remedy of return of the child; (4) a preference for a child to have a permanent family even if that family is not in the state of origin and a concomitant effort to effectuate intercountry adoptions according to sound and ethical adoption practices; and (5) the recognition of the importance of mutual assistance and co-operation by states in order to protect children on a worldwide scale.

The Hague Conference on Private International Law has played an important role not only in creating the Hague Conventions but also in superintending their development. Each of the Conventions was negotiated in the context of extensive background reports developed by the Permanent Bureau of the Hague Conference, and each was accompanied by a thorough Explanatory Report, prepared by the Rapporteur for the relevant Special Commission. The Explanatory Reports are particularly important because there is no supranational institution to provide authoritative answers to interpretive questions that arise under the Convention, as for example, the European Court of Justice does for issues arising under the Brussels Convention. Thus, interpretation of the Convention occurs through national law by national courts as understood within a particular tradition and culture. But the Conventions have strived to create autonomous terms, such as 'habitual residence', 'custody rights', 'protective measures', and 'accredited bodies', and the concepts are now reflected as international law. In addition, the text of the treaties and the Explanatory Reports expresses guidelines for interpretation by emphasizing each of the Conventions' objectives and the need to render decision compatible with those objectives. Uniformity of interpretation will be difficult, and experience with the Abduction Convention demonstrates the kind of problems that lie ahead. With these concerns in mind, the Hague Conference has exercised a stewardship role with respect to the Conventions and has convened a number of Special Commissions concerning the oversight of those Children's Conventions in force as a

---

[109] See Dyer, n 1 above, at 625.
[110] See Marilia Sardenberg, *Comments on the Globalization of Child Law*, in GLOBALIZATION OF CHILD LAW, n 27 above, at 17.

means of sharing collective knowledge and experiences. As we enter into the next millennium, the Hague Children's Conventions are likely to become even more important as a means for resolving transnational disputes concerning children; and the Hague Conference will need to assume an even more significant role to ensure that the Conventions continue to function effectively.

E
Epilogues

28
Individual Rights and Family Relationships

SANFORD N. KATZ

INTRODUCTION

The family law issues that dominated the last half of the twentieth century in the United States and which the American contributors discuss,
paralleled those in Britain, although some have predated the British experience by several years. In a way, the United States may have been the
experimental laboratory for Britain. During the past forty years, laws regulating family relationships have changed, sometimes dramatically. The
evidence is strong that in some areas family law is in a period of transition; in others it has been virtually transformed.

It is curious that in American culture and indeed in the law, itself, 'the
family' is referred to as 'essential to the evolution and growth of a viable
society . . . [as well as] one of the basic processes for the control of human
behavior.'[1] Consequently, the state endows it with a great deal of power.
The impression is that it is a legally recognized institution, like a corporation or a labor union, which can sue and be sued. In fact, the family as such
does not have a separate legal identity. Rather, it is the individual's relationship with other family members, like a husband's relationship with his
wife, and a parent's relationship with his or her child, and so on, which the
law recognizes and regulates, and with which family law is concerned.

To me the most important event that has occurred in family law that has
affected family relationships in the last fifty years, and a theme that runs
through many of the chapters in this book, is the recognition and protection of individual rights. Professor Barron, discussing adults, and Professor Woodhouse, discussing children, have shown how the emphasis on
individual rights in the family developed within a constitutional framework through a series of United States Supreme Court cases during the
last half of the twentieth century.

At first blush, the focus on individual rights may seem to diminish family relationships, perhaps even pitting one family member against
another. Professor Milton Regan has described its effect on the marriage
relationship as defining it as being 'alone together.'[2] Treating marriage
simply as an association of two individuals who are together, but who

---

[1] JOSEPH GOLDSTEIN and JAY KATZ, THE FAMILY AND THE LAW 1 (1965).
[2] See MILTON C. REGAN, JR, ALONE TOGETHER: LAW AND THE MEANINGS OF MARRIAGE (1999).

maintain their individual persona and legal identity,[3] certainly can lead to a relationship that Professor Mary Ann Glendon has characterized as one of 'alienation, powerlessness, and dependency.'[4] However, there is another way of looking at individual rights in marriage. That is, that the individual not only is concerned with his or her own rights, which have received constitutional protection, but is also respectful and supportive of the individual rights of his or her spouse. As the concept of individual rights becomes firmly established in the American culture, family behavior patterns are certain to change. By viewing individual rights in marriage in terms of mutual respect, the sense of community, so forcefully argued for by Professor Glendon, need not be destroyed.[5] In fact, it may be strengthened.

What is the future of marriage? Will it continue to be the centerpiece for creating a family? Have the definitions that emphasize individual rights minimized marriage? Has it become easier to establish relationships like marriage or substitutes for it? In the new century, will marriage be just another kind of adult relationship, differing from others because of its religious significance and its formal requirements? These are questions that will be asked in the decades to come, and for which I have no immediate answers. However, I have chosen to conclude this book by discussing some of the implications of the emphasis on individual rights on family relationships, especially the marriage relationship. I believe this emphasis on individual rights is a positive development, leading to a new concept of the marriage relationship.

MARRIAGE AS PARTNERSHIP

'Marriage,' wrote Justice Field in the 1888 case of *Maynard v Hill*,[6] 'as creating the most important relation in life, as having more to do with the morals and civilization of a people than any other institution, has always been subject to the control of the legislature.'[7] If Justice Field's statement

---

[3] In describing the marital relation in *Eisenstadt v Baird*, 405 US 438 (1972), Justice Brennan wrote: 'The marital couple is not an independent entity with a mind and heart of its own, but an association of two individuals each with a separate intellectual and emotional make-up.' *ibid* at 453.

[4] 'Despite the rhetoric of partnership and community, concrete legal changes . . . [in marriage and informal unions] have moved in the direction of emphasis on the separate and equal individuality of the family members—most decisively in the United States. . . . Stamped on the reverse side of the coinage of individual liberty, family privacy, and sex equality are alienation, powerlessness, and dependency.' MARY ANN GLENDON, THE TRANSFORMATION OF FAMILY LAW: STATE, LAW AND FAMILY IN THE UNITED STATES AND WESTERN EUROPE 147 (1989).   [5] *ibid* at 143–7.

[6] 125 US 190 (1888).   [7] *ibid* at 205.

is interpreted to mean that regulation of marriage rests with the legislature, and that marriage is a reflection of a society's traditions, the activities of the state legislatures and of the federal congress during the last quarter of the past century certainly support the point. Fifty-four years after *Maynard* was decided, Chief Justice Warren wrote in *Loving v Virginia*,[8] the United States Supreme Court case that struck down Virginia's miscegenation statute:

The freedom to marry has long been recognized as one of the vital personal rights essential to the orderly pursuit of happiness of free men.

Marriage is one of the 'basic civil rights of man,' fundamental to our very existence and survival.[9]

Yet history has shown that marriage is hardly an absolute fundamental right. Throughout the century state legislatures have imposed restrictions relating to formalities, age, mental competence, number, and the couple's biological relationship. Each restriction has been based on society's view of and purposes for marriage. One trend that has been discernible during the past thirty years has been a legislative and judicial preference for promoting marriage. This has been manifested in the states by lowering the age at which people may marry, removing health requirements, limiting prison officials from refusing prisoners permission to marry, and interpreting family relationships in such a way as to allow a marriage between relatives. In the context of decedent's estates litigation, the preference for marriage has been reflected in the application of presumptions and the putative spouse doctrine.[10] On the federal level, marital status has been preferred in matters dealing with certain economic benefits and immigration.

At mid-century, marriage was a status regulated by the state and although considered a special kind of contract, it had not yet taken on the characteristics of a partnership that would later define it.[11] Marriage was a union of a man and a woman in which the man held the dominant position. The law created the fiction of 'oneness' which meant that the husband and wife were one, and in reality, the husband was the 'one.' Upon marriage, by operation of law, a wife assumed the domicile of her husband whether she had ever lived there or not. Spouses enjoyed certain testimonial privileges in litigation, presumably because of society's

---

[8] 388 US 1 (1967).

[9] *ibid* at 12, quoting *Skinner v Oklahoma ex rel. Williamson*, 316 US 535, 541 (1942).

[10] My co-authors Walter O. Weyrauch and Frances Olsen and I have written: 'Presumptions are based on popular feelings and predispopsitions reduced to rules of evidence. They carry considerable persuasive weight with the courts. The presumption of marriage, for exammple, is said to be one of the strongest in law.' WALTER O. WEYRAUCH *et al*, FAMILY LAW: LEGAL CONCEPTS AND CHANGING HUMAN RELATIONSHIPS 171 (1994).

[11] See Sanford N. Katz, Marriage as Partnership, 73 NOTRE DAME L REV 1251 (1998).

interest in preserving trust and loyalty in the marital relationship. Spouses could not sue each other in tort, because of the fiction that such an action would be like suing oneself. Such a restriction was based on the idealized view that legal action between spouses would cause a strain in the marriage, and also that recovery for one spouse would benefit the other. The assumption was that married couples pooled their assets. In reality, however, interspousal immunity had more to do with benefiting insurance companies than with preventing a breach in marital harmony.[12]

That the law favored the man in marriage by providing him more advantages, or stated another way, by disadvantaging the woman, has a long history in the common law and can be seen in a variety of contemporary laws. A husband's interest in his wife had possessory characteristics. For example, because of a husband's entitlement to his wife's sexual and domestic services, he could recover for loss of both should she be injured by a tortfeasor. A woman had no such right.[13] A husband could demand sexual relations with his wife, and if upon her refusal he forced himself on her, she was without a civil remedy. In addition, the state could not seek a criminal indictment. If a wife committed adultery, she may have been deprived of alimony. The same was not true for the husband.

Both law and society promoted the dependency of wives on their husbands and actually promoted gender-role stereotypes. In addition to losing their domicile by operation of law, as already mentioned, wives lost their identity when they married and assumed their husband's name, neither voluntarily nor because of any legal requirement, but because of custom or bureaucratic rules. It would be unusual for title in real property to be recorded as John Smith and Mary Jones, husband and wife, as tenancy by the entirety with rights of survivorship. The deed would have to read John Smith and Mary Smith as husband and wife. Credit cards were normally issued in a wife's married name, like Mrs John Smith. If a woman was known as Mrs Mary Smith, the assumption was that she was a widow or a divorced woman. This may seem trivial, but it reflects a wife's dependency on her husband. It made the woman who sought to

---

[12] See Weyrauch, n 10 above, at 317.

[13] In *Gates v Foley*, 247 So 2d 40 (Fla 1971), the Supreme Court of Florida held that a wife was entitled to an action for loss of consortium based on a third party's injuring her husband. The court wrote: '[T]he unity concept of marriage has in a large part given way to the partner concept whereby a married woman stands as an equal to her husband in the eyes of the law. By giving the wife a separate equal existence, the law created a new interest in the wife which should not be left unprotected by the courts. Medieval concepts which have no justification in our present society should be rejected. We therefore hold that deprivation to the wife of the husband's companionship, affection and sexual relation (or consortium . . .) constitutes a real injury to the marital relationship and one which should be compensable at law if due to the negligence of another.' *ibid* at 41.

maintain her own identity by using her own name seem like an oddity. To be called an 'independent woman' had negative connotations.

To define marriage as a true partnership changed the nature of the relationship. Although the word 'partnership' had been used to describe marriage in the past, it really referred to the civil nature of the marriage relationship and not the modern idea of contract.[14] Legally, the partnership would be inconsistent with the oneness of the relationship. By necessity, the partnership concept required marriage to be a contract of two individuals who maintained their individuality. The new legal definition of marriage, which allows individuals to set their own terms of the marriage relationship (within certain limits) developed after mid-century and has continued. It has had important implications for the state's laws regulating the establishment, administration, and reorganization of marriage.

ANTENUPTIAL AGREEMENTS

The idea that marriage was a state-regulated status meant a couple could not customize their relationship and expect the state to enforce their own rules governing it. From the state's perspective, a marriage was a contract, but it was more like a contract of adhesion than one privately negotiated. The state, not the parties, dictated the terms. Laws regulating the enforcement of antenuptial agreements can illustrate this. Until the case of *Posner v Posner*,[15] antenuptial agreements were valid as long as they dealt with the assignment of property upon death of the parties. Courts would not enforce them if they attempted to deal with divorce, or if they regulated marital conduct during marriage in such a way as to deviate from the traditional roles of husbands and wives and the view of marriage as an independent economic unit. In other words, a man could not contract away his right to support his wife and children during marriage. Nor could the couple state that they respected each other's privacy and each could have a separate sexual life or no sexual life at all. They could not set their own terms for evaluating whether their marriage was successful or not and what would constitute termination, for example that they no longer loved each other.

The Florida Supreme Court in *Posner* recognized the changes that had occurred in society, and enforced an antenuptial agreement that provided for the assignment of property upon divorce according to the couple's

---

[14] The 19th-c case of *Ponder v Graham*, 4 Fla 23 (1851) illustrates this point. In discussing *Ponder*, Walter O. Weyrauch, Frances Olsen, and I have written: 'To call marriage a contract in 1851 did not in any sense imply that the parties should be free to set the particular terms of the contract or that notions of laissez-faire should govern the marriage relation.' See WEYRAUCH n 10 above, at 89.   [15] 233 So 2d 381 (Fla 1970).

terms. Other jurisdictions followed Florida so that today the scope of an antenuptial agreement can include almost all aspects of married life including child rearing, which judges feel is within the sphere of parental control, not theirs. However, courts still remain reluctant to cede power to parents with regard to the assignment of children upon divorce. In that situation judges would not be policing an ongoing or intact family, but a divorced one, which historically has been their domain and one which they have felt, rightly or wrongly, needed to be supervised.

Contemporary antenuptial agreement law has built-in safeguards to protect the vulnerable, and that is why antenuptial agreements differ from commercial contracts. Before signing an agreement, each party must fully disclose their assets to each other so that not only must the process by which the agreement was entered into be fair, but the terms must be reasonable. Those requirements deviate from conventional contract law. Also, while unconscionability is a defense in an action to enforce a commercial contract, the standard for applying it is different in antenuptial agreement litigation. In a case where the enforcement of an antenuptial agreement would result in a wife's being destitute or at an enormous disadvantage, the defense of unconscionability can be raised successfully to defeat enforcement. In the commercial world, whether enforcement of the contract will work a hardship on one of the parties is irrelevant. Privately negotiated commercial contracts are meant to be enforced if they were entered into free of fraud, misrepresentation, or coercion.

MARRIAGE AS A FUNDAMENTAL RIGHT

I have already mentioned that marriage is regarded as a fundamental right protected by the United States Constitution, but that it would be misleading to consider it an absolute right because of the number of state-imposed restrictions. Professor Wadlington has written about the restrictions, and Professor Barron has discussed the place of marriage within a constitutional framework, concluding his chapter with an analysis of *Baker v State of Vermont*,[16] the same-sex marriage case decided by the Vermont Supreme Court in 1999. It is important to note that Professor Barron's discussion emphasizes how the development of the protection of individual rights by the United States Supreme Court has had an impact on marriage. At the end of the twentieth century, we cannot claim what Graveson wrote in 1957, 'Despite the changes of the past century the family, rather than the individual remains the unit of English

---

[16] 744 A2d 864 (Vt 2000).

society.'[17] It is quite the reverse. Within marriage, certainly, it is the individual, not the union that receives protection. This helps to explain the abortion decisions, which Professor Annas discusses. It is the woman who controls her body, not the man who impregnated her. As between the competing interests of the protection of maternal health and the protection of fetal life, the former trumped the latter.

Of all the state controls over the entry into marriage, the sex requirement has been given the most attention by legislatures, legal literature, and the popular press in the last decade. In fact, litigation testing the legality of that requirement was not new. The first major case on the validity of a state statute restricting marriage to persons of different sexes was *Baker v Nelson*[18] in 1971 when the Minnesota Supreme Court held that its state marriage law did not violate the Fourteenth Amendment to the United States Constitution. Other attempts were made in Kentucky and Washington to strike down laws restricting marriage licenses to couples of different sexes.[19] Whether a state constitution or the federal constitution was relied upon, the result was the same: persons of the same sex could not marry each other. As Professor Barron points out, the closest proponents of same-sex marriage have come to being successful was in Hawaii[20] and Vermont.[21] But even in those two states, the highest courts were unwilling to make new law. In a certain sense by turning over the issue to the Vermont legislature for resolution, the ultimate outcome of the Vermont case, the Vermont Supreme Court was following the substance of Justice Field's statement that marriage concerns morals, and the legislature is the proper institution to regulate it. The conclusion that can be drawn thus far is that society's interest in preserving marriage as a heterosexual relationship because of culture, tradition, and the morals of a people, outweighs the harm that individuals in a same-sex relationship would suffer being refused permission to marry. If same-sex couples are given the same benefits that flow from marriage except for the label, opponents of same-sex marriage argue that same-sex couples will not suffer any meaningful or practical discrimination.

The Vermont experience illustrates that even a state with a reputation for openness and respect for individual's freedom, which some might label as politically progressive, was reluctant to chart a new direction for family law. That court's response should give advocates of same-sex

---

[17] R. H. Graveson, *The Future of Family Law*, in R. H. Graveson and F. R. Crane (eds), A CENTURY OF FAMILY LAW 413 (1957).

[18] 191 NW2d 185 (Minn. 1971).

[19] See *Jones v Hallahan*, 501 SW2d 588 (Ky Ct App 1973) and *Singer v Hara*, 11 Wash App 247, 522 P2d 1187, *rev denied*, 84 Wash 2d 1008 (1974).

[20] See *Baehr v Miike*, 950 P2d 1234 (1997).

[21] See *Baker v State of Vermont*, 744 A2d 864 (Vt 2000).

marriage pause. If the highest court in Vermont felt it was not the proper forum to change the state's laws, perhaps because the people of Vermont were not ready to support that kind of decision, it is hard to imagine that the United States Supreme Court would act differently. If the statement that the Supreme Court follows election results means that the Supreme Court acts after the public has expressed itself, there may be something in the expression, although crudely stated. United States Supreme Court decisions on social issues often, certainly not always, follow, not lead society. It has been said that when the Court decided *Loving v Virginia*[22] and *Orr v Orr*,[23] many states had already repealed anti-miscegenation laws or statutes restricting alimony to women. In the case of same-sex marriage, events of the next few decades may shape the law of marriage, not the reverse.

In a certain sense it is unfortunate that Vermont chose to defer to its state legislature instead of providing the plaintiffs with the recognition they sought and the immediate relief for which they argued. Had the Supreme Court of Vermont decided that restricting marriage to heterosexual couples violated the common benefits clause of its state constitution and that the plaintiffs in *Baker* should be issued a license to marry immediately, Vermont could have been the laboratory for same-sex marriage law. The marriage law that the legislature would have had to enact would have given guidance to other states. In addition certain questions that have been posed by those opposing same-sex marriage might have been answered. For example, would Vermont have become the magnet for same-sex couples who wanted to marry, and turn Vermont into a 'same-sex marriage mill' similar to the experience of Nevada in the 1950s when, because of the availability of 'quickie divorces,' it became the 'divorce mill'? Would Vermont citizens find it offensive to have same-sex couples marrying, living together, and forming a family through adoption? Instead, the Vermont legislature enacted a law, which resembled marriage as well as providing procedures and substantive rights for the terms of the civil relationship.[24]

It should be mentioned, however, as Professor Barron stresses, that the Supreme Court of Vermont chose to ground both the rationale and holding in *Baker* entirely on the Vermont constitution and not on the equal

---

[22] 388 US 1 (1967).   [23] 440 US 268 (1979).

[24] The law the Vermont legislature enacted, An Act Relating to Civil Unions, is broader in scope than the Reciprocal Benficiaries Act enacted in 1998 by Hawaii. See Haw Rev Stat § 572C (Supp 1998). See generally Sanford N. Katz, *Emerging Models for Alternatives to Marriage*, 33 Fam LQ 663 (1999). The American press has reported that of the small number of same-sex couples who have registered their civil unions in Vermont, most have been out-of-state residents who have returned to their home state after registering.

protection clause of the United States Constitution. Other states with different constitutions could respond differently, thus allowing for a diversity of approaches to same-sex marriage laws in the United States. However, if a same-sex couple married in Vermont, and later moved to another state where the legality of the couple's marriage was raised in some kind of litigation, the issue of recognition or non-recognition could be tested either under conflict of law rules or by the application of the federal Defense of Marriage Act.[25]

It is impossible to catalogue here all the implications on law generally for removing the restriction of the sex of the persons in marriage laws. Certainly from medieval English law onwards, the model for marriage was a heterosexual relationship established in church by an exchange of vows. It was clearly an unequal relationship because of the superior position of the male under the common law. All the legal presumptions about the validity of marriage and the legitimacy of children were, and still are, based on a heterosexual relationship linked to sexual relationships and procreation. It should be mentioned, however, that other legal aspects of marriage are based on society's desire to support and protect values of loyalty, confidentiality, and trust which have nothing to do with the sexual identity of the marriage partners.

DOMESTIC PARTNERSHIP ACTS

In the absence of marriage laws that allow same-sex partners to marry, domestic partnership statutes have been enacted in a number of cities and a few states to accommodate them.[26] Whether these laws are a temporary effort or a permanent solution to the same-sex marriage issue remains to be seen. The early laws were designed to provide economic benefits as well as certain privileges like visitation rights in various institutions to domestic partners of city or state employees (depending on the statute). Some are still limited to these matters. However, domestic partnership laws are beginning to cover more aspects of a couple's life than the extension of employee benefits. Mutual economic dependency is being added. More and more these laws are taking on the characteristics of formal marriage. Yet until domestic partnerships are socially and

---

[25] In 1996 the United States Congress enacted the Defense of Marriage Act, which defines marriage under federal law as 'a legal union between one man and one woman as husband and wife, and the word "spouse" refers only to a person of the opposite sex who is a husband or a wife.' In addition, the Act states that no American jurisdiction must recognize a same-sex marriage entered into in another American jurisdiction. See 28 USCA § 1738 C (West Supp 1997).

[26] For a discussion of domestic partnership laws, see Katz, n 24 above.

legally recognized as having established a 'family,' they will not have achieved the status of marriage.

Some city domestic partnership laws are more restrictive than the state marriage laws in which the city is located. For example, the Domestic Partnership Act in the City of Cambridge, Massachusetts[27] limits registration eligibility to couples over the age of 18 years old, and requires the couple to live together, consider themselves a family and be committed to a mutually supportive relationship. The Massachusetts marriage law has no such requirements. The San Francisco Recognition of Domestic Partners Law[28] precludes a domestic partner from entering into a new partnership for a period of six months after the termination of the relationship. American marriage laws do not require such waiting periods. It appears that as more and more jurisdictions, whether city or state, enact domestic partnership laws, these laws look more and more like the ideal marriage, not the functional marriage that is rarely, if ever, defined in a statute.

Domestic partnership laws may have received their impetus from advocates for same-sex marriage, but their legal antecedent was the 1989 Danish law[29] on the one hand and cases that recognized the legality of cohabitation contracts on the other hand. The first major contract cohabitation case was *Marvin v Marvin*,[30] decided by the California Supreme Court in 1976. That court held that two adults who lived together and shared their lives, one supporting the other financially or otherwise, could have a relationship that could be defined in a number of ways so as to provide the partners with a legal remedy at the termination of the relationship. What made *Marvin* so important, even groundbreaking, was that California did not recognize common law marriage, yet the couple in *Marvin* came as close to living in a common law marriage relationship as one possibly could. Also, missing in the opinion is any phrase that restricts cohabitation contracts to heterosexual couples. Within the next two decades after *Marvin*, cohabitation contracts became a common vehicle for non-marital couples living together to define their relationship. It could be accomplished formally through a written contract, or informally by a court's finding a contract after examining the couple's conduct. Some jurisdictions succeeded in regulating cohabitation contracts by enacting legislation requiring that certain formalities be met in order for them to be valid. That cohabitation contracts and domestic partnerships should be legislatively regulated illustrates the

[27] See City of Cambridge Mun Code § 2.119.

[28] See San Francisco, Cal, Admin Code §§ 62.1–62.8 (1991).

[29] An English translation of The Danish Legislation on Same-Sex Marriage (followed by a discussion of it) can be found in Weyrauch, n 10 above, at 566–7.

[30] 557 P 2d 106 (Cal 1976).

extent to which the state (here, meaning government) wishes to control not only marriage, but also marriage-like relationships.

DOMESTIC VIOLENCE

The unity of marriage and family privacy, two interrelated concepts, had the effect of masking any number of harmful acts against wives and children, some of which were justified and state sanctioned in the name of family governance. Treating each family member as a person with individual rights changed that. It is interesting to note that children received the protection of the state before wives. Perhaps this occurred because children were thought to be more vulnerable than adult wives, or maybe because the idea of the oneness of marriage was so secure not only in the law on the books, but also the law in action.

Under the common law, husbands and fathers could chastise their wives and children. Theoretically, wives were assumed to be able to protect themselves or even able to leave their abusive husbands by returning to their families. Children had no such escape. So basic to American society was the notion of family privacy and so fundamental in family law was the duty of parents to control their children and to teach them 'right conduct', that they were given wide latitude in terms of punishing them. Indeed, the most common defense raised by a parent who was either sued civilly or criminally prosecuted was parental immunity. It was radical for the state to begin to mandate the reporting of child abuse and neglect in the 1960s. There was no such mandated reporting of spousal abuse by physicians or hospital emergency room staff.

At mid-century, the remedy a wife had if her husband abused or assaulted her was divorce. It took about thirty years for women to have protection from violent men, particularly husbands, that was almost equal to children's protection from their abusing parents. Just as all states have mandatory child abuse reporting statutes, all states now have laws protecting women from abusing husbands. In addition, state stalking laws can protect women, although their effectiveness is often questioned. The important point is that the state is now recognizing women as individuals with their own identity and with the legal protection from bodily injury that any other adult in society enjoys. No longer is the state, through the absence of laws, supporting the vulnerability of women against violent men. Indeed, the Violence Against Women Act which Congress passed in 1994[31] is important

---

[31] See Pub OL No 103–322, 108 Stat 1902 (1994). In *United States v Morrison*, 2000 WL 574361 (2000), the United States Supreme Court invalidated the civil rights remedy under the Act, this not allowing a victim to seek relief in a federal court.

for the representing congressional recognition of a family law problem that, like child abuse, has become a national public health issue.

RULES OF EVIDENCE

The abandonment of the concept that a husband and wife were one has had an impact on litigation. Even though most Americans never are involved in litigation, the rules of evidence can be used as an indicator of the law's view on human behavior and family relationships. In other words, the law of evidence reflects a certain, sometimes old-fashioned or outdated, perception of how and why people act and react the way they do. Regarding the marital relationship, the rules of evidence may indeed be a manifestation of an ideal: husbands and wives should be in a relationship that is based on loyalty and trust, and one in which confidentiality is recognized and supported. For the most part, this ideal has been maintained, and the changes that have occurred were designed to protect the victim in the relationship or family.

One of the fundamental evidentiary rules dealing with marriage is that in a criminal case one spouse may not testify against the other while they are married, even if the marriage occurred a day before trial. This disqualification rule remains unchanged. There is no such privilege in civil cases even if the testimony may be highly destructive to the marital relationship. Another fundamental evidentiary rule is that private conversations between spouses are privileged and neither spouse can waive the privilege.[32]

What do these rules of evidence offer us in terms of describing what the law is saying about marriage and about the parent–child relationship? Professor Regan's insights are particularly helpful. He has written:

[T]he adverse testimony privilege seeks to prevent spousal betrayal of trust. There are other forms of betrayal, however, that may be just as searing. Adultery, for instance, can be a source of great anguish that destroys a marriage. We may want society to discourage such conduct. Using the law to do so, however, may pose problems. Recriminalizing or vigorously enforcing laws against adultery would require state monitoring and investigation of sexual matters on a scale that most people would regard inappropriate and threatening. Similarly, making divorce available only on fault grounds may send a message that marriage is an important commitment. Such a legal regime, however, would require state inquiry into and assessment of marital conduct in intimate detail. By contrast . . .

---

[32] For a discussion of these privileges, see PAUL LIACOS, MARK S. BRODIN, and MICHAEL AVERY, HANDBOOK OF MASSACHUSETTS EVIDENCE 766–74 (7th edn 1999).

the adverse testimony privilege promotes an internal stance toward marriage by depriving the state of an opportunity to foment discord between spouses.[33]

Yet when there is discord, for example in cases of domestic violence or divorce, the state is not deprived of such an opportunity. Also, in some states in cases where children's financial support or safety is concerned, the marital testimonial privilege is not honored. In those matters, the individual rights of children rights trump those of parents.

DIVORCE

The assignment of property upon divorce underwent fundamental changes during the 1960s and 1970s, the decades in which no-fault divorce and equitable distribution of property were introduced into state divorce laws. The title theory of property that had governed divorce before then, summarized by the slogan, 'He who owns property, gets it,' was literally correct.

Although the Uniform Marriage and Divorce Act promulgated by the Commissioners of Uniform State Laws in 1970 was adopted in whole or in part by only eight states, it nevertheless prompted a national divorce reform movement that lasted at least a decade. I believe it is responsible for changing the way legislators, judges, and lawyers think about divorce, and paved the way for the American Law Institute's Principles of the Law of Family Dissolution described by Professor Blumberg.

Equitable distribution of property, now in one way or another the method of assigning property after divorce in all states except the eight community property jurisdictions, was designed to recognize the importance of the individual spouse's contribution to the common enterprise called marriage. As Professor Blumberg states, throughout the first half of the twentieth century, husbands and wives were thought to, and perhaps for the most part did, inhabit separate spheres: a husband 'earned the bacon,' and the wife cooked it and cared for the children. Yet the wife's contribution to the domestic enterprise was thought not to have monetary value. Indeed, a wife's household services were considered part of her spousal obligation, and as in the pre-existing rule in the law of contracts, she could not expect to be compensated for them by a husband's promise either during marriage or upon divorce. State divorce statutes, borrowing from the Uniform Marriage and Divorce Act, changed that and now the contribution of a spouse as a homemaker is considered in making an assignment of property.[34]

---

[33] REGAN, n 2 above, at 201–2.

[34] Section 307 of the Uniform Marriage and Divorce Act reads: '. . . The court shall also consider the contribution or dissipation of each party in the acquisition, preservation,

Perhaps the most innovative feature of equitable distribution in addition to its looking behind the title of property to determine ownership and its assignment, is its consideration of what Professor Charles Reich called 'the new property': one's profession or job, how it was acquired, its present and future value, and the right to receive income from it.[35] Indeed, at the beginning of the twenty-first century, the most important aspect of property distribution upon divorce in addition to tangible property consists of job-related rights like salaries, pensions, insurance, and health benefits. As Professor Mary Ann Glendon has pointed out, 'the emphasis has shifted from rights in traditional property to the issue of rights in spouses' earning power and benefits.'[36] Without a focus on the individual, none of these innovations would have been thinkable.

CONCLUSION

In writing about the nineteenth century in Britain, Professor R. H. Graveson stated, 'The change in the legal position of the married woman . . . is one of the most outstanding features in both law and society.'[37] It has taken almost a century for an American to be able to write a statement similar to that one. There is no doubt that the married woman has achieved greater freedom and a certain sense of equality with men in marriage, but there are miles to go before true equality in marriage and fairness in divorce is achieved. The progress that has been made has been due in large part to married women being treated as individuals, not as appendages to their husbands.

Sometimes the words 'individual rights' have been associated with 'individualism.' There is a difference. The definition of 'individualism' is the 'belief in the primary importance of the individual and personal independence.'[38] 'Individual rights' refers to the relationship of the individual to the state wherein the individual's interests take precedence over the

---

depreciation, or appreciation in value of the respective estates, and the contribution of a spouse as a homemaker or to the family unit.' UNIF MARRIAGE AND DIVORCE ACT, §307 (ALTERNATIVE A), 9 A ULA 238 (1973).

[35] In 1964, Professor Charles Reich wrote: '[T]oday more and more of our wealth takes the form of rights or status rather than of tangible goods. An individual's profession or occupation is a prime example. To many others, a job with a particular employer is the principal form of wealth. A profession or a job is frequently far more valuable than a house or a bank account, for a new house can be bought, and a new bank account created, once a profession or job is secure. For the jobless, their status as governmentally assisted or insured persons may be the main source of subsistence.' Charles Reich, *The New Property*, 73 YALE L J 733, 738 (1964).

[36] See MARY ANN GLENDON, THE TRANSFORMATION OF FAMILY LAW 135 (1996).

[37] R. H. Graveson, *The Background of the Century* in A CENTURY OF FAMILY LAW, n 16 above, at 1.

[38] See THE AMERICAN HERITAGE DICTIONARY 427 (3rd edn 1994).

state's. In family law, the progress made in protecting individual rights, especially those of women and children, through the interpretation of the due process and equal protection clauses of the United States Constitution, has required membership in the family to be redefined. No longer does a family have to be a 'source of oppression and subordination.'[39] Yet until gender roles in marriage are determined by choice of the spouses instead of being socially imposed, we can expect some inequality and unfairness, regardless of the law.

It would not necessarily be ideal if marriage were a true union, where the individual lost his or her identity. Fortunately, that is neither humanly nor practically possible. We have seen how the language and practice of 'union' and 'oneness' have affected married women, making them almost invisible. So long as marriage remains a relationship of two individuals, decisions cannot be resolved by majority vote. The best that can be hoped for is that the good will, trust, mutual understanding, and reasonableness of a married couple whose marriage is founded on love will lead to a respect for and support of each spouse's individual rights. Now that there has been such success in the protection of individual rights, the challenge in the new century will be to reconcile these victories with the stability of the family as a social unit. From my observation of my children's and students' generation, I am optimistic.

[39] See Katharine T. Bartlett, *Feminism and Family Law*, 33 Fam LQ 475, 499 (1999).

29

The End of an Era?

JOHN EEKELAAR

With remarkable consistency, the foregoing contributions have revealed that family life and family law underwent such significant change during the last quarter of the twentieth century that the form of family law as a whole in the 1950s was closer to that of the 1890s than to that of the 1980s. I wish to ponder three questions: *what* is the nature of this change? *how* significant is it? *why* did it come about? From this it might be possible to anticipate where we are headed, though such are the vicissitudes of social life that I prefer to leave that attempt to others.

Historically, an individual's rights and duties, his or her social role, depended on the individual's relationship to social institutions.[1] Being married and being born into a marriage was as important as social class or religious affiliation in determining the nature of an individual's social relationships. But the one common feature which links the analyses of the present, not only by our contributors, but by many contemporary analysts,[2] is the perception that the *individual* has now emerged as the focus of concern, the driver of policy and the source of rights, rather than larger social groups, so that, for example, rights are conferred directly on the individual rather than being derived from the individual's association with such groups. But consider the following, written in 1861:

Archaic law . . . is full . . . of the clearest indications that society in primitive times was not what it is assumed to be at present, a collection of *individuals*. In fact . . . it was *an aggregation of families*. The contrast may be most forcibly expressed by saying that the unit of an ancient society was the Family, of a modern society, the Individual.[3]

Sir Henry Maine then famously summed up his review of the development of law from ancient times:

The word Status may be usefully employed to construct a formula expressing the law of progress thus indicated which, whatever be its value, seems to me to be sufficiently ascertained. All the forms of Status taken notice of in the Law of Persons were derived from, and to some extent are still coloured by, the powers and privileges anciently residing in the Family. If then we employ Status . . . to signify these personal conditions only, . . . we may say that the movement of the progressive societies has hitherto been a movement from Status to Contract.[4]

---

[1] Milton C. Regan, *Family Law and the Pursuit of Intimacy* (NYUP, 1993) 26.
[2] *ibid*; Francis Fukuyama, *The Great Disruption* (Profile Books, 1999); Thomas M. Franck, *The Empowered Self: Law and Society in the Age of Individualism* (Oxford University Press, 1999).
[3] Sir Henry Maine, *Ancient Law* (Oxford University Press, 1931) 104. Emphases in original.
[4] *ibid* 141.

It is possible that Maine failed to observe the continued role of status in Victorian England, or that, for him (as for others) certain persons (such as married women) were simply not seen as 'individuals'. This might serve as a caution to us, lest we too are blind to the individuality of some people (children, for example). Yet it may be that Maine was fundamentally correct in observing the gradual erosion of status over time. Have we now reached, or almost reached, the point when status, like fossil fuels may do, has run out, and individuals have lost any remnant of the power and protection which status, derived from relationship to social institutions, can provide? To determine whether this is plausible, and what its significance may be, it is necessary to cast a long look backwards.

FROM INSTRUMENTALISM TO WELFARISM

Consider the following legal structures.

- Serfs, although not slaves, were legally tied to the lord's land as 'their function is to cultivate their lord's demesne'.[5]
- Under medieval law, guardianship and paternal power were seen 'merely as profitable rights' to the guardian or father; '[the law] had only sanctioned them when they could be made profitable [to the guardian or father]'.[6]
- The legal remedy against someone who abducted a child was grounded on the damage caused to the father's interest in the child's potential marriage, or (in later times) in the father's interest in the child's 'services'.
- Many rules introduced by the Church over the first and part of the second millennium concerning marriage (especially the restrictions on it) altered previous strategies of heirship, resulting in vast movement of property away from families to the Church.[7]
- Marriage among the landed classes became a central means of consolidating land holdings and forming alliances between lineages, while by the end of the seventeenth century 'the husband and father for a time became the family despot, benevolent or malign according to temperament or inclination'.[8]

---

[5] F. Pollock and F. W. Maitland, *The History of English Law* (Cambridge University Press, 1968) i. 414.

[6] *ibid* ii. 444.

[7] Jack Goody, *The Development of the Family and Marriage in Europe* (Cambridge University Press, 1983) esp. 214–21.

[8] Lawrence Stone, *The Family, Sex and Marriage in England 1500–1800* (Weidenfeld & Nicolson, 1977) 158.

- Under the *ancien régime*, a father had virtually unfettered discretion over his children. 'He could make use of them for all the operations that were intended to further his *état*.'[9]
- The Tudor poor law, developed throughout subsequent centuries, required the poor, and their children, to use their labour for the benefit of others.

The duties which such legal structures and institutions impose subordinate the interests of the duty-holders to those empowered to enforce the duties. Such legal institutions are typical of what I call *instrumental* relationships, in which duties are simply manifestations of the power of others to further their interests. Although it is not supposed that these examples alone establish the case, I suggest they are representative of an era when status relationships were primarily instrumental. It is important to appreciate that this refers to legal and institutional *structures* and not to actual behaviour, so does not imply *necessary* hostility, indifference, or even exploitation between parties to such relationships. Indeed, there may be a social expectation that the party with the legal power is solicitous of the interests of those over whom he exercises power. Even Robert Filmer's advocacy of the absolute power of monarchs over their subjects, and of fathers over their children, in *Patriarcha*,[10] recognized that kings and fathers should benefit those subjected to them. *But there was no legal constraint on their power*; nor was it thought that there should be any: 'The father of a family governs by no other law than by his own will ... there is no nation that allows children any action or remedy for being unjustly governed; and yet, for all this, every father is bound by the law of nature to do his best for the preservation of his family.'[11]

John Locke's *Second Treatise of Civil Government* (1690) expressed parental power differently. For him, the power 'arises from that duty which is incumbent on them—to take care of their offspring during the imperfect state of childhood'.[12] Its purpose was to benefit children.[13] The idea that power over people derived from the people, and could only be *legitimately* exercised in their interests, was a persistent theme of Enlightenment writers like Rousseau, Diderot, and Priestley.[14] Kant's injunction against treating people as means rather than ends, indeed,

---

[9] Jacques Donzelot, *The Policing of Families* (New York, Pantheon, 1979) 49.

[10] Written at some time before his death in 1653; first published in 1680.

[11] *Patriarcha*, ch III, section 1.

[12] Locke, *Second Treatise of Civil Government*, para 58; also para 170.

[13] This analysis of parental power was the same as that adopted by the House of Lords in *Gillick v Wisbech Area Health Authority* [1986] AC 112.

[14] See David Williams (ed), *The Enlightenment* (Cambridge University Press, 1999) Introduction.

the whole Enlightenment project, found concrete expression in the slow evolution of legal controls over the way people used their power over others to ensure that they used it for the benefit of, or at least not in ways harmful to, those others. This may be called *welfarism*. Early examples are found in legislation protecting child apprentices (no longer to be freely exploited for others' interests) and regulating other forms of child labour. It is essential to understand that, unlike revolutionary Communism, and its Jacobin forebears, which sought to destroy existing social structures and replace them by a centralized welfarist state, the welfarism which emerged from enlightened thought generally accepted existing social structures, but sought to control their exercise. Thus the Custody of Infants Act 1839 for the first time allowed courts to override the father's right to the custody of their children; the Poor Law Amendment Act 1844 allowed an unmarried mother to seek an order against the father for the support of herself and her child, and the legal obligation of husbands to support their wives slowly developed throughout the nineteenth century, reaching full fruition only in 1971.[15] So, under welfarism, protective devices were linked to institutions, and much of family law revolved around defining an individual's connection with an institution (for example, marriage or legitimate birth) through which individuals' interests were safeguarded. But there is a dark side to this. The agents exercising these institutional powers, whether family members, welfare authorities, or courts, were in a position to formulate their own conceptions of what was beneficial to those subject to institutional protection. They could therefore impose a version of that benefit which promoted their own interests or communal goals. Welfarism could be instrumentalism in a new guise. Donzelot,[16] writing of France, captured the essence of this process when he described the tutelary complex as 'governance through families' by a combination of philanthropical, welfare, educational, and medical services, a process which began in the early nineteenth century, and which had its origins in the 'preservation of children' literature of the Enlightenment period. Writing in the 1970s, Donzelot perceived this process to be still in full flow.

---

[15] Eekelaar, Ch 18 of this volume.

[16] n 9 above. See also C. van Nijnatten, 'Authority Relations in Families and Child Welfare in The Netherlands and England: New Styles of Governance', (2000) 14 *Int J Law, Policy & Fam* 107, drawing on Foucault's analysis.

THE WELFARIST ASCENDANCY

On this view, in the United Kingdom at least, the 1970s represents the apogee of a process which had unfolded, intermittently but relentlessly, since the Enlightenment.[17] One might have thought that the occurrence of two devastating wars within the first half of the twentieth century would have been so disruptive that the onward sweep of welfarism would have been checked or transformed. Yet the evidence does not support this. Comparative studies of the impact of both the first and the second world wars have emphasized the relatively minor degree to which the wars had long-term effects on social institutions.[18] The increased employment of women during the wars was regarded, by the women and by men, as exceptional, and division of labour according to traditional gender patterns resumed when peace was restored. Indeed, the post-war societies tended to give *added* emphasis to 'traditiona.' family patterns, despite short-term rises in marriage breakdown.[19] There were a variety of reasons: the wars depleted the ranks of younger males; people tended to respond to the depredations of wartime by accentuating the security provided by traditional roles; the post-war economies needed to provide openings for returned veterans; and, after World War II, psychological theory developed from observations of child evacuees emphasized the importance to children of the maternal bond. Lewis[20] describes the assumption made in the Beveridge Report on 'traditional' family roles. More importantly, from the perspective of the present analysis, she observes that even the sweeping social security reforms of the Attlee Government had their roots in the Liberal measures at the beginning of the century.

The essential continuity between immediate post-war developments in family law and their historic origins can be easily demonstrated. Beginning with child welfare and protection, the emphasis placed in the Curtis Report (1946)[21] on the importance of a child's family ties, especially with its mother, did represent an important shift from nineteenth-century ideas, which had persisted until then, that deprived children were best served by severing those links.[22] But, as Masson[23] demonstrates, this did

[17] This view agrees with that which Grossberg expresses for the United States in Ch 1 of this volume.

[18] See Richard Wall and Jay Winter, Introduction, in R. Wall and J. Winter (eds), *The Upheaval of War: Family Work and Welfare in Europe 1914–1918* (Cambridge University Press, 1988); Harold L. Smith, 'The Effect of the War on the Status of Women', in *War and Social Change: British Society in the Second World War* (Manchester University Press, 1986).

[19] Susan Pedersen, *Family, Dependence and the Origins of the Welfare State: Britain and France 1914–45* (Cambridge University Press, 1993) ch 2.   [20] In Ch 4 of this volume.

[21] See Masson, Ch 26 of this volume.

[22] This idea was most spectacularly manifested in the English practice of emigrating children to the colonies, and American policies of moving children into the interior.

[23] Masson, Ch 26 of this volume. See also the persistence of secrecy in adoption: Katz, at 280 of this volume.

not imply any lessening of the state supervision over children and families which had begun from the late nineteenth century. On the contrary, the establishment of children's officers and the placing of duties on local authorities reaffirmed its role within an optimistic vision of social casework. When it was felt that parents were hindering the realization of the authorities' view of their children's interests, the Children Act 1975 increased local authorities' powers, making adoption easier to arrange and widening the circumstances when they could assume parental rights under a procedure instituted first in 1889.

The legal position between married persons in the decades immediately following World War II was not much different from that pertaining in the late nineteenth century after the Married Women's Property Act 1882 had separated a wife's property from her husband's.[24] Smart[25] has demonstrated how the Morton Commission in 1956 sought to entrench the matrimonial offence doctrine because it thought this marital regime was better for everyone concerned, and throughout the 1960s courts retained the discretionary power to grant or refuse divorces to erring petitioners depending on the judges' view of their moral worth, just as they had in the nineteenth century.[26] The matrimonial offence doctrine ensured that the parties' welfare was determined by the institutional demands of marriage. Although the husband was bound to provide his wife with the necessities of life, this was discharged by providing her with a home, and it was her duty to live there unless the husband was being unreasonable. If the husband was ill-treating her, she might be able to obtain divorce if the requisite grounds were satisfied, but this was available only in the High Court with its deterrent costs and procedures.[27] Even if she obtained a divorce, she would lose her accommodation, and had no access to the husband's property. Most women had to make do with the meagre remedies of the magistrates' courts, with no freedom to remarry. But protection slowly grew. The husband lost his sole right to decide where the couple should live.[28] Spouses were enabled to sue one another in tort in 1962.[29] The Matrimonial Homes Act 1967 tried to give wives protection against alienation of the home by the husband. Very slowly, during the 1960s, courts would exercise their 'inherent jurisdiction' to expel violent husbands from their homes, but this could only be done within the context of matrimonial proceedings, thus restricting

---

[24] Douglas, Ch 10 of this volume. See R. H. Graveson and C. R. Crane (eds), *A Century of Family Law* (Sweet & Maxwell, 1957), especially chs 5 and 6 by C. A. Morrison.

[25] In Ch 16 of this volume.

[26] The story of the divorce jurisdiction is told in John Eekelaar, 'A Jurisdiction in Search of a Mission: Matrimonial Proceedings in England and Wales', (1994) 57 *Modern Law Review* 839.					[27] See Maclean, Ch 24 of this volume.

[28] *Dunn v Dunn* [1949] P 98.			[29] Law Reform (Husband and Wife) Act 1962.

this protection to married persons.[30] But the most significant protection came with the introduction of the reformed divorce law in 1971. It is, however, notable that in most cases, the protection still depended on the status of the parties as married persons. Even when provisions were extended beyond marriage, as when the Domestic Violence and Matrimonial Proceedings Act 1976 broke the linkage between the jurisdiction to exclude a partner from the home and matrimonial proceedings, thus extending the protection to the unmarried, some connection with marriage was maintained through the requirement that, if unmarried parties were to benefit, they must be living 'as man and wife'. A similar story can be told with regard to succession rights. Shortly before World War II, certain persons within a family relationship to a deceased testator could apply to a court for an order for maintenance out of the estate if the testator had failed to make reasonable financial provision for their maintenance.[31] After limited extension of these powers to cases of intestacy in 1952,[32] an Act of 1975 gave courts the same powers to redistribute property in favour of a surviving spouse as they had by then acquired in the case of divorce.[33] The major beneficiary of this welfarist legislation was the surviving *spouse*. Other dependants (including a child or any other person who was being maintained by the deceased immediately before his death) could only be awarded a sum which was necessary for their maintenance. The common thread between these developments is that the traditional family institutions are perceived as being the channel for beneficent behaviour. Welfarism at its height had not essentially dissolved the social structures fashioned through the ages.

THE POST-WELFARIST DISPENSATION: FROM BENEFICENCE TO EMPOWERMENT

We now need to consider whether the developments of the last quarter of the century reflect a *qualitative* change in the structure of family law from the overall direction it had been taking over almost the preceding two centuries. It seems as if this may be occurring, but, like any contemporary

---

[30] But in one important respect a wife was less well protected than her unmarried counterpart, for it was not until 1991 that the vagaries of the case-law system swept away the marital rape immunity: *R v R* [1991] 4 All ER 481. But sentencing practice continued to view rape by a stranger more severely than rape by a partner: Philip N. S. Rumney, 'When Rape Isn't Rape: Court of Appeal Sentencing Practice in Cases of Marital and Relationship Rape', (1999) 19 *Oxford Journal of Legal Studies* 243.

[31] Inheritance (Family Provision) Act 1938. For a full account see S. M. Cretney, *Law, Law Reform and the Family* (Oxford University Press, 1998) ch 10.

[32] Intestates' Estates Act 1952.

[33] Inheritance (Provision of Family and Dependants) Act 1975.

event, it is difficult to detect its deep nature. It is easy to point to demographic change;[34] decline in marriage, increase in divorce; numbers of one-
parent families and single householders; higher economic activity by
women; all factors labelled by Fukuyama: 'The Great Disruption'. But it is
harder to assess how these events have affected the nature of family law.

Let us consider first the kinds of legal and institutional changes which
have occurred. A good place to start is child welfare law in England and
Wales, because this was the subject of intensive rethinking during the
1980s, and the restructuring was quite dramatic. The additional legal
powers local authorities had acquired in the 1970s were removed; the
optimistic vision of social casework as a means for directing families
towards more contented futures within existing social frameworks disappeared. The driving concepts were: *empowerment*, *participation* (or *partnership*) and *responsibility*. While the Curtis Report of 1946 spoke of the
responsibilities of the *state*, the new language was of 'allowing' parents
to 'undertake' *their* 'natural and legal responsibility' to care for their children.[35] Social workers were essentially to play a managerial role, presenting options, and co-ordinating other services when risks to children
became unacceptable. Distinctions, obliterated durin;3 the welfarist
ascendancy, between children who do wrong and those who are victims
of wrong, reappeared, and parents were once again held to account
('blamed') for failing to perform their role responsibly. If we turn to welfare law more generally, we find that within both the United States and
the United Kingdom, overall direction of income policy for mothers has
been one of encouraging movement from welfare dependency to work, to
relieve welfare budgets, it is true, but also on the assumption that women
in employment have more control over their destinies.[36]

Remarkably, parallel features can be found in private law. Although
the 1971 divorce reform was instituted with the object of relieving hardship, the fact that it removed the barrier against consensual divorce, hitherto thought indispensable as a safeguard to marriage, coupled with the
'special procedure', reducing the process to a paper application, meant
that parties could in effect decide on the exit to their marriages.[37] As
importantly, it became usual for parties to settle their financial and
property arrangements by consent, a development encouraged by the
Matrimonial Proceedings and Property Act 1984. However, it was the
mediation movement of the 1980s and 1990s[38] which raised self-

[34] See Gibson, Ch 2 and Morrison, Ch 3 of this volume.
[35] *Review of Child Care Law: Report to Ministers of an Interdepartmental Working Party* (Her
Majesty's Stationery Office, 1985), para 2.8; Masson, Ch 26 of this volume; van Nijnatten,
n 16 above.   [36] See Friedman and Rein, Ch 5 and Lewis, Ch 4 of this volume.
[37] Maclean, Ch 24 and Smart, Ch 16 of this volume.
[38] See Maclean, Ch 24 of this volume.

determination to a new principle, speaking of restoring to the parties the 'ownership' of their own agreements.[39] The extent to which courts will exercise any residual 'welfarist' role in supervising agreements reached on the basis of legal advice is now minimal.[40] Similarly, the Children Act 1989 itself severely limited the role of the courts in overseeing the agreed arrangements made between divorcing parents about their children. Suggestions made towards the end of the century to expand the opportunities for parties to 'control' their post-divorce lives by prenuptial or nuptial contracts[41] take this approach still further, though here, as in other matters (considered below) the movement is much further advanced in the United Sates.

But the move towards 'empowerment' goes still deeper than this. It explains the resurgence of 'rights' remarked on by Dewar and Parker as characteristic of the new, 'complex' era.[42] It also explains the tendency towards rules and away from discretion, for discretion is associated with assessments by third parties of the subjects' welfare, whereas claims to rights appeal to established rules or principles. Possessors of rights are empowered; they need not wait on a third person's evaluation of their needs to achieve the ends they seek. Here it seems that the United States has moved further than England and Wales. Hence it has been argued that married women should be *entitled* to shares in the marital property, either during the marriage, or, if not, then certainly after its dissolution.[43] Many have argued that unmarried cohabitants should have better property rights than they currently do (and it is probably only a matter of time before this is conceded[44]), or that the police should not desist from using the criminal law against men who abuse their wives; the women are entitled to its protection.[45] This sets up a painful paradox, however, for prosecution contrary to the wishes of the victim appears to disempower her.

---

[39] Though it was disingenuous in claiming a unique capacity to achieve this, since an agreement reached through negotiation by lawyers can equally be said to be 'owned' by the parties: John Eekelaar, Mavis Maclean, and Sarah Beinart, *Family Lawyers* (Hart Publishing, 2000).

[40] *Dinch v Dinch* [1987] 1 WLR 252; *Harris v Manahan* [1996] 4 All ER 454; *Xydhias v Xydhias* [1999] 2 All ER 386.

[41] *Supporting Families: A Consultation Document* (The Stationery Office, 1998).

[42] In Ch 6 of this volume. This does not mean that 'rights' were not important before, as Dewar and Parker explain. Indeed, the welfare state sought to ground welfare benefits in entitlement, not charity. But the centralist state still decided what welfare rights people had. The shift from the culture of dependency which that created is very clear in the Social Security Secretary's description of the new approach: 'Our new contract will require people to attend an interview as a condition of receiving a benefit, and to consider the options available to them . . . The Single Gateway will make sure that people understand the opportunities and advice available.' *The Independent Review*, 10 Feb 1999.

[43] Blumberg, Ch 17 and Eekelaar, Ch 18 of this volume.

[44] Douglas, Ch 10 of this volume.

[45] Schneider, Ch 21 and Dobash and Dobash, Ch 22 of this volume.

However, it can be argued that the contradiction is illusory because domestic violence itself disempowers the victim, and it is possible that this can be changed only through state action.[46]

Men have also claimed to be beneficiaries, arguing for entitlements to contact children when they are not living with them, which the courts have acceded to, albeit often claiming that it is the child's right. The possibility of a certain degree of empowerment for children was held out in the *Gillick* case,[47] and in the provisions of the Children Act 1989 permitting them to seek leave to bring certain applications in their own name.[48] However, neither development resulted in significant empowerment of children,[49] and at the beginning of 2000 the age of consent for homosexual relations was higher (18) than for heterosexual relations (16). In England and Wales, therefore, the hold of welfarism and its connections with pre-existing family forms survives; but the sound of the tread of claims for rights and empowerment is unmistakable.

We can see where this might lead by taking a closer look at the American experience. Possibly because welfarism had not taken such a deep hold there as in England and Wales, the challenge to traditional forms from the ideologies of rights and empowerment was more dramatic. For many years the battle has centred on the issue of abortion.[50] In England and Wales, the potentially explosive conflict between the rights of women to control their reproductive capacity and communal concerns characterized also as questions of rights have been submerged under a blandly paternalist welfarism controlled by doctors.[51] More recently, controversies over rights in the United States have centred on the rights of homosexuals to marry.[52] No similar claims have been seriously put forward in the United Kingdom which, at the beginning of the twenty-first century, was embroiled in a controversy over whether the ban on local authorities 'promoting' in schools the acceptability of homosexuality as a 'pretended' form of family life should be lifted.[53] However, there has been some debate as to whether there should be any controls over individuals' wishes to become

---

[46] See Cheryl Hanna, 'No Right to Choose: Mandated Victim Participation in Domestic Violence Prosecutions', (1996) 109 *Harvard Law Rev* 1850.

[47] *Gillick v West Norfolk and Wisbech AHA* [1986] AC 112.

[48] Freeman, Ch 20 of this volume. *re-(Residence Order: Application for Leave)* [2000] 1 FLR 780.

[49] *ibid*. It is, however, claimed that children now play a decisive part in decision-making within families: *Independent*, 31 July 2000.

[50] Grossberg, Ch 1 of this volume, quoting Eva R. Rubin: 'The fetus has become the symbol of larger concerns—family dissolution, morality, secularism.'

[51] John Eekelaar, 'Families and Children' in C. McCrudden and G. Chambers (eds), *Individual Rights and the Law in Britain* (Oxford University Press, 1994) 321.

[52] See Barron, Ch 12 of this volume.

[53] Local Government Act 1988, s 28. The Blair Government's attempts to repeal this provision provoked intemperate national debate, and three defeats in the House of Lords. See *The Times*, 24 Mar 2000 and 25 July 2000.

parents either through artificial reproductive technology or through surrogacy arrangements. The general wish that these should be kept out of
commercial interests has prevailed, out of considerations for the welfare of
children and indeed the participants,[54] in contrast to the United States.[55]

The potential consequences of a thoroughgoing replacement of welfarism by empowerment are therefore great. The present direction might
be seen as a return to earlier times, before welfarism took its twentieth-
century forms. For example, the insistence that it is the responsibility of
parents rather than the state to care for and control their children has distinct echoes of pre-welfarist policy. But there is an important difference.
The drive for empowerment has not only threatened to displace welfarism; it has undermined the institutions upon which welfarism has been
built. Smart[56] has described the transformation the institution of marriage
underwent between the late 1950s and the end of the century. This transformation was accompanied by nothing less than the destruction of
marriage's related institution: legitimacy. It is significant that the last legislation expressly upholding the institution of legitimacy was the Legitimacy
Act 1959. This removed the prohibition against legitimation by subsequent
marriage to a child born to a woman who was currently married to someone other than the father. Shortly afterwards (in 1966) the Law Commission
held out the prospect of thousands of such legitimations as an argument in
favour of liberalizing the divorce law.[57] But subsequent legislation, in
1969[58] and 1987,[59] for all but a few matters[60] equalized the position of
marital and non-marital children. Just as the institution of marriage
declined in its importance as a source of defining obligations between
adults, so the institution of legitimacy became virtually redundant as the
means through which children's rights were instantiated.

As Glendon has observed,[61] the law of succession over this period
rapidly improved the position of wives as against the children of the
marriage.[62] Yet, this attempt to breathe new meaning into the institution

---

[54] See Deech, Ch 8 of this volume.   [55] See Katz, Ch 13 of this volume.

[56] In Ch 16 of this volume.

[57] Law Commission, *Reform of the Grounds of Divorce: the Field of Choice*, Cmnd 3123, 1966.

[58] Family Law Reform Act 1969. This followed the report of the Russell Committee, which
had no inhibitions in its use of language: 'Subject to the modification effected by the Legitimacy Act 1926 . . . neither the bastard nor any issue of the bastard has any right to participate on the intestacy of either parent of the bastard': *Report of the Committee on the Law of
Succession in relation to Illegitimate Persons*, Cmnd 3051, 1966.

[59] Family Law Reform Act 1987.

[60] One is the absence of parental responsibility for unmarried fathers: see Douglas, Ch 10
and Freeman, Ch 20 of this volume; the other is the inability of a child to acquire UK nationality from its unmarried father.

[61] Mary Ann Glendon, *The Transformation of Family Law* (University of Chicago Press, 1989).

[62] For an account of this process in England and Wales, see Stephen Cretney, *Law, Law
Reform and the Family* (Oxford University Press, 1998) ch 10.

of marriage seems doomed. We have seen that the fact of being, or having been, married *in itself* now has relatively few legal consequences as
regards distribution of assets on separation;[63] rather, it is the actual relationship of parenthood which matters more.[64] Other legal benefits of marriage are becoming harder to discern. So it may be asked why it should
be necessary to acquire the status in order to acquire the rights which
empowerment indicates should belong to individuals *as individuals,* and
some jurisdictions have gone far in conferring such rights on *de facto*
cohabitants. England and Wales have hesitated to push far in this direction however,[65] though measures such as the Law Reform (Succession)
Act 1995 (giving limited rights to a surviving cohabitant to claim, for
maintenance, from the estate of a deceased partner), certain legislation on
family violence,[66] and succession to protected tenancies have moved in
that direction. While it might seem ironic that some homosexuals and
transsexuals, presently denied access to marriage in England, should
wish to enter a status which is falling into decline, the demand is yet
another consequence of the drive for empowerment: at least while the
status is the only way to achieve certain rights, these rights should not be
withheld (it is argued) simply on *institutional* grounds.

This scepticism of the role of institutions has led to a tendency for
individuals to negotiate rights and responsibilities more on a personal
basis, without necessary reference to an institutional source. Fukuyama
calls this 'moral miniaturization'.[67] The establishment in some US states
of 'covenant' marriage, which retains for its participants the legal consequences of 'traditional' marriage, is a singular example of this process.[68] But it is reflected also in the expansion, and uncertainty, as to
what is to count as the family unit itself. The House of Lords' decision
in 1999 that a committed, longstanding homosexual relationship fell
within the definition of a family for purposes of succession to protected tenancies[69] might appear a simple case in comparison to possible
claims by persons (whether of the same or the opposite sex) who have
simply experienced a sexual relationship, but not lived together, to
similar protection by the law. Equally, it may be asked whether people
who simply share a household, but do not enjoy a sexual, or other intimate relationship, should be subject to a special normative regime.[70]
And if that is allowed, it becomes hard to see any institutional linkage

---

[63] Eekelaar, Ch 18 of this volume.   [64] Douglas, Ch 10 of this volume.   [65] *ibid.*
[66] Family Law Act 1996, Part IV.   [67] Francis Fukuyama, n 2 above.
[68] See Wadlington, Ch 11 of this volume, describing (at 251) various other proposals for
creating marriage *à la carte*.
[69] *Fitzpatrick v Sterling Housing Association* [1999] 4 All ER 705. For the equivalent in the
US, see Grossberg, Ch 1 of this volume.
[70] Such people are considered 'associated persons' for the purposes of certain remedies
under the Family Law Act 1996.

at all. Rights and duties appear to arise from a range of individual-specific factual situations.

It is not difficult to see how the state might view the uncertainty and fluidity of these developments with anxiety. One response has been to attempt to revitalize the traditional institutions. This can have an air of desperation about it, as in the British Government's proposals to have the benefits of marriage taught in schools,[71] and to produce 'a statement of the rights and responsibilities of marriage' which would be 'made available through [marriage] register offices, churches and other places of worship and other bodies providing advice to married people'.[72] But the strategy of linking the idea of empowerment with that of responsibility is important. Citizens are to be given their rights, but are expected to exercise them responsibly. In this way, the illusion of empowerment is created, while the state keeps control over how the power is exercised. An early example was the strengthening (on both sides of the Atlantic) of fathers' child support obligations. While people may be more free to leave marriages, or to produce children outside marriage, the responsibility for the costs of bringing up children will not be easily avoided. Parents with the sole care of a child have been placed under heavy pressure to allow visits by the other parent; they are expected to conform to the two-parent norm. Further examples are the plans to require any person initiating divorce proceedings to attend an information meeting, designed to underline parents' responsibilities to their children, and to one another,[73] and legislation allowing courts to issue parental supervision orders requiring parents of disruptive children to attend guidance or counselling sessions.[74] There is a mixture of techniques used, but the overt use of persuasion, or the incorporation of duties into contracts, are calculated to give the impression that the decisions are ultimately those of the citizen, an exercise of choice, though the reality may be different.

THE PROBLEM OF AUTHORITY

It is no wonder, then, that the contemporary scene can seem so confusing. The contrast between endeavours to determine what *institutions* required of individuals (as in the application of the laws of nullity and fault-based divorce) and the multitude of ways of trying to make individuals act in a

---

[71] See 'Teachers told to praise marriage': *The Times*, 1 Sept 1999. The guidance was to emphasize the importance of marriage 'and stable relationships', but the Government has had difficulty in securing the support of politicians who believe the directive should give greater pre-eminence to marriage: *The Times* 24 Mar 2000.

[72] *Supporting Families* (the Stationery Office, 1998) 32.

[73] See Smart, Ch 16 of this volume.   [74] Crime and Disorder Act 1998, s 8.

'responsible' way towards those with respect to whom they appear to have special responsibility could not be greater. But how significant is it? The answer to this may depend on its causes. The mere assertion that modern individualism has generated a selfish generation[75] tells us little. After all, as we have seen, the Victorians, too, thought the age of individualism had arrived, and how does one measure selfishness? It is necessary therefore to consider the reasons for changing patterns of behaviour. Many have been suggested, including industrialization; the widespread availability of female contraception since the 1960s; the access of women to the labour market, at the expense of men; even the information revolution. But these need not necessarily have shaken institutions which, by now, were for the most part surrounded by sufficient controls that they had to be exercised in a reasonably benevolent fashion. Why was it that it was precisely when marriage assumed its most benign form that its popularity should so dramatically falter? Why should people not always uphold marriage as an institution in which each partner (irrespective of the presence of children) mutually subordinates their individual interests to one another,[76] or accept that judges or social workers can always be trusted to understand and promote people's interests?

What seems to have occurred is a loss of confidence in *institutions*. This may be part of a general decline in trust in public figures and even in domestic partners.[77] Yet why should everyone suddenly have become so distrustful? It may be we have had our confidence undermined by revelations of domestic violence between adults, and of child abuse within families and in institutional settings. These may all have played a part, but a more subtle process may have occurred. Perhaps the widespread dissemination of knowledge through the physical and social sciences, through psychology and anthropology, and the media (including investigative journalism and satire), has removed the *mystique* upon which institutional authority, and the morality associated with it, relies[78] and has revealed the institutions as the creatures of individuals who themselves were self-interested and fallible. Whether or not individuals have in fact

[75] See esp the discussion in Lewis in Ch 4 of this volume.

[76] Milton Regan calls this the 'internal stance' to relationships, in contrast to an 'external' stance wherein each party measures the value of the relationship by reference to the extent to which they benefit from it: *Alone Together: Law and the Meanings of Marriage* (1999).

[77] See Carl E. Schneider, 'Family Law in the Age of Distrust', (1999) 33 *Family Law Quarterly* 447.

[78] The 1960s in Britain were particularly notable for disseminating scepticism about established institutional values. A notable example was the 1967 BBC Reith Lectures in which the social anthropologist Edmund Leach declared: 'Morality is specified by culture; what you *ought* to do depends on who you are and where you are'; and that, 'far from being the basis of the good society, the family, with its narrow privacy and tawdry secrets, is the source of all our discontents': *A Runaway World?* (BBC, 1967).

become less willing to enter commitments to one another,[79] they became less convinced that their moral and social decisions should be circumscribed by the institutions of the law.[80]

Put another way, the problem can be seen as one of *the legitimacy of authority*. Respect for existing institutions is diminishing. But that simply raises the problem as to the legitimacy of alternative norms promoting individual empowerment. The United States constitution has proved a fertile source for such norms.[81] In Britain, legitimacy for the evolving law rests on the democratic mandate through the parliamentary process. However, many of the changes had been fed into that process from the Law Commission, a statutory law reform body, thus arguably introducing a disproportionate influence of academic and legal opinion into the reform process.[82] This tension erupted into public confrontation in 1995 when proposals from the Commission to rationalize the civil remedies available in cases of domestic violence, which the Commission (and the Government) had thought uncontroversial, were berated by some politicians and the right-wing press for apparently treating married and unmarried couples in the same way, occasioning personal attacks on individual Law Commissioners and resulting in the withdrawal of the proposals.

Other sources of legitimation of law have become increasingly important. Although the European Economic Community, which the United Kingdom entered in 1973, is primarily an economic association, its effects on employment law have probably influenced family life. The law of the European Union is directly effective within member states, with the consequence that it overrides conflicting domestic law, whether found in common law or statute law, and the European Court of Justice (ECJ) is the final court of appeal. Article 119 of the foundational Treaty of Rome required that equal pay should be given for equal work, and this was expanded by the Equal Treatment Directive 1975 to include equal pay for work of equal value. The ECJ has held that this allowed an employee to bring an action directly against her employers if they were in breach.[83] The Directive has also been important in safeguarding employment of pregnant women.[84] But the Court has not extended this

---

[79] This is inherently a difficult proposition to demonstrate empirically, partly because it is difficult to compare the *nature* of personal commitments in modern society with those entered into under social pressures which no longer exist.

[80] See Smart, Ch 16 of this volume.

[81] See the discussion of the 'right of privacy' and the concept of 'liberty' in the Fourteenth Amendment by Barron in Ch 12 of this volume.

[82] For an account of the relationship between the Commission, the Government and the parliamentary process, see 'The Law Commission: True Dawns and False Dawns' in Stephen Cretney, *Law, Law Reform and the Family* (Oxford University Press, 1998) Ch 1.

[83] *Defrenne v Sabena* [1976] ECR 455; *Jenkins v Kingsgate* [1980] ECR 911.

[84] *Webb v EMO* [1994] IRLR 482.

protection to same-sex partners.[85] While European Union law provides a normative source beyond national norms, and can be said to represent something of a European consensus, its 'democratic' credentials are not transparent, and its legitimacy in popular consciousness by no means assured.

The European Convention on Human Rights was an earlier international instrument, dating from 1951. Its provisions, and the decisions of the European Court of Human Rights (ECHR), are not directly applicable in UK law, though the Government has always amended domestic law where necessary to bring it in line with ECHR decisions. Four articles are of special importance to family law: article 8, which states that 'everyone has the right to respect for his private and family life, his home and his correspondence'; article 12, which states that 'men and women of marriageable age have the right to marry and to found a family, according to the national laws governing the exercise of this right'; article 6, which states that, 'in the determination of his civil rights and obligations ... everyone is entitled to a fair and public hearing within a reasonable time by an independent and impartial tribunal established by law'; and article 14, which insists that the enjoyment of the rights and freedoms of the Convention 'shall be secured without discrimination on any ground such as sex ... birth or other status'.

The influence of the Convention on UK family law began to be felt from the early 1980s when the imminence of an adverse decision[86] led to the removal of local authorities' discretion to determine whether parents should be permitted to have contact with their children who were in state care.[87] Other decisions which have had direct consequences have been *Campbell and Cozens v UK*[88] (leading to the abolition of corporal punishment in state schools), *Gaskin v UK*[89] (dealing with disclosure of confidential records of children in state care), and *Dudgeon v UK*,[90] (leading to the decriminalization of homosexuality in Northern Ireland). Convention norms became important again towards the end of the century, when the ECHR held that two boys, both aged 11 at the time of their trial, who had been convicted through 'adult' criminal proceedings of the murder of the 2-year-old James Bulger, had been denied a fair trial, and that their sentences (which had been extended by the Home Secretary) must be fixed by judges, not politicians.[91] The apparent immunity granted by English courts against actions for negligence for social work 'policy' decisions

---

[85] *Grant v South-West Trains Ltd* [1998] All ER (EC) 193. This may change in view of the extension in the Treaty of Amsterdam of the definition of discrimination to cover sexual orientation.   [86] *WOB and R v UK* (1988) 10 EHRR 29.
[87] Health and Social Services and Social Security Adjudications Act 1983.
[88] (1982) 4 EHRR 293.   [89] (1989) 12 EHRR 36.   [90] (1982) 4 EHRR 149.
[91] *T and V v UK*, 16 Dec 1999.

seemed also to be unlikely to be upheld by the Court.[92] In 1999, the Court ruled that the acquittal of a stepfather on a criminal charge for severely beating a 9-year-old child with a garden cane demonstrated the failure of English law's permission to allow a parent to administer 'reasonable chastisement' to protect the child's right to protection against 'torture or inhuman and degrading treatment' guaranteed by article 3.[93]

On other matters, however, the Convention has had less influence. It bears the hallmarks of its immediate post-war origins in its linkage of the right to found a family to the right to marry. In particular, a series of cases in which transsexuals have sought to challenge the refusal of English law to reassign the legal sexual identity of a post-operative transsexual have upheld the law, thus effectively denying transsexuals a right to marry in their new sexual identity, holding that the lack of consensus among participants to the Convention allowed states a margin of appreciation in the matter, at least for the time being.[94] Indeed, although Convention jurisprudence includes non-marital relationships which produce children within the concept of 'family' life,[95] the court maintains a traditional view of family life, and same-sex relationships are more likely to be thought to fall under 'private' life.[96] In this respect, English law has gone further.[97] The UN Convention on the Rights of the Child seems to have had little *direct* impact on UK family law, although it is sometimes referred to by judges in support of a decision.[98] Yet the Convention's emphasis on parental responsibilities, and on the right of the child to be heard, have a strong resonance in the contemporaneous Children

[92] *Osman v UK* (1998) 5 BHRC 293. Although this case concerned the police service, its reasoning appears to cover the immunity given to social services in *X v Bedfordshire CC* [1995] 3 All ER 353. A change of direction in the courts following *Osman* appears to have occurred in *Barrett v Enfield LBC* [1999] 3 All ER 193 and *S v Gloucestershire CC* [2000] 3 All ER 347.

[93] *A v UK* (1999) 27 EHRR 611. The Government has responded by issuing a Consultation Paper, *Protecting Children, Supporting Parents: A Consultation Document on the Physical Punishment of Children* (Department of Health, 2000). This does not propose the complete criminalization of physical punishment of children, but suggests that it would be sufficient to meet the Convention's requirements if the concept of 'reasonable chastisement' was defined more precisely, by for example making express reference to the age, condition, and circumstances of the child and the means by which the punishment was inflicted.

[94] See Douglas, Ch 10 of this volume; *Rees v UK* (1987) 9 EHRR 56; *Cossey v UK* (1991) 13 EHRR 622; *Sheffield & Horsham v UK* [1998] 3 FCR 141.

[95] *Keegan v Ireland* (1994) 18 EHRR 342.

[96] *Kerkhoven v The Netherlands*, App No 15666/89 (Commission). In *X, Y and Z v UK* (1997) 4 EHRR 143, the Court accepted that a female to male post-operative transsexual living with his female partner and children she had conceived by artificial means enjoyed 'family life', but only because the transsexual, although legally still a female, 'was living in society as a man' and the situation was 'indistinguishable from the *traditional notion* of family life' (166, emphasis supplied).   [97] *Fitzpatrick v Sterling Housing Association* [1999] 4 All ER 705.

[98] For example, *Re R (a minor) (contact)* [1993] 2 FLR 762, where Butler-Sloss LJ referred to the Convention as underlining the right of a child to have a relationship with both its parents.

Act 1989. However, it is the European Convention which has the greater potential for guiding English family law in the future because the Human Rights Act 1998 has incorporated it into domestic law as from October 2000. If a court finds domestic law to be in conflict with the Act, it may make a 'declaration of incompatibility', carrying the expectation (but no more) of swift amendment through Parliament. The most fruitful source for development is likely to be the right to respect for family and private life.[99]

In this appeal to normative principles lying beyond positive law, the present age bears a close resemblance to the Enlightenment itself. Then, current orthodoxies were challenged by ideas of natural rights, which were held to repose in the people rather than their rulers. The later writers of the period like the Marquis de Condorcet and Marie de Gouges in France and Mary Wollstonecroft in England extended this to radical visions of equality which embraced women and slaves. It may be that the present ferment of critical self-examination, similar to that of the Enlightenment, is a form of renewal of the open-ended search instigated during that time for the proper relationship between the individual and society which had been overcome by the nineteenth-century reaction against the French revolution and the long dominance of Hegelian and Marxist thought. With a few exceptions, such as Tom Paine's *Rights of Man*, the Enlightenment thinkers sought to transform rather than destroy existing social institutions. Does the present wave of social critique go further? The changes of behaviour chronicled in this volume suggest that it might. But there are many continuities. The controversies over gay marriage are at least controversies over the institution of marriage, not demands for its abolition. English law, at the century's end, provided no institutional framework for same-sex relationships, and had still failed to respond in a comprehensive way to heterosexual unmarried cohabitation. The goal of individual empowerment was itself strongly threatened by a communitarian reaction and an attempt to instil 'responsible' behaviour into citizens. This looks very much like the 'governance through families'[100] characteristic of the welfarist era. Might this lead to a replication of a reaction in the twenty-first century similar to the nationalistic and romantic nineteenth-century response to Enlightenment universalism? It might. The enhancement of

---

[99] The United Kingdom is also party to the International Covenant on Civil and Political Rights. An extensive review has concluded that 'UK law and practice largely comply with Articles 23 and 24 of the ICCPR' [concerning protection of 'the family' and the right to marry with free consent; and the right of children to protection without discrimination]: David Harris and Sarah Joseph, 'Family and Child Rights', in *The International Covenant on Civil and Political Rights and United Kingdom Law* (Clarendon Press, 1995).

[100] Donzelot, n 9 above.

state powers to remove children permanently from (mostly poor) families in the American Adoption and Safe Families Act 1997, described by Guggenheim in Chapter 25, could suggest so. But, unlike the position at the end of the eighteenth century, this time the attempt to impose, or retain, tutelary supervision over family life has to confront the powerful discourse of empowerment and the expectations it raises. Which will gain the upper hand, only our successors will know.

Index

The index lists proper names and legislation which appear in the text.
Case references are selective.
Page references to US contributions are given in italics; references in plain type are to the
English contributions.